MW01170378

SAINT GERMAIN
PROPHECY TO THE NATIONS

B O O K I

ELIZABETH CLARE PROPHET

PEARLS OF WISDOM
TEACHINGS OF THE ASCENDED MASTERS
Mark L. Prophet • Elizabeth Clare Prophet
VOLUME THIRTY-ONE • 1988

SUMMIT UNIVERSITY PRESS®

Saint Germain
Prophecy to the Nations
Elizabeth Clare Prophet

Pearls of Wisdom 1988
Volume Thirty-One Book One

Published by
The Summit Lighthouse®
for Church Universal and Triumphant®

LIBRARY OF CONGRESS CATALOG CARD NUMBER: 89-61842

INTERNATIONAL STANDARD BOOK NUMBER: 0-922729-00-X

Printed in the United States of America

Summit University Press®
First Printing

Page xii: The Messenger Elizabeth Clare Prophet,
photograph by Harry Langdon
Page xiii: The Messenger Mark L. Prophet,
photograph by Porter Studio

Contents

II

III

IV

V

VI

VII

VIII

IX

X

Saint Germain Stumps America

1

2

3

Saint Germain Stumps Portugal

Saint Germain Stumps America

21

An Easter Retreat
March 30 – April 3, 1988
Royal Teton Ranch, Montana

I

II

III

IV

V

VI

VII

Letters to the Field

The Messenger Elizabeth Clare Prophet

The Messenger Mark L. Prophet

The Chart of Your Divine Self

There are three figures represented in the Chart, which we will refer to as the upper figure, the middle figure, and the lower figure.

The upper figure is the I AM Presence, the I AM THAT I AM, the individualization of God's presence for every son and daughter of the Most High.

The Divine Monad consists of the I AM Presence surrounded by the spheres (color rings) of light that comprise the Causal Body. This is the body of First Cause that contains within it man's "treasure laid up in heaven"—words and works, thoughts and feelings of virtue, attainment, and light—pure energies of love that have risen from the plane of action in time and space as the result of man's judicious exercise of free will and his harmonious qualification of the stream of life that issues forth from the heart of the Presence and descends to the level of the Christ Self, thence to invigorate and enliven the embodied soul.

The middle figure in the Chart is the Mediator between God and man, called the Holy Christ Self, the Real Self, or the Christ consciousness. It has also been referred to as the Higher Mental Body or one's Higher Consciousness.

This Inner Teacher overshadows the lower self, which consists of the soul evolving through the four planes of Matter using the vehicles of the four lower bodies (the etheric, or memory, body; the mental body; the emotional, or desire, body; and the physical body) to balance karma and fulfill the divine plan.

The three figures of the Chart correspond to the Trinity of Father (the upper figure), Son (the middle figure), and Holy Spirit (the lower figure). The latter is the intended temple of the Holy Spirit, whose sacred fire is indicated in the enfolding violet flame. The lower figure corresponds to you as a disciple on the Path. Your soul is the nonpermanent aspect of being, which is made permanent through the ritual of the ascension.

The ascension is the process whereby the soul, having balanced her karma and fulfilled her divine plan, merges first with the Christ consciousness and then with the living Presence of the I AM THAT I AM. Once the ascension has taken place, the soul, the nonpermanent aspect of being, becomes the Incorruptible One, a permanent atom in the Body of God. The Chart of Your Divine Self is therefore a diagram of yourself—past, present, and future.

The lower figure represents the son of man or child of the Light evolving beneath his own 'Tree of Life'. This is how you should visualize yourself standing in the violet flame, which you invoke daily in the name of the I AM Presence and your Holy Christ Self in order to purify your four lower bodies in preparation for the ritual of the alchemical marriage—your soul's union with the Beloved, your Holy Christ Self.

The lower figure is surrounded by a tube of light, which is projected from the heart of the I AM Presence in answer to your call. It is a cylinder of white light that sustains a force-field of protection 24 hours a day, so long as you guard it in harmony. It is also invoked daily with the "Heart, Head and Hand Decrees" and may be reinforced as needed.

The threefold flame of Life is the divine spark sent from the I AM Presence as the gift of life, consciousness, and free will. It is sealed in the secret chamber of the heart that through the Love, Wisdom and Power of the Godhead anchored therein the soul may fulfill her reason for being in the physical plane. Also called the Christ flame and the liberty flame, or fleur-de-lis, it is the spark of a man's Divinity, his potential for Christhood.

The silver (or crystal) cord is the stream of life, or "lifestream," that descends from the heart of the I AM Presence to the Holy Christ Self to nourish and sustain (through the chakras) the soul and its vehicles of expression in time and space. It is over this 'umbilical' cord that the energy of the Presence flows, entering the being of man at the crown and giving impetus for the pulsation of the threefold flame as well as the physical heartbeat.

When a round of the soul's incarnation in Matter-form is finished, the I AM Presence withdraws the silver cord, whereupon the threefold flame returns to the level of the Christ, and the soul clothed in the etheric garment gravitates to the highest level of her attainment where she is schooled between embodiments until her final incarnation when the great law decrees she shall go out no more.

The dove of the Holy Spirit descending from the heart of the Father is shown just above the head of the Christ. When the son of man puts on and becomes the Christ consciousness as Jesus did, he merges with the Holy Christ Self. The Holy Spirit is upon him and the words of the Father, the beloved I AM Presence, are spoken, "This is my beloved Son in whom I AM well pleased" (Matt. 3:17).

A more detailed explanation of the Chart of Your Divine Self is given in *The Lost Teachings of Jesus* and *Climb the Highest Mountain* by Mark L. Prophet and Elizabeth Clare Prophet.

THE CHART OF YOUR DIVINE SELF

I

PROPHECY FOR THE 1990S

by
Elizabeth Clare Prophet

1

Challenge, Crisis and Opportunity:
The Handwriting in the Skies

What lies ahead for North America?

In order to chart the future I bring you a message from Saint Germain on prophecy—prophecy as the handwriting in the skies, which comes to us as the astrology of the United States, Canada and the world.

Before I begin to discuss astrology as prophecy, I will give you a unique perspective on your destiny in the Piscean and Aquarian ages, your relationship to God, your divine inheritance and your karma. And I will tell you about the Ascended Master Saint Germain, who has given me as a means of alchemical change the prognostications I will set forth, so that we can save ourselves from the fate of our karma—in time.

As a Messenger of God I am the servant of God's Light within you. And the servant is not greater than his lord.[1] My Lord is the Christ of Jesus and the Christ of you, who are one and the same. For John the Beloved wrote that that Christ was and is "the true Light, which lighteth *every* man that cometh into the world."[2] Therefore I come as a servant of that Light—your Light, my Light, your Christ, my Christ.

N.B. "Prophecy for the 1990s I" is based on a lecture given by Elizabeth Clare Prophet April 16, 1988, Toronto Airport Hilton, Mississauga, Ontario, Canada, updated for publication in the 1988 *Pearls of Wisdom*.

In my writings and lectures I have taught that the successive revelations of God in the ages of Aries, Pisces and Aquarius have been the unveiling of his Person as Father, Son and Holy Spirit. These Three, who are One, are depicted in the Chart of Your Divine Self (p. *xvi*) so that you can visualize your inner divinity as the Father, the I AM Presence (upper figure), and as the Son, the Holy Christ Self (middle figure), and as your soul providing the temple for the Holy Spirit here below (lower figure), abiding beneath the shadow of the Almighty and the only begotten Son, the Universal Christ.

The Chart shows how you look when you invoke the violet flame of the Holy Spirit for soul purification. It also shows your tube of light around you, which you invoke for the protection of your soul and your four lower bodies (not shown on the Chart).

These are energy fields, four interpenetrating sheaths of consciousness, each vibrating in its own dimension, described as the etheric, mental, astral and physical. These four lower bodies surround the soul and are her vehicles of expression in the material world of form. They envelop not only the nuclei of persons but also of planets—demarcating the etheric plane, the mental plane, the astral plane and the physical plane.

And so you have a physical body. You have a mind, which is your mental body. You have emotions, which manifest in your astral, or desire, body. And you have an etheric body, the highest vibrating of the four, which is also called the memory body and the envelope of the soul.

They are like "wheels within wheels." Or you might think of them as interpenetrating colanders. When the "holes" are lined up, it means that your four lower bodies are in sync. They are aligned with the blueprint of your lifestream that is sustained by your Holy Christ Self, enabling the light to flow out unobstructed from your spiritual centers (called chakras) to bless and heal all life.

But most of us don't have our "holes" lined up. We're out of alignment with our Real Self and so we don't experience the full benefit of our just portion of the Light that descends over the crystal cord (shown on the Chart) from our Mighty I AM Presence.

The problem we have to deal with if we are to emerge from earth's schoolroom as an integrated personality in God is this: During our stay on this planet we have gotten our spiritual pores clogged up with a lot of human karma and astral effluvia (i.e., the dust and debris of the misqualified energy of the centuries). In addition, each of us is carrying a percentage of the total planetary karma in our four lower bodies. As we have misqualified

God's pure life-stream of energy perpetually flowing from our I AM Presence for our use here below, it has accumulated in the subconscious as rings on our tree of life and in the collective unconscious of the race. Like it or not, we *are* bearing one another's karmic burden, simply because we are a part of this evolution. And that, too, is our karma!

So as we come to the end of the two-thousand-year dispensation that is known as the age of Pisces, we are reaping the karma of that cycle as well as previous cycles since the last major cataclysm when God through Nature cleared the planet (though not entirely) in the sinking of Atlantis, otherwise known as the Noachian deluge.

This twelve-thousand-year accumulation of our sowings is boomeranging upon the nations and upon every one of us. I sometimes think that the shock factor of so many changes all around us and the crumbling of the old order neutralizes the soul's sensitivity to the darkness and the danger that is oncoming. It is not surprising, for Paul said:

> The day of the Lord so cometh as a thief in the night.
>
> For when they shall say, Peace and safety; then sudden destruction cometh upon them, as travail upon a woman with child; and they shall not escape [their karma].
>
> But ye, brethren, are not in Darkness, that that day should overtake you as a thief.
>
> Ye are all the children of Light, and the children of the Day: we are not of the Night, nor of Darkness.
>
> Therefore let us not sleep, as do others; but let us watch and be sober. For they that sleep sleep in the night; and they that be drunken are drunken in the night.
>
> But let us, who are of the Day, be sober, putting on the breastplate of faith and love; and for an helmet, the hope of salvation.
>
> For God hath not appointed us to wrath, but to obtain salvation by our Lord Jesus Christ.[3]

Karma is never a punishment, although those on the receiving end of it may experience it as such. Karma is the effect of whatever thoughts, feelings, words and deeds we have set in motion through our freewill qualification of God's energy, freely given. Most of us have set in motion good causes that have produced a harvest of good effects, which are stored in the spheres of Light of the Causal Body, the "heaven-world" surrounding our Mighty I AM Presence, shown on the Chart.

But we have also been putting out negative vibrations and then recycling those same negatives as they have come full circle. And we've been doing it for a long time. Too long. Often we have sown error unwittingly, witlessly, in ignorance of Cosmic Law; and we must admit that sometimes we have wittingly, witfully directed harm toward other parts of life. And now the Great Law requires us to pay the price for our willful wrongdoings. We must pay our karmic debts.

Nevertheless, by the grace of our Lord we may pray, "Father, forgive us our trespasses against the Law of thy Bountiful Love, even as we do wholeheartedly, unreservedly forgive those who have trespassed against us."[4]

Jesus came to demonstrate the path of personal Christhood so that the children of the Light could follow in his footsteps throughout the Piscean age and beyond. And he saw to it that it was a path that they could walk and work. But the knowledge of this path was not preserved for them by Church or State. Having no teachers to teach them the Christian mysteries that Jesus imparted to his disciples, they have missed the point of their soul's calling from God to walk and work this path that our Lord taught by example.

It was God's grand design that his children fulfill this calling to a personal Christhood in this two-thousand-year cycle of the Piscean dispensation: "But as many as received him, to them gave he power to become the sons of God, even to them that believe on his name: which were born, not of blood, nor of the will of the flesh, nor of the will of man, but of God."[5]

For all who would work out their own salvation with fear and trembling,[6] as Paul admonished the followers of Christ at Philippi, God gave the dispensation of individual Sonship through the Mighty I AM Presence and Holy Christ Self. This is the path of discipleship leading to the embodiment of one's Christhood.

But the wolves in sheep's clothing,[7] the embodied fallen angels who have occupied positions of power and authority in Church and State, have taken away the true teachings and the sacred mysteries of our Lord and Saviour Jesus Christ lest in lawfully exercising his Power, Wisdom and Love we should overcome them and cast them out of the temples of God and man.

And so we are as shorn lambs—scattered sheep whose Shepherd the Evil One did smite.[8] We are ill-equipped for our mission in this new age because we do not have the fullness of the self-knowledge, what the early Christians called gnosis,[9] of the Universal Christ that the Lord intended us to have when we should enter the two-thousand-year dispensation of Aquarius at hand.

The Violet Flame Can Mitigate Prophecy

Jeremiah prophesied the coming of THE LORD OUR RIGHTEOUSNESS,[10] who would divide the way of Good and Evil within us. This Lord, this Reality, is your beloved Holy Christ Self, and mine. For there is but one Christ and one Lord, whose Presence is individualized for every son and daughter of God. Our self-awareness in and through this Christ has been identified in New Age terms as each one's "Higher Consciousness."

If you would realize this power of the Presence of God within you, then you as one and I as one, multiplied by the LORD—the Mighty I AM Presence, *who is one LORD*—can join forces with the Power-Wisdom-Love of the Trinity in the Great Central Sun. And we, representing the nations of Canada and the United States, can join forces with the Lightbearers of all of North America as we call upon the heavenly hosts to turn the tide of the karmic retribution calculated to come upon the planet in our time.

I believe, because the Ascended Master Saint Germain has told me so, that if millions of people call upon the LORD,[11] call upon his name I AM THAT I AM, to invoke the intercession of the Seven Archangels and the violet flame of the Holy Spirit, we can turn the tide, we can make the difference.

The violet fire is the all-consuming fire that Moses declared to be the very nature of God.[12] And the violet light is God's light. John the Beloved, who was the Messenger of Jesus, declared the Lord's message: "God is Light, and in him is no darkness at all.... If we walk in the Light, as he is in the Light, we have fellowship one with another, and the blood of Jesus Christ his Son cleanseth us from all sin."[13]

John saw the violet light, he declared the violet light, and he walked in the violet light. John knew that the blood of Jesus was the Light of Alpha and Omega. And he also knew that when we call upon the blood of Jesus Christ to cleanse us from all sin, that Light has the power of the Holy Ghost to transmute the cause and core of sin and the karma which is the penalty for that sin.

The violet flame is the key to world transmutation—it works in microcosmic and macrocosmic worlds, from the smallest particle of matter to molecule to mind to materialization in man and mundane circles. The violet flame can alter, mitigate or turn back prophecy entirely. The violet flame is God's gift to us under the sponsorship of the Ascended Master Saint Germain.

The violet flame is the Seventh Ray aspect of the Holy Spirit. When you invoke it in the name of your I AM Presence, your Holy

Christ Self and Saint Germain, it is directed by Archangel Zadkiel
and Holy Amethyst's angels into the untoward conditions of the
personal and planetary out-of-alignment state that are the result of
mankind's misapplication of the universal laws of God's harmony.

This means that all negative karma—cause, effect, record
and memory—can and must, if we are to survive our wrong sowings, literally be transmuted. Through our application of the violet
flame, the energy we have invested in our miscreations (yes, we
can really be called miscreants!) is demagnetized (or stripped) of
its negative vibration and recharged with the positive polarity of
the Godhead; thereby it is transformed and restored to its original
blueprint and Alpha-Omega (yang-yin) balance. The white light,
the violet light and all lights of the rainbow rays are used in
healing because they sustain this Alpha-Omega polarity for each
color and band in the spectrum.

Now, the key to effective transmutation in our worlds is to
transmute that wave of returning personal and planetary karma
before it "breaks" on the shore of our physical hearth and home—
before it precipitates from the astral to the physical plane. If we
can do this by our invocations to the Holy Spirit to saturate the
earth and ourselves with the violet fire and the violet light, we can
avert personal and planetary disaster.

And this is precisely why I am stumping the nations with
Saint Germain's message for the Coming Revolution in Higher
Consciousness. Because we the people united as one in the heart of
God invoking the violet flame *can do something!*

Concerning this question of prophecy and the violet flame,
Archangel Michael said on February 4, 1988, in Tucson, Arizona:

> To enter the New Age does demand new thought and a
> new understanding of prophecy and a realization that the
> karma of a planet that could descend may yet be stayed by
> the heart, head and hand of those who determine to keep
> the flame of Life and recognize that the all-consuming
> power of God released in the violet flame by millions upon
> earth can in this hour, even in a twinkling of an eye, be the
> last trump of the Death and Hell [whence] the forces of
> Darkness [ascend out of the bottomless pit to torment the
> children of the Light].
>
> Where the sons and daughters of God do not cry out
> unto the LORD, the LORD, then, does not come suddenly in-
> to his temple. As has been explained to you, it is a question
> of free will; and our respect for that gift is an ultimate one.
>
> Therefore, the lessons of free will are considered by the

Almighty One to be of greater value than even the preservation of a civilization.[14]

The Law of Karma, which determines the laws of the octaves, says that just as we have the freedom to do what we will
in the physical octave, so the responsibility of freedom is also
accorded us to bear the consequences of our words and deeds. It is
incumbent upon us to call to the hosts of the Lord to intercede in
our behalf, especially where our exercise of this freedom has
gotten us in trouble.

In fact, by divine decree the hosts of the Lord will not come
into our lives and get us out of the mess we've made unless we call
upon them to "Take command of this situation in God's name!"
God's angels are under orders not to interfere in our lives unless
and until we tell them to. They simply will not interfere unless you
call to God for help. So you see, free will *is* the supreme law of this
universe.

I have experimented enough with the alchemy of the violet
flame to know that you can defeat the negative aspects of your
karma through invocations to God and the heavenly hosts for this
divine intercession.

Divine intercession has always been God's solution to man's
nonresolution. Examples abound in the Old Testament of prophets
warning the people of what would happen if they did not repent
from their out-of-alignment state, bend the knee and bow to God's
laws. God always gave the people an out, yet they seldom took it.
But when they did, as in the case of the prophet Jonah foretelling
the destruction of Nineveh, the people repented from their evil
ways and the prophecy did not come to pass.[15]

In Medjugorje, Yugoslavia, Mother Mary has appeared to six
teenagers since 1981, warning of coming calamities. The Blessed
Mother has said that some of these could be mitigated through
prayer and fasting. She has also revealed that because of the
response to her messages, one of the calamities has been averted.
This is a confirmation of what the Ascended Masters have been
teaching us since the early 1950s. And it gives us great hope even as
it goads our souls to more earnest prayer.

None of us knows what we will face tomorrow, next week or
next year. The future is the unknown—but not entirely. When we
stop and think about it, the sudden destruction that comes upon a
people has often been predictable. Had they studied the times and
the trends and been students of their own history and the laws of
Mother Nature, they could have foretold their future. The givens
and the knowns were there. That's why you often hear the

expression "I might have known this would happen." And indeed people do. Their souls know beforehand. But the reasoning mind locked in its own labyrinthian logic cannot see the straight line of causal relationships leading to only one inevitable conclusion.

One thing is certain: at the end of the age of Pisces we're seeing a summing up. The LORD God has required of the angel of records, who is known as the Keeper of the Scrolls, a reckoning of our karmic accounts.

There *is* a Book of Life. It is a record of the soul's history and a ledger of her karmic accounts. We are accountable for our thoughts and feelings, our motives and our acts in every lifetime we have spent on earth since we left the ancient Mystery School called Eden. Either we meet and overtake that karma with the all-consuming sacred fire of God or it will overtake us as calamity and cataclysm, as economic collapse and nuclear war, as disease and death.

What Is Prophecy?

Prophecy is exhortation—God exhorting us to right action through his messengers. It is teaching—the Holy Spirit teaching us, enlightening us to God-centeredness. It is warning—the Ascended Masters warning us of those things that shall surely come to pass if we do nothing.

Prophecy is delivered to us by those Higher Intelligences who guide the planetary spheres and their evolutions. They read our karma as the handwriting in the skies and they tell us what will come upon us and our generation if we do not obey the laws of God.

The sources of prophecy available to us today are:

(1) The Old and New Testaments, especially the prophets and the message of Jesus on the Great Tribulation in Matthew 24 and 25, Mark 13 and Luke 21, and the Book of Revelation.

(2) Mother Mary's prophecies to the children at Fátima in 1917 and to the teenagers in Medjugorje, Yugoslavia, from 1981 to the present. They contain an update on the prophecies of scripture and what the Blessed Virgin has projected as karmic retribution for the second half of the twentieth century.

(3) The writings of Nostradamus, the sixteenth-century French seer about whom I have spoken and written since late 1986. Saint Germain gave me the correct interpretations of key quatrains that apply to the twentieth century and the superpowers. He told me that to a certain extent the prophet has been misread by well-meaning commentators who have unwittingly inserted their world view into their interpretations, thus casting an incorrect light on current history.[16]

(4) The dictations of the Ascended Masters, which come to us directly through the agency of the Holy Spirit and have been delivered through Mark Prophet and me since 1958. These are delivered through the mantle of the Messengership, which Saint Germain bestowed upon us at the conclusion of our training under El Morya. This "mantle" is a unique electromagnetic forcefield placed over our auras whereby the Ascended Masters speak through us not only prophecy for our time but also the teachings of the ancient adepts of East and West as they should have been handed down to us through religious tradition. We must remember that the prophecies of the Ascended Masters, like Old Testament prophecies, are not final. They can always be mitigated or turned back if the people change their ways.

(5) Astrology, which is an accurate means of plotting the cycles of returning karma according to the cycles of the planets. The Ascended Masters Saint Germain and El Morya have instructed me in the uses of astrology to chart both personal and planetary karma.

Prophecy, then, predicts returning karma. But prophecy can be altered, mitigated or entirely turned back at any time before that 'mist' becomes the 'crystal'—before the energy of karma is precipitated in the physical plane as a sudden destruction that cometh upon us.

You may think that this is impossible, but Jesus said, and I believe it: "With men it is impossible but not with God: for with God all things are possible."[17] With God we can turn back the unformed before it crystallizes into the formed. Just so, with God we can turn back returning karma before it hits us as tornado, flood or fire—by invoking the violet fire of the Holy Spirit and directing it through our chakras into vortices of misqualified energy to transmute that returning karma before it manifests.

The violet flame is the universal solvent. God gave us a portion of his fire—fire for fire—when he gave us the divine spark, which is the threefold flame that burns on the altar of our hearts (shown on the Chart). Because we have this divine spark we can direct the violet flame in the name of our Mighty I AM Presence and Holy Christ Self into personal, national and international problems.

For instance, we can apply it to our mutual problem of acid rain, a source of pollution that has industrial as well as political causes. President Ronald Reagan, I am ashamed to say, has betrayed the people of both the United States and Canada by not doing something about it during his eight years in office. Congress is responsible as well. Many lawmakers, such as Democratic Sen. Robert Byrd, resist taking a stand on the issue.

The fish, lakes and streams and all of Nature and elemental life are our responsibility. We as citizens of planet earth must bear the karma for our pollution of the environment. And whose pollution is it? Are we the ones who have built the smokestacks and poured out the chemical putrefication into the waters? If not, then unless we challenge those who do and demand they give to us—we the people of the United States and Canada united, some 270 million strong—an accounting of their deeds against Nature and all humanity, the Great Law will hold us jointly accountable for their crimes, because we did nothing.

We have to be willing to do without those products that are produced at Nature's expense and at the expense of our future and our children's future and their opportunity to be healthy on a healthy planet. The people must unite to challenge the forces of greed working through those who line their pockets at the expense of the environment—this environment that is so precious to the people of Light because the balance of natural forces delivers to us the prana, the spiritual energy and the earth currents we must have in our four lower bodies to fulfill our divine plan while we are in embodiment.

We must realize that environmental pollution is not the fault of all North Americans. It is the fault of the few—the power elite in every country in the Northern Hemisphere. And some of the leaders we have elected do not represent us but they represent only the interests of unscrupulous business.

We the Lightbearers in the United States and Canada must overcome the barriers that separate us. We must challenge the fallen angels who have embodied in our midst ever since Archangel Michael and his legions cast them out of the octaves of Light![18] We must not deny the embrace of brother and brother, sister and sister, Canadian and American, simply because we fear, for instance, that free trade will open the door to the taking over of Canada's industry or to the flooding of our markets.[19]

We should rather fear our mutual control by big business and the power brokers. We should watch out for their divisive tactics, separating us by suspicion of one another when *they* are the spoilers of our oneness. Rather, let's unite and work together to defeat the common enemy, who most of all fears people-power—especially when that power is God's power invoked for the Victory.

I say, "Lightbearers of the world, unite!"

2

Saint Germain:
Nine Incarnations to Victory

The Ascended Master Saint Germain, together with his twin flame, the Ascended Lady Master Portia, is the Hierarch of the Aquarian Age. He is the great sponsor of Freedom's flame while Portia is the sponsor of the flame of Justice. Freedom and Justice are the yin and yang of the Seventh Ray of Aquarius and together with Mercy they provide the foundation for all other attributes of God to be outpictured in the Seventh Dispensation.

If we really want to understand Saint Germain's prophecies, we should take a look at some of his past lives on earth and how he both heralded and heeded prophecy to the benefit of himself and his age.

Saint Germain took his ascension on May 1, 1684, at the conclusion of his life as Francis Bacon. He and Portia became the Lord and Lady of the Seventh Ray upon their coronation on May 1, 1954, as hierarchs of the New Age. They serve as magnificent examples of the path of Seventh-Ray Christhood and its qualities: freedom, justice and mercy. Throughout Saint Germain's incarnations—as ruler, priest, prophet, defender of the Christ, scientist and discoverer—he was engaged in a relentless effort to return the souls of Light who came to earth with Sanat Kumara to the worship of their Great God Source.

Ruler of a Golden-Age Civilization

Over fifty thousand years ago, Saint Germain was the ruler of a golden-age civilization in a fertile country where the Sahara Desert now is. As king-emperor, Saint Germain was a master of the ancient wisdom and of the knowledge of the Matter spheres, and the people looked to him as the standard for their own emerging Godhood. His empire reached a height of beauty, symmetry and perfection unexceeded in the physical octave.

As the people of this civilization became more interested in the pleasures of the senses than in the larger creative plan of the Great God Self, a cosmic council instructed the ruler to withdraw from his empire; henceforth their karma would be their guru. The king held a great banquet for his councillors and public servants. His 576 guests each received a crystal goblet filled with an elixir that was "pure electronic essence."

This elixir was Saint Germain's gift of soul-protection to them so that when their opportunity would come again in the age of Aquarius to bring back that golden-age civilization, they would remember their I AM Presence and they would become a sign to all people that God can and shall dwell with his people when they make their minds and hearts and souls a fitting habitation for his Spirit. Some of you may experience a quickening of your soul memory and the opening of your inner sight whereby you will know that you were at that banquet more than fifty thousand years ago.

During the banquet a Cosmic Master, identifying himself solely by the word *Victory* upon his brow, addressed the assembly. He warned the people of the crisis they had brought upon themselves by their faithlessness, rebuked them for their neglect of their Great God Source, and prophesied that the empire would come under the rule of a visiting prince who would be seeking to marry the king's daughter.

The king and his family withdrew seven days later to the golden-etheric-city counterpart of the civilization. The prince arrived the next day and took over without opposition.[20]

High Priest of the Violet Flame Temple on Atlantis

As high priest of the Violet Flame Temple on the mainland of Atlantis thirteen thousand years ago, Saint Germain sustained by his invocations and his Causal Body a pillar of fire, a veritable fountain of violet singing flame, which magnetized people from near and far, who came to be set free from every binding condition of body, mind and soul. This they achieved by self-effort through the offering of invocations and the practice of Seventh Ray rituals to the sacred fire.

Those who officiated at the altar of the Violet Flame Temple were schooled in the universal priesthood of the Order of Melchizedek at Lord Zadkiel's retreat, the Temple of Purification, which stood where the island of Cuba now is. This priesthood combines the perfect religion and the perfect science. It was here that both Saint Germain and Jesus received the anointing, spoken by Zadkiel himself: "Thou art a priest for ever after the order of Melchizedek."[21]

The Prophet Samuel

In the eleventh century B.C., Saint Germain was embodied as the prophet Samuel. He was an outstanding religious leader in a time of great apostasy, serving as the last of Israel's judges and the first of her prophets. In those days the judges did not simply arbitrate disputes; they were charismatic leaders who were believed to have direct access to God and who could rally the tribes of Israel against oppressors.

Samuel was the messenger of God's liberation of the seed of Abraham from bondage to the corrupt priests, the sons of Eli, and from the Philistines, who had slaughtered the Israelites in battle. He is traditionally named alongside Moses as a great intercessor. When the nation faced continuing threats from the Philistines, he courageously led the people in a spiritual revival, exhorting them to "return unto the LORD with all your hearts" and to "put away the strange gods."[22] The people repented and beseeched Samuel not to cease calling upon the LORD to save them. As he was praying and offering sacrifices, a violent thunderstorm was unleashed, allowing the Israelites to overtake their enemies. The Philistines never rose again in the days of Samuel.

The prophet spent the rest of his life administering justice throughout the land. When he grew old, he appointed his sons to be judges over Israel; but they were corrupt and the people demanded that Samuel give them "a king to judge us like all the nations."[23] Deeply grieved, he prayed to the LORD and received the direction that he must carry out the mandate of the people. The LORD told him, "They have not rejected thee, but they have rejected me, that I should not reign over them."[24]

Samuel warned the Israelites of the dangers that would befall them through their rulers, but they still clamored for a king. Thus he anointed Saul as their leader and charged him and the people to always obey the voice of the LORD. But when Saul proved to be an unfaithful servant, Samuel pronounced the LORD's judgment upon him for his disobedience and secretly anointed David as king. When the prophet died, he was buried at Ramah; all of Israel mourned his passing.

Joseph, the Father of Jesus

Saint Germain was also embodied as Saint Joseph, the father of Jesus and husband of Mary. There are few references to him in the New Testament. The Bible traces his lineage back to David. It also recounts how when the angel of the Lord warned him in a dream that Herod planned to kill Jesus, Joseph heeded the warning and took his family to Egypt, returning after Herod's death. Joseph is said to have been a carpenter and is thought to have passed on before Jesus began his public ministry. In Catholic tradition, Saint Joseph is revered as Patron of the Universal Church and his feast is celebrated on March 19.

The sixteenth-century mystic Teresa of Avila was greatly devoted to Saint Joseph and chose him as the patron of her order. She wrote, "I don't recall up to this day ever having petitioned him for anything that he has failed to grant. . . . With this glorious saint I have experience that he helps in all our needs and that the Lord wants us to understand that just as he was subject to St. Joseph on earth—for since bearing the title of father, being the Lord's tutor, Joseph could give the Child command—so in heaven God does whatever he commands."[25]

In a dictation delivered through me on May 6, 1979, the Ascended Master Jesus said that Saint Joseph taught him much more than the sacred labor of carpentry: "He taught me the sacred labor of the alchemy of the Holy Ghost, the changing of the water into wine. Truly I am the son of Joseph, the great miracle alchemist of all time. And truly my works show forth his handiwork and the blessed grace of my mother."

Where history has not preserved the record, the Ascended Masters have from time to time given us glimpses into the life of the Holy Family. One such story was dictated by Mother Mary to Mark Prophet in 1968:

> I recall one morning when beloved Jesus was yet a small lad that he came to me with a very hard piece of wood that he was trying to whittle. He desired that I should persuade Joseph to exchange it for a softer piece, one that would lend itself more easily to molding. I sat him on my knee, and I proceeded to explain to him that there was an ingrained quality that of old had been placed within trees making one to possess a harder quality and another a softer quality. I told him that the soft wood would easily mar and that, were he to use it, the little image that he sought to whittle would not endure the knocks and tumbles that might later come to it, whereas a carving made of hard wood would endure more substantially.
>
> I also told him that the wood enjoyed being shapened by his hands and that the only difference between the soft and the hard wood would be that of a greater use of

patience on his part. He brushed back his hair which had fallen across his eyes and, with great and quick gentleness, planted a kiss upon both of my cheeks. I noticed a trace of a tear in one eye as he dashed away to continue his work of shaping the hard wood.[26]

In another dictation Mother Mary told us that Saint Joseph "did father and nourish the Christ Child and therefore set the pace of the age of Pisces." The Blessed Mother said: "May all of you who are of the Masculine Ray in this life remember his example in all of his lifetimes and know that your stature in God can be modeled after this role model of one who dared to defend Woman, who dared to raise up that Manchild, and stand as the protector not only of a family but of an entire area of a planet, until that one could fulfill his Christhood."[27]

Saint Alban

In the late third century, Saint Germain was embodied as Saint Alban, the first martyr of Britain. Alban lived in England during the persecution of Christians under the Roman emperor Diocletian. He was a pagan who had served in the Roman army and settled in the town of Verulamium, later renamed St. Albans. Alban hid a fugitive Christian priest named Amphibalus, who converted him. When soldiers came to search for him, Alban allowed the priest to escape and disguised himself in the cleric's garb.

Once his deed was discovered, Alban was scourged and sentenced to death. Legend says that so great a multitude gathered to witness his execution that they could not pass over a narrow bridge that had to be crossed. Alban prayed and the river parted to give passage to the crowd, whereupon his appointed executioner was converted and begged to die in his place. The request was denied and he was beheaded along with Alban.

Teacher of Proclus

Saint Germain worked from inner planes as the Master Teacher behind the Neoplatonists. He inspired the Greek philosopher Proclus (c. A.D. 410–485), the highly honored head of Plato's Academy at Athens. Under the Master's tutelage, Proclus based his philosophy upon the principle that there is only one true reality—the "One," which is God, or the Godhead, the final goal of all life's efforts. Proclus's writings extended to almost every department of learning, from philosophy and astronomy to

mathematics and grammar. He acknowledged that his enlightenment and philosophy came from above and he believed himself to
be one through whom divine revelation reached mankind.

Merlin

In the fifth century, Saint Germain was embodied as Merlin—
alchemist, prophet and counsellor at the court of King Arthur. In
a land splintered by warring chieftains and riven by Saxon
invaders, Merlin led Arthur through twelve battles (which were
actually twelve initiations) to unite the kingdom of Britain. He
worked side by side with the king to establish the sacred fellowship
of the Round Table. Under the guidance of Merlin and Arthur,
Camelot was a mystery school where the knights and ladies pursued the inner unfoldment of the mysteries of the Holy Grail and a
path of personal Christhood.

In some traditions, Merlin is described as a godly sage who
studied the stars and whose prophecies were recorded by seventy
secretaries. The *Prophecies of Merlin,* which deals with events
extending from Arthur's time into the distant future, was popular
in the Middle Ages.

Roger Bacon

Saint Germain was Roger Bacon (1220–1292), philosopher,
Franciscan monk, educational reformer and experimental scientist. In an era in which either theology or logic or both dictated the
parameters of science, he promoted the experimental method,
declared his belief that the world was round, and castigated the
scholars and scientists of his day for their narrow-mindedness.
"True knowledge stems not from the authority of others, nor from
a blind allegiance to antiquated dogmas,"[28] he said. Bacon eventually left his position as a lecturer at the University of Paris and
entered the Franciscan Order of Friars Minor.

In his day Bacon was renowned for his exhaustive investiga-
tions into alchemy, optics, mathematics and languages. He is
viewed as the forerunner of modern science and a prophet of
modern technology. He predicted the hot-air balloon, a flying
machine, spectacles, the telescope, the microscope, the elevator,
and mechanically propelled ships and carriages, and wrote of
them as if he had actually seen them.

True to the flame that Saint Germain had borne throughout
his incarnations, Roger Bacon was the outspoken defender of
freedom—a stand for which he paid the price more than once. As
Bacon said:

I believe that humanity shall accept as an axiom for its conduct the principle for which I have laid down my life—the right to investigate. It is the credo of free men—this opportunity to try, this privilege to err, this courage to experiment anew. We scientists of the human spirit shall experiment, experiment, ever experiment. Through centuries of trial and error, through agonies of research...let us experiment with laws and customs, with money systems and governments, until we chart the one true course—until we find the majesty of our proper orbit as the planets above have found theirs.[29]

His scientific and philosophical world view, his bold attacks on the theologians of his day, and his study of alchemy and astrology led to charges of "heresies and novelties," for which he was imprisoned for fourteen years by his fellow Franciscans. But to those who followed after him, Bacon was "doctor mirabilis" ("wonderful teacher"), an epithet by which he has been known down the centuries.

Christopher Columbus

Saint Germain was also embodied as Christopher Columbus (1451–1506), discoverer of America. Over two centuries before Columbus sailed, Roger Bacon himself had set the stage for Columbus's voyage to the New World when he stated in his *Opus Majus* that "the sea between the end of Spain on the west and the beginning of India on the east is navigable in a very few days if the wind is favorable."[30] Although the statement was incorrect in that the land to the west of Spain was not India, it was instrumental in Columbus' discovery. He quoted the passage in a 1498 letter to King Ferdinand and Queen Isabella and said that his 1492 voyage had been inspired in part by this visionary statement.

Columbus believed that God had made him to be "the messenger of the new heaven and the new earth of which He spake in the Apocalypse of St. John, after having spoken of it by the mouth of Isaiah."[31] "In the carrying out of this enterprise of the Indies," he wrote to King Ferdinand and Queen Isabella in 1502, "neither reason nor mathematics nor maps were any use to me: fully accomplished were the words of Isaiah."[32] He was referring to the prophecy recorded in Isaiah 11:10–12 that the Lord would "recover the remnant of his people...and shall assemble the outcasts of Israel, and gather together the dispersed of Judah from the four corners of the earth."

He was certain that he had been divinely selected for his mission. He studied the biblical prophets, writing passages relating to his mission in a book of his own making entitled *Las Proficias,* or *The Prophecies*—in its complete form, *The Book of Prophecies concerning the Discovery of the Indies and the Recovery of Jerusalem.* Although the point is seldom stressed, it is a fact so rooted in history that even *Encyclopaedia Britannica* says unequivocally that "Columbus discovered America by prophecy rather than by astronomy."[33]

Francis Bacon

As Francis Bacon (1561–1626), he was philosopher, statesman, essayist and literary master. Bacon, who has been called the greatest mind the West ever produced, is known as the father of inductive reasoning and the scientific method, which to a great degree are responsible for the age of technology in which we now live. He foreknew that only applied science could free the masses from human misery and the drudgery of sheer survival in order that they might seek a higher spirituality they once knew.

"The Great Instauration" (meaning the great restoration after decay, lapse, or dilapidation) was his formula to change "the whole wide world." He first conceived of the concept as a boy and, when he later crystallized it in his 1607 book by the same name, it launched the English Renaissance.

Over the years Bacon gathered around himself a group of writers who were responsible for almost all of the Elizabethan literature. Some of these were part of a "secret society" he called "The Knights of the Helmet" that had as its goal the advancement of learning by expanding the English language and creating a new literature written not in Latin but in words that Englishmen could understand. Bacon also organized the translation of the King James Version of the Bible, determined that the common people should have the benefit of reading God's Word for themselves.

Ciphers discovered in the 1890s in the original printings of the Shakespearean plays and in the works of Bacon and other Elizabethan authors reveal that Bacon wrote Shakespeare's plays and that he was the son of Queen Elizabeth and Lord Leicester. His mother, however, fearful of an untimely loss of power, refused to acknowledge him as her heir.

Toward the end of his life Bacon was persecuted and went unrecognized for his manifold talents. He is said to have died in 1626 but some have claimed that he secretly lived in Europe for a time after that. Triumphing over circumstances that would have destroyed lesser men, his soul entered the ritual of the ascension from etheric octaves on May 1, 1684.

The Wonderman of Europe

Desiring above all else to liberate God's people, Saint Germain sought and was granted a dispensation from the Lords of Karma to return to earth in a physical body. He appeared as "le Comte de Saint Germain," a "miraculous" gentleman who dazzled the courts of eighteenth- and nineteenth-century Europe, where they called him "The Wonderman."

He was an alchemist, scholar, linguist, poet, musician, artist, raconteur and diplomat admired throughout the courts of Europe for his adeptship. He was known for such feats as removing the flaws in diamonds and other precious stones and writing the same verses of poetry simultaneously with both hands. Voltaire described him as the "man who never dies and who knows everything."[34]

The count is mentioned in the letters of Frederick the Great, Voltaire, Horace Walpole and Casanova, and in newspapers of the day. Madame du Hausset, femme de chambre to Madame de Pompadour, wrote of him at some length in her memoirs.

Working behind the scenes, Saint Germain attempted to effect a smooth transition from monarchy to representative government and to prevent the bloodshed of the French Revolution. But his counsel was ignored. In a final attempt to unite Europe, he backed Napoleon, who misused the Master's power to his own demise.

Previously Saint Germain had turned his attention to the New World. He became the sponsoring Master of the United States of America and of her first president, inspiring the Declaration of Independence and the Constitution. He also inspired many of the labor-saving devices of the twentieth-century to further his goal of liberating mankind from drudgery that they might devote themselves to the pursuit of God-realization.[35]

Saint Germain comes into our midst with a tremendous prophecy for our time. This prophecy is for the fulfillment of our reason for being—our union with God, our ascension. This we achieve through balancing our karma, reuniting with our twin flame and fulfilling our divine plan upon earth.

And that prophecy, my friends, includes the reading of the handwriting on the wall.

3

My Vision of the Four Horsemen:
The Black Horse and the Astrology of Economic Collapse

God gave his Revelation to Jesus Christ so that his servants might know beforehand "things which must shortly come to pass." Our Lord delivered this Revelation to his apostle John the Beloved, "sent and signified by his angel."[36]

The Book of Revelation is God's gift to all who have answered his call to walk the path of initiation unto Christhood in the footsteps of our Elder Brother Jesus Christ. Its 22 chapters are a study in the psychology of the soul and the soul's testings under the hierarchy of the Great White Brotherhood. These she must master on her homeward path leading to reunion with Alpha and Omega, the Father-Mother God.

Mother Mary has taught me how to chart the 404 verses that make up the chapters of Revelation on the 12 lines of the "Cosmic Clock."[37] The Blessed Mother told me to place one verse on each line of the Clock, beginning with the 12 o'clock line. This results in a single spiral of $33\frac{2}{3}$ turns, which reveal a path of initiation that each soul in her season must pass through in the temples of the 12 Hierarchies of the Sun if she would ascend to God.

Mother Mary teaches us in her New Age astrology that at any point in time and space in any century, the soul on the path of reunion with God may experience in sequence, one after the other, the initiations encoded in the 22 chapters of Revelation; these correspond to the symbology of the 22 letters of the Hebrew alphabet.

According to their soul pattern, evolution and attainment, Lightbearers of the world are experiencing all of the leaves of Revelation; and each of those leaves is tumbling in its time and space, though not necessarily in the same dimension, for we are multidimensional beings.

Revelation portrays the juxtaposition of the soul and the collective planetary evolution between the forces of Light and

Darkness as these are engaged in Armageddon. The outcome of this warfare of the spirit is either the soul's resurrection unto eternal life or her final judgment. By free will the soul must choose either the path of initiation under the Lamb of God and his hosts or the path of Lucifer and the fallen angels in their rebellion against the LORD God and his Christ.

The Book of Revelation is an outline of these two paths and a prophecy of the outcome of freewill choices made—to be or not to be—each step of the way. Through a preordained series of lifetimes God gives each soul the opportunity (1) to serve the LORD and glorify him in her members or (2) to deify the ego, the synthetic self and the carnal mind while swearing enmity with God and his Christ and making war with the remnant of the seed of the Divine Mother.[38]

At the end of this cycle of opportunity the Keeper of the Scrolls reads the soul's record before the Ancient of Days, who sits on the great white throne at the Court of the Sacred Fire; and before the Four Beasts and the Twenty-four Elders "every man is judged according to his works."[39]

In the course of dealing with personal and planetary psychology and the karma of the cycles, the soul will encounter the Four Horsemen of the Apocalypse. These initiators, among others, provide the karmic testing to all. The subject of this chapter is their advancement on the world scene today and the vision God gave me of their doings (with Saint Germain at my side) in September 1986.

Let us read from chapters 5 and 6 of the Book of Revelation so that we can enter, as John the Revelator did, this prophecy and this path of our souls' initiation:

> And I saw in the right hand of him that sat on the throne a book written within and on the backside, sealed with seven seals.
>
> And I saw a strong angel proclaiming with a loud voice, Who is worthy to open the book, and to loose the seals thereof?
>
> And no man in heaven, nor in earth, neither under the earth, was able to open the book, neither to look thereon.
>
> And I wept much, because no man was found worthy to open and to read the book, neither to look thereon . . . .
>
> And I saw when the Lamb opened one of the seals, and I heard, as it were the noise of thunder, one of the four beasts saying, Come![40]
>
> And I saw, and behold a white horse: and he that sat on him had a bow; and a crown was given unto him: and he went forth conquering, and to conquer.

And when he had opened the second seal, I heard the second beast say, Come!

And there went out another horse that was red: and power was given to him that sat thereon to take peace from the earth, and that they should kill one another: and there was given unto him a great sword.

And when he had opened the third seal, I heard the third beast say, Come! And I beheld, and lo a black horse; and he that sat on him had a pair of balances in his hand.

And I heard a voice in the midst of the four beasts say, A measure of wheat for a penny, and three measures of barley for a penny; and see thou hurt not the oil and the wine.

And when he had opened the fourth seal, I heard the voice of the fourth beast say, Come!

And I looked, and behold a pale horse: and his name that sat on him was Death, and Hell followed with him. And power was given unto them over the fourth part of the earth, to kill with sword, and with hunger, and with death, and with the beasts of the earth.[41]

What, then, is the seven-sealed book?

Well, first of all, you are the seven-sealed book! You have seven spiritual centers called chakras lined up in your etheric body from the base of the spine to the crown. These are the seven sealed doors that open to the temple of Being when the soul is ready for the initiations of Christhood. Only the Lamb of God can open the seven-sealed book.

When the Lamb opens each of the first four seals he shows John the Revelator the Four Horsemen, who go out one by one when the command, "Come!" is given by the Four Beasts in succession. These Four Cosmic Forces who guard the throne of God and the Lamb are described in chapter 4 as the Lion, the Calf, the Man and the Flying Eagle.

Who are the Four Horsemen and their riders? They are the harbingers of personal and planetary karma. They come in every century bearing that karma and they are literally the embodiment of it. Hence, there is a certain foreboding with the mere mention of their names. The dread of their day is in the psyche of the race. For when their time is come, the opportunity for transmutation of world karma is no more. The mist has become the crystal and the violet flame does not mitigate or turn back the crystallized karma of a planetary evolution that did not act in time to restore balance to its inner and outer ecosystem. Even the LORD God does not abrogate his own laws of karmic retribution, which bear abundant mercy until the Lawgiver does declare to a recalcitrant mankind: "Thus far and no farther!"

My vision of the Four Horsemen is the sign that time is running out. Therefore we who understand the exercise of the science of the spoken Word through prayer and dynamic decree must make haste to intercede on behalf of those who know not what they do: "Father, forgive them! Father, forgive us!"

When God first showed me these Four Horsemen in September 1986, the thunder of their hoofbeats preceded them. They were moving toward me in a straight line. Those nearest me signified imminent karma; those at a greater distance signified that which was yet to be. I heard the awful roar of their approach, and it made me rise up and take notice that there was a great happening in our nation.

When I saw them I had the impression that their crisscrossing of the United States would encompass a five-year period. But we know that the days of the Lord's prophecy can be shortened or lengthened for the elect's sake[42] by the Holy Spirit.

The Four Horsemen are cloaked. I cannot see their faces. They are leaning over their horses, man and beast one as they gallop through the night. The night is bright. It is illumined by a full moon, whose magnetic pull on the emotions signifies that the astral bodies of mankind are vulnerable to their karma. But despite the brightness of the night, the riders are dark silhouettes against an age of spiritual darkness that is illumined only by the borrowed light of materialism, sensual pleasure, and a technology of which the people are not the masters.

The Four Horsemen represent the four lower bodies of a planet and a people—each one measuring and empowered by the very karma they deliver upon the nations. In our analysis of the astrology of Canada and the United States we will discover what these Four Horsemen portend.

When I first beheld them, the Four Horsemen were well on their way and had been for some time, whereas John wrote his vision at the moment of the opening of the first, second, third and fourth seals. So as I see them, they are descending from other dimensions into the nexus of history. Karmic history, rather than Revelation 6, now dictates the order of their appearing.

The first horse I saw was not the white horse as noted by John but the black horse, the third in his sequence. This immense and awesome creature was twelve feet from me, and his coat shone a black-silvery-green in the moonlight. This horseman is regarded as the one who delivers famine upon the earth, and so he does. But

famine comes through economic problems as well as adverse
weather conditions and improper food distribution. As I watched,
Saint Germain explained that the role of this horseman was to
deliver the karma for the abuse of the economies of the nations.

The voice "in the midst of the four beasts" sounds like an
auctioneer in the marketplace auctioning off our wheat, our barley
and our grains, the staff of life: "A measure of wheat for a penny,
and three measures of barley for a penny." And the warning is given
to hurt not "the oil and the wine," for we need both the wine of the
Spirit (Father) for our spiritual life and the oil of the earth (Mother)
for our material existence to keep the gears of civilization running.

The scarcity of commodities prophesied shows that the value
of the people's sacred labor, hence their self-worth, is being compromised by those who make merchandise of men, those who take
the profits that belong to the farmers, the laborers and the working people. So the black horseman delivers the karma of the
manipulators of the economies of the nations and of the abundant
life God gave us.

The result of this manipulation by the archdeceivers of mankind is world famine. The prices the "auctioneer" is quoting are
famine prices. According to *The Interpreter's Bible,* in the first
century a measure of wheat for a penny would have been eight to
sixteen times the normal price and three measures of barley for a
penny would have also been "likewise far out of line."[43]

What we are seeing, then, is an establishment of the power
elite that has sucked up the light, the energy and the lifeblood of
the people. And because the people have disobeyed the laws of
God by giving their people-power to leaders who would use it to
betray them, they are vulnerable to the rape of soul and body. The
people have fallen prey to the divide-and-conquer tactics of devils
incarnate, who line them up in opposing camps according to the
isms of the fallen angels, setting brother against brother East
and West when they should unite under the banner of Micah, the
Angel of Unity.

The age of Aquarius is a time when Lightbearers must unite
to defeat these enemies wherever and whenever and through
whomever they strike. We have to take control of our money
supply, our interest rates, our banking houses and the life-force
of the nations. This is a global problem. But global problems are
not beyond the reach of the people. To effectively challenge the
forces of Darkness that have invaded our planet we must call upon
the LORD, the I AM THAT I AM, and invoke the intercession of
the Archangels and the heavenly hosts.

Divine intervention is the key to our deliverance in this age, but that doesn't mean we just sit and wait for the Faithful and True and the armies of heaven to come to the rescue, galloping in on their white horses. By all means, we should invoke the King of kings and Lord of lords,[44] but we must also work the works of God here on earth by actively challenging, point-counterpoint, those who misrepresent "we the people" in their citadels of power worldwide.

The black horseman is the first to deliver his karma into the physical octave. The second and the third horsemen, the white and the red, follow close behind ready to deliver theirs. And the last in line, the pale horseman, is at a great distance. His karma is not yet due.

What do these four riders bring? The black horseman brings economic debacle, "a pair of balances in his hand," weighing the commodities of nations and the karma of souls. The white horseman brings war, with bow and crown, "conquering and to conquer." This rider represents (among other eventualities) the United States engaged in wars small and great outside her borders. The red horseman, to whom is given a great sword and the power to take peace from the earth, also brings war. The red rider represents (among other eventualities) the Soviet Union engaged in wars outside her borders. Death rides the pale horse and Hell follows. And Death is as Death does: The Two kill with sword, famine and plague.

One month after I received this vision, at Thanksgiving 1986, Saint Germain said:

> Economic debacle is foreseen. Prepare. Setbacks will be sudden. Be not lulled by the heyday. Many Band-Aids upon the economy, the money system, the banking houses. These will not prevent the collapse of nations and banking houses built on sands of human greed, ambition, and manipulation of the lifeblood of the people of God.
>
> For they shall not prevail who have built their empires on the backs of the children of God who bear in their bodies the very Blood of Christ. . . .
>
> The law of karma is inexorable, irrevocable, saving where the violet flame, the sacred fire, does consume [mankind's karma].[45]

As the vision progressed into 1987, from time to time I would see the black horseman. One October evening in 1987 I was making calls at the altar of our chapel at the Royal Teton Ranch for the healing of the economies of the nations. I looked up and

saw the black horseman directly in front of me. I raised my right
hand and called to Almighty God to stop the black horse. The
horse reared up on its hind legs and was frozen in his stance by the
Right Hand of God. I knew that the moment the horse came down,
there would be a crisis in the economy.

Then on October 3, 1987, before anyone had an inkling of the
stock market crash to come, Saint Germain said in New York City,
"Thus, the 'spiritual wickedness in high places' of this city . . . is a
manipulation in money matters beyond conception. And therefore
I say, Woe! Woe! Woe! Let the judgments descend upon those who
manipulate the abundant life of a people of God and subject them
to a slavery untold far beyond that of the Egyptian taskmasters!"[46]

Saint Germain then delivered "The Speaking of the LORD
God:"

> And the golden-calf civilization does go down! And the
> Cain civilization is judged! For no longer is the Cain civili-
> zation protected by the mark of Cain. It is no more.

> And therefore, let the fallen ones know that the hour is
> come that they must pay the price for the shedding of the
> blood of the holy innocents and of the sons of God and of the
> prophets and of the Christs. Therefore, let them tremble! For
> I come into their citadel of international power and moneyed
> interests. And I AM, of the LORD God, do declare unto you
> that through my Archangels they shall know the judgment.[47]

That was the third of October; on the sixth the market
plunged a record 91.55 points.

At 3 a.m. EST Monday, October 19, I was awakened by Saint
Germain. I saw the black horse come down on all four hooves, race
around me and go beyond me, the white horse galloping after.
There was no stopping either of them. I knew that the karma of
the economies of the nations had descended. And that war would
be next. On that day the market dropped 508 points, the biggest
drop in history, and the United States destroyed two Iranian oil
platforms.

The horsemen are moving toward the present, each in his
turn. As the days pass and the sands in the hourglass fall, we
must prepare ourselves to face the karma they will surely deliver
according to the commands of the Four Beasts.

There is a cycle when the horsemen can be held back and
there is a cycle when they cannot. Day by day the moving vision of
the Four Horsemen is before me. When I tell people what I see,
they don't seem to comprehend what I am saying. They have

already been lulled into a false peace. I call it karma stupefaction. If they feel uneasy, they cover it over with their pleasures, their businesses, their livelihoods, their concerns and their families. And, I am sorry to say, the Lightbearers are not galvanized. They sit around and talk about past lives instead of getting together in the zeal of the LORD to shout their dynamic decrees and then go out and challenge evildoers with the fire of the ancient prophets.

People ask me if I am concerned, if I feel that the situation is "really intense." I am profoundly concerned. And it *is* intense. This is why I am delivering this message at my stumps across North America and Europe. I will speak it wherever I am heard.

Invocation of the Violet Flame

In my book *The Science of the Spoken Word* I teach you how to invoke the violet flame.[48] I would like to invite you to give a dynamic decree with me so you can see what it's like to call forth the violet flame from the heart of God. But first, just so we all know what we're talking about, I'd like to give a word of explanation.

An invocation is "the act or process of petitioning for help or support; a prayer of entreaty (as at the beginning of a service of worship)."[49] In our usage it is also "a calling upon the authority of God to ratify our righteous use of the violet flame on earth as in heaven."

"To invoke" is "to petition the Lord for help, to call to his Archangels for support"; "to make of him an earnest request for his grace and mercy, to solicit divine intercession"; and "to call forth by incantation."[50] An "incantation" is "a written or recited formula of words designed to produce a particular effect," and "to incant" is "to recite" or "to utter."[51]

The ritual of spiritual invocation therefore requires the exercise of the spoken Word. When we raise up our voices to praise the Lord and to offer prayers in the name of Jesus Christ, we are exercising the throat chakra. This chakra, the power center, corresponds to the First Ray of God's will, protection and perfection, and our supreme faith in his Word. The color of this chakra and ray is a beautiful sapphire blue; the diamond and the sapphire are its corresponding gemstones.

Through this chakra we receive from our Mighty I AM Presence the gift of speech, which is the empowerment to create by the science of the spoken Word. Without it we would be powerless to invoke divine intercession. By its masterful use we may bless all life as instruments of the Word of our Father-Mother God.

Saint Germain said on May 28, 1986: "We must have the physical sounding of the Word. This is the purpose of the dynamic decree as the most efficient and accelerated means of forestalling those things coming upon the earth or upon the individual as the outplaying of karma."[52]

This is what the violet flame is all about. That's why I have put together four 90-minute violet flame cassettes, *Save the World with Violet Flame! by Saint Germain 1–4* (along with booklets containing all the words).[53] I recommend that you use these violet flame cassettes daily for your soul's advancement on the path and for the healing of our diseased planet, starting with cassette 1 until you become proficient and can work up to greater speeds on tapes 2, 3 and 4.

So let's give a dynamic decree as our invocation to God and to Arcturus and Victoria, God's manifestation as Elohim on the Seventh Ray. This call is delivered through the throat chakra as a "worded formula," if you will, that unlocks the light, energy and consciousness of the violet flame from our Father-Mother God personified in the twin flames of Arcturus and Victoria. For theirs is the consciousness of God that ensouls the age of Aquarius and the seventh dispensation at the Elohimic level, the same level from which the creation was brought forth as recorded in the Book of Genesis.

Please turn in your books to decree number 70.18, "Arcturus, Blessed Being Bright." If you knew just how powerful and accessible the Elohim are and how you can experience the consciousness of God as Elohim on the Seventh Ray when you call forth their tremendous momentum of the violet flame, I can assure you that you would not miss a day of calling to them!

I want you to have these song and decree tapes so you can play them in your homes, offices and cars, and on your headsets while exercising and traveling, in order to flood the world with violet flame and break down the artificial barriers between Lightbearers. Before we can bear the freedom flame of Aquarius to the world, we the people of North America must first come together in our hearts, because we are a people of the heart.

You can give this decree to Arcturus to saturate the Nature kingdom and Mother Earth with the violet transmuting flame. It is well that we give it on behalf of elemental life, the fiery salamanders, sylphs, undines and gnomes who are Nature's keepers of fire, air, water and earth. These elementals are charged by God with keeping the balance of forces in the earth, but they are bowed down with the weight of mankind's pollution of the elements as well as by the karma of man's inhumanity to man. To lighten their load and brighten our auras let us give this invocation to the Elohim Arcturus and Victoria and their decree which follows.

Arcturus, Blessed Being Bright

Beloved Mighty Victorious Presence of God I AM in me, thou immortal unfed flame of Christ-love burning within my heart, Holy Christ Selves of all mankind, beloved mighty Elohim Arcturus and Victoria, beloved Saint Germain and Portia, Zadkiel and Holy Amethyst, the Lords of Karma, Omri-Tas, Ruler of the Violet Planet, and 144,000 priests of the sacred fire from the heart of the violet planet, beloved Great Divine Director, Zarathustra, Melchizedek and Kuan Yin, all great beings, powers and activities of Light serving the Violet Flame, beloved Lanello, the entire Spirit of the Great White Brotherhood and the World Mother, elemental life—fire, air, water and earth!

In the name and by the magnetic power of the Presence of God which I AM and by the magnetic power of the sacred fire vested in me, I invoke the mighty presence and power of your full-gathered momentum of service to the Light of God that never fails, and I command that it be directed throughout all mankind, elemental life and the angelic hosts serving earth's evolutions.

Blaze thy dazzling light of a thousand suns throughout the earth and transmute all that is not of the Light into the God-victorious, light all-glorious, flaming Jesus Christ perfection.

In thy name, O God, I decree:

    1. O Arcturus, blessed being bright,
        Flood, flood, flood our world with Light;
        Bring forth perfection everywhere,
        Hear, O hear our earnest prayer.

Refrain: Charge us with thy Violet Flame,
        Charge, O charge us in God's name;
        Anchor in us all secure,
        Cosmic radiance, make us pure.

    2. O Arcturus, blessed Elohim,
        Let thy Light all through us stream;
        Complement our souls with Love
        From thy stronghold up above.

    3. O Arcturus, Violet Flame's great Master,
        Keep us safe from all disaster;
        Secure us in the cosmic stream,
        Help expand God's loving dream.

4. O Arcturus, dearest Lord of might,
    By thy star radiance beaming bright,
    Fill us with thy cosmic Light,
    Raise, O raise us to thy height.

Astrology's Prophecy on the Economy

I would like to review for you prophecies for the 1990s concerning the economy that I gave in San Francisco on February 13, 1988. But first let me repeat once and for all that these prophecies do not have to happen! Wherever I deliver Saint Germain's prophecy, this is the message: God has given you the power to change yourself and your world. Use it!

When we can read the handwriting in the skies and then calculate the geometry of our karma outlined in our astrology, we can make incisive calls to the Seven Archangels and other great beings of Light to enter our worlds on the precise lines and degrees of both positive and negative aspects in our astrological charts. For, you see, your chart is an extension of yourself. Like the rings of Saturn or the belt of Orion, your chart is with you wherever you go.

And so we can call to our Mighty I AM Presence and Holy Christ Self and to Saint Germain and Portia to direct the violet flame into all positive and negative portents of our astrology for the maximum resolution of our karma and the balancing of relationships. And once we get on top of our own worlds, with the violet singing flame, as it is called, we can be God's instruments to mitigate or entirely transmute world karma.

Personal and national charts, when accurately read, are a means of predicting and interpreting coming events—providing we do so by the gifts of the Holy Spirit. But just as important, they give us the information we need to formulate a specific prayer for the Ascended Masters and angelic hosts to stand between us and a calamity foreseen.

Remember, the Magi predicted the date and place of Jesus' birth in Bethlehem by their knowledge of astronomy and astrology. And by that prediction they, instead of Herod, who would have killed the child, arrived at the scene to bless the "King of the Jews." (Herod had told the wise men to "bring him word" when they found the young child, but God warned them in a dream not to return to Herod; and "they departed into their own country another way."[54])

The period we are entering is unique, both in its opportunity for progress and in its potential for destruction. We stand on the pinnacle of an age; and which way the age shall go, whether it shall be known as the golden age of Aquarius or the dark age of Aquarius, depends on the decisions we the people of North America make in the coming days.

The first series of predictions deals with the economy. As I noted earlier, Saint Germain predicted economic debacle on Thanksgiving 1986. At that time, astrological indicators of an economic downturn were also evident, something I pointed out in my July 4, 1987 address. Then on October 3, 1987, Saint Germain pronounced the judgment on Wall Street, and we saw the fateful crash of October 19.

Although government figures are optimistic, the state of the economy (especially the record levels of debt) and astrology show that we are in for a major economic crisis. And historically, the Canadian economy and dollar have closely followed the U.S. economy and dollar. If crisis hits the United States, it will hit Canada too. Like it or not, the power elite who are "doing in" the U.S. economy are tied to the power elite in Canada and every other country. Their network spans the continents.

On February 22–23, 1988, there was a major conjunction* of four planets in Capricorn: Mars, Saturn, Uranus and Neptune (fig. 1). Mars moved on, but the three larger planets will continue to form a series of conjunctions in Capricorn until February 1991.

Saturn-Uranus-Neptune conjunctions are extremely rare. The last one took place in 1307 in Scorpio. It was the primary astrological impulse for the Black Death in the fourteenth century, which eventually killed one-third of the population of Europe. The current conjunction in Capricorn marks the formal starting point of a period of upheaval and change on the planet.

Capricorn is an earth sign governed by the planet Saturn. It tends to limit or bring to an end unrealistic behavior. Capricorn is associated with hard times, difficult challenges, recessions and depressions, delays, lack of opportunity, and limitation or loss of freedom due to increased governmental authority. Under its influence, people are often pessimistic and depressed; they become the victims of their own sense of limitation.

The onset of the Great Depression was marked by a conjunction of five planets in Capricorn on December 31, 1929. Since Neptune entered Capricorn in January 1984, oil prices have fallen and the dollar has declined. This illustrates the effect of just one of the large, outer planets in Capricorn.

*An exact conjunction occurs when planets occupy the same degree of the zodiac. The orb, or space in which a conjunction is effective, is 10 degrees. Conjunctions combine planetary influences and start a cycle of experience.

Conjunction of Mars, Saturn, Uranus and Neptune in Capricorn
February 22-23, 1988

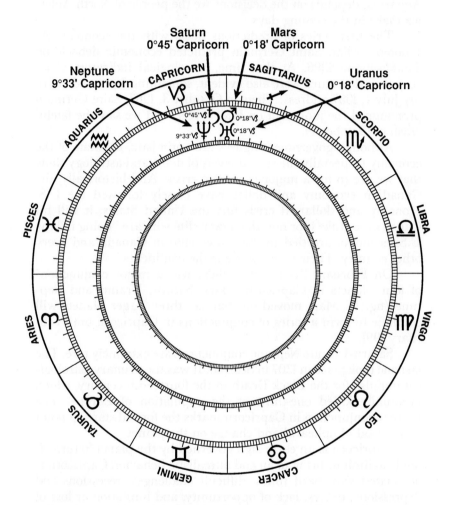

FIGURE 1 On February 22-23, 1988, Mars, Saturn, Uranus and Neptune formed a conjunction that marked the formal beginning of a period of upheaval and change on the planet. This conjunction occurred in two steps. On February 22 at 3:49 p.m. EST, Mars made an exact conjunction to Uranus at 0°18′ Capricorn. Then, at 8:01 a.m. EST on the 23rd, Mars made an exact conjunction to Saturn at 0°45′ Capricorn. Neptune was at 9°33′ Capricorn. A conjunction occurs when two or more planets occupy the same degree of the zodiac, although aspects need not be exact to be within the "orb of influence." I usually allow a 10° orb for major aspects. A rare Saturn-Uranus-Neptune conjunction is the core of this configuration. The last one occurred in 1307 and was the primary astrological impulse for the Black Death.

The February 1988 conjunction in Capricorn marks the beginning of the second leg of the economic downturn that began October 19, 1987, with the stock market crash. During this downturn the era of financial expansion related to oil and international finance will come to a halt and, with the exception of one last expansionary period when Saturn and Uranus return to Sagittarius between May and December of 1988, national economies will contract.

In the years following this conjunction, nations will become conservative and reactionary, there will be massive debt liquidation, the real price of commodities will fall, and a pessimistic mood will sweep the earth. The potential for war is great and the United States government will be in danger of being destroyed or reformed beyond recognition.

When you know that economic collapse and war are possibilities, you should position yourself strategically in time and space and in your Higher Consciousness. And from the point of greatest strength, you should direct the Light of God through your chakras into conditions like this that could manifest in the physical plane. I advise you to prepare yourself spiritually, psychologically and physically for whatever may happen. And then pronounce the fiat in your heart to Almighty God *that you will get to the light of your Christhood at the end of the tunnel of personal and planetary darkness that you are passing through.*

The next big drop in the stock market as well as in the economy is likely to come around November 13, 1989, when Saturn makes its exact conjunction to Neptune at 10° Capricorn and both make an exact opposition* to Jupiter at 10° Cancer.

This configuration, as we shall see, will have a special significance for Canada. It will also affect more than the United States stock market. It will be a critical factor in triggering major debt liquidation and could lead to the dissolution of much of the Western banking system.

After all, how long can the Federal Reserve system crank out more and more paper dollars before those paper dollars become worth less and less until they are "worthless"? You can only slice the pie so many times before it's no longer sliceable!

The Capricorn conjunctions beginning in February 1988 tell us that a testing and an initiation of our planet is at hand. The Maha Chohan said on February 21, 1988, in Beverly Hills, California:

---

*An exact opposition occurs when planets are 180 degrees apart from each other in the zodiac. The orb, or space in which an opposition is effective, is 10 degrees. Oppositions show either union and cooperation or separation and conflict.

I am known as the Maha Chohan; and therefore, beloved, understand that I represent to you not only the Holy Spirit but the initiations of that Spirit.

I have come, then, to deliver to this city the mandate of the Holy Spirit . . . .

Blessed ones, you have heard the interpretation of the four planets in Capricorn. One must understand that they represent the deliverance of the Holy Spirit's initiations to a planet; and as the result of the consequences of the violation of the Holy Ghost in little children, in Nature and [in] the defilement of the body and the soul, you will see that *unless these things are turned around and a people invoke the Light of their God and fulfill the Law of Love, those things projected will come to pass.*

This [astrological] configuration is the testing of the four lower bodies of a planet and a people.[55]

There are other Capricorn conjunctions in the 1990s that will have a major effect on the world. On January 11, 1994, seven planets*—Mars, Venus, Neptune, the Moon, the Sun, Uranus and Mercury—will form a tight "megaconjunction" in Capricorn (fig. 2). Another configuration that adds to the intensity of this conjunction is the square† of Saturn, the planet which rules Capricorn, in Aquarius to Pluto in Scorpio.

Under the influence of this conjunction we could experience economic and military challenges. We could see a dramatic loss of political liberty throughout the world, the establishment of dictatorships, widespread plague and famine, and danger from radioactivity, possibly from nuclear war.

The Ascended Lady Master Kuan Yin told us that we can call for the mitigation of the influence of these astrological configurations by a renewed dispensation of the violet flame. On February 14, 1988, the day after I had delivered an address on astrology from 1988 through the 1990s, Kuan Yin said in San Francisco:

I come to you this evening representing the Lords of Karma and I come, beloved, to tell you that this is the hour when you may appeal to the Lords of Karma for a dispensation of Mercy's flame, [which is the] violet flame, when you make the request to use that dispensation specifically for the mitigation, turning back, [or] transmutation of those prophecies told to you last evening.

---

*Astrologers acknowledge that the Sun and Moon are not planets, but they sometimes refer to them as such for convenience. †An exact square occurs when planets are 90 degrees apart from each other in the zodiac. The orb, or space in which a square is effective, is 10 degrees. Squares generate tension, which may be creative or destructive.

Megaconjunction of Seven Planets in Capricorn
January 11, 1994

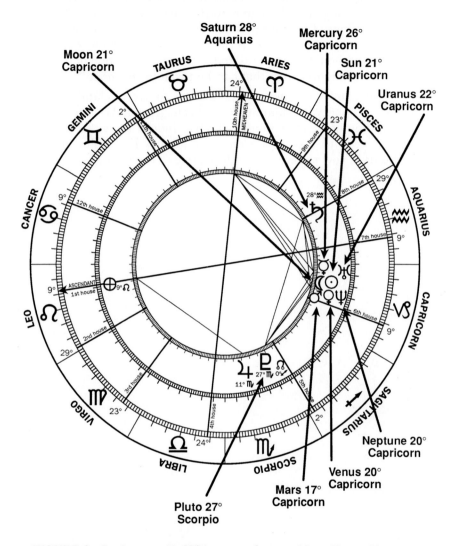

FIGURE 2 On January 11, 1994, seven planets—Mars, Venus, Neptune, the Moon, the Sun, Uranus and Mercury—will form a very tight "megaconjunction" in Capricorn. All seven planets will fall between 17° and 26° Capricorn. A nearly exact square of Saturn, the ruler of Capricorn, at 28° Aquarius to Pluto at 27° Scorpio is likely to intensify the conjunction's negative potential. This conjunction could trigger economic and military challenges in the extreme, the dramatic loss of political liberty throughout the world, the establishment of dictatorships, widespread plague and famine and danger from radioactivity, possibly from nuclear war.

Therefore, all who will join me in the Bodhisattva vow for the saving of Lightbearers in the earth, to you I say, the extraordinary Light of the violet flame is given to those who will direct it and invest it in the saving of that which could be lost without that impetus and in the transmutation of the karma of Lightbearers that can be taken in this hour.[56]

Opportunity has never been greater to avert calamity. Nor has the prophecy of calamity ever been greater. We need this dispensation of Mercy's flame, which is indeed the violet flame. And we need to take action on it by joining Kuan Yin in her Bodhisattva vow to save the Lightbearers of the world!

4

A Prophecy of War:

He that hath ears to hear, let him hear and act in time!

Astrology shows that the period between February 1988 and December 1992 will be a time of karmic summing up. We are likely to see the reform, disruption or dissolution of economic and political systems, revolution, major cataclysm and war.

As you ponder these prophecies, remember that prophecy is sent by God so that those who have ears to hear *will hear* and *will act* in time. They must act to save their souls through supplications to God and they must act to mitigate that prophecy, or turn it back entirely, through prayers to the Holy Spirit for the conversion of mankind to the Lord.

When the prophets of Israel and Judah warned the people of Yahweh's judgments they would say, "If you do not repent of your indulgences, your going after pleasure and selfish pursuits and the murdering of your firstborn, if you do not take care of the poor, the LORD will deliver these calamities upon you."

In the words of the prophet Ezekiel:

> Therefore I will judge you, O house of Israel, every one according to his ways, saith the Lord GOD. Repent, and turn yourselves from all your transgressions; so iniquity shall not be your ruin.
>
> Cast away from you all your transgressions, whereby ye have transgressed; and make you a new heart and a new spirit: for why will ye die, O house of Israel?
>
> For I have no pleasure in the death of him that dieth, saith the Lord GOD: wherefore turn yourselves, and live ye.[57]

And in the words of the prophet Isaiah:

> Wash you, make you clean; put away the evil of your doings from before mine eyes; cease to do evil;

Learn to do well; seek judgment, relieve the oppressed, judge the fatherless, plead for the widow.

Come now, and let us reason together, saith the LORD: though your sins be as scarlet, they shall be as white as snow; though they be red like crimson, they shall be as wool.

If ye be willing and obedient, ye shall eat the good of the land:

But if ye refuse and rebel, ye shall be devoured with the sword: for the mouth of the LORD hath spoken it.[58]

God delivered the karma of Israel and Judah by allowing neighboring states such as Assyria and Babylonia to invade them. Jeremiah said, "Thus saith the LORD, . . . I will give all Judah into the hand of the king of Babylon, and he shall carry them captive into Babylon, and shall slay them with the sword."[59]

History records and akasha will verify that when the children of the Light disobey their Father-Mother God they become vulnerable to "the rulers of the darkness of this world"[60] and reap the karmic consequences. When they do not obey Jesus' Great Commandment: "Thou shalt love the Lord thy God with all thy heart, and with all thy soul, and with all thy mind," and the second, which is like unto it, "Thou shalt love thy neighbour as thyself,"[61] then karma becomes their Teacher.

Karma brings back to our doorstep exactly what we send out. Karma is our unredeemed energy coming for redemption. It is the untransmuted coming for transmutation. It is the unresolved coming for resolution.

Karma teaches us our violations of the laws of physics and metaphysics, of chemistry and spiritual alchemy, and of the balance of forces yang and yin. Any state of mind or being that compromises the equilibrium of the Masculine and Feminine polarity of God within us, any out-of-alignment state in our four lower bodies, begets its own karma that sooner or later will require its own resolution. The law of karma is God's law. It is inexorable. Therefore we say, "Even so, LORD God Almighty, true and righteous are thy judgments."[62]

I would like to tell you that I deliver the prophecies of Saint Germain as I receive them, looking neither to the Right nor to the Left. I am neither liberal nor conservative, nor do I position myself in the middle of the road. Some people ask me why I don't confine myself to spiritual topics, why I speak on political issues. Well, I am a prophet and I come in the tradition of the prophets of Israel and Judah, who spoke out in the midst of political and social upheaval as well as spiritual crisis. They rebuked kings, counsellors, priests, family, friends and enemies alike. And they told the people exactly what they had to do to get on the right side of God and his laws.

Popularity was not their concern. Neither is it mine. Like Jesus, they made themselves of no reputation and took on the form of a servant.[63] But their reputation has followed them to the present. And the voices of these servants of God and of the people still resound in the Holy City.

O Israel, O Judah revisited in this wilderness land, will you not hear, will you not hear?

The Unpopular Prophet

I love the ancient prophets. As a child I turned to them for consolation—and wisdom. They stood apart as gurus fierce and uncompromising in their courage. I was in awe of them. They were my heroes. Today I walk in their shadow, as I would walk in the shadow of the Almighty, a student of their words and their works. God's spokesmen they were as they stood before the mighty men of old, the Nephilim kings, the false prophets and the betrayers of the people—and still stood—until their calling was through.

I want to tell you about Jeremiah. My heart goes out to him. He prophesied death and destruction in a time when people wanted to hear about peace, not war. And he went unheeded for 40 years.

It was a time of upheaval in the Near East—the fall of the Assyrian Empire in 612 B.C. and the rise of the Babylonian empire. The twelve tribes had split into two kingdoms: Israel in the north and Judah in the south, with two capitals, Samaria and Jerusalem. Israel had fallen to the Assyrians in 721 B.C. and most of its inhabitants had been deported. Judah had been a vassal of Assyria and had assimilated its pagan religious practices. When Assyria fell in 612 B.C., Judah gained independence—but only until 609 B.C., when she became an Egyptian vassal.

Jeremiah was called by God to challenge the popular pagan practices. The people had erected altars to a host of foreign gods, whom they worshiped alongside Yahweh. And the fertility cult's sacred prostitution was practiced in the temple at Jerusalem.

To this day the children of God haven't stopped going after idols or misqualifying the sacred fire of God's altar.

Who are you worshipping today? You're worshipping fallen angels—the stars, the celebrities, the rich and the powerful, few having any morality, any principles or any God in them. Your idolatry even extends to yourselves, your materialism and your pleasure cult. You worship sex. You have made a god of it. And these idols that you have placed before your God must come tumbling down!

Jeremiah also challenged social injustice: immorality, official corruption, stealing, murder and lying, as well as oppressing of strangers, orphans and widows. Some of the people even partook of the pagan practice of human sacrifice, making "their sons and daughters pass through fire in honour of Molech."[64]

Child sacrifice—otherwise known as abortion. To deny life is to deny God incarnate. Family planning using scientific methods of birth control is one thing, and it's a good thing, but the practice of abortion as a means of birth control is fraught with the most severe karma and the most severe judgment of Almighty God.

What is abortion? It is the abortion of the divine plan of a soul whose body temple is being nurtured in the womb. God as a living potential, Christ as a living potential, is in that child from the moment of conception. When a father and a mother sacrifice their child to the god of lust, they are killing a part of themselves. Abortion is the greatest crime that has ever been committed by a people against their God.

I believe abortion to be first-degree murder of God. In an interview I gave at Camelot, our headquarters in Los Angeles, in January 1982 I said:

> Abortion is first-degree murder of God. Human government since Noah has existed to protect human life. The nation or the government that creates legislation allowing murder is doomed to go down. It will go down by cataclysm; it will go down by economic collapse. But it *will* go down because it is not consistent with the laws of universal Life.
>
> Now that is a fiat of Almighty God. I didn't originate it but it has the power of the Holy Spirit. It will come to pass. And if America does not refute legalized, tax-supported murder, the judgment will come as surely as it came upon Israel and Judah and every other nation who has murdered its firstborn.[65]

Saint Germain said of that statement:

> Out of the mouth of the Messenger I spoke this day, before a television camera, the pronouncement of God's judgment upon any nation that enacts a law authorizing murder through abortion. The nation that allows these laws to rest upon the books, and therefore to govern life itself, is judged. And unless it be overturned, cataclysm [will be, as it] has always been, the judgment upon those who have defended death, through their own selfishness and self-intent, rather than life in the sacrificial sense.[66]

Twenty-two million abortions, twenty-two million flames snuffed out since 1973—this alone makes America vulnerable to all the prophecies I am speaking about. God help us! God forgive those who know not what they do! And God judge the wicked who do!

Enter Jeremiah. Sent by Yahweh to spark a spiritual revolution.

Sometime around 609 B.C., God directed Jeremiah to go out to the entry of the Gate of the Potsherds, toward the high place of Topheth in the Valley of Ben-hinnom, where the people of Judah practiced child sacrifice, to speak these words:

> Kings of Judah, citizens of Jerusalem! Listen to the word of Yahweh! Yahweh Sabaoth, the God of Israel, says this: I am bringing down such a disaster on this place that the ears of every one who hears of it will ring.
>
> This is because they have abandoned me, have profaned this place, have offered incense here to alien gods [Nephilim gods, fallen angels in their midst] which neither they, nor their ancestors, nor the kings of Judah, ever knew before. They have filled this place with the blood of the innocent.
>
> They have built high places for Baal to burn their sons there, which I had never ordered or decreed; which had never entered my thoughts.
>
> So now the days are coming—it is Yahweh who speaks—when people will no longer call this place Topheth, or the Valley of Ben-hinnom, but Valley of Slaughter.
>
> Because of this place, I mean to drain Judah and Jerusalem of sound advice; I will make them fall by the sword before their enemies, fall by the hand of people determined to kill them; I will give their corpses as food to the birds of heaven and the beasts of earth.
>
> And I will make this city a desolation, a derision; every passer-by will be appalled at it, and whistle in amazement at such calamity.
>
> I will make them eat the flesh of their own sons and daughters: they shall eat each other during the siege, in the shortage to which their enemies, in their determination to kill them, will reduce them.[67]

No sooner had Jeremiah unleashed the words of Yahweh than Pashhur, chief of the temple police, had him arrested, beaten and put in the stocks. The next day, when Pashhur had Jeremiah taken out of the stocks, Jeremiah said to him, "Not Pashhur but Terror is Yahweh's name for you. For Yahweh says this, 'I am going to hand you over to terror, you and all your friends; they shall fall by the sword of their enemies; your own eyes shall see it.' "[68]

The people continued their pagan practices while worshiping Yahweh in the temple, believing they would be protected from his wrath by outer ritual. Jeremiah challenged them, saying their rote performance was not a substitute for moral and ethical conduct. He charged them with a lack of true spirituality and a real relationship with God.

Standing in the gate of the temple, Jeremiah pronounced:

> Yahweh Sabaoth, the God of Israel, says this: Amend your behaviour and your actions and I will stay with you here in this place. Put no trust in delusive words like these: This is the sanctuary of Yahweh, the sanctuary of Yahweh, the sanctuary of Yahweh!. . .
>
> Yet here you are, trusting in delusive words, to no purpose!
>
> Steal, would you, murder, commit adultery, perjure yourselves, burn incense to Baal, follow alien gods that you do not know?—
>
> And then come presenting yourselves in this temple that bears my name, saying: Now we are safe—safe to go on committing all these abominations! Do you take this temple that bears my name for a robbers' den? I, at any rate, am not blind—it is Yahweh who speaks.[69]

Jeremiah did not like prophesying war. But that is exactly what he saw. He said: "I am in anguish! I writhe in pain! Walls of my heart! My heart is throbbing! I cannot keep quiet, for I have heard the trumpet call and the cry of war."[70]

Jeremiah lamented. He said: "Ah, Lord GOD [I AM THAT I AM],. . . here are the prophets telling them, 'You will not see the sword, famine will not touch you; I promise you unbroken peace in this place.' "[71] What did the false prophets cry? "Peace, peace," when there was no peace. Jeremiah said, "They have healed the wound of my people lightly."[72]

They tried to heal the wound of the people with shallow words without going to the root of the problem. The people, who wanted a shortcut to deliverance, refused to come to grips with the judgment that Jeremiah prophesied. They would not bend the knee before their own karma and they were too proud to ask for God's mercy to intercede between themselves and that karma.

Pointing to Israel's exile because of her faithlessness and worship of idols, Jeremiah preached the imminent judgment of

God upon the nation of Judah for its sinfulness. He warned that if the people did not turn wholeheartedly to their God in time, they would meet the same fate as Israel at the hands of an "evil from the North."[73]

Jeremiah's sermons caused an uproar and for a time he was barred from the temple in Jerusalem. He was shunned and ridiculed. His friends deserted him and members of his family betrayed him. The people of his hometown threatened to kill him if he did not cease prophesying "in the name of Yahweh."

In 605 B.C. Babylon defeated Egypt and Judah became a Babylonian vassal. Jeremiah's prophecies spoke of Babylon as the instrument of "a great destruction" by which the LORD would punish Judah for her sins: "Because you have not obeyed my words, behold, I will send for all the tribes of the North, says the LORD, and for Nebuchadnezzar, the king of Babylon, my servant, and I will bring them against this land and its inhabitants, and against all these nations round about. . . . This whole land shall become a ruin and a waste, and these nations shall serve the king of Babylon seventy years."[74]

This is an example of how God chastises a holy people, a chosen people and the seed of Christ, by allowing their karma to descend upon them through pagan nations. Even those who do not worship Yahweh become Yahweh's instrument for the judgment of his people.

About 599 B.C., King Jehoiakim of Judah made a bid for independence. He went against Jeremiah's advice, which was to submit and avoid destruction. In 598 Nebuchadnezzar sent an army to Jerusalem. Jehoiakim died or was assassinated before the Babylonians arrived. His son Jehoiachin surrendered without a fight. Nebuchadnezzar stripped the temple of ornaments, emptied the treasury, carried the king and 3,000 of Jerusalem's leading citizens into exile and placed Zedekiah, Jehoiachin's uncle, on the throne. By the standards of the time, Nebuchadnezzar was lenient with Judah.

But his invasion was not enough; Judah still had not learned her lesson. The people continued to listen to the false prophets of peace, Jeremiah's most influential and troublesome enemies. These played a crucial role in bringing about the wholly unnecessary destruction of Judah.

Rather than admit that Jeremiah had been right all along, they tried to show that this first phase of the Babylonian captivity was but a temporary setback by which God was testing the people. Promising them a glorious future, they enflamed the people to revolt against Babylon, while Jeremiah told them to submit to

Babylon, God's instrument of judgment upon them. The people heard what they wanted to hear. They wanted reassurances of peace. So they listened to the prophets of peace.

As a symbolic gesture, Jeremiah placed a wooden yoke on his neck, saying that Judah should serve the king of Babylon since God had appointed him to rule over them as punishment for Judah's many sins. God said, "Any nation or kingdom that will not submit to Nebuchadnezzar king of Babylon, and will not bow its neck to the yoke of the king of Babylon, I shall punish with sword, famine and plague—it is Yahweh who speaks—until I have delivered it into his power."[75]

But Hananiah, a leading prophet and priest, openly challenged Jeremiah. He said that within two years the LORD would break the power of Babylon and restore the captives. He illustrated his point by taking the wooden yoke off Jeremiah's neck and breaking it.

Jeremiah rebuked Hananiah. He said, "Yahweh says this: You can break wooden yokes? Right, I will make them iron yokes instead! For Yahweh Sabaoth, the God of Israel, says this: An iron yoke is what I now lay on the necks of all these nations to subject them to Nebuchadnezzar king of Babylon." Jeremiah said to Hananiah, "Yahweh [I AM THAT I AM] has not sent you; and thanks to you this people are now relying on what is false."[76] Jeremiah prophesied that Hananiah would die that year. He died within two months.

In 589 B.C., Judah's King Zedekiah was pressured into joining a rebellion against Babylon. Nebuchadnezzar marched swiftly to Judah, destroyed all the fortified cities, and in 588 laid siege to the Holy City, Jerusalem. During the seige, which lasted for nearly one and a half years, "famine was raging in the city and there was no food for the populace."[77]

In 587, the Babylonian soldiers entered the city. They killed Zedekiah's sons before his eyes, blinded him and led him and many of his people into exile. They burned the Temple of Solomon, the pride of Israel for nearly 400 years, and reduced Jerusalem and the walled cities of Judah to ruins.

Today, as in the sixth century B.C., the world has gone after the prophets of peace. I have traveled around the world to deliver the message of Saint Germain; and in some of the places where I have spoken, to my astonishment, people have gotten up and left without even hearing what I had to say. But Saint Germain said to me, "They have not rejected you, they have rejected me."[78] And that's the saddest part.

I am not attached—either to myself or to the message. But I am very attached to Saint Germain and to the saving of souls. I bring you this message because I love you and because I am concerned about you, each one.

You may wonder how I, not knowing you personally, can be sincere in my statement. I assure you that I can be and that I am. I feel a very real heart tie to everyone in whom there burns a desire to serve God. And you who have that sacred fire within your heart and that love of Truth and Freedom, *I know you, I am a part of you.* I meditate upon your hearts and souls daily, I pray for you and I have done so all of my life.

I ask you, then, whether you agree or disagree with what you've heard so far, to bear with me to the end. I don't ask you to accept it. I ask you only to consider it. I don't ask you to convert to my belief system but only to understand that I come as your sister on the Path and as your friend to give you this message from my heart.

Prophecy at Fátima and Medjugorje

At Fátima, Portugal, in 1917, Mother Mary prophesied war for our time when she gave three shepherd children a secret in three parts. The first and second concerned World War II and the rise of the Soviet Union. Before giving the children the first secret, the Blessed Mother gave them a vision of Hell. Then she said:

> You have seen hell where the souls of poor sinners go. To save them, God wishes to establish in the world devotion to my Immaculate Heart. If what I say to you is done, many souls will be saved and there will be peace. The war is going to end [World War I]; but if people do not cease offending God, a worse one will break out during the pontificate of Pius XI. When you see a night illumined by an unknown light, know that this is the great sign given you by God that he is about to punish the world for its crimes, by means of war, famine, and persecutions of the Church and of the Holy Father.[*]
>
> To prevent this, I shall come to ask for the consecration of Russia to my Immaculate Heart, and the Communion of Reparation on the First Saturdays. If my requests are heeded, Russia will be converted, and there will be peace; if not, she will spread her errors throughout the world, causing

[*]On the evening of January 25, 1938, the night was illumined by an ominous red glow that lit the entire sky. It lasted for five hours and was seen throughout Europe, part of America, Asia and Africa. Scientists tried to explain it as an extraordinary manifestation of the aurora borealis. On March 14, 1938, Hitler made his triumphal march into Vienna, annexing Austria, and on September 1, 1939, he invaded Poland.

wars and persecutions of the Church. The good will be martyred, the Holy Father will have much to suffer, various nations will be annihilated. In the end, my Immaculate Heart will triumph. The Holy Father will consecrate Russia to me, and she will be converted, and a period of peace will be granted to the world."[79]

In her six visitations Mother Mary told the children to recite the rosary every day "to obtain peace for the world."

On June 13, 1929, Our Lady appeared to Sister Lucia, the eldest of the shepherd children, and said, "The moment has come in which God asks the Holy Father, in union with all the bishops of the world, to make the consecration of Russia to my Immaculate Heart, promising to save it by this means."[80]

Although the popes have made various consecrations, including Pope John Paul II's consecration of the world to the Immaculate Heart of Mary on March 25, 1984, they have never followed the Blessed Mother's instructions for the consecration of Russia as communicated to them through Lucia. In 1987, Lucia told an Argentine journalist that Russia had not been properly consecrated and that unless there was a worldwide conversion featuring prayer and sacrifice, all nations would fall under Communist rule.[81]

Even if the pope were to correctly consecrate Russia to Mother Mary's Immaculate Heart, it may already be too late. In 1931 Lucia received a vision of Jesus. He said, "They have not chosen to heed my command....They will do it, but it will be late. Russia will already have spread her errors throughout the world, provoking wars and persecutions against the Church; the Holy Father will have much to suffer."[82]

The third Fátima secret was to be revealed by 1960. But the popes, ignoring the Blessed Mother's directive, have never disclosed it. However, in 1963 a German periodical, *Neues Europa,* published what it called an "extract" of the third secret:

> A great chastisement will come over all mankind; not today or tomorrow but in the second half of the twentieth century....Humanity has not developed as God desired. Mankind has been sacrilegious and has trampled under foot the wondrous Blessing of God. No longer does Order reign anywhere. Even in the highest places Satan reigns and directs the course of things. Satan will succeed in infiltrating into the highest positions in the Church. Satan will succeed in sowing confusion in the minds of scientists who design weapons that can destroy great portions of mankind

in short periods. Satan will gain hold of heads of nations and will cause these destructive weapons to be mass produced.

If mankind will not oppose these evils, I will be obliged to let the Arm of my Son drop in vengeance. If the chief rulers of the world and of the Church will not actively oppose these evils, I will ask God my Father to bring His Justice to bear on mankind. Then will God punish mankind even more severely and heavily than He did at the time of the great deluge. The great and powerful will perish the same as the lowly and meek. But a time of very severe Trial is also coming for the Church. Cardinals will oppose Cardinals and Bishops will oppose Bishops. Satan will enter into their very midst. In Rome also will occur great changes. What is rotten will fall and what falls must not be retained. The Church will be obscured and all the world will be thrown into great confusion.

The great, great war will come in the second half of the twentieth century. Fire and smoke will drop from heaven and the waters of the ocean will turn to steam throwing their foam to the very sky. Whatever is standing will be overturned. Millions of people will die. Those surviving will envy the dead. Distress, misery and desolation will be found the world over. The time is drawing nearer and the abyss is ever deepening and there will be no escape; the good will die with the wicked, the great with the lowly, the Prince of the Church with the wicked, the rulers of the nation with their people. Death will reign everywhere, raised to triumph by erring men, the helpers of Satan who will be the masters of the earth. These evils will come at a time when no one expects it, nevertheless it must come as punishment and revenge in accordance with God's plan.

The age of ages is coming, the end of all ends if mankind will not repent and be converted and if this conversion does not come from rulers of the world and of the Church. Woe and greater woe to mankind if conversion does not occur.

Later, however, those who survive those trials, if they will repent and will call upon God in submission to His Will and become true followers of Jesus Christ my Son, I will gather them and become their intercessor. But woe and more woe if that conversion does not occur.[83]

The authenticity of the *Neues Europa* quote has been challenged. Some analysts say that it is much longer than the secret Sister Lucia wrote out for the pope.

However, in 1980, according to the German magazine *Stimme des Glaubens,* Pope John Paul II told a group of German Catholics who asked him about the third secret that "because of the seriousness of its contents" and because it might encourage Communist coups, the popes had chosen not to reveal the secret. "If there is a message in which it is said that the oceans will flood entire sections of the earth; that, from one moment to the other, millions of people will perish...there is no longer any point in really wanting to publish this secret message."[84]

Now, I ask you, why would the pope allude to such calamities if they were not a part of the third secret?

John Paul then took his rosary and said, "Here is the remedy against all evil! Pray, pray and ask for nothing else. Put everything in the hands of the Mother of God!"[85]

I must say that by not telling us the third secret, the pope has deprived us of the message Mother Mary wanted us to have so that we could prepare for the "great chastisement" and the "great, great war" and offer prayers and penances to avert it. It is incomprehensible to me how succeeding popes could disobey the Blessed Mother's directive. However, I judge them not.

Another clue to the content of the third secret came from Sister Lucia. She said that the third secret could be found in the Gospel and the Apocalypse.[86] For example, the ride of the Four Horsemen and the prophecy that "every mountain and island were moved out of their places,"[87] do correspond to the *Neues Europa* quote as well as to the pope's allusion to the content of the third secret.

Mother Mary said on May 15, 1983, dictating through me, "The day is at hand and far spent, and the prophecies of Fátima will surely come to pass in the full ferocity of karmic law if the body of God outside the Church does not reject the infamy within and stand for the victory and the fullness of the descent of the Son of God."[88]

The meaning is clear: If Catholics within the Church will not take their stand against the Church hierarchy's abuse of power and money and their sacred trust, then Christians outside of the Church must do so.

In 1972 Mother Mary gave me her rosary for the New Age. First she outlined her eight 45-minute services, one for each day of the week and two for Sunday. These are the Teaching Mysteries, the Love Mysteries, the Joyful Mysteries, the Healing Mysteries, the Initiatic Mysteries, the Glorious Mysteries, the Miracle Mysteries and the Masterful Mysteries. Then she gave me her five

Love-Ray mysteries for weeknight evenings, and finally her 15-minute Child's Rosary, all of which are available on cassette.[89]

These prayer vigils with Mother Mary are centered upon the recitation of the Hail Mary in this manner:

> Hail, Mary, full of grace
>   The Lord is with thee.
> Blessed art thou among women
>   and blessed is the fruit
>   of thy womb, Jesus.
>
> Holy Mary, Mother of God,
> Pray for us, Sons and Daughters of God,
> Now and at the hour of our Victory
> Over sin, disease, and death.

Mother Mary explained that we are no longer sinners once we have confessed and repented of our sins, and we should not forever label ourselves so. And we need her most not in the hour of death (which is not real in any case) but in the moment of our victory over the forces of sin, disease and death, who assail our souls' ascent to God every step of the way—in life and in death.

In the rosaries, the Hail Mary and the Our Father (called the "I AM Lord's Prayer" in its New Age version) are alternated with verses of scripture taken from the Gospels, the epistles and Revelation. They also include the "Transfiguring Affirmations of Jesus the Christ," the Gloria Patri, "The Keeper's Daily Prayer" (a modern-day Apostles' Creed) and hymns to Mother Mary. Our Hail Mary is our salutation to the Mother Flame in Mother Mary as well as in the sacred fire of the Feminine Ray that rises upon the spinal altar. The rosary is our key to union with the Divine Mother East and West by the Immaculate Heart of Mary—in which we trust.

On June 25, 1981, Mother Mary began a series of appearances to four girls and two boys in Medjugorje, Yugoslavia. She has been appearing daily ever since. She is giving each of them 10 messages, or secrets, concerning the future of the world. These secrets are to be announced three days before they happen. I have no reason to doubt the authenticity of Mother Mary's messages to these six teenagers.

One of the visionaries, Mirjana, is now 23 years old. Regarding the secrets, she has said: "At times, I can hardly cope with it when I seriously think of it."[90] She tells us, "The ninth and tenth secrets are serious. They concern chastisement for the sins of the world. Punishment is inevitable, for we cannot expect the whole world to be converted. The punishment can be diminished by prayer and penance, but it cannot be eliminated."[91]

The events predicted by the Blessed Virgin are near, Mirjana says. Therefore she proclaims to the world, "Hurry, be converted; open your hearts to God."[92]

Dictating through me on February 26, 1988, in Lisbon, Portugal, Archangel Gabriel explained why the Medjugorje secrets are not to be revealed until three days before they happen. He said, "As you know, not unto this hour has any pope. . .so revealed that third secret of Fátima; and this is why Mother Mary appeared again at Medjugorje to the children. But this time those secrets could not be revealed on time [for the nations to act], for the very karma of the Church itself in not delivering her first messages."[93]

I might add to this that it is also the karma of the people who have not heeded even the first Fátima messages and repented and been converted in an all-out devotion to Almighty God.

Saint Thérèse of Lisieux, dictating in Mexicali, Mexico, on February 6, 1988, said:

> We say to you that a Body of Light upon earth is needed immediately in order to stay the hand of world destruction! Many of you are acquainted, then, with the prophecies of Fátima and of Medjugorje and need not have these rehearsed to you. The days are growing short that this prophecy may be turned around and transmuted.
>
> If you could see what the Messenger sees, I assure you that you would make this calling, this election a daily priority in your lives: to offer the calls to the violet flame and the rosary to Saint Michael the Archangel and to Mother Mary. Recognize, beloved, that it will take millions who will invoke the violet flame to transmute world karma.[94]

On February 4, 1988, Archangel Michael said, "Beloved hearts, the 'great war' prophesied can yet be turned back! Let it be done, then, by those who have heard, those who are of the wise ones who will understand."[95]

But on March 1, 1988, Mother Mary, dictating through me during a seminar at Fátima, Portugal, said:

> Blessed hearts, the Fátima message has not changed. You must understand this. Though I have dictated [on my] desire to turn it around and in some areas there has been a mitigation, what is the true cause of this prophecy continuing is that those to whom it has been given, those who have occupied the chair of Peter, these have chosen not to relate it

to the heads of state of free nations. They have chosen not to call congresses of the faithful across all lines of religious belief to warn, to organize, to summon and to rally the forces of freedom worldwide from the beginning to defeat the ugly beast of World Communism. And thus it has grown and it has become a planetary dragon. . . .

Therefore, beloved, it is certainly a truth that in this age my Son will not allow these deprivations of the Light [of the Divine Mother] in the earth to continue. Know, then, beloved, that the hour is long past that this judgment should have taken place. But for the faithful who have given the rosary, but for yourselves whose calls have been powerful and an immense barrier to the acceleration of World Communism, all these things should have already come to pass.

Nevertheless, in the interim greater preparations have been made by these forces of the fallen ones. Therefore, beloved, it must be unmistakable in your awareness that the plan for Europe is no ordinary war. You may not think back on World War II and say to yourselves, "I will stay and hold the balance and somehow survive" or "I will get out at the last minute."

Blessed ones, if (and I say if, for nothing is final until it is physical), but if and when such a war should take place, it should be a blitzkrieg such as none has ever seen. And this lightning war should descend as chemical death, as biological/bacteriological death along with those forces of modern weapons and warfare. Understand, therefore, that should it take place the devastation would be almost instantaneous.[96]

Nostradamus Predicts Nuclear War

Turning our attention to other prophecies, we find that the quatrains of Nostradamus predict war for the twentieth century. A number of these quatrains (which I have discussed in greater detail in my book *Saint Germain On Prophecy*) describe what could only be nuclear war. Quatrain VI.97 reads:

> At forty-five degrees the sky will burn,
> Fire to approach the great new city:
> In an instant a great scattered flame will leap up,
> When one will want to demand proof of the Normans.[97]

Saint Germain showed me that Nostradamus was describing a nuclear airburst from a warhead aimed at New York City at a 45-degree angle. A line from quatrain I.64 reads, "They will think they have seen the Sun at night."[98] In 1945 civilians who unknowingly saw an atomic explosion said it "was just like the sun had come up and then suddenly gone down again."[99]

Quatrain V.8 says:

> There will be unleashed live fire, hidden death,
> Horrible and frightful within the globes,
> By night the city reduced to dust by the fleet,
> The city afire, the enemy amenable.[100]

In a nuclear war the United States and the Soviet Union are most likely to be the protagonists. Modern commentators incorrectly believe that Nostradamus predicted an alliance between the United States and the Soviet Union against an Arab conqueror. Because of this interpretation many in the New Age movement do not believe that the Soviets could be an enemy.

However, the theory of an Arab conqueror is illogical since today the Arabs cannot even defeat Israel, much less the superpowers. And the theory of a U.S.-Soviet alliance is based on a mistranslation of quatrain II.89, which reads in English:

> One day the two great masters will be friends,
> Their great power will be seen increased:
> The new land will be at its high peak,
> To the bloody one the number recounted.[101]

The "two great masters" are the United States and the USSR. The "new land" is the United States at the height of her power. Here is the mistranslation: The first line, "One day the two great masters will be friends," reads in French, *"Un jour seront demis les deux grands maîtres."* Nostradamus used the word *demis,* which means "halved." Commentators arbitrarily changed it to *d'amis,* meaning "friends." Why? Simply because the word *halved* made no sense to them.

In fact, that is exactly what Nostradamus meant. The United States and the Soviet Union *are* halved. They are divided in half ideologically, karmically and astrologically. They are locked in global competition. They are enemies.

In addition, the United States has halved her power by giving or selling to the Soviet Union the technology that gives her the power to destroy the West.

I am asking you not to blame the American people for the arms race. It is the international bankers and industrialists who have armed both sides of the wars of this century. We have seen it most recently in the Iran-Iraq war.

But did you know that Western bankers and industrialists

financed both Hitler and the Bolsheviks? Well, you ought to know it. Antony Sutton, in his book *Wall Street and the Rise of Hitler*, proves that Hitler and the SS, the Nazi elite troops, were funded in part by "affiliates or subsidiaries of U.S. firms, including Henry Ford in 1922."[102]

Sutton has documented that General Electric made payments to Hitler in 1933 and that Standard Oil of New Jersey and International Telephone and Telegraph made subsidiary payments to Heinrich Himmler, the most ruthless of the Nazi leaders, all the way up to 1944.

Sutton further demonstrates that "U.S. multi-nationals under the control of Wall Street profited handsomely from Hitler's military construction program in the 1930s and at least until 1942."[103] Bankers and industrialists also gave financial, material and diplomatic support to the Bolsheviks and enabled them to consolidate the revolution and create the Soviet slave state.*

American companies provided the Soviets with the technology and money they needed to build their war machine that holds us hostage today, all of us!

In his three-volume work, *Western Technology and Soviet Economic Development*, Sutton proves that the Soviet Union has almost no indigenously developed technology and that 90 to 95 percent of it comes from the West, two-thirds from the United States.[104]

The Chase Bank and the United States government's Ex-Im Bank financed the Kama truck factory situated along the Kama River in central Russia. Military vehicles from the Kama truck factory are used by Soviet troops in Afghanistan.[105] And the Mujahidin, our brothers, are taking on the entire Soviet empire with their bare hands—they are the ones these capitalists have betrayed.[106]

Ford and Austin built the Gorki truck factory. And did you know that trucks from Gorki transported war materials along the Ho Chi Minh Trail in Vietnam?[107] A hundred thousand Americans and others were killed in Korea and Vietnam by our own technology in Communist hands!

Wake up, Canada! Wake up, America!

I'm talking about the betrayers of mankind. I'm talking about fallen angels cast out of heaven into the earth who are another breed with another agenda. They're not out to save your life! They're out to steal your Light! And war is one of the principal means they use to achieve their ends of population

---

*For further information on capitalist support of Communists, see "The Abdication of America's Destiny Part 2," published in Book I of this volume, p. 180.

control. So we have to disallow and disavow their war machines, their war efforts, and all that they have been building for their war games toward the world destruction of the Lightbearers for tens of thousands of years.

Did you know that Soviet missiles couldn't even hit Washington, D.C., until they bought U.S. technology for their guidance systems? Now they can hit the South Portico of the White House.

The trade continues today. Western and Japanese banks have lent the Soviet Union nearly $100 billion since 1985.[108]

Our Brothers and Sisters in Tibet

This is the same power elite that trades with China at the expense of our brothers and sisters in Tibet who are being exterminated as we sit here tonight—while we enjoy Constitutional guarantees of freedom of religion, freedom of speech, freedom of the press and freedom of assembly. Through starvation, forced labor, torture, execution, sterilization and even incentives for marriages between Chinese and Tibetans, the Chinese are wiping out an entire race and its ancient culture.

The wrath of God and his righteous indignation well up inside of me for the saving of those saints out of the East, those Lightbearers in whom the threefold flame (the divine spark) has not gone out reincarnation after reincarnation! These Tibetans who have taken their stand in defense of Truth have been murdered not once but hundreds of times over throughout the long period of our struggle on this planet. And the politicians from Jimmy Carter to Ronald Reagan play right along with the Communist game.

Since they invaded Tibet in 1950 the Red Chinese armies have killed 1.2 million Tibetans.[109] John F. Avedon, in his study of the Chinese occupation, *In Exile from the Land of Snows,* describes the atrocities as reported by the Geneva-based International Commission of Jurists:

> The obliteration of entire villages was compounded by hundreds of public executions, carried out to intimidate the surviving population. The methods employed included crucifixion, dismemberment, vivisection, beheading, burying, burning and scalding alive, dragging the victims to death behind galloping horses and pushing them from airplanes; children were forced to shoot their parents, disciples their religious teachers. Everywhere monasteries were prime targets. Monks were compelled to publicly copulate with nuns and desecrate sacred images before being sent to a growing string of labor camps in Amdo and Gansu.[110]

One in 10 Tibetans has been imprisoned by the Chinese at one time or another.[111] Today, estimates of political prisoners range from 20,000 to 100,000. The gentle Tibetans, who have kept the flame of the Buddha for centuries, are being neglected and betrayed by the president of the United States, Ronald Reagan!

If you have ever wondered where hell is, I will tell you. It is inside every nation where World Communism has prevailed— prevailed with the help of their partners in crimes committed against humanity: the international bankers, the industrialists, the financiers and our representatives in Washington.

The Chinese not only practice physical genocide but cultural genocide as well. They have destroyed 6,254 monasteries. The number of Tibetan monks has been reduced from 100,000 in 1957 to 4,000 today.

Since 1978 the United States government has held that Tibet is a part of China. President Reagan has refused to condemn the Chinese government! I am ashamed to say that this man represents me as the head of my country. He refused to condemn the latest Chinese crackdown in Tibet, in October 1987 and March 1988. Instead the Reagan administration has made every effort to strengthen ties with China, stepping up economic, technological and military aid to Beijing.

Just as the power elite of the United States created Russia's military-industrial complex in the twenties and thirties, so it is now creating China's. U.S. trade with China is expected to reach nine billion dollars in 1988 and American businessmen have invested three billion dollars there since 1979.[112]

Any of you see these billions returning to your pockets? Are you making any money on this deal with China? Where's all the money going? And when the big boys make bad investments and the Savings and Loans fail, the Fed cranks out more money; and since the Canadian dollar follows the American dollar, your money in the bank is worth less.

Who does the man in the White House represent? Not only the capitalists and the international bankers. He also represents the Communists, who have the same agenda as the monopoly capitalists—control. One thing is certain: The man in the White House doesn't represent you and me. He doesn't represent the little people of the world.

Who, then, is going to represent them? When you see a job that's got to be done and no one to do it—guess who? *We* have to represent the little people—before God, at our altars, by writing articles, books, letters to the editor, by demonstrations and interviews, by going after our representatives in government and our friends and neighbors, and by getting attention to our cause any way we can. And we can't stop until we know that our brothers and sisters in every nation are protected against all forms of tyranny.

We, the Lightbearers of the world, cannot allow ourselves to be divided by conflicts created by the power elite, capitalist or Communist.

Saint Germain said on February 27, 1988, "Unfortunately, the entrenched forces of Darkness in Washington and New York almost parallel those in Moscow and in the nations' capitals of Europe. Therefore, wherever the betrayers of the Word are, know, then, that it is the Lightbearers of the nations who must unite."[113]

We have to unite against the forces of tyranny wherever we find them and against the karma of their wars now returning.

The Astrology of War

Astrology, another source of prophecy, also predicts war in the coming decade. Let us look at how these predictions affect Canada and the world.

French astrologers Henri-Joseph Gouchon and Claude Ganeau discovered three major cycles of peace and war based on the zodiacal proximity of the five outer planets—Jupiter through Pluto—to each other. As astrologer Charles Harvey explains, Gouchon "found that by calculating the total angular separation between each of the pairs of the outer planets" (Jupiter-Saturn, Jupiter-Uranus, etc.) on an annual basis "and then plotting the results on a graph, the resulting curve showed a striking correspondence with the main periods of international crisis and, most impressively, major and sustained 'lows' for the period 1914–18 and 1944–45."[114] Astrologer André Barbault called this the "Cyclical Index." The Korean War, the Suez Crisis and the Vietnam War also correlate with a negative slope on the graph.

Ganeau developed two cycles—the "Index of Cyclic Equilibrium" and the "Index of Cyclical Variation"—which are variations of the Cyclical Index.

All three indexes have successfully predicted positive periods of harmony, growth, optimism and peace and negative periods of destabilization, disruption and decay. In the late 1980s and early 1990s these indexes will be in the depths of their negative cycle, indicating conflict of the magnitude of past world wars.[115]

In February 1988, as part of the larger Capricorn configuration, Saturn and Uranus formed a conjunction at 0° Capricorn. Historically, Saturn-Uranus conjunctions, squares and oppositions have heralded war, even without the presence of other complicating factors such as those we have discussed.

The United States and the Soviet Union will both be affected by the Capricorn configurations in their natal charts. Pressure increases between January 1988 and October 1991, when Pluto conjoins the Soviet Union's natal Sun and opposes the United States natal Sun (fig. 3).

This is the first time this has happened since the Soviet Union was born at 3:00 p.m., November 7, 1917. This is a period when war, if it's going to happen, is likely to break out between the superpowers.

But even if the United States and the Soviet Union do not go to war, they will still have to deal with a mortal challenge to their nations, their leadership and the foundations of their governments.

On November 26, 1989, Mars will conjoin the Moon, Pluto and the Soviet Sun (fig. 4). This configuration could trigger war between the superpowers, but not necessarily right away. Since Pluto is a slow-moving planet that takes 248 years to orbit the Sun, the effect of a Pluto conjunction can take anywhere from a few months to several years to appear.

On October 2, 1987, speaking in New York City, El Morya said that if the United States did not develop the capability to turn back incoming nuclear warheads before 24 months had passed, there would be a reckoning and a confrontation.[116] November 26, 1989, is nearly 26 months from October 2, 1987. At the time I took that dictation I was not familiar with this astrology. The research was done later—in fact the dictation, in part, prompted it.

The Capricorn megaconjunction on January 11, 1994, which I mentioned when discussing the economy, is also capable of igniting war.

On July 17, 1999, November 14, 1999, and May 13, 2000, we will have exact squares between Saturn in Taurus and Uranus in Aquarius. Again, conjunctions, squares and oppositions between Saturn and Uranus coincide with major wars.

Another indicator of war is the peak of the sunspot cycle. The term "sunspot cycle" refers to the cyclic increase and decrease in the number of sunspots on the surface of the sun. The cycle reaches its peak (i.e., maximum) about every 11 years. Biologist Marsha Adams, an expert on the relationship between sunspots and earthquakes, compared the outbreak of wars with sunspot cycles going back to the 1700s. She found that wars tend to occur about three years after the peak of a sunspot cycle, although they occasionally occur before. The current cycle, which is expected to reach its maximum in late 1989 or early 1990, is rising faster than previous cycles and indications are that it may be the largest on record.

Transiting Pluto Conjoined the Soviet Union's Sun and Opposed the United States Sun
January 1988-October 1991

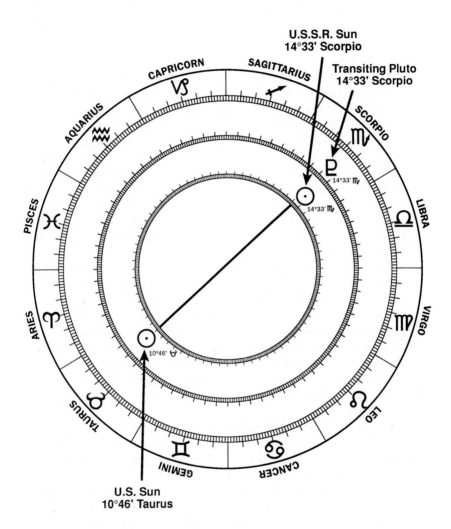

FIGURE 3   As Pluto transits between 12° and 18° Scorpio from January 1988 to October 1991, it will make three exact conjunctions with the Soviet Union's Sun at 14° Scorpio opposed to the United States natal Sun at 10° Taurus. This is the first time in the history of the Soviet Union that this configuration has taken place since Pluto takes 248 years to orbit the Sun. Pluto transits of this sort are associated with the outbreak of wars and with mortal challenges other than war. Even if the United States and the Soviet Union do not go to war, they will face severe challenges that could include economic problems, power struggles, civil unrest and terrorism.

Transiting Pluto, Mars and Moon
Conjoined the Soviet Union's Sun and
Opposed the United States Sun
November 26, 1989

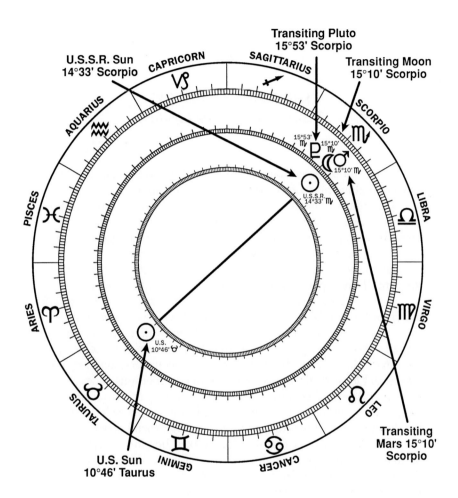

FIGURE 4 On November 26, 1989, the Moon will make exact conjunctions to transiting Mars at 15°10′ Scorpio (10:48 a.m. EST) and transiting Pluto at 15°53′ Scorpio (12:16 p.m. EST), forming a Moon-Mars-Pluto conjunction at 15° Scorpio within one and a half degrees of the Soviet Sun at 14°33′ Scorpio. The conjunction of Pluto, Mars and the Moon with the Soviet natal Sun will oppose the United States natal Sun at 10°46′ Taurus. This is one of several configurations that has the potential to ignite a war between the superpowers at any time between January 1988 and October 1991.

5

Canada's Astrology:
Discover Your True Identity!

How, then, does Canada fit into the framework of coming astrological events? Let's take a look at her birth chart.

Canada was born at midnight, July 1, 1867, the day and hour she became a Dominion. In the chart drawn for this date (fig. 5) Canada's natal Sun is at 8° Cancer in the fourth house. A fourth-house Sun usually shows material success. Uranus, also at 8° Cancer in the fourth house, makes a nearly exact conjunction with the Sun. This aspect marks Canadians as a unique people.

A Sun-Uranus conjunction gives the stimulus to freedom and individuality and is a catalyst for genius. It endows Canadians with the capacity to be individualistic and innovative. It shows that Canada should prosper through developing the genius of her people—in cutting-edge technologies, such as electronics, aviation, computers and mass communications, and in new methods of developing human and natural resources, especially primary economic activities such as farming, fisheries, forestries and mining—as well as through the development of an Aquarian or New Age social order.

The Sun-Uranus conjunction makes beneficial trines* with Saturn at 17° Scorpio and Jupiter at 7° Pisces, the planetary pair that governs the coordinates of the physical universe—time and space, respectively. Canada is fortunate to have Jupiter and Saturn trine her Sun and Uranus (fig. 6). The ancients called Jupiter and Saturn "the great chronocrators," or rulers of time, because the cycles of conjunctions between the two planets subdivide time into large units with observable political and economic cycles.

Saturn, in addition to governing time, rules the government, the constitution and the laws. Saturn rules people who are employed by national, state and local governments. It rules the ability to organize, to crystallize aspirations and to take practical

---

*An exact trine occurs when planets are 120 degrees apart from each other in the zodiac. The orb, or space in which a trine is effective, is 10 degrees. Trines permit a harmonious interaction between planetary influences.

Dominion of Canada
Birth Chart
July 1, 1867, 12:00 a.m.

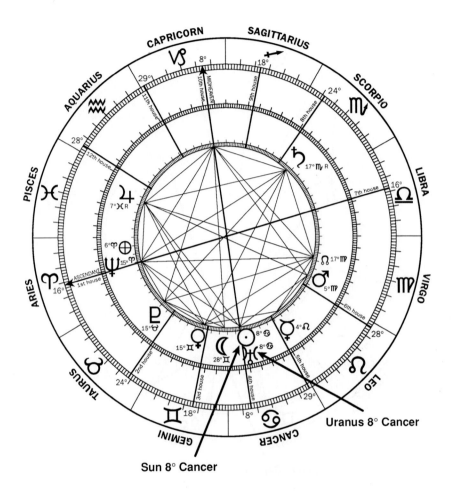

Sun 8° Cancer

Uranus 8° Cancer

FIGURE 5 The Dominion of Canada was created by the British North America Act, which took effect at midnight July 1, 1867, in Ottawa, Ontario. Canada's Sun is at 8° Cancer in the fourth house of agriculture, mining and real estate. A fourth house Sun usually shows material success. The Sun and Uranus make a nearly exact conjunction at 8° Cancer, which marks Canadians as a unique people. This conjunction gives the stimulus to freedom and individuality and endows Canadians with the capacity to be highly individualistic and innovative. It shows that Canada should prosper through developing the genius of her people—in cutting edge technologies and primary economic activities such as farming, fishing, forestry and mining—as well as through establishing an Aquarian (or New Age) social order.

Jupiter and Saturn Trine the Sun and Uranus
in Canada's Birth Chart

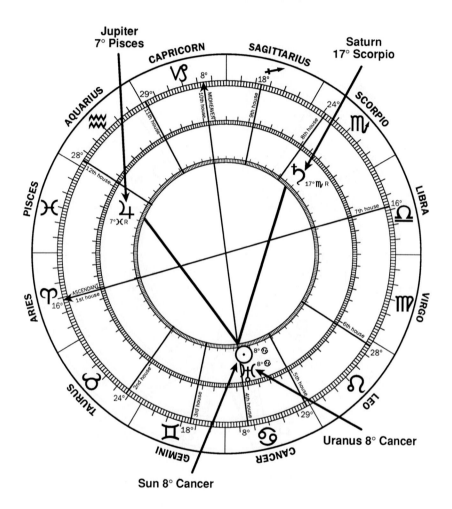

FIGURE 6 Canada's Sun-Uranus conjunction at 8° Cancer receives beneficial trines from Saturn at 17° Scorpio and Jupiter at 7° Pisces. These four bodies provide the framework for Canada to be an economic, cultural, political and spiritual world power. Saturn rules the ability to organize and to take practical action leading to the fulfillment of long-term goals. Jupiter governs the capacity to grow and expand spiritually and materially. It rules honest character, religion, law, culture and foreign affairs. Saturn's trine to the Sun and Uranus shows Canada's obligation to play a responsible and evolutionary role in world affairs. Jupiter's trine shows that Canada has a mission to use her material and spiritual resources for the benefit of her own people and the betterment of the people of other nations.

action leading to the fulfillment of long-term goals. It rules tradition, prudence and stability, and land, agriculture and resources. It also rules karma, delays and restrictions. In sum, Saturn is a yang force.

Jupiter is a yin force. In addition to governing space, Jupiter rules the capacity to grow and expand spiritually and materially. It rules optimism, good judgment and honest character; people and places associated with law, religion and education, hence judges and the judiciary; ministers and churches; lawmakers and elected assemblies; and teachers and educational institutions. Jupiter also rules foreign and cultural relations and good fortune. All of these we see at a keen level of development in Canada.

Saturn is essentially conservative; Jupiter is liberal. Having these planets in harmonious aspect to the Sun and Uranus brings about the conditions necessary for a harmonious, integrated expression of all the elements that we have discussed thus far.

Furthermore, Jupiter in Pisces in the twelfth house trine the Sun shows that Canada has the capacity and mission to use her material and spiritual resources for the benefit of her own people and for the betterment of the people of other nations. Saturn in Scorpio in the seventh house trine the Sun and Uranus shows Canada's ability and obligation to play a responsible and evolutionary role in international and economic affairs.

These four planets—the Sun, Uranus, Jupiter and Saturn—provide the framework for Canada to be an economic, cultural, political and spiritual world power.

Now, remember, astrology is not predestination. Astrology shows opportunity. For people to realize the potential greatness in their charts, they must have the will and determination to make it happen. Sometimes we see in wealthy families that the founder who built the company is successful because he takes nothing for granted except hard work. Succeeding generations, taking everything for granted, accomplish less and less and finally end up with nothing.

When you realize what a great inheritance you Canadians have from your collective Causal Bodies, you have to be careful to forge and reforge your identity and build on a solid foundation of Christ Truth, year upon year. You must never take for granted the abundance of opportunity that is given to you but ride it—ride the proud wave of your Canadian heritage right to your victory!

Canada's Birth Chart: The Challenges

Let's take a look at the challenges to Canada's expression of her vast potential. First, Canada's natal Neptune at 15° Aries in the twelfth house is conjoined her Ascendant at 16° Aries. Both are square to her Sun and Uranus in Cancer in the fourth house (fig. 7).

This square has a number of effects. It can increase the national level of intuition, idealism and religious and artistic inspiration. It can intensify the impulse of enlightened democratic rule. And it can refine and elevate all aspects of national life.

However, the impulse of Neptune is difficult for a person or nation to accurately express. In practice, the positive influences of Neptune are manifest only to the degree that the person or, in this case, the nation is spiritually developed and grounded.

Now, unless she fully integrates the positive aspects in her chart, Canada is likely to experience problems under the influence of this square. These problems would include Canada's inability to act effectively to fulfill her reason for being due to an inability to understand who and what she is—in short, an identity crisis.

Without spiritual luminaries among the people who know who God is and where he abides within their temples, who understand the glorious nature of the indwelling Presence in profound humility and never in spiritual pride, there is an absence of a sense of national identity, there is an identity crisis.

Where does anyone find identity if it's not in the divine spark centered in the heart? What other identity is permanent about ourselves except the God flame? *That* must be our fiery destiny.

An identity crisis arising from a square such as Canada's Sun-Uranus-Neptune-Ascendant square is often accompanied by illusion, confusion and diffusion of energies and the inability to formulate practical goals. Without vision the people perish.[117] They cannot agree on national purpose. They are unable to solve their problems. Under this square you are also likely to see peculiar problems that block goals or delay their fulfillment, the tendency to fantasize and dream instead of act, opposition from hidden enemies, as well as an undeservedly bad reputation and social unrest.

The square we are discussing is related to other configurations that amplify its effects. Neptune forms one corner of a relatively rare configuration that is called a Yod, or a Finger of God. This occurs when two planets that are sextile (60° apart) are both quincunx (150° apart from) a third planet. They form an acute, fingerlike isosceles triangle in space.

In Canada's chart, Neptune at 15° Aries forms a sextile to Venus at 15° Gemini, and both form a quincunx to Saturn at 17° Scorpio in the seventh house (fig. 8). This configuration can extend Neptunian confusion and deception into domestic and international economic affairs and foreign relations. It can generate anxiety

Neptune Conjoined the Ascendant
Square the Sun and Uranus
in Canada's Birth Chart

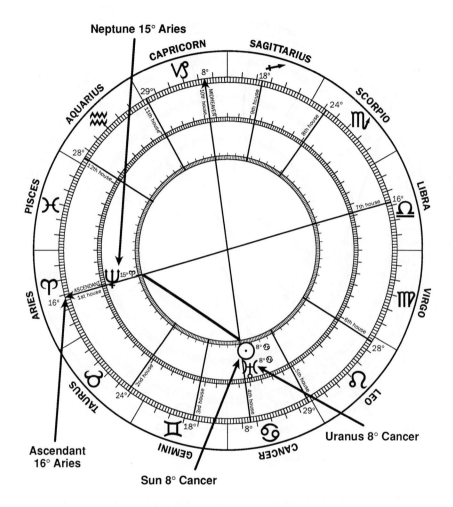

FIGURE 7 Canada's Neptune at 15° Aries conjoined the Ascendant at 16° Aries makes a square to the Sun and Uranus conjoined at 8° Cancer. This aspect can increase the national level of intuition, idealism and religious and artistic inspiration. It can also refine and elevate all aspects of Canada's national life. But in practice, the positive influences of Neptune are manifest only to the degree that the nation is spiritually developed and grounded. Without a strong spiritual foundation, Canada is likely to experience an identity crisis accompanied by illusion, confusion and the inability to formulate practical goals. Canada may also suffer from an undeservedly bad reputation and loss from hidden enemies such as spies.

Finger of God Bisected by Pluto
in Canada's Birth Chart

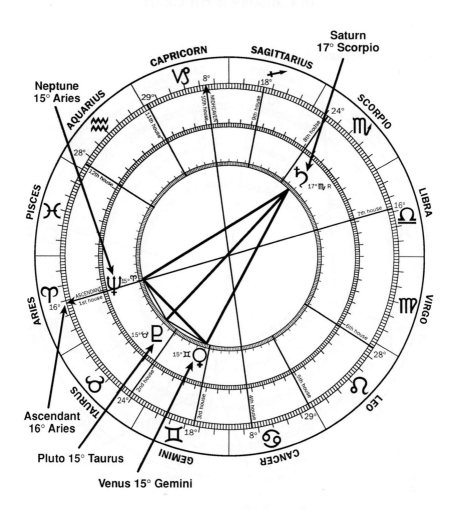

FIGURE 8   Canada has a relatively rare configuration known as a Finger
of God (an acute isosceles triangle) formed by a conjunction of Neptune at
15° Aries and the Ascendant at 16° Aries sextile (60° apart from) Venus at
15° Gemini all quincunx (150° apart from) Saturn at 17° Scorpio. This
configuration shows the potential for confusion and deception in domestic
and international economic affairs as well as for periodic recessions and
depressions. The Finger of God is bisected by the opposition of Pluto at 15°
Taurus to Saturn at 17° Scorpio. This opposition is indicative of an
obnoxious bureaucracy and shows the tendency of power elites to thwart
the will of the people. It was related to the delay in the repatriation of the
Canadian Constitution and is associated with mass destiny and serious
karmic problems such as the outbreak of war.

about Canada's fuzzy self-image, social standing and reputation. It can also disorganize Canada's economy, block the formulation and passage of sound domestic and international economic policy and lead to periodic economic recessions and depressions.

The Finger of God is bisected by an opposition between Saturn at 17° Scorpio in the seventh house, and Pluto at 15° Taurus in the first house (fig. 8). This opposition makes it difficult for Canada to express the highest elements of the Finger of God. It tends to block the expression of the true will and personality of the body politic. This will usually be due to the intrusion of domestic and international power elites.

The Saturn-Pluto opposition is indicative of an obnoxious bureaucracy. It can cause delays and difficulties in the government, and trigger and aggravate constitutional crises. It was directly related to the long delay in repatriation of the Canadian Constitution. This opposition, along with one between Mars and Jupiter, can also tend to give some Canadians an aggressive, harsh, vindictive, combative, blindly ambitious and acquisitive nature.

Saturn-Pluto oppositions are often associated with mass destiny and serious karmic problems such as the outbreak of wars. Since this opposition is nearly exact and falls in the first and seventh houses, it could lead to the cataclysmic destruction of the government as a vehicle of expression of the people through war, economic circumstances or other reasons. Canada will soon face a major challenge when this opposition is powerfully activated.

Now let's look at the Mars-Jupiter opposition. Mars at 5° Virgo in the sixth house opposed to Jupiter at 7° Pisces in the twelfth house shows, among other things, a talented labor force, but one that is aggressive and inclined to go on strike even when it is not warranted or in the interests of the nation (fig. 9).

Finally, the Moon is at 28° Gemini in the third house. On the positive side, a Gemini Moon in the third house shows skill in all forms of communication and the ability to unify diverse aspects of the people into a productive, healthy body. It is also indicative of bilingualism.

Canada's Moon is generally well aspected. But the negative elements of Gemini, the loss of energy and inability to achieve goals due to divisiveness, are clearly evident. The divisions in Canadian society go back to the square of Neptune to the Sun and Uranus at 8° Cancer. The Moon rules Cancer. Thus, the afflictions of the Sun and Uranus can be transferred to the Moon.

When the Sun, which represents national identity and will, is weakened by the square of Neptune, the center of gravity of the

Mars Opposed to Jupiter
in Canada's Birth Chart

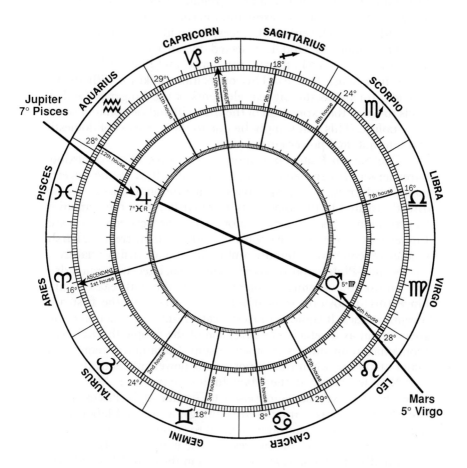

FIGURE 9   Canada's Mars at 5° Virgo in the sixth house (which rules the work force and the civil service) opposed to Jupiter at 7° Pisces in the twelfth house (which rules covert activity, public charities, welfare and prisons or self-imprisoning behavior) shows that she has a talented labor force, but one that is aggressive and inclined to go on strike even when it is not warranted or in the interests of the nation.

Key for Planetary Symbols			
☉ Sun	♀ Venus	♄ Saturn	♇ Pluto
☽ Moon	♂ Mars	♅ Uranus	☊ North Node
☿ Mercury	♃ Jupiter	♆ Neptune	⊕ Part of Fortune

nation is weakened. Consequently, the parts of the whole break out into more or less nonintegratable pieces. The individuality of Canadian ethnic groups that should be expressed in their unique Christhood becomes instead a separatist, insular exclusivity, denying the larger profile of all peoples as Canadians first, which is essential in coalescing national unity and purpose. This effect is amplified by the opposition of Pluto to Saturn, which reduces the ability of the people to focus and express their true personality.

Let's not see these aspects as "obstacles." Let's see them as the creative tension that tests the mettle of a man, a woman, a child, and compels us to put forth our best and highest self. There's always a creative tension that is a part of the birth process—whether of a nation or of a child from its mother's womb. And is not the cry of the newborn the "Eureka!" of the Greek scientist Archimedes, "I have found it!"

And so, along with the good signs come some testers and teasers to see if you can pass your initiations, endure to the end and receive the crown of victory for your winning of Canada's destiny and your own. You have to summon all of your strength, your self-knowledge, your experience, your will, and that sacrificial staying power to be sure that you win—when the fates are betting on your winning and when they're not.

If the forces of Antichrist were to meet in council to determine how to defeat the Christhood of the people of Canada, the first thing they would do is study the astrological charts of the nation and of her citizens to determine the national, individual and collective points of karmic vulnerability. Then they would work to break down the leadership as well as the rank and file wherever they could.

Become the Capstone!

It is my opinion that in this age, our civilization must meet the challenge to transcend itself. The historian Arnold Toynbee, after studying the rise and fall of the world's civilizations, concluded that all nations are required to self-transcend through a spiritualization, or "etherialization." And unless that happen, unless a nation merit the endowment of a flame, it is subject to entering a "time of troubles" followed by disintegration.

Nations, as people, come to the hour of self-transcendence when all of the foundation and body of the pyramid they have built is focused in that moment of quintessence in the capstone, thence to give birth to a golden age. If the components of society are not ready for self-transcendence, the civilization cannot meet this initiation of the Universal Christ. Failure to pass that initiation effectively halts the forward march of progress—spiritually and industrially.

As we look at the two thousand years of the age of Pisces, we have to admit a certain loss of our soul-identity in the sense of our soul's evolution on the path of personal Christhood. We were the victims of the compromise of Jesus' real teachings by the wolves in sheep's clothing who early on took control of the Church of Rome and eliminated all rival groups that threatened their citadel of control. By taking away the key to self-knowledge and the sacred mysteries taught by Jesus to his disciples and carried on through the tradition of the Gnostics, the orthodox Church hierarchy deprived an entire age of the right to fulfill their reason for being.[118]

Thus, as we come to the moment of supreme challenge to the national identities of Canada and the United States, we have to face the fact that our people have not yet solved the equation of being itself, or of being in God. Christ must become the chief cornerstone of our identity in God before we can realize the spiritual identity of our nationhood and offer our collective attainment on the world altar.

Very few people really know what it means to be developed spiritually. Spiritual development comes from the raising up of the Mother Flame in the temple, the expansion of the Light in the seven chakras and the balancing of the threefold flame of the heart so that our hearts may become the chalice for the Sacred Heart of Jesus. In short, to develop oneself spiritually one must be self-disciplined on a path of discipleship under Jesus Christ and the Ascended Masters until, being perfected daily in Love, the soul is ready for the Holy Christ Self to enter her temple and reign.

The path leading to the soul's reunion with God at the conclusion of this life is a path of mysticism, of meditating upon the inner Light, of serving the inner Light until one is wholly assimilated by that Light.

The "white fire core" of every nation is composed of a nucleus of spiritual devotees (their outer religious affiliation matters not) who sustain a conscious contact with the Presence of God, who exercise the science of the spoken Word in prayer, mantra, affirmation, dynamic decree and recitation of holy scriptures, who lead a life of physical and moral purity, put God and his kingdom first, and in love sublimate their wills to his own.

Not only are they servants of God, but they are also the selfless servants of the people in all walks of life. They lead a holy interior life, sometimes unbeknownst even to their loved ones. By their words and their works these souls collectively create a chalice of Light, though they may not be aware of one another or even know on the outer that they serve under the hierarchy of the Great White Brotherhood.

This chalice is a real and tangible Holy Grail that can be seen centered over the nation in the etheric octave. It is made up of the combined energies of devotion of this white fire core and contains the Light of the Seven Rays of the Holy Spirit that nourishes the souls and the divine plan of a people. The lives of these saints and the spiritual fruits thereof demonstrate the real meaning of being a Keeper of the Flame of Life for oneself, one's family, one's community, one's country, and one's world.

I was thinking about the spiritual destiny of the United States on my spring 1988 tour stumping for the Coming Revolution in Higher Consciousness, and I realized that the hour had come for America to place the capstone on the pyramid. We see this pyramid on the reverse side of the Great Seal of the United States.

When you examine a U.S. dollar bill, you see that on the back of it are printed both sides of the Great Seal. The front side of the seal displays an eagle with a shield in front of it, holding an olive branch in its right talon and arrows in its left. The reverse of the seal is a pyramid with its capstone suspended above it. Within the capstone is an eye emanating rays of light.

Charles Thomson, the Secretary of Congress, and artist William Barton were appointed to design the Great Seal in 1782. They described the pyramid as signifying "Strength and Duration" and wrote that "the Eye...allude[s] to the many signal interpositions of providence in favor of the American cause."[119]

After the first die of the Great Seal was cut from brass in 1782, the design on the seal's reverse was seldom used, until 1934, when Franklin D. Roosevelt put the Great Seal on the back of the dollar bill.

The eye within the capstone is the All-Seeing Eye of God and represents the third-eye chakra. The crown chakra at the apex of the capstone marks the point through which we pass to unite with God.

And so the placing of the capstone on the pyramid is a spiritual initiation. But as you look at the capstone and you look at its volume, it is a very small percentage of the pyramid. If the pyramid represents the population of the nation, the capstone would comprise .018 percent of the total population. So if the population of any nation—including the United States or Canada— is represented in the pyramid, we see that the people and the substructures of a civilization are the foundation. As the pyramid rises, the components are the more educated, the professionals and the architects of all phases of life.

I figured out percentage-wise by volume that the number of people required for the placing of the capstone on the United States is a mere 45,218. The leadership in every field occupy the top half of the pyramid. The capstone consists of the forerunners of the future, the spiritually enlightened, and coincidentally those with the least karma who are nearest to the individual process of etherealization, or what we call the ascension, i.e., the acceleration unto the light of the I AM THAT I AM whereby the soul passes through the crown chakra unto oneness with the Great God Self.

So if you take the symbol of the pyramid for Canada, taking .018 percent of your population of 25,334,000, you can see that 4,629 people is all you need to make up your "white fire core" who could become the components of the capstone. So, not all of the people of a nation have to carry a spiritual fire in order for that nation to meet the requirements for self-transcendence, or etherealization, but only the number represented in the volume of the capstone. But unless that percentage—a white fire core—carry that spiritual fire, and unless they know it is their calling from God to do so, the nation could be lost because there were not enough people to form the critical mass necessary to sustain the collective divine spark.

In all past ages and civilizations it was the holy orders, the religious of East and West, who kept the flame and the watch through prayers, devotions and a spiritual life and became the capstone of their nations' great pyramid, thereby enabling the builders, the families and those carrying the larger community responsibilities not only to balance their karma and fulfill their reason for being but also, in so doing, to share in the nation's self-transcending cycles ignited by the flame-bearers.

My beloved brothers and sisters, Canadians and Americans, each of you must decide, one by one, if you are to be a keeper of the Flame of your nation. And if you are, you will begin right where you are. And as your capacity to keep the Flame increases, you will mount the steps of the pyramid, taking the place of those who were the white stones, the first strong and enduring components of the capstone, so that they may pass on to higher octaves and other pyramids.

And when you rise in consciousness to the top of your civilization's pyramid, you raise up the entire nation even as you keep that Flame. That is why Saint Germain founded his Keepers of the Flame Fraternity.

Addressing those who would "make their energies count" on behalf of "all who have ever lived to defend the flame of freedom," Saint Germain once explained:

To be a Keeper of the Flame is to be a torchbearer of the age. To be a Keeper of the Flame is to run with the fires of the resurrection, that all life might be regenerated in the flame of Reality.

The crumbling of the old order and the building of the new take place simultaneously. Some identify with the downward spiral and some with the upward spiral. Keepers of the Flame recognize that this is a time for the gathering of the sheaves of consciousness. This is a time when men must reap the sowings of the past. This is a time when the foundation of a golden age must be built. . . .

It is time for men and women mature in judgment, capable in leadership, humble before God and possessed with a profound vision of the consequences of mankind's turning from their God, to make the decision to come together in the communion of the flame under the aegis of the Great White Brotherhood to sponsor the revolution of the ages—the revolution of Light, Love and the Victory of the Flame. . . .

This is a time to pursue the dharma of a planet and a people with a passionate devotion to the blueprint of Life and to the divine plan for all.[120]

You can decide whether you want to be affiliated with the Keepers of the Flame Fraternity. You don't have to join in order to be a component of your nation's capstone. But if you do become one of Saint Germain's Keepers of the Flame, you will be helping to fulfill Jesus' call for ten thousand Keepers of the Flame from North America this year in order to prevent the descent of returning karma as war or cataclysm upon North America. Jesus told us that the spiritual defenses must come from that white fire core of dedicated Keepers of the Flame and their daily invocation of the protection of North America.

In his dictation given May 28, 1987, Jesus said:

I am sent by the Father for the quickening now of ten thousand saints in the City Foursquare that I mark as North America.

Blessed hearts, it is to these states and nations of the lost tribes regathered that I come, even as I sent my apostles to the lost sheep of the house of Israel. . . .

Blessed ones, this North America, a place consecrated by Love to the reunion of souls with God, is a place where if the Lightbearers would respond and *make the Call,* even as

I call you this night, there should be established even the white light over a continent to protect it from those calamities of the Four Horsemen, which could indeed appear for want of mediators in the earth.

Understand, beloved, that the mediators who must stand between a people and a planet and their karma must be in physical embodiment. If you will read my words, you will find that they say, *"As long as I AM in the world, I AM the light of the world."*. . . Recognize, then, that the Call to be the Divine Mediator must be answered ere the earth changes that must come about take their toll in a cataclysmic way or perhaps in war, even that war prophesied by my Mother at Fátima.[121]

Notice that beloved Jesus spoke of the United States and Canada as the "City Foursquare that I mark as North America." When these two countries are viewed as one on the map, they look like a giant "city foursquare."[122] Let's take the eraser of the violet flame held in the hand of the Ascended Master Saint Germain, which looks just like a giant chalkboard eraser, and erase the artificial barriers to our universal oneness in God!

That doesn't mean we have to lose our identity as separate nations. It means we wise up and don't let ourselves be manipulated into bickering and squabbling. Let's wise up—let's be wise as serpents and harmless as doves[123]—and hold in check the manipulators of our money, our blood, our crops, our children, our resources, our jobs, our minds and our souls. Because they're out there and they've been the spoilers in the earth for tens of thousands of years every time the sons and daughters of God have gotten a good thing going.

But today the people are unmasking them and they have nowhere to hide! What they have done in secret with the economies of the nations is being shouted from the housetops. And their judgment is nigh.

Let us bear one another's burden. Let keepers of the flame of freedom in the United States and Canada communicate with one another on their problems and relate to one another as sister nations and sister cities. Let us all pray together on these problems at set times and let us do what we know how to do best: summon the legions of Light to challenge in the name of God those who move in our midst to the detriment of the Light and the Lightbearer in embodiment.

This is how the spiritual lines of our defense run: our call and heaven's answer combine to bring about the defeat of the consciousness of Evil on earth. This is God's victory, our victory that is imminent. Let none dash from our lips this cup of victory. My beloved, it is in our hands. And by God's grace and in invocation to his name, we can defeat these prophecies together.

So as you look at Canada's astrology, the mandate cannot escape you. For your nation to make it, you must see that the nation is spiritually developed and grounded through you. Don't look around for someone else to keep the Flame for you. For one day every citizen of Canada will have to take his turn to keep the Flame if he would endow the lesser endowed with the mission and the message of opportunity for self-transcendence. All who would pass through the point of Light to behold the flaming ones must first keep their Flame on earth.

God is speaking to you personally. You need to seize that torch of illumination of the Goddess of Liberty and run with it and be certain that you are one of the components of the capstone of your nation.

Canada's Future

With both the positive and negative potentialities in mind, let us look at Canada in the context of coming astrological configurations.

As you recall, I pointed out that in the next few years there will be major economic, political, environmental and military challenges for the entire world. Some of these are triggered by a series of Capricorn conjunctions that began with the February 23, 1988 conjunction of Mars, Saturn, Uranus and Neptune in Capricorn.

So that you can appreciate the significance of the Capricorn conjunctions in relation to Canada's chart, let me say a word about the places in which these conjunctions will fall—Canada's ninth house, tenth house and Midheaven. The ninth house rules foreign affairs, higher education, cultural affairs and religion. The tenth house rules the nation's chief executive, government, constitution, the party in power, the nation's reputation and public standing, and its honor, ideals and achievement.

Canada's Midheaven, the point highest in the sky when the nation was born, is its tenth-house cusp. The Midheaven is a concentrated expression of tenth-house affairs. More than any other point in the chart, it reveals the nation's reason for being and her mission. Canada's Midheaven is at 8° Capricorn directly opposed to the Sun and Uranus in Cancer.

For the first time in Canada's history, on January 8, 1988, transiting Neptune in Capricorn conjoined Canada's Midheaven at 8° Capricorn and opposed her Sun and Uranus at 8° Cancer (fig. 10). This means that Canada is entering a new and crucial phase of her life and development.

Canada is due to come of age as a nation and play a leading

Transiting Neptune Conjoined Canada's Midheaven and Opposed to Canada's Sun and Uranus
January 8, 1988

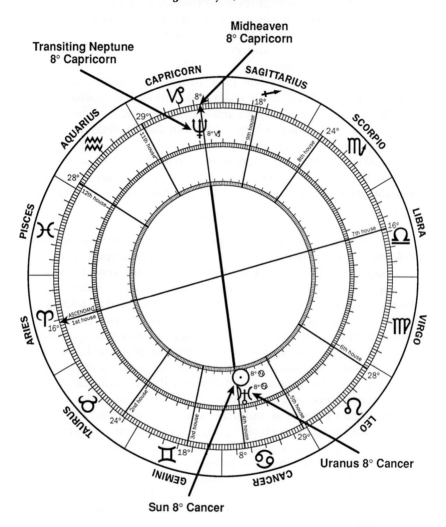

Midheaven
8° Capricorn

Transiting Neptune
8° Capricorn

Uranus 8° Cancer

Sun 8° Cancer

FIGURE 10   On January 8, 1988, Canada entered a new and crucial phase of her development. For the first time in the nation's history, Neptune (the planet of spiritual growth) conjoined Canada's Midheaven (ruling national policy, purpose and reputation) at 8° Capricorn and opposed her Sun and Uranus conjoined at 8° Cancer. Canada is due to come of age as a nation and play a leading role on the world stage. To do so, Canada must mature spiritually and crystallize her true identity, her true Christhood. She must demonstrate the correct uses of power, transcend the Neptunian conditions that have partially incapacitated her, and allow her highest spiritual impulses to direct the course of government policy.

role on the world stage. The fact that this coincides with a time of momentous world changes adds to the significance of these transits. Canada must come of age spiritually, and all who are called must lead the way! She must crystallize her identity, her true Christhood. She must demonstrate the correct uses of power, transcend the Neptunian conditions in her birth chart that have partially incapacitated her, and allow her highest spiritual impulses to direct the course of government policy. I will discuss the consequences of Canada's failure to do so in a moment.

But let's get back to the Capricorn conjunctions and how they affect Canada's chart. As I previously mentioned, Saturn-Uranus-Neptune conjunctions are extremely rare. They set in motion forces that change the course of history. Their immediate influence may last decades; their long-term influence, centuries. These three planets form the backbone of the six-planet Capricorn conjunctions of late 1989 and 1990 (fig. 11). These conjunctions will have a depressing effect on the government, economy and people of Canada as well as the rest of the world, unless these have worked diligently to build their nations on a foundation of reality.

On November 13, 1989, Saturn and Neptune will make an exact conjunction at 10° Capricorn (fig. 12). This falls in Canada's tenth house conjoined her Midheaven at 8° Capricorn. Saturn and Neptune will also form an opposition to Canada's Sun-Uranus conjunction at 8° Cancer conjoined transiting Jupiter at 10° Cancer in the fourth house. All of these planets, plus the Midheaven, square Canada's Neptune at 15° Aries conjoined her Ascendant at 16° Aries, forming a 45°-45°-90° triangle called a T-square.

By this date Canada should have completely integrated into her national psyche the positive elements of the trines of Jupiter in Pisces and Saturn in Scorpio that are in her birth chart and be capable of expressing the highest attributes defined in her chart. If Canada is unable to do that, the November 13, 1989 configuration, which could eventually cause the dissolution of the economy, stock market and even the government of the United States, could have a similar but more powerful effect in Canada.

There could be a social, economic and political cataclysm of considerable duration. At the very least, the government in power will be threatened. More likely, the Canadian form of government could be drastically and unpredictably altered for the worse. Since Saturn and Neptune are slow-moving planets that conjoin each other only about every thirty-six years, it could be three to six months or even longer before the effects of this Saturn-Neptune conjunction are felt.

Conjunction of Six Planets in Capricorn
Near Canada's Midheaven
December 27, 1989

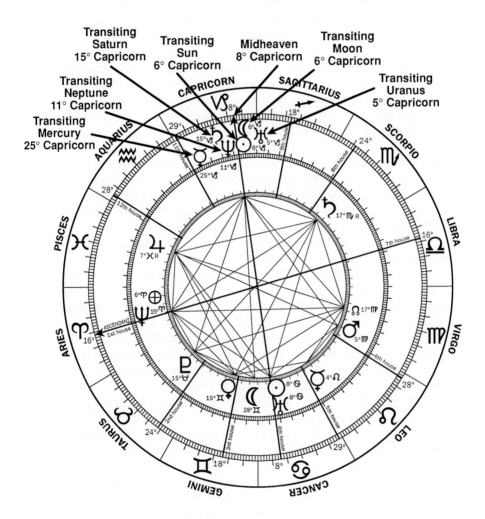

FIGURE 11 The first of several six-planet conjunctions in Capricorn that take place in 1989-90 will occur on December 27, 1989. The planets in these conjunctions are close to Canada's Midheaven and are likely to have a depressing effect on her government, economy and people. A conjunction of Saturn, Uranus and Neptune forms the nucleus of the six-planet Capricorn conjunctions. Saturn-Uranus-Neptune conjunctions are rare and set in motion forces that change the course of history. Their immediate influence may last decades; their long-term influence, centuries.

Transiting Saturn and Neptune Form a T-Square
in Canada's Birth Chart
November 13, 1989

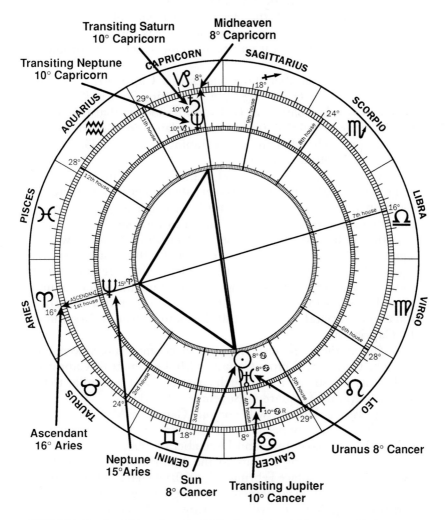

FIGURE 12 On November 13, 1989, Saturn and Neptune will form an exact conjunction at 10° Capricorn in Canada's tenth house. It will also conjoin Canada's Midheaven at 8° Capricorn and oppose her Sun and Uranus at 8° Cancer and transiting Jupiter at 10° Cancer. All of these planets, plus the Midheaven, will square Canada's Neptune at 15° Aries conjoined her Ascendant at 16° Aries. These planets form a right triangle, called a T-square. This configuration indicates that Canada could experience social, economic and political cataclysm and her government could be drastically altered for the worse. Since Saturn and Neptune are slow-moving planets, it could be three to six months or longer before the effects of this Saturn-Neptune conjunction are felt.

November 13, 1989, could mark the onset of a major economic downturn and of political changes leading to a great loss of individual freedom. If the negative elements of international karma associated with this configuration break through into physical manifestation, then it will be difficult to solve the problems that may arise.

There are a number of reasons for this. Capricorn is ruled by Saturn and its effects are long-term. Transiting Pluto at 15° Taurus opposes Canada's Saturn at 17° Scorpio, showing that the activation of serious karmic problems is related to the transits of Saturn—precisely what we see beginning November 13, 1989, in the Saturn-Neptune conjunction.

At the same time, Pluto and Mars transiting in Scorpio will conjoin Canada's Saturn and exacerbate the negative potential of the Saturn-in-Capricorn configuration enough to call into question the continued existence of Canada as we know her today.

In addition, during this period transiting Neptune will be square to Canada's natal Neptune in the twelfth house. Neptune square Neptune can precipitate problems that are difficult to solve. (Israel, for example, which has been unable to formulate a workable policy for the occupied territories, is currently beset by a square of her natal Neptune at 10° Libra to transiting Neptune at 10° Capricorn.)

And if the previously mentioned configurations were not enough, Uranus will cross Canada's Midheaven at 8° Capricorn and create a T-square in her birth chart that will be similar to the Saturn-Neptune T-square of November 13, 1989.

Transiting Uranus will conjoin Canada's Midheaven and form nearly exact oppositions to Canada's Sun and Uranus in Cancer in February, June and December of 1990. The first of the three conjunctions of Uranus to the Midheaven is particularly explosive. It takes place February 11, 1990, when transiting Mars at 9° Capricorn will be conjoined transiting Uranus at 8° Capricorn and transiting Neptune will be nearby at 13° Capricorn, and all three will square Canada's natal Neptune and oppose her natal Sun and Uranus. These planets form a T-square. In its most extreme expression this configuration could lead to a violent overthrow of the government.

The squares to Neptune show a mounting force from within of treachery and intrigue by hidden enemies and possibly by agents from foreign countries as well. The Capricorn challenges go on, but I think you get the point.

The most powerful indicators of war in the next few years are the triple conjunction of Saturn and Uranus on February 12, June 26, and October 18, 1988, the peaking sunspot cycle and the Capricorn megaconjunction of 1994. The transit of Pluto in Scorpio conjoined the Soviet natal Sun at 14° Scorpio and opposed to the U.S. natal Sun at 10° Taurus shows that the United States and the Soviet Union are likely to be combatants during this time of extreme tension.

If the superpowers go to war, Canada will almost certainly be an integral participant for three reasons. Canada and the United States are physically close to each other, share common values and a common defense. If there is a general East-West conflict, Canada will most likely be attacked in the opening moments. But even if the United States and the Soviet Union do not go to war, Canada's astrology is such that she could go to war or experience a mortal challenge equal to war.

On November 27, 1989, about two weeks after the Saturn-Neptune conjunction that powerfully aspects Canada's government and economy, there will be a strong planetary indicator that Canada could soon enter a war. Transiting Pluto and transiting Mars will form an exact conjunction at 15° Scorpio, only two degrees from Canada's Saturn at 17° Scorpio in the seventh house and opposed to Canada's natal Pluto at 15° Taurus in the first house (fig. 13).

Pluto will be moving quickly at that time and will make its exact conjunction with Canada's Saturn at 17° Scorpio on February 13, 1990 (fig. 14). The Mars-Saturn-Pluto combination in Scorpio and Taurus triggers long-term, life-and-death battles. Since the conjunction falls in Canada's seventh house, which rules war, the prospect for international battles is even higher.

Pluto will still be conjoined Canada's Saturn on February 11, 1990, that explosive day when transiting Uranus will conjoin Canada's Midheaven at 8° Capricorn with transiting Mars at 9° Capricorn and transiting Neptune at 13° Capricorn close by. These planets will oppose Canada's Sun-Uranus conjunction at 8° Cancer square Canada's Neptune at 15° Aries and Ascendant at 16° Aries, forming a T-square almost identical to the November 13, 1989 T-square shown in figure 12. In addition, on February 9, 1990, an eclipse of the Moon in Leo will activate a configuration in the birth charts of the United States and the Soviet Union and could trigger a war between the superpowers sometime thereafter.[124]

Pluto will be part of other intense placings that indicate a high probability of war, including two other conjunctions with Canada's Saturn on October 25, 1990, and June 13, 1991.

Transiting Mars and Pluto Activate
the Bisected Finger of God in Canada's Birth Chart
November 27, 1989

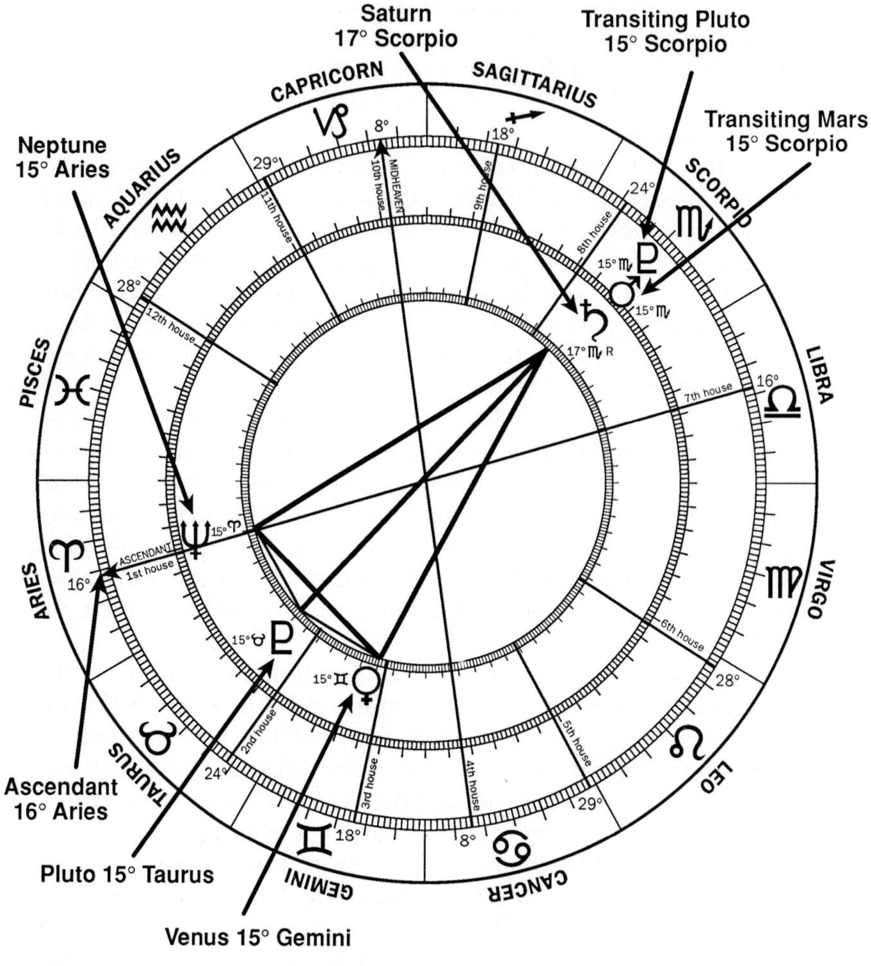

FIGURE 13   On November 27, 1989, transiting Mars (the planet of war) and transiting Pluto (the planet of widespread death and destruction) will form an exact conjunction at 15° Scorpio. This conjunction will activate Canada's bisected Finger of God formed by Saturn, Pluto, Venus, Neptune and the Ascendant. The conjunction of transiting Mars and Pluto falls only 2° from Canada's Saturn (the planet of karmic circumstances) at 17° Scorpio (in the seventh house of war) and opposed to Canada's Pluto at 15° Taurus (in the first house of the nation as a whole). The quincunx of transiting Mars and Pluto to Venus shows the abrogation of peace agreements. The quincunx of transiting Mars and Pluto to Neptune shows international intrigue. Thus, Canada could be embroiled in a deadly war anytime in the succeeding 24 months.

Transiting Pluto Makes an Exact Conjunction
with Canada's Natal Saturn
February 13, 1990

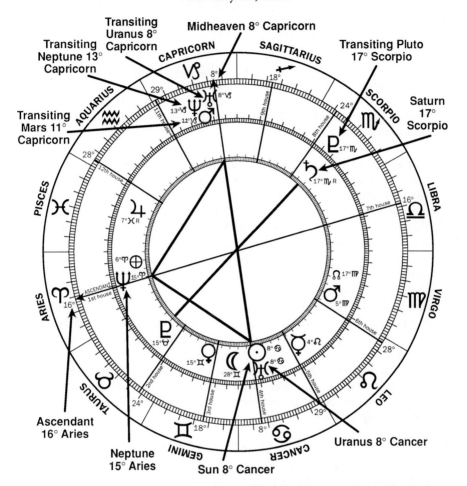

FIGURE 14 On February 13, 1990, transiting Pluto will form an exact conjunction to Canada's Saturn at 17° Scorpio and an opposition to her Pluto at 15° Taurus. This occurs just two days after transiting Uranus exactly conjoins Canada's Midheaven at 8° Capricorn with Mars at 11° Capricorn and Neptune at 13° Capricorn close by. These planets form a T-square with Canada's Sun and Uranus at 8° Cancer, her Neptune at 15° Aries and her Ascendant at 16° Aries. The combined effect of the two configurations has the potential to ignite a war. They link the body that represents Canada's identity (the Sun) with the planets of war (Mars), karmic circumstances (Saturn), sudden events (Uranus), intrigue (Neptune) and widespread death and destruction (Pluto) in an explosive combination. In addition, a lunar eclipse on February 9, 1990, impacts the U.S. and Soviet charts and could trigger a war between the superpowers sometime thereafter.

It is clear that Canada will be profoundly impacted by the
karmic challenges affecting the United States and the rest of the
world in the 1990s. What we covered today, however, outlines the
basic challenges that the people of Canada must meet in the days
and months ahead.

Canada will definitely need enlightened leadership and the
intervention of the hosts of the Lord during this cycle! And I have
confidence that the people of Canada can, if they will, provide the
leadership and that the faithful can, if they will, pray for divine
intervention.

I know that every aspect of the astrological predictions of
Canada's karma can be defeated. But what's more important is
that you know it and that you seize the torch of the Goddess of
Liberty and run with it as a Keeper of the Flame and a runner in
the race for God's victory and ours in the City Foursquare!
Whatever else you do, make it your central goal in life to be one of
the components of the capstone of your nation's pyramid.

You need a running momentum to head off these configurations so they don't come upon you standing still. You need to use
the violet flame daily to quicken the people of your nation to
invoke such a conflagration of violet flame that would be sufficient
to turn the tide of oncoming karma. By the grace of God and your
free will enjoining the hosts of the Lord in this battle daily it can
be done.

But only you can answer the call from God to be the keepers
of his Flame of your nation. Only you can give answer and defeat
the fates whose writings are there in the night sky for those who
will look up and see.

What Happens Next?

Let us return to the Book of Revelation and see what is in
store after the ride of the Four Horsemen.

After the Four Horsemen are unleashed by the Four Beasts in
succession with their resounding "Come!" the Lamb opens the
fifth seal. And John said, "I saw under the altar the souls of them
that were slain for the Word of God, and for the testimony which
they held: And they cried with a loud voice, saying, How long,
O Lord, holy and true, dost thou not judge and avenge our blood
on them that dwell on the earth?" [125]

The millions of souls who have been slain for the Word of
God in this century are a grim reminder of the pale horseman,
whose name is Death and who, with Hell following after him,
rides through our century as he has ridden through others.

"White robes were given unto every one of them; and it was said unto them, that they should rest yet for a little season, until their fellowservants also and their brethren, that should be killed as they were, should be fulfilled."[126]

Therefore there are those who wait in the etheric octave (the heaven world) who have the white robes, who in these centuries and decades have been slain for Truth and for Freedom and for the cause of the Faithful and True, the representative of the Great White Brotherhood whose armies follow him "upon white horses, clothed in fine linen, white and clean."[127] And it is our turn, we who are in embodiment upon earth, we who are also a part of this Great White Brotherhood, to make our mark in time, in space. And we must repeat together the words of Abraham Lincoln "that these dead shall not have died in vain."[128] And let us say in this hour that they shall not have died in vain because we will pick up their swords and wield them as the sacred Word.

We will enjoin the legions of the Ancient of Days to march with us. We will challenge the forces of Antichrist in the name I AM THAT I AM. And we will make good the sacrifices that the soldiers of the cross have made before us.

Though the darkest hour may precede the dawn, this is the hour for the victory of the Light on earth.

What does Revelation say is coming, then?

I beheld when he had opened the sixth seal, and, lo, there was a great earthquake; and the sun became black as sackcloth of hair, and the moon became as blood;

And the stars of heaven fell unto the earth, even as a fig tree casteth her untimely figs, when she is shaken of a mighty wind.[129]

The stars of heaven who fell unto the earth, and still fall, are the fallen angels who were cast out of the octaves of Light by Archangel Michael and his hosts in "the war in heaven" chronicled in Revelation 12. To this day Archangel Michael executes the LORD's judgment upon the rebel angels who were recast in the mold of mortals when they were confined to earth bodies on planet earth after their defeat.

The LORD's first judgment upon them was that they were no longer allowed to occupy the heavenly realms. His second judgment, which has now fallen due, is that unless they bend the knee and confess the Universal Christ, the Manchild brought forth by the Woman clothed with the Sun, and are converted to God under his Law and his Will, they will no longer be allowed to occupy the realms of earth or any other planetary system. For the cycles of their opportunity to repent are up. And the LORD has declared: "It is finished!"

Unless they cease and desist from their perpetual warfare against the seed of Woman, they will no longer be the stars in our governments, in our houses of banking and commerce or in our media and entertainment industries. Their time is up. Therefore it is lawful that we call to Jesus Christ and Archangel Michael for their judgment.

> And the heaven departed as a scroll when it is rolled together; and every mountain and island were moved out of their places.
>
> And the kings of the earth, and the great men, and the rich men, and the chief captains, and the mighty men, and every bondman, and every free man, hid themselves in the dens and in the rocks of the mountains;
>
> And said to the mountains and rocks, Fall on us, and hide us from the face of him that sitteth on the throne, and from the wrath of the Lamb:
>
> For the great day of his wrath is come; and who shall be able to stand?[130]

This prophecy bespeaks planetary cataclysm as the sign of the LORD's judgment. Whether it will be in the physical octave, as many have predicted earthquake, including Edgar Cayce, Nostradamus and Jesus, whether it will be on the astral plane as Peter saw the elements melt with a fervent heat,[131] whether it will be in the mental body as the chaos of the mind, whether it will be on the etheric plane or on all four remains to be seen. It is a prophecy of turbulence in our time, and we should take it both literally and figuratively; for it is taking place and will continue to take place in the four lower bodies of the planetary evolution and the planet itself until the planetary alchemy for the transition to Aquarius is accomplished.

Sealing of the Servants of God

> And after these things I saw four angels standing on the four corners of the earth, holding the four winds of the earth, that the wind should not blow on the earth, nor on the sea, nor on any tree.
>
> And I saw another angel ascending from the east, having the seal of the living God: and he cried with a loud

voice to the four angels, to whom it was given to hurt the earth and the sea,

Saying, Hurt not the earth, neither the sea, nor the trees, till we have sealed the servants of our God in their foreheads.

And I heard the number of them which were sealed: and there were sealed an hundred and forty and four thousand of all the tribes of the children of Israel.[132]

Saint Germain has sent me across the nations for this sealing of the servants of God in their foreheads. This sealing is accomplished by means of the 'Emerald Matrix'.

What is the Emerald Matrix? It is a Chatham emerald which, although a laboratory-grown crystal, has the molecular structure of a real emerald. I understand it is made from sowing "seeds" of a mined emerald in chemicals in a tray. It took this three-inch by two-inch emerald nine months to "grow." A friend of Light brought it to me under the direction of Saint Germain.

And so I have invited my audiences to come before me single file after the concluding dictation of the evening, and I touch the Emerald Matrix to their brows. Many people feel the powerful current enter their bodies. Some do not. The variable is the individual's own light-energy-consciousness at the time. The constant is that beloved Saint Germain and the Great Law allow you to receive only that which is the necessary and safe requirement of your lifestream. And of course it is your free will and a very private decision whether to come to the altar or not.

I call it an Emerald Matrix because it is a molecular pattern in crystal that Saint Germain can use to transfer the ray of Light for the sealing of the servants of God. This ray passes from his heart through my heart chakra through this crystal and is anchored in your third-eye chakra.

Your third eye is the spiritual center of 'single-eyed' vision at the brow of the forehead. Called a chakra, the third eye corresponds to the Fifth Ray, whose color frequency is green, or emerald. It is the ray of the abundant life and the means whereby you bring into physical manifestation, or precipitate, your needs— i.e., all that is necessary for you to fulfill your divine plan and to serve to set life free.

The key here is that the molecular structure of the emerald has the capacity to condense and transmit an extraordinary 'charge' of the sacred fire.

The meaning of the sealing is this: A great upheaval coming upon the earth is prophesied for our time. The angel who ascends

from the east cries to the angels guarding the four quadrants of
Matter, "Wait. Let us seal the servants of our God in their
foreheads [i.e., let us seal the sacred fire of the Divine Mother in
their third eye] that their souls might be protected, that their vision
might be opened to know those things that will shortly come to
pass, that their minds might be made one with the Mind of God
through his name I AM THAT I AM, that they might remember
their point of origin in God and their true identity as his sons and
daughters through the Universal Christ. Let their electromagnetic
field be sealed, that they might be protected wherever they may be
found meeting the challenge of personal and planetary karma and
the forces of Armageddon already unleashed upon the planet."

Thus I have been called, as the Messenger of the Great White
Brotherhood, to be the forerunner of "the angel ascending from
the east" (the east symbolizes the origin of the Sacred Mysteries
and the dawn of Christ illumination for the evolutions of earth),
"having the seal of the living God."

And Saint Germain has sent me all over the world stumping
for the Coming Revolution in Higher Consciousness, delivering
the message of the Ascended Masters—which is for the opening of
the third eye, the mind and the heart—so that God's servants may
be sealed. This sealing is the conclusion of my presentation
wherever I deliver the prophecy of Saint Germain and the lost
teachings of Jesus.

Interestingly, the initiation of the sealing of the servants of
God in their foreheads is also the restoration of the dispensations
of the ages of Taurus, Aries, Pisces and Aquarius. It is the sealing
of their memory in God. It is the quickening of their remembrance
not only of prophecy but also of the LORD's judgments, which have
been written in the past and which may be projected on the screen
of life in the future.

The sealing awakens individual accountability for action,
reaction and interaction, past, present and future: karma. It
awakens the need to give and receive mercy. The sealing is the
confirmation of Divine Justice whereby we are no longer afraid,
for our God is with us—Emmanuel[133]—and we will call upon him
and he will answer us in time of trouble.[134]

We, then, as the sealed servants, can face the future with
confidence in him and challenge that proud wave of returning
karma and say to it, "Thus far and no farther!" That is the
authority that God has given you as his sons and daughters. Take it
and run with it.

The dictation by Saint Germain that was delivered following this lecture is published in Book II, pp. 401–8. Throughout these notes *PoW* is the abbreviation for *Pearls of Wisdom*. (1) John 13:16; 15:20.* (2) John 1:9. (3) I Thess. 5:2–9. (4) Luke 11:1–4; Matt. 6:9–13; see the Lord's Prayer. (5) John 1:12, 13. (6) Phil. 2:12. (7) Matt. 7:15. (8) Zech. 13:7; Matt. 26:31. (9) The Greek word *gnosis* means literally "knowledge"; it is also translated as "understanding," "insight," or "acquaintance." As used by the early Christian gnostics of the second century, *gnosis* was not rational or intellectual knowledge but self-knowledge—that is, knowledge of God or knowledge of the self as God; the "acquaintance" with, or recognition of, the divine element that constitutes the Real Self. (10) Jer. 23:5, 6; 33:15, 16. (11) Gen. 4:26; 12:8; 26:25; I Sam. 12:17–20; II Sam. 22:4, 7; Pss. 4:3; 18:3, 6; 50:15; 55:16–18; 86:3, 5–7; 99:6; 118:5; 145:18–20; Jer. 29:12; Joel 2:32; Acts 2:21; Rom. 10:12, 13. (12) Deut. 4:24. (13) I John 1:5, 7. (14) See p. 136. (15) Jon. 3:1–10. See also II Chron. 15:1–19; 29–32. (16) See Elizabeth Clare Prophet, "Nostradamus: The Four Horsemen," in *Saint Germain On Prophecy*, Book Two, $5.95 (add $.50 for postage). (17) Mark 10:27. (18) See Rev. 12. For Enoch's revelations and warnings about the fallen angels called Watchers, with exegesis and exposé by Elizabeth Clare Prophet, see *Forbidden Mysteries of Enoch: The Untold Story of Men and Angels*, containing all the Enoch texts, including the Book of Enoch and the Book of the Secrets of Enoch, $12.95 (add $1.00 for postage). (19) For information on political and economic border problems between the United States and Canada, see p. 400 n. 5. (20) Godfré Ray King, *Unveiled Mysteries* (Chicago: Saint Germain Press, 1934), pp. 33–71. (21) Gen. 14:18, 19; Ps. 110:4; Heb. 5:6, 10; 6:20; 7. (22) I Sam. 7:3. (23) I Sam. 8:5. (24) I Sam. 8:7. (25) *The Collected Works of St. Teresa of Avila*, vol. 1, *The Book of Her Life, Spiritual Testimonies, Soliloquies*, trans. Kieran Kavanaugh and Otilio Rodriguez (Washington, D.C.: ICS Publications, 1976), pp. 79–80. (26) Mother Mary, March 3, 1968, 1968 *PoW*, Book I, p. 37. (27) See p. 220. (28) Henry Thomas and Dana Lee Thomas, *Living Biographies of Great Scientists* (Garden City, N.Y.: Nelson Doubleday, 1941), p. 15. (29) Ibid., p. 20. (30) David Wallechinsky, Amy Wallace, and Irving Wallace, *The Book of Predictions* (New York: William Morrow and Co., 1980), p. 346. (31) Clements R. Markham, *Life of Christopher Columbus* (London: George Philip and Son, 1892), pp. 207–8. (32) *Encyclopaedia Britannica*, 15th ed., s.v. "Columbus, Christopher." (33) Ibid. (34) Voltaire, *Œuvres*. Lettre cxviii., ed. Beuchot, lviii., p. 360, quoted in Isabel Cooper-Oakley, *The Count of Saint Germain* (Blauvelt, N.Y.: Rudolf Steiner Publications, 1970), p. 96. (35) For further information on the embodiments of Saint Germain and his sponsorship of the United States, see "The Mystical Origins of the United States of America," in *Saint Germain On Alchemy*, pp. 101–26; *Saint Germain On Prophecy*, Book One. (36) Rev. 1:1. (37) For teachings on the Cosmic Clock see pp. 479 n. 5, 501 n. 2. (38) Rev. 12:17. (39) Rev. 20:12, 13. (40) The Revised Standard Version and the Jerusalem Bible omit the words "and see" which appear in the King James Version after the word "Come" in Rev. 6: 1, 3, 5 and 7. *The Interpreter's Bible* says that the additional words "and see" "are not well attested." "Come!" is a command upon which the horses appear in turn. The words "and see" are extraneous and change the meaning of the verses. Consequently, they are omitted in this citation of the King James Version. (41) Rev. 6:1–8, King James Version. Compare with the Jerusalem Bible translation: "Then I saw the Lamb break one of the seven seals, and I heard one of the four animals shout in a voice like thunder, 'Come.' Immediately a white horse appeared, and the rider on it was holding a bow; he was given the victor's crown and he went away, to go from victory to victory. When he broke the second seal, I heard the second animal shout, 'Come.' And out came another horse, bright red, and its rider was given this duty: to take away peace from the earth and set people killing each other. He was given a huge sword. When he broke the third seal, I heard the third animal shout, 'Come.' Immediately a black horse appeared, and its rider was holding a pair of scales; and I seemed to hear a voice shout from among the four animals and say, 'A ration of corn for a day's wages, and three rations of barley for a day's wages, but do not tamper with the oil or the wine.' When he broke the fourth seal, I heard the

*Bible references are to the King James Version unless otherwise noted.

voice of the fourth animal shout, 'Come.' Immediately another horse appeared, deathly pale, and its rider was called Plague, and Hades followed at his heels. They were given authority over a quarter of the earth, to kill by the sword, by famine, by plague and wild beasts." **(42)** Matt. 24:22; Mark 13:20. **(43)** George Arthur Buttrick et al., eds., *The Interpreter's Bible,* 12 vols. (Nashville, Tenn.: Abingdon Press, 1951–57), 12:412. **(44)** Rev. 19:11–16. **(45)** Saint Germain, November 27, 1986, 1986 *PoW,* Book II, pp. 647, 648; *Saint Germain On Prophecy,* Book Four, pp. 207, 208. **(46)** Saint Germain, October 3, 1987, 1987 *PoW,* Book I, pp. 484–85. **(47)** Ibid., pp. 487–88. **(48)** Mark L. Prophet and Elizabeth Clare Prophet, *The Science of the Spoken Word,* $7.95 (add $1.00 for postage). **(49)** See *Webster's Ninth New Collegiate Dictionary,* s.v. "invocation." **(50)** Ibid., s.v. "invoke." **(51)** Ibid., s.v. "incantation," "incant." **(52)** Saint Germain, May 28, 1986, 1986 *PoW,* Book II, p. 521; *Saint Germain On Prophecy,* Book Four, p. 166. **(53)** *Save the World with Violet Flame!* by Saint Germain 1–4 released by Elizabeth Clare Prophet, audiocassettes including booklets: cassette 1, B88019; cassette 2, B88034; cassette 3, B88083; cassette 4, B88117; $5.95 each (add $.75 each for postage); see pp. 400 n. 6, 560 n. 1. **(54)** Matt. 2:7–12. **(55)** See p. 225. **(56)** See p. 209. **(57)** Ezek. 18:30–32. **(58)** Isa. 1:16–20. **(59)** Jer. 20:4. **(60)** Eph. 6:12. **(61)** Matt. 22:37, 39. **(62)** Rev. 16:7. **(63)** Phil. 2:7. **(64)** Jer. 32:35, Jerusalem Bible. **(65)** Biblical references to child sacrifice: Lev. 18:21; 20:2–5; Deut. 12:31; 18:10; II Kings 16:3; 17:17; 21:6; 23:10; II Chron. 28:3; 33:6; Ps. 106:37, 38; Jer. 7:31, 32; 19:1–6; 32:35; Ezek. 16:20, 21, 36; 20:26, 31; 23:37–39; Isa. 57:5; Amos 5:25, 26; Mic. 6:7. **(66)** Saint Germain, January 6, 1982, 1982 *PoW,* Book I, p. 179. **(67)** Jer. 19:3–9, Jerusalem Bible. **(68)** Jer. 20:3, 4, Jerusalem Bible. **(69)** Jer. 7:3, 4, 8–11, Jerusalem Bible. **(70)** Jer. 4:19, Jerusalem Bible. **(71)** Jer. 14:13, Jerusalem Bible. **(72)** Jer. 6:14, Revised Standard Version. **(73)** Jer. 4:6. **(74)** Jer. 25:8, 9, 11, Revised Standard Version. **(75)** Jer. 27:8, 9, Jerusalem Bible. **(76)** Jer. 28:13–15, Jerusalem Bible. **(77)** Jer. 52:6, Jerusalem Bible. **(78)** I Sam. 8:7. **(79)** *Fatima in Lucia's Own Words: Sister Lucia's Memoirs,* ed. Louis Kondor, trans. Dominican Nuns of Perpetual Rosary (Fátima, Portugal: Postulation Centre, 1976), p. 162. **(80)** Ibid., p. 200. **(81)** Robert A. S. Sullivan, "Russia Is Not Yet Properly Consecrated," *The Fatima Crusader,* March–May 1988, p. 29. **(82)** "The Race Against the Clock," *Fatima Crusader,* October–December 1985, p. S-9. **(83)** Louis Emerich, *Neues Europa,* 15 October 1963. **(84)** Pope John Paul II, November 1980, printed in *Stimme des Glaubens;* quoted in "Pope John Paul II and the Third Secret of Fatima," *The Maryfaithful,* May–June 1986, p. 12. **(85)** Ibid. **(86)** Frère Michel de la Sainte Trinité, "The Third Secret Revealed . . . ," *Fatima Crusader,* June–July 1986, p. 23. **(87)** Rev. 6:14. **(88)** Mother Mary, May 15, 1983, 1983 *PoW,* p. 546. **(89)** *Mother Mary's Scriptural Rosary for the New Age* is published on 8-audiocassette album A8048 and in the book *My Soul Doth Magnify the Lord!* by Mark L. Prophet and Elizabeth Clare Prophet, $7.95 (add $1.00 postage); *A Child's Rosary to Mother Mary,* 15-minute scriptural rosaries published on 4 audiocassette albums, 3 cassettes per album; Album 1 (A7864): John, James, Jude; Album 2 (A7905): Paul to the Hebrews; Album 3 (A7934): Paul to the Galatians; Album 4 (A8045): Paul to the Corinthians; $9.95 each (add $.90 each for postage). **(90)** Center for Peace, *Medjugorje Newsletter 1-86,* p. 1. **(91)** René Laurentin and Ljudevit Rupčić, *Is the Virgin Mary Appearing at Medjugorje?* (Washington, D.C.: The Word Among Us Press, n.d.), p. 143. **(92)** Ibid. **(93)** See p. 243. **(94)** See p. 140. **(95)** See p. 136. **(96)** See pp. 315–16. **(97)** Edgar Leoni, *Nostradamus and His Prophecies* (New York: Bell Publishing Company, 1961), p. 309. **(98)** Ibid., p. 149. **(99)** Edward Teller and Allen Brown, *The Legacy of Hiroshima* (Garden City, N.Y.: Doubleday and Co., 1962), p. 5. **(100)** Leoni, *Nostradamus,* p. 253. **(101)** Ibid., p. 187. **(102)** Antony C. Sutton, *Wall Street and the Rise of Hitler* (Seal Beach, Calif.: '76 Press, 1976), p. 163. **(103)** Ibid. **(104)** Antony C. Sutton, *Western Technology and Soviet Economic Development,* vol. 1, *1917 to 1930;* vol. 2, *1930 to 1945;* vol. 3, *1945 to 1965* (Stanford, Calif.: Hoover Institution Press, 1968–73). **(105)** Antony C. Sutton, *The Best Enemy Money Can Buy* (Billings, Mont.: Liberty House Press, 1986), pp. 24–25, 28, 247. **(106)** Even though the Soviets withdrew most of their troops from

Afghanistan in February, 1989, American officials charge that the Soviets have sent their former puppet government in Afghanistan $250 to $300 million a month in military supplies since their "withdrawal." See "U.S. Must Reassess Afghan Policy," *Wall Street Journal,* 18 October 1989; Robert Pear, "U.S. Asserts Soviet Advisers Are Fighting in Afghanistan," *New York Times,* 8 October 1989. **(107)** Antony C. Sutton, *National Suicide: Military Aid to the Soviet Union* (New Rochelle, N.Y.: Arlington House, 1973), p. 257. **(108)** Toby Roth, "Big Bankers Lending Billions to Moscow," *Conservative Digest,* February 1988, p. 82. **(109)** John F. Avedon, "The U.S. Must Speak Up for Tibet," *New York Times,* 10 October 1987. **(110)** John F. Avedon, *In Exile from the Land of Snows* (New York: Vintage Books, 1986), p. 48. **(111)** 18 June 1987, *Congressional Record,* 100th Cong., 1st sess., H5229. **(112)** "Who May Cry for Tibet?" *New York Times,* 9 March 1988. **(113)** See p. 282. **(114)** Michael Baigent, Nicholas Campion, and Charles Harvey, *Mundane Astrology* (Wellingborough, Northamptonshire, England: The Aquarian Press, 1984), p. 169. **(115)** Baigent, Campion, and Harvey, *Mundane Astrology,* pp. 169–74. **(116)** El Morya, October 2, 1987, 1987 *PoW,* Book I, pp. 474, 480. **(117)** Prov. 29:18. **(118)** See Mark L. Prophet and Elizabeth Clare Prophet, "The Romanization of Christ and Christianity" and "The Age of Apostasy and an Angry God Is Not Over," in *The Lost Teachings of Jesus II,* pp. 57–68; and "The Making of a Cult Leader," a December 11, 1988 sermon by Elizabeth Clare Prophet available on two 90-min. audiocassettes, $13.00 (add $.95 for postage), K88045–6. **(119)** Charles Thomson and William Barton, "Remarks and Explanations," quoted in Robert Hieronimus, *America's Secret Destiny: Spiritual Vision & the Founding of a Nation* (Rochester, Vt.: Destiny Books, 1989), p. 54. **(120)** Saint Germain, "A Pledge from the Knight Commander," in brochure *Keepers of the Flame: A Fraternity of Sons and Daughters of God Dedicated to the Freedom and Enlightenment of Humanity,* pp. 33, 34. **(121)** Jesus Christ, April 19, 1987, 1987 *PoW,* Book I, pp. 269, 274. **(122)** Rev. 21:16. **(123)** Matt. 10:16. **(124)** See Elizabeth Clare Prophet, November 26, 1989, 1989 *PoW,* pp. 725–44. **(125)** Rev. 6:9, 10. **(126)** Rev. 6:11. **(127)** Rev. 19:11–16. **(128)** Abraham Lincoln, Gettysburg Address, November 19, 1863. **(129)** Rev. 6:12, 13. **(130)** Rev. 6:14–17. **(131)** II Pet. 3:10, 12. **(132)** Rev. 7:1–4. **(133)** Isa. 7:14; Matt. 1:23. **(134)** Pss. 50:15; 91:15; 107:6, 13, 19, 28.

Notes

Pearls of Wisdom®
published by The Summit Lighthouse

| Vol. 31 No. 1 | Beloved El Morya | January 3, 1988 |

New Year's Retreat
at the Royal Teton Ranch

I
My Candidacy for President
of the United States of America
"I Run in the Race in the Hearts of My Chelas"

Hail, Chelas of the Will of God!

I salute you from the heart of Darjeeling and from the heart
of this nation's capital, for I have not deserted the ship of state.

Ladies and gentlemen, Keepers of the Flame, Lightbearers
of the world, I declare to you in this hour my candidacy for president of the United States of America! [46-sec. applause]

Chelas of my heart, any number of the ascended hierarchy
should so choose to declare their candidacy and do desire as the
fervor of your hearts also desires to see occupy the highest office
of this land one who does truly understand and espouse the will of
God, his wisdom and infinite compassion.

Therefore, you who are my chelas, come, then, and let me
reason with you as to how I shall accomplish my goal. In the flame
of dedication to the God-government of Sirius made manifest in
America, I bid you be seated tall now as members of the I AM Race.

Blessed hearts, there are proverbs in many nations which so
state that the leadership of the people is that which they deserve.
Let us examine, then, the science of this proverb. Is it not the
concept of the coordinate in the earth? Therefore, if you do have
my Diamond Heart and the Diamond Heart of Mary in your
heart, if you do radiate such devotion to the will of God, shall you
not deserve capable leadership of the same quality of heart?

So it is, beloved—the people have magnetized candidates on the Right, on the Left, in two parties and more, and these candidates are indeed profiles in mediocrity. They have risen from "the system," from the entertainment world; they have risen from the educational houses; they have come out of this continent, fed by a food not adequate for heroes and conquerors. These are the products of a modern America, not like the one founded upon those great principles of individualism as in the profile of your first president, George Washington.

Thus, beloved, flanking me this night are the Messengers Godfre[1] and Lanello, and in their hearts and in mine is a reaffirmation of our loyalty to and our upholding of the office of Messenger of the Great White Brotherhood, whose mantle is upon the one through whom we speak.

Therefore, beloved, we come to affirm that mantle as one which you may call upon for the profile of courage that must manifest as a point/counterpoint to that of mediocrity, which shall not win a war or the fight in the economy for balance, nor shall it win in space, in time, in the center of the earth or in the heart of man. [For] leadership is born of a certain 'all-chemistry' of God[2] that was once the very fire and flavor of this nation under God, the Mighty I AM Presence.

I come, then, seriously to declare my candidacy, yet my candidacy must come under cosmic law. What can I do, then? By the Order of the Diamond Heart[3] I raise up profiles of courage, profiles in you—in each and every one of you my chelas who does pledge to become a part of that Order, a true manifestation of leadership by the Holy Christ Self.

Therefore, I run for office and I truly run in the race in the hearts of all of my true chelas.

I myself come into you and unto you, beloved—in your hearts—to define and to set forth such an archetypal pattern of holy Christhood of the leadership of The LORD Our Righteousness that in you shall be the grooming of my heart to take your place in positions of leadership great and small. These are spiritual, beloved, and leadership as it pertains to the spiritual path: the spiritual path of discipleship unto individual Christhood.

You who then cheer when I declare my candidacy, you may vote for me and you may vote me into office *by becoming myself on earth.* Your vote for me, then, is a vote of confidence in the will of God, in that holy Christhood whereby each and every one does grow in the stature, the nobility of the will of God, the wisdom, the study.

And therefore, beloved, it is not a leaping to enter the

political race to which I call you or myself but to the raising up of those whose hearts are so like Godfre's, so like those of us who have occupied this office, that you will be the ensign in the earth, the mandate of the people whereby it may be said in heaven and on earth: this people does deserve in the highest temporal office of the land that highest representative of Maitreya and of the Great White Brotherhood.

Therefore, beloved, as I run for office I shall look to raise up those who may qualify for our sponsorship. Thus far we say, we are the sponsors of right action. Therefore, let right action be illumined, be championed and be taught as to what that *Awareness/Action*⁴ may be in this land.

Blessed hearts, when the people know what is right action and when the people demand that both parties contain that roster of right action as a party platform, then the candidates of both parties and the single candidate who does win must pledge to precipitate that right action by law, by the proper bills, by taking the helm of the ship of state.

Blessed hearts, the people must not sleep, for once having the correct platform, they must demand that those who have promised fulfill. To break one's word concerning what one's actions will be in occupying this office, beloved, is a crime against Almighty God, the state and the people. Therefore, know and understand that those presidents who arrive and fulfill not their campaign promises ought to be subject to impeachment.

This nation has gone soft on soft ice cream and all manner of sweets. It is a pity that the loss of life, the loss of nationhood, the loss of God-government should have so much to do with the dietary intake of drugs and the fare of rock music and the toxins in the food and all manner of chemicals in the earth, the water and the air.

Thus, the chemical warfare inflicted from without is also from within as those who are afflicted, beloved, have no longer the spine to rise up and reject their overlords worldwide who have put upon them that which has caused such a densification of their brains, which are already subject to limitation by genetic engineering by the fallen ones and the people's own karma.

Thus, beloved, my plan for this year is that what a president ought to be should be reflected in the mien, in the visage, in the action, in the manner of speech and reasoning, in the deliberation, the counsel and the honor of those who are chelas of El Morya and those who are truly disciples unto individual Christhood.

I would speak, then, of certain of those Keepers of the Flame who have thought that in serving our cause they could circumvent the laws of man and thereby also circumvent the laws of God. Blessed hearts, this is an utter mockery of our path and our goal. If you are the Light of the world and a city [set upon the mountain of God] that cannot be hid, *and you are,* then recognize that (for the most part) your aura has a light that is of far greater intensity than that of those with whom you associate, by the very fact of your decree momentum if not by your "attainment," which means *the action of retaining the Christ Light* within you.

Therefore, each time you circumvent decency, honesty, kindness, comfort and that which is appropriate according to the actions and decorum which have been espoused by Godfre and others, you do despite and disservice to our cause and our movement.

This tendency, beloved, is seen not alone in isolated cases. The idea that you are a chela has somehow made some of you to believe that you are also favorite sons and favorite-son candidates; but instead you make yourselves candidates for the very mockery of the Law that you say you espouse. And therefore we say that those who accept the call of Christhood under Jesus[5] must recognize that in that calling and in that path they must exhibit tenfold the integrity and the cosmic honor flame, the credibility that is expected of normal citizens: Your lives must be impeccable. They must be exemplary.

Understand, beloved, that not only are the angels looking, your I AM Presence and Holy Christ Self, but your neighbors are also looking; and therefore many of you have caused embarrassment to ourselves, to this organization and to its leadership by actions which simply belie all that you have been taught. If you begin at the beginning of [such mockery of the Law, with] squabbles and discords among the brethren, you will see that such a display of pettiness can in no way attract others to your faith. This must cease!

I speak of mediocre examples that have been set by various individuals in this Community, in its headquarters, in Glastonbury and throughout this state. It is a shame that when we secure dispensations from the Central Sun that you should take them so lightly and not recognize that these do not come again so easily and that for every misuse of our Teaching and our Path and for every bad example, you give to us a mountain of karma to balance.

Blessed hearts, you cheer with joy my declaration of candidacy. Perhaps you would run with me. Perhaps you would vote for me. I say to you, vote for me as being in you. Vote for me as being yourself and say, "What would Morya do in this situation?"

Some of you have fantastic notions as to what the Darjeeling Council would do in the situations that must be decided in the halls of the federal, state and local governments. Some of you would be considerably surprised to know that your opinion of what the right step and the right measure is may not be our opinion or our counsel.

Therefore, none can pocket or place in a slot El Morya or the members of the Darjeeling Council. We have made our statement long ago that we are neither Left nor Right nor middle of the road but we do espouse Truth wherever we find it[6] and we are determined to find that Truth in the hearts of our chelas and in their actions.

Let there be no shame, then, and let there be the withdrawing of the dissimulation of the Word, whether by human bickering or competitiveness or simply an absence of the expression of Divine Love throughout this worldwide Community. I would see chelas who have a sense of upholding the reputation of the Great White Brotherhood in the earth. I would have you be, everywhere you go, the sublime profile of those who have the courage to express their hearts and yet know that unless the expression of the heart be prompted truly by the Holy Spirit, it will not achieve the desired goal.

Therefore, in the great silence of Gautama Buddha and the power of his meditation, there is a pulsation throughout the world of the balance of the threefold flame and of the mind in individual and national self-rule—self-rule for him that would keep the city and the citadel of our retreat.

Hasten, then, hasten to leap up three steps at a time on this flight! Beloved, you dare not any longer allow our garment to trail in the mud of human foolishness.

Therefore, I comment on the words of the Messenger which I placed in her heart concerning those who become farther and farther afield from the will of God and know it not. Why do ye know it not?

Blessed hearts, the receptacle of the Diamond Heart, the receptacle of the heart of Saint Germain, your own threefold flame, is the measure and standard of right consciousness. Few are right all of the time but many believe that they are right at least some of the time, if not all of the time.

Thus, each and every one in his own way becomes highly opinionated and when his stubbornness of mind does therefore enter the realm of spiritual matters where fantasy and the psychic enter in, some of our own who might have been our best servants are found simply out in the field, not centered where the action is.

I speak of the fields of this property and beyond and not of the general field of our membership, which has many fiery hearts who are realistic while others dabble in any number of ways and paths and communications purported to be from our octave.

Blessed ones, many say that it is easy to receive channelings from Saint Germain and others. Well, you may think it is easy from this level, and so it is, to contact other minds disembodied. What is difficult, beloved, is that at our level the dispensation to train a Messenger, to raise up one clothed with a certain inner garment whereby you may trust our delivery of the Word, requires an enormous placement, upon the altar of God and on the line of battle, of our lives, our causal bodies, our ascended state, our very beings. The dispensation, therefore, for the Messengership does not come easily to us.

And I will tell you what determines the continuity of the office: it is whether or not the hearers of the Word assimilate the Word, embody it, implement it and whether or not the worded release does have the effect of changing a society, a civilization and a planet for the better, and finally, whether or not the delivery and the mission and the organization we sponsor do produce the fruit of the annual ascension that is called for.

It is beloved Godfre who elected to take his ascension on this night, 1939. Blessed ones, the requirement for that ascension for that year had to be fulfilled, and thus it has been a tradition ever since, that on New Year's Eve some one individual on the planet does take his ascension, therefore attaining that immortal Life that does again warrant the dispensation of the office and mantle of Messenger of the Great White Brotherhood continuing.

As we desire to do more for you and through you, we are therefore limited by each and every individual's use or misuse of our communication, and the karma we dread most is the karma of neglect when the Word is neglected, when the instructions are so carefully given and people go out and develop a totally independent "tack," if you will, as *their* approach, as *their* unique solution to the solving of the world's problems.

As we come together, then, in winter in the white fire core of Being and our Retreat, it is a time for deliberation. It is a time for the review of Alpha's proclamation and the Wesak address, of Alpha's dictation on July 5th and even those deliveries that have come from the Lord of the World on the New Year's Eves past.[7]

Thus, I say to you, beloved, as I run for office as president of the United States of America, one son of Hierarchy, one daughter one day may be myself in form to be elected to that office, but it will come about only if you raise up that Spirit of Christ in yourself uniquely, holding and keeping the Flame whereby heaven will be compelled not only to send you such souls of Light but to see to it that one becomes the leader of this nation.

In the meantime, beloved, this year and the election which follows, all of the speeches and campaigning that will take place, being a period of grave darkness, is a time and a space for the keeping of the flame of America and of the office of the president, that the very mantle itself be able to be called forth again. For at this time, when some of you, and certainly not all, may be involved in the small problems that affect your households or your interactions in business and with one another, that which is being deliberated by the Karmic Board and the Council of Sirius is whether or not the mantle of the office of president of the United States shall indeed fall upon the one who is elected.

Blessed ones, if one not worthy is elected, there may come to pass, as it were, the "headless horseman," an individual in office who does not bear the mantle and sponsorship of the Great White Brotherhood. I can assure you that should this occur, it will be the darkest day in America's history since Saint Germain did anoint George Washington to that office.

The deliberation, then, is ongoing as to whether or not that mantle should fall upon one who does not hold the office but who is capable of keeping the flame of that office in our name. Thus, when I tell you that I declare my candidacy, I am telling you that I am searching for the chela who will make himself/herself worthy to bear that mantle should the day and hour come on Inauguration Day that the one who takes the oath of office does not receive the corresponding spiritual mantle.

Blessed hearts, you remember the years when Godfre was in embodiment in America. In those years there were some who occupied that office who were truly not worthy. That mantle could not be borne by them, yet it did still rest above them though they never did integrate with it. Thus, it was beloved Godfre while he was in embodiment who did keep the flame for that office.

One wonders in reading the history of the nation how the nation has survived her presidents. It is because of the heart and the fire of the people! Whereas one may have borne the spiritual flame of the office while the wrong one occupied it, millions of hearts bore a portion because of the profile and the image of Christ they outpictured in some measure. Thus, almost as though by the 'collective' or 'community' consciousness of this nation has that office been upheld. Unfortunately, this is no longer the case in this day and age and those who occupy positions of leadership do so in an utter betrayal of the founding principles and the spiritual light from on high.

Understand, beloved, that there is a parallel here to the call that has been sent to you to become a part of the Order of the Diamond Heart of Mary and Morya. Here we see that many Keepers of the Flame bearing a portion and becoming a greater portion daily of that Diamond Heart can secure the spiritual grants and dispensations that flow through the office of the Messenger for the saving of the Lightbearers of the world and, if not for the saving of a nation, then for the saving of the opportunity of a nation to rise again.

Consider this which I have said, beloved. Some nations have been lost on earth and their dispensations are not retrievable. They will not rise again, not in this particular thousand years of cycles. In the case of America, as Saint Germain's dispensation has been given, a portion of it has already been lost with his exit from the nation's capital.[8]

Understand, then, beloved, that all those who raise up the Diamond Heart in the spiritual path for the maintenance and the holding of the balance of karma in the earth may also hold a portion of the mantle of the office of the president and in so doing, beloved, being a part of my heart, you are not only running for office but "occupying"[9] until a people may bridge the gap of their neglect and ignorance and once again by the momentum of your heart, by the magnet of the Central Sun and that diamond, come to a realization of who and what they want to be in that office.

And when they again come of age, to the age of courage,* beloved, then it is your magnet, your profile, your presence, your right action that will be the nucleus whereby a people once again deserve a Son of God in office.

Blessed hearts, understand the deeper meaning of the dispensations of God to earth and know that so long as Alpha does remain extending to each one of you his Mantle and his Presence for a fiery mission and purpose, we say, *Onward courage!* [30-sec. applause]

---

*courage: cœur-âge, the age of the heart's emboldening by the full flowering of the threefold flame

Delivered New Year's Eve, December 31, 1987, at the **Royal Teton Ranch. (1)** The Ascended Master Godfre was embodied as George Washington and the Messenger Guy W. Ballard (born July 28, 1878; ascended December 31, 1939). **(2) 'All-chemistry' of God.** See *Saint Germain On Alchemy,* pp. 7, 38. **(3) Order of the Diamond Heart.** See 1987 *Pearls of Wisdom,* vol. 30, pp. 633–37; 638, n. 11; 640, 641, 644–46. **(4) Awareness/Action.** See 1985 *Pearls of Wisdom,* vol. 28, p. 94; 1987 *Pearls of Wisdom,* vol. 30, p. 32. **(5)** See 1987 *Pearls of Wisdom,* vol. 30, pp. 269–76, 491–98, 577–82, 601–6. **(6)** See El Morya, *A White Paper from the Darjeeling Council Table,* in *Lords of the Seven Rays,* Book Two, pp. 53–64; and *Encyclical on World Good Will,* in *Morya,* pp. 121–23. **(7)** See 1987 *Pearls of Wisdom,* vol. 30, pp. 239–49, 379–93, 1–15. **(8)** See 1987 *Pearls of Wisdom,* vol. 30, pp. 611–12, 615, 617. **(9)** Luke 19:13.

Pearls of Wisdom®

published by The Summit Lighthouse

| Vol. 31 No. 2 | Beloved Gautama Buddha | January 10, 1988 |

New Year's Retreat
at the Royal Teton Ranch

II

Once Upon a Footstep
"The Way Out for 1988"

A Tapestry of the Great Buddha Sanat Kumara

My Blessed Ones,

I AM in the heart of the world even as I hold the world in my hands.

One may guide the totality of a sphere, yet the individual parts may continue on the merry road of destiny. Free will within the confines of karmic law appears to mankind as a shrinking box closing in around them. By prior exercise of free will, limitation upon limitation is built in to what once was a magnanimous gift of the Infinite whereby infinity as a conscious reality could be bestowed upon the manifest creation.

Expand, O concentric spheres—crystal spheres of the etheric crystal of a planetary idea, ideation, blueprint!

Once upon a time the mist became the crystal. How evident is the crystallization of the mist, even in the crystal that is found in the earth. Thus, a mystery is unveiled in the heart of the rock, and by science it is known that in the nucleus of every atom of every molecule a "fire" does burn.

As the fire is sealed in the heart of crystal, as it were a prisoner of form, time, space, dimension, so is the divine spark within your heart encased, not alone by the density of physical temple but by karmic skeins woven over and again as a gnarled knitting without pattern or precision.

Thus, as you would not hold up to the light or place in contest the knitting of your astral body, I say to you, beloved, let the threads be unraveled and wound again into separate balls of their various vibrations and colorations. Let the Divine Mother within you raise up a soul who begins anew the process of creation even in the very moment of the darkest hour when the world as a box is closing in for those who have not the vision of the mist that has become the crystal.

Perceive, then, the aura of the crystal sphere.* Perceive an ovoid that does manifest as an energy field around a sun center. Where you see this physical crystal sphere, you must visualize an identical one in another dimension to the side of it. Thus wherever there is one there is always two, one the unmanifest, one the manifest, Alpha/Omega.

For some the world is a toy and they have toyed with earth's energies recklessly, wantonly. They have not understood the world they build, in which they encase themselves.

Now the Avalokiteśvara Buddha, now the Buddha-behind-the-Buddha, does appear before you in a sphere of light, and the tear in his eye, beloved, reminds of the depth of feeling of this Presence of God who does know and experience that for some the weaving of the tangled gnarl of astral body and the wanton misuse of energy is, as it were, the coffin built by the misappropriation in base ignorance of the gift of free will and the gift of fire crystallized in the mist become matter.

Some shall ne'er escape the cave they have created round themselves!

Thus, our God does shed a tear, and we in the profound pain of knowing the parts of the whole of earth must also agonize in this hour when the Law nor the Grace nor the Mercy nor the Justice of it can afford these, who are gods surely in their own domain, any way out save the reigniting of the flame of the heart. For the flame is able to burn until that flame may crack the encasement and by the flame, the heat thereof, the atomic energy thereof, clear a path that the soul may escape.

But, beloved, wherewith shall the soul be known or know of the process of escape?

The soul who has already used the ritual of denial as "back-knitting" and backbiting thus to erect the enclosure wherein there is darkness and extreme anguish and fear—for there is no candle within to light the way—[that soul shares] the plight of many who have gone forth, sowers in the earth oblivious to their accountability for using good seed, sowing it in good vibration, harvesting,

*The Messenger, seated before the altar during the dictation, holds a crystal sphere of a 33.66-centimeter circumference.

then, in a mighty trump of victory as the sound of Archangels and their legions welcome home the Son of God who is become the All even in the all of this temporal life and world.

How much more perfectly can elemental life render the imagery of the crystallization of the Divine One encased in form? See, then, the condition of those who have sown in Darkness. See, then, the condition of the Son of God: though encased in the same similar form, the same conditions and laws of physics limiting his comings and his goings, in him we see that a god is born and not an anti-God, but a living God-Man, a *Man*ifestation of this Law of the One.

Therefore, I AM THAT I AM the God in the earth, the God-Manifestation! I AM part of every particle yet not limited by any. I may enjoy myself in all of my bodies manifest as *bhikkhus*,* sisters of the holy orders, all Keepers of the Flame. Therefore I AM everywhere in the Consciousness of God in the divine spark within you!

And the Avalokiteśvara God-ideation streaming forth in this hour does heighten sense and solar sense-awareness of the predicament of Life—Life that is God encased in form seeking to save that which is lost and Life that has become trapped by its own law and gift of free will.

How, then, shall Life escape if there be no individuality to cry out for that escape—or if there be individuality left at all, if that one has no ability or knowledge to make the call?

If I, then, should hurl by the power of God this crystal sphere into the Infinite, either Elohim should catch it and it transcend time to be the infinite crystal or it should find surcease of pain in the highest rock upon the hills and mountains of this area, only to be shattered and in that shattering discover the breaking of the mold of chaos. And the fire released should consume, then, a Darkness sown by the profligate ones, the proud, the ungodly, the profane, and they and their own creation should be consumed by their wanton misuse of fire.

The liberation of Life is a mercy unto Life. Life as God impelling, compelling does therefore seek an end to the Death matrix imposed upon it. Those who have identified with this matrix, having built it, continue on their merry way until their creation does undo themselves, disqualifying them forevermore as co-creators.

Things are coming to a head! This is the heart of my message.

Those found at the nexus where the mist becomes the crystal, they, then, shall sit in the seat of the Mediator, Universal Light

bhikkhu [Pali, from Sanskrit *bhiksu*]: Buddhist monk, religious mendicant.

who is Christ the LORD. At the very moment where crystal is the mist and mist is becoming that crystal, there is a realization of God—of the Word, of the power of Spirit, the wisdom of Love, and immortality. And in the very same nexus, as it is a figure-eight flow between these spheres, so the crystal ascending back to the mist is an accelerating spiral of ascension's flame abuilding within you, right within your heart, the secret chamber thereof.

Therefore, to experience Life descending and ascending at the very same point of the nexus, this is the experience, this is the self-knowledge of equilibrium, cosmic equilibrium, and at that point [the *laya* center] one can be and know oneself as God above, God below, God in the center of the flow, holding the balance for cosmos, retaining the flame, guarding the flame here in Matter.

How art thou the Buddha now, O chela of my heart? Thou art verily, for I AM the transparent sphere of Body of First Cause, of etheric blueprint. Thou art a crystallization of Alpha, aye. There-fore, we are one.

We are one because the heart flames, thine own and mine, are one at the nexus. I would be in your heart as you would be in my heart in this year 1988, the symbol of the 88 being twin flames establishing, as Above, so below, this crystal sphere.

Blessed hearts, if you know it not in this hour, you shall come to know it indeed, that the necessity of establishing co-measure-ment by the crystal of self with myself does become more urgent, more obvious. Therefore, I say to you these comforting words for that hour of a soul's desperation, encased in a case of karmic limitation: Come unto me, for I would be with thee. I would be thy heart. I would strengthen thy heart chakra to be the Diamond Heart even of Mary, Morya and the blessed saints of Jesus' own longing and desiring.

Thou hast need of me, beloved, beyond ken in this moment. Therefore, I supply a way of endurance in this octave, a contem-plation upon my form or image, reestablishing again and again truly—truly the equilibrium by the balance that is already mine, that I choose to make thine by secret overlay of Electronic Presence, impelling the divine spark within thee to pulsate to the rhythm of eternal Life of my heart, which flame I keep for all the world.

Thus, my beloved, may this pattern of the divine image of threefold flame and very presence of that tripartite fire be to you the point of magnetization of the God Flame whereby the bird of the soul shall break the encasement and transcend all karmic limitation *by Oneness with the living Guru.*

For those, then, bound without a flame in the darkness of their creation there is only one escape! It is the path of the Master/ disciple relationship. When does one know how far one has removed oneself to the coldness of outer space, far, far from the sun and central sun of being? One does not know, for all darkness is relative whereas the Light is absolute.

Thus, beloved, in the unknowing state, not knowing oneself but thinking one knows oneself, it is best, it is advisable, it is the better part of wisdom to choose the mantle of Padma Sambhava placed upon our Messenger for good cause, for ancient service and discipleship unto this Holy One of the East.[1] Take recourse in the mantle, knowing that it does take thee to the heart of Maitreya and the Western Shamballa, my abode,[2] and to Sanat Kumara and the Avalokiteśvara and to the Great One of Mercy, Kuan Yin.

Therefore, beloved, we do place in the crystal of the earth a mantle of Guru that is necessary physically to save that which is lost. It is the Avalokiteśvara consciousness that does descend upon you in this hour taking you into the great spheres and spheres upon spheres of his causal body that you might feel the heartbeat irregular of a planet off course, that you might know the heartbeat of God, listen to its sound only, accepting no other rhythm or sound that could jolt or take your inner system of Light from the true sound of the music of the spheres.

Peace, beloved. Peace, beloved. As these are trying times for chelas, these are also trying times for the one who wears our mantle, who must feel perpetually the agitation, the sorrow and the abject evil in form on planet earth and even imported from other systems.

In this moment and hour of transition when you are impelled and magnetized by the central sun of Helios and Vesta, know, then, that the supreme acceleration which we would bear to your beings is an absolute necessity for survival. As time narrows to become infinity, so options also narrow, and one realizes that at the point of destiny in the nexus where time and space meet eternity and are neutralized by it, only the single choice is acceptable. There are no longer five hundred options or two hundred or three or four. One right word is acceptable, one right act, one right choice: to be all Light, to pour in the cups many, waiting to be filled, all Light.

In the time of greatest darkness of war and turbulence, those who gather in our mountain must also know that the pause to ascend by the Seventh Ray is the key to being in an octave and a vibration of safety. Thus, contemplate the Grand Teton, for we go there, this entire company, in an exercise—an exercise of soul flight swift to the heart of the mountain in time of necessity or danger.

Let the mind become an arrow! Let the arrow be in the hand of the Archer, thy Christ. Let the bow be pulled.

Blessed hearts, see how, suddenly, the arrow of self now working in the field where one is taken and another is left[3] does fly straight to the heart of the etheric octave from the physical crystal sphere to the etheric [sphere] through the single opening, the only open door, the nexus where "thy heart/my Heart one" provides the tunnel of Light.

The arrow does fly and you are in an instant in a violet flame chamber hitherto undescribed, for there are many chambers in the mountain whose existence has not been chronicled or revealed.

Visualize, then, the vast violet flame chamber, sufficient to contain all Keepers of the Flame of the earth and many more, a vast chamber of amethyst and quartz crystal, stalactites, stalagmites. Thus, one senses descending from above, rising from beneath pillars of violet flame crystallized in the rock as so many ancient teeth of ancient dragon of Eastern wisdom.

Understand that violet flame, violet ray is the frequency of the true and perfect vibration of planet earth. Is, then, the violet planet the etheric sphere of this physical earth? Contemplate the mystery and determine to be at the nexus of the etheric sphere of planet earth. Then understand the beloved Presence, the devoted Presence of Omri-Tas and priests of the sacred fire of the violet planet who serve with the elemental beings and angels in a planetary abode which, being etheric, is, as it were, in its own counterpart of a quasi-physical manifestation, though not physical as you understand it. This, then, is a journey in transitions.

As you are able to still yourselves of the night of New Year's Eve, will you not be reminded by my image or statue that the contemplation of the One and the meditation of the arrow's flight—the repeating of the visualization of the arrow's flight instantaneous to the violet flame chamber—is, as it were, a physical exercise. The mind becomes agile, the soul follows, embraced and braced by the desire body desiring a haven of safety and surcease from world pain, desiring to have such a cave of light of violet flame crystal.

Where there is the desiring, beloved, is there not the counterpart reality? Can you desire anything [of God-Good] that does not already exist in the heart of God and in the heart of the mountain?

Blessed ones, it is a pity but understandable that only in time of greatest planetary distress do the many realize the increase of desire for spiritual attainment, co-measurement and a fully conscious existence in the etheric octave. Be it so, we understand. Where there is the breaking up of the crystallization of darkness, so worlds of manifestation are rearranged and some are shattered.

Thus, to fly to the heart of the mountain, to be able to come and go at will, is this not your desiring? And does not your security or lack of it, does not your insecurity and suffering derive from the box of karmic limitation?

And as you realize that you live on the surface of the earth and you contemplate millions of years of records, there does dawn in you the idea that some who could not make the transition to the etheric octave in full conscious retention of identity did flee inside the earth to escape the madness of the false gods on the surface of the planet and in the skies, and in so fleeing, finding therein a means of life, did remain, some evolving to a higher level and some 'devolving' to a subhuman level.

Thus, layers of evolution upon planet earth are, as it were, honeycombed, and in past ages many came to the same conclusion that you have come to, that the most dangerous place to be in this solar system is on the surface of the physical planet. What with pollution, manipulation, unseen forces and unwelcome visitors, is it not so?

Thus, O thus, in the Avalokiteśvara whose compassion is an infinite love beyond one's comprehension, is it not in that awareness, is it not in that joy of the heart of that One that you discover a true allegiance to becoming immortal? And that immortality, beloved, that quest sparked by a dead and dying world has given many an impetus to simply enter the invulnerable, untouchable octaves of Light.

Whatever, then, does impel thy ascent, daily seek the purification of the heart, that all thy sayings, doings, comings and goings (and as thou dost stand as watchman at the nexus) are conceived and executed in the purest motive, the purest desiring, the purest Be-ness, the purest hope, the purest faith, the purest charity. Let the purity and the clarity of the crystal, stream through life, stream through the coursings of thy soul!

It is lawful to desire to ascend. Once one has fulfilled, then, the establishing of this goal and entered the Lords of the Seven Rays' goal-fittedness program, there does occur—once peace of mind is found in the sense of continuity of being—the desiring to be God, not as escape but, as Morya was wont to say, "for the very love of Thee."[4]

For the very love of the Divine Lover, for this cause thou shalt desire to enter into the Allness of God, and for this cause alone I say to thee: Thou shalt ascend! Thou shalt ascend! Thou shalt ascend the holy mountain of God until once upon a footstep, after many thousands of footsteps, the next step, beloved, shall be the crossing over (unnoticed of thy soul) from physical to etheric octave—no death, no dying, simply mounting until the fulfillment is come.

Keeping on keeping on is a profound statement. It is made by all who have experienced the wonders of that moment when the very next step on the Path has been to reenter eternity whence thou didst descend.

Truly, then, the grandeur of life immortal is thine inheritance and the very definite option of free will unto those who know the ropes, who know that the key to the transcending of oneself, to the pulling of oneself up by one's bootstraps, is to place not one hand but both hands in the hands of the Guru. Now, this is the sign to remember, forming therefore the great sphere of light.

Let it be, then. As your hands come together, so make this form of the circle that I make in this hour. The circle of your hands coming together may reach above and take my hands. My hands, then, embracing and holding the upper sphere, your hands embracing the lower, our hands meet now at that point of the nexus.*

You may visualize this calmly and sweetly and know two hands holding two hands is the closed circuit. In that moment, beloved, you realize that alternating with the current and the flash of light, you are disciple, you are Guru. Each time for a single moment you experience the self as Guru, you then return to the self as disciple, determined to retain by conscious attainment and mindhood, *mindhood,* a greater and greater portion of the Great Guru above.

Thus, beloved, applying this comparison to the one who wears the mantle of Padma Sambhava, here we have placed the preponderance of the self as Guru below with the disciple above. Thus, the disciple who wears the mantle experiences discipleship in heaven, a tough course of chelaship in the inner retreats, and Guruship on earth, a most challenging enterprise, a most challenging enterprise...

Each and every one of you, then, must determine to pass the initiations of Christhood on earth, pulling and tugging, magnetizing by wisdom and astuteness and love the Higher Self here below and then with the fortitude of the crystal, meeting

---

*The Messenger's arms are raised above her head forming a circle, fingertips touching, as though holding the lower crystal sphere, then parted as her hands reach up to take the hands of the "Buddha-behind-the-Buddha."

every foe and enemy of that Christhood.

Nothing shall prevail against thee, my beloved, when the crystal does become thy aura. Is the crystal not, then, the Deathless Solar Body? O call to be and dwell in that Deathless Solar Body, more sure than space suit or any conveyance of capsule or module.

Blessed ones, when you wear your Deathless Solar Body, you are prepared for any journey or flight. You are in training for that soaring to the amethyst crystal cave room at the Grand Teton.

O beloved, when we say this, then does Reality disclose that many who study our words have neglected the weaving of the Deathless Solar Body.[5] Now then, being called to the Order of the Diamond Heart, this Diamond Heart being composed of millions of facets of good deeds and exact and exacting words, you understand that this is a comparable path of initiation to that of the weaving of the Deathless Solar Body. For that weaving is composed of an infinite number of stitches, and if this were physical, it would be a very thick knitting, inches thick. For after all, it is the soul's garment unto eternal Life. The sphere of light of the base chakra provides the yarn for this knitting and it is fully abundant unless squandered in unholy and ungodly action.

Thus, beloved, attentiveness, *attentiveness* is more realizable in the Order of the Diamond Heart, for one becomes instantly conscious by the Gurus of this Order when one is not creating a facet of diamond mirror. One by one, as octagon crystals, they form a Diamond Heart that grows and grows within you. One is conscious, then, [through the Mind of the Guru] when one does not create this faceted, this mirrorlike piece of the mosaic of the Diamond Heart.

Thus, it is as though the building of the Diamond Heart were more concrete and to the soul a safer measure of progress [than the weaving of the Deathless Solar Body]. One can pursue both courses, for it is the action [of "Diamond-Heartedness"] whereby the weaving of this garment takes place for thy wedding day, wedded eternally to immortal Light.

By action, by word, as you go about the business of the Father/Mother God, you are weaving and knitting that garment; and the astral that was disappears. It is displaced, for this Body [the Deathless Solar Body] is Light. It has infinite strength, resilience, mother-of-pearl radiance. Know and see the beauty of this garment. Treasure it. It is the weaving of many lifetimes. Some weave slowly, some fast. Some return to their knitting in every spare moment. Some set it aside for years.

O beloved, it is an hour of eternity. Eternity knocks and

comes to you in the personification of Avalokiteśvara. The pressure of his Presence of Light surrounds me and all. All keepers of the Light in the earth know his Presence of comfort and know that in saving that which is lost, this Presence of the God Buddha does therefore recognize those led astray not originally of their own volition yet certainly at some level by freewill consent.

Thus, those yet bound by the snarls of the fallen ones (who have no continuity of being) whose judgment was pronounced at the throne of God before and in the Presence of Enoch,[6] for these bound ones, yet subject to fallen ones who are still enslaving others, there is the hope and the present possibility, while there is yet time and space, for them to choose to be and to be rescued by that One who does extend Himself throughout all of the darkest depths of miscreation.

Thus it is a moment and a nexus. Thus it is an hour that you may also reach out through the Presence of Avalokiteśvara to save that which can be saved. We are still on that course as we were a year ago and aeons ago.[7] Nevertheless, the priority of the hour is the saving of one's own soul. That in itself is the great challenge and, as you have been told, a mighty work of the ages. In that saving, if it is truly a saving, the better portion of thyself does live in the etheric sphere that is the cause behind the manifestation of the crystal.

Once you have centered yourself in that etheric sphere, the crystal that is below that is also the extension of thyself in Matter may now become a habitation, a proving ground for many who may derive a sense of source, a sense of causal body within thine own. For those who have lost the way or even lost the flame or lost the thread of contact with Hierarchy, your crystal here below becomes that haven longed for, that single log cabin in the vast stretches of the land of snows and endless hills and mountains, rivers and streams. And the one candle in the window of that cabin is thine own, burning strong in the physical plane.

Thus, this activity here in America's wilderness, situated at its borders, is that haven, is that bourne, is that only crystal they shall enter until they do so enter it and begin the process which I have described.

You, then, are all a part of one etheric sphere. All of your service and love and causal bodies do comprise the upper sphere in this place for this organization. As the sphere is expanded, as you lend the momentum not only of your causal body and Christhood but of a purified etheric body, it does become not only more pure and perfect but more relevant to that which is below. And therefore, more and more among those who have lost the Way by forfeiture [of free will, of the divine spark] may then be drawn to it, may once again see that upper sphere reflected in the crystal sphere of the organization here below, and in one glance, one glimpse, see and know their point of origin and the day and the hour where they left off being in the higher octaves.

This is a great gift, beloved, for your service does re-create, then, the reality of upper spheres and other worlds, quickening a memory, providing a nexus which is wider when many form this together. In that opening, then, they [those who have lost the Way] may surely through your services and in these dictations actually rise to experience briefly the higher octave, nevermore to forget but only to be haunted, haunted in the divine sense that that *presence* of heaven does not leave them or leave their memory until they utterly reject it.

Free will reigns supreme unto the end of opportunity when the individual has lost all opportunity by abuse [of the Law and the Light]. Thus, the day when opportunity runs out for the individual is the day when, as a co-creator, his creation of Death does overtake him [as the sorcerer's apprentice] and, as it has been explained to you, it is the day of the second death,[8] when that soul-identity [dissolving in the sacred fire] disappears with finality from the graph of time and space and the heaven-world.

From the heart of Avalokiteśvara I release to you, then, the thoughtform for the year 1988: This thoughtform is a vast tapestry where the Great Buddha Sanat Kumara—and Buddha upon Buddha of the mind of the Avalokiteśvara—is in the center surrounded by Buddhas of various octaves, and hierarchies and bodhisattvas, bhikkhus, brothers and sisters. Thus, this great tapestry, which is imprinted within each and every lifestream at the mental level, the mental belt of the planet, does show pictorially the way of the Guru/chela relationship and how it has been translated in the earth through the path of Padma that leads to Maitreya that leads to my heart.

This tapestry, then, becomes alive and living, and it is open on all sides so that in the out-of-the-body state, almost in the dream state of desiring an escape, the soul may step forth from the body and enter the tapestry. Those devotees of God Buddha at the extreme edges of the tapestry are those to whom earth's evolutions may most easily relate. Thus, beloved, it is possible for the individual to choose to enter the tapestry,* which becomes for him, then, a teeming cosmos of [ascended and unascended] beings all on the Path, all a part of this becoming, all approaching

*through the Diamond Heart of the Ascended Master closest to his own vibration and path

the heart of Sanat Kumara and in that heart finding the nexus and the point of self-transcendence unto the One.

The thoughtform of the year is the living, breathing reality of the etheric octave itself and the place of the mystery schools that pertain to this Path. Thus, beloved, by impressing this thought-form and these images in the psyche, in the inner finer bodies, by fire and water, by air and earth, by every form of element, [the Solar Logoi have seen to it that] the soul may find the way out, heed the Call, make the call and extricate herself—by two hands placed in two other hands extended from Above—from the shrinking box of karmic experience or karmic finality.

Blessed hearts, our beloved God, our beloved Avalokiteśvara in the heart of the Solar Logoi have conceived this thoughtform as "The Way Out for 1988." May the knowledge of the path of the bodhisattvas, the disciples unto Christhood, the sisters and brothers of mercy, of wisdom, of golden ages be made known, become popular, until all who count in the earth because they count themselves worthy shall be buzzing with talk of Maitreya's Mystery School—that special place shown on the tapestry where the outline of the mountains surrounding this our retreat and the river and the valley floor are unmistakable—and with talk of the great boon that on the way to the heart of Sanat Kumara one can pass through the Mystery School that is physical for the refinement and the refiner's fire. For when the Messenger does suddenly come into his temple, who shall stand in the day of that fire?[9]

I know who shall stand. It is those among you who fear not our fire but understand the intensity of it through our Mantle and Messenger that must at all times be measured by our co-measurement of the urgency of the hour.

Blessed hearts, in sending you my blessings for a God-filled new year, I say to you: Thy ascent is urgent! Accelerate now, for the mist and the crystal spheres are converging.

I return to the point of the nexus where I AM everywhere in the heart of the living ones of God. Fear not, beloved. Naught can assail thee when thy garment is without rent, thy purity without compromise, thy integrity the integration with God, with God, with God.

Delivered New Year's Eve, December 31, 1987, at the **Royal Teton Ranch.** (1) On the bestowal of the **mantle of Guru** upon the Messenger Elizabeth Clare Prophet, see Padma Sambhava, July 2, 1977, "The Great Synthesis—the Mother as Guru," 90-min. audiocassette B7745, $6.50 (add $.50 postage). (2) **The Western Shamballa** is Gautama Buddha's etheric retreat centered at the Heart of the Inner Retreat at the Royal Teton Ranch, Montana. It is an extension of Shamballa, his retreat located above the Gobi Desert. See 1981 *Pearls of Wisdom,* vol. 24, pp. 226, 227. (3) Matt. 24:40, 41; Luke 17: 34–36. (4) Thomas More, *English Works,* 1557. See *Lords of the Seven Rays,* Book One, pp. 38–39. (5) **Deathless Solar Body.** See Serapis Bey, *Dossier on the Ascension,* pp. 154–59; 1987 *Pearls of Wisdom,* vol. 30, p. 622; 1984 *Pearls of Wisdom,* vol. 27, pp. 2, 3–4, 564, 565, 568. (6) I Enoch 14–16. (7) See 1987 *Pearls of Wisdom,* vol. 30, pp. 1–15. (8) **Second death.** Rev. 2:11; 20:6, 11–15; 21:8. See *The Lost Teachings of Jesus II,* pp. 75, 117–19. (9) Mal. 3:1–3.

Pearls of Wisdom®
published by The Summit Lighthouse

Vol. 31 No. 3	Beloved Omri-Tas	January 17, 1988

New Year's Retreat
at the Royal Teton Ranch

III

Be the Spark That Ignites a Cosmos!
The Violet Flame Is the Key to Physical Survival

Keepers of the Flame of the Violet Planet on Earth,

I AM your Omri-Tas and I am welcome in this place by violet flame leaping from the ground about to become violet flame flowers, immortelles!

Because you are and because you keep the flame of the Seventh Ray on earth, we of the violet planet may transmit over the figure-eight spiral from our sphere of light into the earth body the momentum of our service on the Seventh Ray on the violet planet. So long as the violet flame is tended on earth, so long shall we be able to multiply it and thereby forestall the intensity of the impact of mankind's own returning karma.

Thus, I greet you in this New Year, as earth cycles are counted, with an expression of gratitude and a torch of opportunity. We are come, then, legions of angels and, of course, the 144,000 priests of the sacred fire of the violet planet, whose names unknown (yet whose numbers having been sung) remain to you a concept of a cosmic reinforcement of sacred fire not unlike the priesthood of the Order of Melchizedek.

For, you see, beloved ones, even the order of that priesthood and Melchizedek himself did have their point of origination in this sector of cosmos upon the violet planet. And all who have become a part of that order have spent some time with our evolutions and legions of Light even while in embodiment. For those who are so endued with the Spirit of Cosmic Freedom, those who have such a fervor of devotion to Saint Germain qualify themselves automatically to receive our ministration as well as our invitation to be guests in the chambers of our retreats upon the violet planet.

Therefore, welcome, old friends and new, children and those preparing for the return to the infinite Light. For wherever you may be on the path of grace, know that the moment and the hour does come when by your service to the Seventh Ray you may take a retreat of rest and re-creation in the Light* with our planet.

Blessed hearts, we are not far removed but we are not of this physical wavelength. Therefore, you will not see in the heavens a violet flame body and planet. But by the very pressure and presence of the violet flame in your aura, you will feel and know our evolutions, servitors of Light, and elementals of tremendous stature and attainment. And do you know, beloved, that when you feel them and understand their support, you will come to the realization that each and every one who does abide there from the three kingdoms of the Sons of God, Elohim and Archangelic, all are dedicated to the endowment of earth with the full-gathered momentum of our violet sphere.

Year upon year, millennium upon millennium, we attend, therefore, the coming of age of the children of the Sun on earth. We dare not endow this planet with our momentum while she is in the state of discord and darkness perpetuated by the fallen angels, for to give them [mankind] the violet flame is to give them the key to longevity, eternal youth and immortal life. Even when *you* invoke the violet flame we stand guard to seal it and to dispense it to those who will not take freedom and the violet flame as a liberty to desecrate life. For the violet flame, as any other flame of the sacred fire, when contacting misqualified substance of the human or fallen angel creation, does also activate that negative karma that it may come to light and by free will be cast into the sacred fire.

Thus, as you joyously give the calls to the violet flame, know that we stand guard. And there is a cosmic science that does attend through angel attendants all evolutions of all spheres who begin to understand the science of the spoken Word and who become so fervent and zealous in its use that often their decree momentum and the mastery thereof does exceed their mastery of their emotions, feelings, thoughts, words and deeds.

Therefore, beloved, each time there is a victory of God-mastery within the individual and a balancing of chakras, of the threefold flame and of the four lower bodies, there we find a more secure abode for the release of a greater and greater momentum

*Christ consciousness of the Seventh Ray

and intensity not only of the violet flame but of the pure white fire, sacred fire itself.

Thus, understand that reservoirs of violet flame invoked by you do exist even on this planet. They are sealed in openings in the mountains beneath the surface of the earth. These violet flame reservoirs are held for those hours and moments when individuals whose hearts are pure in their allegiance to God truly have need of this Power, Wisdom and Love, this Presence of our God who is a consuming fire.[1] The day will come, then, when according to the just and holy and righteous judgments of our God, this violet flame shall also be released [to mankind at large], but it shall be done according to cosmic science and cosmic law.

Our concerns, therefore, as we enter this year when perforce world karma does increase as the water levels of the astral plane also rise, are how to increase transmutation without violating cosmic law and the dispensations that have been forthcoming in the proclamation of Alpha and in the words of Gautama Buddha.[2]

Therefore, know, beloved, that the violet flame can increase mightily through the hearts of all Lightbearers. The Holy Christ Self is in God-control and therefore you cannot invoke too much violet flame. A sufficiency is released to you physically, portion by portion. But the Holy Christ Self does keep a mighty reservoir of light. Therefore, in the days and hours of thy need, flood tides of violet flame may descend.

Insofar as the Lightbearers and the Keepers of the Flame are daily transmuting their karma and building magnificent auras, concentric spheres of the many-faceted colors of the violet flame, there is a message that is beamed to all the earth; and those who have not used the violet flame, those who have not come into the understanding of that flame begin to realize that that presence is the key to physical survival. The violet flame is the most physical flame,[3] and it does correspond to the earth body.

Inasmuch as all dispensations and support forthcoming from the Great White Brotherhood in 1987 have been confined to the Lightbearers of the earth, we must see, then, how every single Lightbearer may become a sending station of violet flame in all seven chakras and the secret chamber of the heart—through the hands, through the feet, through the spleen itself.[4]

Therefore, we set before you the goal of letting all of thy life and thy body, thy temple and thy being become a violet flame sphere. As you so commit yourself to this action, beloved, you will understand swiftly that it is necessary on a commensurate level to increase the blue flame and the spheres of blue flame and never to neglect the putting on of the whole armour of God,[5] which is undoubtedly a physical/spiritual protection but does consist of all of the virtues intended to be outpictured by yourselves.

Virtues are like studded stars, gemstones and crystals that have been sewn by angels to your garments. Virtues exemplified by the Blessed Mary you may see in the gemstones upon her hands.[6] Blessed hearts, these virtues are your protection. They are the basic building blocks of good character. As El Morya has referred to this, I shall also say, neglect not the perfecting of the soul and the purity of heart.[7]

When you examine motive, beloved, sometimes you will suddenly be ashamed, for you will realize that some deed rendered to another was in fact self-serving. Some who have not received praise, affection or compassion in childhood have a need and a desire to be approved of by others, and therefore, in that starving for approval, they will perform all manner of acts and deeds not in the purity of the love of God but in the desire to be seen, to be looked upon and, above all, to receive someone's friendship, someone's kind word.

Blessed hearts, one may look upon psychology and momentums developed from childhood, but one ought not to be so taken up or taken aback by these conditions. Remember, there is a ball of wax of the human consciousness, and remember that from the hour of thy declaration with thy twin flame to be the immortal one, there have been organized false hierarchies to defeat thy Christhood. They would if they could in each lifetime undo the full-gathered momentum of thy self in God—self-esteem and integrity, a sense of independence, a sense of strength and power that in standing for principle one may stand alone but one is always all one with God.

As life proceeds and one witnesses the futility of compromise, there is a return to the strength garnered in previous lifetimes. Beloved, understand that those who have wronged you in this life or who may have wronged you in the past are, one and all, triggered as tools of the sinister force for the demeaning of oneself, for the debasement, for the lowering of one's vibration and, of course, for the springing of the ultimate trap: self-condemnation.

I speak of these things because they all inhibit the intensity and the increase of the power of the violet flame within you. One may in true humility and not false humility admit before God and one's friends one's errors. But this is not an ongoing process. Once confessed, forgiven and forsaken, draw the line and reenter thy Christhood. Do not forevermore be tattooed with the sins of the past as though these are a stain that can never be erased.

We seek the remolding of consciousness, of self-awareness. For [unless this be the goal of chelaship] the habit patterns of human consciousness would endure far beyond the day of the transmutation of the very actions which established the human patterns in the beginning. It is as though one had utterly transmuted all of the noxious poisons of the weed of the field but had not put to the torch the weed itself. And as the tree has grown crooked and gnarled, so may the individual be, at the astral level.

Blessed ones, the violet flame can penetrate bone substance itself to render supple again all of thy body and inner being to be remolded in the fullness of the stature of Christ!

You are not creatures, prisoners of habit, but you must know this. You must see it and you must not let the enemy take a victory when you know you have put behind you momentums of the past that are no longer a part of you. Do not let individuals in this or previous lifetimes get the victory over you as you retain the residual momentums of reaction to those circumstances when you knew not the fullness of the Law.

I give you a very stern message, without prolonging any further this comment, that you must look at your momentums. You must study the teaching on momentum given to you in *The Lost Teachings of Jesus*[8] as well as in the *Corona Class Lessons* on the subject of habit.[9] You must put down those [untoward] momentums and re-create the new momentum! Where there is a groove in consciousness, fill it in with light and begin again as you would be as your Christ Self is. Do not wait until the breaking of the mold of this lifetime to re-create yourself in God. It is a daily rejoicing to know that you are a co-creator with God and that with the violet flame all things are possible in God!

The violet flame truly allows you to perform, as it were, a cosmic surgery—and this is never by a momentum that may be fed into the subconscious by all of the popular tape recordings that are available to you as to how you can become a better person and overcome procrastination and all manner of burdensome addictions. Blessed hearts, these tapes are for those who are computerized and do not have a threefold flame. They are for those who have merely a human personality that has built upon itself incarnation after incarnation without integration with any flame or Spirit of God.

Therefore, all the world is gone after the latest fad in consciousness development, in the success fad that is now at hand,

and it is indeed a success fad, beloved hearts. Be not trapped or entrapped. For I would tell you the cosmic secret, that every Ascended Master dictation that has ever gone forth through our Two Witnesses upon earth does contain within it the power of Elohim for the re-creation of oneself. It is not without forethought that we have released to you the *Only Mark* series.[10] It is not without consideration that we have made available to you year upon year the audio- and videotapes of our dictations.

Once you have carefully listened to them and *consciously* entered into that spiral and *consciously* made the decision to incorporate that teaching, that sacred fire, that cup of light into your being until you have willed thereby to become a manifestation of your Higher Self—when you have accomplished this and taken your notes and you thoroughly consent by *conscious free will* to the content, then know, beloved, that that *conscious consent* has involved your Holy Christ Self, your threefold flame and your I AM Presence.

At that moment, then, you may play these tapes [continuously on an auto-reverse tape player] in your home, you may play them in a special room or even in the background, and you will be weaving, by the repetition of the sound, the Word, the rhythm and the teaching, your Deathless Solar Body. This is with a *conscious cooperation and re-creation in God.*

Blessed ones, anything that comes from the human level, no matter how positive the statements are, does always embody the entire karma, electronic belt and subconscious of the individual through whom it has come. This is why we have released to you in our decrees worded cups of light, mantras out of the pure octaves of Spirit, out of the causal bodies of the Ascended Masters. The decrees, then, are the most valuable gift because they are cups of our God-attainment, of our conscious willing to be free on a certain ray through a certain chakra over a certain human or dark condition which we faced and which you now face.

Decrees are the highest prayers on earth because they are dictated by the Ascended Masters, save for those which may come down through the Eastern tradition of the Himalayas, from Sanat Kumara or Gautama Buddha or Maitreya or the true adept and unascended Master. Beloved hearts, that which is in your decree books does become to you the access to the infinite Light. It is only by a conscious entering in to this worded mantra that you are a conscious creator with God and re-create yourself, not only in Matter as a human personality, but you are re-creating yourself fit to dwell in the octaves of Spirit, weaving that Deathless Solar Body.

Therefore, in a time when so many come with their wares, offering you a means to attainment, mastery, success and money, personality and glory and friends, relationships and conquests in male and female activity, beloved ones, understand that you have been given and provided with all that you require to make your ascension and to do so swiftly at such time or in such an hour when you may be called, and that day no man may knoweth save the Father and the Son.

Blessed hearts, realize, then, that those who sell their wares in the programming of consciousness do so with a tremendous momentum of knowledge of advertising, of their subliminal messages, their "subliminal seduction,"[11] as it has been called. This is not so with our Ascended Master activity. We lay before you a table in the wilderness, and on that table are the most magnificent fruits of paradise and all manner of meats and substances that are assimilated at all levels of being. These are offered to the wise and to those who know, to the disciples and the initiates who perceive that there must be a profound reason and purpose in all that we do and who do not miss the opportunity to enter in to that tremendous aura that does enshroud with light all those who enter in.

Thus, I come to speak to you of our concern of the year: How, then, to diminish karma in the earth, how to allow the Lightbearers, who have the dispensation, to account for planetary momentums as they send forth the violet flame for transmutation.

Blessed ones, where people continue to repeat their old sins and abrogations of the Law, it is not possible continually to douse the fires of hell with the violet flame. The violet flame is a principled, cosmic action. It does move in as God himself, as Archangel Zadkiel himself, to consume the errors of the children of the Sun who have gone astray under the influence of the fallen angels, the false gurus. It is a flame of forgiveness accorded by the Father to his own. It was not the gift to the seed of the wicked who plotted the death of those children of the Sun.

Therefore, you see, beloved, if you send forth violet flame for the transmutation of conditions created by the seed of the wicked, those conditions may not [necessarily] be transmuted, according to cosmic law. For these fallen ones and those who have gone after them as idolaters must suffer their own karma. For these have never bent the knee. They have never bowed to the Lord Sanat Kumara. They have never admitted their wrong. The only wrong they have ever admitted to is a miscalculation of judgment whereupon they did not succeed or get away with their plots of Darkness.

Therefore, beloved, if you spend your time sending violet

flame in defense of the cause of the Watcher or the fallen ones or the schemes they have perpetrated against mankind, you may, therefore, deprive the Lightbearer of the fullness of the measure of violet flame that is his spiritual birthright and also enter into a karma-making spiral. Therefore, heed the dispensations and know that it has been spoken, that it has been said and that it has been written that there is no dispensation forthcoming to the evildoers who continue in their anti-Christ activities.

How, then, to increase Light? Beloved hearts, to call for the violet flame to expand in the hearts of all those who give their devout love and allegiance to the Godhead, this is wisdom. And inasmuch as millions and millions of barrels of violet flame, as it were, as barrels of oil coming as a balm of Gilead to the children of the Sun, are necessary and needed, I am certain that you will not run out of the necessity to give the calls for all who are the servants of God in the earth and who truly have espoused a path of doing good to others, helping others and being positive individuals in society.

Thus, beloved, by that increase of the violet flame in all who are of the issue of God, it is our vision and our determination that planet earth shall have a greater momentum of the violet flame to hold up the tent of America,[12] to hold up the nations. In this way, beloved, those who come into the violet flame by your calls will also come into the vision of their I AM Presence and their Holy Christ Self, and they will begin to realize that the hour must come and the hour now is when the seed of the wicked must go down.

Inasmuch as they have implanted themselves in the structure of civilization itself, it is inevitable that in some quarters and in some levels major change take place. You have seen therefore the signs in the heavens and the signs on Wall Street of conditions in the economy that do not augur well for America or the world.[13] You have seen the frantic and frenetic movement of those who control international banking and the money systems and the currencies of the nations, moving almost in a stepped-up film in fast motion here and there and everywhere to create more money to stop the inevitable descent of karma.

Blessed ones, think how ludicrous this is: Can paper money forestall the karma of the seed of the wicked?

Thus, we counsel you again to remember the safety in gold. We counsel you to consider wisely how you shall use those funds that are already in your hands and how you will not plight your troth with a money system, with an investment system that you cannot control and that you cannot trust. I trust that all of you have put behind you the days when you have used your decrees to call for the raising of your investments or your stocks. Understand, beloved, that it is in some respects wishful thinking because it does interfere again with the karmic law of those who are controlling those stocks and those corporations who do not have the good karma.

In bygone days many of you have sent good light after darkness and fed into such corporations a momentum of your light. Thank God for the Christ-discrimination of your own Holy Christ Self who has not permitted it, for without this mediatorship many of you would have made serious karma by sending light into quarters where that light is of no avail. For the Law of God has spoken in the beginning and it is written in the annals of Enoch that this Watcher must come to naught and that the Nephilim gods are judged in the end, as well as their offspring and their giants.[14] To see the end, then, of the era of the seed of the wicked is to behold the dawn of a golden age.

Know, then, that as you call for the judgment of a civilization of Cain and of the fallen angels, you must be prepared to see the consequences of the call. And therefore, it is necessary to buy time for yourselves and for this Community. So the cycles of the elect have been extended as Saint Germain announced it.[15]

Understand, beloved, that the securing of oneself by the violet flame is powerful, even as the violet flame judgment is powerful. The very violet flame in the earth is a judgment of the totalitarian movements and of dictatorships.

When you stand before the altar of God, therefore, and demand the judgments of the fallen ones, whether in Wall Street, Washington or Moscow, you must understand that at any moment and hour your calls may become instantaneously physical, and you must ask yourselves, Are you ready for that physical judgment to descend? And I daresay that most of you are not prepared for what the LORD God is prepared to deliver in answer to your calls.

Therefore, our recommendation to you is that you accelerate the Seventh Ray consciousness. For that Seventh Ray momentum of violet flame in your auras will literally make you a part of the etheric octave, beginning to become a part of the higher sphere. And if you will journey on the etheric plane to that chamber of the cave of violet flame at the Grand Teton,[16] you will also come to the realization that you are indeed day by day becoming part of the fire itself, even as the seraphim of God who are a part of your being and do pass through you daily as you call to them are a part of that fire. What a grace and gift of mercy, seraphim and violet flame angels purifying you and preparing you for heaven's ascent!

Blessed ones, secure in the violet flame means to be secure in the earth and in the earth body and in all ways that pertain to the physical body and its needs. This must be the first order of business for this entire year for Keepers of the Flame. Let us see, then, twenty-four months dedicated to the absolute physical survival of Keepers of the Flame.

Heed, then, the words of Saint Germain.[17] Heed, then, the words of El Morya.[18] For the strength of your union is here. And this is a physical place where cosmic law does allow us to preserve the life of Keepers of the Flame, whereas in other parts of the world and in other areas, beloved, it is not so. And therefore, think not that you can simply pick a place anywhere on the face of planet earth. For if indeed that which you call for is to come to pass—that is, the binding of Death and Hell and the casting of Death and Hell into the lake of sacred fire as it is prophesied in Revelation[19]—then you must be out of the way when these events do become physical.

Cycles have turned at inner levels. There is an acceleration of the evil intent of the enemy. Do not cease to call for the judgment of that enemy—the enemy of oneself as one's own dweller on the threshold, the enemy of nations as the International Capitalist/Communist Conspiracy. But remember, beloved, that all the while the call is being made, the Cosmic Christs and the Great Silent Watchers with your own Holy Christ Self, by the computer of the Mind of God, are taking those calls and locking them into a fiery coil, and they are prepared to release them when and at such time the Cosmic Council does so decree it by events in the earth.

That which could precipitate untimely war or cataclysm or economic collapse is the absence of violet flame in the earth. We see, then, that the answer of our call to the Messenger to send forth violet flame song and decree tapes does become a means of the awakening of all souls on the planet. Let all who hear these tapes awaken, then, whether to everlasting life through the Seventh Ray dispensations of the age, whether to everlasting contempt[20] as they gnash their teeth[21] against the Holy Ghost and the sound of angels singing and of voices of saints and of Keepers of the Flame decreeing.

Blessed hearts, so it shall be. For the fire of the awakening of the age is indeed the violet flame, and as you embody it you become without any question the instruments of those angels who come to awaken all. For they must be roused that they might make their choices and in so choosing determine whether, to the right or the left, they shall stand midst the Tree of Life or midst the darkness of Death and Hell.

Blessed ones, anticipating and seeing what the new year shall bring, I counsel you that those Keepers of the Flame who take the violet flame as the most necessary security in life will indeed survive, endure and conquer. But those who neglect once again our counsel, as some have neglected our words in the past, they will find that the tides of human karma shall sweep them out of the way, and they shall be helpless to face the adversity of that which is coming upon the earth.

The violet flame is the key and the love of the violet flame does unlock that secret place of the Most High shown to you last evening. And that chamber of the Royal Teton Retreat is indeed a place prepared for you, beloved.

And therefore, I, Omri-Tas, would tell you that in answer to my call the Messenger has assembled here these focuses of amethyst crystal. They are as silent sentinels at the altar. Each one does bear an elemental of the violet flame who has been a part of the building of these crystals. They are assembled here as the silent guard of the gnomes of the earth and the rock.

They are assembled for you. For all of these violet flame crystals that are upon this altar are here for you to take with you at the conclusion of this conference on the condition that this violet flame crystal be upon an altar dedicated to the Great White Brotherhood as the centerpiece, as the chalice, that this altar have above it the Chart of the I AM Presence, that it have the portraits of Jesus and Saint Germain, that it have upon it the image of the Two Witnesses,[22] who stand for you in the night and in the day, in the physical and in the spiritual octaves. To this you may add your favorite saints or the statues of those whom you love, such as the Lord of the World.

If you will keep this altar in a place where other activities are not going on such as television or the playing of rock music or social activities, if you will keep it sealed and use it as the place of your invocation, I can promise you that the violet flame will increase and increase and increase in these chalices of crystal. Understand, beloved, that when that altar is sealed (and it may be very small in a closet), then you will know that an altar sealed and tended daily does have a momentum that does build.

Blessed ones, the search to find this amethyst crystal resulted in the acquiring of all that was available at the moment on the market. Thus, I have so instructed our representatives to continue to assemble amethyst crystal to be placed on our altar throughout our conferences that you might have with you a living crystal charged with the devotions and the holiness of the violet flame angels of the violet planet.

Remember always that your heart is the violet flame heart of Saint Germain and Omri-Tas if you will it so, that the key crystal is the threefold flame and the beating heart.

Beloved ones, I pour into this our chalice, our Messenger, a gift of violet flame, sealed in the physical and in the higher octaves. And therefore, by the authority of the Cosmic Council, we do send her on a mission to Europe, one final mission, then, so selected to be Lisbon, Portugal. And therefore to that place shall she bear the living violet flame that the Lightbearers of Europe, those who may come to these shores and those who remain, might be given an extraordinary impetus of Light in this day and age to yet retrieve that continent.

Blessed ones, as Saint Germain has no further dispensation for that continent and as the dispensations may be given only to the Lightbearers,[23] so, consistent with that cosmic edict, we do send her there to celebrate the ascension day weekend of your own beloved Lanello as he shall pour forth from his own causal body the gift also of the violet flame.

Thus, beloved, that which has been in the heart of the Messenger and the Keepers of the Flame of Europe for a long, long time does open in this year, and it is indeed a bright spot, sealing, then, Pisces, sealing, then, Aquarius. I tell you, beloved, the victory of the Light on earth can come, for there are sufficient Lightbearers to hold the balance in world change.

May you not underestimate the need for planetary alchemical transmutation. The chemicalization in the earth is for the purging of all ancient records. If you begin to consider the transmutation of the records of Lemuria and Atlantis and all of the evil perpetrated by the fallen ones and then you realize that their connections are to the entire physical cosmos, you will no longer wonder or doubt what we are about. For we are about the grand conflagration of the Matter cosmos!

Let earth, then, be the spark that ignites a cosmos with violet flame until all is consumed that is unreal and the Matter cosmos does stand again to be the chalice of the Spirit cosmos, and heaven and earth and Spirit/Matter come into the divine union. And all those who have Christhood may stand at the nexus of the ascending and descending currents for eternity upon eternity upon eternity.

Inasmuch as they [the fallen ones] have chosen earth for the battleground, so we draw the line here. And we with you, beloved Keepers of the Flame, do stand on that line with the Lords of the Seven Rays, the line where Light meets Darkness and swallows it up by the all-consuming fire of God's own Seventh Ray! In this seventh day of creation it is re-creation by Elohim of the All!

Now hasten to be God-centered and know that when you are in the eye of God, you shall experience all things and retain permanent integration in the permanent atom of being.

Onward to the mount of ascension, to the valleys where souls must needs be rescued. Go forth, O Messenger! Go forth, O staff of the Messenger! Go forth, O Keepers of the Flame! Stump America and stump the fallen ones! We are with you, millions of angels strong. Therefore, fear not but remember, the Mantle and Presence of our Alpha be upon you always.

By the sign of the violet flame cross of fire, I seal you in my amethyst heart.

"The Summit Lighthouse Sheds Its Radiance O'er All the World to Manifest as Pearls of Wisdom." This dictation by **Omri-Tas** was **delivered** through the Messenger of the Great White Brotherhood Elizabeth Clare Prophet on **New Year's Day, January 1, 1988,** during the 5-day New Year's Retreat at the **Royal Teton Ranch, Montana. (1)** Deut. 4:24; 9:3; Heb. 12:29. **(2) Dispensations confined to the Lightbearers.** In his May 13, 1987 Wesak address, Gautama Buddha read from "A Proclamation" by Alpha, which announced that "no new dispensation is forthcoming on this Wesak 1987 for the planet as a whole, but the dispensation [that is forthcoming] is a mathematical formula to each individual according to his own inner attainment. . . . There is not an Ascended Master who is given a new dispensation for the saving of a planet but every Ascended Master is given a dispensation to assist the true chela of the Light." See Gautama Buddha, "For the Alignment of a World—'A Proclamation' by Alpha," 1987 *Pearls of Wisdom,* vol. 30, no. 24, pp. 242–49. **(3) The violet flame as a physical flame.** See 1984 *Pearls of Wisdom,* vol. 27, no. 61, p. 553, or *The Lost Teachings of Jesus II,* pp. 479–80; 1987 *Pearls of Wisdom,* vol. 30, nos. 6, 22, pp. 92, 221. **(4)** The hands, feet, and spleen represent the five **secret-ray chakras** as emanating points for the light of the five concentric rings surrounding the heart. On the five secret-ray rings around the heart, see 1987 *Pearls of Wisdom,* vol. 30, no. 56, pp. 492, 495. **(5)** Eph. 6:11–17. **(6) Gemstones upon the hands of Mother Mary.** On November 27, 1830, Mother Mary appeared to 24-year-old Catherine Labouré, a novice with the Sisters of Charity in Paris. In her account of the visitation Catherine reported, "I saw rings on her fingers, three rings to each finger, the largest one near the base of the finger, one of medium size in the middle, the smallest one at the tip. Each ring was set with gems, some more beautiful than others; the larger gems emitted greater rays and the smaller gems, smaller rays." Catherine said Mother Mary explained to her that the gems "are the symbols of the graces I shed upon those who ask for them. . . . The gems from which rays do not fall are the graces for which souls forget to ask." In this apparition, the Blessed Mother detailed for Catherine the images she wanted placed on the front and back of what has come to be known as the "Miraculous Medal." She instructed Catherine that the medal was to be worn around the neck and said, "Graces will abound for those who wear it with confidence." See John J. Delaney, ed., *A Woman Clothed with the Sun* (Garden City, N.Y.: Doubleday & Co., Image Books, 1960), pp. 77–78. **(7) El Morya on integrity, good character and purity of heart.** See pp. 3–6; 1986 *Pearls of Wisdom,* vol. 29, no. 80, pp. 700–703. **(8)** See **"Momentum,"** in *The Lost Teachings of Jesus I,* Summit University Press, pp. 121–67, $14.95 (add $1.00 for postage), or 90-min.

audiocassette B8073, $6.50 (add $.50 for postage). **(9)** See Jesus and Kuthumi, **"Habit,"** in *Corona Class Lessons,* Summit University Press, pp. 257–303, $12.95 (add $1.00 for postage); Elizabeth Clare Prophet, *On the Mother I,* including lectures on the six Corona Class Lessons on habit, 12 hrs., A8260, $50.00 (add $1.30 for postage). **(10)** The *Only Mark* audiocassette series begins with the final dictation given through the Messenger Mark L. Prophet, February 18, 1973, and continues back to 1958 to include every Ascended Master dictation delivered by him. Fourteen albums (four 90-min. audiocassettes each) published to date, $26.00 each (for postage add $1.15 for the first, $.25 for each additional album). The newest release, *Only Mark 14,* includes dictations given October 1969–December 1969 by Saint Germain, the Angel Deva of the Jade Temple, the Great Divine Director, Pallas Athena, Archangel Chamuel, Sanat Kumara, El Morya, Casimir Poseidon, God Meru, Zarathustra, Paul the Venetian, the Maha Chohan and Jesus. **(11)** On **subliminal seduction** in the media, see Wilson Bryan Key's exposés *Subliminal Seduction: Ad Media's Manipulation of a Not So Innocent America, Media Sexploitation, The Clam-Plate Orgy* (New York: New American Library, 1973, 1976, 1980); and "Subliminal Seduction: Selling Products to the Subconscious Mind," "Dr. Wilson Bryan Key: The Sherlock of Subliminal Advertising," and "True Confessions of the Admen," *Heart: For the Coming Revolution in Higher Consciousness* (Spring 1983). **(12)** See the Goddess of Liberty, February 8, 1987, "The Tent of the LORD," 1987 *Pearls of Wisdom,* vol. 30, no. 8, pp. 107–8. **(13) Prophecy on the economy.** For Elizabeth Clare Prophet's lecture on prophecy, including her analysis of what coming astrological configurations portend for the economy; her vision of the Four Horsemen given to her by Saint Germain, with an update on the black horse, which delivers the economic karma of the nations; and teaching on how we can undo untoward prophecy through calls for Divine Intervention, see "Halloween Prophecy 1987," October 31, 1987, on two videocassettes, 4 hrs. 26 min., GP87063, $39.95 (add $1.20 for postage), or on three 90-min. audiocassettes, B87079–81, $19.50 (add $.80 for postage). **(14) The judgment of the Watchers (fallen angels) and their offspring.** I Enoch 1:3–6; 10:1–20; 12:5–7; 13:1–3; 14:1–7; 16; 19; 66:4–15; 67:2–5; 92:5–16; 105:13–17. See Elizabeth Clare Prophet, *Forbidden Mysteries of Enoch: The Untold Story of Men and Angels,* containing all the Enoch texts, including the Book of Enoch and the Book of the Secrets of Enoch. **(15)** See 1987 *Pearls of Wisdom,* vol. 30, no. 55, p. 484. **(16)** See pp. 14, 17. **(17) Saint Germain's warnings to prepare for survival.** See Saint Germain, November 27, 1986, "A Prophecy of Karma of the United States of America," 1986 *Pearls of Wisdom,* vol. 29, no. 75, pp. 647–49, or *Saint Germain On Prophecy,* Book Four, pp. 207–9; 1987 *Pearls of Wisdom,* vol. 30, nos. 2, 22, 37, pp. 34, 221, 224, 225, 371. **(18) Twenty-four months.** In his dictation delivered in New York City, October 2, 1987, El Morya warned: "Ere twenty-four months have passed, be it known to you that this nation must have the capacity to turn back any and all missiles, warheads incoming whether by intent or by accident. Where there is no defense you invite the bear into your own haven. . . . Ere twenty-four months pass, beloved, there shall be a reckoning and a confrontation unless something is done" ("24 Months: The Enemy Does Not Sleep," 1987 *Pearls of Wisdom,* vol. 30, no. 54, pp. 473–81). See also 1987 *Pearls of Wisdom,* vol. 30, no. 46, p. 439; 1985 *Pearls of Wisdom,* vol. 28, no. 30, pp. 388, 389–90, 396. **(19)** Rev. 20:14. **(20)** Dan. 12:2. **(21) Gnashing of teeth.** Pss. 35:15, 16; 37:12; 112:9, 10; Matt. 13:41, 42, 49, 50; 22:11–13; 24:48–51; 25:30; Luke 13:23–28; Acts 7:54–59. **(22)** The Messengers Mark L. Prophet and Elizabeth Clare Prophet received the anointing from Saint Germain to occupy the offices of the **Two Witnesses** foretold in Daniel 12:5 and Revelation 11:3–12: ". . . And they shall prophesy a thousand two hundred and threescore days [i.e., cycles whose length is unknown], clothed in sackcloth. These are the two olive trees, and the two candlesticks standing before the God of the earth," Lord Gautama Buddha. In 1973 Mark L. Prophet took his ascension and is known as the Ascended Master Lanello. Thus, the Messengers continue their service as the "other two, the one on this side of the bank of the river and the other on that side of the bank of the river," as Daniel described in his vision. **(23)** See 1987 *Pearls of Wisdom,* nos. 25, 37, pp. 254–55, 372–73.

Pearls of Wisdom®

published by The Summit Lighthouse

| Vol. 31 No. 4 | *Beloved Sanat Kumara* | *January 24, 1988* |

New Year's Retreat
at the Royal Teton Ranch

IV
The Warning
Darkness May Come at Any Hour and Any Day

Ho! Let the Word of the LORD be upon his own! And let it descend as the extreme unction upon those who this day throughout the earth stand before the Lord God to give answer as to their deeds, as to the motive of their hearts, and therefore let whatever unction may be accorded unto them by the earth representatives of the LORD be now delivered.

For the hour is come when all must give account before the living witness, before the altar of the Most High God, before the threefold flame within their hearts.

Therefore, the infamy that is upon the earth does receive the blinding Light of my own heart. For I AM the Great Guru descended now with my legions of Light and angels of record, who shall render unto me an accounting of the opportunity that has been made of all souls who have descended into these Matter spheres.

For the line has been drawn, and that line is drawn, and therefore the tide of evil has reached a mark wherefore and whereby it shall not exceed it, but those who have brought it to that level shall themselves be judged.

And if, therefore, the pots be not found to be filled with Light to hold that line, blessed ones, that line shall be kept in the etheric octave and yet in the earth there shall be weeping and gnashing of teeth.

I, the Lord Sanat Kumara, greet the troops of Saint Germain

and those who march with the seraphim of God. I commend you for your Light and Calling and I warn you where there is an absence of diligence in the shoring up of the Light in your members and in your chakras against the day of your own testing and initiation.

For you are called to my service, you are called to the Great White Brotherhood because in ancient times one and all have stood against the enemy and the adversary and in some moment of past time have been put down by these archdeceivers. For they have garnered the Light of the Divine Mother and they have used it against civilization upon civilization against the children of the Sun.

Therefore, let the sons of God in the earth know that you prepare for the most extreme confrontation with these fallen ones, who desire nothing else and nothing less than to mete upon you Death and Hell and the destruction of the soul.

Therefore, I say to you, be prepared! Enter the sacred fiery heart and never let down your guard, for when you come to that moment of challenge, I tell you the breath of life does hang in the balance and the very thread itself.

And therefore let the garment of God be upon you by diligence daily. Let the sword never be put down. Let the shield be around you, and know, beloved, that those who would inherit the kingdom of God, the full consciousness of Godhood with me, must stand before those who have challenged my office and the offices of the least of these little ones who have no defense but are as lambs who have been shorn even of their coat of wool.

Blessed ones, the very forcefield and the aura of the sons of God can be in the earth the full power of the Great Central Sun Magnet. Therefore, I say unto you, invoke the Great Central Sun Magnet and know how serious and how complete are the fourteen-month dispensations of Serapis Bey. Each and every fourteen-month cycle, you are calling to the Great Central Sun for the amplification of one of the spheres of the causal body by the power of ascension's flame.[1]

Therefore, on the first of the secret rays you have walked now these ten months since the changing of the cycles. Blessed ones, understand that this is for your ultimate protection, and we have explained to you that the initiations of the five secret rays, which have succeeded those of the seven, are most difficult. For here is the place of the violation of the heart. Here are the rings of light that surround the heart and are closest to the I AM Presence, and it is these five secret rays which the fallen ones and the Watchers have violated to the utter destruction of planetary bodies.

Blessed ones, it is not alone nuclear war but the very splitting and sawing asunder of planets themselves. This is the destruction that was wrought in those days when in the physical Matter universe the Sons of God with full Christ attainment had not descended.[2]

Now with the descending of the Sons of God and angels of high hierarchical position such as the Archeia Mother Mary, there has been therefore the rescue mission of the children of the Sun these two thousand years and longer. And with the walking of Enoch in the earth and with the coming of the Ancient of Days, my own mantle into the physical octave long ago, there has been intercession while our shepherds have gone forth to teach and to bring the children of the Sun into a path of individual Christhood that they might put on divine Sonship.

This is the purpose of Maitreya's Mystery School, which we now convoke, and therefore the Lords of the Seven Rays descend this day to take their place as instructors of those who understand and must understand that you come to our halls of learning for the single purpose of Christed realization and the living incarnation of the Word.[3] *Lo, I AM THAT I AM!* and I tell you the hour is now, as has been told to you.

Let there be, therefore, the watch and the alertness of the Light. For it is not enough to bask in the Light or to give your decrees but [there must be] that supreme sense of diligence, that instinct that is ready to pounce when the fallen ones unleash a tirade of darkness out of the pits through their alien individuals, through their spacecraft. For they come suddenly as thieves in the night to tear from you the sacred love tryst and the spirit of Community; and, beloved ones, they stand apart and away, not revealing the terror of their night and their hellfire until that hour and the moment when they determine to deliver it suddenly as a blitzkrieg upon the planetary body.

Therefore, those of you who have not stood against Antichrist nose to nose, as one would say, do not have the sense of recollection of what it means to be in peace and all in the bliss of God, minding your business and living your life as good individuals, suddenly to have the chaos of the underworld unleashed. Those who have experienced world wars and been in the midst of battle, they do know and they recall.

Therefore I say, sleep not but be watchful, for this descent of Darkness in your midst may come at any hour and any day! It may come to assail you and set aside your mission. I do not come to incite fear but I speak of the realism of the hour, and the realism is that even the sons of God who have that Christhood just above them as a mantle of Light do not sense the urgency of claiming it in the full path of God-mastery.

Therefore, the Lords of Karma have so asked me that I might deliver unto you that warning whereby the vigil be kept in your heart and whereby moment by moment you sense yourselves ready with the Archangels, ready with the hosts of the Light, ready to meet Armageddon should it cross your path even at this Inner Retreat.

I speak not necessarily at all of nuclear war. I speak of those skirmishes where the fallen ones come to destroy a single living soul, a potential God, one necessary to the mandala of Light. Blessed hearts, these encounters are sprung precisely when the victims are unawares, and this unawareness is also calculated—as they do inundate you with all types of rays and forces of manifestation—subtly to put you to sleep and cause you to be not centered in the heart of Alpha and Omega.

Blessed ones, there are some who will not cross over to see the "Promised Land"[4] for the very reason of their not taking seriously the messages we have been giving year in and year out. I must speak again, for the hour is short.

Therefore, earth stands on the pinnacle of entering a great golden age: earth stands on the precipice of being taken down into the abyss. And in this hour it is truly the vigil of the hearts of the Lightbearers that does count.

Therefore, weigh the expenditure of time and money always. The expenditure of thy life before the altar of God is most vital in [meeting] the necessities of daily existence and the economics of life. This [initiation] is a close parallel to the altar experience. But all other projects and plans must be set aside for the fire of the heart, for the path of the ascension, for that which is most essential.

When you are prepared as Saint Germain has told you to be, beloved, there shall be no necessity to be burdened and the enemy therefore does fear. For the enemy is a coward. The enemy is the ultimate coward! And therefore, beloved, know that the Light of God that does not fail when raised up by you is feared. Thus, it is a "power play" at intergalactic levels by the fallen ones against the Sons of God.

We here now gathered in this assembly and company for this convocation therefore do say to you that we can hold the balance in the physical octave only through you. This is the Law day by day and hour by hour, and when you are taken suddenly unawares, I tell you it is the momentum of your heart and the momentum of your aura and the magnetism of your "Life-field"[5] that does make the difference. For we may enter in with the speed of light to save those who are under the attack of the fallen ones whereas those who are sometime frequenters of our chapels and our services and now-and-then decreers, these place themselves in the worst jeopardy of all.

Beloved ones, between the Dark and the Daylight is a twilight zone of terror, and therefore I say, enter into the white fire core of Being! Place yourself in zeal upon a course of decrees for some period of time, and place yourself diligently before the diet that has been presented to you[6] to see what you can make of it for the balancing of your lifestream in the physical octave.

Beloved ones, you will require a mind that is sharper than a two-edged sword, a heart that may beat and not become disoriented by the panic of the fallen ones and the changing earth conditions. You will require all of your forces summoned unto the Victory from the heart of the I AM Presence.

Let the vessels be brought! Let all vessels that can be found be brought to the altar that we might pour our oil into them and fill them full that there shall be no oil wanting in the day when the fire must be kept on the altar of being.[7]

You are the vessels. Let the vessels be emptied. For I, Sanat Kumara, would fill them with my oil of gladness, my oil of praise and thanksgiving, my oil of everlasting Life! I would see you get the Victory here and now! Blessed hearts, it does mean the Victory of a cosmos.

Therefore, I require you now to be seated in silence in my heart.

I make known to you this day, inasmuch as this is a branch of the Great White Brotherhood sponsored by the level of my office with the Seven Holy Kumaras, that in this hour there is the withdrawal of the Brotherhood of Mount Shasta[8] from the retreat physical of Mount Shasta. This entire brotherhood, therefore, does withdraw and does transfer their forcefield and focus both in[to] the Grand Teton and in[to] another area of the Northern Rockies.

Blessed hearts, this announcement is a sign unto you and let it be a sign unto every heart and let it be known from within. I give you, therefore, this report that you might accommodate and understand your position as the pillars in the temple of our God.

Therefore, deliberations at the Royal Teton Retreat continue, beloved, and we express gratitude for the light released and the calls given. We, therefore, call to each and every one of you and those who are the creative sons and daughters of God to put your hearts together, to know and to understand how there might be executed a proliferation of the *Word* and of the *Warning* and of the *Message* that has gone forth.

Let it be so, then, by the release (through the use of such supply as is available to you) of this message that comes from the heart of Saint Germain, that has been shouted from the housetops, delivered by the Messenger and by yourselves wherever you might be received. Let it go forth, then, for the people of the earth must have the warning as they had that warning in the days of Noah, and Noah did preach one hundred years.⁹

Therefore, the Hierarchy was determined (as the Hierarchy is determined today) that earth might have a full preparation and the Lightbearers be cut free. Understand, then, the mockery that was upon Noah and how he was mocked perpetually, imagine, for a century of time, warning the people of the flood that was to come.

Therefore, let it be known that that warning must sound as the drawing of a line that shall divide the Real from the Unreal, that those who respond shall respond, those who shall not respond shall not.

This is the work of the evangels of the LORD, the angel messengers* which you are, who go before the face of my Presence. For you are the evangels of the Archangels and of the Seven Holy Kumaras and of the Lord of the World and the living Saviour Jesus Christ, Maitreya and Kuthumi.

Therefore, know the I AM THAT I AM and know that living Word and know that I AM able to stand in your midst in this hour. And by the power of the fire of my office, I therefore may transfer to you that momentum of light that is yours for the sealing and the protection, but only that which may be borne by you without discord, without disobedience to the law of your inner members.

Therefore, I say hasten! Hasten to present this body, brain, mind and heart, this substance of the chalice that you own in this octave. Hasten to present it, then, the living sacrifice in order that you might never again, never again, *never again by the grace of God* be found wanting in the hour when the enemy does knock at thy door, coming as friend but in reality bearing the witness of Death and Hell.

Remember the archdeceivers. Remember the archdeceivers, beloved ones. Remember those who have come as friend only to destroy the Lightbearers, the creative servants and those who are in the very midst of bringing forth the divine music of God. See

---

*angel: from Greek *angelos*, lit., messenger; evangel: from Greek *eu-* good + *angelos*.

this portrayal in the life of Mozart. See it again in the lives of many others, how those who have presented themselves as friend of the sons of God have been their ultimate betrayers.

Therefore, know that when the enemy speaks peace but does amass his implements of war you must be ready—you must be ready for this one who has smiled the smile of Death and kissed with the kiss of Death.

Know, then, O beloved, that you do have a right to live and to live forevermore in God, and we prepare you for everlasting Life and for the conquest of the Matter spheres. This is not a message of fear; I repeat it to you. It is a message of quickening and awakening that you might have lawful concern but never anxiety, that you might use the violet flame and that you might see yourself with equanimity in the earth as a fiery instrument of the Lord God!

Therefore, I say unto the seed of the wicked who attack the representatives of Sanat Kumara, *Woe! Woe! Woe!* Let your judgments be upon you! For you have assailed the house of the Mother and upon you therefor shall be the return current of that hate and hate creation and that death wish, and it shall be upon you in this hour. *Woe! Woe! Woe!*

And therefore, I say, go down! Go down and be reduced by the percentages of the darkness that you have sought to move upon those who have served you lifetime after lifetime!

Therefore, I, Sanat Kumara, draw my circle, my circle of Light, around this body of Lightbearers of which you shall ne'er be a part wherever you may walk on the face of this earth, and I draw my circle of Light around this Retreat and Ranch such as it is intended to be in the final drawing of the lines of the boundary.

Therefore, beloved, let all who come upon that circle of fire feel and know the wall of Light,[10] and let those who are sensitive in this activity know that when you cross the line and enter, you have passed through the wall of Light of Sanat Kumara, of Lady Master Venus, of the Holy Kumaras, of our legions of Light. And therefore, it is maintained as a wall of Light; and may you internalize it, may you invoke it, and may you know that the tube of Light is the sealing now of the whole house of Israel, of all who are Real in the divine identification!

I AM THAT I AM Sanat Kumara! I will not leave my own in the earth. I shall not leave them to become the fodder of those who have determined to make mincemeat of the children of the Sun! I AM determined, therefore, by the power and the authority of this scepter to raise up among you true shepherds and Christed ones!

All is set in position for you so to become. Therefore, beware the pitfalls of pride and ambition. Beware the pitfalls, beloved, and heed the word of my Messenger, who has truly the mantle and the training to point out to you those subtle burdens that are upon you that prevent you from being a transparency for the living Word of God.

Without faith in the living Guru, it is impossible to please God. This is the meaning of that which is recorded in scripture: Without faith it is impossible to please God.[11] It is the faith in the living Christ of Jesus and in those who have worn the mantle of Guru throughout the ages that enables you to fulfill that which is pleasing unto the LORD. You will not see of your own that which must be cast out[12] and this is why those who have rejected all gurus [i.e., enlightened teachers] become the incarnation of pride, intellectual pride, Luciferian pride and the sense of superiority on the Path.

I say, my angels have come to tear from you the mask[13] and the garments of spiritual pride that block your true attainment on the Path. Know and understand this, beloved, that the voices subtle of the fallen angels so mock our own that many have thought they have received visitations of ourselves and do take their dictations from, supposedly, Maitreya or Jesus or Saint Germain or the Archangels.

They have been beguiled and fooled by these fallen ones and by the false hierarchies misrepresenting the Great White Brother-hood. And in each and every case, slowly but surely, those fallen ones, speaking to them and whispering in their ear, will deliver a message of flattery as to their supposed attainment and their being chosen and set aside for an extraordinary mission, et cetera.

Beloved ones, those who will not bend the knee before the living Presence of Sanat Kumara throughout the hierarchy of the Great White Brotherhood have no part with this path or the ascension in the Light, and therefore they remain outside the courts of Maitreya's Mystery School as of old in days of Lemuria and Atlantis.

And they would gnash their teeth and they would rush against the Lightbearers [if they could], even as in the stoning of Saint Stephen,[14] and move against those who had the Holy Ghost, and they would claw them and would tear from them their very garments! For beloved, they have come again in the land, and they have stood apart, and they both fear and hate the Messenger and the path of the ascension.

They claim to have it all, but I tell you they have not the wedding garment and we say unto them worldwide: Friend, how camest thou in without the wedding garment?[15] And without that wedding garment, there is no transition to higher octaves. Though they may misuse the mantras to attract to themselves a light and a glamour of sanctity, they have it not. Go not their way! For I tell you the false teachers in the land are many.

I will isolate for you one false-hierarchy impostor of Lord Himalaya, that Swami Rama that does preach out of the United States and does pass his wares. This individual is corrupt and a fallen one to the very extent and boundaries of this kingdom. And therefore I say, *Woe! Woe! Woe!* unto this Swami Rama and all who are like him and with him, the false hierarchies out of India who have come as fallen angels, taken bodies of that blessed nation and therefore moved against her people.

And therefore, they may use the light of the Mother to establish the *siddhis*[16] and physical powers, but they have not the light of the Father, the I AM Presence, and not the sponsorship of the Great White Brotherhood. And the silly women and the silly men who have gone after them worshiping them will come to challenge the Messenger, "Why do you not proclaim this one? Why do you not proclaim Krishnamurti? Why do you not proclaim this and that and the other one who is supposed to be the Christ of the age?"

I tell you, go not after them, for you have the Christ in your being! You have the kingdom of God within you![17] You have my flame within you! You have your heart-to-heart contact with me and through me to all of the ascended hosts of the Great White Brotherhood!

I have come for the saving of your beings of Light, and many of you have joined me as we came to planet earth long ago for the saving of these evolutions. Have you lost and forgotten your First Love? This is the hour to remember it with the full intensity and fire of your being, beloved. This is the hour to know that souls are being gobbled up by these false gurus!

Let it come to pass, therefore, that *they are exposed! they are exposed! they are exposed!* as you name them now and demand the cutting free of all true Lightbearers who have been fastened to them by manipulation and, yes, by direct black magic.

I say the hour is come for the false hierarchs, impostors of my name Sanat Kumara, to go down in the earth; and as my Son Jesus has proclaimed to you to declare their judgment, so I proclaim it this day!

Let the word go forth from this mountain of God. Let it go forth in the name of Elijah and Elisha, in the name of John the

Baptist and Jesus Christ: and therefore let that fallen one who has turned aside the path of freedom, even that Sun Myung Moon, go down! *Woe! Woe! Woe!*

I say before all the false gurus of the nation, let them go down now! For the children of the Light have the right to be cut free, have the right to become Keepers of the Flame of Life of Sanat Kumara, have a right to take their stand!

Let all those who are the sentinels of freedom in the earth therefore keep the watch. Let all seraphim of God receive my command now, issued unto the holy one, Justinius. Go forth and surround these Keepers of the Flame, four in number. I charge you, millions of seraphim from the Great Central Sun, keep the flame of Life and cosmic purity to the north, to the south, to the east, to the west in the turning of these sons and daughters of God and children of the Light!

Let all who are such, all who have the threefold flame of God and the worship thereof hear, then, this day: I send to you from the Great Central Sun four seraphim of God to keep thee in all thy ways. Command them in the name of Jesus Christ and send them on your missions. They come to protect you and seal you from that encroachment in your beings of the toxins and pollutions of world karma that are descending from the hour of midnight of New Year's.

Therefore, as the days pass and as you carve a light and as you hollow out a flame in the midst of planetary darkness, the darkness does increase and your light does increase and the flame of your dynamic decrees does uphold a nation. Therefore, to assist you in continuing the mighty work begun at this conference, I send these seraphim with you, beloved.

Let it be known that Ra Mu does stand with me upon this platform, that ancient one who has spoken even from the heart of Mount Shasta,[18] and therefore the sounding of the tone of Ra Mu has to do with the changing of earth cycles in the Pacific Basin, has to do with Lemuria and the engines of Mu of the fallen ones and the Light of the Divine Mother being raised up.

Both the binding of the Darkness and the raising of the Light itself, beloved, do portend alchemical change. Therefore, let the violet flame, let the sacred fire go forth and let utter transmutation take place for the consuming of that which could cause physical disturbance in the earth.

I tell you, beloved, you are gathered from all mystery schools of ancient Lemuria and Atlantis. You have known the Path, you have known the way of Community and you have known the interlopers who have sought to enter our communities and temples of Light. You have seen them then. You have seen them again today. I say, They shall not pass! They shall not enter this Community! And if they so do, they shall be bound instantaneously in answer to your call. Let it be done, I say! Let the full power of the seraphim of God maintain the watch.

And now our beloved Mother Mary would have me say to you that her concern for the souls of the earth is indeed grave, and she does, therefore, ask you with a plea of her heart once again to give that call of the rosary[19] and that single judgment call of the raising of the right hand of the Blessed Virgin, even the Cosmic Virgin, to give it once a day with your fifteen-minute rosary that she might have the authority to act on a twenty-four-hour basis for the binding and the judgment of those who go after the new souls of Light and the children of the Sun.

And therefore, our mission is to save all Lightbearers of the earth. Blessed ones, I count on your assistance and I count on it firmly and ultimately. May I have your word and may that word resound worldwide in this hour from the hearts of all Keepers of the Flame? ["Yes!"]

I, Sanat Kumara, have spoken unto you and I call now my Son Sean to this altar. [Rev. Sean C. Prophet kneels at the altar.]

Now, as you kneel before the God and Goddess Meru in the temple of Lake Titicaca, I, Sanat Kumara, say unto you, receive the mantle and authority of your father, Mark Prophet, and know that I stand before you and I seal you this day from the wiles of Death and Hell as I have sent my angel to prevent them from prevailing over you and your own this very night.

Therefore I say, receive, then, my anointing and know that all who shall send Darkness and the death wish upon you and the force of Hell shall deal with Sanat Kumara, and their death wish shall be instantaneously returned upon them. Therefore, assume that role and know that you go forth in the fullness of that mantle of Mark Prophet. Seize it now and divide the waters of Jordan![20]

Who, then, shall proclaim the Word of the LORD? Who shall proclaim the coming of the Prophet? I proclaim it, and I seal you now with the full protection of your office and mantle, and I say you shall live to fulfill your fiery destiny. Fear not. Death and Hell shall not prevail over thee.

And by this mantle you may also decree it so for all of thy members of this household and all members of this Community; and all Keepers of the Flame worldwide may appeal to me through your mantle for this protection against the wiles of

Death and Hell and against the inordinate inroads that have been made by the fallen ones against those new Lightbearers that have been entering in as the fallen ones have attacked them. Therefore, this day hence they have no power! For the Prophet is in the land and he shall go forth.

Therefore, let all acknowledge their own Christhood. Let all acknowledge the mantle of their own I AM Presence and use it! Beloved ones, hear me! For the mantle that is not exercised is the mantle, therefore, that may be seized from you by the fallen ones. Exercise and revere the mantle. Let none trample upon it.

Go forth, then, and fulfill that divine calling. And so I say it to you and I say it to all, let the will of God be made known and let all other things be set aside for the fulfillment of that mission.

I commend you to the keeping of the Diamond Heart of Mary and Morya that this Messenger through whom I speak may be with you all the days that she has called forth to extend her service upon this planet. For this Messenger has vowed not to take her leave of the planet until all Lightbearers destined to ascend under this dispensation have already ascended to heaven, and then and only then shall she be the last to enter that open portal and then it be shut. May it so come to pass, beloved, because you have realized the necessity of being the Diamond Heart in this octave.

In the name of the living Witness, I have come. In the name of the living Witness, I now ascend to higher octaves for the concerns of the planetary problem of Evil and these fallen ones marching.

So therefore, I summon you Oromasis and Diana, Aries and Thor, Neptune and Luara, Virgo and Pelleur, Elohim of God from the Great Central Sun. Come forth now in the Victory of the God Flame! Come forth now and overturn the fallen ones and set back their timetables of war and attack on the economy! Let them be set back! Let their Darkness be reduced! I decree it in the name of the living God. I decree it, for there are Keepers of the Flame in the earth.

Therefore, I AM THAT I AM. *Therefore,* let the Light go forth in this hour, and I say to all you who are betrayers of the Word: this day you are judged before the Divine Mother Mary and it is done! It is done in the name of the Father and of the Son and of the Holy Spirit. It is done in the name of the Divine Mother, in the name Brahma, Vishnu and Shiva, in the name Brahman and the Word. So I stand. So you stand. And we are the coordinates of the Infinite Fire, as Above so below. It is done!

"The Summit Lighthouse Sheds Its Radiance O'er All the World to Manifest as Pearls of Wisdom." This dictation by **Sanat Kumara** was **delivered** through the Messenger of the Great White Brotherhood Elizabeth Clare Prophet on **Saturday, January 2, 1988,** during the 5-day New Year's Retreat at the **Royal Teton Ranch, Montana. (1) Serapis Bey's fourteen-month cycles.** At winter solstice 1978, Serapis Bey inaugurated the fourteen-month cycles of ascension's flame released from the Great Causal Body of Life. See Serapis Bey, October 28, 1984, "Initiation from the Emerald Sphere," and Elizabeth Clare Prophet, "Fourteen-Month Cycles of the Initiation of the Christed Ones through the Spheres of the Great Causal Body," 1984 *Pearls of Wisdom,* vol. 27, no. 56, pp. 487–93, 495–510; Serapis Bey, December 28, 1985, "The Descent of the Mighty Blue Sphere," 1986 *Pearls of Wisdom,* vol. 29, no. 15, pp. 125–27. On February 28, 1987, Serapis Bey announced, "I, Serapis, inaugurate fourteen months of planetary initiation in the First Secret Ray" as the first of "five [fourteen-month] rounds in the five secret rays." **(2) The destruction of planetary bodies. Maldek,** once a planet in our solar system, was destroyed when its lifewaves waged a war ending in nuclear annihilation. The asteroid belt between Mars and Jupiter is the remains of this planet. A group of asteroids closer to the sun is the record and remains of the planet **Hedron,** overtaken by the pleasure cult of its lifewaves who, when reincarnated on earth, became known for their cult of hedonism. According to author Zecharia Sitchin's study and interpretation of Babylonian creation myths, a planet called **Tiamat** was split in half when it collided with the satellites of Marduk ("the Twelfth Planet"), a large planet drawn into this solar system by the gravitational pull of Neptune. Sitchin says that Tiamat's upper half, along with her chief satellite, became Earth and her moon and that her lower half, shattered by Marduk during its second orbit, became the asteroid belt between Mars and Jupiter. See Mark L. Prophet and Elizabeth Clare Prophet, *The Lost Teachings of Jesus I,* pp. 367–68; Zecharia Sitchin, *The 12th Planet* (New York: Avon Books, 1976), pp. 210–34, 255–56; Zecharia Sitchin, *The Stairway to Heaven* (New York: St. Martin's Press, 1980), pp. 88–90. **(3)** Winter Quarter of Summit University, January 4 to March 27, 1988, the first quarter to be held at the Royal Teton Ranch, is sponsored by the Lords of the Seven Rays. **(4)** Moses' karma for killing the Egyptian taskmaster was that he could not enter the Promised Land, Exod. 2:11, 12. See also Num. 20:12; 27:12–14; Deut. 32:48–52; 34:1–5. **(5) The Life-field,** or L-field, is an invisible electrodynamic field which surrounds all living things and is said to exist prior to the birth of the physical organism. This "field of life" correlates with differences in human emotions, health, disease, and aging, and interacts with the electromagnetic state of the environment. For teachings on the **aura,** see Kuthumi, *Studies of the Human Aura,* and Djwal Kul, *Intermediate Studies of the Human Aura;* also published as *The Human Aura.* **(6)** During the New Year's Retreat, the Messenger lectured on the **macrobiotic diet,** including how human behavior and physical and mental health relate to the condition of the body's organs and what foods are beneficial to the organs. The diet was given by Sanat Kumara to the Lightbearers and, among others, to Lord Lanto when he was embodied as the Yellow Emperor (c.2704 B.C.). The principles of macrobiotics are based on *The Yellow Emperor's Classic of Internal Medicine* (the *Nei Ching*), the oldest known book of Chinese medicine. See Elizabeth Clare Prophet, January 3 and 4, 1988, three audiocassettes, B88010–12, $19.50 (add $.80 for postage). **(7)** II Kings 4:1–7. **(8) The Brotherhood of Mount Shasta,** an ancient hierarchy of priests and priestesses who tended the flame of the Mother on the altars of Mu (Lemuria) before the sinking of that continent, is a brotherhood composed of ascended and unascended Masters who are devotees of the Buddha and his light and who until this hour have kept the flame of purity in Mount Shasta. **(9)** Gen. 5:32; 7:6. **(10)** Zech. 2:5. **(11)** Heb. 11:6. **(12)** Matt. 7:3–5; Luke 6:41, 42. **(13)** Read "Removing the Mask," in *The Lost Teachings of Jesus I,* pp. 3–19. **(14)** Acts 7:54–59. **(15)** Matt. 22:11–14. **(16)** *siddhis* [Sanskrit]: supernatural powers acquired through the practice of yoga, such as clairaudience, clairvoyance, levitation, supremacy over the body and mind, knowledge of a previous birth, dominion over the elements, vision of perfected beings, and the power of making oneself invisible. **(17)** Luke 17:20, 21; 21:8. **(18)** See Ra Mu, July 7, 1975, "I AM Ra Mu," in *The Great White Brotherhood in the Culture, History and Religion of America,* pp. 209–14; on 90-min. audiocassette B7531, $6.50 (add $.50 for postage). Ra Mu also dictated at Camelot, Los Angeles, on November 28, 1981, "You Becoming the All—For Thou Art Mother Also," on 90-min. audiocassette B8269, $6.50 (add $.50 for postage). **(19)** See *A Child's Rosary to Mother Mary*—15-minute scriptural rosaries published on 4 audiocassette albums, 3 cassettes per album; Album 1 (A7864): John, James, Jude; Album 2 (A7905): Paul to the Hebrews; Album 3 (A7934): Paul to the Galatians; Album 4 (A8045): Paul to the Corinthians, $9.95 each (add $.90 each for postage). **(20)** II Kings 2:1–15.

Avalokiteśvara [Sanskrit, "the lord who sees" or "the lord who hears the sounds of the world" or "the lord who is seen"], known in China as the feminine being Kuan Yin or Kuan Shih Yin and in Japan as Kannon, Kwannon, or Kwanzeon. In Mahayana Buddhism, Avalokiteśvara is the bodhisattva of infinite compassion and mercy; a bodhisattva is literally a "being of wisdom" who is destined to become a Buddha but has foregone the bliss of Nirvana with a vow to save every being on earth. Avalokiteśvara is a divine emanation of the Dhyani Buddha Amitābha, who embodies the quality of compassion in its highest sense. As one of the most popular and beloved Buddhist figures, Avalokiteśvara's attributes and miracles are recounted in many scriptures *(sutras).* His assistance is invoked often, especially for protection from natural disasters and calamities, to resolve personal and family problems, and to bestow children. The Surangama Sutra records that Avalokiteśvara has the power to appear in thirty-two different bodily forms, according to the different types of beings he is trying to save, and that he has the power to bestow fourteen kinds of fearlessness. Devotees invoke Avalokiteśvara's power and merciful intercession through the mantra OM MANI PADME HUM ("Hail to the jewel in the lotus!"). The worship of Avalokiteśvara can be traced back to the second century in China and was well established in Tibet by the seventh century. Tibetan Buddhists believe that Avalokiteśvara is incarnated in each Dalai Lama (the spiritual and temporal ruler of Tibet; the fourteenth Dalai Lama was forced to flee the country following the 1959 Tibetan uprising against the Chinese). Avalokiteśvara is often portrayed with a thousand arms and varying numbers of eyes, heads and hands, sometimes with an eye in the palm of each hand. In this form he is looking in all directions, sensing the afflictions of mankind and striving to alleviate them. His female consort is the White Tara, who is said to have been born of a tear shed by him in compassion for the distress of sentient beings. In his 1987 New Year's Eve address, Gautama Buddha said, "It is an hour that you may also reach out through the Presence of Avalokiteśvara to save that which can be saved." See Pearl no. 2, pp. 10, 11, 13, 15, 18, 19, 20.

Pearls of Wisdom®
published by The Summit Lighthouse

| Vol. 31 No. 5 | Beloved Surya | January 31, 1988 |

New Year's Retreat
at the Royal Teton Ranch

V
Passing Through
A Grid of Light—a Course of Deliverance and Self-Mastery

In the great depths of the Pacific Ocean there is a grand processioning this night as ancient ones, priests of the sacred fire, walk sandaled and robed in white the breadth and length of the Pacific Basin under the sea on what was once Lemuria. Blessed ones, it is an ancient ceremony rekindled by great Masters of Light, their adepts and chelas.

This processioning with torches held is a ritual for the holding of the balance out of our retreat. For I am Surya of the Sun and my Son Cuzco does maintain the retreat for the holding of the balance in the earth and in earth changes.[1] Therefore, one hears the vibration of peace, the vibration of the Divine Mother. Thus for a holy purpose are there come, then, those ancient ones.

You heard described the march of the Ancient of Days and the armies of heaven in the nation's capital.[2] So it is that much activity does take place at inner levels on planet earth for the sealing, for the saving, for the calling Home of souls of Light for the finishing in order that new beginnings might begin.

I have come from the Sun, figuratively in my chariot, journeying across infinity.[3] I come, as always, in the fire of the Buddhic Mind for the liberation of souls—their liberation to be fully in the highest octaves and in physical matter the incarnation of God.

I AM God's awareness of himself as Surya, as the God of the Sun-radiance. I AM part of the Light of the Central Sun wherever lifewaves receive it.

I enter earth, then, bearing a momentum of calm and peace as with Peace and Aloha we seek the stilling of the mind's agitation, the anxiety of the emotions, that for a moment in an interval of stillness some might behold Reality, even the reality of our beloved Babaji, who has been suspended within this hall and court for some time, floating in the lotus posture, beaming intense and fiery love.

So he has come forth and has not, as some have conceived, incarnated in recent time. Remaining at the interval and the nexus [between the crystal spheres of the Spirit/Matter Cosmos], this unascended Master of the Himalayas does come to demonstrate to you what is the victory of the Mother Flame, how ascension's flame as a buoyant fount of light may become the lotus pad.

By the fire of Mother rising, then, one can be suspended at her fountain of light, even as there is the sign of Old Faithful, of the Holy Spirit piercing the sky with the fierceness of conveyance of earth's fire and a transmission to all of the secret awareness that the rising Mother Flame and the sacred fire can easily defy all laws of gravity contrived by grave karmic difficulties borne by evolutions benighted and ignorant in understanding, having not, then, the cubic dimensions that do convey a cosmic approach to life.

"Passing through," they say. I pass through and so do you, beloved. We have come from other stars and spheres, and to the Central Sun, our Home, we return.

Therefore, to quiet a turbulent earth is our motive. Where hearts are pure, does not purity flow? Let the fount, then, be purged at its source, in each level of awareness.

Come, Goddess of Purity! Come, Cuzco and Queen of Light! Come, Goddess of Light out the Central Sun! Out of the ancient retreats of the Andes, across the island chains of the Pacific, around the fire ring,[4] let there be a stilling.

Come, O hierarchs of elemental life! Come, Oromasis and Diana! Come, Neptune and Luara! Come, Virgo and Pelleur! Come, then, sweet ones of Light! Come, sweet ones of Light, come!* Come also, Aries and Thor! Release the fullness of Mind of God in all quadrants.

We set a grid of Light† on the buoyant joy of the rising of song and praise. We set a course of deliverance and a course of self-mastery. All, then, are quickened to the awareness in this place of Arthur of a weariness, an utter weariness of being subject unto the veils of flesh and the out-of-control, out-of-alignment state. So long it seems thou art a prisoner of the vessel. No longer, then, for

*Beloved Surya is coaxing shy elementals to accompany their hierarchs at his call.
†grid of Cosmic Christ consciousness

in the twinkling of the eye of God there is a moment of recognition
that contrary to all outer appearances thou art the Master within.

Attune for a moment to thy higher being who is Master of
Life, thy God Reality, and then to the plane of pure Spirit where
I AM THAT I AM is individualization of pure God Light. You
can shinny up and down this pole of being at will by the mind's
flight, by the song of the heart. You need not be encased in form
except in a pendulum swing as light enters and light is released.

Therefore consciousness, moment by moment, may ascend to
God and return in such speed of light and proportion of cosmic
consciousness as to make one aware continually and perpetually
of oneself in a form that is no longer a prison house, of oneself in
the higher octaves, breathing in, entering in to great causal
body spheres.

I speak to release, then, the heart of fire of Himalaya, whose
Electronic Presence does radiate through this hall. Lord Himalaya,
I salute thee from the heart of the Central Sun and the God Star!
I salute thee, O blessed one and Manu of Light, for thy members
are ascending, truly those of thy root race! Therefore, we come to
infire them with a level of permanence that is white light, and this
white light shall make permanent every purest thought and virtue,
kindness good, and deeds well done.

Visualize, then, rising from you pink roses of light signifying
the completion of tasks and a light-heartedness in the midst of the
weight of this world's karma. Thou hast no part with it! Weary
not in being upon it, for thou art always in the Central Sun, and
my angels are beholding thy faces as before the face of the
Father[5] they affirm his holiness in thine own visage.

Know this, beloved, that this is not concrete form but only a
mirage in itself, substance worn as coalesced water, fire and
earth, as air breathed upon it. Thou hast, then, a vessel for the
movement, for the being, for the action, for the glorious creativity
of highest manifestation.

In the resilience of thy spirit, then, ascend the mountain of
God and descend by the suppleness of movement and a poet's
heart capturing delicate strings and sounds and new calls of the
new bird not heard in the physical octave.

By all these things I convey to you, beloved, a freedom beyond
freedom yet known, a coming and a going as easily as thy soul's
flight at night to the etheric octave, where the presence of loved
ones and so many sons and daughters of God does remind you that
whereas on earth there may be those committed to the dark and the
dark ones, all of cosmos' spirit is filled with endless processionings

of souls who by the ritual of their movement sustain the coordinates of the very manifest creation.

Out of the *Ungrund* there does come therefore the *Grund*.[6] Know, beloved, that nothing cannot come forth from something, but rather from something grand and glorious there does descend the very issue, the very presence, the very perfectionment and precipitation *here and now* of the inner glory!

Live in this truth! Live in this joy, beloved, and therefore the weariness shall take flight and a crystal consciousness, a rippling of light-forms, even through thy present grid of identity, shall provide thy soul with a lilt and a laughter, a steadiness and a sternness, a love unabated, a Truth that equates with principles of a cosmic geometry that do define and realign all matter and thy being.

Blessed hearts, you appear as naked, thinking that you are but this form. The extension of thy being goes far beyond this physical receptacle, and therefore see how the grid of Light of a great blue causal body does surround thee now as the Great Divine Director does step forth to consecrate spheres as of fine blue lines of force, establishing a forcefield whereby the momentum of dynamic decree and the release of light shall be as garlands hung upon a latticework and so precise, beloved, as to be an instrument as an aeolian harp through which the winds do play and upon which many angels play.

Hearts of living fire, it is well to distance thyself for a moment from the political struggles of the hour. It is well to take the great inbreath of God and to feel the expansion of that Holy Spirit within, to know who thou art and who is God and the oneness of thy life with purest rose of counterpart, twin flame, and all who are a part of Sanat Kumara's mandala, as ye are.

Let all who are a part of this Community worldwide, then, see themselves as holding a vast *antahkarana*.* As children play with string games upon their fingers and make intricate weavings, so each one of you is a finger in time and space somewhere on earth, positioned not by chance but by Love, not by force but by the Divine Will, not by cunning calculations but by the vastness of the eternal knowing of the Mind of God.

Therefore all become coordinates whereby strings of light are strung upon earth. O what joy! For these strings are of finest cord of light as harp and violin strings to be plucked, always resonating and sounding a great inner music that does emit from the very center of the earth and the great causal body formed of the entire Spirit of the Great White Brotherhood, including yourselves, who

---

antahkarana [Sanskrit 'internal sense organ']: the web of Life; the net of light spanning Spirit and Matter, connecting and sensitizing the whole of creation within itself and to the heart of God.

are a part of the hierarchy of this planet from the central fire of
the earth to the spiritual sun of all serving here.

Know, then, that a sound is released, and wherever there is a
harmonic convergence of chakras well tuned, balanced Alpha
and Omega, spinning centers of light, these sounds resonate,
these sounds pass through for the neutralization of all discordant
sound in the earth that does drag down civilization and children
of the Sun to lower levels of nonidentity.

I come, then, as God of the Sun, expanding Sun-awareness
from center to periphery to beyond the physical planet. I come
endowing life and matter with a new impetus of a charging and a
charging again and a charging again with inmost vibration to
realign, to draw back to the divine rhythm and the divine sound.
This is my effort for and on behalf of all Lightbearers who know
me now and see my face as the smiling white-fire/blue-fire sun.

As I beam upon each Lightbearer of the planet home, so
there is the response, and mirrored in my eyes the soul does
behold himself/herself and I behold my own. Therefore, look
into the pool of the infinite above you, not beneath. See the divine
reflection of thy God.

Know, then, that we who take the dispensations of the
Cosmic Council have studied ways and means to contribute light,
consistent with cosmic law. Therefore, this light does lighten the
way of the Lightbearer and by its very presence does reduce and
reduce and reduce those who are the dwellers in darkness, the
bearers in darkness, the servants of darkness.

Light, then, comes for the expansion of the Lightbearer's
heart flame, for the diminishing of those who have made nonuse
of that flame. Therefore, consistent with the judgment of the
fallen one, this grid of Light of earth is come. Consistent with the
assistance to the Lightbearer,[7] this grid of Light is now intensifying and quivering. Happy are ye who have been resonators of the
Word in this place this day by the Diamond Heart of Morya
multiplied and Mary's thrice blessed in love!

Now in Wisdom's fount drink, for Maitreya's Mystery School
is active again[8] and the LORD, the Good Cosmic Christ, has come
to claim his own. While I busy myself about (with my legions of
Light) the securing of these harpstrings Lemurian for a planet and
while priests continue to procession, so come, Maitreya, come,
speak to thine own. Let them hear, then, thy song of Life, thy
sweet mystery, as there is a meditation on the music and the sound
of this single keynote. [intonations, 20 seconds]
["Ah! Sweet Mystery of Life" by Victor Herbert played as a meditation.]

"The Summit Lighthouse Sheds Its Radiance O'er All the World to Manifest as Pearls of Wisdom." This dictation by **Surya** was **delivered** through the Messenger of the Great White Brotherhood Elizabeth Clare Prophet on **Saturday, January 2, 1988,** during the 5-day New Year's Retreat at the **Royal Teton Ranch, Montana. (1) The retreat of the Ascended Master Cuzco** at Viti Levu in the Fiji Islands in the South Pacific is dedicated to the holding of the balance of the forces in the earth, including the adjustment of the earth to the weight of karmic effluvia and the guarding of the earth on its axis and in orbit, by the use of computers and scientific instruments. On December 23, 1973, Cuzco said that his retreat "is concerned with such matters as planetary cataclysm, its possibility, its prevention, with the straightening of the axis of the earth, with climatic conditions and with the evolutions of souls migrating from one continent to another in order to gain awareness of all of the facets of the Christ consciousness in preparation for mastery. As I stand in my retreat, cosmic instruments available to me enable me to perceive the aura of any individual lifestream walking the earth at any place, at any hour of the day or night. For it is my responsibility to determine whether the energy, the weight of darkness, released through the aura of the individual increases the total karmic weight of a planet, and thereby increases the possibility of cataclysm. . . . I come to show you that the preservation of a planet, a people, of lifewaves and root races is most scientific and is carried on by the Ascended Masters for this one purpose—to preserve the opportunity for evolution. For, you see, if the planet earth were destroyed it would take thousands, tens of thousands of years for your souls to complete their evolution on other planetary homes amongst other lifewaves at different levels of evolution. Therefore, Hierarchy is concerned with the preservation of the platform of planet earth." **(2)** See Archangel Uriel, November 25, 1987, "The Promise of Thy Deliverance," 1987 *Pearls of Wisdom,* vol. 30, no. 78, p. 597. See also 1987 *Pearls of Wisdom,* vol. 30, no. 47, pp. 443–45. **(3) Surya and his chariot.** In Hindu lore and religion Surya, the sun or sun god, is traditionally depicted seated on a lotus in a chariot of gold drawn by seven horses or by a single horse with seven heads. The Sanskrit word *surya* comes from the root *sur* or *svar* 'to shine', and Surya's brilliance is portrayed by rays of light surrounding his head. The sun god's charioteer is the legless Aruna, the deity of the dawn, who rides in front of Surya, using his body to shelter the world from the sun god's rays. One of the most famous temples dedicated to Surya is the colossal thirteenth-century Surya Deula (Sun Temple) at Konarak in the state of Orissa; the 100-foot high temple and its hall are designed in the shape of a giant chariot borne on twelve carved stone wheels and drawn by seven stone horses. **(4) Ring of Fire:** a string or belt of active volcanoes which encircles the Pacific Ocean at or near the margins of the continents of North and South America, Asia and Australia. **(5)** Matt. 18:10. **(6)** *Ungrund:* German term meaning groundless; introduced by the German mystic Jakob Boehme (1575–1624) to refer to the Abyss, which is also God, that lies behind the world as its source and explanation, or the undifferentiated Absolute that is ineffable; sometimes defined as pure potentiality. *Grund:* German for ground, foundation, basis, reason. The comparison between the *Ungrund* and the *Grund* here is to the unformed and the formed. **(7)** See Gautama Buddha, May 13, 1987, "For the Alignment of a World— 'A Proclamation' by Alpha," 1987 *Pearls of Wisdom,* vol. 30, no. 24, pp. 242–49. **(8) Maitreya's Mystery School.** In his May 31, 1984 dictation, Jesus said that Lord Maitreya "desires me, as his pupil, to announce to you that he is dedicating this Heart of the Inner Retreat and this entire property as the Mystery School of Maitreya in this age. . . . You realize that the Mystery School of Maitreya was called the Garden of Eden. All of the Ascended Masters' endeavors and the schools of the Himalayas of the centuries have been to the end that this might occur from the etheric octave unto the physical—that the Mystery School might once again receive the souls of Light who have gone forth therefrom, now who are ready to return, to submit, to bend the knee before the Cosmic Christ. . . . Maitreya truly is more physical today than ever before since the Garden of Eden." See "The Mystery School of Lord Maitreya," 1984 *Pearls of Wisdom,* vol. 27, no. 36, pp. 316–17, 324.

Pearls of Wisdom®
published by The Summit Lighthouse

Vol. 31 No. 6	Beloved Lord Maitreya	February 7, 1988

New Year's Retreat
at the Royal Teton Ranch
VI
Welcome to the Mystery School!
In the Secret Place of the Crystal Cave

My Beloved Sons and Daughters,

I reenter the physical octave through the blessedness of thy being, thy desiring to know the Truth, to study the Truth, to be the Truth.

Hail, O Thou Cosmic Christ! Lo, I AM THAT I AM Maitreya. I call my Sons, Lords of the Seven Rays: Make thy Presence known here! Let the trees, the rock, the frozen earth and stream know the warmth of thy compassionate Presence.

O my beloved Seven, O Lord [the Maha Chohan], thou who art the Representative of the Holy Spirit, welcome, then, and welcome thine own students, for they have truly desired to enter in.

Therefore, the golden fount of illumination's flame is seen to dance as flames licking the hillsides, and an aurora of golden light pulsating does create an atmosphere of a Sun Presence as though the earth were already a sun star—and the indigo blues of the night and the power of the First Ray and the sparkling and the bursting of the fireworks within.

Blessed hearts, it is a celebration of earth by elemental life who come to meet you, to welcome you to their land, to their place where they are nurtured by the Divine Mother. And the etheric octave and the retreat of Lady Master Venus[1] does draw nigh as you yourselves have somewhat entered the etheric octave of your being.

It is good, then, to commune in love and to prepare to enter the equations of the teaching of the Path. Thereby to be forewarned is to be forearmed, and in being forearmed, beloved, you shall be truly prepared to meet the Adversary within and without and to meet me on the way of forest path, mountain fastnesses and in the heart of the valley and the hearth of home and fire.

Welcome, ye! Welcome, all who have determined to gather on the mount! Let those who have come for lesser reasons be purged of their lesser reasons, for I, Maitreya, quicken a golden illumination flame in every heart who has come. This flame must be expanded else it shall decrease. To increase illumination as illumined action does rid oneself of the grumpiness of human ignorance that stubs its toe or thumb for want of inner equilibrium of illumination's golden plume.

The gentleness of those out of the East and those from ancient civilizations is apparent. Now you see in the realm of the Second Ray so many hearts at so many levels a part of this thoughtform of the year—the bodhisattvas, the blessed students and disciples,[2] all, then, having locked within their hearts the divine image of Buddha; and Buddha, the smiling one, the meditating one, does twinkle his eyes in a merriment, then.

Do not take yourself too seriously, he says. Do not be too seriously burdened with all illusions in the world. Though they be strong illusions, it is well to pause to remember they are not real, nor all the engines of war or rumors thereof. They are not real but only set in place as props, as bad dreams, that those who see and know Reality might draw the sword and pierce that set, that backdrop in life, and in so piercing it, excise all of the poisons and the manipulations of those fallen ones. They cannot stand unless some believe they are real. Thus, Evil has no permanent reality except the reality given to it.

We come as withdrawers, this may be our name. Withdrawers all, our aim. Withdraw the light from the fight, there is no fight! Bind the Darkness in its way, it cannot hold sway! There is a moment of joy in the release of light from all of your chakras at the point and the place prepared.

Blessed hearts, these hordes of darkness do tremble at the gentle footsteps of Lord Confucius, Lord Lanto; and my own Presence does cause them to fall back in dismay and faint as the Holy Ghost may therefore judge them in the Presence of the Cosmic Christ. They are breathless, for there is no breath of life save that from the Maha Chohan. For they have already ruined their breath by noxious weeds of earth.

O uncommon Light, O uncommon ones, I, Maitreya, salute you, for thou hast come long, long way from the days of Lemuria!

Throw off thy weariness in the long trek of thy return. Thou art Home. Thou art Home in light, and illumination's glow as the fire in the heart of the mountain does set the backdrop for the Buddha of the Ruby Ray.

Look, then, on inner plane at the mount you have called Himalaya[3]—it looks as though the entire side of the mountain should open as a vast door; and in the heart of the mountain is a blazing illumination's flame and seated in this flame, beloved, is the transparent Buddha of the Ruby Ray. How beautiful!

And therefore, all inside the mountains of earth, those which have been chosen by the Gods, there are manifestations of Light unknown and unheard of. Yet the waters under the earth and the fires therein, the heat that has been sealed, all these receive the charge and vibration of the holy ones of God. Earth conceived in holiness has been rendered profane by the fallen ones, but we shall endure in holiness and love.

I take from you, then, if you will release it, wrong desire. I release in you an upward mounting spiral of illumination's flame intertwining with resurrection's flame. Therefore, let all of the energies of thy being mount and rise and spiral in this hour.

Welcome to the Mystery School, called in the outer Summit University. But within, beloved, as depicted in the Roerich painting on the covers of *The Lost Teachings of Jesus,*[4] there is that inner gathering, there is that inner oneness in the secret place of the rock, in the secret place of the crystal cave, in the inner dwelling place.

Therefore, enter the chakra of the Eighth Ray—the eight-petaled chakra, secret chamber of the heart—the heart of the mountain, the heart of Himalaya, and know that in planes slightly above the physical there are pathways to be entered. And there is a coursing of tunnels and caves and compartments within earth's crust that have been prepared for thy meditation one upon one with the beloved Buddha.

Therefore, I make my trek now to the Heart of the Inner Retreat, physically there, and in the etheric Western Shamballa I bow before the Lord of the World, Gautama Buddha, who welcomes me and all members of this Community to an era of enlightenment unprecedented in an era of outer darkness that has not been exceeded.

Thus, we keep the home fires burning, and the warmth of our love, the kindling fire of our wisdom does return to you, beloved, the spark of the divine consciousness and the divine intelligence which was thine in the beginning and has atrophied, whereby the fullness of its use is not thine own in this hour.

I shall seal my delivery with you, then, by inviting you to decree with me for golden illumination's flame that you might have the momentum of my Presence on the path of overcoming.

Being the Coming Buddha, then, I am come into your temple. Just as there is prophesied in the West the Second Coming of Christ, so there is prophesied in the East the Coming of Maitreya. The significance is the descent of the Buddha who is Cosmic Christ into your heart. It is not delayed, it is ready.

I AM here, beloved. I would enter. As the chamber is emptied and then filled again, emptied and then filled again by the fire breath of illumination's flame, know that in your process of processioning through the inner canyons of being, mounting, then, the spiral staircase to the heart, I am with you, and in a moment of recognition [we experience] the divine awareness of we two in the heart of hearts communing.

Thus, develop the listening ear, the All-Seeing Eye of God, the sensitivity of touch and the breathing in of the sacred breath. Develop all senses as spiritual senses, thereby sharpening the outer, and let the fire of the Divine Mother rising consume all unnecessary bag and baggage of a self, a former self, that the self that is yet to be might be entered into and known by the soul.

Thus, upon you are placed now, one and all of this Community and those who study with us in this hour, the neophyte's golden robe, a simple, natural garment the color of a golden yellow. Thus, wear it with joy on inner levels and be unencumbered by any other necessity of adornment.

You will see, then, at inner levels and on the etheric octave devotees of the Buddha. Some of these are out of their body in hours of sleep, some have risen to the etheric octaves.

Blessed hearts, many of the Tibetan Buddhists pause to listen to my message to those of the West. These are disciples who always enter the etheric octave or chambers of the mental belt. They have sustained a pillar of my flame. See what has come upon them[5]—the hordes of night and those who have become so by the vicious indoctrination of Mao's Communism and that even more fanatical than that of the Western Communists.

Blessed hearts, know, then, that when the pillar of fire is raised up, there must be an inner chamber and the ability of the soul to rise to the etheric octaves. Thus, we count this mystery school as the opportunity of all souls gathered here to master the science of the Word and therefore to deliver the death blow and the death knell to every force of Evil that has moved against our temples, our mystery schools and our retreats.

For the Lord God himself has decreed: They shall not pass! They shall not pass! Rather that the earth itself should not endure than levels of our disciples again and again be brutalized and massacred, tormented and tortured and the light put out of our Community.

Thus, from the heart of Alpha, from the heart of the Lord God is your sign and authority to demand the judgment of all those seed of the wicked embodied in the earth who have persecuted in Church and State the children of the Sun, that they be bound and judged by angels of Light. This authority to call forth their judgment, beloved, is given to you from your beloved Alpha.[6] Take it, then.

Have mercy, O God within you! Have mercy, O God within you! *Have mercy, O God within you,* for the Tibetans who have held a tradition unto my coming!

Blessed hearts, see to it that these, *these,* these shall not have died in vain. And therefore stand in the earth in this hour to redeem their name, their service and their life by the call of the judgment upon all those who have agreed to their takeover, including those in the United States, the president thereof and the Department of State.[7] I say, that Department of State is also judged, whereupon let the woes be on them and all who are with them in vibration!

I, Maitreya, say, there is room in the earth for me. Thus, there is no room for Antichrist.

My hand is raised. Let your right hand also be raised, and by the power of the Great Call let the judgment descend. I decree it once. I decree it twice. I decree it thrice. Let them be bound and let it be by the fullness of the intensity of the Mind of Buddha in all disciples of the Light.

Therefore, pray with me now for golden illumination's flame to pierce the night of ignorance and quicken hearts to defend their Victory. There are those who take their stand to defend Freedom. I say, Defend your Victory in the heart of the Cosmic Christ!

(Please take your decree books. Decree number 20.13. Together:)

Golden Flame from the Central Sun

In the name of the beloved mighty victorious Presence of God, I AM in me, Holy Christ Selves of all earth's evolutions, beloved Alpha and Omega, beloved Helios and Vesta, beloved Great Central Sun messengers, all Cosmic Beings, powers, activities, and legions of Light, the beloved

God and Goddess Meru, and all who serve Illumination's
flame, beloved Lanello, the entire Spirit of the Great White
Brotherhood and the World Mother, elemental life—fire,
air, water, and earth! I decree:

> Golden flame from the Central Sun, (3x)
> Expand thy Light through me today! (3x)
> Golden flame from the Central Sun, (3x)
> Transmute all wrong Illumination's way! (3x)
> Golden flame from the Central Sun, (3x)
> Direct our youth into action God's way! (3x)
> Golden flame from the Central Sun, (3x)
> Illumination's flame, fore'er hold sway! (3x)
> Golden flame from the Central Sun, (3x)
> Illumine the earth by Christ-command! (3x)
> Golden flame from the Central Sun, (3x)
> Thy beauteous power I now demand! (3x)

> Take dominion now,
> To thy Light I bow;
> I AM thy dazzling Light,
> Golden flame so bright.
> Grateful for thy ray
> Sent to me each day,
> Fill me through and through
> Until there's only you!

I live, move, and have my being within a mighty pillar
of Illumination's golden flame from the heart of God in the
Great Central Sun and my very own individualized Mighty
I AM Presence, beloved Alpha and Omega, beloved Helios
and Vesta, and all who serve God's victorious golden Light
radiance which blesses and heals, illumines and seals me
and all mankind forever in the Light of God that never,
never, never fails.

Golden Victorious Light

In the name of the beloved mighty victorious Presence
of God, I AM in me, Holy Christ Selves of all mankind,
beloved Mighty Victory, beloved Lanello, the entire Spirit
of the Great White Brotherhood and the World Mother,
elemental life—fire, air, water, and earth! I decree:

I AM the golden victorious Light, the full-orbed flame
of Illumination from the heart of God that refuses to

accept any concept of limitation concerning my eternal reason for being here and now made manifest in the chalice of the present hour.

I AM the radiation of that Victory which sweeps across the face of the earth, removing barriers by the power of Faith that will not be denied its immortal birthright.

I AM the flame of Illumination that sweeps all continents, awakening peoples of every walk of life from the lethargy and sleep of the ages to a vital, breathing awareness of the wisdom that transcends dogma, sense consciousness, and personality functions, threading the eye of the needle with the thread of light-determination whose sewings upon the garments of the Lord of Creation produce elevation, consummation, radiation, purification, and freedom for every man, woman, and child upon this planet.

> *O world, awake,
> Your dusty selves now shake;
> Purify and rectify,
> New ways of thought to make! *(10x)

Decree for Brotherhood

Out of the One,
Thou, God, hast spun
All of the races of men.
By thy Great Law
Do thou now draw
All to their God Source again.

Take away hate;
By Love abate
All mankind's vicious intent.
Show thy great power
Every hour
Of love and compassion God sent.

I AM, I AM, I AM
Divine Love sending forth
The wonderful feeling of true divine healing,
Unguents of Light now sealing
All of the schisms of men.

Stop all division!
By God-precision
Love is the hallowed law—key.

Ultimate peace,
Make all war cease,
Let the children of men now go free!
Stop mankind's friction,
All their predictions
Tearing bless'd heart from heart.
By God-direction
Produce now perfection
In thy great family—one heart.

And in full Faith I consciously accept this manifest, manifest, manifest! (3x) right here and now with full Power, eternally sustained, all-powerfully active, ever expanding, and world enfolding until all are wholly ascended in the Light and free!
Beloved I AM! Beloved I AM! Beloved I AM!

Did you hear the affirmation "Beloved I AM"? You are saying, I am belov'd of God. Beloved, I AM. Beloved, I AM. Beloved, I AM. If I am the beloved of God and you are the beloved of God, then we are one in the Divine All. In this oneness of consummate Being, know that I shall give thee to drink of the same fount from which I gave Jesus to drink.

Therefore, beloved, enter in to the mainstream of cosmic life and put behind thee the past streams of consciousness that no longer are useful or fruitful.

In the heart of the yellow rose, I AM and I remain *Maitreya! Vajra! Vajra! Vajra!*

This dictation was **delivered January 2, 1988,** at the **Royal Teton Ranch.** (1) See Sanat Kumara, "The Retreat of the Divine Mother at the Royal Teton Ranch," 1986 *Pearls of Wisdom,* vol. 29, pp. 70–72. (2) See pp. 19–20. (3) **Himalaya,** named by the Messenger, is a 6,316-foot mountain (unnamed on the Miner U.S. Geological Survey map of the area) on the Royal Teton Ranch property just across Mol Heron Creek from the Ranch Headquarters. (4) *Treasure in the Mountain,* by Nicholas Roerich. (5) **Chinese takeover of Tibet and destruction of Tibetan culture.** Tibet, once an independent and predominately Buddhist nation ruled by the Dalai Lama, who acted as both spiritual and temporal head, was invaded by the Communist Chinese in 1950. Since then, the Dalai Lama has fled into exile, 1.2 million Tibetans have been killed or starved to death by the Chinese, and 6,254 monasteries—the centers for Tibetan cultural, educational and religious life—have been destroyed. The number of Tibetan monks (100,000 in 1957) has been reduced to 4,000, with only 10 to 15 new monks allowed to enter a monastery each year. Sacred art and statuary have been melted into bullion or sold for foreign exchange, and an estimated 60 percent of Tibet's religious and historical literature has been burned. The Chinese have forced abortions and sterilizations on Tibetan women and used a policy of population transfer to create a Tibetan underclass by importing millions of Chinese, who now outnumber native Tibetans 7.5 million to 6 million. Estimates of political prisoners range from 20,000 to 100,000. Northeast Tibet has the largest prison camp complex in the world, the Amdo Gulag, capable of holding 10 million prisoners. For an account of the disasters that were prophesied to befall Tibet during the middle of the Kali Yuga (the last and worst of the four world ages), including an invasion by China, the destruction of monasteries, and desecration of sacred scriptures, see the teachings of Padma Sambhava in *The Legend of the Great Stupa* (Berkeley: Dharma Publishing, 1973), pp. 15–16, 49–59. (6) See 1987 *Pearls of Wisdom,* vol. 30, no. 38, p. 387. (For note 7 see Pearl 8.)

Pearls of Wisdom®
published by The Summit Lighthouse

Vol. 31 No. 7	Elizabeth Clare Prophet	February 14, 1988

New Year's Retreat
at the Royal Teton Ranch

VII
The Race for Space
America, Accept the Challenge
to Master Time and Space for Saint Germain!

What is uppermost in our minds concerning the survival of freedom upon earth is the race for space. Whoever gains control of space will have a decisive military advantage for 50 years and perhaps indefinitely.[1]

Saint Germain has called for 50 years of peace,[2] and with those 50 years he is convinced that he can bring the planet and her people into a golden age. Yet moment by moment, as we are gathered here at this conference, the Soviets are racing to dominate space.

Their purpose is to gain enough of a military advantage to deny the United States access to space. They are putting in place their own version of Star Wars—a ground- and space-based missile defense system that will have the capability to intercept ballistic missiles, cruise missiles and aircraft, destroy satellites in orbit, and prevent other nations from deploying satellites. It may also have an offensive military capability.

The Soviet Union is winning the race for space. On December 29, 1987, the Feast Day of Saint Thomas Becket,[3] NASA reported that the test of the space shuttle's booster on December 23, which was thought to have been a success, turned out to be a failure. As a result, the space shuttle's next mission, scheduled for June 2, 1988, will be delayed until August 4, 1988. In contrast, also on December 29, 1987, Soviet cosmonaut Yuri Romanenko broke the endurance record for space flight by remaining aboard the Mir space station for 326 days.

On October 5, 1987, *Time*'s cover headline read "Moscow Takes the Lead." Their story was called "Surging Ahead: The Soviets Overtake the U.S. as the No. 1 Spacefaring Nation." There is considerable evidence of Soviet leadership in space. Moscow has become the space capital of the world. Seminars once given at the Goddard Space Flight Center in Greenbelt, Maryland, are now given in Moscow. Every year since 1967 the Soviets have launched more vehicles into space than the United States. For example, in 1986 the Soviets conducted 91 launches with only one failure. The United States was successful in only six of nine launches.

The great discrepancy in the number of launches reflects, in part, different space philosophies. The United States tends to launch a small number of state-of-the-art satellites. The Soviets launch many more satellites using less-advanced technologies.

The United States, for instance, has chosen to launch a small number of technically sophisticated reconnaissance satellites with long operational lives. The Soviets have been able to achieve comparable and in some cases superior peacetime reconnaissance using larger numbers of cheaper, less-sophisticated satellites with shorter operational lives. Thus, they tend to launch more missions.

But even after allowing for the Soviets' need to carry out more launches to perform comparable missions, it is clear that the Soviets have maintained a much more aggressive space program than the United States for at least a decade and that the U.S. program is in a serious slump.

Soviet cosmonauts have logged 14 man-years in space; U.S. astronauts less than five. The Soviets have two permanent space stations in orbit—the Salyut 7 and the Mir. They will launch two new modules for the Mir in 1988 and intend to build larger stations. NASA isn't even planning to launch a space station until the mid-1990s. Even then its value will be questionable unless the United States develops a coherent space policy and a well-defined mission for it.

NASA had a space station called Skylab in orbit from 1973 until 1979 but never quite knew what to do with it. As a result, it was often unoccupied and Skylab II, a duplicate, was donated to the Smithsonian Institution rather than being launched because, as T. A. Heppenheimer, a space reporter and member of the American Institute of Aeronautics and Astronautics, points out, "NASA could not find work enough for its space crews to justify launching [it] and supporting it with astronaut-carrying flights."[4]

As we know, the projections of world karma being delivered by the Four Horsemen as well as the astrology for America and the Soviet Union do not allow us the indulgence to wait until the 1990s to put up a space station. Our people are afflicted with euphoria and euphemisms, procrastination and psychic nonsense. And we have assembled at this conference for the breaking of the spine of that astral beast of national suicide and the downward beat of rock music and drugs that has lulled the people to sleep as though they were in the last days of Atlantis, unaware of what was coming upon them.

The Soviets are undertaking more missions and more complex missions than the United States. In July of this year they are planning an ambitious launch of two spacecraft to Mars. One will fly above the Martian moon Phobos, then drop a lander vehicle to collect data on the moon's soil. If it is successful, the second spacecraft may take off to explore Mars' second moon, Diemos. In 1992 the Soviets plan to launch a spacecraft to analyze soil from Mars and by the late 1990s they want to follow up with a robot probe that will walk the planet's surface over a year's time to gather soil samples.

We know that Martians embodied on this planet today carry the consciousness of war. The ancient warlords of Japan are an example of those who descended from the false hierarchy of Mars. Not only does the exploration of Mars advance the technology of the Soviets but it also probes the astral belt and opens up the astral records of war that spill out into the solar system and pollute Earth. Each time we have had an encounter with Mars through space exploration we have seen the increase on Earth of Martian consciousness and Martian misuses of the base chakra of the Divine Mother, turning the sacred fire to war—thus the appearance of nuclear, chemical and biological weapons that have been used in past ages in rival wars of the gods on Mars, Maldek, Hedron and Earth.[5]

I submit that the real reason the Soviets are going to Mars (not necessarily consciously) is to link up vibrationally with the false hierarchy of that planet on the physical as well as on the astral plane, much of that false hierarchy already being on Earth. I believe that there are aliens who assist the Soviets in their space program—aiding and abetting the cause of World Communism to maintain control of the Lightbearers of Earth—and that some of these are also connected with the Martian evolution, who, after rendering their own planet uninhabitable, reincarnated on Earth and other dense spheres bearing the contaminating karma of war.

The Soviets now have an enormous advantage in "lift capacity"—the amount of weight a vehicle can carry into space. Lift capacity is a critical index of a space program's vitality. A nation with a large lift capacity can undertake more complex missions because it can launch a larger payload. It can also deploy systems faster and more cheaply.

For example, with their large lift capacity the Soviets could in a single launch deploy numerous satellites. The United States has a smaller lift capacity and therefore it would take much longer to deploy a comparable number of satellites. The ability to launch large numbers of satellites is a crucial element in a strategic defense system.

The Soviets' heavy-lift capacity will enable them to launch not only satellites for strategic defense but also powerful space-based laser platforms. The United States is not expected to have a comparable capability until large rockets now being developed come on line sometime between 1995 and 2000.

The Energia, pictured in *Time*'s story on space, is the largest of the Soviets' heavy-lift vehicles. It can lift a 100-ton payload. It is similar but not identical to the old U.S. Saturn 5 rocket, which was developed for the Apollo program that put man on the moon in the 1960s. The Saturn 5 was capable of lifting 90 tons into space. The U.S. program has slipped so badly since the Apollo program ended in 1972 that the shuttle booster, which can only lift a 30-ton payload, is now our largest lift vehicle. It has been grounded since the Challenger exploded.

The problems we have in space are not technological. They are political and conceptual. According to Dr. Robin Ranger, Bradley Resident Fellow at the Heritage Foundation, U.S. space policy suffers from a "curious disconnect."

The problem is twofold. First, he says, U.S. space policy "has suffered from a lack of realistic strategic goals, that is to say, a set of objectives that make military or commercial or scientific sense. There's been a tendency to define the space program as putting a man on the moon or building a manned space shuttle." But, he points out, "we haven't said, 'What do we need? We need access to space the same way you want to access the sea for oceanographic research and for naval purposes, both in peacetime and in conflict situations.'"

"Paradoxically," says Dr. Ranger, "the other failure has really been at a more mundane level where we have simply failed to ask, 'What kinds of things should we be building to get the kind of access to space we want?'"

The turning point in the race for space came in the early seventies as the Apollo program began to wind down. At the urging of NASA, the United States decided to cut back on its existing launch vehicles, cancel development of almost all of its new class of expendable launch vehicles, and put all of its resources into the space shuttle program.

"NASA was an agency in search of a mission to preserve its budget and work force after the end of the Apollo program," says Dr. Ranger. It had a big budget and payroll and wanted to preserve them. So it began to promote the concept of the space shuttle and overestimated the shuttle's capabilities and underestimated its costs. But in order to insure the viability of the shuttle program, they went a step further and, according to Dr. Ranger, said, "What we must do is destroy anything that could possibly compete with the shuttle program."[6] So they destroyed the Saturn system and with it our heavy-lift capability. This, as we shall see, would have profound consequences in the race for space—especially in the near-term military sphere.

The United States still leads the Soviets in a number of key technologies needed for space missions, including computers and data processing, but we are in danger of losing even that lead. Assuming it will take the Soviets some time to overcome weaknesses in these areas, they can still gain complete military dominance of space in the mid-1990s—primarily due to four capabilities that the U.S. lacks: a heavy-lift capacity, an ability to launch numerous missions in a short period of time (known as surge capacity), an anti-satellite capability, and a coherent military doctrine which guides the Soviets toward their goals.

Today the U.S. space program is disorganized, demoralized, underfunded, torn by power struggles within NASA and between the military services and, worst of all, without a mission.

That description fits the stumbling blocks we find on the six o'clock line as we chart our national astrology and psychology on the Cosmic Clock.[7] Disorder, disorganization, demoralization, absence of supply, power struggles, infighting, as well as a loss of vision, direction, the sense of mission, a lack of goals, goal-fittedness, the will to be, to win and to survive—all of these are a perversion of the attributes of God-harmony and God-integration, the Law of the Abundant Life and the cosmic honor flame which demonstrates the power of the hierarchy of Cancer and of individuals and states who pass their initiations of Christhood under that sign on the six o'clock line.

These perversions of the Divine Mother are embodied by the

false hierarchy of Cancer and are amplified by today's full moon in Cancer.

The six o'clock line of the Cosmic Clock is the position not only of the Divine Mother but also of the Great Guru Sanat Kumara, who by ancient tradition in the Far East appears as the leader of the armies of heaven under the name Karttikeya. Our relationship to the Great Guru Sanat Kumara on the six o'clock line is directly related to our ability to raise the sacred fire of the base-of-the-spine chakra (i.e., the Kundalini) to the point of the third eye (nourishing each chakra on the way) for the vision that we need.

We are in a profound dilemma at this moment and we have met our nemesis on the six o'clock line with the initiations which our souls are facing. The six o'clock line is the line of the base chakra, and the base chakra of the people is afflicted in this nation. America is a nation reincarnated from the land of Lemuria and of the Divine Mother. It is because of the absence of our adoration of the Divine Mother in our body temples, in our beings, in our lives that we are being overtaken by an enemy who is misusing the light, the science, and the technology of the Divine Mother.

In addition to our weakness on the six o'clock line, the second opposition to our space program is that in order to master space one must have the mind of the Buddha. In achieving the mind of the Buddha, we manifest a mastery of space. In achieving the mind of the Divine Mother who is Guru, we achieve the mastery of time. We have demonstrated the mastery of time and space in our space program for over 25 years now. But our dharma mandates that we dominate space *first*, and we are allowing the Soviets to undermine in the physical plane the protection of Archangel Michael and the hosts of the LORD that we invoke.

Once upon a time we had vision and a decisive purpose in space. In October 1960, in the midst of his campaign for the presidency, John F. Kennedy declared, "We are in a strategic space race with the Russians and we have been losing. . . . Control of space will be decided in the next decade. If the Soviets control space they can control Earth, as in the past centuries the nations that controlled the seas dominated the continents."[8]

As it turns out, it will be the 1990s, not the 1960s, which will probably decide the race for space. We did not lose in the 1960s because President Kennedy determined we would not. He also determined that we would land on the moon and we became the first to do so. As a result, by the late 1960s the United States had a clear lead in space. No president since has determined to make our leadership in space a national priority, placing all else subordinate to it.

If the Soviets achieve military dominance of space, they will be able to use that advantage to keep us from putting up our space-based missile defense system. What's more, they will be able to keep us from deploying new satellites in space and could destroy those that are already in orbit. They will be able to shoot down any ballistic missile fired at them from anywhere on the planet. Therefore, all nuclear arsenals but theirs will be obsolete. They will be able to attack anyone with impunity and will enjoy global military dominance. They could then control the political, social, economic and cultural life of every nation on earth.

Therefore, we the citizens of the United States of America could very well see within 10 years a totalitarian power with weapons in the sky dictating to us the terms of our everyday life, our military and our economy unless we can find a president who will win the race for space.

People get the type of leader they deserve; El Morya was saying this to us in his New Year's Eve dictation.[9] According to that concept, if we want better leaders, we must change ourselves. If we raise up the living Christ within us, then we deserve to have an anointed one for our president. If we desire to have Sanat Kumara champion us in the battle of Armageddon, then we must bend the knee before him, not merely in an outer demonstration or ritual but truly in our heart of hearts in a fearless surrender to God and to his will, knowing that this is the only way out of the human dilemma.

The United States must achieve military dominance in space. Not in order to act aggressively, but in order to develop enough strength and mobility to prevent any aggressor from attacking—and if they do attack, to insure that our nation will suffer as little damage as possible and a minimum loss of life.

The lessons of history, even in our own lifetime (witness Hitler's attack on Britain in World War II), tell us that a nation unprepared to defend itself will be attacked; if seriously unprepared (like Poland in 1939), it will be defeated, plundered and enslaved.

Twenty-four hundred years ago, the ancient Chinese military strategist Sun Tzu wrote, "When the enemy's envoys speak in humble terms but he continues his preparations, he will advance." This is happening before our very eyes as the Soviets continue their preparations for war while signing the INF Treaty—and there is much more happening behind the Iron Curtain that our government knows and isn't telling, as we will see later in this lecture.

We cannot ignore reality. If we want peace, we must objectively assess the world as it is (not the world as we would like it to be) and be prepared to deploy the necessary military forces in space and on the ground to defend our homeland.

Countering the Soviet threat should be the primary objective of our space program. But it's not. One reason is that Pentagon bureaucrats, like all other bureaucrats, have their pet projects.

The military doesn't have a greater role in space because the intense competition for defense budget dollars would require reallocation of money from existing weapons systems—such as fighter aircraft or tanks—into space systems. The various departments in the Pentagon don't want to see resources taken from any of the existing programs—whether or not they are more important than the race for space. In addition, each military service wants to keep the other services from getting the power and prestige that would come with manning a space defense program.

The power struggles between the military services are like the power struggles that come about through sibling rivalry for the affection and approval of the Mother. They also remind me of the power struggles between the fallen ones who long ago extinguished the divine spark within and so they are fierce competitors and vie for territorial supremacy one over the other. Name and fame, money and power are their game. Treating the common people as chattel, they use them as an expendable means to their ends.

We, therefore, must look to this new year with a profound commitment to establish through our hearts the figure-eight flow here of the Buddha and the Mother. What do we find that has been given to us? The Western Shamballa of Gautama over the Heart of the Inner Retreat and the Retreat of the Divine Mother over the entire Royal Teton Ranch.[10] But are we actually drawing down the Light and becoming that Buddha and that Mother in action?

My perception is that our performance is wanting, and the leadership that has been called for by the Brotherhood is not rising up as it could—even in the day-to-day details of running an organization. Too often people passively wait for someone else to tell them what to do instead of exercising the Christed intelligence of the heart. Such passivity derives from the absence of alignment with the Divine Mother, who is intensely active in the defense of her little ones and out of her fiery love arrives at ingenious solutions to their plight.

Leadership comes by the descent of the Christ within you. That Christ within you is the Buddhic mind. We, therefore, focusing the flame of the Divine Mother and the Buddha, raising up the true Shepherd within us, the Holy Christ Self, can demand of cosmos that co-measurement, that co-equality in our leadership.

That is why El Morya told us that he is running for the office of president of the United States of America. He is running through his chelas, who must raise up the standard of leadership and show that "profile of courage," as he said in his dictation.

He wants us to understand that as far as our leaders are concerned, we get what we deserve. And if we know we deserve better, then we will have to be better and we will have to show it in the day-by-day application of our joint heirship with Christ.[11] Then we have to call for the judgment of the interlopers who have stolen the seats of power, calling to the LORD as Mary did to "put down the mighty from their seats"[12] and exalt the Christ and the humble whose inner God Flame is their divine right to rule.

And on the home front we have to enter into such an uncompromising dedication and service to Saint Germain to prepare this headquarters, this Community for Keepers of the Flame, for our staff and for all who are to be a part of it whom El Morya will send us. And this will only happen because people from the field come and help us and are willing to do what is necessary for this headquarters to be established.

Remember the Macedonian cry, "Come over into Macedonia and help us!" and Paul's immediate response when he went to preach the true teachings of Jesus to the Macedonians.[13] As I have and shall continue to answer the call of Keepers of the Flame to stump your cities, so I also give the Macedonian cry to you to come over to the ranch and help build our "Camelot Montana" on the Spring Creek site. Now is the time to start making plans since our EIS is out and the state is close to giving us the green light to move forward with our construction projects.

Thus far Keepers of the Flame from the field have not come forth in sufficient numbers to enable us to do the job that Saint Germain has asked us to do; and many times those who are qualified are the last to volunteer and those least qualified are up front. When jobs require a certain sophistication of training and preparedness, it delays and complicates matters to work with untrained labor.

My awareness of the Soviet threat in space—and of the failure of our government to show us that they have the strength, the will, the wisdom, the vision, and the energy to keep the flame of Life and Liberty in America—is ongoing. I perceive that the American leadership is not committed to a true Master/disciple relationship to Jesus Christ or to Maitreya, nor to Lord Gautama or to their own Holy Christ Self or Saint Germain. When this divine allegiance is wanting at the national level and a people have committed the actions that we have committed and made the karma we have made, then the nation is truly vulnerable to the enemy within and without and to the karma of the age.

The American people are vulnerable today because we have abdicated our responsibility to defend life. We do not defend life in the womb, nor have we as a nation effectively protected our children against those who would destroy their minds and bodies through drugs, violence, child abuse and child pornography.

Since the January 22, 1973 Supreme Court decision legalizing abortion, the opportunity for 20 million souls to fulfill their destiny in the New Age has been aborted in the United States—1.5 million every year, one every 21 seconds. This is the genius and creative potential of Aquarians who are simply not here! Passport to planet earth denied! By a people desensitized to the signs of the times—and the mandate of cosmic law to care for and defend Life that is God in manifestation.

We are also vulnerable because we have neglected our responsibility to defend life and freedom abroad by failing to give substantial support to freedom fighters who are resisting totalitarian encroachments upon their lives and nations by the Soviet Union and the agents of World Communism.

The Challenger disaster brought our karmic vulnerability into sharp focus, but the problem has been developing for years because our people have been inattentive to the call of Saint Germain, the Spirit of Freedom which gave our nation birth. When a people do not individually or collectively deal with their karma, it builds up. The density of karma is ongoing, the weight of our sins is cumulative and it is intensifying. This is reflected in the crises we face today in every area of life—from education to the economy to the space program.

There is no question that the Soviet space program is designed to achieve the military control of space. They say it is for peace, for scientific advancement, for the union of East and West—America and the Soviets in the exploration of space, et cetera, et cetera. This propaganda is just part of the Big Lie. They are racing to achieve that military superiority, to get their weapons into space so that when all is set and in readiness, they can do what they will—launch a first strike or blackmail the West or both.

And one can dominate the world from space. It's no longer a question of half-slave and half-free. It's simply all slave, and when the day comes that the Soviets fully dominate space militarily, it will be very difficult to unseat them. It would take infiltration and sabotage right up to their space stations. We couldn't attack them from the ground because anything that attacks from the ground would be shot down before it even got going.

If the Soviets dominated space, they could greatly increase their surveillance capacity. It is terrible to think about planetary surveillance from space. Just think of it—being monitored in everything you do 24 hours a day from space. It becomes the fulfillment of Orwell's *1984* and far beyond, even beyond our imagination.

Almost all Soviet launches are for military purposes. Their space stations and launch capacity are essential to their military warfare capabilities. The Department of Defense publishes an assessment of Soviet military capabilities called *Soviet Military Power*. It says that "at least 90 percent of [Soviet] launches and satellites are military related and support both offensive and defensive operations. The USSR tries to mask the true nature of most of its space missions by declaring them as scientific." [14]

Thomas Krebs, former Pentagon expert on Soviet space warfare capabilities, whom we interviewed at our Fourth of July conference in the Heart of the Inner Retreat last summer, estimates that only 30 percent of U.S. space launches are for military purposes.

The major media seldom, if ever, explain what the Soviets are doing in space. According to Krebs, their immediate goal is to put up a space-based missile defense system like the one proposed for the United States by High Frontier, an organization headed by retired Lt. Gen. Daniel O. Graham. The system High Frontier proposes has three layers. The first two are ground-based, the third is space-based. The third layer consists of a network of satellites armed with conventional rockets to kill warheads at several phases of their flight, especially during the boost and post-boost phases as they travel through space

In order to deploy such a system, you need a number of components. First, you need a heavy-lift vehicle like the Energia to launch satellites cheaply. You need a large, manned space station like the Mir to service the satellite network. You also need a spaceplane to fly out from the space station to service individual satellites. (The Soviets have already tested a subscale version of a spaceplane of this type and are expected to deploy it by 1990.) And last, you need a military doctrine and a strategy for deployment, which, as I pointed out earlier, the Soviets have had for years.

If the Soviets put up their space-based missile defense system before we do, they will be able to keep us from getting into space. It's as simple as that. They will be able to shoot down anything we put up and we will not be able to do anything about it. The Soviets will have the ultimate checkmate. And they know it. And they're working furiously to make it happen before the West rouses itself from its soft slumber in the euphoria of peace talks, INF talks, disarmament talks, START talks!

Krebs points out that the Soviets are not more technically advanced than the United States. He says the Soviets' superior position comes from "an awful lot of persistence" and "what their vision is for space."

"Way back in the mid-sixties the Soviets set a space doctrine [which] was to gain preeminence in space in order to achieve victory in war," says Krebs. "We, however, have not had an objective in space. We do scientific experiments. We build transportation systems. We went to the moon. . . . But we do not have a military objective in space. . . .

"We haven't decided that space is a military environment— even though we spend billions of dollars on space and even though our forces—ground, sea and air forces—are heavily dependent upon [our space capabilities]. We have not set it as our goal or our mission to defend space and to make sure that we will prevail if there's a war. The Soviets did set that goal."[15]

In essence, the U.S./Soviet space race is the classic case of the tortoise chasing the hare—and then surpassing him. And now the tortoise is about to take a quantum leap that will make it *very* difficult for the hare to catch up.

Does the hare wish to catch up? On February 11, 1988, President Reagan announced a National Space Policy that for the first time committed the United States government to a long-term program of manned exploration of the solar system. Part of the new policy is the development of "Pathfinder" technologies that will make it possible for U.S. astronauts to return to the moon at the turn of the century, establish a permanent base there, and then fly to Mars. The new policy is also designed to spur commercial space exploration.

Does this mean the U.S. space program will now be organized and directed by a sharply defined goal? Not really.

First, President Reagan has announced the policy too late in his second term for it to be institutionalized. And there is no guarantee that the next president will embrace the goals of the new policy. Second, from a military point of view, the program is a case of doing too little too late. It takes a long time to bring space programs from conception to reality. The advances envisioned by the new National Space Policy will take about a decade

to come to fruition. And these are primarily civilian programs—
not military programs.

In the meantime, the Soviets are poised to gain military
dominance. The authoritative *Jane's Spaceflight Directory* says the
current Soviet lead is "almost frightening."[16]

As I have said, one of the factors that could give the Soviets
the edge in time of crisis is their surge capacity. They have
stockpiled large numbers of satellites as well as the vehicles they
need to launch them.

They also have a proven anti-satellite weapons capability—
i.e., they can destroy our satellites in orbit. Gen. John L.
Piotrowski, commander in chief of the U.S. Space Command, told
the Air Force Association's national space symposium on May 22,
1987, "In a crisis the Soviets could significantly increase their
launch rate while...simultaneously reducing our own on-orbit
forces" with "their operational anti-satellite [ASAT] weapon."[17]
That makes the Soviets the only power that can deny others access
to space, he said.

Furthermore, Piotrowski announced on October 23, 1987,
that Soviet ground-based lasers can now destroy U.S. satellites in
low Earth orbit and even damage sensors on satellites in geosta-
tionary orbits 22,300 miles from the Earth.[18] In fact, the Soviets'
ground-based lasers have already been reported to have blinded
U.S. satellites in orbit.

Moreover, satellite radar images from the French space agency
"confirm that a massive Soviet strategic defense program is under
way to develop lasers for both antiballistic missile defense and
antisatellite operations," *Aviation Week and Space Technology* reported in October 1987.

The Soviets have two complexes where the lasers are being
developed—Nurek and Sary Shagan. These sites "form two elements of an array of Soviet antisatellite capabilities that includes
directed energy weapons sites at Semipalatinsk and the anti-
satellite spacecraft launch sites at Tyuratam. These facilities
are positioned longitudinally across the USSR so that virtually
all U.S. low-altitude military spacecraft are within the attack
range of at least one of the sites daily.

"U.S. officials believe the Nurek site, about 25 miles southeast
of the city of Dushanabe, near the Soviet border with Afghanistan,
is being developed as one of the USSR's first operational anti-
satellite laser systems that could counter future U.S. Strategic
Defense Initiative spacecraft and other key U.S. military satellites. Intelligence data indicate that microwave weapons [which

can disable a satellite's or missile's electronics] could also be based at Nurek."[19]

In addition, former intelligence official Steven Trevino says that the Soviets will also soon be able to deny the U.S. access to space with "some radically new technologies that will be coming out in the press in the next few years."[20]

One of the key reasons the Soviets are ahead in space is sabotage. And our people, our government and our media are absolutely unwilling to see or to do anything about it when it parades before their wondering eyes. It's like the monkeys, "See no evil, hear no evil, speak no evil," and that's the prevailing metaphysics of this country: pretend it isn't there, see nothing of war, hear nothing of war, speak nothing of war. Don't look at what the enemy is doing, don't listen to what he's really saying, just think peace, think it hard, see peace, see it with all your mental might, and enter into dialogues of peace—citizen-to-citizen via satellite—and believe with metaphysical faith that peace will come because you have willed it so.

And when you talk about negotiating with the enemy who has vowed to bury you[21] be sure you use that Soviet euphemism for defeating you without a rocket ever being fired—"the peace process." Let this cliché be repeated enough times and all that the Soviets want will be in their pocket and your pocket will be hanging out empty!

Look at the record and tell me what the odds are. Between August 28, 1985, and March 26, 1987, the U.S. lost eight launches, including the space shuttle Challenger.

The list of failures:

• August 28, 1985: an Air Force Titan 34D exploded a few seconds after lift-off from Vandenberg Air Force Base in California.

• January 28, 1986: the space shuttle Challenger blew up 73 seconds after launch from Cape Canaveral in Florida.

• April 18, 1986: Titan 34D exploded five seconds after launch. (Notice they're all exploding just after lift-off.)

• April 25, 1986: a Nike-Orion "sounding rocket" misfired at the White Sands, New Mexico, missile range.

• May 3, 1986: a Delta rocket suffered an electrical failure 71 seconds into launch, causing the rocket to tumble, and was destroyed by ground controllers at Cape Canaveral.

• August 23, 1986: an Aries rocket mysteriously veered off course and was destroyed 50 seconds after launch by ground controllers at White Sands, New Mexico.

• August 28, 1986: a Minuteman III missile launched from an underground silo at Vandenberg was destroyed shortly after launch by ground controllers when it malfunctioned for unknown reasons.

• March 26, 1987: an Atlas-Centaur rocket went out of control 51 seconds after lift-off when it was hit by lightning and was then blown up by range safety officers. It was carrying an $83 million military communications satellite which would have linked the president with the U.S. armed forces abroad.

Let us look at the following videoclips taken from several news sources so you can take notes on these space disasters. They begin with an excerpt from High Frontier's promotional video, "A Defense That Defends."

Narrator: The space shuttle offers us an opportunity to step off the nuclear treadmill and out into the new high frontier of space. Commander John Young.

Comdr. John Young: The space shuttle will be able to do in five to 10 years what it would have taken us 20 to 30 years to do otherwise. We couldn't do it if we didn't have the space shuttle and that payload capability. It will immeasurably improve the defensive capability of the country.

Narrator: If we utilize the extraordinary capabilities of the space shuttle to deploy the system known as High Frontier, America for the first time will be able to defend herself against a Soviet missile attack.

Following is ABC's "Nightline" from January 28, 1986:

Narrator: Lift-off of the 25th space shuttle mission and it has cleared the tower.

Technician #1: Engines beginning throttling down now. Engines at 65 percent, three engines running normally, three good fuel cells, three good APUs. Engines throttling up, three engines now at 104 percent.

Technician #2: Challenger, go with throttle up.

Challenger Astronaut: Roger. Go to throttle up. [Space shuttle Challenger explodes; spectators scream.]

This is CBS News from April 18, 1986:

Dan Rather: The prime unmanned backup now used for putting big U.S. military payloads into space since the Challenger disaster today exploded on takeoff. It was the second straight failure in eight months of a launch of an unmanned Titan 34D rocket from Vandenberg Air Force Base in California; and CBS News was told tonight that, in effect, the United States now has no system for putting big, sophisticated military reconnaissance satellites into orbit.

Here's NBC News of May 3, 1986:

Connie Chung: Good evening. At Cape Canaveral tonight an unmanned Delta rocket exploded just a minute after lift-off. It was the second explosion of a U.S. spacecraft since the Challenger disaster last January. Last month an Air Force Titan rocket exploded. Jay Barbree is at Cape Canaveral and watched as the Delta rocket broke up in flames.

Jay Barbree: NASA's most reliable rocket, an unmanned Delta, blew up shortly after what appeared to be a successful lift-off. The slender rocket climbed into the sky with a $57 million weather satellite in its nose. It flew as it should for one minute and its first set of solid rocket boosters fell away as scheduled. Then it happened. The rocket appeared to swing out of control and debris streamed from the nose of the Delta. The rocket flipped over, breaking up into a fireball.

Now we'll see ABC News from March 26, 1987:

Narrator: The launch had been delayed 14 minutes because of stormy skies accompanied by lightning, but NASA weather experts gave a green light.

Engineer #1: Main engine sequence start ignition—

Narrator: The 137-foot rocket roared off the pad with a backdrop of gray clouds. On board the Atlas-Centaur was an $83 million navy communications satellite called the FLTSATCOM. Lightning is reported to have struck the launch pad 35 seconds after lift-off. The rocket disappeared into the dark clouds and at 51 seconds all communications went dead. The range safety officer then destroyed the vehicle.

This is ABC's "Nightline" from June 9, 1986:

Ted Koppel: The one impetus that we have not been talking about, the one force that hasn't come into this conversation yet is our competition with the Soviet Union. Where do we stand in that competition and what effect is that going to have on the future?

Sen. John Glenn, Former Astronaut: Ted, I think we're dangerously close to being in a perilous situation there because last year, for instance, in 1985, I believe, the Soviets had 97 total launches, that's of all kinds. At the same time we had 22.

Our final clip is CNN News taken from April 4, 1987:

Commentator: Pentagon sources say the Soviets are ready to begin manned testing of two reusable spaceplanes. That closes the only major gap remaining between the Soviet space program and NASA's. CNN's John Holliman has more.

John Holliman: Defense Department sources say the Soviet spaceplane, which has successfully been launched and recovered from orbit four times, will be ready for full-scale manned testing by the end of the decade. These same officials say it will be used to defend the Soviet space station or to attack satellites. Some nonmilitary analysts aren't so sure.

Marsha Smith, Soviet Space Analyst, Congressional Research Service: I think that they do have several more steps to go through before they'll have a functional spaceplane, and whether they plan to use that as a ferry craft for taking crews back and forth to space stations or if they plan to outfit it for military reconnaissance roles, I think it's really up in the air.

John Holliman: In addition to the two-person spaceplane, the Soviets are developing a large shuttle similar to the U.S. version. The Pentagon expects a manned flight by next year, but Smith says it probably won't be operational till 1990. Even though there's disagreement about specifics, there is a general sense among U.S. observers this country is losing the space race to the Soviets.

Narrator: The Soviets have launched seven space stations since 1971. They've kept Salyut 6 continually manned by alternating crews of cosmonauts that remain aloft in excess of 200 days at a time. An entire city, Star Town, exists solely for the training of their strategic rocket forces personnel. The Soviets launch five times as many rockets and place 10 times as much equipment into space as we do. Their commitment is clear, constant and determined.

Marsha Smith: But right now they do have a tremendous lead over the U.S. in this one area of space activities, which is manned Earth orbital operations.

Charles Walker, Former Astronaut: In terms of permanent habitation, permanent capability on orbit, I guess we're at least eight years behind.

Pete Conrad, Former Astronaut: They're working on much larger boosters. They're working on a reusable vehicle and, as best we can tell, they have sort of indicated that they are in fact on their way to Mars.

John Holliman: Conrad said it's up to the president to get America's act together in space, but it's not going to be easy. The U.S. space program is beset with problems, from the Challenger disaster a year ago to last month's Atlas rocket failure. Some space agency supporters in Congress say lack of action by the administration has weakened support for NASA almost to the breaking point.

When I interviewed General Graham at Summit University Forum, he told us that "the odds of a chance succession of [launch] failures [like the one the U.S. experienced], are one in 250 million. You either have to suspect sabotage or you have to believe that one chance in 250 million came about."[22] As former director of the Defense Intelligence Agency and former deputy director of the Central Intelligence Agency, General Graham is highly qualified to make this estimate.

During the same interview, Dr. Dmitry Mikheyev, a Soviet physicist who was expelled from his country, told why he believes the KGB could have destroyed the rockets with a microwave gun. "A microwave creates a beam which penetrates through the skin of a rocket" and scrambles the electronic equipment inside, he said. All the rockets failed within 74 seconds of launch. Mikheyev says that this is during the boost phase when the rockets move slowly and are therefore easy targets.

The Soviets could have easily fired microwave guns at the rockets, he said. After they shoot the rocket, "there is no hole in it. It malfunctions and falls by itself because [its] mechanisms don't function." It is impossible to tell that the circuits were destroyed by microwave because the evidence burns up in the explosion.[23] The microwave guns may have been on Soviet ships or they may have been fired from elsewhere.

Professor Antony Sutton has cited the same figures as Graham. When I interviewed him last summer he said, "Statistically that succession of failures would come about—knowing what we do about the reliability of these rockets—at one in 250 million. Now, if you want to believe that one in 250 million chances is acceptable, then go ahead. I believe fully, and I wrote it within a week of the Challenger going down, that this was clearly sabotage."

An interesting side note is that two Soviet-bloc citizens and a Soviet scientist were working at NASA in 1985, which is the year the string of failures started. The scientist was working in the Aeronautics division on projects involving engine sensor systems and instrumentation control. The Pentagon said their presence there was intended as a gesture of goodwill toward the Soviets.[24] Could they have had anything to do with the sabotage?

Sutton continues: "The second point is that the Soviets always monitor launches from Cape Canaveral from so-called 'fishing' vessels, which are actually electronic espionage vessels. They have these vessels offshore which regularly monitor [launch] communications. About two hours before Challenger left the launchpad, the Soviet vessels took off at flank speed. They left the launch area—that's the first time they've ever done this.

"So that's subsidiary evidence that the Soviets knew that the Challenger launch was going to be a failure. And thirdly, I understand from sources that the KGB had a big party in Moscow the night the Challenger went down."[25]

You realize that the leadership of this nation suffers from fear and spinelessness. Fear enters the psyche on the six o'clock line as it trines with the two o'clock line, the line of Pisces initiations in God-mastery, which may be thwarted by fear, doubt, human questioning, and records of death. Fear enters the psyche on the six o'clock line as it and the two o'clock line also trine with the ten o'clock line, the line of Scorpio initiations in God-vision, which may be thwarted by human selfishness and self-love, including all sensual indulgences and perversions.

The United States is wallowing in the 2/6/10 astrological initiations of Pisces, Cancer, Scorpio. The people perish for want of vision because all of their energy is tied up in their pleasure cult. They cannot see because they will not see. By free will they squander their light and their life-force. Thus their inner sight, or "insight," is nonfunctioning in the third eye, for the energy of the Divine Mother is not raised upon the spinal altar to nourish the upper chakras.

So our leadership is afraid that if they expose the sabotage of our space program to the American people, who would raise a hue and cry, it would ruin their negotiations with the Soviets and they might have to take stern measures against them.

They might have to finally admit that we are in a state of

undeclared war, sever diplomatic relations with the Soviets, send their diplomats packing, put an end to Soviet spying and technology theft, and demand that their subs and "fishing" vessels operating off our coasts go home.

They might even have to declare the Soviets in violation of the United Nations Charter (which commits its members to the cause of peace) and kick the UN and all of its East bloc spies out of the country.

And our leaders might have to withdraw from the ABM Treaty and face up to the equation of realpolitik: that the Soviet Union *is* at war with the United States (whether or not we are fighting back) and that we *are* in a state of national emergency. And our president ought to declare it!

The fact of the matter is that the Soviets have been quietly breaking out of the ABM Treaty for years by deploying a dual-capable air-defense system that can shoot down ballistic missiles as well as defend against aircraft. One of the most blatant violations of the treaty is the construction of a large phased-array radar in Siberia at Krasnoyarsk, which completed the circle of battle management radar coverage of the USSR.

Battle management radars take the longest of any component of a nationwide ABM system to produce—as much as 10 years. The other components—including small, mobile radars such as the Flat Twin and Pawn Shop radars—can be produced quickly once the factories are built and the assembly lines are going.

While the Soviets' dual-capable air-defense system and massive radar capacity are alarming, that's not the whole story. On February 25, 1988, *The Wall Street Journal* said in an editorial, "We hear that Air Force Intelligence has officially concluded the Soviets *have rolled production lines to break out of the ABM treaty and deploy a nationwide anti-missile system, which possibly could be in place by next year.* That Maj. Gen. Schuyler Bissell, head of Air Force Intelligence, briefed the CIA on this conclusion late last week." (emphasis added)

The *Journal* said this Air Force finding is based on two new pieces of evidence:

"First, the Soviets are 'internetting' their early-warning radars. . . . They have conducted 'hand-off exercises' in which the large phased-array radars like the controversial one at Krasnoyarsk pick up targets and alert the Flat Twin and Pawn Shop mobile radars that guide their [ABMs]. This is the key 'battle management' function of an anti-missile system.

"Second, the Soviets are mass producing the Flat Twin and

Pawn Shop radars, though the ABM treaty limits them to two locations. Similarly, they are mass producing the SH-08, a relatively new supersonic [anti-ballistic] missile that intercepts warheads within the atmosphere, with 500 such missiles already produced and 3,000 ultimately projected. The ABM treaty limits each side to only 100 interceptors of all types, and the Soviets also have the SH-04 [ABM], which intercepts above the atmosphere, as well as other interceptors with both anti-aircraft and anti-missile capability."[26]

A seasoned defense expert with access to highly classified information confirmed to us the accuracy of this report and said that further classified information on the subject that was not leaked is more serious still. But even with what we do know, it is now quite obvious that the Soviets are in the final stages of covertly deploying a nationwide ABM system. It is only a matter of time before they get enough mobile radars and anti-ballistic missiles off the assembly line to give them the defensive capability to launch a first strike against the United States without being annihilated in a counterstrike.

It may be difficult to understand how a defense system could be a threat. Defenses are not inherently threatening but they became so in the context of our nuclear strategy. Our strategy is guided by the doctrine of Mutual Assured Destruction (MAD), which says that war is deterred when both sides believe they will be destroyed if either attacks.

According to MAD, defenses which stop nuclear warheads are "destabilizing"—that is, likely to cause nuclear war—since the side that has them can attack without fear of being annihilated in retaliation. This argument has been used against the deployment of strategic defense in the United States for 20 years.

But the Soviets never agreed to abide by the principles of MAD. Rather than live in mutual terror with us, they decided to covertly build themselves a defense system—and talk us out of building our own. When the Soviet system is complete, it will mean they are more likely to launch a nuclear attack against us since they will be able to stop most of our retaliatory missiles. It will also mean they can force political concessions from us and the rest of the world by threatening to use their advantage.

The Soviet ABM system will not be able to stop 100 percent of our missiles. But it will doubtless protect most Soviet military and industrial targets and key civilian areas, which is what they really care about. In combination with their countrywide civil defense already in place, it will give them a decisive advantage.

It could make the difference in their decision to launch a nuclear first strike.

The president *must* issue a mandate to install an ABM defense for the United States. He must realize that MAD was a faulty theory to begin with and that it is no longer applicable to the realities of today. Our scientists and engineers know how to defend the United States, but President Reagan continues to adhere to the outdated, outgrown and outrageous ABM Treaty that has never stopped the Soviets from doing anything they wanted to do!

Nevertheless, it's a good bet Reagan will continue with business as usual. We've seen over the years, in this and past administrations, that no matter what would be the obvious step to take to stop the Soviet advance, if it interferes with the goals of the international bankers, the establishment and the International Capitalist/Communist Conspiracy, you can be certain that step won't be taken.

In fact, the Soviets owe the success of their space program not only to the ironclad commitment of their top leadership to dominate space but also to the transfer of Western technology and money. Yes, they owe it to the "capitalists" and the international bankers. They would never have had the power or the resources to make it on their own. Therefore I desire to deliver to you my lecture on the subject of the International Capitalist/Communist Conspiracy and America's abdication of her role as a Christed nation in history.[27]

The Soviets have been able to buy or steal high technology from the United States. Their space program, says Professor Sutton, "to a great extent started off with German technology" that they acquired when they captured German scientists at the end of World War II. They have gotten a number of important technologies from the United States since then, such as the docking mechanism for the Soyuz space vehicle, semiconductor technology that is critical to electronic guidance systems, and carbon-carbon technology which can be used to make missiles more accurate. Some of this was acquired legally, some of it illegally.

But, says Sutton, if we had not built their technological base—including steel, chemical, and truck factories—patiently over several decades, "they would have no space capacity at all."[28] And I must add, Saint Germain would have his 50 years and more to bring in a golden age of Aquarius.

Did any of the common people give the industrialists and bankers permission to sell our technologies? Did any of us say it was OK? No, not us; the power elite gave them the green light.

And these gods respect no bounds either of nation-states or of morality and they have no relationship of trust with the people of America or of any nation upon whose backs they have built their corporate empires! Yes, the embodied fallen angels of the United States and Western Europe played a major role in building the Soviet military-industrial complex that forms the backbone of the Soviet space program today!

Our government is willing to underwrite loans to the Soviet bloc but it is not willing to do the same for our national security. Congress just trimmed $1.8 billion off the administration's budget request for strategic defense. This seriously hampers a number of strategic defense programs. Furthermore, Secretary of Defense Frank Carlucci is asking the Pentagon to cut about $33 billion from the next defense budget. As a result, two aircraft carriers, additional MX missiles, and the new Midgetman missile might be cut.

As long as the U.S. government is controlled by the betrayers of the living Word in the people, they will continue to support the Soviet Union with our money, our grain, our technology and our light. How long are we going to stand for it?

Well, we're not going to stand for it today because we're going to leap to our feet and give our calls, and call and call and call to Almighty God and his Christ and the entire Spirit of the Great White Brotherhood for the defeat of that International Capitalist/Communist Conspiracy of the alien gods who have for too long enslaved humanity.

Therefore remember, when their house of cards comes tumbling down, you need to be in your right place—the "Place Prepared" *for you*. The only reason I can see for the judgment not having fallen already is that the Lightbearers are not prepared and God's hand of mercy is raised in your defense. Therefore, I am asking for your help to build the Inner Retreat and for your vision to carry out a twofold measure and path: to secure your place in "the wilderness"[29] where you desire to be and to make the calls in the name JESUS CHRIST to see to it that this judgment descends only according to God's will.

As I look into the face of God and the hierarchies of heaven, I know that God has said, "No longer will I allow it." The days are short and we must use them wisely. For the opportunity to turn around the race for space in favor of America and world peace and freedom is fast slipping through our fingers. It takes time to install the defense we need. And time, like the sands in the hourglass, is running out. And the end of the LORD's "striving with flesh" may soon come to pass.

Following is an eight-point agenda of what we must do in space and on the ground right now to give Saint Germain his 50 years of peace.

1) First and foremost, we must protect our military forces against the Soviet threat of a first strike against the United States. As I have established in my book and lectures on Saint Germain On Prophecy and the Defense of Freedom and on Summit University Forums, the centerpiece of Soviet military strategy is to be able to launch a first strike against our military targets[30]—and this is the main reason they want to dominate space. Therefore, we must protect these targets immediately since it will take at least five years to catch up to the Soviets in space.

The best way to do that right now is with low-tech ground-based defenses—the first of a three-layered defense system. We can deploy this layer to defend our ICBMs, submarine and bomber bases, launching pads and command, control and communications facilities within 24 months.

These defense systems, such as swarmjets and high-speed GAU-8 Gatling-type machine guns, would use off-the-shelf technology. The swarmjet fires a cloud of one-inch rockets to destroy a warhead three-fifths of a mile from its target. It is 90 percent effective against the first three warheads coming into range. The GAU-8 Gatling-type machine gun has already been tested successfully against a simulated Soviet warhead.

2) We must deploy a second layer of ground-based defenses for larger areas, including our military bases and cities— and we can do it within three to five years.

These would be sophisticated ABM systems that would use nearly available technology like the Exoatmospheric Reentry Vehicle Interceptor Subsystem (ERIS) and the High Endoatmospheric Defense Interceptor (HEDI). ERIS could use the site at Grand Forks, North Dakota, where we built the Safeguard ABM system, which was dismantled in 1976, and would consist of 10,000 interceptor missiles. These non-nuclear interceptors would be fired into space to destroy a warhead outside the atmosphere. Since ERIS has such a long reach, it could defend much of North America from a single site.

We need 3,000 HEDI interceptors which can be deployed on trucks together with radar and power generators. These would be positioned around key targets. HEDI interceptors are non-nuclear missiles which fly at more than six times the speed of sound to destroy warheads after they enter the atmosphere. Your city could have its own HEDI system defending it. Since HEDI interceptors can be launched directly from their trucks and the Soviets couldn't target them, they would make the Soviets think twice about launching a first strike.

3) In order to neutralize the effect of a Soviet Star Wars system, we can and should deploy a non-nuclear, space-based kinetic kill vehicle (KKV) system consisting of 2,000 satellites. The system could be deployed in five to seven years and would be 50 to 70 percent effective against a full-scale attack of intercontinental ballistic missiles (ICBMs). It could stop an accidental launch fired either by us, the Soviets, any of the other members of the nuclear club, a Qaddafi-like madman or a terrorist.

It is irresponsible in the extreme not to be protected against an accident. The military forces of all nations frequently make mistakes. By the laws of probability, an accidental nuclear attack— a military Chernobyl—is likely to happen sooner or later. While the superpowers have developed elaborate safeguards to prevent an accidental or unauthorized use of nuclear weapons, nuclear weapons accidents actually happen frequently.

Between 1958 and 1966, for instance, the U.S. Air Force had 13 accidents involving nuclear weapons. And from 1965 through 1977, the Navy had 381—about two accidents per month. The details of many of these accidents are unknown today because most of the information is classified.

I would like to underscore that the KKV system is non-nuclear and has a primarily defensive capability. It cannot attack targets on the earth from space, as the Soviets often charge. Each satellite in the system carries anti-missile rockets and a gun which fires a cloud of pellets into the path of an ICBM or a warhead and destroys them by the force of the impact. The only place KKV satellites could attack is in space. They could not penetrate the atmosphere to harm anyone on the ground or attack a missile before it entered space. The KKV system could attack satellites but this capability can hardly be called destabilizing since the Soviets already have a system which can destroy satellites.

As I've already noted, we don't have the proper lift capacity to deploy these satellites quickly. But we can begin deploying them a few at a time with our best available lift vehicles—the space shuttle and the MX booster. Then we must begin immediate development of the ideal systems we need to deploy and maintain the space-based defense system: a fleet of heavy-lift launch vehicles, a large space station, and several spaceplanes and space cruisers to service the satellites and defend them against Soviet spaceplanes and anti-satellite (ASAT) weapons.

4) **By 1994, we can and must deploy the three-layered low-tech strategic defense system.** According to a study by the George C. Marshall Institute, the ground- and space-based layers working together would be 93 percent effective against a Soviet attack of 10,000 warheads and 100,000 decoys and could be deployed at a cost of $121 billion.

5) **In order for a strategic defense system to be legal under existing agreements with the Soviet Union, the United States must immediately:**

a. announce its intention to withdraw from the 1972 ABM Treaty within the prescribed six-month time limit due to repeated Soviet violations of its spirit and letter, and

b. repudiate the understanding between United States Secretary of State George Shultz and Soviet Foreign Minister Eduard Shevardnadze, announced on September 18, 1987, that the United States would abide by the ABM Treaty for an undisclosed period of time, probably seven years.

6) **In order to deter a Soviet attack we must install civil defense for every American.** The Soviets are more likely to attack us because they have civil defense for their population and we have none. An American civil defense system will decrease their confidence in their ability to successfully carry out a first-strike attack. The cost of civil defense for America is approximately $75 billion—about one quarter of our annual defense budget.

7) **We must not only establish a presence in space to stop Soviet weapons but we must also develop the means to defend our satellites against Soviet anti-satellite (ASAT) weapons.** We must develop our own ASAT weapons to deter the Soviets from using theirs. We already have the know-how, we just need to build them.

8) **Finally and most importantly, the president must declare a doctrine for the domination of space, develop a strategy to attain it, and authorize and fund a National Space Force, separate from the other branches of the military, whose sole purpose is to occupy and defend space.**

We must act now to fulfill this agenda and take advantage of the window of opportunity that yet exists. Time is running out to win the race for space.

Let us prepare for Archangel Michael's dictation. I am asking you to sing "Glory and Praise" to the music of "The Soldiers' Chorus" from *Faust,* the keynote of his retreat, and to stand and welcome him.

["Glory and Praise," song 45 from *The Summit Lighthouse Book of Songs,* sung]

Based on a lecture by Elizabeth Clare Prophet **delivered** on **January 3, 1988**, at the **Royal Teton Ranch, Montana,** updated for print as this week's Pearl. (**1**) Personal interview with John Collins, Library of Congress, 1985. (**2**) **Saint Germain's call for 50 years of peace.** See Saint Germain, Feb. 7, 1987, "The Pillar of Violet Flame," and the Goddess of Liberty, Feb. 8, 1987, "The Tent of the LORD," 1987 *Pearls of Wisdom,* vol. 30, nos. 6, 8, pp. 95, 108. (**3**) **Thomas Becket** (1118–1170), English saint and martyr, past incarnation of the Ascended Master El Morya, founder of The Summit Lighthouse. In 1155 he was appointed chancellor of England by King Henry II and became an intimate friend, adviser, and supporter of the king. When Henry nominated Becket to the post of archbishop of Canterbury in 1161, Becket resigned the chancellorship and worked uncompromisingly to protect the Church against Henry's attempts to dominate it, opposing the king on many issues. On Dec. 29, 1170, Becket was brutally murdered inside Canterbury cathedral by four knights who acted on the king's words that he wished to be rid of "this turbulent priest." Becket's tomb at Canterbury quickly became a great shrine and the site of many reported miracles. He was canonized in 1173. (**4**) T. A. Heppenheimer, "The Space Station Nobody Wants," *Reason,* Feb. 1988, p. 22. (**5**) The Ascended Masters teach that Martian misqualified energy manifests through the Martian dweller on the threshold as aggression, anger, arrogance, argumentation, accusation, agitation, apathy and atheism, annihilation, aggravation, aggressive mental suggestion, anti-Americanism, and forces of anti-Father, anti-Mother, anti-Son, and anti-Holy Spirit. (**6**) Telephone interview with Dr. Robin Ranger, Feb. 18, 1988. (**7**) **Cosmic Clock.** See Elizabeth Clare Prophet, "The Cosmic Clock: Psychology for the Aquarian Man and Woman," in *The Great White Brotherhood in the Culture, History and Religion of America,* pp. 173–206; and *The ABC's of Your Psychology on the Cosmic Clock,* 8-audiocassette album, 12 hrs., A85056, 12 lectures. (**8**) David Hobbs, *An Illustrated Guide to Space Warfare* (New York: Prentice Hall Press, 1986), p. 27. (**9**) See El Morya, Dec. 31, 1987, "My Candidacy for President of the United States of America," 1988 *Pearls of Wisdom,* vol. 31, no. 1, pp. 1–2. (**10**) **The Western Shamballa.** See 1988 *Pearls of Wisdom,* vol. 31, no. 2, p. 20, n. 2. **The Retreat of the Divine Mother.** On Dec. 15, 1985, Sanat Kumara announced "the opening of the door of the temple of the Divine Mother and her Inner Retreat" positioned above the entire area of the Royal Teton Ranch. 1986 *Pearls of Wisdom,* vol. 29, no. 10, pp. 70–72. (**11**) Rom. 8:14–17. (**12**) Luke 1:52. (**13**) Acts 16:9, 10. (**14**) Department of Defense, *Soviet Military Power 1987* (Washington, D.C.: Government Printing Office, 1987), p. 53. (**15**) "Thomas H. Krebs on 'Tsar Wars,' " Summit University Forum, June 30, 1987. Videocassettes: 2½ hrs., 2 videos, GP87005, $39.95 (add $1.20 for postage). Two 1-hr. cable TV shows for home use: "A Special Briefing on Soviet Space Warfare Capabilities," HL87009, and "The Race for Space," HL87013, $19.95 each (add $.90 each for postage). Two audiocassettes, 2½ hrs., A87052, $13.00 (add $.80 for postage). (**16**) Gregg Easterbrook, "Big Dumb Rockets," *Newsweek,* 17 Aug. 1987, p. 46. (**17**) Edgar Ulsamer, "At Risk in Space," *Air Force Magazine,* Sept. 1987, p. 132. (**18**) "Soviet Lasers Could Hit Satellites," *Indianapolis News,* 24 Oct. 1987. (**19**) Craig Covault, "Soviet Strategic Laser Sites Imaged by French Spot Satellite," *Aviation Week and Space Technology,* 26 Oct. 1987, p. 26. (**20**) Telephone interview with Steven Trevino, Feb. 18, 1988. (**21**) On Nov. 17, 1956, in an address to ambassadors at the Kremlin, Nikita Khrushchev, First Secretary of the Communist Party of the Soviet Union, said, "Whether you like it or not, history is on our side. We will bury you." Gen. Maj. Jan Sejna, the highest-ranking Communist military figure ever to defect, said on Nov. 28, 1987, at Summit University Forum, "If you take Lenin, Stalin, Khrushchev and Brezhnev, and today Gorbachev, it is the same. Khrushchev said, 'We will bury you,' and Gorbachev said, 'Our system will replace your system.' So what is different?" See note 30 below. (**22**) "Gen. Daniel O. Graham and Dr. Dmitry Mikheyev on Strategic Defense: To Deploy or Not to Deploy," Summit University Forum, July 4, 1987. Videocassettes: 3 hrs., 2 videos, GP87014, $39.95 (add $1.20 for postage). Three 1-hr. cable TV shows for home use: "A Three-Layered Defense—Will It Work?" HL87004; "America's Future in Space," HL87005; "A Scientific or a Political Question?" HL87006, $19.95 each (add $.90 each for postage). Two ½-hr. cable TV shows: "A Three-Layered Defense—Will It Work?" parts I and II, HL87007, HL87008, $10.95 each (add $.90 each for postage). Two audiocassettes, 3 hrs., A87056, $13.00 (add $.80 for postage). (**23**) Ibid. (**24**) *Washington Inquirer,* 26 July 1985. (**25**) "Professor Antony C. Sutton on the Capitalist/Communist Conspiracy," Summit University Forum, July 1, 1987. Videocassettes: 2 hrs., V87009, $29.95 (add $.90 for postage). One-hr. cable TV show for home use: "We Have Built Ourselves an Enemy," HL88004, $19.95 (add $.90 for postage). Two audiocassettes, 2½ hrs., A87054, $13.00 (add $.80 for postage). (**26**) "Breakout," *Wall Street Journal,* 25 Feb. 1988, p. 20. (**27**) The Messenger delivered her lecture "The Abdication of America's Destiny" on Jan. 4, 1988. (**28**) Telephone interview with Prof. Antony C. Sutton, Feb. 18, 1988. (**29**) Rev. 12:6, 14. (**30**) See *Saint Germain On Prophecy,* Summit University Press, $5.95 (add $.50 for postage); "Gen. Jan Sejna and Dr. Joseph Douglass, Jr.: Inside Soviet Military Strategy," Summit University Forum, Nov. 28, 1987. Videocassette: 4 hrs. 42 min., 3 videos, GP88001, $59.95 (add $1.60 for postage). Three audiocassettes, 4 hrs. 41 min., B88016-18, $19.50 (add $.80 for postage).

Pearls of Wisdom®
published by The Summit Lighthouse

Vol. 31 No. 8   *Beloved Archangel Michael*   *February 21, 1988*

New Year's Retreat
at the Royal Teton Ranch
VIII
A Cosmic Urgency
May Your Love and Light Rise to the Occasion

Hail, Legions of the Central Sun! Hail, Lightbearers of the Earth!
I AM in your midst in this hour by the grace of God before whom I kneel and of whom I AM the incarnation of that Word. I AM the I AM THAT I AM and my Presence does fill all the house with my faith and love and goodwill. Therefore, beloved, be seated as I speak to you in this hour.

As there is a national urgency, so there is a cosmic urgency. May your love and light rise to the occasion. I say it again, may your love and light rise to the occasion!

Beloved hearts, you know the words but the actions are wanting. You do not even perceive that you are overcome by lunar energies. You do not even perceive that your absence of a manifest leadership is a point of indecisiveness, betwixt and between, not knowing which way or the other to move or step or speak or do. And thus the fright, as though you were affected like scared rabbits, does render you at times, and I say at times, almost as useless to Hierarchy as the president of the United States has become.

Blessed hearts, this individual ought not to be the example that you follow. But sometimes we see that that is precisely what takes place. As the leader of the nation is indecisive, filled with compromise and lukewarm, so even our chelas go the same way. Though the Messenger has gone stumping to plead with Keepers of the Flame to attend the Saturday night services, yet the reports come in that the attendance yet dwindles.

Blessed hearts, I must repeat to you the warning that has been given: the year opens with ten times the darkness of the latter. And how do we find you? We find you overcome by that darkness instead of piercing the veil, and not in the realization that when the birds of the dawn appear and the sun does crest the land that is the hour to be in invocation before your God.

It does not matter what is the hardship, I can assure you. If Keepers of the Flame do not declare a state of personal emergency in their own lives, the hardship that comes later will be far beyond the price we ask you to pay in this hour.

Therefore, beloved, focus on space. Focus on the dominance in space and continue to give those calls that are needed, profoundly needed, to unravel the snarl of darkness and confusion and entanglements that prevent that shuttle from rising—those rockets to go up, those space stations to be launched. I tell you, if the spines were straight and the light were raised up and people did not mock the Lord God, you would see that the very fire of a people would raise that dominance in space to a perfection that would be admired even by the hierarchies of Light.

What is so sad, beloved, is that it is Saint Germain who has carefully given this technology to this nation only to see it piece by piece, point by point transferred to the enemy.

How, then, do you feel? How, then, do you feel when you are an Ascended Master who has to be told by the Lords of Karma, "No more scientific dispensations until the protection is raised up." Well, at least you know you have already given to a nation the means for its defense and protection and for deterrence. At least you know if the will be there, the technology is already secured.

But, beloved hearts, it is a burden to a heart that you must also share and understand, truly the heart of Saint Germain. And how can there be any greater burden, then, to the Mother's heart, our beloved Mother Mary, than to realize that those who do know of Saint Germain and of every word that he does speak and who do believe all of the teachings cannot yet bring themselves to the point of action and the point of realization of how urgent the hour is and are yet prepared to squander away moments and hours in diversions and absence of focus at the altar?

Blessed ones, change must come about first in the body of Keepers of the Flame worldwide if there is to be change in the nations. As 1988 is upon us, therefore, all that can be considered by you is to gain the new God-mastery to meet the higher levels of planetary darkness and not be defeated by them. For, you see, above all people you will be accountable for that defeat. For you have been carefully nourished and sustained with an abundant teaching now since 1958 as well as in prior Ascended Master dictations and dispensations.

Thus, beloved ones, if it is you who are defeated, you will bear the fullness of accountability because you have the knowledge for the Victory. Whereas those who are ignorant do have the karma of their ignorance, their neglect and their denial, they have not received the great sacred mystery and the transfer of Light of the Word heart to heart since they were babes.

Thus, beloved, with a sword in hand and a scepter, with an armour and a shield, with the power of the call that is astounding even to yourselves, you can have this Victory! But it is not won in silence. It is not won in refraining from the altar.

Blessed ones, the days will come to pass when no Ascended Master or Archangel will be allowed to remind you again, for these reminders have caused some to say the dictations are repetitious. Well, we speak into the very heart and teeth of the repetitious procrastination and disobedience and stubbornness that still remains in the children of Israel and our own blessed and dear chelas.

Dear hearts, the battle can be won instantaneously and in this hour but your position must be one of noncompromise!

Understand, beloved, that it is very difficult for a Messenger to receive and deliver a dictation after doing hours of decree work on the platform. And therefore, when the vessel is ready and you are not ready and we cannot dictate [and she must first lead you in decrees to establish the platform for our release], wherefore shall the Light* descend and into what vessel shall we pour it? If there be none vessels left, then where shall earth appear? One ought to give due concern and pause in consideration of such subjects and not to be perpetually drawn away in this or that new endeavor or involvement or ambition.

It is true, beloved, that the economy and the weight of karma, as written in the astrology, upon that economy ought to give all pause to shudder. And you should be profoundly concerned as to what measures you will take in your own households to deal with that which is prophesied by the configurations of planets in the month of February which does draw nigh.

We have not given these prophecies for your interest, fascination or amusement. We have given them to you for your action, and our representatives have spoken to you for at least five years concerning the coming burdens in the economy. Will you let your house, then, fall all around you by not realizing that the message is given to Lightbearers for the saving of Lightbearers?

*the God consciousness of the archangelic realm

Given, then, the state of consciousness of the world, only those who know the Light and keep the Flame can make the difference. Given, then, the astrology that is the state of consciousness of the world portrayed in the heavens, given the ancient prophecies laid before you of Nostradamus, can you not wonder that there is a certain and grave possibility of that very nuclear war and the "Great War" prophesied by Mother Mary, the blessed Archeia of the Fifth Ray?

Therefore, let it be understood, beloved, if these things appear as a certainty—given the waywardness of mankind's consciousness—and if you are yet told that there is an opening for the turning aside of it and if you reckon with the few numbers, the very few percentages of people on the planet who keep the Flame, will you not realize that each and every hour of your life you are making a decision to be or not to be the Intercessor?

I tell you, beloved, the day will surely come when the sands in the hourglass will run out and we will have to announce to you that there is no turning around of these predictions.

I believe that even some Keepers of the Flame have thought to themselves, "Things will simply turn out well in the end and we will one day hear the dictation that all these things have come to naught." Beloved ones, this is the same delusion from which the nation suffers!

It is important to be realists and it is important to go back now and to study what we have released in 1987 in your Pearls of Wisdom and in 1986. It is important, then, to make decisions that are not foolhardy. It is important not to place your funds in investments in those situations which will simply not pan out when the economy itself is not flowering and is not healthy.

Let all of you come to the realization of what we have said long ago at Camelot: those who watch the movements of the Messenger must understand that these are the signs to be seen and these are the footsteps to be followed. Not in specific explanations, not in revelations of prophecies we have already given to her that are not to be revealed, but in her actions you will note what is the way of the LORD.

Therefore, look at the profile of Moses and of Jesus Christ and Gautama Buddha, of Padma Sambhava. Look at the saints and note their profiles, for in [observing] their actions all who lived in their times might have been surely saved from the fate of their own karma.

In the Victory of the God Flame I commend you to the keeping of that faith upon earth. Truly, then, we desire to see, if not a civilization, then a world consciousness of God endure. Let there not be a losing, then, of all that this planet has been endowed with for thousands of years. Let it be preserved in your hearts. The only way it can be preserved is by action.

Beloved ones of the Light, your assembly on the mountain of God is tremendously needed in this hour and I ask you to prolong your stay to intensify your calls and to make up for the lost hours, to continue this vigil and not to leave this ranch until you have fulfilled a certain calling for a certain invocation of light and dynamic decrees that can turn back those things that are projected upon the year.

Blessed ones, we can reveal and crack wide open the sabotage of the fallen ones through the Soviets, through those inside America. We can crack wide open the UFO conspiracy and those aliens in the midst of the people. It is known in many quarters, beloved, but the people are not being told.

By your fervor to Cyclopea, by your keeping the Watch of Jesus, by your understanding of the urgent need for you to become components of the Diamond Heart for the very preservation of the office and person of the Messenger, by all of this, beloved, and by that entering in you will see how hearts can expand, how hearts can be purged and how a land can be renewed.

Let us come to the realization that if all will hear me throughout this field and [if] all Lightbearers yet coming into this activity [will hear me], that there can be such a marshaling of forces by the power of the spoken Word as either truly to turn around completely this condition or to buy time whereby it can be turned around.

Blessed ones, we are gratified beyond words that Summit University will again become a pillar in this Community, of light and fire, of the dynamic decree and of entering into the heart by illumination's flame, of students who are here truly to assimilate the living Word and to become Christed ones.

Weary not in well doing,[1] beloved, for the Holy Spirit in you is a mighty attainment. Bring that attainment, then, all the way home to the altar of God. If you are weary, pass by the altar for ten minutes and cry unto the LORD and make your fiats for those ten minutes. For those ten minutes count for us, and by your command and your leave we may work tirelessly and with blue lightning through the night.

Blessed ones, you do not need to turn back because you are not able to give a full session of Astreas. Come for twelve minutes, come for three, come for fifteen and stand in King Arthur's Court and know that your voice counts in heaven and on earth. Blessed ones, fewer have turned the tide in the past but the many are waiting to devour this nation. Let them be taken by our bands! We but need the call and the energy!

I, Archangel Michael, stand before you. I stand before you not to judge you but to implore you and to plead with you. We would desire to save the earth for your career, for your future as a son of God, for your leadership in this nation, for your children and their future! We desire you to be all that you are and we desire to see you in those positions of government and the economy where you can speak the truth and the truth itself shall defeat the lie.

Beloved hearts, our desire does not leave off. We are here and we are determined as the blue lightning angels. Blessed hearts, let us have your divine approbation. Let us have your call! Let us have your hearts! We need that witness on earth. For we must stand before the Cosmic Council and we stand before the Lord God. *Do not send us there empty-handed, Keepers of the Flame, I implore you!*

And I AM Michael Archangel, Captain of the Lord's Hosts[2] of the First Ray!

Legions of Light, now march! March throughout this continent and find and cut free those Keepers of the Flame!

So we go forth, beloved, and so we seal you once again in the Diamond Heart of Mary, Morya and that Diamond Heart of faith that is our own. In Victory we stand!

"The Summit Lighthouse Sheds Its Radiance O'er All the World to Manifest as Pearls of Wisdom." This dictation was **delivered** through the Messenger of the Great White Brotherhood Elizabeth Clare Prophet on **Sunday, January 3, 1988,** during the 5-day New Year's Retreat at the **Royal Teton Ranch.** (1) I Cor. 15:58; Gal. 6:9; II Thess. 3:13. (2) Josh. 5:13–15.
Note 7 from Pearl No. 6 by Lord Maitreya:
(7) **U.S. government support for Chinese Communists in Tibet.** The U.S. government has held that China gained sovereignty over Tibet in the 1950 Chinese invasion and takeover and in 1978 recognized Tibet as a part of China. Washington does not recognize the Dalai Lama's government-in-exile in India and has consistently refused the Dalai Lama official State visits. The Reagan administration has also refused to condemn China for its recent atrocities in Tibet. In late September 1987, reports filtered out of Tibet that hundreds of Buddhist monks had staged peaceful protests calling for Tibetan independence. These protests coincided with the Dalai Lama's visit to the U.S., during which he presented a 5-point peace plan to the Congressional Human Rights Caucus. The House passed a resolution supporting him, and leading members of the Congress sent a letter urging China's premier to use the 5-point program as a basis of negotiation with the Dalai Lama. The Communists responded on September 24 by gathering 15,000 Tibetans at a stadium in the capital, Lhasa, sentencing eight to prison and two to death, executing one immediately. On October 1, thousands of Tibetans demonstrated in Lhasa and Chinese police fired into the unarmed crowd. At least thirteen, including some police, were reported killed. Throughout the turmoil the Reagan administration and the U.S. State Department supported Communist China's policies, while the Senate voted to condemn China for their crackdown. On October 6, the State Department voiced strong opposition to the Senate move. The *New York Times* reported that "one State Department official said that any possible benefits of the Senate action for the Tibetan people were 'insufficient to outweigh the almost certain damage to the United States-China bilateral relationship.'"

Pearls of Wisdom®
published by The Summit Lighthouse

Vol. 31 No. 9   *Elizabeth Clare Prophet*   *February 28, 1988*

New Year's Retreat
at the Royal Teton Ranch

IX
The Abdication of America's Destiny
Part 1
*Inasmuch As Ye Have Done It unto One of the Least
of These My Brethren, Ye Have Done It unto Me*

When the Son of man shall come in his glory, and all
the holy angels with him, then shall he sit upon the throne
of his glory:

And before him shall be gathered all nations: and he
shall separate them one from another, as a shepherd divid-
eth his sheep from the goats:

And he shall set the sheep on his right hand, but the
goats on the left.

Then shall the King say unto them on his right hand,
Come, ye blessed of my Father, inherit the kingdom prepared for you from the foundation of the world:

For I was an hungred, and ye gave me meat: I was thirsty,
and ye gave me drink: I was a stranger, and ye took me in:

Naked, and ye clothed me: I was sick, and ye visited
me: I was in prison, and ye came unto me.

Then shall the righteous answer him, saying, Lord,
when saw we thee an hungred, and fed thee? or thirsty, and
gave thee drink?

When saw we thee a stranger, and took thee in? or
naked, and clothed thee?

Or when saw we thee sick, or in prison, and came
unto thee?

And the King shall answer and say unto them, Verily verily I say unto you, Inasmuch as ye have done it unto one of the least of these my brethren, ye have done it unto me.

Then shall he say also unto them on the left hand, Depart from me, ye cursed, into everlasting fire, prepared for the devil and his angels:

For I was an hungred, and ye gave me no meat: I was thirsty, and ye gave me no drink:

I was a stranger, and ye took me not in: naked, and ye clothed me not: sick, and in prison, and ye visited me not.

Then shall they also answer him, saying, Lord, when saw we thee an hungred, or athirst, or a stranger, or naked, or sick, or in prison, and did not minister unto thee?

Then shall he answer them, saying, Verily I say unto you, Inasmuch as ye did it not to one of the least of these, ye did it not to me.

And these shall go away into everlasting punishment: but the righteous into life eternal. [Matthew 25:31–46]

On November 29, 1987, Saint Germain said in Washington, D.C.:

Keepers of the Flame, by your leave I AM sent from the Great Central Sun to stand in the midst of this city as a pillar of violet flame, my aura, then, sealing a destiny— a destiny far spent.

For America has abdicated her role as the nation of Christhood, the eternal Law of God, as the nation wherein The LORD Our Righteousness should raise up a standard, an ensign of the people and a two-edged sword.

Thus, beloved, through your hearts and yours alone, the Lightbearers in all the earth—those who know me and may not know my name but have espoused the Cause of Freedom and of Peace—through them I shall continue to work.[1]

My message to you from the heart of Saint Germain is entitled "The Abdication of America's Destiny."

It is America's destiny to be the Comforter Nation, to fulfill the mandate given through the prophet Isaiah: "Comfort ye, comfort ye—comfort ye my people, saith your God."[2]

Our forefathers founded this nation on the principle of the Comforter. The comfort of the unalienable rights to "Life, Liberty, and the Pursuit of Happiness"[3] is the opportunity to walk the path of individual Christhood and to enjoy the fruits of one's sacred labor in the abundant life.

America is the place set apart from all nations where God's

people were called to raise up an ensign—a sign. That sign is the sign of the I AM Presence, individual Christhood and the banner of Maitreya. It foretells the coming of the standard-bearer. America, individual by individual and heart by heart, is sent by God to be the standard-bearer of the path of individual Christhood, bringing that path to the nations of the world, to all who would receive us, even as one of the least of these the brethren of the Lord.

America is the nation sponsored by the Ascended Masters of the Great White Brotherhood who have come because Saint Germain has raised up his standard of freedom on these shores. Here, then, in an experiment of freedom we gather. We gather together through the Master/disciple relationship under Jesus Christ and the apostles, Moses and the prophets, Gautama Buddha and the bodhisattvas—all of whom trace their lineage to the Ancient of Days, our Lord Sanat Kumara.

America is destined to bring forth the culture of the Divine Mother that was once on Lemuria and Atlantis and in previous golden-age civilizations. The founding pyramid of her civilization is the path of the soul's reunion with the Divine Mother.

The capstone of this pyramid is the highest spiritual teaching of East and West which Gautama Buddha and Jesus Christ taught to their disciples. But in order for the capstone to be placed on the pyramid, that lost teaching must be regained and embodied heart by heart through The LORD Our Righteousness, whom we address as our beloved Holy Christ Self. On this path of the putting on of the garment of the Lord, the sons of God in America must become the living Word if we are to see the sealing of the capstone of this civilization.

Through the teachings of the "Chart of Your Divine Self" which unfold the path of individual Christhood (the path of the bodhisattva), all discover the foundation and the consummation of America's destiny. Saint Germain teaches that Americans are called upon to champion every man's right to joint-heirship, with Jesus Christ, of the Presence of the Great I AM. Under the Master's sponsorship Americans have a destiny, a dharma, if you will, to bear the flame of liberty, the four sacred freedoms and the example of representative government and free enterprise to the nations of the world.

They are sent to teach, working side by side with the people, that those who have the right to govern as "God's overmen" are those who have disciplined themselves before Christ in a sacred labor by which they serve the people and, in the process, balance the threefold flame and transmute personal and planetary karma, thereby earning (by grace) the right to wear the Lord's mantle (his authority to rule).

The true representatives of the people in every race and nation are the anointed of God, i.e., "the Christed ones,"[4] who have raised up the light of the Ancient of Days within their temples. These anointed have come to America's shores to fulfill a soul destiny, and they or their descendants must one day return in spirit or in person to their point of origin to deliver the light of the Goddess of Liberty to their people and their nations.

Without the freedoms we enjoy in America today, protected by law, secured by Divine Right, there is, there can be, no individual path of soul-testing or initiation unto the soul's union with God. Without the freedom to create with God, the entering in to the Word and Work (the Alpha and Omega) of the Lord, there is no living Spirit of America—and by definition, there are no "Americans."

The early Americans compared the colonies to the tribes of Israel—their trials, their tribulations and their God-ordained destiny—and referred to America as the "New Israel." Preachers in the eighteenth and nineteenth centuries developed this theme. They gave their sermons titles like "The Republic of the Israelites: An Example to the American States" and "Traits of Resemblance in the People of the United States of America to Ancient Israel."

Thomas Jefferson said in his second inaugural address delivered in 1805, "I shall need...the favor of that Being in whose hands we are, who led our fathers, as Israel of old, from their native land and planted them in a country flowing with all the necessaries and comforts of life."[5]

Archaeologist Raymond Capt writes, "Our Pilgrim Fathers called themselves the 'Seed of Abraham,' 'God's Servants,' 'Children of Jacob,' 'His Chosen'; they followed after the council of Moses, the lawgiver of Israel and in all their undertakings asked for guidance and the blessings of the God of Abraham, Isaac and Jacob."[6]

God's covenant with Abraham founded the nation of Israel. The LORD commanded our father, the patriarch: "Get thee out of thy country, and from thy kindred, and from thy father's house, unto a land that I will show thee: And I will make of thee a great nation, and I will bless thee, and make thy name great; and thou shalt be a blessing: And I will bless them that bless thee, and curse him that curseth thee: and in thee shall all families of the earth be blessed."[7]

Our forefathers believed that through the founding of the United States of America all families of the earth *would* be blessed. They believed that the American Revolution was fought not just for themselves or for the 13 colonies, but for the whole world. They saw their experiment as a gift to all mankind.

Historian Bernard Bailyn says that "what was essentially involved in the American Revolution was...the realization, the comprehension and fulfillment of the inheritance of liberty and of what was taken to be America's destiny in the context of world history." The Founding Fathers believed, says Bailyn, "that the colonization of British America had been an event designed by the hand of God to satisfy his ultimate aims."[8]

John Adams wrote, "I always consider the settlement of America with reverence and wonder, as the opening of a grand scene and design in Providence for the illumination of the ignorant, and the emancipation of the slavish part of mankind all over the earth."[9]

By 1776, writes Bailyn, "Americans had come to think of themselves as in a special category, uniquely placed by history to capitalize on, to complete and fulfill, the promise of man's existence."[10] "The liberties of mankind and the glory of human nature is in their keeping," John Adams wrote in the year of the Stamp Act. "America was designed by Providence for the theater on which man was to make his true figure, on which science, virtue, liberty, happiness, and glory were to exist in peace."[11]

James Madison wrote in *The Federalist Papers*, "Happily for America, happily we trust for the whole human race, [the leaders of the Revolution] pursued a new and more noble course. They accomplished a revolution which has no parallel in the annals of human society. They reared the fabrics of governments which have no model on the face of the globe."[12]

New England clergyman Lyman Beecher said in a speech given in 1832 that America was "destined to lead the way of moral and political emancipation of the world....It is time she understood her high calling, and were harnessed for the work,"[13] the work that is the Lord's work.

The moving force behind the Revolution and the formation of the United States was Freemasonry. As many as 53 of the 56 signers of the Declaration of Independence were Masons and all but five of the 55 members of the Constitutional Convention were Masons.[14] They were concerned not only about the physical establishment of the new nation but also about the fulfillment of its inner calling.

The purpose of Masonry, writes W. L. Wilmshurst in *The Meaning of Masonry,* is "the expediting of the spiritual evolution of those who aspire to perfect their own nature and transform it into a more god-like quality." The Mason's goal is to become "a just man made perfect, with larger consciousness and faculties, an efficient instrument for use by the Great Architect in His plan of rebuilding the Temple of fallen humanity, and capable of initiating and advancing other men to a participation in the same great work." [15]

The word *Israel* means in Hebrew "he will rule as God" or "prevailing with God." [16] This was the goal of our Founding Fathers for America, the "New Israel," to embody that LORD Our Righteousness, to be the instrument of that one who rules as God—whose coming was prophesied by Jeremiah.

The Ascended Masters have taught us about America's destiny and mission in the world. Saint Germain said on April 13, 1968, "America is, in effect, today the key to the destiny of the world. The Ascended Masters do not actually work for only one nation; they work for the entire human family....My great love for America is because I have felt through the ages since the formation of this land that America had the potential to become a way-shower to the world, a cup of light that would enable the emergent democracies in the world to be able to uphold the teachings and principles of good example which mankind would show forth here in this world." [17]

Again, in June 1977 Saint Germain said, "People of light, accept your mission of the ages! Accept your role as the ones who are the protectors of freedom on earth. This indeed is America's destiny—to teach a way of life that is a form of government whereby each threefold flame and every living soul may commune with God and out of that communion evolve one vote and cast that vote for freedom." [18]

America is meant to teach other nations. On New Year's Eve 1985 Gautama Buddha explained, "The people of this nation have an endowment and a protection from the Master [Saint Germain]....America must come to her original purpose and fulfill it. She has ever been established and sponsored by Saint Germain as the guru nation."

The Lord of the World said the people of America should be "going forth to transfer [Saint Germain's] science, his economy, his religion, his way of life, which represents that of the entire Great White Brotherhood, to every nation....Thus, though the chelas of Saint Germain and of America throughout the world may have in some areas perfected and gone beyond the disciplines of the people in this nation, yet the mantle has not yet been taken from [Americans] to restore the earth to the place of peace and freedom."[19]

Let us sing, then, to Old Glory, the sign of the standard and the standard-bearer and the symbol of our raising up of the Christ and the I AM Presence within every citizen of the world who will claim that banner for the "I AM" Race and for himself as a member of it!

Let us sing to the Star-Spangled Banner that reminds us that we the people enjoy the blessings of the flame of liberty solely because we are endowed by our Creator with a divine spark. Let us sing the anthem of our America that is more than a nation, that is a spirit of oneness shared by people of every land who know their God is with them in the Presence of the I AM THAT I AM, who also went before the children of Israel "a pillar of fire by night."

Yes, the letters of *America* spell out the words *"I AM" Race* as though encoded for our discovery when we should come to see our God face to face not only in the I AM Presence but also in the noble mien of Saint Germain. Yes, we the people of this "common wheel" of Light, hovering with wings of cherubim just above our heads, share an uncommon Light and Destiny as we are gathered on these shores out of every race and nation to prove our reason for being. ["The Star-Spangled Banner" is sung followed by the pledge:]

America, we love you!
America, we love you!
America, we love you!
And our Love is great enough
to hold you eternally victorious in the Light!

(Thank you. Please be seated.)

How and where and when, then, did America abdicate her destiny?

The turning point in America's history was the assassination of Abraham Lincoln at 10:13 p.m., April 14, 1865.

The archetype of America's emergent Christhood through a path of individualism, Abraham Lincoln, was born in humble surroundings in a log cabin in the backwoods of Kentucky. As president he fought to preserve the Union. His secondary goal was to free the Negro slaves, although he said he would not free them at the expense of the Union. He was opposed by business and financial interests in both the North and South.

With his assassination the balance of power shifted from "we the people" to a power elite that has controlled the higher levels of government, the economy and our cultural life ever since. As a result, the Union for which Lincoln gave his life has been steadily subverted in an ongoing revolution that has nearly destroyed the delicate architecture of the American republic with its limited powers, checks and balances, and individual sovereignty. Concurrently, the people of America have become progressively disenfranchised.

The history of the Civil War (1861–65) is complex. Lincoln was opposed not only by the Confederacy but also by Northerners who wanted to trade with the South. Lincoln's blockade of Southern ports hurt Northern moneyed interests who had been making it rich off the war. A coalition of speculators, financiers and a group of congressmen known as the Radical Republicans determined to do anything they could to restore trade—and thus their profits. Lincoln's blockade was also slowly strangling the South. And so, in this matter the Northern bankers had a common interest with Southern Confederate leaders, businessmen and bankers.

Lincoln opposed the financial powers in other ways as well. At the beginning of the war, Lincoln tried to borrow money from national and international bankers to finance the Union Army. According to one source, they wanted to charge him 24 to 36 percent interest.[20] Rather than accept the bankers' terms, he decided to print paper money—greenbacks—which became legal tender. Had Lincoln borrowed money at those usurious rates, the bankers would have essentially owned the United States government at the close of the war.

Next, the bankers proposed a national banking system which would allow them to issue bank notes backed by U.S. government bonds. These notes would be just short of legal tender since the law said that they could be used in payment for all debts except duties on imports. The National Bank Act which incorporated their plan would allow expansion of the money supply through a fractional reserve system: banks could lend out more money than they had on deposit.[21]

After heavy lobbying by bankers led by Jay and Henry Cooke, the act was passed in 1863 and it resulted in a surge of inflation. Furthermore, as economist Murray Rothbard writes, it also "paved the way for the Federal Reserve System by instituting a quasi-central banking type of monetary system."[22]

An undocumented source says that during his second term in office Lincoln planned to repeal the National Bank Act or restrict the powers it had granted bankers. Had Lincoln repealed this privilege, banks would have lost a huge money-making opportunity.

In their book *The Lincoln Conspiracy,* David Balsiger and Charles E. Sellier, Jr., demonstrate that bankers and politicians North and South plotted to eliminate Lincoln. The authors worked from the missing pages of John Wilkes Booth's diary and recently uncovered letters and documents to show that the plot against Lincoln included not only the frustrated racist, John Wilkes Booth, but also Edwin Stanton, Lincoln's secretary of war who coveted the presidency, and greedy bankers who wanted Lincoln out of their way.

Booth talked with financier Judah Benjamin, a Confederate cabinet minister who took him to meet the president of the Confederacy, Jefferson Davis. Davis arranged funds for Booth to conduct trade for the Confederacy and Benjamin arranged for him to meet with important Northern speculators, including Philadelphia financier Jay Cooke.

Cooke invited Booth to a meeting at Astor House in New York. There he met gold and cotton speculators, bankers and industrialists. Among them were Cooke's brother Henry, political boss Thurlow Weed, cotton broker Samuel Noble and the Radical Republican senator Zachariah Chandler.

Balsiger and Sellier point out that for Booth this was a curious situation—"one of the top men in the Confederacy's cabinet had sent him to meet the very bankers who financed Lincoln's war." Booth was dedicated to the victory of the Confederacy and could not understand why important figures from opposing camps were cooperating.

At the meeting Jay Cooke declared, "I will continue to have dealings with the Confederacy. Not out of fear of betrayal, but because, in peace and in war, a businessman must do business, whatever the stakes." At the end of the meeting Cooke told Booth, "There are millions of dollars in profits to be made, and we're being denied our share. We'll be ruined if Lincoln's policies are continued."[23]

The leaders of this alliance, both North and South, hired Booth to kidnap President Lincoln, write Balsiger and Sellier. After failing in six attempts, Booth became desperate and on the night of April 14, 1865, shot the president as he sat with Mrs. Lincoln in the balcony of Ford's Theater.[24]

The country has never been the same.

> *Inasmuch as ye have done it unto one of the least*
> *of these my brethren, ye have done it unto me.*

The Civil War had destroyed the power of the Southern landholding aristocracy and established the Northern industrial powers. "A new plutocracy emerged from the War and Reconstruction, masters of money who were no less self-conscious and no less powerful than the planter aristocracy of the Old South," wrote historians Samuel Eliot Morison and Henry Steele Commager. "The war, which had gone far to flatten out class distinctions in the South, tended to accentuate class differences in the North."[25] This set the stage for the emergence of the Northern banking establishment as a national ruling class.

The era of political chaos which followed Lincoln's assassination was to be instrumental in the rise of this power elite. Lincoln's successor, Andrew Johnson, fought to carry out his lenient reconstruction plan. Echoing Lincoln's sentiments he said, "If a State is to be nursed until it again gets strength, it must be nursed by its friends, not smothered by its enemies."[26]

Lincoln had promised to recognize governments of Southern states that would emancipate their slaves and pledge loyalty to the Constitution and the Union if they were backed by at least 10 percent of the number of voters in the 1860 presidential election. Johnson's plan followed the same basic lines.

The Radical Republicans virulently opposed both plans. Over Johnson's repeated vetoes, they passed their own more extreme reconstruction legislation. With fiery rhetoric they called for the punishment of the South in the name of morality and justice. But their real aim was to see that their own power remained unchallenged.

During the war, the Radicals had passed economic measures benefiting Northern industrialists. They feared that once Southern Democrats reentered the Union and joined forces with the Western lawmakers, their programs and newfound political supremacy would be jeopardized. Some critics also accused the Radical Republicans of wanting to buy up the best Southern land for a nominal price.[27]

Johnson turned out to be as much of an obstacle to the Radicals as Lincoln had been. He declared himself the enemy of their goals of monopoly, centralization of power in a national government, and the unlimited exploitation by corporations of the country's natural resources. "Wherever monopoly attains a foothold," he said, "it is sure to be a source of anger, discord, and trouble."[28] As Professor Howard K. Beale writes, "For the future of industrial America, Johnson's championship of public interest and the common man was far more dangerous than any Southern policy he might conceive."[29]

During his term Johnson took a firm stand against the

attempts of big business to use the federal government to exploit unsettled Western lands. He opposed grants of public lands to railroads and favored reserving them for pioneer farmers. Of interest is his veto of two bills which would have permitted corporations to purchase public lands in Montana and thus monopolize the mineral and coal resources of the state for their own private gain.[30]

The Radical Republicans counterattacked. They set out to strip the presidency of its power and render Congress omnipotent, even if it meant bypassing the Constitution and its system of checks and balances. In March of 1867, Congress passed three bills that were unconstitutional, one of them taking from the president his role as commander in chief.

When Johnson openly defied another of these laws by removing from office his secretary of war, Edwin Stanton, who had been plotting with the Radicals against him, they voted articles of impeachment against him and he missed being convicted by only one vote. After Johnson's term was finished, a more compliant president was elected—Gen. Ulysses S. Grant—who allowed the Radicals to control the executive branch.

While Johnson had been able to slow down the industrialists and protect the powers of the presidency, he could not stop them and the lawmakers they controlled from ushering in a new economic order and an age of big business. Following the Civil War, the robber barons—men such as Jay Gould, John D. Rockefeller, Cornelius Vanderbilt and John Jacob Astor—and other financiers and industrialists seized control of the institutions of the country through their unscrupulously gained wealth.

By definition, a nation's leadership is an elite. It is when this elite becomes self-serving that the problems of the nation arise.

Prior to and during the Revolutionary War (1776–83), the elite had been composed largely of civic-minded individuals. Sociologist C. Wright Mills in his influential study of the American ruling class, *The Power Elite,* said that from the years spanning the Revolution through the beginning of the nineteenth century, America's elite were "political men of education and of administrative experience, and, as Lord Bryce noted, possess a certain 'largeness of view and dignity of character.'"

Mills says that during the next period of time, roughly from Jefferson to Lincoln (1801–65), "no set of men controlled centralized means of power; no small clique dominated economic, much less political affairs.... For this was the period...when the elite was at most a loose coalition."[31]

Nevertheless, a power elite had some control over the government even prior to the Civil War. In 1933 President Franklin Roosevelt, a bona fide member of the Establishment, wrote to Col. Edward House (a Kissinger-like figure), "The real truth of the matter is, as you and I know, that a financial element in the larger centers has owned the Government ever since the days of Andrew Jackson."[32] And that was since the 1830s.

The stage was set and after the assassination of Lincoln the power elite was able to use the government to increase their wealth and power. It was at that point, according to Mills, that "the supremacy of corporate economic power began, in a formal way, with the Congressional elections of 1866."[33]

It is hard to imagine just how unscrupulous this new elite was. Mills, summarizing the words of several of their most severe critics, writes:

> The robber barons, as the tycoons of the post-Civil War era came to be called, descended upon the investing public much as a swarm of women might descend into a bargain basement on Saturday morning. They exploited national resources, waged economic wars among themselves, entered into combinations, made private capital out of the public domain, and used any and every method to achieve their ends. They made agreements with railroads for rebates; they purchased newspapers and bought editors; they killed off competing and independent businesses, and employed lawyers of skill and statesmen of repute to sustain their rights and secure their privileges.
>
> There *is* something demonic about these lords of creation; it is not merely rhetoric to call them robber barons. Perhaps there is no straightforward economic way to accumulate $100 million for private use; although, of course, along the way the unstraightforward ways can be delegated and the appropriator's hands kept clean. If all the big money is not easy money, all the easy money that is safe is big. It is better, so the image runs, to take one dime from each of ten million people at the point of a corporation than $100,000 from each of ten banks at the point of a gun. It is also safer.[34]

The financial moguls of the late nineteenth and early twentieth centuries made a conscious effort to seize the power of the nation's institutions as a means of enriching themselves. They recognized that they could not gain great wealth any other way.

They also realized that they had to neutralize or circumvent the constitutional and legal barriers to their activities.

There emerged a set of unspoken rules by which they operated which were, oddly enough, written down in 1906 by power-elite financier Frederick Clemson Howe in his book entitled *Confessions of a Monopolist.* Howe wrote:

These are the rules of big business. They have superseded the teachings of our parents and are reducible to a simple maxim: Get a monopoly; let Society work for you: and remember that the best of all business is politics, for a legislative grant, franchise, subsidy or tax exemption is worth more than a Kimberley or Comstock lode [these were fabulously rich diamond and silver lodes, respectively] since it does not require any labor, either mental or physical, for its exploitation. . . .

Mr. Rockefeller may think he made his hundreds of millions by economy, by saving on his gas bills, but he didn't. He managed to get the people of the globe to work for him.[35]

Professor Antony C. Sutton comments on the modus operandi of the power elite in his book *Wall Street and FDR:*

Old John D. Rockefeller and his 19th century fellow-capitalists were convinced of one absolute truth: that no great monetary wealth could be accumulated under the impartial rules of a competitive laissez-faire society, [that] the only sure road to the acquisition of massive wealth was monopoly: drive out your competitors, reduce competition, eliminate laissez-faire, and above all get state protection for your industry through compliant politicians and government regulation. This last avenue yields a legal monopoly, and a legal monopoly always leads to wealth. . . .

This robber baron schema is also, under different labels, the socialist plan. The difference between a corporate state monopoly and a socialist state monopoly is essentially only the identity of the group controlling the power structure. The essence of socialism is monopoly control by the state using hired planners and academic sponges. On the other hand, Rockefeller, Morgan, and their corporate friends aimed to acquire and control *their* monopoly and to maximize its profits through influence in the state political apparatus; this, while it still needs hired planners and academic sponges, is a discreet and far more subtle process than outright state ownership under socialism....

Success for the Rockefeller gambit has depended particularly upon focusing public attention upon largely irrelevant and superficial historical creations, such as the myth of a struggle between capitalists and communists, and careful cultivation of political forces by big business. We call this phenomenon of corporate legal monopoly—market control acquired by using political influence—by the name of corporate socialism.[36]

Howe, the monopolist, recognized that there was a profound difference between free market capitalism and the capitalism he and his fellow capitalists practiced. He wrote:

This is the story of something for nothing—of making the other fellow pay. This making the other fellow pay, of getting something for nothing, explains the lust for franchises, mining rights, tariff privileges, railway control, tax evasions. All these things mean monopoly, and all monopoly is bottomed on legislation....

Monopoly and corruption are cause and effect. Together, they work in Congress, in our Commonwealths, in our municipalities. It is always so. It always has been so. Privilege gives birth to corruption, just as the poisonous sewer breeds disease. Equal chance, a fair field and no favors, the "square deal" are never corrupt. They do not appear in legislative halls nor in Council Chambers. For these things mean labor for labor, value for value, something for something. This is why the little business man, the retail and wholesale dealer, the jobber, and the manufacturer are not the business men whose business corrupts politics.[37]

What we are seeing here is the compromise of a nation conceived in the heart of the Goddess of Liberty founded upon a dispensation of tremendous moment from the causal body of Saint Germain. We see those of ulterior motives denying her ensoulment by the original Founding Fathers, who had been chosen and picked by the Master, sponsored as his initiates and disciples.

We see that light of Aquarius in the Master/disciple relationship becoming America. We see the movement of people from the 13 colonies across a continent. We see coming to life the green shoot of a new hope for millennia of freedom by the power and presence of Saint Germain.

Yet in the shadows, not perceived, there are lurking those who have not that original light, have no heart tie to the Ascended

Master of the seventh age and dispensation and are not sponsored
by him, for they came not bearing the kindling light of freedom.
They affirm, "We are the law, we bow to no other." Such as these
have no direct access to the Light of the I AM THAT I AM, for
they long ago extinguished the divine spark in their absolute
rebellion against Almighty God and the Christ of His offspring.

They see the people of Light coming from all over the world
impelled by the Spirit of Freedom. They see them bearing the
flame of the I AM Presence to America's shores to fulfill a grand
experiment in freedom. They see them becoming a part of the
great tapestry of America, stitch by stitch, life by life, hard won.

They watch and wait and they move in to control, to subjugate, once again to elevate themselves. They assume the posture
of a royal dynasty—not as "noblesse oblige" but as "mon droit,"
my right—an elitist corps. They think they are a privileged class
because of their heavenly origins. But they descended not in grace
as world saviours but as falling stars—fallen angels, so named
"Watchers" by our father Enoch.[38]

They have come to subjugate and enslave the Christ of all
people. They know that it is the light of the people that produces
and multiplies the wealth and the health of the economy. They
have come to live off of that light and to make all Americans—all
who are of the Race of the I AM THAT I AM—pawns in their
monopoly games.

Inasmuch as ye have done it unto one of the least
of these my brethren, ye have done it unto me.

And so they moved in to control the money system in order to
siphon off that light. As Sutton notes in *Wall Street and FDR*, "In
modern America the most significant illustration of society as a
whole working for the few is the 1913 Federal Reserve Act. The
Federal Reserve System is, in effect, a private banking monopoly,
not answerable to Congress or the public, but with legal monopoly
control over money supply without let or hindrance or even audit
by the General Accounting Office. It was irresponsible manipulation of money supply by this Federal Reserve System that brought
about the inflation of the 1920s, the 1929 Depression, and so the
presumed requirement for a Roosevelt New Deal."[39]

In his work *The War on Gold*, Sutton explains:

The groundwork for the Federal Reserve System was
laid at an unpublicized meeting at the J. P. Morgan Country
Club on Jekyll Island, Georgia, in November 1910. Senator
Nelson Aldrich, bankers Frank Vanderlip (president of
National City Bank and representing Rockefeller and Kuhn

Loeb interests), Henry P. Davison (senior partner of J. P. Morgan), and Charles D. Norton (president of Morgan's First National Bank), met in secret to decide how to foist a central bank system on the United States. Others at the meeting were Paul Moritz Warburg, the German banker, and Benjamin Strong (a Morgan banker who later became first Governor of the Federal Reserve Bank of New York).

Out of the Jekyll Island cabal came the basic bill passed by Congress and signed into law by President Woodrow Wilson as the Federal Reserve Act of 1913. Under the earlier sub-Treasury system, bankers had no control over the money supply in the United States and, even less to their liking, none over currency issues.[40]

Thus we have inherited from these masterminds meeting in secret behind closed doors the central banking system. Jekyll Island participant Frank Vanderlip in his autobiography, *From Farmboy to Financier,* had no compunctions about revealing the purpose of the Jekyll Island meeting. He wrote, "Our secret expedition to Jekyll Island was the occasion of the actual conception of what eventually became the Federal Reserve System. The essential points of the Aldrich Plan [Senator Aldrich's proposed legislation for a central banking system] were all contained in the Federal Reserve Act as it was passed."[41]

The power elite came to dominate both the Republican and Democratic parties. They elected and defeated presidents, especially in the post-Civil War days, and simply bought senators and judges. They gained control of the media and set the national agenda and the tone of the debate on the issues.

But ultimately, it was the American people who were at fault. They allowed these men to control them instead of electing those who would follow the principles of the Founding Fathers. Lincoln once said, "If destruction be our lot, we must ourselves be its author and finisher. As a nation of freemen, we must live through all time, or die by suicide."[42]

America, we have got to get in there and kick out the power brokers! It's the moneyed interests who have been responsible for the wars of this century. It's the capitalists who have built up Nazi Germany and the Communists and betrayed the people of light around the world.

Unless we stop them, in the name of Almighty God, we, too, will have abdicated even our right to decide the life or death of our nation. If we allow them to kill our nation, it may be suicide by proxy, but it will still be suicide. If this nation is destroyed by others because we do nothing, it will be just the same as if we had destroyed it ourselves. If we want to fulfill our destiny, it's time we realize who the real culprits are and stop allowing them to use our nation as the means to their world takeover!

Civilizations do fall for lack of leadership and the real cause of their collapse is always self-destruction. Historian Arnold Toynbee conducted an exhaustive study of the world's civilizations. He recognized that a civilization cannot continue to grow unless it can successfully respond to all challenges.

This parallels the life of the individual. When you cease to be able to meet all challenges to your identity, to your life, to your personhood, to your path and to your soul, you will cease to grow and you will wither away.

Toynbee also concluded that as a civilization evolves, more of its challenges are internal rather than external. He wrote in his monumental work, *A Study of History*, "It has to reckon less and less with challenges delivered by external forces and demanding responses on an outer battlefield, and more and more with challenges that are presented by itself to itself in an inner arena."[43]

"The criterion of growth," he says, "is progress towards self-determination,"[44] unencumbered by either internal or external challenges because one is meeting both. Growth is dependent upon creativity—ingenuity, the ability to put down those forces that assail one's highest calling—"perpetual flexibility and spontaneity," as Toynbee defines it.[45] And this is precisely what we need when we are fighting for our highest reality.

The ability of a nation to defend itself against external and internal challenges depends on comparable spiritual development. "Real progress," wrote Toynbee, "is found to consist in a process defined as 'etherialization', an overcoming of material obstacles which releases the energies of the society to make responses to challenges which henceforth are internal rather than external, spiritual rather than material."[46] If a society cannot etherialize, or spiritually transcend itself, then the civilization breaks down and enters what he calls a "time of troubles" preceding its ultimate dissolution.

What we see here is that nations go through the identical phases of initiation as do individuals. First we must deal with the objective enemy who is without and then we turn to deal with the psychology of the subjective enemy who is within. Nations, as people, come to the hour of self-transcendence when all of the foundation and body of the pyramid that they have built is focused in that moment of quintessence in the capstone in the

All-Seeing Eye of God, thence to give birth to a golden age.

If the components of society, which are made up of the complex components of individual psyches, are not ready for self-transcendence, the civilization cannot meet this initiation of the Universal Christ which must be self-realized in the corporate body of the national will. Failure to pass one's initiation at the hour appointed by the law of cycles effectively halts the forward march of progress—spiritually and industrially.

Yet life cannot stand still. The law of motion governs stars and cells and the body politic and the heartbeat of freedom and the spirit of a people. That which ceases to breathe the breath of immortal Life or to be endowed with creative fires from the altars of God, that which ceases to experience growth ceases to entertain Be-ness. Whether it is the individual who abdicates his path of personal Christhood or a nation (as a collective of individuals) that abdicates hers, without the Holy Christ Flame fanned and hard won as the centerpiece of existence there is *no* integrating factor for the continuity of Life anywhere—period.

One of Toynbee's most important conclusions is that civilizations die by suicide and not by invasion. "The most that an alien enemy has achieved," he says, "has been to give an expiring suicide his *coup de grâce*"[47]—that is, the final blow that brings death to a sufferer.

When, individual by individual, a nation abdicates a path in the Master/disciple relationship under Jesus Christ, then the nation as a whole must flounder and fall. In the light of this understanding of histories of all civilizations, we can see why Jesus called us on May 28, 1987, to the path of the ascension through the path of Love and self-givingness—to be world teachers and to claim the mantle of Mediator on behalf of those who know not the way to go.

We can see why on that same date he called for ten thousand Keepers of the Flame who will invoke the Light (through prayer and invocation and dynamic decrees) that will stand between a people, a world, a continent and their own returning karma.[48]

We can see why he has cried unto us and called us to be his disciples, even naming the date of November 1, 1987, when we must begin in earnest to realize that path of individual Christhood:[49] It is because there must be Lightbearers in a nation who fulfill this chemistry, this alchemy at this hour when a nation must transcend herself or enter the deceleration spiral of a suicidal recession.

America has come to the Y: to choose to embrace the living Christ for the glorification of the God Self and the giving of the light unto others for God Self-determination *or* to choose not to be and to take what light one has for the glorification of the not-self, thus entering the left-hand path of the enslavement of souls to Antichrist under the tyranny of fallen angels.

You recall that Jesus in his Last Judgment set the sheep to his right hand but the goats to his left. "The blessed of the Father" take the right-hand path of the glory of God, the Divine Ego; "the cursed" take the left of the glory of the human ego. The judgment of the latter pronounced by the Son of God was "Inasmuch as ye did it not to one of the least of these, ye did it not to me."

When the power elite rose up in America, it was for the glorification of their identity as a proud race of fallen ones. This was to be accomplished through the taking of the light—that is, the money, i.e., the value of the sacred labor—of the people. The shift was from one nation under God to a plurality of monopolies under the Luciferian hierarchy of the Eastern establishment. We had been taken and taken over by the Watchers and the agenda of their false hierarchy of America which was to be the abdication of America's destiny as designed by Providence.

Inasmuch as ye have done it unto one of the least
of these my brethren, ye have done it unto me.

The fulcrum for change, change for the better or for the worse, is a civilization's leadership. Toynbee sees two types of leadership classes: the creative minority and the dominant minority. Here we see the creative minority as the sons and daughters of God, co-creators with him; the dominant minority as those arch-deceivers who subjugate the people by the abuse of power.

Toynbee explains that the creative minority have the ability to lead civilization up the mountain of self-transcendence. We see these leaders as the Founding Fathers, the Masons, the Light-bearers, those, both Christian and Jew, who knew they were the descendants of Israel. A society's transfiguration, says Toynbee, comes only as its people imitate this creative minority.

Thus, El Morya wants the profile of your Christhood and of the leadership of the I AM Presence with and in you to shine. He wants your example to be an image of what the people deserve to have raised up in the highest office in the land.

Toynbee observed that when the creative minority lose their creativity and become oppressive—when they let the threefold flame go out and the divine spark—they degenerate into a dominant minority which rules by force. Thus, those who in heaven were the guardian spirits of our grace fell into disgrace when they descended to earth to lust after the daughters of men.[50] This creative minority became the oppressors of the sons of God in the earth. And the Lightbearers are displaced by the fallen ones who come in their cunning with their serpent schemes and their plots of takeover—and they are well-organized plots.

As it is written, "The dragon was wroth with the woman, and went to make war with the remnant of her seed, which keep the commandments of God, and have the testimony of Jesus Christ."[51] Therefore the Lightbearers, off guard, not fully integrated on the path of initiation for want of a true path of the religion of the Divine Mother, a true path of a God-government and a God-economy understood and taught to them by true shepherds, are set aside and displaced by those in whom no candle burns.

In reaction to the oppression of the dominant minority, Toynbee says, the people withdraw their allegiance to their leaders and no longer seek to imitate them. This schism between the people and their leaders marks the disintegration of the civilization and heralds an epoch in which it is no longer able to adequately respond to challenges.

Today, Western civilization is the preeminent world civilization and America is its leader. Since Lincoln was assassinated a dominant minority concerned solely with the interests of the ruling class has gradually replaced the creative minority in America. With the advent of this New Year of ever-new challenges to our integrity as individual sons of God, my friends, that transition is virtually complete. And the people, untutored by the heart of Christ, continue to allow their leaders to make decisions that are not in the best interests of their nation or their world.

As a result of this change in leadership, which has brought the United States under the dominant sinister force of an elite inner circle comprised of the powerful Watchers, America has been taken step by step on the road leading to the abdication of her Divine Destiny—complete in the twentieth century!

> *Verily I say unto you, Inasmuch as ye did it not*
> *to one of the least of these, ye did it not to me.*
> *And these shall go away into everlasting punishment:*
> *but the righteous into life eternal.*

[to be continued]

"The Summit Lighthouse Sheds Its Radiance O'er All the World to Manifest as Pearls of Wisdom."
Based on a lecture by Elizabeth Clare Prophet delivered on Monday, January 4, 1988, at the Royal Teton Ranch, Montana, updated for print as this week's Pearl.

(1) Saint Germain, November 29, 1987, "It Is the Last Time," 1987 *Pearls of Wisdom,* vol. 30, no. 81, p. 611. (2) Isa. 40:1. (3) Declaration of Independence, July 4, 1776. (4) The word *Christ* is derived from the Greek *Christos,* meaning "anointed," from *chriein,* "to anoint." (5) U.S. Congress, *Inaugural Addresses of the Presidents of the United States from George Washington 1789 to Richard Milhous Nixon 1973,* 93d Cong., 1st sess., 1974, H. Doc. 93–208, p. 21. (6) E. Raymond Capt, *Our Great Seal: The Symbols of Our Heritage and Our Destiny* (Thousand Oaks, Calif.: Artisan Sales, 1979), p. 65. (7) Gen. 12:1–3. (8) Bernard Bailyn, *The Ideological Origins of the American Revolution* (Cambridge: Harvard University Press, Belknap Press, 1967), pp. 19, 32. (9) John Adams, "A Dissertation on the Canon and Feudal Law," quoted in Capt, *Our Great Seal,* p. 85. (10) Bailyn, *Ideological Origins of the American Revolution,* p. 20. (11) *Diary and Autobiography of John Adams,* quoted in Bailyn, *Ideological Origins of the American Revolution,* p. 20. (12) James Madison, *The Federalist Papers,* No. 14. (13) Capt, *Our Great Seal,* p. 85. (14) "The Mystical Origins of the United States of America," in *Saint Germain On Alchemy: For the Adept in the Aquarian Age* (Livingston, Mont.: Summit University Press, I985), p. 131. (15) Ibid., pp. 124–25. (16) James Strong, "Dictionary of the Hebrew Bible," in *The Exhaustive Concordance of the Bible* (Nashville: Abingdon Press, 1894), p. 53; Alexander Cruden, *Cruden's Unabridged Concordance* (Grand Rapids, Mich.: Baker Book House, n.d.), p. 581. (17) Saint Germain, April 13, 1968, "The Grand Adventure," 1977 *Pearls of Wisdom,* vol. 20, no. 32, pp. 152, 151. (18) Saint Germain, June 11, 1977, "Message to America and the People of Earth," 1977 *Pearls of Wisdom,* vol. 20, no. 31, p. 146. (19) Gautama Buddha, January 1, 1986, "The Teaching Is for the Many," 1986 *Pearls of Wisdom,* vol. 29, no. 21, pp. 191, 190. (20) *Appleton Cyclopedia,* 1861, p. 296. (21) Herman E. Krooss, ed., *Documentary History of Banking and Currency in the United States* (Edgemont, Pa.: Chelsea House Publishers, 1969), 2:1392–93. (22) Murray N. Rothbard, *The Mystery of Banking* (n.p.: Richardson & Snyder, 1983), p. 224. (23) David Balsiger and Charles E. Sellier, Jr., *The Lincoln Conspiracy* (Los Angeles: Schick Sunn Classic Books, 1977), pp. 58–62. (24) Ibid., pp. 108–9. (25) Samuel Eliot Morison and Henry Steele Commager, *The Growth of the American Republic* (New York: Oxford University Press, 1962), 2:17. (26) Kenneth W. Leish, ed., *The American Heritage Pictorial History of the Presidents of the United States* (New York: American Heritage Publishing Co., 1968), 1:432–33, 429. (27) Claude G. Bowers, *The Tragic Era: The Revolution after Lincoln* (Cambridge, Mass.: Houghton Mifflin Co., 1929), p. 20. (28) Howard K. Beale, *The Critical Year: A Study of Andrew Johnson and Reconstruction* (1930; reprint, New York: Frederick Ungar Publishing Co., 1958), p. 264. (29) Ibid., p. 218. (30) Ibid., pp. 265, 269–71. (31) C. Wright Mills, *The Power Elite* (New York: Oxford University Press, 1956), pp. 270–71. (32) President Franklin Delano Roosevelt to Col. Edward Mandell House, November 21, 1933, quoted in Antony C. Sutton, *Wall Street and FDR* (New Rochelle, N.Y.: Arlington House Publishers, 1975), p. 13. (33) Mills, *The Power Elite,* p. 271. (34) Ibid., p. 95. (35) Antony C. Sutton, *Wall Street and the Bolshevik Revolution* (New Rochelle, N.Y.: Arlington House Publishers, 1974), p. 16; Sutton, *Wall Street and FDR,* p. 73. (36) Sutton, *Wall Street and FDR,* pp. 72–73. (37) Frederic C. Howe, *Confessions of a Monopolist,* quoted in

Sutton, *Wall Street and FDR,* pp. 73–74. **(38)** I Enoch 10:10–20; 12; 14:1, 2; 15:1–8; 16. See Elizabeth Clare Prophet, *Forbidden Mysteries of Enoch: The Untold Story of Men and Angels* (Livingston, Mont.: Summit University Press, 1983), containing all the Enoch texts, including the Book of Enoch and the Book of the Secrets of Enoch. **(39)** Sutton, *Wall Street and FDR,* p. 75. **(40)** Antony C. Sutton, *The War on Gold* (Seal Beach, Calif.: '76 Press, 1977), p. 84. **(41)** Ibid. **(42)** Abraham Lincoln, "The Perpetuation of Our Political Institutions," address at the Young Men's Lyceum, Springfield, Illinois, January 27, 1838. **(43)** Arnold J. Toynbee, *A Study of History,* abr. of vols. 1–6, abr. D. C. Somervell (New York: Oxford University Press, 1947), p. 208. **(44)** Ibid. **(45)** Ibid., p. 278. **(46)** Arnold J. Toynbee, *A Study of History,* abr. of vols. 7–10, abr. D. C. Somervell (New York: Oxford University Press, 1957), p. 364. **(47)** Toynbee, *Study of History,* abr. of vols. 1–6, p. 272. **(48)** Jesus Christ, May 28, 1987, "The Call to the Path of the Ascension," 1987 *Pearls of Wisdom,* vol. 30, no. 27, pp. 269–76. **(49)** Jesus Christ, November 1, 1987, "The Day of Thy Christhood," 1987 *Pearls of Wisdom,* vol. 30, no. 74, p. 578. **(50)** Gen. 6:4; I Enoch 7. **(51)** Rev. 12:17.

Pearls of Wisdom®
published by The Summit Lighthouse

Vol. 31 No. 10	Beloved Saint Germain	March 6, 1988

New Year's Retreat
at the Royal Teton Ranch

X

There Is a Fire on the Mountain
The Victory Is Nigh

As long as there is a fire on the mountain, so long shall hearts endure in a flame of hope—a hope that yet casts forth a light and a fire all-consuming to devour all Death and Hell that would array itself upon the nations.

Therefore, let the fire burn on in the holy mountain of God in the hearts of Keepers of the Flame. For this fire on the mountain that is now white fire, now golden yellow, violet or blue, now emerald green or ruby or in the power of the purple or the aquamarine, this fire that does embrace all rainbow rays of God and the secret rays, beloved—*this fire* does cause us to think upon the coming of the Ancient of Days, when a spiritual fire was first kindled at Shamballa, the place prepared for our Lord.

There it was, beloved, that the magnificence of the Flaming One did appear, and all at once the great glow of fire in the earth did signal to all life and all cosmos that earth had received a new impetus for freedom—and if freedom, then the choice once again to choose to receive the engrafted Word,* to be reignited by the flame of that Flaming One who had come. Thus, field and stream and flower and mountain and those burdened by the weight of a night of darkness all felt the glow and the fire, and once again earth was in the running for the path of initiation unto Christhood and Buddhahood.

Blessed hearts, today it is as though it were the hour of "the Second Coming," the second coming of our Lord Sanat Kumara.

*James 1:21

It has been long time since a people spread abroad on the earth have spoken his name or sung to his flame. How I love to join you in singing to that wondrous fiery flame of *Finlandia** and thereby [through its vibration] to enter even the heart of the earth where for a time in periods when barbarians would rise again, the sons of Light would abide until renewed opportunity should come once again to pursue the children of God on the surface in an attempt to quicken them to separate themselves out from the creations of the mass mind.

Thus, beloved, in cycles since the coming of Sanat Kumara have the Lightbearers served with intensity midst civilizations, and then again, even without taking the ascension, they have been required to retreat while in the planetary plan there was an out-picturing of the forces of chemicalization and upheaval generated by the intense karma made within the nations and perpetrated upon them by these fallen ones.

Therefore, I have chosen for you to hear a certain sequence of scenarios that have occurred in these centuries that you might see that the enemy never sleeps and never stops.† Their plans are imitations of the Great White Brotherhood point/counterpoint, as you have been told.

When you amass all of these crimes of the fallen ones against humanity and the sons of God, surely, as the one who ought to sit in the seat of judge of this nation does not and as you yourself sit in that seat, by Christ-discrimination it is evident that the hour prophesied in Enoch—of the ultimate judgment of the Watchers and their seed and also of the Nephilim gods who would not bend the knee before the Lord—is come. Thus, beloved, they need not commit any more crimes to be judged guilty as charged by the Divine Mother or to be summoned to the Court of the Sacred Fire.

Blessed ones, this is not a simple matter. To withdraw these evolutions from the earth planet would leave such caverns and openings in the earth, as the misqualified substance of their karma was removed, as to unbalance and unhinge a planetary body. If you begin to think how entrenched these fallen ones are everywhere, [you will understand why] it has been the deci-sion of the Cosmic Council to leave a civilization to remain intact while yet some and the many should find the path of the ascen-sion and the way back to Maitreya's Mystery School. Thus, beloved, choices made by cosmic councils are not compromises. They are always and always a putting forth of grace to those

---

*See "Our Beloved Sanat Kumara," sung to the melody of *Finlandia* by Jean Sibelius, song 546 in *The Summit Lighthouse Book of Songs;* no. 51 in *Mantras of the Ascended Masters for the Initiation of the Chakras.*
†This dictation was delivered through the Messenger Elizabeth Clare Prophet following her lecture "The Abdication of America's Destiny," given at Saint Germain's behest Sunday evening, January 4, 1988, at the Royal Teton Ranch, published as last week's Pearl of Wisdom.

emerging, those awakening, those fervent hearts.

Therefore, we come not to make predictions per se or declarations but to tell you that as the violet flame intensifies on behalf of the people of God and as the weight of world condemnation put upon them by the fallen angels, those Luciferians, is transmuted and every burden and vestige thereof, these pillars of violet flame in the earth can be a grid of Light whereby the outcome even of their judgment and removal may be far less discomfiting and disturbing to the planet.

I remind you, then, of the great teaching given to the Messenger: For every black magician that is taken, there must be a Christed one, one in whom there dwells the living Christ, to fill that vacuum, to fill that vacancy lest the very vacancy itself become, as in physics, a means for the undoing and the imbalancing of a planet. Nature abhors a vacuum; it will either be filled by the Christed ones or an even greater evil.

Therefore you have come to the Mystery School and you are being given mighty teachings and very strong reasons as to why you should pursue with haste the integration with the fire of the mountain. The fire upon the mountain that is burning is a source of sacred fire to all peoples of the earth who shall turn to serve their God. It is a source and a force to negate all misuse of nuclear power. The fire must burn on. It must increase. It must have many hearts nourishing it.

Dare we think that one day in the near future there will be this many who are gathered here in surplus of the necessities of the service of the day-to-day activities of this headquarters who on a rotating basis could give the perpetual ritual of the twenty-four hours, fulfilling the need of the Great Divine Director for the filling in of the planetary body with the momentum of the mighty blue sphere?

Blessed ones, stadiums fill for weekly sports events worldwide. It is not impossible that Keepers of the Flame should suddenly be raised up by miracle, by call of my heart—of Saint Germain—by call of all hearts, for it is in keeping with the will of God. Fear not, then, for these Keepers of the Flame who are called shall raise up a Light to also defend the integrity of the land and the organization.

Let us all, then, incline our ears to the Lord Sanat Kumara and rest our heads upon his breast, that we might know again the heartbeat that we knew in the very bosom of Abraham, that we might hear it again, as Abraham's heart was indeed a vessel of the Ancient of Days.

As we turn our gaze to the earth, we see momentums continuing as begun. Momentums of Evil keep rolling; momentums of Light, they are on the increase. In many areas the momentums of Evil have been decelerated by the calls of the Keeper of the Flame but, beloved hearts, as the karma descends daily, this adds fuel to the hellfires that move across the earth.

When in battle, standing against relentless forces, the commander in chief can only say,

Keep on, brave knights and ladies!
Keep on, Lightbearers—
Torches through the night
    and the heart's devotion to the fight
To win!

When at any hour of the day or night, somehow the enemy convinces any child of God at the emotional level that the hour is futile and the battle is lost, this is a seed sown and received of individual spiritual suicide.

One must fortify oneself for the victory with the sword of Serapis, with the fire of the Divine Mother he embraces. One must have the resilience of springtime to be able to soar into the heavens and the earth, beneath the streams and under the earth, to frolic with undines and to know the grace of salamanders.

Blessed ones, the battle is not to the rigid but to the strong who bend with the waves and the wind and know themselves blending into the seas and the higher atmosphere! In the heart of Helios and Vesta they soar as on a trajectory and return to the place of service recharged. There is no fear of death or the future in those who understand themselves as a movement, a wave of light, if you will, passing through time and space in this sphere.

I, Saint Germain, come to stretch the mind this way and that and the heart as well, to give the soul pause to realize that she is not shrouded in mourning garb but may walk from these and enter the bridal gown, the veil itself signifying the sealing of that which was rent and the restoration of a virgin consciousness in the heart of Mary.

Let us not allow world karma and world condemnation to weigh heavy upon our ranks. When the violet flame is handy on tape and in the heart, I AM there. Let it play and sing! Let it pass through the crystals and the rock. Let it become the lining between the marrow and the bone. Let it become the inner cell walls and a part of the arteries and veins. Let the mind be a conflagration of violet flame preceding the infilling of illumination's golden flame.

One must displace matter where one is! One must enter into infinity, for in the infinite sense of life you can lose nothing in the fight but only gain sphere upon sphere of integrity, integration with Krishna's heart! The Lord Christ in many manifestations does come.

Beloved ones, this year is truly a year of testing, *self-testing*, I would add, whereby you may see against the backdrop of events and challenges to be met where is the standard and where is the measure of a self, of a man, of a woman, of a child. Is it not good to stretch oneself a mile high and to know the glistening ice on the peaks and to descend swiftly to the center of the mountain to find the fire of the Ruby Ray Buddha?

Blessed hearts, I bring comfort and I say, the hourly and daily calling in the name of the Lord for the judgment of the betrayers of mankind is at hand! Let the judgment descend, I say! For so long as it is delayed, so long will they continue the slaughter of the Lightbearers, the sweet peoples of the earth. How long must they lay down their lives? No longer than you allow it, for the cup of the wrath of the [indignation of the] LORD God is filled.*

I say, then, violet flame side by side with the judgment call, this, then, is the opening of space, space unknown. You open a place before you; you think it is a singular space, but in that space there is a squaring of space itself until compartment upon compartment can be retrieved. Space and time may be not what you think they are but coordinates that can be adapted by the mastery of the heart of Christ within you for uses to confuse, outrun and outdo these fallen angels.

They have had their day. *They* have nothing left. They are as shrinking heads, already shrunken, as some vestige of the past that an ancient tribe might put upon a totem pole. Blessed ones, believe me, they are self-emptied, and the power of Hell that uses them can also be beaten, for our Lord Sanat Kumara is truly here, *here* in the planet, *here* occupying where you are, *here* and there, everywhere; and the force of the anti-Mind dare not cross his path. Therefore, when giving the judgment call, any judgment call, precede it with the words, "In the name I AM THAT I AM Sanat Kumara, Gautama Buddha, Lord Maitreya, Jesus Christ, Elohim, I decree."

Let the powers of all octaves and angelic and archangelic hosts answer the call of the sons and daughters of God and the children of the Light for the binding and the judgment of this seed of the wicked, thereby preventing their further proliferation of war and chaos. Let the hour of the enlightenment of a people come.

All of the foregoing which I have said to you [in past dictations] regarding preparation does remain the need of the hour. I simply come to carry your consciousness, as I would carry the Christ Child, over the river of the astral plane to take you to the heart of the living God. The living God is in your midst and not far from you.

Receive my heart, beloved—all of my gratitude for your givingness. To all Keepers of the Flame of the world, I say: for this

*Isa. 51:17, 22, 23; Jer. 25:15–18, 27–29; Rev. 14:8–10; 16:19

1988 I extend myself to you. Please extend yourselves to me in fervent decree daily that we might save many more than might have been saved were it not for your presence.

Omri-Tas, Omri-Tas beloved, Omri-Tas, kiss my own with your violet flame. Seal them, caress them, embolden them. Take them now and let them know the secret chambers of the violet flame. It has no bounds but carries the soul to her infinite habitation in God here and now, wherever, whenever.

For I AM Saint Germain, and I AM in the consciousness of God, yet I am exactly in this court of my beloved Arthur, exactly where you are. Death is not even a portal into this place. It* is achieved by entering the fullness of Life *here and now.*

This transition in consciousness is the greatest armour and protection for the Day of Vengeance of our God which is coming upon the seed of the wicked, which is concurrently the day of the Liberty unto his own. Therefore, Goddess of Liberty, thou who dost bless this company, let thy light descend and thy stars illumine their way.

With hands extended, with heart embracing your own, I remind you of duty, urgency, sacrifice and unlimited strength from my heart in swift answer to your call. Let the message go forth and let it be heard!

I AM Saint Germain, standing in the midst of the fire in the mountain of God for the victory of America's destiny! O "I AM" Race, come to me! I AM your Knight Commander! Come to me, O beloved, and receive the fire of my heart, the co-measurement and ultimately the adjustment where you, too, shall stand with me in the center of the flaming flame that is neither quenched nor shall it quench thee, for our God is a consuming fire[†]—consuming all unlike himself. Thou art natives of fire; therefore, thou art like him.

Therefore, from the fire we have come, to the fire we return. Let it be by increments won daily, for the victory is nigh, beloved, the victory is nigh. Let them, then, be judged for all of their crimes, and let the records of their crimes be also bound that these crimes shall not fall upon the people of Light as a planetary debt to the universe.

So, beloved, they have managed to make you accountable for their monetary debts, but if you say the word, they shall never make you accountable for their crimes against humanity. This, then, is a singular and very important key. Take it and turn back upon them their infamy. It is the hour, it is the Law. So be it. So be it.

My love forever goes with you. I AM in your heart Saint Germain, beloved of my own and hierarch of Aquarius. Portia and her angels adorn you with comfort flowers to comfort, comfort ye my people.

*Entering here in the consciousness of God   †Deut. 4:24; 9:3; Heb. 12:29

Church Universal and Triumphant®

January 19, 1988

My Beloved Sons and Daughters,

These precious Pearls of Wisdom are the Body and Blood of Christ that pours through me from the Ascended Masters to you morsel by morsel, drop by drop to nourish your souls and shore up your fiery spirits as you daily weave the Deathless Solar Body--your wedding garment of immortal light substance whereby in due course the Lord shall take you to be His bride.

And if by His grace and leave I have realized a Christhood that I might give for thee and for America in the ritual of the Fifteenth Rosary, then know that as my life is His--and thine--my body and my blood one with His does also flow in the confluent stream of His Word:

Take, eat and drink of this communion cup of the Pearls of Wisdom, for they are also my life that is given easily, sweetly, and tenderly for thee. And as you drink from the same fount from which I have drunk, you too shall be the cup of Christ's Love to the world.

I pray you will resolve this year of 1988 never to be without your Pearls, and to enter that state of listening grace and perpetual prayer which our Lord speaks of in <u>Prayer and Meditation:</u>

Prayer without ceasing is the key to a release of radiant streams of God-energy that focus in the chalice of your being. The garnering of this energy will in time make the Son to become one with the Father, for these energies are powerful and they are life. . . . (p. 18)

BOX A, LIVINGSTON, MONTANA 59047-1390 (406) 222-8300

How frequently I found during my own mission that by going up into the mountains to pray, getting away from the madding crowd, or curling up in one end of a ship, I was able to renew my strength and perform a greater ministry of service and healing. All who would follow in my footsteps must understand that unless they are able to contact the Great Source of Life and continually renew their strength, their mission will not be carried forth in the manner desired by God. . . . (p. 9)

Let us decree that each individual soul, expressing the greatness of the Divine Self, may learn the precious art of weaving the golden flow of the shuttle of attention between himself and his God, between the Son and the Father, between Darkness and Light. Thus shall Light inhabit Darkness and dispel it and bring to all the wedding garments of eternal purpose that cause the holy spiritual Bride of the Church to say, "Behold, the Bridegroom cometh!" (p. 32)

As we--you and I, Beloved--are now fully One in the Diamond Heart of Jesus and in the Order of the Diamond Heart established to His name by Mother Mary and El Morya, I ask you to send me your heart's love offering to keep the Pearls coming in a steady stream of crystal light--from the heart of Jesus and the Servant-Sons in heaven through our Christhood on earth to your own emergent God-Identity.

All my love,

Mother

P.S. On the top line of your Pearls of Wisdom address label, you will find in parentheses the expiration date of your subscription. It is based on the date and amount of your last love offering for the Pearls of Wisdom. To be certain that you never miss a single one of the Masters' weekly dictations, please renew your subscription six weeks before the expiration date.

February 1, 1988

Beloved Keepers of the Flame of America and Lightbearers
of the World,

Significant are the events, political, economic and
spiritual, which have taken place since I wrote to you on September 18 of my mission to stump America for Saint Germain's
Coming Revolution in Higher Consciousness--the mission to
which we have all been preparing for lifetimes, the mission
in which we are truly one and which we share heartbeat
by heartbeat.

A year ago Thanksgiving Saint Germain said, speaking through me at the Airport Hilton in Los Angeles:

The hour is come, then, that the most important
reason for being of the Messenger is to make the call
and to keep the vigil that there be not an acceleration,
indeed a mud slide of forces, toward an end precipitated before the LORD's timetable be fulfilled. For when
the fallen angels see the coming of the LORD and the
enlightenment of his people on the horizon, they
attempt to precipitate darkness in the land even before
its [karmic] due date. (Pearls of Wisdom, vol. 29,
no. 75, p. 654)

Without Saint Germain and the violet flame there is,
there can be, no new age and no new opportunity in Aquarius.
Saint Germain is the living Spirit of America. His mind, his
heart, his fiery presence have endowed this nation with an
aura of the seventh age--the Seventh Ray and Dispensation.

Without the continuing sponsorship of Saint Germain
as the Hierarch of the Aquarian Age, without the dispensation
of being able to call forth the violet flame (which many of us

take for granted as though it were a right rather than a gift of grace that can be lost through neglect or abuse), there is no ongoing path of initiation on the Seventh Ray, the Flame of Freedom on earth is in jeopardy and the alchemy of change necessary for the golden age of Aquarius to appear will not come about. That's why our winter Stump in cities of Utah, Nevada, Arizona, Mexico, California and Portugal puts us on the road once again so that we may quicken the hearts of God's people to the name of Saint Germain and to the greatest Friend of Freedom earth has known in the last two thousand years and more.

On November 25, 1987, in Washington, D.C., Archangel Zadkiel placed before us a vision of "all of America covered by violet flame"--"the vision whereby you see what destiny America can deliver unto the nations." If this is not accomplished, Zadkiel said we will see instead "the third vision of George Washington. . . . You will see warfare and bloodshed upon this very continent and soil. . . . And you will see as hope against hope the failing of those of America to turn back that nightmare of the Great War.

"You will see, then, that the only deliverance that can come to a people so unprepared as this to face a world war is Divine Intervention. . . . Therefore, see and know, beloved, that what kind of victory shall be your own is truly your choice and choosing in this hour" (Pearls of Wisdom, vol. 30, no. 77, pp. 591, 593).

Hearing these words as I received this dictation-- even as I am also a listener--I was reinfired with Jesus' call of May 28:

Blessed hearts, I have come, then, to make a plea to you and to send my Messenger abroad across this continent for the gathering of ten thousand who will call themselves Keepers of the Flame of Life and who will understand that I, Jesus, have called them. (Kansas City, Kansas, Pearls of Wisdom, vol. 30, no. 27, p. 273)

Obedient, then, to my reason for being and yours, I am making the call for world transmutation and teaching others to do the same. One with your own striving hearts, I am keeping the vigil for Freedom and Peace on earth, and night after night delivering the message of Divine Reality as I watch the Holy Spirit quicken souls, awakening those who sleep, teaching those who are teachable how to exercise the science of the spoken Word for their own souls' liberation and for the victory of planet earth. Seeing your loving faces and feeling your support--your incomparable devotion to Saint Germain and to me personally--was and remains the treasure of the Stump experience for me.

My Beloved Sons and Daughters, there is simply no one like you on the face of the earth! Don't ever forget: you are the salt of the earth and the light of the city set on the mountain of God.

Because of You there's a song of Jesus' Love in my heart. Because of your dauntless courage I am mightily encouraged to keep on keeping on--on the stumping trail for our dearest Saint Germain.

One of the great highlights of our fall 1987 Stump was Saint Germain's delivery On Prophecy in lecture format and dictation on Saturday night, October 3, in New York City. Here the Master told America what we're going to do and what we have to do to secure our borders, our people, our cities, our military installations against that surprise Soviet first-strike attack which Saint Germain said we should be prepared for in his November 27, 1986, address. He, as well as the LORD God, whose powerful voice came upon us that night, prophesied the judgment of the moneyed interests of Wall Street:

And therefore I say, Woe! Woe! Woe!* Let the judgments descend upon those who manipulate the abundant Life of a people of God and subject them to a slavery untold far beyond that of the Egyptian taskmasters!. . .

I say unto all purveyors of drugs and all who poison the minds and souls and bodies of youth eternal everywhere:

Woe! Woe! Woe!

So the pronouncement of the judgment of Almighty God be upon you. So by the spirit of the Prophet does there descend now that karma upon those who are the destroyers in the earth!

And let the archdeceivers of the people in their nests in the nations' capitals now tremble, for the LORD God Almighty does walk the earth!

---

*The interpretation of the scriptural pronunciation of the deprecatory woes is: Let the woes of your own karma be upon you! When the woes are pronounced three times the LORD God is declaring them in the name and by the power of the Trinity--Father, Son, and Holy Spirit.

For the LORD God Almighty is come and the Divine Mother does enter and does take dominion in the Matter universe. . . .

Hear me, people of earth! I say to you, bind, then, the oppressor! For the hour is come for the judgment of the fallen ones in the earth who would push you to the brink of war and economic collapse and famine and plague. . . .

The golden-calf civilization does go down! And the Cain civilization is judged! For no longer is the Cain civilization protected by the mark of Cain. It is no more. . . .

Therefore, let them tremble! For I come into their citadel of international power and moneyed interests. And I AM, of the LORD God, do declare unto you that through my Archangels they shall know the judgment. (Pearls of Wisdom, vol. 30, no. 55, pp. 485–86, 487, 488)

With scarcely a delay factor from the spoken Word from on high to the crystallization of these judgments, on October 6 the Dow Jones Industrial Average fell a record 91.55 points. In fact, the two weeks following his dictation the Dow registered back-to-back its two biggest weekly declines, falling a record 158 points October 5–9 and then dropping another 235 points October 12–16. Then on "Black Monday," October 19, the market crashed. The Dow fell more than 508 points--the largest decline since the crash of October 29, 1929, that had signaled the onset of the Great Depression.

That night Vesta, dictating in Toledo, prophesied regarding the stock market, "Yes, there can be a rise again, beloved, but never as steady as before. Thus, the sudden setbacks are experienced. Prepare, then. . ." (Pearls of Wisdom, vol. 30, no. 65, p. 545). Since then the market has been extremely volatile, registering dramatic rallies and precipitous declines.

The dictation of El Morya delivered in New York the night before Saint Germain's had given us a solemn warning that "ere twenty-four months have passed,. . . this nation must have the capacity to turn back any and all missiles, warheads incoming whether by intent or by accident. Where there is no defense you invite the bear into your own haven. . . . Ere twenty-four months pass, beloved, there shall be a reckoning and a confrontation unless something is done" (Pearls of Wisdom, vol. 30, no. 54, pp. 474, 480).

Something can still be done, beloved, but it's going to take all of our hearts' decree power to break the stranglehold the International Capitalist/Communist Conspiracy has on the government, the economy and the people of America.

Here is what we can do. There is still time if we can mobilize our people to mobilize our leaders. Since in America, the leaders follow the people instead of the other way around!

1) First and foremost, we can deploy defenses for our ICBMs, submarine and bomber bases and command, control and communications facilities within 24 months. These would be low-tech defenses such as swarmjets and high-speed GAU-8 Gatling-type machine guns. The swarmjet fires a cloud of one-inch rockets to destroy a warhead three-fifths of a mile from its target. It is 90 percent effective against the first three warheads coming into range. The GAU-8 Gatling-type machine gun has already been tested successfully against a simulated Soviet warhead.

2) We can deploy defenses for our military bases and cities within three to five years.

These would be systems which use nearly available technology like the Exoatmospheric Reentry Vehicle Interceptor Subsystem (ERIS) and the High Endoatmospheric Defense Interceptor (HEDI). ERIS would use the old Safeguard site at Grand Forks, North Dakota, and consist of 10,000 interceptor missiles. These non-nuclear interceptors would be fired out into space to destroy a warhead outside the atmosphere. Since ERIS has such a long reach, it could defend much of North America from a single site.

We need 3,000 HEDI interceptors which can be deployed on trucks together with radar and power generators. These would be positioned around key targets. HEDI interceptors are non-nuclear missiles which fly at more than six times the speed of sound to destroy warheads after they enter the atmosphere. Your city could have its own HEDI system defending it. Since they could be launched directly from their trucks and the Soviets couldn't target them, they would make the Soviets think twice about launching a first strike.

(The prevailing MAD doctrine of Mutual Assured Destruction holds that defenses make war more likely because they make the person who has them more confident and thus more likely to attack. It says that without defenses, neither side will launch a first strike because they are afraid of retaliation upon their cities and people. But, as I have shown in my Saint Germain On Prophecy lectures, the Soviets are defending their people and their missiles. Therefore, MAD is no longer valid and we are in danger.)

3) **We can deploy a non-nuclear, space-based Kinetic-Kill Vehicle (KKV) system consisting of 2,000 satellites in five to seven years.** This would be 50 to 70 percent effective against a full-scale attack of intercontinental ballistic missiles (ICBMs). It could stop an accidental launch fired either by us or the Soviets. It is non-nuclear and could harm no one.

Each satellite in the KKV system carries anti-missile rockets and a gun which fires a cloud of pellets into the path of an ICBM. Since missiles are fragile, even one hole punched in the skin would mean that the missile would self-destruct upon reentering the atmosphere. These satellites would be incapable of harming anyone on the ground or of attacking a missile before it exited the atmosphere. Thus, any Soviet claims that a KKV is an offensive weapon are false.

4) **This low-tech strategic defense would cost $121 billion. It can be fully in place by 1994.** Its three layers would be 93 percent effective against a Soviet attack of 10,000 warheads and 100,000 decoys, according to a study by the George C. Marshall Institute.

5) **We can install civil defense for every American at a minimum cost of $75 billion.**

In order for a strategic defense system to be legal under existing agreements with the Soviet Union, the United States must immediately:

a. Announce its intention to withdraw from the 1972 ABM Treaty within the prescribed six-month time limit due to repeated Soviet violations of its spirit and letter.

b. Repudiate the understanding between United States Secretary of State George Shultz and Soviet Foreign Minister Eduard Shevardnadze that the United States would abide by the ABM Treaty for an undisclosed period of time, probably seven years.

Thus, the warnings, the admonishments, the prophecy, the teaching, the comfort and consolation continued night after night throughout the fall as we stumped the East Coast and Midwest until the fateful moment when in almost disbelief we heard Saint Germain announce his withdrawal from the nation's capital.

Stunned and grieved, Keepers of the Flame in attendance determined to continue their prayer vigil throughout Monday at the Rakoczy Mansion, the Washington, D.C., Teaching Center. But by midnight Monday, November 30, his withdrawal was complete.

Had there been another time in the history of our memory, our association with the Knight Commander that he was so felt by his absence? It was as though all at once we suddenly knew just who and what he was and is--by his absence, by the nonpresence of that spirit and light and lilt and joy and fiery devotion to freedom in Washington. How we have come to take for granted the Spirit of the LORD embodied in Saint Germain as something that is just the quality of American life, the vibration that is everywhere apparent in every nook and cranny of nature and our city streets.

Prior to Saint Germain's dictation at the Capital Hilton, there was not a place you could go in the United States of America or her territories and possessions where you couldn't meet Saint Germain face to face, where the very soil wouldn't rise in the violet flame to greet his every footstep.

It dawned on me twenty-four hours later. Saint Germain had left the city because the nation through her president had chosen Mikhail Gorbachev in his stead; had chosen to dialogue with the false hierarchy of Antichrist to sign a treaty for the removal of the best defense and the best deterrent Europe will ever have against nuclear blackmail or conventional, chemical and biological warfare waged by invading Warsaw Pact land forces; had chosen to deny substantial aid to the Contras, his freedom fighters, blessed hearts of the Virgin Mary in Central America, and to give to the Communist/Soviet-backed Sandinista regime the benefit of the doubt in their peace ovations, buying them time to regroup and raise up a 600,000-man army as Ortega has vowed to do.

Clearly, the nation had not chosen Saint Germain, his flame, his solution--his heart. He donned his purple cape, wrapped it around himself and was seen leaving the city-- walking toward the Northern Rockies and a citadel of freedom where the vote of confidence in his leadership for America and Aquarius is unanimous.

The Master had told us that Holy Amethyst with violet flame angels, priests and priestesses of the Seventh Ray would be moving about the city igniting violet flame camp-fires as the sign of the "hundred circling camps" for "a consuming action and a quickening of souls." He said that many of the Hierarchy, ascended and unascended, had volunteered to remain in the city and keep the vigil in his stead, including the Ascended Master Godfre, who on July 14, 1987, announced in Washington that he would ride his white horse up and down the streets of the capital hour by hour speaking to the people. But though we were comforted by ten thousand-times-ten thousand legions of angels led by the Lord Christ moving with legions of Sanat Kumara, the Ancient of Days, who also marched through the city, without Saint Germain it just wasn't the same.

On December 8, 1987, as the nation watched, the General Secretary of the Soviet Communist Party received a twenty-one-gun salute on the south lawn of the White House. As the Army Old Guard Fife and Drum Corps played for Mikhail Gorbachev and his entourage, we saw not one but two betrayers of our national identity--glad-handing, making speeches and signing away America's future and her destiny in the conquest of time and space.

For it is not only the enemy who speaks peace but continues to arm while preparing to strike that is the threat-- but it is also the head of state who, setting aside our own military and strategic preparedness, gives the enemy all of the ground and the rope and the technology and the money and the moral support that allows him to achieve his ends! He, too, as the accomplice in this Great Deceit, is the greatest enemy the nation has ever known since the discovery of America by Christopher Columbus (Saint Germain) and the anointing of our first president, George Washington, by none other than that same blessed Brother of Light.

As I write this letter to you at Saint Germain's altar, where I pray for you daily, beloved, I am moved to tears, which blur the image of the Master that hangs on the wall above his amethyst crystal. The pain in my heart and the grief that I have at once for our beloved Saint Germain, for you who are his dearest friends on earth, for the nation America that is still the hope of Hierarchy--the hope of all oppressed peoples of the world and of all who have given their lives for the cause of freedom--is profound and beyond words.

Every now and then when I contemplate the long history that has brought us to this hour, I experience this agony of soul. But day by day and hour by hour, my choice is to transmute this "world pain" and to channel it into a fiercely determined stand for you and for Saint Germain and the cause to which we have pledged ourselves with every breath and hour of opportunity that Life still holds out for us.

Yes, beloved, the Life who is God still affords us a supreme opportunity and that indeed by the grace of Saint Germain and his beloved twin flame, Portia. They have not cried halt nor retreat nor have they condemned any one of us for our mistakes or errors or human foibles, but they have called all Lightbearers of the world to unite and defeat the forces of tyranny and Death and Hell and the karma being delivered by the Four Horsemen who stalk the planet, the plains and the city streets.

As I pointed out in my "Halloween Prophecy" delivered in Minneapolis, there will be a conjunction of Mars, Saturn, Uranus, and Neptune in Capricorn during the last week of February. I would like to remind you that this conjunction signals the formal starting point of a period of upheaval and change on the planet.

This is a time when we can expect that the era of financial expansion related to oil and international finance will come to a halt and, with the exception of one last brief expansionary period, national economies, including our own, are likely to contract. The predictions of planetary karma and the Four Horsemen are that nations will become conservative and reactionary, that there will be massive debt liquidation, and that a pessimistic mood will sweep the earth. Only the Word, The Faithful and True and his armies can deliver us--but our deliverance will come to pass only if we make the call and renew that call DAILY.

Due to a number of karmic factors--including that which is written in the skies in this Capricorn conjunction and the transit of Pluto in Scorpio in close contact to the United States' and Soviet Union's Sun--1988 to 1992 will be a time of karmic summing up. During this period we are likely to see the karma of persons and nations manifest as the disruption or dissolution of economic and political systems. We're likely to see revolution, major cataclysm, and war.

If ever there was a time to mount our forces in violet flame and Astrea decrees, in the giving of the Archangel

Michael Rosary and Jesus' Watch, beloved of my heart, that time is now--today, not tomorrow!

As Omri-Tas told us on January 1, 1988:

> That which could precipitate untimely war or cataclysm or economic collapse is the absence of violet flame in the earth. . . . By that increase of the violet flame in all who are of the issue of God, it is our vision and our determination that planet earth shall have a greater momentum of the violet flame to hold up "the tent of America," to hold up the nations. (Royal Teton Ranch, Pearls of Wisdom, vol. 31, no. 3, pp. 30, 28)

As we daily watch the decisions of our nation's leadership move us inexorably toward that confrontation with the planetary karma of the fallen angels and of the whole world that has gone after their false prophecy, I can hardly believe, much less accept, that what is taking place before our very eyes is actually happening in our lifetime--while we are in embodiment, yes, while we occupy space and time on earth and claim our divine inheritance as well as our human rights.

We see the mujahidin poised to drive the Soviet Union out of Afghanistan and our government willfully believing the lie that the Soviets would really like to leave--if only the United States would agree to stop aiding the freedom fighters. And our government is prepared to comply. Nasra Dullah, a Soviet soldier who joined the freedom fighters, says that "Mikhail Gorbachev is just talking. He is just the same as Joseph Stalin was." And the mujahidin know it.

If the Soviet Union wants to leave Afghanistan, all they have to do is pack up and go home. They do not need U.S. assistance to help them "save face" before they withdraw, as has been suggested to some of our naive diplomats. But the Afghans do need our full support and continuing supply of arms just to be sure those Soviet rascals don't move back in after a mock retreat like the stunt they pulled in the takeover of Hungary in 1956. You may recall that following the Hungarian uprising of October 23, 1956, the Soviets withdrew their troops to the frontier, signed an armistice, and called a meeting to negotiate the final withdrawal of their troops from Hungary. Then they arrested the Hungarian diplomats who were to negotiate the withdrawal and on the night of November 3–4 invaded Hungary with five thousand tanks and a quarter of a million troops!

How's that for the promise of peace and the kiss of death! Our leaders don't want to know the Truth. All they care about is their place in history. Well, they shall have it! But not as they have plotted it. "For it shall come to pass. . . . thus saith the LORD. God is not mocked: for whatsoever a man soweth that shall he also reap!"

We see Nicaragua at <u>the</u> turning point. The Sandinista economy is in shambles. There are such serious shortages that the people almost cannot live. It is fast becoming a revolutionary situation. The people generally hold the Sandinistas responsible for the state of the economy. At the same time, the Contras are having enough successes in the field so that the Sandinistas have done something they vowed never to do-- negotiate directly with the Contras. Should the Contras press ahead--and receive adequate military, economic, and diplomatic support--they could lead a popular uprising that would topple the Sandinistas <u>and</u> consolidate the revolution for freedom begun in Nicaragua in 1979.

But President Reagan just asked Congress for a measly $36 million in aid for the Contras, of which a mere $3.6 million is slated for military aid. Meanwhile, in the first half of 1987 the Soviets shipped $300 million worth of military goods to Managua and shipments are continuing. Thus, we may soon see the Sandinistas complete their planned expansion of their army to 600,000 soldiers! If that happens, we can anticipate war and revolution sweeping onto American soil-- just as Saint Germain has prophesied.

<u>Now is the acceptable time</u> to make Saint Germain's words come true:

I pray the Father of all victory and light and freedom, come swiftly, then, to bind the spoilers in North and South America! Come quickly, then, and let the fire of freedom emerge in the hearts of those who dare to challenge tyranny, dictatorship and murder in Nicaragua!

O God, deliver these, as they are as the early American patriots taking upon themselves the responsibility to defend a nation against the usurpers of the seat of God-government that belongs to the people, is of and by the people of Nicaragua, who demand their freedom this day. And I say, they shall have it!

And I challenge <u>you</u>, Keepers of the Flame, to prove me right. I challenge <u>you</u> as prophets in the earth this day. For my mantle of prophecy descends upon you now, beloved. Seize it. Wear it. Use it. For this nation must be filled with the prophets of the Almighty whose prophesying is in the affirmation of the prophecy itself.

To affirm the victory is a fiat of the LORD's prophecy. Therefore, let those who dare, go, then, to the side of those freedom fighters and say at their side the rosary to Archangel Michael. Let those who dare, go in their finer bodies as others may go in the physical. (July 4, 1986, Camelot, Los Angeles; <u>Pearls of Wisdom,</u> vol. 29, no. 64, p. 558)

<u>Now is the acceptable time</u> to start a violet flame bonfire in the center of Managua and Washington, D.C.--and in the hearts of the Contras and all Lightbearers of Central America!

Keepers of the Flame--Our voices can be instruments of God's power if we raise them, if we raise them, <u>if we raise them</u> on high and give a mighty shout to the Hosts of the LORD to: <u>Charge, Charge, Charge and Let Victory Be Proclaimed!</u>

Let's do it. It's now or never!

The forces of Antichrist have an agenda, Alpha has dictated to us his agenda, but the leadership of America and the free world have none. They have failed to heed the prophet Aleksandr Solzhenitsyn and the countless defectors who have come forth out of the Soviet Union, the Eastern bloc and even the South American Marxist regimes to tell us exactly what the program and the timetable is for planetary takeover nation by nation by the forces of World Communism who are fully supplied and financially underwritten by Western capitalists with <u>our</u> money, <u>our</u> industry, <u>our</u> labor of love for <u>our</u> nation--and by the light that flows from our hearts as the blood of Christ.

Gen. Maj. Jan Sejna, the highest-ranking Communist military figure ever to defect, was my guest on Summit University Forum during our Thanksgiving seminar in Washington, D.C. I had been waiting to interview him for four years and it was the most astounding Summit University Forum of my entire career. (This unbelievable 4-3/4 hour interview is now available on three videocassettes, $59.95, and three audiocassettes, $19.50, and it should be shouted from the housetops.)

Along with Dr. Joseph Douglass, Jr., a leading expert on national security, General Sejna outlined the Soviets' long-range strategic plan whose centerpiece is a surprise nuclear attack on the United States. During the interview General Sejna told us bluntly: "The major target was, is, and will be the United States. Because, as Khrushchev told us--and they repeat this--the United States is the major stone in the way of Communism. Once the stone is away, as Khrushchev said, the door for Communism in Europe and elsewhere is open."

General Sejna told a rapt audience at the Capital Hilton that at the start of the nuclear age Soviet military preparations were defensive in nature because they lacked the strength for offensive operations against the United States. The turning point came in 1963 as the Soviet nuclear forces became more powerful. "Since then," said Sejna, "everything has been prepared for a surprise [nuclear] attack" on the United States.

Dr. Douglass, after an exhaustive study of Soviet military literature, has come to the same conclusion. "I think General Sejna certainly captured the essence of their strategy when he said their strategy is to strike first," said Douglass. "The Soviets really focus on preparing to fight and win a nuclear war. There's no question about it. . . . When you look at nuclear war and the Soviet approach to war, it's going to be very different from what people in the West see and think about. It is extremely serious. The Soviets believe it is possible to win a nuclear war. . . . The objective in war--and we are in a sense at war today--is to get the other side to relax its preparedness, to disarm."

Saint Germain, Send Violet Flame to All Life on Earth!

What will it take to stop this awful nightmare that gets more awful by the day as we have to listen to the sheer idiocy and hypocrisy that comes out of the mouth of our leaders, our congressmen and, yes, those unmentionable, unbelievably boring, ill-equipped, ill-prepared presidential candidates?

I can tell you that I don't know what it will take to turn around the nation and the nations. I don't know what sword can cut the Gordian knot that the false hierarchy is tying as a noose around the neck of the American people, but I do know that I for one, and each one of us for one, must daily give the allness of our life, our strength, our energy, our endowed genius and creativity to the reversing of the tide of this conspiracy of Darkness that is closing in.

To "spend and be spent," as the apostle Paul said describing his daily offering of himself to God, to give what we are and what we have in a supreme effort, to know that we have given the last drop of life that is ours to give, to do this, to do this is the only way that we can truly know whether the measure of our individual life's contribution multiplied by the gift of each one of us and squared by the Law of the One can or could have made the difference.

We are called to be intercessors between God's people and the rising levels of planetary karma. Our father Abraham was also called to be the intercessor before the Lightbearers of his time. Out of his own heart he said to the LORD who had spoken to him of the impending destruction of Sodom and Gomorrah, "Wilt thou also destroy the righteous with the wicked?. . . Wilt thou also destroy and not spare the place for the fifty righteous that are therein. . . . Shall not the Judge of all the earth do right?"

And it is written in Genesis 18 that the LORD said, "If I find in Sodom fifty righteous within the city, then I will spare all the place for their sakes."

But Abraham was worried. Suppose five of the fifty should be wanting? Suppose only forty would be found there or thirty or twenty or ten? What would it take to save the wicked cities of the plain taken over to lust, wantonness, the perversion of the life-force and the idolatry of aliens (the false gods of the UFO), the cities of sorcery and incantation, of communing with foul spirits, rife with the perversions of the Seventh Ray and the Seventh Ray dispensations which God was ready to deliver to a people in that hour as he is ready to deliver them to us today? Truly the cities of the earth in many quarters are no different today than Sodom and Gomorrah and some are worse. The same sins of Atlantis are to be found in the cities of our nation and every nation.

And did not the Great Divine Director tell us in 1966 that the accumulation of darkness "has risen higher than ever before in history. In fact, it was only seventy-five percent this high when the decision was made to overthrow in the time of Noah the civilizations then existing" (Los Angeles, Pearls of Wisdom, vol. 12, p. 263). Serapis Bey told us on November 1, 1987, "The abuses of this light [of the base-of-the-spine chakra] have reached a level beyond the abuses that were practiced against the Divine Mother both on Lemuria and in Atlantis" (Minneapolis, Pearls of Wisdom, vol. 30, no. 75, p. 583).

And on January 3 of this year Archangel Michael said, "I must repeat to you the warning that has been given: the year opens with ten times that darkness of the latter. And how do we find you? We find you overcome by that darkness instead of piercing the veil, and not in the realization that when the birds of the dawn appear and the sun does crest the land that is the hour to be in invocation before your God" (Royal Teton Ranch, Pearls of Wisdom, vol. 31, no. 8).

Even so, the LORD gave his word to Abraham, "I will not destroy it for ten's sake." But it came to pass that the emissaries of the LORD who encountered the wickedness of the men of the city at Lot's door pronounced the judgment: "We will destroy this place, because the cry of them is waxen great before the face of the LORD; and the LORD hath sent us to destroy it" (Gen. 19:13). And so we read that the LORD rained upon Sodom and Gomorrah "brimstone and fire" from the LORD out of heaven "and he overthrew those cities, and all the plain, and all the inhabitants of the cities, and that which grew upon the ground...."

The akashic records show, Mark Prophet taught, and Zecharia Sitchin has confirmed that Sodom and Gomorrah were destroyed by nuclear weapons unleashed at the hand of the alien gods, allowed by the Law and the LORD; for the wickedness of men's hearts and deeds did not allow the intercession of Almighty God before the conspiracy of the gods--even when that conspiracy was directed against God's own people. Four people were escorted out of the city by the LORD's emissaries--Lot, his wife and two daughters. Even his sons-in-law did not heed him.

Keepers of the Flame, thank God we are not yet at this point of the reckoning--the reckoning of accounts by the Lords of Karma of the evil of the fallen angels in our midst. Thank God for the intercessions and dispensations that give us yet time and space to act decisively.

Because Saint Germain knows the modus operandi of these false hierarchies, he has explained to us that when the enemies of Christ see that the enlightenment of the people is nigh at hand, they attempt to precipitate darkness even before the karmic due date. This he explained in his November 27, 1986, dictation. He spoke of the unpredictability of the sinister force when confronted by the light and why he was assigning to us his angels to warn and direct us personally even as the angel of the LORD also came to him and told him to take the child and the mother to flee into Egypt, saying:

Do you understand, beloved, that this x-factor is the reason that you cannot depend upon preestablished dates but only upon the angel of the LORD who also came to me? And when he told me to take the Child and the Mother to flee into Egypt, so we left immediately.

I, therefore, Saint Germain, assign to your heart, to the head of every household, to the mother, and even to the child, my angels who will warn and direct you personally, Keepers of the Flame. These are sent to those who are loyal to God, who have become a part of this fraternity that I have long desired to see in every nation.

Beloved ones, angels may knock but you may not hear if you are surfeited in noise, if you allow yourselves to be tossed and tumbled by responsibilities or interruptions. Therefore, listen. You must take fifteen minutes before retiring at night, establish the circle of fire round the place where you rest. Give certain decrees and let all the house be silent as you meditate without interruption upon Almighty God, your Mighty I AM Presence.

Then call to me. Let my angels deliver you to the Royal Teton Retreat, where you may be instructed. Then take note, upon awakening, of the first voices, the first messages that come into your mind. Try the spirits, of course, and always, but be attentive. For a thousand angels cannot alert you to your destiny if you are not tuned in, if you are not listening.

Let your aura be an electromagnetic field of the Seventh Ray. For in the Seventh Ray violet flame is the alchemy of communication between octaves. Let your aura be sealed by the tube of light and the action of Archangel Michael. Let your receptivity be pure because your heart is pure. Inordinate desire for money or things or other distractions clouds the reasoning of the Logos within you. Thus, the mind that is at peace with God, unattached to the consequences of the human and willing to follow when called, will surely hear my angels.

Beloved ones, cast out fear and doubt. Cast out whatever is the prevention of thy Godhood. Let God be your Guru. But remember this--that the I AM THAT I AM is self-revealed in the course of events and in his movement through the Messenger of God. Therefore, do not <u>ask</u> the Messenger but <u>watch</u> the Messenger. Then understand how your priorities may be parallel. I can tell you, beloved, that the movement of the Messenger to the mountain of God is, in fact, contrary to that which she would choose to do, which would be to go out into all the world and preach again and again this Teaching.

And therefore, sometimes you must understand that the pure reason of God for your life may not be in agreement with your heart's desirings or inclinations. And the key, beloved, is the law of cycles. Thus Ecclesiastes wrote that there is a time to sow, a time to reap, a time to live and a time to die. There is a time to take up arms and a time to lay down arms, a time to marry and be with child and a time to remain in the holiness of God for a purpose. All things in their season will lead you to the harvest of a life that has been balanced in all equations. (Los Angeles, <u>Pearls of Wisdom,</u> vol. 29, no. 75, pp. 654–56)

Beloved, all of the above and all that I wrote to you in my letter of September 18, 1987, concerning my Stump to the cities of America is why I'm on the road again stumping for Saint Germain's Revolution in Higher Consciousness.

Therefore, I'm writing to ask you for your dynamic decrees offered on behalf of the Lightbearers of the cities and states and countries wheresoever the LORD does go before us in our mission.

I'm asking you to keep the vigil with me in your town and the towns near you and to ardently keep the flame for the cities where we have already stumped together and for future cities and towns of North America where I may be called to come by Saint Germain because there be found there, "peradventure, ten righteous" who are rightly dividing the word of Truth, rightly applying the Law of the One in the exercise of the science of the spoken Word for the cause of Saint Germain and America's freedom continuing, that she might fulfill her destiny on behalf of all nations of the earth.

I am also asking you to lay upon Saint Germain's altar at the Inner Retreat at least a $33 love offering as your heart's alchemy for the Stump and pray that it might be multiplied by the power of the ten thousand times ten thousand--by grace, by intercession and by the dispensations from on high to keep open the door for God's divine plan to be fulfilled through many stalwart souls who see and know the right but have been rendered powerless to do anything about the dark ones--because they have not and know not the Lost Teachings of our Lord and Saviour Jesus Christ or the science of invocation through the name of God I AM THAT I AM.

Therefore, to assist you to keep the flame for Saint Germain, to attune with Saint Germain's angels whom he has assigned to you, to assist you in your spiritual and physical preparations and to be counted as the righteous of God on earth, I have prepared for you with my beloved staff the first 93-minute cassette of violet flame songs and decrees as I promised Saint Germain and you that I would do immediately following the New Year's conference.

Whether or not you send me your alchemical $33 or more, I am committed unconditionally to you--to see to it that this tape (with the printed words to all of the songs and decrees that are on it) is in your hands just as soon as they can be duplicated, printed, and mailed. This tape can be used by anyone in the whole wide world--regardless of their church affiliation or path or guru. Saint Germain belongs to everyone! Everyone is entitled to know him, to love him, and to receive his help in time of trouble! Therefore, all of the decrees are simply given, slowly with depth of feeling and good articulation, recited at King Arthur's Court--our temporary chapel at the ranch (so named by Lanello in his Christmas dictation).

That you should offer these decrees and songs daily from your heart directly to the heart of Saint Germain to use your love and devotion and energy for the saving of opportunity for America is my desire and my imploring to you in this hour. Therefore, I shall not ask but I shall without shame beg you. I shall not tell you, but without equivocation I will by the mantle of the Guru command you in the name of Christ to decree and sing and pray on your knees with this tape daily for thirty-three days for the alchemy of America's Great Awakening and for the victory of God in your own private life and karmic circumstance.

This prayer vigil shall be dedicated to your personal divine plan and to our stumping until we have secured those ten thousand new Keepers of the Flame which beloved Jesus called for on May 28, 1987. You will rejoice with me to know that approximately 11 percent of that figure have joined the fraternity since Jesus called! Praise the LORD and Hallelujah, Amen!

If the percentages invoked by Abraham are any gauge, then we know that the LORD would have spared Sodom and Gomorrah for one-fifth of the number proposed by Abraham-- ten out of fifty. We should then mount our efforts and not rest until we see one-fifth of ten thousand securely ensconced on their violet flame lotus pad offering to qualify the crystal stream of life flowing over their crystal cords as a stream of violet flame that shall conjoin with all other streams flowing from the hearts of the Lightbearers of the world who similarly pledge to this thirty-three-day spiral of victory for Saint Germain.

Thus, we shall visualize a mighty river--truly the River of Life--moving through America, even as the Great Mother Ganges has flowed through India for thousands of years, delivering the blessings of the Divine Mother to her people. And we won't stop till the "new" ten thousand added to the "old" Keepers of the Flame are marching with The Faithful and True and his armies across the nations!

The decrees and songs on this cassette are given exactly as I would lead them for brand-new people who might walk into my lectures off the street never having heard of Saint Germain or the violet flame. They are excellent for children of all ages, from tiny newborns to full adulthood, and for members of your family or your friends whom you may invite to pray with you for the LORD's emissaries, his mighty Archangels and seraphim and cherubim, to come to our aid.

But most of all, the measured, heartfelt and devotional tone of these calls offered with strength and expression and a genuine communion with all of the saints robed in white who comprise the entire Spirit of the Great White Brotherhood is good for Keepers of the Flame and Lightbearers of long standing who are accustomed to give decrees rapidly and by force of habit may have lost the connection to each precious word that is a cup of light in our songs and decrees--who in their fiery zeal may have forgotten what it is like to savor each and every phrase as the sweet fruits of the Buddha and to use the cadences of the decrees to carry your inmost thoughts and feelings, your soul's confession and your spirit's yearning to see God face to face, to talk with Him and hear His Word spoken on the return current of your love.

Although it is well to be able to sit still and offer a joyous violet flame song and decree session without interruption and in full concentration, <u>one should not fail to miss one's daily devotions with the Seventh-Ray Masters for want of time.</u> You can decree and sing along with these tapes to fulfill Saint Germain's request that you make a fifteen-minute preparation for retiring at night to establish the circle of fire around the place where you rest. You can sing along and decree along while preparing for your day in the morning, in your car on the way to work or on errands, on headsets while you exercise or use public transportation or perform routine chores, et cetera.

The elementals and nature spirits love to decree with you and they will gather with your violet flame angels wherever and whenever you pause even for a fifteen-minute slice of the tape. Fifteen minutes six times a day is another way of approaching the fulfillment of your thirty-three-day alchemy. (After all, even the Moslems pray five times a day! Can we who have been given so great a salvation do any less?)

What I hope to accomplish with this prayer vigil is an experiment in the flame of Aquarius whereby all of us can see and know at the end of that thirty-three-day period just what such a concerted effort, just what such a mandate from our hearts unto the LORD can bring to bear upon the national and international scene. <u>If we expect change, we have to be the instruments of change.</u> If we want greater dispensations from the Great White Brotherhood at this year's Fourth of July conference, then we have to give the energy and the devotion on time and ahead of time. We must be the spirit sparks that ignite the bonfires of dispensation on the altars of the LORD-- in heaven as well as on earth.

I repeat: these violet flame tapes are for everyone, not just members of the Keepers of the Flame Fraternity or those affiliated with our organization. Saint Germain and his gift of the violet flame to the people of planet earth is the sign of Aquarius sent and sealed and delivered by the Seventh Angel whose coming is made known to us in Revelation 10:7, of whom it was prophesied by Jesus through his angel to his servant John: "When he shall begin to sound, the mystery of God should be finished, as he hath declared to his servants the prophets."

The Seventh Angel, Saint Germain, is sounding in the land not only through his dictations delivered through his servants "the Prophets" as we are called to be his Two Witnesses in this era but also through each and every one of you! Each time you sound the Word, each time you decree in the name of God I AM, each time you sound the AUM or sing a song of the violet flame, you are the instrument and the voice of the Seventh Angel. And as he is sounding in the earth through us, so the acceleration of the prophecy may be fulfilled that the mysteries of God may be finished.

On May 30, 1987, Saint Germain said:

I AM hopeful, in the profoundest sense of the word, that you will hear my cry and know this: that God our Father has truly entrusted to my heart an opportunity to save this nation under God, not I alone but many Masters of Light. There is a special, special blessing he gives to my heart that is a catalyst and necessary, and yet I cannot bring it forth without friends on earth. . . .

The chime of an ancient bell now sounds. One of my angels called by Portia does begin this chiming. It will sound in the ear of every true son and daughter of Liberty as though he or she does hear a liberty bell that long ago rang on other spheres. This chiming, beloved, shall continue as the inner Call. And if it stop its chiming, beloved, Cosmos shall know that I, Saint Germain, have no longer opportunity to rescue the Lightbearer.

Therefore, beloved, let the giving of the violet flame on behalf of those who respond and hear be continuous as a vigil unto the seventh age. So long as there are those who respond, even a single heart reciting my violet flame mantra in each twenty-four-hour cycle, Opportunity's door shall remain open and the chime shall be heard. (Kansas City, Kansas, Pearls of Wisdom, vol. 30, no. 29, pp. 291–92)

When you sing with the violet flame angels our song "O Saint Germain, Send Violet Flame," you will hear the chime we are sounding in honor of the perpetual chiming of the ancient bell. May you let it resound through your chakras, even as it is heard in the great cathedrals.

To all of you who lovingly respond to my call to keep the thirty-three-day vigil with Mother Liberty and Saint Germain for America, for the Lightbearers of the world and for the cutting free of Jesus' ten thousand Keepers of the Flame, to you who support our stumping for the Coming Revolution this winter with a $33 love offering--and never ending until the victory--I will automatically send you the second 90-plus-minute violet flame song and decree tape.

When you receive it, you will then have twice as many decrees and songs to choose from and you can alternate the two cassettes for Seventh Ray meditations on the Seventh-Ray Masters in your group get-togethers. These tapes will also suffice for new people's Saturday night Saint Germain services and for those who are not able to attend but desire to keep the Saturday night vigil at home. Each cassette will be complete in itself with a folder containing all the words to all the songs and decrees on it, and when we have finally finished the number of cassettes planned we will put all of the words into a single booklet.

Thus, from the very first cassette for new people you may wish to send these cassettes to your new-age friends. If you wish to purchase them in quantity, they will be 33 percent off for ten or more ($3.95 each) with a price break for quantities of the booklets. And so we multiply our devotions and our actions as sponsors of Saint Germain's Stump to America--by the sound of the Word!

It is my hope that you will give these songs and decrees with the goal of memorizing them--every single word emblazoned upon the atoms and cells, even the tiny electrons and the nuclei of atoms, upon the brain and central nervous system so that all of your being may truly become that "pillar of fire" Saint Germain called us to be. When you know these songs and decrees by heart, the violet singing flame will sing in you all the day and through the night. Even so, as you give the mantra, beloved, you become the mantra and the mantra becomes you!

Beloved Saint Germain's decrees are truly his mandate to the people of earth. Let us become the mandate and let others receive freely of the Master's lifestream, of his River of Life, even as we make ourselves the instruments and the fulfillment yet in this day and age of Saint Germain's dream for America. Above all, let us not forget his words of November 27, 1986:

> Seek ye first the kingdom of God and his righteousness. Seek ye first to live, to endure, to survive the age. And know that it is possible to live through the worst of prophecy.
>
> I may speak it, but I am not the origin of prophecy! Every living soul upon this earth and fallen angels and godless ones--all are harbingers of that which must descend. For the law of karma is inexorable, irrevocable, <u>saving where the violet flame, the sacred fire, does consume it.</u>
>
> Thus, the LORD has said, "Be pillars of fire." (<u>Pearls of Wisdom,</u> vol. 29, no. 75, p. 648)

In closing, I would like to express my supreme gratitude to all Keepers of the Flame who made possible by hard work and joy-filled sacrifice the many victories of our East Coast Stump and our New York and Washington seminars. To all of you who have been working for many weeks now to prepare Utah, Nevada, Arizona, Mexico, California and Portugal for our coming, I know what it takes to get ready for the coming of the Lightbearers and all of the countless details that go into making our Stumps the great experience in higher consciousness that they are for the many strangers who come to our gates who are undoubtedly angels, whom it is our privilege "to entertain" (Heb. 13:2).

I wish to thank all of you who contributed your $33 alchemy in 1987. Your hearts' love offerings made all the difference in our being able to break even on our mission. Moreover, I wish to say a heartfelt thanks for your receiving and giving "Watch With Me," Jesus' Vigil of the Hours. This vigil truly brightened up the Christmas and New Year's season and left in you an extra-special fire from Jesus' heart, a diamond that sparkles and twinkles at me as I think of you in my meditations and see you across the miles! I look forward to receiving your mail recounting the healings and miracles and victories that have taken place in your life already as the result of your keeping the watch.

As beloved Omri-Tas recounts in his New Year's Day dictation, I answered his call in preparation for his coming and assembled upon our new altar at King Arthur's Court large amethyst crystals which were lined up, as he says, like silent sentinels throughout the New Year's Retreat together with their elementals. These crystal "chalices" were filled with the light and forcefield of a conference and taken home by Keepers of the Flame on condition that they place the crystal on an altar dedicated to the Great White Brotherhood, on which the violet flame crystal would be the centerpiece, "a living crystal chalice," with the focus of the Chart of the I AM Presence and the portraits of Jesus and Saint Germain as well as the image of the Two Witnesses. Each one then can add his own individual choice of favorite saints or statues such as one of the Lord of the World.

I'm happy to tell you that we have replenished our supply of most magnificent violet flame amethyst crystal from Seventh Ray focuses of South America and therefore will have these available at the San Francisco seminar for Keepers of the Flame. I'm looking forward to seeing a thousand stalwart souls in San Francisco, and many angels and elementals joining the throng of our voices enveloped in violet flame.

Please be sure to come! For although I would like to return to California again, I have a feeling that I will not be returning for some time. This is an opportunity to conclude our Lemurian cycles, our Lemurian karma, and to fulfill the fountain of light of Camelot by sending the call to all Light-bearers who still have not heard the message of their I AM Presence and the path of their reunion with God.

The signs of alchemical change from the temples of Lemuria were noted in the dictations of the New Year's Retreat. Surya told us on January 2: "In the great depths of the Pacific Ocean there is a grand processioning this night as ancient ones, priests of the sacred fire, walk sandaled and robed in white the breadth and length of the Pacific Basin under the sea on what was once Lemuria. Blessed ones, it is an ancient ceremony rekindled by great Masters of Light, their adepts and chelas. . . . Much activity does take place at inner levels on planet earth for the sealing, for the saving, for the calling Home of souls of Light for the finishing in order that new beginnings might begin" (Royal Teton Ranch, Pearls of Wisdom, vol. 31, no. 5, p. 49).

Earlier that day Sanat Kumara announced "the with-drawal of the Brotherhood of Mount Shasta from the retreat physical of Mount Shasta. This entire brotherhood, therefore, does withdraw and does transfer their forcefield and focus both in[to] the Grand Teton and in[to] another area of the

Northern Rockies. Blessed hearts, this announcement is a sign unto you and let it be a sign unto every heart and let it be known from within. I give you, therefore, this report that you might accommodate and understand your position as the pillars in the temple of our God" (Royal Teton Ranch, <u>Pearls of Wisdom,</u> vol. 31, no. 4, p. 39).

My Chelas--I was there when the nuclear blast, heat and light hit Sodom and Gomorrah. I looked on from afar-- and paid the price. I know it can happen again. I know the Supreme Judge wills to preserve the righteous. But they must prove their righteousness by being prepared <u>in</u> <u>Spirit and</u> <u>in</u> <u>Matter.</u> O make haste to retreat to the mountain of your I AM Presence!

Decree and pray!

Decree and pray!

Decree and pray!

And stand steadfast in your calling to be intercessors for God's people.

I love you with all my heart,

Guru Ma

P.S. Here at the ranch, matters are rapidly drawing to a conclusion with the completion of the draft version of the Environmental Impact Statement being prepared by the State of Montana. We have now been informed that the document, comprising more than 100 pages, has been sent to the printer and should be released within two weeks. We believe this exhaustive study will lay to rest once and for all the many environmental questions and concerns raised by such groups as the Upper Yellowstone Defense Fund and Yellowstone National Park.

Once the document is distributed, 30 to 45 days will be allowed for public comment and another public meeting will be held--after which a final EIS will be issued and action will be taken on all our pending permit applications. But the environmental groups have threatened to take legal action to attempt to stall us even more.

Now is the time to be vigilant and push forward to the victory--so keep us in your decrees and prayers daily. Our future and your future depend on it! We will be sending you a full report just as soon as the draft EIS is released.

P.P.S. Easter Conclave dates at the Royal Teton Ranch: Wednesday, March 30 – Sunday, April 3, 1988, with prayer vigils before and after at King Arthur's Court. We meet "where the eagles gather."

Circle your calendar for June 29 through the Fourth of July to be sure and be at the ranch. Complete conference dates will include forums and seminars both before and after those dates.

Stump the U.S.A.
with Mother!

*"Blessed hearts, I have come, then,
to make a plea to you and to send my
Messenger abroad across this continent
for the gathering of ten thousand who
will call themselves Keepers of the Flame
of Life and who will understand that I,
Jesus, have called them."*

Kansas City
May 28, 1987

*"Pass that torch and
let us stand
Defenders of Freedom
in this land!"*

Lightbearers of America, Unite!

Please mark a cosmic cross of white fire over your house!

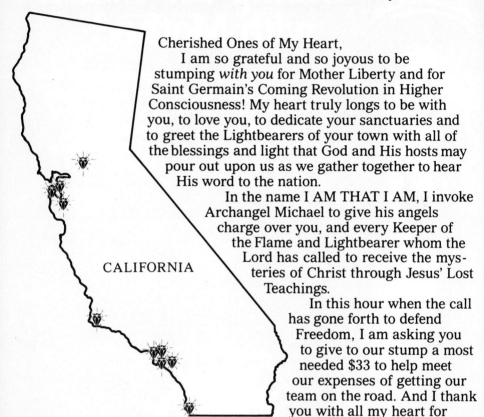

CALIFORNIA

Cherished Ones of My Heart,
 I am so grateful and so joyous to be stumping *with you* for Mother Liberty and for Saint Germain's Coming Revolution in Higher Consciousness! My heart truly longs to be with you, to love you, to dedicate your sanctuaries and to greet the Lightbearers of your town with all of the blessings and light that God and His hosts may pour out upon us as we gather together to hear His word to the nation.
 In the name I AM THAT I AM, I invoke Archangel Michael to give his angels charge over you, and every Keeper of the Flame and Lightbearer whom the Lord has called to receive the mysteries of Christ through Jesus' Lost Teachings.
 In this hour when the call has gone forth to defend Freedom, I am asking you to give to our stump a most needed $33 to help meet our expenses of getting our team on the road. And I thank you with all my heart for your most dedicated service to the Cause of Freedom and for your faithful support of beloved Alpha's agenda at the ranch, in your home town and throughout America.
 I am seeing *you* in the Light of God that never fails. Remember Morya's words, "From the beginning we were winning!"

 All my Love forever,

NEVADA

UTAH

ARIZONA

MEXICO

PORTUGAL

"I am upholding the torch of Liberty in the heart of

"

_____
Your town   Your state

♡ Beloved Mother,
        Here is my bouquet of
      violet posies to help precipitate
      the victory of Saint Germain's
Coming Revolution in Higher Consciousness!

I AM sending $ _____

Name _____
(please print)

Address _____

_____

P.S.   Please let me see your blessed face so I can know you better and visualize you in my heart as one of "my favorite chelas" for the victory of the stump in Salt Lake City, Las Vegas, Phoenix, Tucson, Mexicali, Mexico, Anaheim, North Hollywood, Berkeley, San Francisco, Sacramento, San Jose, Santa Barbara, Beverly Hills, Long Beach, San Diego, and Lisbon, Portugal!

I am keeping a strong vigil with you, using this form with your photo in my daily invocations at Saint Germain's altar.

The Love of God never fails and his Love is "a burning and a shining light" in your heart!

"My Favorite Chela"

May I have your autograph? ➡

P.P.S.   They tell me "All good things must come to an end." Not so with the stump! The stump goes on forever. Shiva never stops doing his cosmic dance and you never stop preaching the Word because you know that only by preaching the Word will the end of your karma come. As Jesus said, "And this gospel of the kingdom shall be preached in all the world for a witness unto all nations; and then shall the end come."

We know the "end" is the   end of our karma and of the fulfillment of the Age of Pisces—the end of many cycles leading to the Beginning of a New Era and a New Age. It is the coming of age of the soul for a new going out on the Path of Attainment.

Praise the Lord for this wondrous opportunity to fulfill His will.

Ma

Pearls of Wisdom®
published by The Summit Lighthouse

| *Vol. 31 No. 11* | *Beloved Lady Master Nada* | *March 13, 1988* |

Saint Germain Stumps America
1
So Great an Open Door
The True Initiation of Jesus Christ

O Infinite Light of the Love Ray, by the star of Christos I summon legions of angels of the Lord Christ to descend for comfort and healing to a people who have lost the way, led by the blind leaders of the blind taking them into arteries and byways not central to the path of the living Christ.

Let the false hierarchy of Antichrist go down, I say, in the name of Jesus Christ, and let the Lightbearers be raised up!

Angels of the Holy City, surround this place in concentric rings of light. Let the Diamond Heart of Mary be centered in this place and let healing be the power that does indeed, by the hand of Mary and Raphael, exorcise those things which have come to pass which ought not to be. Yet how an unenlightened free will can be led astray by subtlety. O beloved, the way of the fallen angels has gone too far and too long!

What will you do, then, with knowledge vouchsafed to you? Know you not that knowledge unused does dissipate? The fire of the mind must be disciplined. Therefore, put out those things that would take from you your love tryst with your Lord—the alchemical marriage in this life and your return to higher octaves, your home.

When you have found the reason for Divine Love—when Love has come into your heart as God—then, beloved, rejoice, for it is the greatest treasure! For out of that love is born the Sacred Heart of Jesus in you and out of that heart that is pierced the Light* does flow for healing.

Therefore, the Light essence as Alpha and Omega is the real and living communion cup. Drink ye all of it. Have courage, blessed hearts. Be not those who are set aside, having heard, been

*essence of Christ

entertained and then the cares of this world overtake them.[1]

My Lord Jesus is searching for his own.[2] He does know them, he does know you. Do you know him truly as the Ascended Master Jesus Christ, as the one who does place his aura around you—now as a swaddling garment as you be babes in Christ, then again as the mantle given to Elisha, who also went forth to smite the waters of the Jordan?[3]

Blessed ones, the Path is open. One step at a time measured and in the rhythm of the Divine Word does increase until one day you will look back at this moment and say, "How glad I am that I heard and as a hearer of the Word became a doer!"

The Lord hath need of thee. Remember when the Lord needed the foal of an ass? Were you there? Some of you were there on Palm Sunday. You were there laying the branches, crying out the hosannas, and what did those Pharisees say who have returned to the temples today to imprison the light of Christ in you—what did they say? "Silence your disciples." And what did the Lord say? "If these should hold their peace, the very stones should cry out."[4]

Now then, beloved, he who is master and alchemist of fire and rock, do you not know that the very elementals themselves should have acclaimed him had not the people done so, and does not the spirit of Nature cry out for the shedding of blood whether of innocent Abel[5] or of those slain in these hours?

Know, then, that earth herself will convulse in repudiation of millions of deaths, the slaying of the firstborn in the abortion of life, the abuse of the child who is destroyed in the mind and the psyche. Blessed hearts, these things did come to pass in ancient Judah and Israel.[6] Did not Jeremiah prophesy? Aye, indeed he did.

You have reincarnated to the present hour. Will you not feel the fire of determination of the heart and the spine, and this day put down those fallen ones—fallen Atlanteans who come again to lead the youth astray as pied pipers with their so-called music out of hell? Thus the rhythm of the beat of rock music does as easily lower the energy of the spine as you have raised it by mantra and sacred science.

Blessed hearts, it is a sin against the Holy Ghost to allow unsuspecting children to be violated in their bodies by chemicals—and then their souls, their souls, beloved, are split and sawn asunder. You do not understand how delicate are the chakras and the soul itself and how affected is its integration with the body by the presence of chemicals.

Thus, beloved, in a nation where there is lethargy and indulgence let the good people of the heart of Christ rally! Let them be fearless to denounce leaders in Church and State who limit their expression of the Divinity and of the Divine Lawgiver.

Sometimes the people are so enamored of their leaders that they accept their wickedness as though somehow it were a craft or an art. As Morya would say, Let us call a spade a spade. Let us denounce it and call upon the Archangels to defend us!

Blessed hearts, you have recourse to the living God. You have been taught basic principles. As Christ is the chief cornerstone of your temple, so he is the foundation of the New Age, and by that door, that open door of the living Ascended Master, and by your acknowledgment of the Christ of his heart he does transfer to you that heart and you discover what is the true initiation of Jesus Christ that can come to you when you kneel in prayer alone.

Thus, beloved, it is an hour of such opportunity and acceleration. In two thousand years there has not returned to the planet so great an open door. You yourselves have waited and languished through the dark ages, through the ages of limitation, religious persecution, wars upon wars, embodying on the battlefields of life, powerless and helpless to move against tyrants.

Suddenly total freedom is in your hands! Will you let it slip through as water or will you prepare a cup and hold not only the water but the fire itself?

Padma, come, then, out of the East! Come, then, Maitreya! Come, then, Kuan Yin! Teach the way of Confucius and Lord Lanto. Show the Path, then, that these may garner a fire, that these might propel a light and turn around a dying world.

Therefore, beloved, I am sent by Jesus to manifest the intensity of the Ruby Ray for a purging action in this state. Those responsible in Church and State for depravity and violence continuing must also stand before the Court of the Sacred Fire. Those who represent the people must be fearless to act for and on behalf of their highest Christhood. With leadership is the responsibility to bear the mantle of Jesus. Earn it, beloved. He is ready to bestow it. The time is very short.

Thus, in this moment there is a processioning of angels of the Holy Spirit. Blessed ones, as the sin against the Holy Ghost, the violation of the sacred fire in the Holy of Holies of life, the altar and the innocents, is not forgiven,[7] so the judgment of the Holy Ghost is a sacred fire of God beyond the judgment of the Son.

Know, then, that the path of the Third Ray of Divine Love, the path of the Holy Spirit and the heart is come in this hour. Be touched, then, and feel what is the Sacred Heart of Jesus. [6-sec. pause] Feel the presence and the pressure of that heart of your Lord. Know, then, that this heart presents the path of the Ruby Ray. It can be walked and it can be known; and when that love intensifies, you will see how it acts as a sword to cleave asunder the Real from the unreal in self and society.

Fear not, beloved, for the coming of the New Age portends the tearing down. As Mother Mary said, let that which is torn down be set aside.[8] We will build anew. The beginning of the mission of the individual life, as with the ancient prophets, always begins with the tearing down and then the building again.[9]

Those things that are no part of thy Reality will easily slip away. Your desires shall transcend the old desires. You shall hunger and thirst for the cup—that cup of the elixir of Life that an angel or Master may extend to you on the mountainside. You shall hunger for the fruits of the Spirit. Your desiring shall be to be clothed upon with robes of righteousness.

Your treasures shall be virtues star-studded and your desire will be to heal, to be healed, to know the mysteries, to embody them and to be so enamored of the Christ, so clothed upon by him, so one in his heart as to go out and deliver a people and a nation founded and consecrated by God to be the exemplar nation where each individual under his own I AM Presence and Holy Christ Self should know the Lord,[10] should commune in him and therefore raise up the sign to all the earth that the Second Coming of Christ truly is [takes place] each time he finds the receptive heart and temple.

These things are real and as you cherish and desire such service, know, then, thy reward is with thee. It is time to set the course of a life and to determine to endure in his service for the saving of life and souls.

You who are worthy, you who are able, accept the love of my heart. I have known you long and therefore because of my tie to this people, I am sent to this place. [24-sec. pause]

I release sacred fire in each one for the quickening of the crown, for Jesus desires that you should be endued with his mind and consciousness. Let that mind be in you.[11] Let that heart be in you. Let that Presence be in you. Let his angels into your home and life. Know the living and tangible awareness of angels ministering unto you and of the Lord Christ a regular guest at your table.

I release light to the capacity of your souls and I step aside as Saint Germain, faithful to his promise, does stand here now to seal the servants of God in the forehead.[12] Therefore come, beloved, receive him. His heart's devotion to your own is truly an infinity of the Seventh Ray.

I, Nada, bow to the Light within you, to the pink rose of the heart that is budding and blossoming in you now. I am your friend on the Path. Call in time of trouble and I will also answer. [16-sec. pause]

*Purusha. Purusha. Purusha.**

[Parousia. Parousia. Parousia.†]

Purusha: Sanskrit, lit. man; soul or spirit, the animating principle in man, the Spirit as passive as distinct from the Prakriti, or creative force. †*Parousia:* Greek, lit. presence, being near, coming; advent or return, Second Coming of Christ. It is possible that the Sanskrit and Greek words converge in the Divine Word to exemplify the Second Coming of Christ as the raising up of the Divine Principle in the heart of every individual.

Delivered following the Messenger's Jan. 30, 1988 Stump in Salt Lake City, Utah. For notes, see Pearl 12.

Pearls of Wisdom®

published by The Summit Lighthouse

Vol. 31 No. 12   *Beloved Serapis Bey*   *March 20, 1988*

Saint Germain Stumps America

2

A Temple of the Divine Mother

The Initiation of the Cosmic Cross of White Fire

From the Temple of Luxor, Egypt, I, Serapis, greet the devotees of the Divine Mother in this place, for I am arcing a light of pure white fire from Luxor to this city where the cosmic cross of white fire has been invoked this day by our Messenger.

Therefore, observe how in answer to the call of the one sent that cosmic cross of white fire is in this city and therefore firmly planted in the ground unto the highest atmosphere as the sign and the reminder that every soul in his hour and in his time does come to the nexus of the cross where God in man meet and the Four Cosmic Forces are balanced.

Thus the initiation of the cosmic cross of white fire is before you in this site and city where in ancient days there was once a temple of the Divine Mother. There ensued wars of the gods and then a precipitous decline during eras when mankind entered into depravity.

Blessed ones, the temple of the Mother that was once here and her shrine are nowhere apparent except if one consider the earmarks of the misuse and misqualification of the Divine Mother in these gambling houses, in these places where people come for sensual pleasure. For through the gambling entity and all else that ensues around it, controlled by the money beast and often by organized crime, there is the stealing of the light of the base chakra and its channeling therefore into the fallen ones of the earth. For that which one surrenders to the money beast and the gambling entity may not be returned to that individual, for it is lost.

Thus, the sign of the cosmic cross of white fire does portend and foretell even at inner levels to every soul of this city that one cannot serve the Divine Mother and the Moloch[1] of human greed.

Therefore, beloved, choose ye this day *whether to* enter the fiery coil of the ascension of the Divine Mother (and therefore to deprive those vultures of the astral plane of their booty, who wait to take your light) and thus to focus within your being a counter-force of ascension's rising flame that thereby the momentum of gambling may not spread further throughout the nations of the earth, fed and fueled by the money beast and the rationalization "Let us do evil that good may come;[2] let us use the funds for state projects and education," all feeding again and again upon the credulity, the wishful thinking that one can acquire attainment by Lady Luck—*or whether to* go the way of the squandering of the Divine Mother's light and abundant life within you!

Blessed ones, the Divine Mother Fortuna herself, Goddess of Supply, Lakshmi in Eastern terms,[3] does give both abundance and light, does take nothing from you but allows you to raise up that which is pure and perfect.

Thus, I declare, I AM Serapis Bey, Hierarch of Ascension's Temple and Lord of the Fourth Ray. I look upon what once was a mystery school, a secondary focus of the great Mother temple of Lemuria, and I say to you, beloved, let the restoration come within the heart and within the soul.

Therefore, in the name of the living Word the Divine Mother does challenge in this place and all areas of the nation those fallen ones that have gone after her children to take from them the light of their chakras by all manner of diversion.

Significant work at inner levels has preceded the coming of the Messenger by her calls and those of Keepers of the Flame, of our staff and those who are around the world. Therefore, beloved, one may see a waning of the power of the money beast, but those who are tied to that money beast on Wall Street may find themselves too late disentangled from its clutches.

See to it, therefore, that you recognize that the hour of the judgment of Evil is come, and let yourselves become disentangled from all forces known or unknown anywhere upon this planet that take light and give nothing in return but illusion. Thus, by being a part of them, you create and multiply illusion; and in a state of illusion the people of God cannot defend liberty nor expand the threefold flame within their hearts.

Consider how it is, then, that spiritual seekers and those who have naught to do with that which is taking place within this very building[4] have assembled themselves, been surrounded with angels and a tube of light. Veritably, you may see in this very forcefield angels ascending and descending out of heaven into the earth. Thus, the consciousness of the heights of God and the depths of darkness may coexist. And in the heart of a living soul who knows her Lord, you may find there the crystal that is the nucleus of the ascension coil in *you* and *you* and *you* each one.

Blessed hearts, is earth not a crossroads of many lifestreams pursuing the paths of free will? Yet, I say, they are indeed not free, beloved, but they follow that which they have been taught and the blind leaders of the blind.

I say to each and every one of you, take the proffered gift of the teachings and identify yourself as a true shepherd, leading by example, self-knowledge and the enlightenment of the Holy Ghost. Let it be said of you that you have seen the Light and you have seen the Darkness and you have chosen to embody the Light and to cast out the Darkness. Let a city and a nation and a planet go free! For the hearts of Light within this city are many. Many noble hearts are here as they are in every city.

Therefore, we have come with joy to give unto those who would drink of our cup the cool, clear waters that flow in the well of Luxor. We have come, beloved, to remind you that you also are called in this life to make your ascension. I, Serapis, am impelled by the cosmic law to appear and to speak wherever there is a sufficiency of souls who are those whose names are written in the Book of Life and upon whose record there is written the hour of the ascension for the twentieth century and the next.

Therefore, beloved, understand that it is a day and an age when all can be fulfilled. There is a path to be known and a soul that can fly. Take my treatise, a *Dossier on the Ascension;* learn of me and know me,[5] for I am the defender of Cosmic Christ purity in each one of your chakras. I would acquaint you with the Divine Mother East and West. I would show you that the disciplines for the ascension are not beyond either your ken or your doing.

Blessed ones, nothing is too hard for thee when the desire is pure and the light does shine. Thus, step by step we mount the thirty-three steps and in the ascension temple you may hear the strains of the "Triumphal March" that Verdi wrote down for *Aïda.* That triumphal march is the sounding of the tone of your victorious incarnation in this life. Know, then, that Christ in you is able to tutor and raise up your soul. Give yourself lovingly, freely to the embrace of the blessed Lamb who is come to claim you for your victory.

I AM Serapis, pleased, then, to apprise you that wherever there is the arc of the Mother from Luxor, there is the gathering of the seraphim led by Justinius, Captain of Seraphic Bands! Therefore, he is sounding. Let the sound be heard now as I cede my place to Saint Germain, who calls you to the altar to receive the sealing of the third eye, the sealing of the servants of God in their foreheads. Go with God, beloved, and go with God as Father and Mother.

"The Summit Lighthouse Sheds Its Radiance O'er All the World to Manifest as Pearls of Wisdom." This dictation by **Serapis Bey** was **delivered** by Elizabeth Clare Prophet on **Monday, February 1, 1988,** at the Dunes Hotel, **Las Vegas, Nevada,** where she was stumping for Saint Germain's Coming Revolution in Higher Consciousness. (**1**) **Moloch.** Ancient Semitic deity to whom children were offered as a propitiatory sacrifice by their parents (see Lev. 18:21; 20:2–5; II Kings 23:10; Jer. 32:35; Amos 5:26; Acts 7:43); a tyrannical power propitiated by human subservience. (**2**) Rom. 3:7, 8. (**3**) In Hinduism, **Lakshmi** is the goddess of wisdom, i.e., 'wise dominion', hence of wealth, good fortune and abundance. She is the consort of Vishnu, the Preserver, second person of the Hindu Trinity. (**4**) The **Dunes Hotel** where Serapis Bey dictated is located on the Strip in Las Vegas and is frequented for its gambling facilities by nearly 70,000 people annually. The Dunes houses two large casinos open 24 hours a day containing over 5,000 slot machines and numerous gaming tables. The main casino, off the hotel lobby, is situated so that people must walk through it to get to other parts of the hotel. (**5**) For dictations by and teaching on **Serapis Bey,** see *Dossier on the Ascension,* $5.95 (add $.50 for postage); and *Lords of the Seven Rays: Mirror of Consciousness,* Book One, pp. 149–81; Book Two, pp. 135–68, $5.95 (add $.50 for postage).

Notes from Pearl No. 11 by Nada:
(**1**) **Parable of the sower.** Matt. 13:3–8, 18–23; Mark 4:3–8, 13–20; Luke 8:4–8, 11–15. (**2**) **The call to discipleship under Jesus Christ.** See Jesus Christ, 1987 *Pearls of Wisdom,* vol. 30: "The Call to the Path of the Ascension," no. 27, pp. 269–76; "The Call of the Cosmic Christ: Discipleship unto the Ascended Master Jesus Christ," no. 56, pp. 491–98; "The Day of Thy Christhood: Keep the Flame of Eternal Life," no. 74, pp. 577–82; "Comfort Ye My People! I, Jesus, Prophesy the Certain Day of Your Victory," no. 79, pp. 601–6. See also dictation by Jesus Christ, February 28, 1988, given in Lisbon, Portugal, on 93-min. audiocassette B88042, $6.50 (add $.50 for postage). (**3**) II Kings 2:1–15. (**4**) Luke 19:28–40. (**5**) Gen. 4:8–12. (**6**) **Child sacrifice denounced by the prophets.** Jer. 7:31, 32; 19:1–6; 32:35; Ezek. 16:20, 21, 36; 20:26, 31; 23:37–39; Isa. 57:5; Amos 5:25, 26; Mic. 6:7. (**7**) Matt. 12:31, 32; Mark 3:28, 29. (**8**) See Mother Mary, April 21, 1987, "The Old Order Must Pass Away," 1987 *Pearls of Wisdom,* vol. 30, no. 21, pp. 209–10, 213, 214–15. (**9**) "Then the LORD put forth his hand, and touched my mouth. And the LORD said unto me, Behold, I have put my words in thy mouth. See, I have this day set thee over the nations and over the kingdoms, to root out, and to pull down, and to destroy, and to throw down, to build, and to plant." Jer. 1:9, 10. (**10**) Mic. 4:4, 5; Jer. 31:33, 34; Heb. 8:10, 11. (**11**) Phil. 2:5. (**12**) **Emerald matrix blessing.** Following the Messenger's delivery of Saint Germain's Prophecy, the Lost Teachings of Jesus and a concluding dictation by an Ascended Master, those attending pass before the altar to receive Saint Germain's transfer of light to the third-eye chakra by the "emerald matrix" as she touches their brow with a laboratory "grown" emerald crystal. This is the "sealing of the servants of God in their foreheads" prophesied in Revelation 7:1–8.

Pearls of Wisdom®

published by The Summit Lighthouse

| *Vol. 31 No. 13* | *The Beloved Great Divine Director* | *March 27, 1988* |

Saint Germain Stumps America

3

Holding the Balance of Light in the Earth

Multiplied by the Power of the 10,000 Times 10,000

From out of the Cave of Light in the heart of the Himalayas[1] I who am called the Master R salute you, sons and daughters of Aquarius.

I send light from the Himalayas to the Andes where the Masculine and Feminine Ray enter the earth respectively.[2] I send light for the inner balancing of the earth in consideration of mankind's karma and those changes that could come to pass.

The balance of light that I am able to anchor within you because you have tarried to be a vessel of light and prepared your bodies is considerable indeed, and therefore for your most gracious attendance, for your listening grace, I am thankful.

As the sponsor of Saint Germain I am in search of those who will understand the mission, the great mission of my son, and who will comprehend that the holding of the balance of Light[3] in the earth depends upon those who hear the call and take it finally in this life as a serious election in the heart of Maitreya, the Cosmic Christ.

Blessed ones, with physical vessels in the earth who understand the meaning of the crystallization of the God Flame in this form, we can move across the earth and hold a majesty of light. As you become, then, pillars in the temple of the God who is on earth even as he is in heaven, earth can see the mitigation and transmutation that is called for in this hour.

May you who have heard and understood go forth to manifest the dream of God for the age of gold! May you know that by perseverance and constancy you may enter into a relationship of trust with one or more of the Ascended Masters beginning with my son Saint Germain.

Realize, beloved, that the Master/disciple relationship, or that which is called the Guru/chela relationship, is one that can be sustained only by the flame of trust—trust in the guarding of the light. For the light is power and when it is not guarded but misqualified in an unguarded moment, that light simply goes to feed the sinister force upon this planet. Thus, when in a moment of anger or a sudden flash of envy the light given is turned to a lesser vibration, there are always those brothers of the shadow waiting to take it from you.

Thus, trust must be the hallmark of our devotion to those students of the Light.* We love all who take up this teaching, but to enter in to a guarded relationship whereby that Light is transferred for the healing of nations we must, then, see a responsibility that is mature and that has the understanding that we deal with cosmic forces and it is the misuse of these forces that has in the past brought calamity and the sinking of continents.⁴

You live in an era, beloved, when the ancient karma sown in the rock and the mountain, even of this vicinity, comes due for balance. Let it be balanced by a violet flame conflagration.

Understand, therefore, that those who are ascended lead you on the path of the ascension, and those who come in their spacecraft lead you on a byway of technological transcendence but have not the ability to initiate you in the Christic light of the higher dimensions.

Therefore, seek ye first the kingdom of God within.⁵ Those who are the sons and daughters of the Great Central Sun and of the God Star⁶ know where their allegiance lies and know that their source of power and salvation lies solely within their I AM Presence and their Christ Self.

We reinforce and multiply what light you are able to externalize in the weeks and months and days ahead. This, though you are diligent daily, is, however, not sufficient to the fulfillment of earth's destiny. Thus, as you serve and give the call we do multiply it by a dispensation of the Cosmic Christ known as the power of the ten thousand-times-ten thousand.⁷

Thus, as I speak to you I use these hands [of the Messenger] to direct light into this area, anchoring light rays into the mountains themselves for a stabilization. For I too would buy for you and for Saint Germain time and cycles for the perfecting of the law and for that golden age to come.⁸

The world can receive the violet flame as the gift of your

*Christ consciousness

hearts. Know you, beloved, what six hundred souls of Light such as those who have gathered here this evening can do, not alone for this state and nation but for a planet?

I tell you, were six hundred to gather even weekly for four hours of violet flame, what changes you would see would astonish you. For there is a geometrization of that God Flame, and the number who gather is squared and then multiplied by the power of the ten thousand-times-ten thousand.

So we desire to see the thousands gather in the cities of America and this is the need of the hour. To that end, then, may you understand of just what great worth is your heart and soul and your chalice in the earth in this hour.

Would to God that the people who so love the Light would capture this spark of Liberty, this sign of the Godhead of creativity descending in the dawning hours of the age of Aquarius. Would to God that the people en masse would rise up to overthrow not only their karma but also their oppressors who keep them bound to a round of darkness in Church and State worldwide.

Beloved, the world is upon the verge of the ushering in of such an age of enlightenment! The gentle turning of each individual toward his God, toward his I AM Presence, with that meditation and utter love, I tell you, in the twinkling of the All-Seeing Eye of God you would see what change upon planet earth!

Thus, engage not in wishful thinking but in dynamic decrees and see what you can do and draw forth from your causal body. Out of the treasures of all lifetimes which you have stored in heaven, you can endow earth with such a victory and in the very process, beloved, balance a heap of karma and enter in to a path of true adeptship—for true adeptship is not won except in the balance of karma itself.

I am known as the Great Divine Director, for I do direct the planetary energies out of the mighty blue sphere above. Therefore, the light descends through the hearts of gold. Through the lovers of light, I send light. This light that you receive now, beloved, is a quickening and it shall work in your members for forty-eight hours from this moment. If during this cycle you will take these decrees and calls and give them as frequently as your life allows, I, remaining with you, will give you a charge and a multiplication factor not available in the ordinary sense.

Therefore, beloved, it is by my love of Saint Germain and his love of your particular lifestreams that I give you my heart. All of heaven stands poised and waiting for the response of the Lightbearers of the world.

Therefore, in Saint Germain's name I say to one and to all, Lightbearers of the world, unite in the Seventh Ray and Age! Establish thou it! For you are by reason of your embodiment on earth the authority as to what shall take place upon this planet.

I seal you in Saint Germain's Maltese cross, the sign of your alchemy.[9] May you pursue it and be God-victorious for all evolutions of earth.

My Light, my Love upon you always. I AM the Master R.

This dictation by the **Great Divine Director** was **delivered** by Elizabeth Clare Prophet on **Wednesday, February 3, 1988,** following her lecture at the Sheraton Phoenix, **Arizona,** where she was stumping for Saint Germain's Coming Revolution in Higher Consciousness. (1) **The Cave of Light** is the retreat of the Great Divine Director, the Master R, in India. (2) **The Masculine Ray for the planet** is focused in the Himalayas by Lord Himalaya, Manu of the fourth root race. **The Feminine Ray** is focused at Lake Titicaca in the Andes through the God and Goddess Meru, Manus of the sixth root race. (3) **Holding the balance of light in the earth** means to gather the sacred fire around the coil of being and to expand it in the aura through prayers, decrees, mantras and meditation—holiness and harmony. This white light, as the energy of God, gains momentum through constancy of devotion, becoming the magnet and the vessel for the individual attainment and self-mastery of God self-realized. This Light is, then, more than the energy of God: it is the Higher Consciousness of God whereby one is becoming the integrated personality in God—the awareness of self in and as the embodiment of the Christ Self. This is achieved in the daily exercise of putting on the garment of the Lord until, by the light-emanation of the Word and Work of the Lord, the soul, tracing the ray back to the Source, is become that Source. In this capacity she is no longer a child of God but a mature Son of God—truly the Sun of the I AM THAT I AM in radiant manifestation. This is the alchemical marriage and the crystallization of the God Flame. It is, then, by becoming the full incarnation of the Light, or Christ consciousness, that one ultimately holds the balance in the earth of the light (energy of God) and the Light (his consciousness). Hence the distinction between the terms *light* and *Light* is that when lowercased, *light* refers to the energy of God magnetized by the soul through many lifetimes of weaving the Deathless Solar Body. When uppercased, *Light* denotes the Christ, the Word self-realized. In order for the Lightbearers—those who bear the Light of the Christ consciousness—to hold the balance of the light/Light in the earth they must be pursuing the parallel goals of invoking the "light," as the universal radiance and energy of God, and becoming the "Light," as the embodied Christ, by a disciplined path of discipleship under the Lord Jesus Christ and the Ascended Masters. The path of the Ascended Masters is essential to the achievement of both goals as they are called for in this dictation by the Great Divine Director. Only thus can the earth be saved. (4) On the sinking of **Lemuria and Atlantis,** see Mark L. Prophet and Elizabeth Clare Prophet, *Climb the Highest Mountain,* 2nd ed., pp. 91–92, 97–98, 132, 493–95, 581 n. 140, 582 n. 144; *The Lost Teachings of Jesus II,* pp. 260–61, 262–64, 312–13, 480–81. (5) Matt. 6:33; Luke 12:31; 17:21; Gospel of Thomas, logion 3. (6) **The God Star.** The Ascended Masters' term for the binary star Sirius, which is the galactic seat of God-government and focus of the Great Central Sun, representing with its companion sun the Guru/chela relationship; called the "Dog Star" by astronomers. (7) **The power of the ten thousand-times-ten thousand.** See Lord Maitreya, July 1, 1961, "The Christ Consciousness," 1984 *Pearls of Wisdom,* vol. 27, no. 7, p. 63; and Mark L. Prophet and Elizabeth Clare Prophet, "The Power of the Ten Thousand Times Ten Thousand," in *The Science of the Spoken Word,* pp. 78–79. (8) On February 7, 1987, Saint Germain said, "I ask you to buy **fifty years of peace** for me and I will show you what the heavenly hosts working through you may do to save this planet utterly from disease and death and war" (1987 *Pearls of Wisdom,* vol. 30, no. 6, p. 95). (9) **The Maltese cross.** See *Saint Germain On Alchemy,* pp. 268–70, 275–76, 277–84, or *Climb the Highest Mountain,* 2nd ed., pp. 288–89, 293, 294–99.

Pearls of Wisdom®
published by The Summit Lighthouse

| Vol. 31 No. 14 | Beloved Archangel Michael | April 3, 1988 |

Saint Germain Stumps America

4

An Archangel's Power of Deliverance
The Liberation of Souls and the New-Age Movement

Hail, Sons and Daughters of God! Hail, Legions of Light!

I AM Michael Archangel descended into this form and place to address you, O people of fiery hearts whose allegiance is to the Law of the One that is Divine Love.

I AM the defender of your faith in the power of God to deliver you at every hand. I AM the defender of the light of Freedom in this nation and all nations wheresoever a people have conspired in the heart of Mother Liberty to raise up that light of Freedom. I come to this town, then, for the binding and the purging of all forces not of the Light that would assail the children of the Sun and the New Age movement of Saint Germain.

Come, therefore, legions of my bands! Let there be the clearing of the ancient records here. Let there be a clearing, then, of that false theology whereby the spirits that "mutter and peep" and have naught to do with the Holy Ghost do take on those who are the "religious" but without a flame.

Therefore, beloved, I am in the nation in an hour of peril and I speak to you of the name and the heart Saint Germain, for I go forth before him for the clearing of the way.

I AM indeed an Archangel endued with the power of God. For, lo, with Gabriel, with Jophiel, with Chamuel, with Raphael, with Uriel, with Zadkiel, I stand in the Presence of God!

Blessed ones, the call to me is your certain deliverance from planes of ignorance and old bondage. The call for the deliverance of Freedom in the earth is another question.

Beloved hearts, we the Archangels move across the face of
the earth, speaking in the hearts of many, for we are also cosmic
teachers. We desire awareness and a quickening, and for that
purpose we must open the continents of the air, of the mind itself,
that you might know that to enter the New Age does demand new
thought and a new understanding of prophecy and a realization
that the karma of a planet that could descend may yet be stayed
by the heart, head and hand of those who determine to keep the
flame of Life and recognize that the all-consuming power of God
released in the violet flame by millions upon earth can in this
hour, even in a twinkling of an eye, be the last trump of the Death
and Hell of the forces of Darkness.

Where the sons and daughters of God do not cry out unto the
LORD, the LORD, then, does not come suddenly into his temple.[1]
As has been explained to you, it is a question of free will; and our
respect for that gift is an ultimate one.

Therefore, the lessons of free will are considered by the
Almighty One to be of greater value than even the preservation of
a civilization. You need only look for proof of this statement in the
sinking of continents where the flame of God has been violated
and his laws abrogated. In that way, beloved, all have a record in
the subconscious of what are the consequences of the misuse of the
sacred fire in the seven chakras and on the seven rays; and therefore the lessons learned afford individuals the opportunity to move
forward on the ladder of initiation, to balance karma and not to
repeat their mistakes of previous incarnations in future lives.

Beloved hearts, the "great war" prophesied[2] can yet be turned
back! Let it be done, then, by those who have heard, those who are
of the wise ones who will understand.

Let there be an infusion of light and the setting aside of
phony money and phony ones in the banking houses who have
made a merchandise of the souls of my people.

I AM the defender of your hearts and souls, and, yes, I come
for the binding of those entities that assail the mind and warp the
consciousness and blur the Divine Reality of a golden age that is
on the horizon, even as the sun crests the hills at the dawn!

Therefore, beloved, it is a time for all due seriousness for
those who know that they are mature sons and daughters of God.
Enter into the path of keeping the flame, I say! Call unto the
angelic hosts and invoke the violet flame daily. It is necessary,
beloved, else, I will tell you, certain cataclysms will not be averted.
It is no longer a question of hundreds but of millions of lifestreams
who must hear the call of the Archangels who come in the defense

of the God of Freedom to the earth, who is Saint Germain.

Therefore, for the clearing of the way in this town, beloved, you shall see a purging action and a cleansing. Be not concerned that elemental life and the beings of Nature take on this task, for where I do appear through my Messenger, *know*, then, that the power of God does also descend; and therefore the beings of Light who serve to set aright the balance of cosmic forces do minister. For my Word that is fire becomes spoken and therefore does move in the physical octave, and you yourselves keeping this flame of the First Ray by the call to me may know an extraordinary liberation.

I remind you that in 1961 I appeared in Boston and I delivered a dictation through the Messenger Mark Prophet and I set the fiery coil for the liberation of this Messenger and her ascent the spiral of Being, her training as a Messenger. And from that one dictation she did arrive at that place of the full balancing of her karma in this life.

Therefore, know the power of an Archangel who has come to rescue you in this hour, and know that I sponsor you and I release the coil that can be your deliverance and that of your twin flame! You need but claim it, accept it and rise to your mission in life, for the hour is short!

My legions of Light have formed a vast circle of fire around this city. Know, then, that when the LORD God does speak through me and I speak through the Messenger, by the law of octaves that light does descend. It is for the holding of the balance and for the purging of all persecution of the Divine Mother in the earth—the Divine Mother who does reside in each and every one of you.

For the Divine Feminine must be raised up in you and I AM the defender of that Woman within you. And you shall see the clothing of the Son of God within you, you shall know all things that must be made known unto you if you receive that light that is delivered.

Therefore, the power of Helios and Vesta is released! And not an erg more may I deliver, for it is by cosmic dispensation that we speak.

Therefore, I seal you with the cosmic cross of white fire, and my blue flame sword is plunged into the earth as the sign of an Archangel that has come!

Purusha![3]

Delivered following the Messenger's Feb. 4, 1988 Stump at the Tucson Hilton East, Arizona. **(1)** Mal. 3:1. **(2)** In 1963 the German newspaper *Neues Europa* printed a supposed extract of the third secret given by Mother Mary at Fátima, Portugal, July 13, 1917. It read in part, "The great, great war will come in the second half of the twentieth century." See also *Saint Germain On Prophecy*, Book Two, pp. 18–78, 93–142; Elizabeth Clare Prophet, October 31, 1987, "Halloween Prophecy 1987," two videocassettes, 4½ hrs., GP87063, $39.95 (add $1.20 postage), or on three 90-min. audiocassettes, A87079, $19.50 (add $.80 postage). **(3)** Purusha. See 1988 *Pearls of Wisdom*, vol. 31, no. 11, p. 126 note.

THE RADIANT WORD
A Divine Mediatorship

Excerpt of a dictation given in Boston, April 22, 1961
by Beloved Archangel Michael through the Messenger Mark L. Prophet

...I tell you, people of Boston, mankind need the protection of the Ascended Masters, mankind need the protection of the ascended hosts! And they need the services we of the archangelic realm are able to render them. For our service was unparalleled and unheard of by mankind, until this dispensation came forth by which we are able in this age to speak directly to mankind once again as in the past ages....

Blessed and beloved ones, there is no night through which the light of God cannot penetrate. There is no condition in your physical bodies through which the light of God cannot penetrate. There is no particular illness or densification of gross substance through which the light of God cannot strike its power and immediately, on the instant, set it free from all discordant manifestations and flood absolute Christ-perfection into full manifestation, on the instant!...

God intends that the protection of the great, transcendent Niagara of light which flows down from their [mankind's] own God Presence shall be a tangible substance of Ascended Master light which shall so fortify them against all the hordes of darkness and shadow that nothing, and I say *nothing*, shall pass through!

Individuals have accepted into their consciousness the idea that the tube of light can be easily rent. And because they have *thought* that the tube of light could be easily rent, it has become so....When they shall realize that this great power of light, flowing down from their own God Presence over their head and radiating out around them, is a Niagara— a torrent of light from the heart of God, from their own God Presence, which cannot be penetrated—and they shall so qualify that wall of light, I tell you, man shall have a freedom which he has not known before!...

In the name of God, the Almighty I AM Presence, I blaze my cosmic sword of blue flame through the city of Boston! I reach it out through the entire Eastern seaboard, and I stretch it forth for the protection of America this night *against the hordes of war!* I say that the power of war shall not be able to destroy this nation....

Blessed and beloved ones, some of you are of advancing years, and it will not be long before you shall vacate your body temples. Some of you shall do so by the ascension and some shall enter the realms of our world in the other manner called death.

I say to you, if you doubt that I am speaking through this Messenger this night, I will make you one promise: If you will call to me secretly within your heart and ask me to come to you at that hour, I, Michael, will materialize to you at the hour of your passing and you will see me as I AM. And I will promise you that I will help to cut you free from the remaining portions of your karma and will help you to enter the realms of light with less of the attendant pain which results from human fear in passing.

This is a privilege and a gift I give you from my heart. I flood it forth to the people of Boston and to those throughout the world who have the faith to accept it and to realize that God walks and talks with men today in the same manner as of old....

This dictation is printed in 1982 *Pearls of Wisdom*, vol. 25, pp. 431–34.

Pearls of Wisdom®

published by The Summit Lighthouse

| *Vol. 31 No. 15* | *Beloved Saint Thérèse of Lisieux* | *April 10, 1988* |

Saint Germain Stumps America

5

Outside the Church

Part I

O my beloved, I have desired to speak to you, and in my prayers unto the Father he has answered me, and by the leave of our Blessed Mother I am come this night in my Ascended Master Light Body that you might see me and know me as I AM—your sister of Light in octaves fair, yet very near.

This night I come bearing white roses in honor of the Blessed Virgin Mary. I come in her name and it is to deliver to you the outpouring of my heart for the holy Church and for the orders of the religious and the priests.

For I would tell you, beloved, that for want of true shepherds these orders are waning, and there is not a replenishment in the Church because the councils and those who direct its destiny have chosen not to receive your sister and mine who serves as your Messenger, who was also embodied in this Church as Saint Catherine of Siena and also as the beloved Clare, sister of Francis.

Therefore, understand, beloved, that we who have given our Light* for the victory of this institution are forced to step on the outside, even as Mother Mary has done to deliver her message of the age through these Messengers, although she does continue to speak to those children within the Church wherever they may be reached.[1]

Beloved ones, the teaching of the New Age has come forth and it has not been received by this hierarchy. Yet, understand that the people themselves are destined to be the Light of the true Church, which is the temple of man.

And know ye not that ye are all brides of Christ? Know ye

*Christhood

not, then, that the mighty work of the ages is the building of this true temple and therefore [is], wherever you are, to be the votive light on the altar of the true Church, the Church in heaven that is the Church Universal and Triumphant?

Blessed hearts, let millions rally in this hour to the cause of our beloved Saint Joseph.[2] Blessed hearts, he would save both Church and State and yet must now do so on the outside of both. For as of old, heads of state nation by nation have not heard* his call, and those who represent the people† have not received the gift of the violet flame.

There are saints in heaven, numberless numbers, and those not yet ascended waiting in the etheric octave. Many of these have graduated out of the Church and yet did not make their full ascension because they lacked the knowledge and use of the violet flame and the gift of the science of the spoken Word.

Beloved, I direct you, then, to the deliberation of all of our hearts who have sought again and again to bring this Truth into the Church. We say to you that a Body of Light upon earth is needed immediately in order to stay the hand of world destruction! Many of you are acquainted, then, with the prophecies of Fátima and of Medjugorje and need not have these rehearsed to you. The days are growing short that this prophecy may be turned around and transmuted.

If you could see what the Messenger sees, I assure you that you would make this calling, this election[3] a daily priority in your lives: to offer the calls to the violet flame and the rosary to Saint Michael the Archangel and to Mother Mary.[4] Recognize, beloved, that it will take millions who will invoke the violet flame to transmute world karma.

Thus, we who have waited long can wait no longer for the Church to receive a teaching, to send it forth and to use it! O beloved, the power has been in their hands and many years ago they could have taken the mystery of the Chart of the I AM Presence and placed it upon every altar. I tell you, beloved, we have wept at inner levels. And the cause for the tears on the statues of Mother Mary[5] are for the sorrow in her heart that the release of Jesus Christ and Saint Germain has not turned the world around and prepared the way for the entering in of a golden age.

While‡ there are those who will, then, raise up the light and make the call, you are indeed buying time for us to give us another day and another day to turn back the forces of world destruction. May the hearts, the great and devoted hearts, of the people of this

---

*have not heeded   †who are in a position to lead them in the path of righteousness for his name's sake
‡as long as

nation and all of Latin America now rise to the occasion and receive the teaching and know that it is the daily prayer and dynamic decrees that shall support a world revolution of Light.

Blessed ones, I can assure you that those of us who have ascended or are waiting the ascension from the etheric octave do move toward those of Light and pure hearts; and as we offer our prayers and angels take them to the throne of the Father, we spend all of our days helping those who have Light,* who have an open heart to receive this teaching, helping you to rearrange your lives so that you can give your all for the destiny of planet earth.

Blessed ones, I give to your heart my vibration. I reveal to you the purity of this message. You need not endless writings or channelings of fascination to the human ego. You need the most direct route to be an intercessor on behalf of humanity.

They are ignorant, and we say, "Father, forgive them, they know not what they do."[6] But the true children of the Light and the sons and daughters of God who have lived in past ages and known this Truth, it is they who are called. It is *you* who are called, for you have already recognized our Presence and been drawn to this vibration this evening.

Blessed hearts, I tell you, the hour is perilous indeed! Let it be that you remember that the "great war" has been prophesied at both Fátima and Medjugorje. Let it be mitigated, let it be consumed!

Blessed hearts, while there is life and hope and while the courses continue, there is day by day the intercession of your lifestream. This is my plea to you and this is my call. While the representatives of the governments of the nations betray the people and many of the clergy also betray them, let the people en masse rise up to save the world by the violet flame and by the fervent call.

We must go, then, into the streets. We must go to the hearts of those who have received us in past ages and received the Lord. We must go to those who may not have name or fame or money or power or position but who recognize that the ultimate power is in their I AM Presence and Holy Christ Self.

Let those who hear me know that I too see and I too shed a tear with Mother Mary at those things that are on the brink of becoming physical upon earth. In this hour, then, I pour out my heart to you, and the very heart of the Messenger does receive the sensation of my burden and my plea. To your hearts I call, for you are on earth and in embodiment, and we can act mightily with angelic hosts to intervene if you will but make the call.

*Christ-Self-awareness

Now receive the blessing of the Sacred Heart of Jesus and the Immaculate Heart of Mary.

Many saints who are your brothers and sisters have placed themselves at this altar this night that you might feel the kinship and the oneness with those you have known in past lives who have gone on before you. They are your wayshowers. And many of you in this room have been told by Gabriel the Archangel that you were to make your ascension in this life. Let it be so that you understand that this is not a predestination but it is a calling to which you direct all of your strength and energy and your discipleship unto the heart of our beloved Jesus Christ.

In the heart of my Lord, I AM one with you each and every day, for I do spend all of my heaven on earth.[7]

I seal you with the white roses of the ascension of the Blessed Mother and I embrace you as a sister of Light and Love.

This dictation by **Saint Thérèse of Lisieux** was **delivered** by the Messenger Elizabeth Clare Prophet following her **Saturday, February 6, 1988** Stump at the Holiday Inn Mexicali, **Mexico.** (1) **Mother Mary's appearances at Medjugorje.** Since June 25, 1981, Mother Mary has appeared almost daily to six youths in the village of Medjugorje, Yugoslavia, with messages stressing peace, conversion, prayer, fasting, penance and a sacramental life. According to the youths, the apparitions will continue to occur until Mother Mary has given each of them 10 secrets concerning future events. These will be revealed to the public three days before the events are to occur. See the Messenger's "Fátima Update" Part II, published with Part I, four 90-min. audio-cassettes K87033–36, $26 (add $.80 postage); and "Halloween Prophecy 1987" (see 1988 *Pearls of Wisdom,* p. 137, n. 2). (2) **Saint Joseph** was an embodiment of Saint Germain. (3) II Pet. 1:10. (4) See *Save the World with Violet Flame! by Saint Germain,* 92-min. audiocassette of violet flame decrees and songs, B88019, $5.95 (add $.50 postage); *Archangel Michael's Rosary for Armageddon,* 36-pg. booklet and 91-min. audiocassette, $5 (add $.80 postage); Mary's Scriptural Rosary for the New Age in *My Soul Doth Magnify the Lord!* $7.95 (add $1 postage); *A Child's Rosary to Mother Mary,* 15-min. scriptural rosaries on 4 audiocassette albums, A7864, A7905, A7934, A8045, $9.95 ea. (add $.90 ea. postage). (5) **Weeping statues.** See 1987 *Pearls of Wisdom,* vol. 30, no. 65, p. 546, n. 6. (6) Luke 23:34. (7) **Thérèse of Lisieux** (1873–1897), French Carmelite nun, known as the Little Flower of Jesus. Born Marie-Françoise-Thérèse Martin, January 2, 1873, in Alençon, France. At 14, Thérèse had such an ardent desire to enter the convent that on a pilgrimage to Rome with her father she boldly asked Pope Leo XIII during a public audience for his permission to enter the Carmel at age 15. He responded that she would enter "if God wills it." The next year her request was granted by the bishop of Bayeux and on April 9, 1888, she entered the Carmel at Lisieux where she took the name Sister Thérèse of the Child Jesus and the Holy Face. She became acting mistress of novices in 1893 and considered it her mission to teach souls her "little way," the way of "spiritual childhood, the way of trust and absolute self-surrender." Her path was a path of love, for, she wrote, "it is only love which makes us acceptable to God." Her favorite works were those of Saint John of the Cross, the Gospels and *The Imitation of Christ.* Thérèse developed tuberculosis and during the final months of her life she was racked with pain. She said that this was a time of great spiritual trials. Thérèse died September 30, 1897, at the age of 24. Undaunted in her love for Christ, her last words were, "My God, I love you!" Her autobiography, written at the direction of her prioress and published after her death as *Story of a Soul: The Autobiography of St. Thérèse of Lisieux,* became one of the most widely read spiritual books. Two of the statements for which Thérèse is most remembered are "I want to spend my heaven in doing good on earth" and "After my death I will let fall a shower of roses," for she foresaw that her activity after her death would be far reaching and her mission of "making others love God as I love him" would continue. Statues of the saint portray her carrying a bouquet of roses. Thérèse was canonized on May 17, 1925, less than 28 years after her death. In 1927 she was declared patroness of foreign missions and of all works for Russia. Her feast day is October 1. The Ascended Lady Master Thérèse of Lisieux also dictated through the Messenger Elizabeth Clare Prophet on October 25, 1981 (see "A Bird That Takes Flight," 1981 *Pearls of Wisdom,* vol. 24, no. 44, pp. 447–52). Her life story is depicted in the 1986 film *Thérèse.*

Pearls of Wisdom®
published by The Summit Lighthouse

| Vol. 31 No. 16 | Beloved Cyclopea | April 17, 1988 |

Saint Germain Stumps America

6

The Sealing of the Lightbearers
"Get Thee Hence, O Beloved of the Light!"

I AM Elohim of the Fifth Ray. Cyclopea I am called, and the Divine Mother Elohim of this ray is Virginia.

Therefore, out of the Fifth Ray of Divine Science we descend on that mission for the stabilization of the planetary body and sheaths of interpenetrating light. We come also for the adjustment of cycles in those who elect to be qualifiers of light by the All-Seeing Eye of God, those who elect to be infilled with light and know not as yet how treacherous are the ways of the astral plane and its denizens. We come to cut you free!

Many years ago we came for the sealing of this coast against certain earthquakes then projected. That mission to which Elohim were sent and in which we sent our Messenger was fulfilled and sealed, and this state and coast did therefore receive a dispensation granted of opportunity for that open door to remain open unto those who would elect under the ministry of the Ascended Masters to come into a higher light and vibration. In these past years we have declared that certain mission sealed[1] and directed our Messenger and movement to establish a headquarters in Montana and so it was done.[2]

Our coming in this hour, then, by the God of very gods is to seal the Lightbearer one by one individually, to give assistance and to aid. Concerning those predictions of that which may come to pass in the earth in this coast,[3] be it understood that planetary karma shall take its course. The only divine intervention that may be forthcoming is that intervention invoked by those below. Thus, it is an hour to wrap one's cloak about oneself by the fire infolding itself and to remember when in days of old Abraham did say, "We seek no continuing city here."[4]

Let the Lightbearer raise up the light and be raised up! And in that rising light let him see and know as the watchman on the wall of the night of earth's Dark Cycle that where the star of the Divine Mother does appear so there is the gathering of his own Christhood and fellow members of that divine design, even that mandala of the eternal Buddhas and Christed ones.

Get thee hence, then, O beloved of the Light! For the dispensation is a saving grace unto those who bear the pillar of fire in the earth and move up and down the earth with angels of Light for the holding of that balance.

Karma, then, as you have been told, may be mitigated. Nevertheless, remember the call and the warning, for there has not been a prophet or a saint of God who in one lifetime or another has not been called to move himself to a place that is chosen for him to be that individualization of the God Flame.

Therefore, we Elohim of God come for a sealing of those who are the anointed and accept our anointing. We have no partiality but serve the Light in those who serve the Light.* It is, then, quite simple that the law of God does honor the righteous who make righteous use of the law and the energy and the Presence of our God.

Hear, O elemental life! Receive, then, our balance as you hold the balance in this area of a planet, as you endow the very earth itself with more violet fire and the emerald ray for the keeping and the protection of these souls of Light.

Thus, beloved, let us for a moment turn our attention from time and space and to the higher octaves. Let us be suspended and above the earth. Let us together climb a spiral staircase and see, as the watchman of the night does see in his watch—see, then, a planet and understand how one shall endure and pass through, as though passing through walls of glass and time and space, in his finer body into those wavelengths and vibrations that do carry one and transport one.

Blessed ones, the attachment to mortality itself, to fixed places and fixations in time and space is a result of karma. Seeing and knowing and being the vibrancy of the will of God in action will be for you the gentleness and at times the overwhelming power of the Holy Spirit that does take you to those places and other years and centuries past and future where you are given to know the Truth and to feel, even now as I AM with you, the gentle

*the Christ consciousness

pressure at the brow whereby there is a softening and a quickening of the inner vision of thy life.

It is not necessary to wait until the proverbial hour of the one drowning to see one's past come before one or one's future. In the calmness of meditation and the light you can know the will of God. Therefore, disassociate oneself from the conundrums of time and space and "Will or will it not take place?"

But, beloved, to find the key, the goal and the Path and to follow it unerringly does in fact eliminate a decision to be or not to be in this or that place; for then you are moved by angels of the Lord and emissaries from on high and the service of thy God does impel thee to that point in life where the cosmic cross of white fire does find you in the center, in the heart—the Sacred Heart of thy Christ.

In the Universal Christ consciousness is thy salvation! Be uplifted and set apart from the fantasies of this world. Be uplifted as you raise up that Light! So if that Light be raised up in thee, O gentle ones, O gentle hearts, so thou shalt know the spherical union while yet here in these veils of time.

In the All find the uniqueness of thy embodiment of the All. In the bliss that I impart in this hour be thou healed of fear and doubt, recrimination, self-condemnation!

I come, then, a comforter in light. I come in the Presence Elohim. I fill all the world and the children of the Sun with an inner knowingness that transcends all these things in the bliss of God's love.

I AM thy vision, I AM thy certain knowing, I AM the action past, present, future rolled in one as the Be-ness, *the Be-ness of the All* descending drop by drop as dew of the morn upon the fragrant flowers unfolding now in thy chakras.

Sweep all the earth, angels of our bands and elemental beings! Sweep the seas and the sky, the stars and the patterns! Bless the tiny feet of children playing. Clear the way for the coming of the Christed one!

O blessed mothers and fathers, it is indeed the hour of Divine Opportunity. Let some usher in the New Age who have seen a brilliant light and may stand in dignity before their Presence in the Individed One to attain a co-measurement of that light, becoming it and therefore being found in the secret place of the Most High God, sealed in the crystal chamber of my heart.

I AM Elohim and that which I have spoken is known within the soul and deciphered, each one according to his own path. My Christ/thy Christ shall unfold the mystery of Being, beloved.

Fear not, I AM with thee. Elohim I AM.
I AM sealing you now in precipitation's flame of Holy Science
wed to Religion.
Alpha/Omega! Cloven tongues of fire! I seal thee now.
ELOHIM

"The Summit Lighthouse Sheds Its Radiance O'er All the World to Manifest as Pearls of Wisdom."
This dictation by **Cyclopea** was **delivered** by the Messenger Elizabeth Clare Prophet following her **Monday, February 8, 1988** lecture at the Inn at the Park Hotel, **Anaheim, California,** where she was stumping for Saint Germain's Coming Revolution in Higher Consciousness.
(1) The sealing of the West Coast against cataclysm. On August 5, 1973, the Elohim of Purity delivered a dictation in Santa Barbara, California, announcing: "The fire of purity is released from the Elohim as the sealing action of this coast, the sealing at subterranean levels beneath the sea, beneath the land. And the light fills those areas where formerly darkness dwelled. And the light seals this coast for a time and a half a time that the flame of the Divine Mother might appear, that Wisdom might teach her children, that the renaissance of the true culture of the Divine Mother might come forth." On March 9, 1975, the Elohim of Peace, dictating in Los Angeles, said: "I anchor now electrodes beneath the Central Sun magnet, holding this city in fire again for a time and a time and half a time so that those who would be the law may prove the law." The Elohim also delivered a dispensation of the Lord Christ and the Four and Twenty Elders that the image and pattern of the soul of Jesus in the hour of the crucifixion and "as that soul was crying out in the Garden of Gethsemane in prayer, holding the balance for mankind," be sealed "as an electronic forcefield in the seat-of-the-soul chakra [Los Angeles is the seat-of-the-soul chakra of America], in the fiery heart at the etheric plane of the city of Los Angeles. And it is sealed this day in all who have prepared the heart chakra and the seat-of-the-soul chakra as the dwelling place of the Most High God. . . . You are, then, sealed by an arc of light in the heart of the Elohim of Peace. And all who will take that arc and make of it the Ark of the Covenant will walk the earth with that sacred-fire thread, evermore one with the Elohim, evermore drawing the energies of the Elohim. So this is holding the balance against cataclysm. There can be no cataclysm as long as you are one in God, as long as mankind pledge to serve and work beneath his rod. . . . So we prepare that this city might receive the greatest influx of light. . . that can be afforded in this hour, the greatest light that has been anchored here since the time of Lemuria when all sang praise and hosanna to the Mother Flame." A week later, on March 16, 1975, the Elohim Hercules returned to Los Angeles and said: "We are determined to save this planet. We are determined that no energy coils will challenge the life that is God's love. We are determined to give our all. . . . Watch how Terra is reborn in the sphere of the consciousness of Hercules and Amazonia. Watch, then, for the rumbling in the hills. Watch for the adjustment of the elements and elemental life. Watch and pray and be the focal point of balance. I AM the balance of the law for a point of energy you call Earth and I AM the balance of the law of commeasurement whereby you stand one foot upon earth, one foot in heaven." Cyclopea is announcing in this dictation that the purpose of the dispensation for the sealing of the West Coast has been fulfilled. He is letting the Lightbearers (who have held the balance as instruments of Elohim) know that the times and half a time given have expired, even as the mission of the Two Witnesses in Los Angeles which they have supported has been accomplished. See *Spoken by Elohim* (1978 *Pearls of Wisdom,* vol. 21, nos. 8-10), pp. 40, 45, 46, 48, 54; also on cassette MTG7310 and on 4-audiocassette album *The Seven Elohim in the Power of the Spoken Word,* cassette B7636. **(2)** From 1976 through 1986 the international headquarters of Church Universal and Triumphant was located in Pasadena and Malibu, California. The Keepers of the Flame have also maintained a Motherhouse and Teaching Center in Santa Barbara (1969–83) and Teaching Centers in downtown Los Angeles (1976–83) and San Francisco (1976 to the present). In 1981 the Church purchased the Royal Teton Ranch in Park County, Montana, and moved its headquarters there in 1986 and 1987. Teaching Centers or Study Groups remain in the following locations in California: Alhambra, Bakersfield, Gridley, Gualala, Lakewood, Lancaster, Los Angeles, Los Osos, Menlo Park/Palo Alto, Palm Desert, Pasadena, Redding, Riverside, Sacramento, San Diego, San Francisco, San Jose, San Luis Obispo, Santa Ana, Santa Barbara, Santa Cruz, Stockton, Tarzana, and Victorville/Barstow. **(3) Predictions of earth changes on the West Coast.** See *Saint Germain On Prophecy,* Book Two, pp. 143, 146–47, 150–51; Book Three, pp. 54–56, 66. **(4)** Gen. 12:1, 2; Heb. 13:14.

Pearls of Wisdom®

published by The Summit Lighthouse

Vol. 31 No. 17	Beloved Archangel Gabriel	April 24, 1988

Saint Germain Stumps America

7

To Open the Way of the Divine Mother

I Announce the Opportunity for the Ascension

Hail, Sons and Daughters of God! Hail, Legions of Light!

I AM Gabriel, which stand in the Presence of God![1] I have descended to this city and place for the calling Home of the Light, for the raising up of that Light in the servant-sons upon earth.

Therefore, O ye daughters of Jerusalem, *blaze forth thy Light!* For I AM in the earth and I AM come the Archangel of the Annunciation. And I come to open the way for the Divine Mother and her return. And therefore, for the clearing of the highway of our God, for the making way for the Divine Mother, let the judgment descend upon the force of anti-Light moving against her little ones!

I, Gabriel, come, sent by God for the dividing of the way of Light and Darkness and the Real from the Unreal. I *pierce* the illusion, then, of all those who believe that they are well and increased with goods when beneath all this there is the filthiness and there is the lack and the absence of the filling of the cup of Light.[2] I come before the hour when none can turn back the LORD's appearance, none can turn back the white fire as the wrath of the Most High God.

Therefore, I, Gabriel, am sent to you, O ye people of this state and way, for a quickening, for an awakening, for the clap and the thunder and the lightning from on high, as in the Holy of Holies the Light is released for a chemicalization in the earth that all that is of the Light might prevail.

Blessed hearts, the hour is come for world change and for the

melting of the elements with a fervent heat of sacred fire.³ Therefore, when you invoke that fire and become it, you move in the
Spirit of God; but when you leave yourselves empty, therefore you
are open to be tumbled and tossed and turned in the wave of
oncoming karma.

Blessed hearts of the Light, we have sent this Messenger for
decades up and down these coasts and cities. Know, then, that the
hour of the Divine Appearing of the LORD within you is upon you.
May you see the Light and know the Light and realize that change
is due upon a planet and upon a people who have walked in
ignorance and not sought the Light of divine illumination.

Happy are ye who have come to a fount of illumination so
raised up in this place. Happy are ye whose chakras delight in the
law of God and who receive the Blessed Virgin and know that the
Immaculate Divine Mother is also thine own. For out of the Cosmic
Womb, Omega, thou hast come forth for a fiery destiny. What will
ye? Set it aside for the paltry pleasures of an age—an age revisited
and relived ad nauseam in all past civilizations?

You are made for greater things and callings. Therefore, I,
Gabriel, announce to you the hour and the opportunity for the
ascension. And by that power of the Holy Spirit, even by the
power of the cosmic dance, *Shiva! Shiva! Shiva! shatter,* then,
even the matrix of that desire that is untoward that leads not to
Life but Death. And therefore, let the sweet smell of death and the
success cult be cast aside as the Divine Reality of thy God does
descend before thee as a fire infolding itself.⁴

Ye are called and called again and called again, O beloved of
the Light! Hear, then, and know that the Divine Light shall surely
come upon a planet and a people. And as the harvest is nigh,
lifetime by lifetime sow good fruits while there is yet the sowing
and the reaping, that in this world and in the world to come the
harvest of abundant treasure might find thee in the abundance of
the abundant Life; and therefore a cup which runneth over may
feed the millions of the unwashed masses.

In the living light of the morning star, as we have gone before
prophets and apostles of old and as they have gone before the face
of the Archangels proclaiming our Word to a people, so we come
again that you might know that the LORD's Spirit is in the land
through his Archangels, sent and signified by a Messenger whom
you may see and know and touch and understand to be your sister
of Light.

O come out from among them and release yourselves from all
folly! For anyone who may be decided and decide himself to enter
the fiery coil can be the instrument of the saving of a world. So

may the Daystar from on high[5] that has visited your forefathers of old be upon you and may the call be heard and answered, for the answer must be forthcoming from those upon earth who will then receive the emissaries of God and thereby know the presence of our comfort. Our consolation upon a people is an immensity out of the Immensity.

O ye who do the will of God, blessed art thou amongst all people. And ye who know not the joy of the alignment with the fiery coil of Being, know, then, that I, Gabriel, come in this hour with mercy and peace, understanding and grace to all who will receive me in their homes.

I AM the Angel of visitation. Lo, I AM come! For it is a reprieve and a surcease for the servants of God that they might know the loving care of one who calls you Home, for it is the hour of thy coming.

Will you not, then, cry unto the One:

"O my Father, O my Mother, I AM coming Home. I AM thy Son, long chosen to go forth in veils of maya. Now I wield the sword, flaming sword of Light, and I pierce all unreality that the children of Light might step through the veil and know thee face to face.

"I remember my ancient calling, O my Father, O my Mother, to shepherd, to succor life, to give comfort. I shall be, then, the [instrument of the] Divine Helper, for I have seen the LORD's Spirit this night in the person of thy servant, Gabriel."

Thus, beloved, heaven does pierce the night and enter earth's octaves in strange and mysterious ways, so they say. My coming is as miraculous and no more so than the natural extension of the branch of the Tree of Life to touch and bless the head of a child most holy. Let the children of the earth who are the holy ones of God receive me, for their hearts are pure, these little ones.

O you who can be cosmic sponsors of life on earth, care for the innocents, care for the children; for in them is thy joy, thy peace and thy holiness preserved. And inasmuch as ye have done it unto one of the least of these my brethren, ye have done it unto me.[6]

I seal you with the cosmic cross of white fire unto the day of your destiny and your path of initiation.

O thou beauteous white rose of the Divine Mother, unfold in these hearts that they may not lose the touch of peace and the kiss of a Mother's love. Unto her heart I return with the swiftness of the infinite arrow shot from the bow of the Infinite Archer.

Delivered following the Messenger's February 9, 1988 Stump at the Sheraton Universal Hotel, North Hollywood, Calif. (1) Luke 1:19. The angels of the LORD which "stand in the Presence of God" are "sent from God" as his messengers to transmit the Light (Christ consciousness) of that I AM THAT I AM to his sons and daughters for the accomplishment of those dispensations which they announce. Unto Moses was revealed the I AM Presence through "the angel of the LORD who appeared unto him in a flame of fire," which was the actual presence and personification of the I AM THAT I AM by Archangel Michael (Exod. 3:2). (2) Rev. 3:16–18. (3) II Pet. 3:10, 12. (4) Ezek. 1:4. (5) II Pet. 1:19. (6) Matt. 18:5, 6; 25:40; Mark 9:41, 42; Luke 17:1, 2.

THE RADIANT WORD
THE POWER OF THE 10,000 TIMES 10,000*

Excerpt from a dictation given in Washington, D.C., July 1, 1961
by Beloved Lord Maitreya through the Messenger Mark L. Prophet

...The greatest word of power that has ever been uttered was spoken into your consciousness within the framework of your being when the voice of God in you spoke and said, "Behold, I AM!"

This being, which is the fiber of you, this existence of immortality, did not begin to be yesterday, nor shall it cease to be today, nor shall it cease to be forever. Anchor in yourself, therefore, a sense of the immortal consciousness of God and the immortal consciousness of Love....

I, Maitreya, say to you today that the Ascended Masters, in the great deliberations and the councils of the Great White Brotherhood, have determined that human tyranny has too long held sway over the mass mind. Therefore we have asked for a great petition whereby the student body today shall be given that which is known as *the full power of the ten thousand-times-ten thousand*. From this day henceforward, every decree that you utter shall be increased by the power of the ten thousand-times-ten thousand!

I, Maitreya, declare that those who give decrees from this day forward shall be creating a tremendous, impelling, swiftly moving acceleration which shall sweep through the earthly consciousness of mankind and compel this earth free.

It is determined by the Great Cosmic Law that this earth shall not submit to the tyranny of human consciousness—which, in itself, while it is intelligent substance to a degree, is not Ascended Master discriminating intelligence. Therefore, it has *no* power! It has *no* power! It has *no* power! And I say that you must cut yourself free from that consciousness by a conscious, joyful entering in to our thought by entering in to the thought of God about you.

You are thought of by God. Each and every lifestream here is a part of God. Each of you has a doorway to enter into God's consciousness. Each of you can expand the flame of the sacred fire on the altar of your own being. And no other lifestream can do it for you. No Ascended Master can do it for you. No one can do it for you, in the final analysis, but your own God Presence and Holy Christ Self.

We can and we *do* give you our love! We can and we *do* give you our energy! We can and we *do* give you our strength! And we guide you and we direct you and we deliberate in our councils to bring to the earth and all of its environs the great enfolding love of the infinite Cosmic Christ intelligence and the All-Father/Mother God.

But, blessed and beloved ones, it is up to individuals to determine that they shall be *one* with God, *one* with Life, *one* with beauty, *one* with the Buddha, *one* with the Buddha of their own unfolding divinity, *one* with the mantrams of the Spirit—until they in God-victory are a part of God forevermore....

*Mentioned in Pearl no. 13, p. 132.

This dictation by Lord Maitreya is printed in 1984 *Pearls of Wisdom,* vol. 27, no. 7, pp. 59–64. See also Mark L. Prophet and Elizabeth Clare Prophet, "The Power of the Ten Thousand-Times-Ten Thousand," in *The Science of the Spoken Word,* pp. 78–79.

Saint Germain Stumps America

8

To Embody a New Vibration
The Golden Yellow Light and Gem of Illumination

Holy Ones of God,

Be raised up to the crown of life, for I, Lanto, am sent to you that you might know the true path of the bodhisattva,[1] that you might enter grace by a gentle light of illumination, a piercing light that does also fracture ignorance and the bondage of Old Night.

And therefore, as light does increase in the crown chakra, cracks in the ceiling appear that there might be above the devotee of wisdom's flame a vaulted ceiling, geometric, of crystal manifestation. And out of the cave and into the crystalline chamber, so the soul may emerge in clusters of other crystallized ones discovering the fire infolding itself within.

Therefore, in the mountains of the north (as it has been said and told by our bands) there is the gathering of souls beneath the surface of the earth with adepts ascended. In your finer bodies you may go there to learn of me and of my embodiment of the Christ Teaching long, long ago prior to the Christian era; for in every age there have been forerunners of the next. And many thousands of years before the dawn of that light does reach an outer humanity through the adepts, there are those who keep the flame within the secret chambers of the earth and within certain mountains.

Blessed ones, the Lost Teachings of the living Christ are sent to you and signified by his angel in the release of the Revelation to John.[2] Happy are ye in illumination's golden flame of God-happiness when through self-knowledge you take dominion and know the joy of life never known before.

In this hour, then, of the Lord's descent, even that notable day of the LORD,[3] prepare ye, for thy God is nigh. Therefore, let the little children take the bells and sound them as in ancient days in the temples of the Far East the tinkling bells denoted the quiet footsteps of gentle, sandaled ones coming to an altar where a flame kindled without signified the hour for the flame meditation within.

I am the one, then, the Lord of the Second Ray, who does come to teach you the way of the inner Light. Let that inner Light glow that far-off worlds might know that bands of devotees have determined to embody a new vibration: the vibration of Buddha, the vibration of the Lord of the World, the vibration of Christos.

O how illumination as a dawn of presence, quietude and yet power magnificent does come upon the individual, and there is a surcease of all outer noise, ignominy and those who live for outer titillations. And there is a fire that draws one in even to the secret chamber of the heart where the light of Christ is the Presence all-knowing.[4] Come into that science of the New Age. Come into the heart of hearts.

Beloved, so near and yet so far are many who walk the path of a New Age dispensation from the Divine Reality. As thin as parchment is the distance between thy heart and the Inner Splendor. O blessed ones, by a change of vibration, by wisdom and a light raised up, you, then, know the inner Presence and become it.

By this inner peace and the tranquility of spheres upon spheres of Light—of Light's meditation and mantra—come to know how the golden-robed brothers of our bands do walk up and down the land, and the bell tinkles, memories are kindled and souls are awakened. And they make their way, processioning, then, with Shiva[5] to the Grand Teton, to the heart of that inner retreat.[6]

It is an hour, beloved, as in all past cycles of earth changes, when in their finer bodies souls of Light find those places in higher octaves and begin to merge with a new vibration and dispensation.

It is the message of Lord Gautama, it is the message of Maitreya we bring in these days together. For this ancient city [Berkeley] is the recipient of the arcing of light of the ancient Eastern teachings also sealed in the caves of the Himalayas.

Know thyself. Know thyself as a God-man, as a God-woman. Know thyself truly as an intermediary, a facilitator in this hour of transition. With a little bit of attentiveness to the science of mantra, with a little bit of withdrawal from the things of this world, you can begin to evidence a visage, a countenance, of peace and a certain level of mastery and wisdom.

As you study the dictations of the Masters of the Second Ray published through our Messengers in abundance, you will become aware of your soul ascending, carried aloft on the gentle fountain of the Mother Light rising.*

Know, then, the way of the Ascended Masters who lead you so gently into a new awareness of self; and by violet flame with the wisdom of wisdom's yellow fires, there is transmutation by illumination. True illumination of Christos and Buddha is always become illumined action. Those who are true to Truth herself as the living goddess and patroness of all that is true in life must by the inner love of that living flame of Truth become doers, changers, reorganizers.

O yes, those of the wisdom ray do balance that wisdom by the brilliance of the sapphire power of God's will and the intense rose of love. Thus, in this threefold flame, I did teach my disciples in ancient China and did also teach Lord Confucius the way of the revealing of the inner Light, letting that Light shine, then, from my heart.[7]

Thus, those who were with me had impressed upon the memory a goal, that goal to raise up the flame of Liberty, that threefold flame of the heart, and to do so until that Light in such a shining splendor would call Home all those who are of the Ancient of Days, of Sanat Kumara.

Know thy inheritance, O beloved. Know that thou art called. And in this evening together in communion and harmony, surely you have contributed a jewel of light fashioned of your heart's love as a focus that will not be set aside, a golden gem that is a sign of hope to elemental life who must hold the balance in this area.

Blessed are ye who understand the fulcrum of the individualization of the God Flame and yourself as instrumental in the raising of the consciousness of an age. Where God is, where the stream of Life is, I, Lanto, say with Confucius with me, let that stream become the golden yellow light! Let all who follow it to its source know that in wisdom's fount there is the peace which always passes understanding,[8] there is the unfoldment of the complete gnosis of Self.

Thus, knowledge of the within as a geometry, as an alchemy to be, *that must be,* does unfold that flower, petal by petal, of the crown chakra. And I predict to you, each one who will come with me this night guided by Jophiel's angels of the Second Ray, that you shall know and have an illumination, sponsored as well by the Goddess of Wisdom, that will carry you far in holding the light of Lake Titicaca, of Meru and the Feminine Ray of the planet now come to the fore.[9]

*the sacred fire, Kundalini, rising on the spinal altar, balancing the chakras with the Mother Light

Know, then, wisdom's love, wisdom's alchemy. Play thy part, beloved, for many souls who know not and cannot in this hour respond to me or my Messenger depend on you to keep the flame.

Keep the flame, then, of golden illumination, and let thy crown be truly a crown of victory. Thus, in the annals of the centuries and the millennia, let thy name be remembered as one who contributed to the confluent stream of the Self-awareness of an evolution in the heart of Buddha, Buddha, Buddha.

AUM Buddha. AUM Buddha.

"The Summit Lighthouse Sheds Its Radiance O'er All the World to Manifest as Pearls of Wisdom." This dictation by **Lord Lanto** was **delivered** by Elizabeth Clare Prophet following her **Thurs., Feb. 11, 1988** lecture at the Berkeley House, **Berkeley, Calif.,** where she was stumping for Saint Germain's Coming Revolution in Higher Consciousness. (1) **Bodhisattva.** See 1988 *Pearls of Wisdom,* vol. 31, no. 4, p. 48. (2) Rev. 1:1. (3) Isa. 61:1–2; 63:4; Joel 2:28–32; Acts 2:1–21. (4) For teachings on the **secret chamber of the heart** see Djwal Kul, *Intermediate Studies of the Human Aura,* pp. 38–41, 84. (5) **Shiva** [Sanskrit "auspicious"] is the Third Person of the Trinity of the Godhead in Hinduism, the Holy Spirit, the Lord of Love, who outpictures the dual aspect of the Destroyer and the Restorer of the universe. He is worshipped as the fearsome and auspicious one who drives away sin, disease, death, and demons of delusion. See *A Trilogy On the Threefold Flame of Life,* in *Saint Germain On Alchemy,* Book Three, pp. 319–20; Mark L. Prophet and Elizabeth Clare Prophet, *The Lost Teachings of Jesus II,* pp. 145–46; Jesus and Kuthumi, *Corona Class Lessons,* pp. 189, 424–25. (6) **The Royal Teton Retreat,** congruent with the Grand Teton near Jackson Hole, Wyoming, is the principal retreat of the Great White Brotherhood on the North American continent. This physical/etheric retreat is an ancient focus of great light where the seven rays of the Elohim and Archangels are enshrined. The Lords of Karma, Gautama Buddha, and all members of the Great White Brotherhood frequent this gathering place of the Ascended Masters and their disciples while also maintaining the specialized functions of their own retreats. Customarily the Lords of Karma meet at the Royal Teton Retreat twice a year, at winter and summer solstice, to review petitions from unascended mankind and to grant dispensations for their assistance. Conclaves attended by thousands of lifestreams from every continent, who journey there in their finer bodies through soul travel while they sleep, are also held at this retreat as well as smaller classes and tutorials. Here also Saint Germain and Lord Lanto with the Ascended Master Confucius (hierarch of the Royal Teton Retreat) are conducting their universities of the Spirit—courses of instruction being given by the Lords of the Seven Rays and the Maha Chohan at their respective retreats for tens of thousands of students who are pursuing the path of self-mastery on the seven rays. See *Lords of the Seven Rays: Mirror of Consciousness,* Book One, pp. 79–80, 89, 92, 95, 96–97, 104–10, 301–5; 1987 *Pearls of Wisdom,* vol. 30, no. 28, pp. 285–86. (7) During his final incarnation before his ascension Lord Lanto's adoration of the threefold flame within his heart was so great that the intense glow of his divine spark could be seen emanating a soft golden glow through his chest. See *Lords of the Seven Rays: Mirror of Consciousness,* Book One, pp. 91–92. (8) Phil. 4:7. (9) **Feminine Ray of the planet.** See 1988 *Pearls of Wisdom,* vol. 31, no. 13, p. 134, n.2.

Pearls of Wisdom®

published by The Summit Lighthouse

Vol. 31 No. 19	Beloved El Morya	May 8, 1988

Saint Germain Stumps America
9
A Sapphire Chalice
Violet Flame for a Measure of Safety

I give myself, a sapphire chalice, to the chelas of the will of God. Fashioned of my heart, this chalice interspersed with diamonds is one that can grow as the chela grows (even as the parent who carries the child may carry a greater weight as the child does grow).

So I, El Morya, looking with utter compassion upon my own, desire in this giving of myself to demonstrate to you the way of the Diamond Heart of God's will.

Therefore, out of the First Ray of the dawn's love for the diamond-shining Mind of God I come to you with lessons to keep you in the facets of the sapphire will of God that you might not sink into lesser vibration, my chelas, in these hours when earth becomes heavier before she shall become lighter—and she *shall* become lighter by your invocation of the violet flame *and only by that invocation.*

Therefore, in making myself a chalice for my chelas, I give myself to be filled by my chelas with the wine, the purple wine of the rich grape of the harvest. Let it be, then, an intense wine of the Spirit that comes forth by your call to the violet flame. Let the chalice of my being, with you, be the wine-bearer of Aquarius, beloved, for something must be done. Something is needed, beloved. Therefore, I propose in my heart to give myself, for what else can one give?

Therefore, I have appealed to beloved Alpha, who has assured me that in the giving of myself to those who espouse the will of God I am consistent with his proclamation of sponsorship of the Lightbearers of the earth.[1]

Blessed hearts, I desire to be a chalice that does overflow with the wine that you distill by your meditations in the white light of the Holy Spirit, and then with the intense imploring and fiery appeal to Mercy, to Kuan Yin, my cohort of Light, there might flow through you such intensity of the violet flame as to provide our beloved Saint Germain with an extraordinary portion, even a reservoir of such violet flame as to increase transmutation and therefore provide that measure of safety that is not now present in the earth.

You tread on thin ice, beloved. This sea of glass, then, becomes a transparency not for heaven but for the pit itself that does exist beneath this city, and therefore see how a surface of glass sustained by the light only of Lightbearers* does hold up a city that has turned toward Darkness.†

Let us reverse the tide, the Lemurian tide of the misuse of the Light‡ of the Divine Mother in holy temples![2] Let there be a turning of the tide, for God is able and God in you is able and I have seen what miracles my chelas have wrought in recent years and centuries. Therefore, it is never too late to begin.

Thus, I AM become a chalice walking—a chalice running when you run! I come, beloved, in the full measure of my heart's devotion to my brother Saint Germain, your own beloved Master whose life, I tell you, is given for you. Therefore, let the full measure of this chalice be given daily, for each day I shall take that which you have deposited in this chalice and place it in the violet flame reservoir of light on the etheric plane. Therefore, beloved, fill and let it be emptied—fill it to overflowing.

Thus, beloved, this my walk with Saint Germain may prove to be that stitch in time of Hercules and Amazonia.[3] It may prove to be such a boon to chelas that they will at last transcend these planetary karmic cycles that have produced a density within them that is not to my liking.

Therefore, *pierce! pierce! pierce!* O blue-flame sapphire light! Blue-lightning angels and devas of the Diamond Heart, come forth, then! For there must be a piercing of this density, that this overflowing wine of violet flame, Holy Spirit, may pour through the cracks and the fissures in the earth and yet give to elemental life the support so necessary.

Blessed hearts, now let us consider how each one does become a facet of the Divine Mother's Diamond Heart and my own. Blessed Mary does stand in this room radiating a healing light. You have tarried long, some longer than in many a year, longer

*pillars of individual Christhood   †toward the left-handed path of the turning of the Light to the subservience of the not-self, its pride, ambition, sensuality and denial of the Christ in the Sons of God
‡God consciousness

than many have attended a church service for lifetimes, and therefore the reward is instantaneous. As the Blessed Mother has perceived needs for healing you know not of, she does anoint you with unguents of healing light. You are so beloved.

O be quickened, O be quickened, beloved! For the victory is nigh. The angels stand guard. But a victory whose cup is not quaffed is not a victory—and there are not in-betweens. Blessed hearts, it is a choice for victory or utter defeat and self-humiliation.

Let the light ascend and the soul will follow suit. Let the soul ascend and millions will follow. Have we not earned our blue-flame ribbons of light? Have we not seen and known the inspiration of millions because we have dared to ascend the mount Horeb and to know God face to face?[4]

Let the uncommon Light be kept by the uncommon souls who do dare to be different.

I now touch by my heart's love and the fire of God's will ten thousand new chelas of the will of God about to enter in. I touch them, beloved, for my love of Jesus and his call for ten thousand new Keepers of the Flame.[5] I touch them and I tell you I am in pursuit of the holy ones of God who know not they are holy until they are told by the Blessed Mother.

Beloved, let the flowers who are the lilies in the earth be quickened and awakened! Let them feel the gentle breezes and have hope again. Do your part, beloved, for I have secured all the dispensation that the Great Law will allow me. Now, will you not give of your heart's Light* that you also might be the recipient from Alpha of a fiery mantle and dispensations that I could not receive?

In your own way, then, seek and find. Call and knock. Receive the answer and know that the door of Darjeeling is opened.[6] Come, then, my beloved, for we have the work of the Divine Mother of all ages to fulfill.

O ancient Divine Mother of Lemurian soil, O Divine Mother, rise again, rise once again! Thy children call thy name, see thy face, know thee once more. Rise, Divine Mother! Carry thy children to the heights of summit peaks! Bear them up and we shall catch them by the Holy Spirit.

O Divine Mother, raise on high the Manchild ere flood tide take him from thee. O Divine Mother, many-armed Kuan Yin, blessed Mary, O Divine Spirit of Omega, O Mother of the World, receive thy children ere it is too late! Seal them in the Immaculate Heart that they may not lose faith or hope or courage.

Let fearlessness flame *pierce*, then, the darkness surrounding

---
*Holy Christ Flame

the children of God! Angels of the Diamond Heart, seal them in the fiery protection of Saint Michael that they may no longer be abused, misused, trodden upon. Father, take them in thine arms.

I AM Morya, so concerned for the little ones and the tender hearts and the little feet and the blessed hands that pray and the lispings of the tiniest child in crib.

I stand before you in this city as I have stood before. I receive you, if you will receive me, on a path of discipleship that shall lead to a practical and swift application of the Law for the defense of Life. Life must needs be defended, beloved. I implore you, defend Life and know your own freedom!

I AM Morya. I seal you by the sign of the First Ray. Know, then, the signet of the blue rose of Sirius.

Purusha.

"The Summit Lighthouse Sheds Its Radiance O'er All the World to Manifest as Pearls of Wisdom." This dictation by **El Morya** was **delivered** by Elizabeth Clare Prophet following her **Friday, February 12, 1988** lecture, "Crystals and Chakras: Chakra Initiations with the Lords of the Seven Rays," at the Sheraton-Palace Hotel, **San Francisco, California,** where she was stumping for Saint Germain's Coming Revolution in Higher Consciousness. **(1) Dispensations confined to the Lightbearers.** See 1988 *Pearls of Wisdom,* vol. 31, no. 3, p. 33, n. 2. **(2) The cult of the Divine Mother on Lemuria and the fall of Mu.** See Mark L. Prophet and Elizabeth Clare Prophet, *Climb the Highest Mountain,* 2d ed., pp. 493–95; *The Lost Teachings of Jesus II,* pp. 260–61. **(3) Hercules and Amazonia's stitch in time.** In a dictation given July 1, 1987, during *FREEDOM 1987* in the Heart of the Inner Retreat, the Elohim Hercules said: "By your presence I send through your body chalices—which I do qualify with sapphire diamond light—a current of the First Ray to summon all earth to divine purpose. [10-second intonation] The sound I have sounded in that instant, beloved, reached the Central Sun and did return as a cosmic stitch in time through this heart. So make thy heart a chalice of God's will and be those who sewed up the garment of earth with a stitch in time. I, Hercules, the cosmic tailor, will sew it through your heart." See 1987 *Pearls of Wisdom,* vol. 30, no. 34, p. 317. **(4)** Exod. 19:3–25; 33:9–11; Deut. 5:2, 4, 5. **(5)** On May 28, 1987, Jesus called for **ten thousand Keepers of the Flame:** "I am sent by the Father for the quickening now of ten thousand saints in the City Foursquare that I mark as North America....Blessed hearts, I have come, then, to make a plea to you and to send my Messenger abroad across this continent for the gathering of ten thousand who will call themselves Keepers of the Flame of Life and who will understand that I, Jesus, have called them....Blessed ones, this North America, a place consecrated by Love to the reunion of souls with God, is a place where if the Lightbearers would respond and *make the Call,* even as I call you this night, there should be established even the white light over a continent to protect it from those calamities of the Four Horsemen, which could indeed appear for want of mediators in the earth. Understand, beloved, that the mediators who must stand between a people and a planet and their karma must be in physical embodiment." On Oct. 2, 1987, El Morya said: "I come in the power that God has given unto me as the Lord of the First Ray to summon the troops and to say to you, the Lord Christ has called for ten thousand Keepers of the Flame. Can he save the city and North America with ten thousand? He has said so, beloved, and I believe him....To be a Keeper of the Flame and to give that daily support in decrees as well as an activism that does display one's heart and thought and mind for a cause—this is the calling of the hour." See 1987 *Pearls of Wisdom,* vol. 30, nos. 27, 54, pp. 269, 273, 274–75, 475. **(6)** El Morya's retreat, the Temple of Good Will, is located on the etheric plane over Darjeeling, India. See Mark L. Prophet and Elizabeth Clare Prophet, *Lords of the Seven Rays: Mirror of Consciousness,* Book One, pp. 68–70, 75; Book Two, pp. 34–35, 39, 46, 301–2, 304–5; and El Morya, *The Chela and the Path,* pp. 36–42, 56, 137.

Pearls of Wisdom®
published by The Summit Lighthouse

Vol. 31 No. 20   *Beloved Saint Germain*   *May 15, 1988*

Saint Germain Stumps America
10
The Law of Self-Transcendence
"What Man Has Done, Man Can Do!"

In the invincible majesty of the light of Freedom, I descend by freewill choice into this city of an ancient light. Therefore, beloved, I am come to greet my own and my own hearts of the living flame of Freedom! Welcome, O beloved, to my heart! [15-sec. applause]

You do me honor, beloved, to provide yourselves a living chalice and a living flame for my descent. Therefore, grateful for every precious gift of your heart to the living Spirit of Cosmic Freedom in the earth, I salute you as compatriots of a cosmos that we ignite for Liberty's flame.

In the oneness of my heart, beloved, I deliver, then, to you the violet flame dispensations accorded me from the Central Sun. Therefore, I AM the multiplier of the good works of all those who are keeping the fires of Freedom worldwide.

Wherever there is a Lightbearer in any clime or nation or race or compartment of consciousness, there am I with the gift of my violet flame this Valentine's Day. My desire is that this gift multiplied by your heart, sent many times over not as a chain letter but as a chain decree, beloved, will therefore be the igniting of wreaths of light around a planet and chains of rosaries of pearls from the heart of the Blessed Virgin Mary.

Blessed ones, *I have heard, I have delivered, I have seen* surely the handwriting in the stars above you.[1] Know, then, beloved, that our awareness of these conditions spans the ages. Surely you realize that in our retreats and by the advanced technology we also use, we have plotted the course of systems of worlds for millennia, both in the past and into the future, for all must one day meet.

The precision with which these cycles occur, beloved, is entirely dependent upon the humanity with which we deal— whether or not an evolution may subject itself unto its own creation or transcend it. This is the question, then: to be or not to be above the Darkness descending, to be or not to be in the center of the Light.

The law of self-transcendence is a gift from the heart of God; so is its understanding and application. Blessed hearts, you have observed how in the animal kingdom there is no self-transcendence but only the redundant repetition of that which is an original matrix with a very slow evolution, if any evolution at all. Realize, then, that the gifts of God are not to be taken for granted. The gifts of God that go unused, therefore, are lost.

Have the sons of God in the earth lost the application of self-transcendence? I should say that in some cases it is so and in some cases it is not. Would to God that all would summon the very power of Be-ness from on high and know the descent of that star of the I AM Presence that, not as falling star of Wormwood but as the descent of light of a cosmos of the Central Sun, does come into your temple with a spiral of light that is for nothing less than the self-transcendence of the individual, of child-man, until he real-izes himself as God-man and God-manifestation!

Thus, beloved, while some forget and some have never known and some have never been inscribed in the memory of God, *you* may determine to write your name in the sky and in the earth and on documents that you will find at the retreat of the Royal Teton as you come while your bodies sleep this night to that area of the Grand Teton, escorted by angels of Archangel Michael, there to see and know how the destiny of nations in this hour can be forged, can be realized, can be raised to a victory by the conserva-tion of that Light-force of the Divine Mother.

Realize, beloved, that the opportunity is unprecedented. When in past ages of the last two thousand years did the individ-ual have the option to enter a path of the ascension unto the Light eternal? When was the option opened to you in general to have my teaching bound and in the bookstalls of the nations?

I tell you, beloved, for the gifts given, for the knowledge imparted, there ought to have been a greater harvest of souls by this hour! How, then, can a people to whom is given so great a salvation,[2] so great a means to an end long sought neglect that gift and that salvation?

I tell you, beloved, though the human consciousness may be

unpredictable, though it may fail to realize and appreciate the potential of Christ within, I say, the soul does know. And I remain the champion of all souls in the age of Aquarius until the Lord God himself should take from me that opportunity, God forbid.

Blessed ones, therefore, we are always gratified when the response to our message and our Messenger does warrant a continued infiring of a locale by the action of a sacred alchemy. O would to God, then, that Keepers of the Flame should rise up en masse in this city to deter cataclysm and earthquake prophesied! Would to God they would see and know that in these hills and beyond to the north, ancient temples of the Divine Mother have records and once stood.

Therefore, know, beloved, that those things which might have been may already have been withdrawn, but the fruits of victory are yet possible to every individual who does know that the hour of his fulfillment is come!

If you, then, acknowledge your individual destiny in this planet and beyond, if you recognize that you have an immortality shining through the veil of Matter, if you know that one day you shall not only transcend yourself but transcend the stars, then believe me that I AM Saint Germain and that I AM here and that I AM the champion of the Light within you and the Master Alchemist who looks for you to be a pupil on the path of that fulfillment!

Blessed ones, the stars of the heavens are the signs of those who have gone before. Make your own star and causal body the signet in this hour of your commitment to your own personal cosmic freedom. Can those who move on a dying world do any less than claim the stars and their own stardom? This is "thy kingdom come on earth as it is in heaven" and this is the will of our Father for you as it was for me!

I am a Master of the Seventh Ray and I have chosen to be that Master for one purpose, that you might see me shining in the splendor of the aura of Aquarius and know that you may achieve the same as I have done. What man has done, man can do! And therefore never, and I say *never*, never allow the mediocrity of the mud slides of the planet to come upon you and to snuff out that hope for God-realization!

When you carry that hope in your heart, there is no tragedy in life, no monotony, no boredom that can take from you that star of hope. God-realization is your reason for being, and your destiny today can be accelerated if you will it so. Therefore, I tell you, keep the flame and study my courses in alchemy,[3] and I will show you how swiftly you can make a difference in the world scene.

Blessed ones, the astrology of the hour to the end of this century is dire, there is no other word for it. You have heard it.[1] The wise who consider these statements will recognize the following: that mastery must come in Spirit and in Matter and that efforts must be taken in all octaves of being.

One does not rest one's case on a hope that enough souls of Light on a planet will deliver the mandate of the violet flame that can be received by the Karmic Board to turn the tide of world history. There is more than violet flame involved, beloved. There is free will.

And there are many in positions of power this day who have amassed power and wealth and armaments and technology whose free will is committed to world destruction. I should not trust my fate to their hands, nor should you. Therefore, the wise will remove themselves to that point in time and space which they discover by meditation and unerring guidance of my angels[4] is the correct place for them to be.

Do not consider, then, that you who have not attained to the levels of an Ascended Master may turn the world around merely by the raising of the right hand. If it were so, beloved, we should long ago have done this through you. What you ultimately can do and must do, in all of the promises you have heard, is to invoke that violet flame and to continue to invoke it and use Archangel Michael's Rosary for Armageddon.[5]

For much will change, much will be set aside. Entire kingdoms may come to their judgment. Yet you must be found out of the way. For this very process to occur, world chemicalization is in order!

Thus, beloved, while you fully believe in a complete and total victory for the Light, you also secure yourselves in the physical octave. You get out of the way of the wave of human karma and the waves which rise in world cataclysm. You secure yourselves, and from a bastion of light, from an inner retreat, you direct waves of light into the earth and know that our angels will save all that can be saved.

Practicality, then, takes into account that God does not interfere with free will, nor do the Ascended Masters, nor do the angels. If some have committed themselves to the vicious plot of creating and spreading a plague such as AIDS upon this planet, blessed hearts, as has been done by nefarious individuals (and this exposé is yet to come), I tell you, where a people is vulnerable, the free will of the powers of darkness may bring upon the nations untold mourning and burden.

But you have an equal gift of free will and an access to unlimited power in your I AM Presence and its direction through the science of the spoken Word. Therefore, the [untoward] effects of another's exercise of free will may be challenged and transmuted by yourselves.

Now, if you see yourselves with my angels as the cosmic clean-up committee of planet earth, well, you have rightly positioned yourselves. The question remains, How much can a people so committed clean up? You see, beloved, there is limitation; otherwise, all should have unlimited powers to alter the course of events to their own design of world history.

Therefore know that free will comes down to the gift of the world that is you. You in the microcosm, as this Messenger has repeated to you often, may raise up such a fire and such a light as to be a conversion point for millions and to be the springboard of your own victory and ascension in the Light.

By the power of persuasion and the enlightenment of the Holy Spirit, you may talk and preach and deliver my message everywhere you go; and you may find, by the miracles of God and by a turning around of a national conscience toward the defense of freedom and of this land, that there may yet be a saving grace that every single prophecy heard this night may be consumed.

Blessed ones, to count on this without taking the necessary physical measures would be tantamount to gambling, and you gamble you know not what, for you know not what will be the response or the free will of all others who have heard it.

Therefore, beloved, we long ago directed our Messengers to found the Inner Retreat at the site in Montana as a place set aside in a wilderness area where those who keep the flame of freedom for earth may do so without suffering the backlash of those energies of civilization into which that light is directed.

Do not think that the fallen ones will take their judgment lying down. They will thrash and react, and those who are in the way will experience, therefore, not only their calamitous judgment but the aftermath of their reactionary measures, as they always use change in the world scene to reinforce another amalgamation of power. Thus, the cyclic rounds of light descending must be received by sons of God who take that light and take their stand and defend the little ones, who are always the victims of the abusers of life in the earth.

Blessed hearts, I trust that I make myself clear. The preparedness at a personal and national level has never been more paramount.[6] Your preparedness in your life can be complete in a matter of months. When you are fully prepared and determined to survive physically in the earth, come what may in all of these predictions and those you have heard elsewhere, you are then a free agent of Saint Germain and you may give your life and heart to this very cause of stopping those conditions in their tracks before they are outpictured, therefore rendering your preparations only a safety valve, a security net, a lifeboat, if you will.

Know this, beloved, that those who are prepared often do not need to avail themselves of their preparations. But it is the absence of preparedness that does make a nation vulnerable. We have tried without success to impress this message upon the leaders of this nation and the leaders of movements and social movements, leaders of churches, and politicians. They have not heard us and the sands in the hourglass run out. We do not have a voice in the earth except through you, and therefore what you do in this hour that is left to you remains your option.

As the day of Saint Valentine is upon us, I give to you, then, a gift from my purple fiery heart, and that purple-fiery-heart matrix, beloved, is an amethyst heart surrounded by tiny diamonds. These diamonds are prayer beads for the counting of the thirty-three steps on the spiral of your initiation and the thirty-three times you give my decrees. This is a living amethyst heart which is as real and tangible on the etheric plane as is anything you have in this physical octave.

These hearts come to you now as with wings. They are superimposed as a focus of my heart over your heart. By this gift of the valentine of my heart, beloved, may you know that our hearts are one and that my heart with your heart, multiplying the action, then, can give you, while there is time, a tremendous impetus to world transmutation as you give the calls to the violet flame—an impetus of the Holy Spirit for the conversion, the turning around, of many hearts to embody the living Spirit of Cosmic Freedom.

This amethyst heart is a lodestone. It gives direction to your footsteps and a roseate glow of the warmth of the love of Mary. Let Love lead the way and deliver your hearts to the highest mountain of consciousness. And from the heart of the earth and inner levels may you so bless a planet that when the dark night of her karma is spent and the skies are clear and the light is shining, you may see a New Day and live unto that New Day and be in a position to be my assistants, guiding and teaching souls in the alchemy of building the new world.

Let the Great Instauration[7] on planet earth begin now. Let the spiritual building take place within and within the heart of the mountains of the Inner Retreat. Let that building, then, be such a magnificent etheric matrix as to render obsolete the old order of decay and dying.

Let us see the sign and the mark of the golden-age man and golden-age woman—of the Aquarian child. Let us see the eternal youth and a light shining from the aura. Let us know that Aquarius is an age of freedom unto full mastery in physical embodiment.

It is an age when the world can be so accelerated as to draw you into higher and higher vibrations until you realize that the old physical nature of the planet has itself been transcended. As you change your diet and outlook and let the sign of the mantra be the Seventh Ray, you will see that the new world is in a higher vibration and octave than the last.

Blessed hearts, I am walking with you into this new world. I take you, each one, by the hand. I am walking with you unto the hour that the natural course of your life on earth is fulfilled, that by the hand I may lead you into the Royal Teton Retreat.

Blessed hearts, the fulfillment of all of the promises of God is upon you. So long as you claim me as your Brother and Friend, I am at your side, and when you give but fifteen minutes of violet flame decrees each day, you allow me to place an extraordinary measure of my Electronic Presence with you. Thus, I am seeking the lamplighters who will ignite a planet with violet flame candles, that all of the stars and the angels may look down upon it and know that a planet has been claimed for Freedom by a people who awakened before it was too late!

O Freedom's Star, be thou the fullness of these causal bodies of Light, these hearts so full of love!

I am sealing you now, beloved, sealing all who have come, come newly to my heart or kept the flame for lifetimes. I seal you in my aura and light, and I am with you unto the fulfillment of the age!

May your choices be to ratify heaven's design and may you know yourself centered in the pillar of violet flame that shall not go out on earth so long as there is the Keeper of the Flame.

I bow to the Light of Almighty God within you each one.

"The Summit Lighthouse Sheds Its Radiance O'er All the World to Manifest as Pearls of Wisdom." This dictation by **Saint Germain** was **delivered** by the Messenger Elizabeth Clare Prophet on **Saturday, February 13, 1988,** at the Sheraton-Palace Hotel, **San Francisco, California,** where she was stumping for Saint Germain's Coming Revolution in Higher Consciousness. (1) Prior to the dictation the Messenger delivered the lecture **"Saint Germain On Prophecy from 1988 through the 1990s—the Astrology of World Karma,"** in which she analyzed current and upcoming astrological configurations and the karmic challenges they portend. Lecture and dictation on 2 videocassettes, 3 hr. 50 min., GP88019, $49.95 (add $1.20 for postage), or 3 audiocassettes, 3 hr. 51 min., A88024, $19.50 (add $.80 for postage). (2) Heb. 2:3. (3) See *Saint Germain On Alchemy,* pocketbook, 540 pages; includes *Studies in Alchemy, Intermediate Studies in Alchemy, A Trilogy On the Threefold Flame of Life,* and the comprehensive glossary *The Alchemy of the Word,* $5.95 (add $.50 for postage). (4) **Saint Germain's angels will warn and direct you.** In his November 27, 1986, Thanksgiving Day dictation given in Los Angeles, Saint Germain said: "I, therefore, Saint Germain, assign to your heart, to the head of every household, to the mother, and even to the child, my angels who will warn and direct you personally, Keepers of the Flame. These are sent to those who are loyal to God, who have become a part of this fraternity that I have long desired to see in every nation. Beloved ones, angels may knock but you may not hear if you are surfeited in noise, if you allow yourselves to be tossed and tumbled by responsibilities or interruptions. Therefore, listen. You must take fifteen minutes before retiring at night, establish the circle of fire round the place where you rest. Give certain decrees and let all the house be silent as you meditate without interruption upon Almighty God, your Mighty I AM Presence. Then call to me. Let my angels deliver you to the Royal Teton Retreat, where you may be instructed. Then take note, upon awakening, of the first voices, the first messages that come into your mind. Try the spirits, of course, and always, but be attentive. For a thousand angels cannot alert you to your destiny if you are not tuned in, if you are not listening. Let your aura be an electromagnetic field of the Seventh Ray. For in the Seventh Ray violet flame is the alchemy of communication between octaves. Let your aura be sealed by the tube of light and the action of Archangel Michael. Let your receptivity be pure because your heart is pure. Inordinate desire for money or things or other distractions clouds the reasoning of the Logos within you. Thus, the mind that is at peace with God, unattached to the consequences of the human and willing to follow when called, will surely hear my angels." See Saint Germain, "A Prophecy of Karma of the United States of America," 1986 *Pearls of Wisdom,* vol. 29, no. 75, p. 655. (5) See 1988 *Pearls of Wisdom,* vol. 31, no. 15, p. 142, n. 4. (6) **Preparedness.** "Economic debacle is foreseen. Prepare. Setbacks will be sudden. Be not lulled by the heyday. . . . Beloved ones, preparedness is the key" (Saint Germain, November 27, 1986, 1986 *Pearls of Wisdom,* vol. 29, no. 75, pp. 647, 648). "Let those around the world hear me then. The hour is coming and now is when the preparation must be complete—the physical preparation, I say. For you are called to be physical and to remain so for the holding of the light in the earth. . . . Prepare the place. And if in your preparing, as Saint Germain has said, world calamity is turned back, averted or mitigated, then you shall see a golden day of opportunity again. . . . Beloved, the months are short. You must know and understand this. Prepare and be at peace. When you are prepared, let the pillars of flame rise from the heart of the earth to the heart of the Great Central Sun through the chakras of each one" (Mother Mary, May 11, 1987, 1987 *Pearls of Wisdom,* vol. 30, no. 23, pp. 231–32, 236). "Blessed hearts, though my message is one of Victory, there is one line that I would leave with you and that is *'Prepare for the worst.'* Therefore, when ready and prepared, you can *'Live for the best'* and continue to roll back the tides of Darkness and go forth to rescue souls. Blessed ones, it is your hour and the hour of your God-mastery of the physical octave—of the mind and especially of the emotions. Therefore I leave to your discernment, beloved ones, what is the necessary preparation for the worst and, in fact, what might be the worst that may be coming upon this planetary body" (Saint Germain, July 4, 1987, 1987 *Pearls of Wisdom,* vol. 30, no. 37, pp. 370–71). "Ere twenty-four months have passed, be it known to you that this nation must have the capacity to turn back any and all missiles, warheads incoming whether by intent or by accident. Where there is no defense you invite the bear into your own haven. . . . With some preparation, all of which is known to the Department of Defense, this nation can permanently deter nuclear war. Let it be done, I say! . . . Ere twenty-four months pass, beloved, there shall be a reckoning and a confrontation unless something is done" (El Morya, October 3, 1987, 1987 *Pearls of Wisdom,* vol. 30, no. 54, pp. 474, 476, 480). (7) Francis Bacon (1561–1626), an embodiment of Saint Germain, called his plan for universal enlightenment **"the Great Instauration."** First conceived when he was a boy of 12 or 13 and then crystallized in the book by the same name in 1607, Bacon's formula for changing "the whole wide world" launched the English Renaissance. See *Saint Germain On Prophecy,* pp. 21–22, 24, Book One; *The Golden Age Prince,* 2-audiocassette album, 3 hr., A83176, $12.95 (add $1.10 for postage). Saint Germain is using the term "Great Instauration" in its New Age sense—the Great Instauration of the Christ consciousness in all Lightbearers of the world for the restoration of the culture of the Divine Mother and the elevation of humanity to a path of co-measurement with the discipleship of the children of God.

Pearls of Wisdom®
published by The Summit Lighthouse

| Vol. 31 No. 21 | Beloved Jesus Christ | May 22, 1988 |

Saint Germain Stumps America

11
Christhood
Present Attainment and the Goal

In the light of the eternal Guru, I am come to you, your Jesus. It is I. Be not afraid. For I rejoice whenever the teachings of my own Beloved Teacher are taught.

I, then, came into this world sent by the One who has sent me, and when I said, "I and my Father are one,"[1] I spake of the All-Father and the living I AM Presence and of his representative, the One who should wear the mantle of Guru. Thus, the One who did send me in the chain of hierarchy of the ancients was none other than Maitreya.

Realize, beloved, that the prophecy of his coming,[2] [which was known] in the time of my incarnation two thousand years ago, was indeed fulfilled in me. I came, then, giving the light, the profile, the incarnation of the Word I AM THAT I AM whose keynote and inner name is Metteyya.

Now know this, beloved, that as I did preach, "He that heareth me heareth not me but the One who sent me,"[3] so I longed for that Universal Light to be the endowment of an age where Christhood could become the walk of all people.

Therefore, beloved, I went to the Himalayas[4] to find that One and that Beloved, to be trained and tutored of him, and so I was. And so I met him in form in the person of many teachers and individuals along the way. And I saw a continuity of a message, a path and a teaching unfold before me, guided by his ever-present hand.

Yes, I knew him face to face, not in embodiment but as that Universal Christ personified. Blessed hearts, the continuity of the message of Maitreya come again is in this hour in you, not in one individual chosen apart, but through you and through that Holy Christ Flame.

Let those, then, who manifest the flame, the flame of loving kindness of Maitreya, be self-revealing, not self-proclaimed. For, beloved, when the Light is, the Light is; and those who have the Light recognize the Light. Those who have it not see me not, hear me not, know me not, nor do they know my Messenger and yours.

Blessed ones, one of the common mockeries of the transmission of the word of Hierarchy from the higher bodies descending finally unto one wearing physical form is that this is "a communication from departed spirits—'dead people,'" as they say. How ludicrous is the carnal mind, yet how vicious is the lie.

Understanding, then, the continuity of my being in all of my bodies and of your continuity of being in all of your bodies, you ascend and descend that scale; you experience me in the seven chakras, for I AM the Light of the world in you as ye are the Light of the world in me.[5] Only thus, by the Master/disciple relationship, is the light Above manifest below and is the light below raised to the equivalency of the light that is Above.

Therefore, this Master/disciple relationship is a self-giving-ness unto the Beloved. It is a mutuality in mercy's flame. And so it is the hour of the coming of Kuan Yin. Therefore know, beloved, that as I have longed to reveal to all the world my relationship to Maitreya, so I have not done so, for the world has not ears to hear, for they have not been taught of this thread of light that is woven through all levels of the lineal descent of the Buddhas, the Christs, the bodhisattvas.

Come unto my heart and know me, then, as the son, the "sonshine" of Maitreya. Know, then, that my mission, going before him, even as John the Baptist went before me, was to clear the way of the coming of this Universal Christ in all sons of God upon earth.

The title Son of God is a level of attainment, beloved, beyond that of child of God. Therefore, I come in this hour to contact those who know you are Sons of God yet who also know that you are not manifesting the fullness of the attainment of the Son of God that you have at inner levels and that you have had in past golden ages.

Blessed ones, the recognition of one's inner attainment and the awareness that by karma or neglect one has not brought forth that Light in this life is surely a moment, a moment of inner recognition, a sense of the gap between a manifest Reality that could be and somehow a vacancy that yet is.

This self-assessment, beloved, is necessary. One may affirm in decree "I AM a Son of God," but there is a level of the incarnation of the Son that one must realize in order to be that absolute decree in manifest actuality. Do not take for granted that your Holy Christ Self will descend into your temple and take over and suddenly a Son of God will appear. This is not the real teaching of the Path.

In the first instance one must study what is that karma that prevents the fullness of the inner attainment from being the working person that you are in form. Then you must assiduously invoke the violet flame for the binding of that interloper who has come to occupy your house, not necessarily with your permission. But he did not knock but entered and when you saw that one in your house, instead of putting him out, you accommodated. I speak of the dweller on the threshold, a self-created not-self, the antithesis of my Christ and thy Christ, truly the antithesis of Maitreya.[6]

Therefore, beloved, as some are, as you would say, wishy-washy, spineless, allowing into their consciousness and their homes the unwanted guests and thoughts and feelings, as some have not the fire of *vajra*[7] and the determination and the zeal of the Lord to expel these unwelcomed inhabitants, so I say to you, beloved, the day is past when you who know you are the Son of God can tolerate or allow compromise any longer. I say it is long past and far spent because I see the cycles of your own personal Cosmic Clock and the planetary clock.

The days are hastening on. Your Christhood is needed for the salvation of your own soul. Do not lose it by dalliance and indulgence with those who, though they may speak words of agreement, have no intention whatsoever of becoming true initiates of our calling.

Blessed ones, while you allow your house to be inhabited by the stranger that is not an angel in disguise, you yourselves will find that you are losing ground and the groundwork laid by us long ago, and you may even be losing your soul in the delusion that you have such attainment that you may be a saviour of another before in actuality you have manifested the fullness of that saviour.

Be on guard! I, Jesus, warn you that in these days it is the hour when antichrists should come,[8] and the dweller on the threshold that is the antithesis of Self is indeed the anti-Christ force. Expel it, then, by the thunderbolt *Vajra! Vajra! Vajra!*

Let the power of God in you, then, seek first things first and know that to be a messiah, a leader of men and nations, this Christ must be firmly ensconced, fixed in your being, integrated with you chakra by chakra. This is the immediate goal. Pursue it daily.

Come not again to me with vacant expressions and a passivity that is a belief which belies the great truth that the divine decree you offer becomes a reality only when *you* become the doer, when *you* get in the driver's seat and know that this day you are begotten of the Lord,[9] this day that *Sambhogakaya*,[10] if you will, shall come and dwell with you and you shall rise in vibration to the occasion and be that one. Let us not confuse, then, the goal with the present attainment but let the present attainment always bear signs of the goal.

Thus, beloved, having so said to you these words, I step aside that Maitreya may occupy this one of his many bodies.

"The Summit Lighthouse Sheds Its Radiance O'er All the World to Manifest as Pearls of Wisdom." **Delivered Feb. 14, 1988,** at the Sheraton-Palace Hotel, **San Francisco, Calif.** Prior to the dictation, the Messenger delivered the lecture **"The Lost Teachings of Jesus and Maitreya on Your Divine Reality."** Lecture and dictation on 2 videocassettes, 3¾ hr., GP88023, $39.95 (add $1.50 postage), or on 3 audiocassettes, A88027, $19.50 (add $1.00 postage). **(1)** John 10:30. **(2) Prophecy of Maitreya's coming.** Buddhist scriptures record that Gautama prophesied the advent of a future Buddha whose name would be Metteyya (Pali; Maitreya in Sanskrit). In the Pali text Mahaparinibbana Suttanta, Gautama tells his chief disciple, Ananda, "In due time another Buddha will arise in the world, a Holy One, a supremely enlightened One. . . . He will reveal to you the same eternal truths which I have taught you. . . . He will proclaim a religious life, wholly perfect and pure; such as I now proclaim." When Ananda asks, "How shall we know him?" Gautama replies, "He will be known as Metteyya, which means 'he whose name is kindness'" (Paul Carus, *The Gospel of Buddha* [La Salle, Ill.: Open Court Publishing Co., 1894], p. 245). *Maitreya* is derived from the Sanskrit *maitri,* which means "friendliness," "benevolence," or "goodwill." Buddhists believe that Maitreya is a bodhisattva residing in Tushita heaven awaiting his final rebirth, which is to occur after the decay of Buddhism. **(3)** "Jesus cried and said, He that believeth on me, believeth not on me, but on Him that sent me. And he that seeth me seeth Him that sent me" John 12:44, 45. See also John 7:16; 14:10. **(4)** See Elizabeth Clare Prophet, *The Lost Years of Jesus.* Now in pocketbook, $5.95 (add $.50 for postage), special offer: $3.95 ea. in quantities of 12 (add $4.25 for postage per dozen); "The Lost Years of Jesus," *Heart: For the Coming Revolution in Higher Consciousness* (Spring 1983), $4.00 (add $.25 for postage). **(5) The Light of the world.** Matt. 5:14–16; John 1:4, 5, 9; 8:12; 9:5; 12:46. **(6) Dweller on the threshold.** A term sometimes used to designate the anti-self, the not-self, the synthetic self, the antithesis of the Real Self, the conglomerate of the self-created ego, ill conceived through the inordinate use of the gift of free will, consisting of the carnal mind and a constellation of misqualified energies, forcefields, focuses, animal magnetism comprising the subconscious mind. For further teaching, see Elizabeth Clare Prophet, Nov. 26, 1987, "The Lost Teachings of Jesus: On the Enemy Within," on two 90-min. audiocassettes, B87097–8, $13.00 (add $.95 for postage); 1983 *Pearls of Wisdom,* vol. 26, nos. 6, 36, 38, pp. 50, 383–91, 429–54; 1985 *Pearls of Wisdom,* vol. 28, nos. 9, 26, pp. 84, 85–93, 97, 350 n. 10; 1986 *Pearls of Wisdom,* vol. 29, no. 22, pp. 199, 203, 210–12; *Saint Germain On Alchemy,* pp. 395–96. **(7) vajra** [Sanskrit]: rendered as thunderbolt or diamond; that which is hard, impenetrable; that which destroys but is itself indestructible; a scepterlike symbol of the thunderbolt, representing the adamantine nature of Truth, used in rituals, especially of exorcism of demons. The *vajra* is thought to cleave through ignorance and therefore symbolizes the indestructible nature of the Buddha's wisdom and the victory of knowledge over illusion. In Vajrayana Buddhism, it is the symbol of *bodhicitta,* or enlightenment. **(8)** I John 2:18, 22; 4:3; II John 7. **(9)** Ps. 2:7; Acts 13:33; Heb. 1:5; 5:5. **(10)** Holy Christ Self.

Pearls of Wisdom®
published by The Summit Lighthouse

| Vol. 31 No. 22 | Beloved Lord Maitreya | May 29, 1988 |

Saint Germain Stumps America
12
Continuity of Life
Keep the Flame

My Beloved,

Out of the compassionate heart of the Buddha I come to you this day in an aura of love—a love that is such splendor in such simplicity as to woo you to the heart of the Divine Mother, who does nourish in you that light eternal.

Therefore in the sweetness of the Mother do the Buddhas come, in the adoration of the Tara, the great Kuan Yin, in all planes and in our incarnations of that Divine One.

Come then, beloved, and know that in the Body of Bliss[1] we tarry for assimilation of the power of Love. And in the conclusion of our meditation as I am releasing to you the fragrance, the essence of my highest being, you will contain the power of Love that you may direct—according to your free will enlightened by your Christhood—into conditions that must be alleviated, that must be allayed for the establishment of a basic continuity of life.

It is the continuity of being midst the turbulence in the earth of earthquake and jarring sensations and frights that come upon people in every walk of life [of which we would speak].

Where there is a continuity of the stream of Life from on high through you, through this thread of contact, through the flowing words of my heart, the Path can be sought and won, the weary can be fed and clothed and given to drink. Continuity of life, beloved, is the need of the hour and that is what is threatened by the prophecies you have heard, by the signs in the heavens.[2]

Know, then, beloved, that where the stream is broken or the thread of contact severed, there, then, souls truly may suffer a

Dark Night and be tossed and tumbled until the Avalokiteśvara may descend with his legions to carry them from their inundation in the astral seas and waves.

Blessed hearts, this is why you are called to keep the flame of Christ, of Maitreya, of Buddha.

Keep the flame of Life, beloved. For in that flame of your heart, some will understand, [some] will come to know me or to know the true Jesus as my Messenger and Son, some will come to know their own Christhood.

Keep the flame, beloved. You are in the earth, flames becoming bodhisattvas and some among you are bodhisattvas.

Note well, beloved, that life deserves your ministering and it is only just that you give it in this hour. Remember, you minister unto a soul becoming the fullness of that Light who by your ministration may even exceed your glory, for which you should give a shout of gratitude to the cosmos.

Remember, then, that you serve not the human lesser self but a soul that is entrapped by that human lesser self. Take care, then, in time-wasting upon the bottomless pit of human desire and appetite that will take not only your wares and teaching and light but yourself if it could.

Seek the devotee who is in straits dire and wield the sword of Maitreya to cut him free. But do not become entangled with those who have no intention of rising but only of keeping you tied in argumentation—and distractions and byways [which take you] from the cries of the little ones who need you now and not tomorrow.

I AM Maitreya, always in the heart of Jesus—always the Buddha within his crown, always the Buddha within his heart.

I AM Maitreya in the earth body, conversing with your soul. Know me, then, in kindness first expressed by you. Then the return current of that kindness expressed by another will reveal to you one of my million smiles through the friend, through the kind ones on earth, the wise ones who know that true kindness is found in the act of one who has cared enough to earn the key to open the door to successive chambers of my retreat.

Come and find me, beloved, for now I retreat to the Himalayas where I hold class continuing. May you experience me in your own discipleship of realizing the One, the Ineffable, the All, the Love—of Aquarius.

This dictation by **Lord Maitreya** was **delivered** by the Messenger Elizabeth Clare Prophet on **Sunday, February 14, 1988,** at the Sheraton-Palace Hotel, **San Francisco. (1) Sambhogakaya** [Sanskrit]: rendered as the Body of Bliss or Glorious Body; second of the three bodies of the Buddha *(trikaya);* the radiant spiritual body in which the Buddha's virtues and accomplishments are manifest; the form that a Buddha characteristically uses to reveal himself in his glory to bodhisattvas, enlightening and inspiring them. According to the teachings of the Ascended Masters, the *Sambhogakaya* is the Holy Christ Self. **(2)** See 1988 *Pearls of Wisdom,* vol. 31, no. 20, p. 166, n. 1.

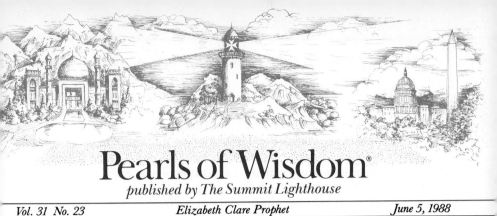

Pearls of Wisdom®
published by The Summit Lighthouse

Vol. 31 No. 23   Elizabeth Clare Prophet   June 5, 1988

New Year's Retreat
at the Royal Teton Ranch

IX
The Abdication of America's Destiny
Part 2
Inasmuch As Ye Have Done It unto One of the Least of These My Brethren, Ye Have Done It unto Me

The United States abdicated her responsibility to provide the abundant life when she went off the gold standard. This happened in stages. On April 5, 1938, President Roosevelt declared a national emergency and said he was depriving American citizens of the right to own gold and use it as a medium of exchange.[1] This is the most hellish and damnable act ever perpetrated against the people of this nation! And they don't even know it!

President Nixon took the final step on August 15, 1971, when he suspended the convertibility of the dollar for gold internationally. We were then fully on the paper standard.[2] In recent years, important steps have been taken towards remonetizing gold. Legislation passed in December 1974 allowed American citizens to own gold. Gold clause contracts, not covered in this legislation, were made legal as of October 28, 1977. And, on December 17, 1985, President Reagan signed the Gold Bullion Coin Act which required the U.S. Treasury to mint and sell gold coins which have limited legal tender status.[3] But other steps must be taken before gold circulates as legal tender in the U.S. economy. Essentially, we are still on the paper standard.

This is a violation of the spirit and the letter of Article I, Section 10 of the Constitution, which says, "No State Shall...make any Thing but gold and silver Coin a Tender in Payment of Debts."

The framers intended Congress to use gold and silver coin as money even though they did not explicitly state that Article I, Section 10 applied to the federal government. This can be demonstrated by the statements of a number of the framers, a text analysis of the Constitution and by Supreme Court decisions. The Founding Fathers' intent is also seen in the actions of the First Congress, which in 1792 created a monetary system based on gold and silver.[4]

At the time the Constitution was being framed, the nation was in the midst of a terrible inflation caused by the expansion of the Continental, a paper currency. During the debate over the wording of Article I, Section 10, Roger Sherman, a delegate to the Constitutional Convention, said he thought this "a favorable crisis for crushing paper money."[5] Thomas Jefferson and John Adams both wrote about the evils of paper money.

But, contrary to the framers' intent, bankers plotted to control the currency. They began, as we saw in Part 1, at Jekyll Island in November 1910. The Federal Reserve Act which they designed gave the banking community control of the nation's money in violation of Article I, Section 8 of the Constitution, which gives to Congress the power "to coin money" and "regulate the value thereof."

Now the Federal Reserve system (the Fed), serving the interests of the banking community, exercises the unilateral right to expand and contract the supply of money and credit and create periods of boom and bust. The ramifications of this state of affairs are almost beyond calculation. Today we could have a financial collapse worse than the Great Depression of the 1930s. And we know that the power elite used the depression to concentrate power in the central government.[6] Doubtless they would like to do the same in the future.

If we have another depression, it will be America's own karma because we the people have turned over our power and our abundant life to the godless dominant minority, the same Watchers, this time coming in the guise of the bankers and their elite rulership over the Federal Reserve system and its 12 member banks.

In turning over control of our monetary system to the fallen ones and allowing them to retain it, we are giving them the power to bring about the decline and ruination of our economy. The Fed's ability to expand credit is what is behind the out-of-control national debt, consumer debt, farm debt, domestic energy loan debt as well as the debt bomb—loans to foreign nations which will likely never be repaid. These debts taken together, especially the over $2 trillion national debt created by deficit spending, are such a major problem that it would take a president of the stature of Abraham Lincoln and greater to turn it around.

The Ascended Masters have explained to us that gold is necessary for the stability of the economies of the nations as well as for the stability of the individual consciousness. On October 10, 1977, the Ascended Master known as the God of Gold said the formation of the Federal Reserve system "must be challenged and reversed because it is no part of the divine plan of the United States. . . . The American people must understand the great fraud that has been perpetrated upon them by this printing of money without backing. The grinding out of money by the printing presses will surely cause the collapse of the economies of the nations. . . . The salvation of the soul of America depends upon the reestablishment of gold."[7]

Let us consider how else America has abdicated her destiny. America abdicated her role to defend freedom by ignoring Hitler until it was too late and by allowing the international bankers to finance the Nazis.

Antony Sutton, in his book *Wall Street and the Rise of Hitler,* proves that Hitler and the SS, the Nazi elite troops, were financed in part by "affiliates or subsidiaries of U.S. firms, including Henry Ford in 1922." Sutton says that General Electric made payments to Hitler in 1933, and that Standard Oil of New Jersey and International Telephone and Telegraph made subsidiary payments to Heinrich Himmler, the most ruthless of the Nazi leaders, up to 1944. He further demonstrates that "U.S. multi-nationals under the control of Wall Street profited handsomely from Hitler's military construction program in the 1930s and at least until 1942."[8]

America, you did not stop these corporations from setting the stage for World War II and the deaths of 41 to 49 million people![9]

If you would like to read the Book of Life this day from the Lords of Karma of the abdication of America's destiny, you will see how the power elite have made a karma and debted it to the United States and to the common people who share the uncommon light of their LORD. You will see how, by not protesting, these people have accepted the karma of the fallen ones and how America is compromised by their evil deeds.

Under the domination of the power elite, America abdicated her role as defender of the oppressed, as the home for the "huddled masses yearning to breathe free," when she turned away Jewish refugees from Hitler's Holocaust and left them to almost certain death.

America could have opened her doors to the refugees but she did not. "A substantial commitment to rescue almost certainly could have saved several hundred thousand [Jews], and done so without compromising the war effort," writes David S. Wyman in *The Abandonment of the Jews.*[10]

Many Americans were unaware of the murder of millions of Jews because the media did not report it. Even though reports were available on the wire services and from foreign correspondents, the major media either failed to cover the Holocaust altogether or else relegated the stories to back pages.[11]

The United States government knew of the Holocaust as early as May of 1942 when the Polish Jewish Labor Bund report revealed that 700,000 Jews had been killed since 1941. "Authenticated information that the Nazis were systematically exterminating European Jewry was made public" by November of 1942, writes Wyman. "President Roosevelt did nothing about the mass murder for fourteen months, then moved only because he was confronted with political pressures he could not avoid."[12]

The State Department did not increase Jewish immigration quotas in response to repeated pleas from refugees and their families. Instead, they actually decreased the number of visas they issued. They did not even ensure that existing quotas were filled. In fact, due to arbitrary State Department restrictions only 10 percent of the immigration quotas—21,000 Jews—were allowed to enter America between Pearl Harbor and V-E Day.[13]

America, did you hear the cry of the 907 German Jewish refugees aboard the *St. Louis?* They fled Germany on May 13, 1939, having purchased Cuban visas. However, the visas were invalid. The German steamship corporation and the Cuban government had collaborated in selling the visas even though they knew the refugees would be denied entry to Cuba.

After being turned out of Havana, the ship cruised up and down the coast of Florida but the United States did not offer asylum. A cable sent from the ship to the American Jewish community read, "We appeal to world Jewry. We are being sent back. How can you be peaceful? How can you be silent? Help! Do everything you can! Some on the ship have committed suicide. Help! Do not allow the ship to go back to Germany!"[14]

Finally the Netherlands, Belgium, England and France agreed to accept the refugees and the *St. Louis* returned to Europe. Most of those that went to England survived. But of those sent to Belgium, the Netherlands and France, between 227 and 667 died in concentration camps during the war.[15]

Such is the treatment of the Jews by the power elite, the fallen ones and the Nephilim gods.

Inasmuch as ye did it not to one
of the least of these, ye did it not to me.

America, *you* have abdicated your destiny and your responsibility to oppose world genocide by the seed of the Wicked One!

Holocaust survivor Elie Wiesel is said to have replied when asked what he had learned about genocide, "You can get away with it."

Well, it happened in Russia before the Nazis ever got started and it has happened all over again in China, Tibet, Cambodia and now Afghanistan; and the American people by abdicating their divine right to self-rule and allowing the godless power elite to reign in their stead *are* allowing its perpetrators to get away with it!

The deaths of World War II are staggering. But Communism has killed far more people in this century than has war. Political science professor R. J. Rummel calculated that over 35 million people have been killed by war in this century, while 95 million have been killed by Communist governments.[16]

Exact figures are difficult to calculate. Totalitarian regimes do not release data on how many people they kill. Rummel estimates that the Soviets killed 39.5 million of their citizens from 1918 to 1953. Historian Robert Conquest made a detailed study of deaths from mass executions, famines and forced collectivization, taking into account demographics, reports from refugees and former prisoners as well as official reports. He estimates that from 1930 to 1950 alone, the Soviet government executed, starved or worked to death 20 million Russians. Conquest says that this figure "is almost certainly too low and might require an increase of 50 per cent or so."[17]

Aleksandr Solzhenitsyn reports that émigré Professor of Statistics Kurganov estimated that 66 million were killed from 1917 to 1959. "We, of course, cannot vouch for his figure, but we have none other that is official," comments Solzhenitsyn. "And just as soon as the official figure is issued the specialists can make the necessary critical comparisons."[18]

In Stalin's dekulakization campaign of the 1930s alone, 10 to 15 million Russian peasants died, according to figures reported by Conquest and Solzhenitsyn.[19] Stalin's object was to break the resistance of an entire class of people and in 1930 he began a campaign to liquidate those he called kulaks but who were in reality the cream of rural Russia. After the peasants started resisting Stalin's forced collectivization, he began calling anyone who was a better peasant than his fellows a kulak.

In Russian, says Solzhenitsyn, "a *kulak* is a miserly, dishonest rural trader who grows rich not by his own labor but through someone else's, through usury and operating as a middleman."[20] Stalin's "kulaks," says Solzhenitsyn, included "all peasants strong in management, strong in work, or even strong merely in convictions." If someone had two stories on his house in a village of one-story houses, he was a kulak. If he was a miller or a blacksmith or a veterinarian, he was a kulak.

There were quotas to meet and the most intelligent and prosperous were rounded up. Sometimes entire villages of hard-working peasants were taken away, even though no one could say precisely who they had been exploiting. The government re-cruited "activists," usually drunkards and ne'er-do-wells, to help identify the kulaks. If a person offended one of the "activists," they took revenge by labeling him a kulak or a *podkulachnik,* a "person aiding the kulaks."

What was the fate of these "enemies of the people"? They were evicted from their land, their property was confiscated and they were herded into carts or sleds or boxcars and taken off to remote northern wastes to die of cold and starvation. Solzhenitsyn tells of one incident in which 10,000 families, or 60 to 70 thousand people, were killed. First they were driven in winter along the ice of the Tom, Ob and Vasyugan rivers.

> In the upper reaches of the Vasyugan and the Tara they were marooned on patches of firm ground in the marshes. *No food or tools were left for them.* The roads were impass-able, and there was no way through to the world outside, except for two brushwood paths....Machine-gunners manned barriers on both paths and let no one through from the death camp. They started dying like flies. Desper-ate people came out to the barriers begging to be let through, and were shot on the spot.[21]

The government sent food barges but since they could not pass the ice, the food was delayed. Every one of the 70,000 died at the hands of the state whose rallying cry is "Workingmen of all countries, unite!"

Whatever the final tally of Soviet citizens murdered by devils incarnate, these millions of Russian citizens who died in "peace-time" unmourned and unsung remain a testament to the Commu-nist war waged throughout this century against the Lightbearers of the world and to the abdication of America's destiny.

> *Inasmuch as ye did it not to one*
> *of the least of these, ye did it not to me.*

The above figures do not take into account the over 7 million liquidated by either the Soviet government or by the Soviet-backed Communist regimes of these nations during and after World War II.[22]

At Yalta in February of 1945, Franklin Roosevelt and Win-ston Churchill agreed to give Stalin control of the East European nations of Bulgaria, Romania, Hungary, and Czechoslovakia. The Allies allowed Russia to maintain control of East Germany and Poland. All told, the Soviets received 100 million citizens as a result of the Yalta agreement. And what did Roosevelt and Churchill get in return for these countries? They got Stalin's promise to enter the war against Japan and to support the United Nations. Who needed Russia against Japan and who needs them in the United Nations!

In line with the Yalta agreement, the Allies also turned over to the Soviets more than 2.25 million Soviet citizens, prisoners of war and Russian exiles, even those with international passports. An estimated 795,000 of them were executed or died in slave-labor camps on their own native soil.[23]

On July 4, 1976, in our nation's capital, Saint Germain spoke of the betrayal at Yalta.

> Again and again the master plan of the ages has been brought forth. And in a moment, a moment's hesitation, a moment being off guard, supply, light, and the projects of the Brotherhood have been lost. In that moment when the Western powers gave way to the black magician Stalin, gave to him Eastern Europe in that very moment when the West was victorious,...I can tell you that in that moment when I saw the spell of the fallen ones reaching out, even on Churchill and Roosevelt and on those who assented to that appeasement, I cried, precious ones.
>
> I cried for mankind and I tell you, Mother Mary cried. You think that Ascended Masters do not weep. I assure you that we weep, and our tears are shed as the tears of a cosmos. I can assure you that that which is done in a moment of weakness may take many, many cycles to undo. And therefore, those who acknowledge and understand the forging of a new world and a free world must realize that day by day decisions are being made and day by day there is the requirement of the flame.
>
> The armies had withdrawn. America was in celebration for a victory. People were off guard. They were too anxious, *too anxious,* and not at all in the vigil. And therefore, from the very light of victory there came the greatest defeat to freedom that has ever been known....
>
> Need I tell you how we wept when Soviet tanks entered Budapest and Hungary? The people, the people in their love of my flame,...were willing to give their lives for freedom—to attack tanks! And America would not come. America would not hear. America would not respond to defend them.[24]

America, you abdicated your destiny to defend freedom in Eastern Europe. You betrayed millions of people and denied them a path of individual Christhood!

Woe to the power elite of this nation! Woe to the fallen ones in the State Department this day! Woe to the president of the United States of America this day for his betrayal of the peoples of Western Europe and the United States in this INF agreement signed with this betrayer of mankind, this visiting "prince" who has come from Moscow!

And the actions of the Soviet Union are attributable at least in part to the United States. She allowed bankers and industrialists to give financial, material and diplomatic support to the Bolsheviks, which enabled them to consolidate the revolution and create the Soviet slave state. Through the faithlessness and machinations of the international bankers, America abdicated her responsibility to defend the nations against Marxist/Leninist Communism.

Capitalists have aided World Communism to foment change and managed conflict starting in 1917 when they gave financial and diplomatic assistance to the Bolsheviks. William Boyce Thompson, director of the Federal Reserve Bank of New York, gave the Bolsheviks $1 million of his own money in 1917.[25] In his book *Wall Street and the Bolshevik Revolution,* Antony Sutton demonstrates a financial link between the Guaranty Trust Company in New York and the Bolsheviks before, during and after the Revolution.

American companies provided the Soviets the technology and money they needed to build their war machine that holds us hostage today. At the same time Lenin was proclaiming that "socialism is electrification," General Electric was lighting up the Soviet Union. In 1928 the International General Electric Company signed an agreement to give the Soviet Union $26 million worth of electrical equipment together with technical assistance in installing it, Sutton reports.[26]

In his three-volume work *Western Technology and Soviet Economic Development,* Sutton shows that the Soviet Union has almost no indigenously developed technology. Ninety to 95 percent of it comes from the West and two-thirds from the United States.[27] We have built the Soviet military-industrial complex, including steel and truck factories that produce military trucks, tanks and rocket launchers. And it continues today. Western and Japanese banks have lent the Soviet Union nearly $100 billion in the last three years.[28]

America, you have allowed the godless power elite to abdicate your destiny to oppose tyranny and thereby you, "we the people," are a party to the slaughter of millions of people perpetrated by the Soviet government since 1917.

You, America, could have prevented these deaths by the simple act of cutting off technology and money to the Communists! You could have forced your allies and the rest of the world to do the same by making compliance with a technology embargo a condition for the economic and military aid you have poured out to the world in this century.

> *Inasmuch as ye have done it unto one of the least*
> *of these my brethren, ye have done it unto me.*

America, you have abdicated your role to defend freedom in China. One billion Chinese are under a Communist government today because you have failed, *failed utterly* to fulfill your destiny to nurture the oppressed peoples of the world. The blame rests upon the betrayers of the people in the United States government for its action and inaction from 1945 to 1948.

In 1945 at the conclusion of World War II, China was in the midst of a civil war. Nationalist forces led by Chiang Kai-shek outnumbered the Communist forces led by Mao Tse-tung five to one. By 1949 the situation was reversed: the Nationalists had retreated to the island of Formosa (Taiwan) and Mao controlled the mainland.

The State Department argued that the Nationalists lost because they were corrupt, brutal and lacked popular support and that the Communists won because the people supported them. They said that we gave the Nationalists all the aid that we could but that we simply could not turn back the force of history and the will of the people. The truth is that while the Nationalists had their flaws they were, without a doubt, preferable to the Communists.

Professor Anthony Kubek of the University of Dallas documents how the Truman administration manipulated the situation: First, Harry Truman forced the Nationalists to form a coalition with the Communists, then he gave them inadequate aid, embargoed it after they had grown to depend on it and finally, when it looked like the Nationalists were going to lose, declared a "hands off" policy and did nothing. It is unclear whether Truman fully understood the effects of his policy, but the clique of Mao supporters whom he appointed to the State Department's Office of Far Eastern Affairs undoubtedly did.[29]

Truman's step-by-step betrayal of the Chinese is worth studying. At the end of 1945 he appointed Gen. George C. Marshall his special representative in China and instructed him to threaten to cut off United States aid unless Chiang declared a truce with Mao and began negotiations to form a coalition government in which the Communists were represented.

Demanding a position in a coalition government is a textbook Communist ploy. Characteristically, after they achieve a splinter position in a government, they go on to eliminate their opponents. Chiang was trying to show his good faith to the Americans, so he not only agreed to a truce but also began reducing his armed forces in the interests of peace and democracy. He deactivated 180 divisions out of a 300-division army and created six divisions with mixed Communist and Nationalist troops. He also began negotiations with Mao to allow him a position in a new government.

In March 1946 the Communists broke the truce by pouring troops into Manchuria. The Nationalists retaliated and continued to advance, reasoning that the truce had been broken by the Communists. The United States blamed Chiang Kai-shek and responded to the incident by embargoing American arms and canceling a $500 million American loan. This was the turning point in the war between the freedom fighters and the Lightbearers of the motherland of China and the Communist hordes under the dominant minority leadership of the ruthless fallen ones.

Henceforth, the Nationalists received little U.S. aid while the Soviets aided Mao's forces. Stalin gave Mao all the weapons and equipment left in Manchuria by 700,000 surrendering Japanese troops at the end of World War II as well as nearly 600 shiploads of unused American lend-lease equipment which we had given the Soviets to fight the Japanese.[30] The United States government did not protest!

Meanwhile, American aid to the Nationalists since 1945 had been a betrayal from start to finish. The State Department tried to convince the American public that they had done everything possible to save the Nationalist government. In 1949, Secretary of State Dean Acheson (a devil incarnate if I ever saw one!) tried to prove that we had given them $2 billion worth of aid between 1945 and 1949 and that further aid would not change the situation. However, Sen. Pat McCarran proved that Acheson's figures were "misleading and false," concluding that United States aid totaled only $110 million.[31] The fact is that after World War II, the U.S. government gave only token aid to the Nationalists and continually undermined them.

(It is noteworthy that while an undergraduate at Yale University, Acheson was a member of Scroll and Key, an elite senior society that is apparently affiliated with Skull and Bones, another society on the Yale campus, many of whose members have played a leading role in providing Western support for the Soviet empire. Although he allegedly became an anti-Communist in 1945, he blocked efforts to fire accused Communists from the State Department in 1949–50. He remarked, "I will not turn my back on Alger

Hiss." As you may recall, Hiss was a high-ranking State Department official who was accused of spying for the Soviet Union and was convicted of perjury and sentenced to five years in prison.)

Under Marshall's embargo the Nationalists could not get gasoline for the air force we had given them. Marshall had equipped 33 of the Nationalists' best divisions with American 30-caliber rifles. Then he embargoed 30-caliber ammunition.

In addition, our lend-lease supplies were inadequate. Col. L. B. Moody said that we didn't send the Nationalists what they really needed, which was small arms and ammunition. What we sent, Moody said, were "billions of moldy cigarettes, blown-up guns and junk bombs and disabled vehicles from the Pacific islands."[32] Furthermore, as Kubek writes, "Lend-lease equipment intended for China [was] either destroyed or dumped into the India Ocean."[33]

America's aid cut-off had disastrous results for the Nationalists. Professor Kubek writes that "General George E. Stratemeyer... testified before the Senate Internal Security Subcommittee that he flew 90,000 Chinese troops north....We promised we would supply them, but the troops were left there, stranded, at the mercy of the Communists. [Stratemeyer testified,] 'They had no ammunition, they had no spare parts, they couldn't fight. They had to live, so the Communists took them over, and those they didn't kill, I think they forced into their services.'"[34]

Under the embargo the Nationalists were running out of everything. The *New York Times* reported on June 22, 1947, that their guns were so worn and burned that "bullets fell through them to the ground."[35] Other arms lacked crucial parts. Professor Kubek says that some gun shipments reached China without bolts. They were therefore useless.

In April of 1948 Congress appropriated $125 million in military aid to the Nationalists. But due to Defense and State Department delays the first shipment of American arms did not arrive in Shanghai until seven months later. By that time it was too late for Chiang Kai-shek.

These aid "mix-ups" are the beginning of a disturbing pattern which we shall see as we trace the history of United States support for anti-Communist resistance movements. One mix-up can be a mistake but we must look for other motives when it happens repeatedly.

The Nationalist forces retreated to Taiwan, completing their withdrawal December 7, 1949. The West hailed Mao as a potential moderate, a Nationalist figure who would not necessarily be aligned with Moscow. But, since the Communists established the People's Republic of China on October 1, 1949 (thanks to the government of the United States of America), they have killed from 33 to 61 million Chinese, according to a report released by the Senate Subcommittee on Internal Security in 1971.[36]

*Inasmuch as ye did it not to one
of the least of these, ye did it not to me.*

America, you have abdicated your fiery destiny to defend the Chinese people and their right to become a sister nation of light, illumination and culture! You, America, sold the Chinese into slavery! You allowed the fallen ones, the power elite, the betrayers of the people in the earth, the spoilers from the beginning to betray the Lightbearers of the motherland of China; and what they could have been is amply seen today on the island of Taiwan, where freedom reigns, where free trade and commerce has built a strong capitalist nation, a free people and those who are able to understand the path of the Master/disciple relationship.

On December 8, 1975, Saint Germain gave a landmark dictation entitled "Freedom for Taiwan." In it he warned, "This is the hour and the century of the turning point for Terra, for her evolutions, and for opportunity. This very year in the elections in America, in world politics, there is the turning." In 1976, Jimmy Carter was elected president and on December 15, 1978, he announced that the United States was establishing diplomatic relations with the People's Republic of China (PRC) after 30 years of nonrecognition.

At the same time, he severed diplomatic relations with the Republic of China on Taiwan, which the U.S. had previously recognized as the sole legal government of China, and agreed to terminate the 1954 Mutual Defense Treaty with Taiwan. No provision was made in the agreement for Chinese treatment of Taiwan and China never pledged to refrain from using force to recover the island. Instead, the PRC reiterated its long-standing position that the "liberation" of Taiwan did not involve the U.S., calling its reunification with Taiwan "China's internal affair."

Congress did not entirely approve of Carter's move and, in April of 1979, it passed the Taiwan Relations Act which promised to provide the arms necessary for Taiwan "to maintain a sufficient self-defense capability." But on August 17, 1982, under the Reagan administration, the U.S. signed a joint communiqué with Peking pledging to gradually reduce arms sales to Taiwan "leading over a period of time to a final resolution."

It remains to be seen when and how Red China will attempt reunification with Taiwan. Clearly, the United States cannot be counted on to intervene. The Taiwanese army is the sole force standing between free China and the fate their brethren on the mainland have already met.

Saint Germain told us of the importance of Taiwan to the cause of Freedom on earth:

Let the sons and daughters of Liberty arise this day! For I am calling you, and this is my message: The fulcrum of light on Terra for the reversing of the tide of the beast of the Orient is Taiwan. Fifteen million souls of light are keeping the flame of Kuan Yin on that island of light. That island of light is an ancient focus of freedom; and it must not be turned over to the Communists. . . . I tell you, children of the Light, if you lose Taiwan, you will lose the greatest concentration of Lightbearers per square mile in any part of the earth. There is no greater concentration.[37]

In recognizing China, Carter ignored not only her treatment of her own people but also her brutal invasion of Tibet. Since they invaded Tibet in 1950, the Red Chinese armies have killed 1.2 million Tibetans.[38] John F. Avedon, in a study of the Chinese occupation called *In Exile from the Land of Snows*, describes the Chinese atrocities as reported by the Geneva-based International Commission of Jurists:

The obliteration of entire villages was compounded by hundreds of public executions, carried out to intimidate the surviving population. The methods employed included crucifixion, dismemberment, vivisection, beheading, burying, burning and scalding alive, dragging the victims to death behind galloping horses and pushing them from airplanes; children were forced to shoot their parents, disciples their religious teachers. Everywhere monasteries were prime targets. Monks were compelled to publicly copulate with nuns and desecrate sacred images before being sent to a growing string of labor camps in Amdo and Gansu.[39]

One in 10 Tibetans has at some time been imprisoned by the Chinese.[40] Today estimates of political prisoners range from 20,000 to 100,000. In northeast Tibet near the Gobi Desert is the biggest network of prison camps in the world, the Amdo Gulag. Reportedly, it is capable of housing up to 10 million political prisoners.

If you have ever wondered where hell is, it is inside every nation where World Communism has prevailed—prevailed with the help of their partners in crimes committed against humanity— international bankers and the industrialists and the financiers.

After consolidating control in Tibet, the Chinese undertook a massive population transfer, encouraging Chinese citizens to emigrate to Tibet by offering them triple salary and other benefits in

an effort to make Tibetans a minority in their own country. Today
there are 7.5 million Chinese occupying a country of 6 million
Tibetans.[41] They are trying to destroy them genetically, to inter-
marry with them, to wipe out the Tibetan people from the face of
the earth, the bearers of the Light of the Buddha. In the 1960s,
the Chinese began a campaign of involuntary sterilization of
Tibetans. Gradually this method was phased out in favor of
inducing Tibetan women to marry Chinese soldiers.[42]

The Chinese not only practice physical genocide but cultural
genocide as well. They have destroyed 6,254 monasteries—the
centers for Tibetan cultural, educational and religious life. The
number of Tibetan monks (100,000 in 1957) has been reduced to
4,000, with only 10 to 15 new monks allowed to enter a monastery
each year. They have burned an estimated 60 percent of Tibet's
religious and historical literature. They have melted down sacred
art and statuary into bullion or sold it in Hong Kong and Tokyo
for foreign exchange.[43] In 1959, the Dalai Lama, Tibet's spiritual
and temporal ruler, was forced to flee into exile in India.

The Chinese do permit the limited worship and practice
of Buddhism in Tibet. But the Dalai Lama says that because of
"direct and indirect restrictions on the teaching and study of
Buddhist philosophy," Buddhism is "being reduced to a blind
faith."[44]

Since many of the 1.2 million Tibetans murdered were members of the intelligentsia, such as monks and teachers, Tibet's
cultural heritage is not being passed on to the next generation.
"For the first time in Tibet's history, there is a 'lost generation,'"
writes Avedon. "They're bitter, depressed and, with all opportunity denied them, lazy."[45]

Since 1978, the U.S. government has held that Tibet is a part
of China. President Reagan does not recognize the Dalai Lama's
government-in-exile in India and has refused him official State
visits. He has also refused to condemn the Chinese government for
its latest repression.

In late September 1987, reports filtered out of Tibet that
hundreds of Buddhist monks had staged peaceful protests calling
for Tibetan independence. These protests coincided with the Dalai
Lama's visit to the U.S., during which he presented a 5-point peace
plan to the Congressional Human Rights Caucus. The House
passed a resolution supporting him, and leading members of the
Congress sent a letter urging China's premier to use the 5-point
program as a basis of negotiation with the Dalai Lama.

The Chinese responded on September 24 by gathering 15,000
Tibetans at a stadium in Lhasa, the capital of Tibet, sentencing

---

eight to prison and two to death, and executing one immediately. In this they demonstrated their utter disdain for the United States government and Congress. On October 1, thousands of Tibetans demonstrated in Lhasa and Chinese police fired AK-47 assault rifles into the unarmed crowd, killing at least 12.

The Senate voted to condemn China for the crackdown but the Reagan administration actually voiced support for China, even though it later backpedaled. On October 6, the State Department announced its strong opposition to the Senate move. The *New York Times* reported that "one State Department official said that any possible benefits of the Senate action for the Tibetan people were 'insufficient to outweigh the almost certain damage to the United States–China bilateral relationship.'" [46] That relationship is based primarily on trade and Western capitalists foreseeing great profits in Chinese markets.

The Reagan administration has made every effort to strengthen ties with China, stepping up economic, technological and military aid to Peking. Just as the United States created Russia's military-industrial complex in the twenties and thirties, so it is now creating China's. United States trade with China is expected to reach $9 billion in 1988 and American businessmen have invested $3 billion there since 1979. [47]

On March 5, the Tibetans again rioted for freedom. The protest began when a monk stood up in Jokhang Temple, the holiest of Tibetan Buddhist shrines, during an annual prayer festival and began chanting slogans for independence. After he was detained, a crowd of several thousand began stoning the police. Three Chinese policemen and five Tibetans, including a 15-year-old monk, were killed, the *New York Times* reported. [48]

These riots coincided with the visit of the Chinese Foreign Minister Wu Xueqian to the United States to discuss increased high-tech trade. But everything was business as usual. State Department spokesman Charles Redman, while he expressed deep concern about human rights in Tibet, reaffirmed the American position that "Tibet is part of the People's Republic of China." [49]

You fallen ones who have entered the halls of government calling yourselves Americans—you have abdicated our destiny in our stead! You are not using trade as a lever to force China to improve conditions in Tibet. You have betrayed the Lightbearers of Tibet and continue to do so with every computer you send to China and every garment you import. Woe! to the fallen ones and the betrayers in the White House and in the State Department.

Inasmuch as ye have done it unto one of the least
of these my brethren, ye have done it unto me.

There is no other parallel in the world as singular and unique as the parallel of the community of the nation of Tibet to this Community of the Holy Spirit. We are in the Northern Rockies. They are on the Tibetan plateau, surrounded by the highest mountains in the world where they have been since ancient times, keeping the flame of Gautama Buddha.

You can see the handwriting on the wall: all spiritual communities and creative minorities must be snuffed out in order for the dominant minority of the power elite to retain control of planet earth. To meet that challenge and that external force to this community, the Ascended Masters have given to us the power of the spoken Word and a direct access by that Word to the hierarchy of the Great White Brotherhood.* They have vested in us as a community the final opportunity of Lightbearers on earth to defeat the false hierarchy; and into this community are being reborn day by day the slain Tibetans, the slain East Europeans, the slain Lightbearers of Mother Russia and all nations. They return here, the freedom fighters who have laid down their lives over and again. You are among them.

And here we are given that final opportunity to say: A spiritual community together with a world body of Lightbearers, all of whom descend from the lineage of Sanat Kumara, can and shall endure and they shall turn around the takeover of a planet by a power elite of this and other systems of worlds.

This is where we stand today. Even the Tibetans of this hour, even the Dalai Lama, whom Mark and I and Keepers of the Flame met with in Dharmsala in 1970, do not have the light or the access or the keys to the science of the spoken Word and the authority that we have been given in our mantle and our sponsorship by the Ascended Masters.

This community is the ensign of the people, each one of you bearing that sign of the I AM Presence and the Christ; and you have come from all spiritual communities of the earth, East and West, of all generations and time. The vindicating of such peoples being murdered today under World Communism can only come through a community such as this in a nation that is free such as ours. I speak to you the truth: What is at stake at this moment is the fate of a planet and beyond.

In Saint Germain's 1975 dictation on Taiwan, he told us of our responsibility to defend freedom throughout the world:

> You must forsake all to defend Terra; or I tell you, you will stand and watch, helpless, as many have done in the

*A spiritual order of Western "saints" and Eastern "masters," described in the Book of Revelation as the saints robed in white, who have mastered the testings and trials of life on earth and earned their immortal freedom. The word "white" refers not to race but to the aura (halo) of white light surrounding their forms.

countries behind the iron curtain. I tell you, they have stood and watched . . . them being torn limb from limb! They have watched them be raped and persecuted. They have watched their bodies maimed and cut apart as they screamed in anguish . . . . I tell you, deliverance will not come unless it be invoked! God cannot act except through you.[50]

Let us hear, then, the continuing abdication of Saint Germain's destiny for America by the betrayal of the fallen ones and the sleepfulness of the people who for want of rallying around the Divine Standard have lost, inch by inch, mile by mile, decade by decade, their options.

During the Korean War from June 25, 1950, to July 27, 1953, 54,000 Americans and over three million Koreans (both North and South) died. Many were killed because the United States, fighting on behalf of South Korea, was under the United Nations Command and under the United Nations flag. There is considerable evidence that the Soviets, who were supporting the North Koreans, used their position at the UN to gain intelligence about American operations and use it to their advantage in the war. The North Koreans knew General MacArthur's plans as fast as he made them. Thus, many Americans died needlessly and we were pushed out of North Korea. Our only achievement was to essentially preserve the pre-war borders. It should have been the war (and it would have been had MacArthur had his way!) to claim and win all of Korea for freedom!*

The Soviets were directing the North Korean war effort. It is a matter of history that by 1949 they had armed the North Korean army with military equipment, a brigade of tanks, and an air force.[51] The U.S. Defense Department released a report May 15, 1954, entitled "The Truth About Soviet Involvement in the Korean War." It quotes testimony of a North Korean major who had been captured as a prisoner of war. He said that he had been in charge of translating orders from Russian advisors to the North Korean army and that orders came from these advisors, and furthermore that "many Russian 'advisors' were attached to the North Korean Army advance headquarters established in June, 1950. They wore civilian clothing . . . and it was forbidden to address them by rank. They were introduced as 'newspaper reporters' but they had supreme authority. They took the lead in making operational and mobilizational plans,

---

*Some scholars today charge that MacArthur wanted to use nuclear weapons on China in order to win the war and that it was therefore necessary for President Truman to remove him. However, history contradicts this. As Dupuy and Dupuy write, "MacArthur was advocating neither the use of the atom bomb nor a land invasion of China. He did want to destroy, by conventional air attack, bases in Manchuria which were being used as springboards for invasion of Korea. He did urge the use of Chinese Nationalist troops in Korea, and also the 'unleashing' of Chiang Kai-shek on the Chinese mainland." Chiang had offered to assist U.S. forces with half a million troops but Truman turned him down. "The United States," continue Dupuy and Dupuy, "had deliberately given up the idea of liberating all of Korea and was seeking merely to restore the status quo in South Korea" (p. 1248).

and in commanding and manipulating troops."[52]

"The North Korean Major identified two of these Russian 'advisors' as Lieutenant General Vasiliev and Colonel Dolgin," the report says. "Vasiliev, he said, apparently was in charge of all movements across the 38th parallel." The report quotes another North Korean prisoner who said he actually heard General Vasiliev give the order to attack on June 25, 1950 (the day North Korea invaded South Korea).[53]

The Soviets were also involved in directing the UN forces. From October 21, 1949, until May 26, 1953, a Soviet officer, Konstantin Zinchenko, was assistant secretary general of the UN in charge of Security Council affairs,[54] which was responsible for application of UN enforcement measures, i.e., military action.

When war broke out, Zinchenko became de facto UN minister of war, communication and information in charge of all legal, military and judicial affairs relating to the subsequent UN operations in Korea. The UN required American commanders on the battlefield to make frequent and detailed reports to UN headquarters. And, according to one undocumented source, reports from General MacArthur in the battlefield went directly to Zinchenko. It wasn't until 1952 that UN Secretary General Trygve Lie began to suspect that Zinchenko was passing MacArthur's information on to the Soviets and directed that reports from the front bypass the Soviet officer.

So we see that, in effect, United States forces fighting in Korea on behalf of the United Nations were under the Soviets, who were also directing the North Korean war effort. This is what the cooperation and the absolute oneness of the international capitalist/communist conspirators brought our nation to.

To my knowledge no one from the president to the Joint Chiefs of Staff to the Congress to the media challenged this mockery of Liberty, this betrayal of her Sons. On the contrary, in addition to Soviet espionage, restrictions placed upon American forces by President Truman, the Joint Chiefs of Staff and the UN undermined the war effort. As military historians R. Ernest Dupuy and Trevor N. Dupuy report, MacArthur was forbidden to conduct aerial reconnaissance north of the Yalu River and was denied a request to bomb the bridges across the Yalu as well as the port of Rachin, through which Soviet war matériel flowed, and to bomb bases in Manchuria from which the North Koreans were preparing their invasion.

These restrictions had a direct effect on the outcome of the war. In October and November of 1950, 180,000 Communist Chinese troops poured across the Yalu River. They could have been stopped had MacArthur been permitted to bomb the bridges. Since aerial reconnaissance had been forbidden, UN forces were unaware of their presence and were ambushed. Four thousand men of the U.S. Eighth Army were killed and American troops were eventually forced to evacuate and retreat back into South Korea.[55]

One feels profound compassion for the Darjeeling Council of the Great White Brotherhood whose chief, our beloved guru El Morya, was himself betrayed by the deafening silence of cowards. As Thomas Becket he wrote to his fellow clergymen from his exile in France: "I have waited; not one has arisen. I have endured; not one has taken a stand. I have been silent; not one has spoken. . . . Let us then, all together, make haste to act so that God's wrath descend not on us as on negligent and idle shepherds, that we be not counted dumb dogs, too feeble to bark."[56]

Is this not also why the Blessed Virgin weeps?

This absurd situation in which United States forces were placed by the UN Command was detailed in the 1979 book *The Eleventh Hour* by Gen. Lewis Walt, who was commander of the Fifth Marine Regiment in Korea:

> As you know, American forces in Korea were under United Nations command. (They still are.*) It first began to dawn on me that something was drastically wrong as a result of my own combat experiences. I was a colonel then and not privy to the frustrations that were besetting our high command.
>
> I think most of us were shocked and angry when General Douglas MacArthur was relieved of his command. We in the Marines were even more shocked and angry when our 1st Marine Division had completed its drive to the Yalu River and then were faced with hordes of Chinese Communist Army forces who were forming and attacking from a UN-imposed sanctuary north of the Yalu.
>
> Both before and after they crossed, we were denied the use of our artillery and air power to prevent their massing for attack into Korea. Our forces were ordered to withdraw to the UN-imposed Demarcation Military Zone line.
>
> Once we manned that line to defend South Korea from further incursions by the North Koreans and Chinese, we had further restrictions placed on our forces. I was a regimental commander on that line from late October, 1952, until the summer of 1953. We were dug-in in trenches and bunkers on a lineal defense line nose to nose with Communist Chinese Forces one-half to three-quarters of a mile away.

*Today Gen. Louis C. Menetrey, four-star commanding general of U.S. forces in Korea, serves as commander in chief of the United Nations Command in Korea.

Artillery, mortar and machine gun fire from the Communists was a constant and deadly harassment. We returned the fire in kind—but were limited in the number of artillery and mortar shells we could fire no matter how intense the enemy action was!

The Chinese also made heavy infantry attacks against our positions and although we were always able to repel these attacks, it was not without considerable casualties on both sides. In an effort to destroy the enemy's ability to make these attacks, we planned numerous offensive attacks against their heavily defended, entrenched and bunkered positions. Time and again we captured their strongholds and could have held them, but each time we were ordered by UN Headquarters Command to relinquish control and fall back to our own lines.[57]

This is how the power elite and the fallen ones have made fodder of the Lightbearers, lined them up on the battlefields of life to fight their no-win wars. It's gone on not century by century but ten thousand years by ten thousand years. It is safe to say that every one of us in this room, including men and women and our children nestled in their beds, has fallen in battles such as these in one century or another.

General Walt continues:

It bothered me deeply that I was required to submit twenty-four hours in advance a detailed plan of attack for approval by UN Command Headquarters. It bothered me because it soon became apparent that each time we attacked, the enemy was waiting for us. Only by a supreme effort and teamwork on the part of my Marines were we able to win our objective and defeat the local enemy forces.

We were literally in a *Catch-22* situation. We could not achieve surprise. We could not retain anything we won. But we could not afford not to attack, for if we had not, the Chinese would have been able to build up their forces to overwhelming numbers which could have then broken through our lines and annihilated our forces. We had to keep them off balance. The Chinese fought under no UN restrictions.

One evening in early March, one of my radiomen intercepted a Communist Chinese message which indicated they were planning a heavy attack against the center of my regimental position shortly after midnight. This time, I did not report this to higher headquarters—for two reasons: first, we had only an indication and weren't sure, but secondly, if it was good information, I intended to take full advantage of it.

At 12:30 A.M., I requested flares from a plane circling overhead. I was in my front line observation post, a radio transmitter in my hand connecting me to nine batteries of artillery and one battery of five-inch rockets. The eerie light of the flares revealed a mass of humanity, over a thousand Chinese soldiers, moving toward our lines and only 600 to 800 yards away. They started a charge and I gave the order to fire. Every Marine on the line opened up and all ten batteries fired simultaneously. It was the end of the world, literally, for those Chinese. They never reached our line.

A lucky radio intercept had saved the lives of many Americans. The next morning, however, a reprimand sizzled down from UN Command Headquarters. I had failed to notify them of the intercept and I had fired too many artillery rounds![58]

America, in your name the power elite has abdicated our destiny—our destiny to defend the flame of freedom burning brightly in the hearts of the blessed peoples of Korea and all of Southeast Asia. America, by subterfuge and betrayal, by intrigue, they have betrayed our countrymen who died needlessly in a no-win war. Will you take the rap for these fallen ones or will you demand the karma be upon them and their own heads in this hour?

America, by the takeover complete of a power elite, more evil than any of those of this or that political persuasion East or West—a power elite who is not even concerned with capitalism or Communism but with absolute world control—by that takeover, our destiny and the very mantle of Saint Germain has been abdicated.

> *Inasmuch as ye have done it unto one of the least*
> *of these my brethren, ye have done it unto me.*

Our responsibility to defend the flame of freedom in Vietnam has been taken from us by the fallen ones. Since the United States evacuated its Saigon embassy in 1975, the Communist government of Vietnam has killed 250,000 of its own people.[59] A minimum of 200,000 people were interned in concentration camps.[60] Another 750,000 Vietnamese fled as refugees,[61] hundreds of thousands of them in boats. Of the boat people from Vietnam and Cambodia, a hundred thousand perished.[62]

The American government did not help them! They perished at sea with the hope of America in their hearts. Yes, America, the one nation, they thought, who would receive them with open arms. America, home of the dispossessed, their ancient Motherland reborn.

In fact, the *San Diego Union* reported in 1975 that on orders from the Ford administration, "U.S. naval vessels have been pulled out of the areas and their commanders forbidden to offer any assistance to South Vietnamese refugees on the grounds that the U.S. evacuation of refugees is over."[63] It was simply not convenient to evacuate any more. It was not convenient to save the oppressed, these huddled masses of the Goddess of Liberty yearning to breathe free.

The Vietnam War (1965–73) had a profound effect on the American psyche. Fifty-six thousand Americans died over a nine-year period in a war that cost the U.S. $141 billion to defend a country that was conquered two years after we pulled out.

On the face of it, it seemed that a great superpower had been defeated by a Third World nation. But some military experts have demonstrated that we had, in essence, won the Vietnam War militarily on several occasions but we lost because we failed to claim and consolidate the victory. Remember the teaching of Mighty Victory: When you have a victory, you must continue to claim it even after the victory is won because the sinister force will never accept your victory. Therefore, the sinister force in the person of the moneyed interests of America, the same who killed Abraham Lincoln, they denied our victory in Vietnam.

The Tet Offensive in which Soviet-backed North Vietnamese forces and Viet Cong guerrillas attacked military bases and towns in South Vietnam beginning January 30, 1968, was a military defeat for the North but a psychological defeat for America. Dupuy and Dupuy point out that the Communist forces "suffered severe casualties and gained neither any substantial new territorial footholds nor increased support among the South Vietnamese."

However, the media portrayed Tet as a crushing defeat for U.S. forces and the American people came to see it as such. Dupuy and Dupuy conclude that "although the Tet Offensive was a tactical military defeat for the Communists...it was a major strategic victory for the North Vietnamese and the Viet Cong."[64]

Military experts have shown that a determined American effort to prosecute the war following Tet could have resulted in quick victory. In fact, Henry Paolucci, professor of government and politics at St. John's University, points out that civilian control of the military had denied victory even earlier. "Had such political restraints not been imposed," he writes, "President Johnson's escalation of the troop level during 1965 would have resulted, no military man doubts, in a complete collapse of the enemy's war effort in the south before the year was over."[65]

Even as late as 1972, we could have won the war had we not lost our political will. "Although by 1972 General Abrams's U.S.

and ARVN [Army of the Republic of Vietnam] forces had virtually won the land war in South Vietnam, drastically curtailing Viet Cong and North Vietnamese operations and inflicting unacceptable casualties on their troops," write Dupuy and Dupuy, "the American public had almost uniformly come to see the U.S. involvement in Vietnam as a tragic mistake."[66]

On January 23, 1973, Henry Kissinger and Le Duc Tho, the North Vietnamese representative, initialed a peace agreement in Paris under which all U.S. forces would leave South Vietnam and American prisoners of war would be released. The North Vietnamese violated the cease fire agreement and continued to attack. On April 30, 1975, South Vietnam surrendered.

American failure in the Vietnam War was based on the power elite's doctrine of limited war as articulated by Henry Kissinger, foremost betrayer of the Christ in all centuries. His ideas provided the framework around which the American war effort was organized. Secretary of Defense Robert MacNamara under Presidents Kennedy and Johnson turned many of Kissinger's theories into policy. Kissinger himself applied them when President Nixon appointed him national security advisor in 1969 and secretary of state in 1973.

Kissinger promoted the doctrine of Serpent in the Garden: "Limited war . . . must be based on the awareness that with the end of our atomic monopoly it is no longer possible to impose unconditional surrender at an acceptable cost," he wrote in his influential 1957 book, *Nuclear Weapons and Foreign Policy*. "The result of a limited war cannot depend on military considerations alone," he continued. "It reflects an ability to harmonize political and military objectives. An attempt to reduce the enemy to impotence would remove the psychological balance which makes it profitable for both sides to keep the war limited."[67] Therefore, Kissinger is saying, the enemy must not be reduced to impotence as this might force him to step over the nuclear threshold. And so, the United States must accept impotence for the good of the world.

Speaking for the fallen ones and the power elite, he is notifying the children of the Light who are without shepherds that you cannot impose unconditional surrender upon the fallen ones cast out of heaven by Archangel Michael, who to this day persecute the seed of the Woman, and he has made that official policy of the United States.

Kissinger insisted that the Soviet Union, which backed the North Vietnamese forces, believed that it *could not* afford to lose the Vietnam War. And he believed that the United States *could* afford to lose it. Thus he said that the United States must not win the war. As he had written in 1957, "There would seem to be no sense in seeking to escape a limited defeat through bringing on the cataclysm of an all-out war, particularly if an all-out war threatens a calamity far transcending the penalties of losing a limited war."[68] In short, he decided we must lose the war in Vietnam to prevent a nuclear holocaust.

Of course, this was based on his opinion of the Soviets and his view of nuclear weapons. History has shown that both are fundamentally flawed. The Soviet Union is not and was not willing to risk nuclear war for Vietnam and she has not abided by Kissinger's hallowed principle of the nuclear age—that both sides must exercise restraint. But the Lightbearers of planet earth have paid for his mistake.

Where are the shepherds? Where are you in America who should have taught and fed and nourished the children of the Light that they could come of age and move this civilization for the saving of nations?

Kissinger wrote in 1957 that public opinion must be "educated to the realities of the nuclear age." Through the Vietnam War, he and the power elite wanted to teach the American people a lesson that we could no longer expect to win wars. Why not? Archangel Michael always wins his wars and we are fighting on his side! The "realities of the nuclear age" that Kissinger wanted to "teach" are that sons and daughters of God and children of the Light must abdicate their fiery destiny and bow and scrape before the power elite until the hour when they are delivered in that coup de grâce at the point of their national suicide.

The Vietnam War was a perfect opportunity for the power elite to teach the American people this doctrine. They had to do it by example since the people would have rejected the philosophy had it been spelled out for them.

The forces in the executive branch adopted Kissinger's philosophy and ensured that the war would be conducted as a limited war. To begin with, it was the first time in history that America fought a war with no strategy for victory, no allegiance to the Great Guru Sanat Kumara or the fiery heart of the angels of Victory. When Clark Clifford took over as secretary of defense under President Johnson in March 1968, he asked to see the plan for victory. As he recounted it, he was told that "there was no plan for victory in the historic American sense."[69]

Limits placed on the military by the executive branch throughout the war fit Kissinger's description of limited war to a T. He had written that "in a limited war between major powers, sanctuary areas immune to attack are almost essential" and that the military doctrine of destroying "enemy communication and industrial centers" would have to be modified.[70]

The Rules of Engagement which specified the conduct of American bombing of North Vietnam were, in effect, a codification of Kissinger's belief system. The text of these rules was declassified in 1985. They allowed the North Vietnamese large sanctuaries and prohibited the bombing of important military and industrial targets. While some of the rules were necessary in that they prevented the killing of civilians and destruction of religious shrines, their primary effect was to greatly hamper the American war effort.

A U.S. Air Force analysis of the rules for January 1966 through November 1969 concluded that "in military eyes, these restrictions had the effect of creating a haven in the northeast quadrant of [North Vietnam] into which the enemy could with impunity import vital war materials, construct sanctuaries for his aircraft, and prop his [anti-aircraft artillery] defenses around the cities of Hanoi and Haiphong."[71]

The rules forbade pilots to attack commercial shipping in the Haiphong Harbor (the most important North Vietnamese port) unless fired upon by the ships. This included the Soviet ships which were supplying the North Vietnamese army with weapons. They were immune to attack throughout the war. Secretary of Defense McNamara justified the restriction to Congress by saying that bombing of the port facilities to interdict Soviet war-supporting material would seriously threaten Soviet shipping.[72]

The Ho Chi Minh Trail was a network of roads and tracks through Laos and Cambodia which allowed North Vietnam to deliver Soviet and Chinese weapons and supplies to its forces in the South. American planes bombed the trail but restrictions blunted that effort. Targets had to be approved by the American Embassy in Vientiane, the capital of Laos. The Air Force reported that "the average time consumed between identification of an area and the clearance to strike was 15.5 days."[73] This removed the elements of surprise and spontaneity from the bombing and allowed the North Vietnamese to operate around it.

Another rule said that trucks carrying supplies along the trail could not be bombed unless they had been positively identified as hostile. The Air Force pointed out that the only trucks using the trail were North Vietnamese and that the time planes spent in identifying the trucks gave them ample time to escape by driving off the road. However, the rules remained in force.[74]

Kissinger admitted in his memoirs that political restrictions had denied victory to the military. In his 1979 book, *The White*

House Years, he wrote that "[General] Westmoreland labored under political restrictions that barred any of the major maneuvers that might have proved decisive—sealing off the Ho Chi Minh Trail in 1967, for example."[75]

The complex set of American restrictions in effect under Nixon-Kissinger from 1968 to 1972 allowed the North Vietnamese to build up a formidable air defense:

American planes could only bomb a surface-to-air missile (SAM) site if it had already fired on them or had activated its radar to fire. Furthermore, they could only target the specific weapon which had fired upon them. The ramifications of this policy were that a SAM site under construction could not be bombed. It could only be bombed after it was armed and dangerous. The Air Force study reveals that "throughout the spring and into the summer of 1971 the Secretary of Defense [Melvin Laird] disapproved all requests for one-time preemptive strikes against the maturing [North Vietnamese] air defense system."[76] This system inflicted heavy losses on American planes when Nixon renewed bombing of North Vietnam in 1972.

The restrictions not only allowed the North Vietnamese to complete their air defense but also let them prepare a massive invasion of over 150,000 troops into South Vietnam which they launched in March 1972.

The American military knew the invasion was coming. Gen. Creighton Abrams requested permission to disrupt preparations for it by air attacks into North Vietnam. The request went to Kissinger, who convened his national security "Senior Review Group." "The Group's recommendation to President Nixon," writes Paolucci, "passed on to him in a Kissinger memo, was that he should 'let Abrams have part of his cake but not the bombing of the North.'" Nixon authorized Abrams to step up bombing in South Vietnam only.[77] When the spring offensive from the North came, American and South Vietnamese soldiers fought bravely but they could not hold the line.

Richard Nixon had been elected in 1968 on a pledge to "end the war and win the peace." Yet the peace treaty was not signed until four years later—after he had been elected to a second term and after 20,000 additional Americans had been killed, 150,000 wounded and another $50 billion spent.[78]

The terms of the January 1973 agreement were virtually identical to a North Vietnamese proposal that Kissinger had rejected in August of 1969. The only significant difference between the terms North Vietnamese representative Xuan Thuy offered Kissinger during secret negotiations in Paris in 1969 and

the terms Kissinger accepted in 1973 with Le Duc Tho was that in
'73, South Vietnamese president Nguyen Van Thieu was not
required to abdicate.[79] This was a moot point since Kissinger
allowed the North to keep 150,000 troops in the South and no one
believed the Thieu government could stand for long without
American support.

Why did Kissinger and Nixon delay three years in signing
what was essentially a surrender agreement? Paolucci makes a
convincing case for his argument that Kissinger wanted to force
America to accept defeat while avoiding a backlash from middle
America against his policy and at the same time negotiating
détente with Moscow.

Nixon went to Moscow for a summit meeting in May of 1972.
Jonathan Schell described the summit in *Time of Illusion:* "For a
moment, as President Nixon proclaimed that 'America's flag flies
over the ancient fortress' while Americans were dying in Southeast Asia in an attempt to counter the Kremlin's influence, the
fighting in Vietnam came to look like something without prece-
dent in military history: a war in which generals on the opposing
sides combined into a joint command."[80]

Limited war was a difficult concept to explain to the American public. As Schell observed, "One might say that it was in the
very nature of the doctrine that it had to be presented mis-
leadingly to the public and the world. For to explain the policy
would be to undermine it."[81]

The doctrine was pounded into American heads by three
more years of war. Paolucci writes that

> from the standpoint of Kissinger's limited-war theory, the
> controlled fighting must be continued until the risks of
> escalation are sufficiently appreciated, at least by one side,
> to make it ready to accept defeat if the other side won't
> settle for a stalemate. . . . [The war] had to continue, accord-
> ing to Kissinger, until the Soviet-American detente he had
> been negotiating was signed, sealed, and institutionalized;
> and then, with Soviet intervention motivated by its desire to
> enjoy the advantages of detente, Hanoi would be forced to
> settle; or, if that couldn't be brought about even with Soviet
> intervention, then we would wisely settle, accepting limited
> defeat. . . rather than risking the survival of mankind once
> more with another massive-retaliation threat.[82]

By 1973, American GIs had taken enough punishment to
teach middle America that we could not expect to win wars
anymore.

And you wonder why the vets of Vietnam have demonstrated and have had so many problems readjusting psychologically to society in America. No wonder Americans grew tired of the senseless fighting and demanded, "Stop the killing." The killing could have ended years earlier if our leaders had had a strategy of victory. Victory was denied in Vietnam—the victory of the light of personal Christhood in the Vietnamese people and in the Americans who fought for them.

Inasmuch as ye have done it unto one of the least
of these my brethren, ye have done it unto me.

America, Jane Fonda, did you hear the cry of the people of Cambodia? An estimated 1 to 3 million Cambodians out of a population of 7 million were murdered or died from disease, malnutrition and forced labor during the four-year Khmer Rouge regime from April 1975 to January 1979.[83]

Where were you? What were you doing from 1975 to 1979? What were you doing when the Communist Khmer Rouge marched into Phnom Penh, the capital of Cambodia, a city of 3 million, and forced the entire population to march into the jungle in an effort to "purify" society?

No preparation had been made for food, water or sanitation. Hospitals were emptied of the sick. Doctors were forced to leave in mid-operation. Those who could not keep pace on the march were clubbed to death or shot. As the days passed, the young children and elderly, the sick, wounded and pregnant were left to die. Whole families committed suicide together rather than face the future. That was Cambodia after the American pullout in Vietnam.

Soldiers of the former regime, professionals of any kind and their families were slaughtered. City dwellers were forced to break ground and construct new villages in the jungle and begin growing rice. Love between unmarried couples was forbidden. Boys and girls caught holding hands were executed. Hunger forced the people to eat grasshoppers, lizards, snakes and tree bark. Those who complained or disobeyed the rules were executed—usually with knives, hoes, sticks and pickaxes. Just before harvest, half a million people were forced to move and build new villages. Famine, disease and malnutrition decimated the country. In 1978 the Vietnamese invaded. They took power in 1979. A civil war continues today.[84]

The media all but ignored the genocide. Depending on whose estimates you accept, between 14 and 43 percent of the Cambodian population died between 1975 and 1979. Analysts William Adams and Michael Joblove did a study of news coverage of the

Cambodian crisis. They found that "added together, all three television networks devoted *less than sixty minutes* to the new society and human rights in Cambodia over the entire four-year Khmer Rouge period....The stories were so sporadic that even the most constant viewers could not be expected to grasp the gravity of the Cambodian crisis."[85]

On our nation's bicentennial, Saint Germain squarely addressed the question of responsibility for our failures in Southeast Asia:

> Listen to my question: Who decided the death of thousands and thousands of Vietnamese after America pulled out? Who decided the death of a million Cambodians who have been lost in the past year?
>
> You say, "The Communists decided their death. *They* murdered them." I say, nay! Nay, it is the free people! It is the people to whom is passed the torch of initiation. You who were not there keeping the flame. Upon you, America, is the burden of this karma. For you knew the intent of the enemy. You knew the doctrine of the enemy. You knew the avowed doctrine of world takeover and world conquest. And you knew the writing of history—that every nation that has been taken over by Communism has murdered the life, the light of the leaders in government, in the military, and in the professions.[86]

On May 15, 1983, Mother Mary warned us that America should not be overcome by guilt for these deeds. She said:

> America still is the exemplar nation, still under the grace and dispensation of Almighty God. Let not past sins of this nation create an aura of guilt, confusion, loss of vision of its destiny. But rather, let the people of America rise up and overthrow that self-condemnation and enter anew into the propagation of the faith in the principles of American freedom, in her Constitution, and all for which she has stood in the defense of the rights of individuals.[87]

Let us take Mother Mary at her word and rise to give the judgment call upon the heads of those who have betrayed our destiny.

I invite you to give your individual calls in this hour upon all the situations that I have placed before you, beginning with the assassination of President Lincoln. I ask you to also call for the judgment upon the condemners of the American people, the very ones who have betrayed us.

In the Name of the I AM THAT I AM,
   I invoke the Electronic Presence of Jesus Christ:
They shall not pass! They shall not pass! They shall not pass!
By the authority of the cosmic cross of white fire
   it shall be:
That all that is directed against the Christ
   within me, within the holy innocents,
   within our beloved Messengers,
   within every son and daughter of God...
Is now turned back
   by the authority of Alpha and Omega,
   by the authority of my Lord and Saviour Jesus Christ,
   by the authority of Saint Germain!

I AM THAT I AM within the center of this temple
   and I declare in the fullness of
   the entire Spirit of the Great White Brotherhood:
That those who, then, practice the black arts
   against the children of the Light...
Are now bound by the hosts of the LORD,
Do now receive the judgment of the Lord Christ
   within me, within Jesus,
   and within every Ascended Master,
Do now receive, then, the full return—
   multiplied by the energy of the Cosmic Christ—
   of their nefarious deeds which they have practiced
   since the very incarnation of the Word!

Lo, I AM a Son of God!
Lo, I AM a Flame of God!
Lo, I stand upon the Rock of the living Word
And I declare with Jesus, the living Son of God:
They shall not pass! They shall not pass! They shall not pass!
Elohim. Elohim. Elohim. [chant]

   Unto the betrayers of the living Word in America and the
world by the fallen ones East and West, the power elite, we say:
   Unto you be your karma this day.
   Woe! Woe! Woe! (4x)
   Unto you, then, be the karma of your sin against the Father,
against the Son, and against the Holy Ghost in my people.
   Woe! Woe! Woe! (3x)

   Let us sing "America the Beautiful." ["America the Beautiful" is sung]
Thank you. Let us sing "God Bless America." ["God Bless America" is sung]

[to be continued]

"The Summit Lighthouse Sheds Its Radiance O'er All the World to Manifest as Pearls of Wisdom."
Based on a lecture by Elizabeth Clare Prophet delivered on Monday, January 4,
1988, at the Royal Teton Ranch, Montana, updated for print as this week's Pearl. For
Part 1, see 1988 *Pearls of Wisdom*, no. 9, pp. 95–116. **(1)** Ron Paul and Lewis
Lehrman, *The Case for Gold: A Minority Report of the U.S. Gold Commission*
(Washington, D.C.: Cato Institute, 1982), p. 129. **(2)** Murray N. Rothbard, *The Mystery of Banking* (n.p.: Richardson & Snyder, 1983), p. 254. **(3)** See "Turning Paper
into Gold: Joe Cobb's Alchemical Formula for a Healthy Economy," *The Coming
Revolution: The Magazine for Higher Consciousness,* Summer 1986. **(4)** Edwin
Vieira, Jr., *Pieces of Eight: The Monetary Powers and Disabilities of the United States
Constitution* (Old Greenwich, Conn.: Devin-Adair, 1983), pp. 15–36. **(5)** *Notes of
Debates in the Federal Convention of 1787 Reported by James Madison* (Athens,
Ohio: Ohio University Press, 1966), p. 542. **(6)** Vieira, *Pieces of Eight,* pp. 237–51.
(7) The God of Gold with the God Tabor, October 10, 1977, "The Flow of Energy in the
City Foursquare: Children of God, Demand and Supply the Abundance of the
Mother!" on 90-min. audiocassette B7808. **(8)** Antony C. Sutton, *Wall Street and the
Rise of Hitler* (Seal Beach, Calif.: '76 Press, 1976), p. 163. **(9)** R. Ernest Dupuy and
Trevor N. Dupuy, *The Encyclopedia of Military History from 3500 B.C. to the Present,*
2d rev. ed. (New York: Harper & Row, 1986), p. 1198. **(10)** David S. Wyman, *The Abandonment of the Jews: America and the Holocaust, 1941–1945* (New York: Pantheon
Books, 1984), p. xiii. **(11)** Ibid., pp. xv, 321. **(12)** Ibid., pp. xiv, 21–22. **(13)** Ibid., p. xiv.
(14) Haskel Lookstein, *Were We Our Brothers' Keepers? The Public Response of
American Jews to the Holocaust, 1938–1944* (New York: Hartmore House, 1985), p. 86.
(15) Gordon Thomas and Max Morgan Witts, *Voyage of the Damned* (New York: Stein
and Day, 1974), pp. 303–4. **(16)** Rummel counted only battle deaths for wars of this
century, not other deaths which occurred during wartime. The 41 to 49 million figure
cited on p. 175 includes all World War II deaths. Fifteen million people died in battle
during World War II. Some estimates of deaths caused by Communist governments
are higher than Rummel's. See R. J. Rummel, "Deadlier than War," *IPA Review,*
August–October 1987, p. 24. **(17)** Robert Conquest, *The Great Terror: Stalin's Purge
of the Thirties,* rev. ed. (New York: Collier Books, 1973), p. 710. **(18)** Aleksandr I.
Solzhenitsyn, *The Gulag Archipelago, 1918–1956: An Experiment in Literary Investigation,* vol. 2, trans. Thomas P. Whitney (New York: Harper & Row, 1975), p. 10.
(19) Conquest, *Great Terror,* p. 713; Aleksandr I. Solzhenitsyn, *The Gulag Archipelago, 1918–1956: An Experiment in Literary Investigation,* vol. 3, trans. Harry Willetts
(New York: Harper & Row, 1978), p. 350. **(20)** Aleksandr I. Solzhenitsyn, *The Gulag
Archipelago, 1918–1956: An Experiment in Literary Investigation,* vol. 1, trans.
Thomas P. Whitney (New York: Harper & Row, 1973), p. 55. **(21)** Solzhenitsyn, *Gulag,*
vol. 3, p. 363; see Solzhenitsyn, *Gulag,* vol. 1, pp. 56–57; Solzhenitsyn, *Gulag,* vol. 3, pp.
351–63. **(22)** Rummel, "Deadlier than War," p. 25. **(23)** Ibid., pp. 27–28. **(24)** Saint
Germain, July 4, 1976, "Our Service in the Next Hundred Years of America's Destiny,"
1977 *Pearls of Wisdom,* vol. 20, no. 50, pp. 239–40. **(25)** Antony C. Sutton, *Wall
Street and the Bolshevik Revolution* (New Rochelle, N.Y.: Arlington House, 1974), pp.
82–83. **(26)** Antony C. Sutton, *Western Technology and Soviet Economic Development, 1917 to 1930* (Stanford, Calif.: Hoover Institution Publications, 1968), p. 198.
(27) See Antony C. Sutton, *Western Technology and Soviet Economic Development,*
vol. 1, 1917 to 1930; vol. 2, 1930 to 1945; vol. 3, 1945 to 1965 (Stanford, Calif.: Hoover
Institution Press, 1968–73). **(28)** Toby Roth, "Big Bankers Lending Billions to
Moscow," *Conservative Digest,* February 1988, p. 82. **(29)** Anthony Kubek, *How the
Far East Was Lost: American Policy and the Creation of Communist China, 1941–
1949* (New York: Twin Circle Publishing, 1972), pp. 321–22, 335. **(30)** Ibid., pp. 337, 387.
(31) Ibid., pp. 397, 406. **(32)** Ibid., p. 405. **(33)** Ibid., p. 396. **(34)** Ibid., p. 401.
(35) Ibid., p. 338. **(36)** U.S. Congress, Senate Committee on the Judiciary, *The
Human Cost of Communism in China,* 92d Cong., 1st sess., 1971, p. 16. An often-quoted figure says Mao killed 34 to 64 million Chinese. This includes those killed by
the Communists prior to 1949. **(37)** Saint Germain, December 8, 1975, "Freedom for
Taiwan," 1977 *Pearls of Wisdom,* vol. 20, no. 46, pp. 216, 223. **(38)** John F. Avedon,
"The U.S. Must Speak Up for Tibet," *New York Times,* 10 October 1987. **(39)** John F.

Avedon, *In Exile from the Land of Snows* (New York: Vintage Books, 1986), p. 48. **(40)** 18 June 1987, *Congressional Record*, 100th Cong., 1st sess., H 5229. **(41)** "Stand Up for Decency in Tibet," *New York Times*, 8 October 1987. **(42)** Avedon, *In Exile*, pp. 266–67. **(43)** 18 June 1987, *Congressional Record*, 100th Cong., 1st sess., H 5229. **(44)** "Documentation," *News Tibet*, September–December 1987, p. 3. **(45)** John F. Avedon, "Tibet Today: Current Conditions and Prospects," p. 12. **(46)** Edward A. Gargan, "Police Station Is Hit in Rioting in Tibet," *New York Times*, 6 March 1988. **(47)** "Who May Cry for Tibet?" *New York Times*, 9 March 1988. **(48)** Edward A. Gargan, "Ominous Wind in Tibet," *New York Times*, 9 March 1988. **(49)** Richard Beeston, "U.S. Airs Concern with China's Wu over Tibet Unrest," *Washington Times*, 8 March 1988. **(50)** Saint Germain, "Freedom for Taiwan," pp. 218, 223. **(51)** Dupuy and Dupuy, *Encyclopedia of Military History*, p. 1241. **(52)** Department of Defense, "The Truth About Soviet Involvement in the Korean War," (Office of Public Information) release Number 465–54, 15 May 1954, p. 5. **(53)** Ibid. **(54)** *The Year Book of the United Nations* (New York: Columbia University Press, 1953). **(55)** Dupuy and Dupuy, *Encyclopedia of Military History*, pp. 1244–48. **(56)** Joseph Vann, ed., *Lives of Saints* (New York: John J. Crawley & Co., 1954), p. 220. **(57)** Lewis W. Walt, *The Eleventh Hour* (Ottawa, Ill.: Caroline House, 1979), pp. 33–34. **(58)** Ibid., pp. 34–35. **(59)** Rummel, "Deadlier than War," pp. 25–27, 29. **(60)** Pham Kim Vinh, *The Vietnamese Holocaust and the Conscience of Civilized Nations* (n.p.: PKV Publications, 1979), p. 67. **(61)** Albert L. Weeks, "Communist Death Toll: 160 Million," *American Freedom Journal*, November 1987, p. 5. **(62)** Rummel, "Deadlier than War," pp. 26–27. **(63)** *San Diego Union*, quoted in Vinh, *Vietnamese Holocaust*, p. 42. **(64)** Dupuy and Dupuy, *Encyclopedia of Military History*, pp. 1211–12. **(65)** Henry Paolucci, *Kissinger's War: 1957–1975* (White Stone, N.Y.: Griffon House Publications, 1980), p. 20. **(66)** Dupuy and Dupuy, *Encyclopedia of Military History*, pp. 1212–13. **(67)** Henry A. Kissinger, *Nuclear Weapons and Foreign Policy* (New York: Harper & Brothers, 1957), p. 145. **(68)** Ibid., p. 146. **(69)** Paolucci, *Kissinger's War*, p. 21. **(70)** Kissinger, *Nuclear Weapons*, p. 227. **(71)** 14 March 1985, *Congressional Record*, S 2983. **(72)** Ibid., S 2984. **(73)** Ibid., S 2987. **(74)** Ibid. **(75)** Henry Kissinger, *The White House Years* quoted in Paolucci, *Kissinger's War*, p. 119. **(76)** 18 March 1985, *Congressional Record*, S 3015–17. **(77)** Paolucci, *Kissinger's War*, p. 121. **(78)** Ibid., pp. 43, 45. **(79)** Stanley Karnow, *Vietnam: A History* (New York: Viking Press, 1983), pp. 597, 648. **(80)** Jonathan Schell, *Time of Illusions*, quoted in Paolucci, *Kissinger's War*, p. 25. **(81)** Ibid., p. 89. **(82)** Ibid., p. 27. **(83)** Rummel, "Deadlier than War," p. 25; Weeks, "Communist Death Toll," p. 5; John Barron and Anthony Paul, *Murder of a Gentle Land* (New York: Reader's Digest Press, 1977), pp. 201–6. **(84)** See Barron and Paul, *Murder of a Gentle Land*. **(85)** William Adams and Michael Joblove, "The Unnewsworthy Holocaust," *Policy Review*, Winter 1980, pp. 59–60. **(86)** Saint Germain, July 4, 1976, "Our Service in the Next Hundred Years of America's Destiny," 1977 *Pearls of Wisdom*, vol. 20, no. 51, pp. 246–47. **(87)** Mother Mary, May 15, 1983, "The Sign of a Great Liberation in the Earth," 1983 *Pearls of Wisdom*, vol. 26, no. 45, pp. 544–45.

Pearls of Wisdom®

published by The Summit Lighthouse

| *Vol. 31 No. 24* | *Beloved Mother Mary* | *June 8, 1988* |

Saint Germain Stumps America

13

Reason for Being

Make Your Calling and Election Sure

I come bearing sacred fire from the altars of heaven on a mission to this city. In my hand, I, Mary, hold, then, fire of the living God that is the fire infolding itself. And as it draws within, retiring to the within, this fire sounds the call for the drawing [together] of those lifestreams who must move on in the cosmic cycles of the Divine Mother. Therefore, follow the fire to the heart of the mountain and know a consuming fire that does descend upon this world to take from it unreality of every kind.

I am your ancient Mother, O beloved, and the 'I' within me that is that universal and divine Woman clothed with the Sun[1] has known you personally heart to heart and in the depths of your soul since you went forth out of the Great Central Sun and the Sun behind the sun with your beloved.

The descent of Lightbearers who truly went after that which was lost is a cosmic drama all its own. Tapestries exist in heaven where[on] angels have outpictured every face and countenance, every pair of Lightbearers that did go after [souls] to save that which was lost in the descending spiral into the mayic illusion.

Blessed hearts, be no longer accustomed, then, to dwelling in this illusion. Sound the note—the note of Harmony, the note of Warning, the note of the Teaching, the note of the Guru and the Divine Mother. Let the souls hear this chime and the chime of the ancient bell sounding, then, for the Seventh Age and Ray.[2]

Let the violet flame, as ribbons of light, contact all hearts who yearn for Kuan Yin, for Saint Germain, for Light eternal. Let those, then, who yearn for the return and are willing submit to the path that does lead Home. [For] I am your Mother initiator with Kuan Yin.

Thus, I place before you the dilemma of a civilization and organisms that crumble from within, beloved, because there is no integrating light or flame or consciousness. However precise or complex the mathematical formula of building in Matter, unless there be a central flame upon the central altar of being, that creation will not endure beyond a certain span, that span determined by the cohesive power of love of the atoms and molecules themselves.

Thus, much of Western civilization has reached the level wherein it must be endowed by the flame of the bodhisattvas else spiral into that [cycle of] degeneration, for it has reached the peak beyond which it cannot ascend without living hearts of fire.

Therefore, in knowing oneself as a flame-bearer (as I am and [as] is the beloved Kuan Yin and those in heavenly octaves) realize that you may choose to endow with the flame of your heart that which you may judge as worthy of extension in time and space or ultimate permanence. By the permanent atom of being of the I AM Presence and the seed atom of the Divine Mother within you, you therefore give life to forces and causes, to persons and the creations of your heart.

Now choose that which must survive coming earth changes. Choose well, for to tend the flame of any endeavor requires all of thy life and love and giving. Choose well, beloved, for to allow the cycles of time to pass and the energy to flow from thy Tree of Life³ into those things that are of nonconsequence to the next two thousand years, this is shortsightedness, to say the least.

It is time to look at the present and measure it against the rod given to John the Beloved.⁴ Measure, then, by co-measurement that which must endure if there is to be a golden age of Aquarius. And begin with thyself, a soul endowing a planet portion for portion, measure by measure, with Light.*

Know, then, beloved, that thy call [answered by the Lords of Karma] to "grace the earth" in embodiment† in this hour, was no small measure or dispensation. Consider, then, the millions to whom life has been denied, for whom life is aborted, and see how that much more precious is opportunity and the shuttle whereby [thy soul enveloped in] light descends and occupies, verily, time and space of this dimension.

Now, beloved, look to the future. Let the consequences of thy life be the fulfillment of the promise of love to thy twin flame, to thy God, to thyself—a trinity indeed! Therefore keep the promise, be faithful and know that separating out from foundations unreal

*with the gift of your Christ consciousness   †i.e., to take embodiment

may take you apart and away from your present geographical location to a place of more permanent vibration, that thou and thy purpose, thy cause and life, shall endure until the fulfillment of [thy] reason for being.

Reason for being, ponder it! Crack the nut. Discover the seed inside and the Sun behind the sun. Know, beloved, that to come apart and retreat, to contemplate the mystery of life and what shall be done with that which remains to you [as the sands] in the hourglass [of a lifetime] is most necessary and the purpose of my coming.

Weigh all things. Study all that we have delivered in the past year and this, for our messages are truly to the point of [necessity for] all who care deeply for the Life that is God within them and the purpose to which their course is set.

Thus, beloved, the cycles are turning and the decade of the nineties does portend for all the initiation of the three-times-three whereby the threefold flame of the Presence, the threefold flame of the Holy Christ Self and the threefold flame upon the altar of your heart must come into alignment by balance. By the power of this three times the three of their union, you, then, can manifest the Power, Wisdom and Love fused in the identity of the Mother within you to meet every challenge, to walk as initiates of the elements and the suns.

Know, then, beloved, that without balance and without preparation for the initiation of that decade, many will be tossed and tumbled and lose their grip on life in this octave. Hold fast what thou hast received![5] It is the calling of Keepers of the Flame. Keep the flame of Life and place not that flame [or] thy soul in harm's way.

When you know, as we have told the Messenger, that you indeed hold the key in consciousness as path and teaching and the gift of knowledge to a new civilization and age, do not place yourself where there is uncertainty of future. There are places where life shall endure and there are places where life shall not. Attunement with the angels of Saint Germain by violet flame harmonies will lift you as the Holy Spirit does take you where you know not[6] and yet where you are guided by a free givingness and movement with warm winds that cycle into the winds of the north.

Thus, I, your Mother, who have been present at your birth, each one, and who will be there when the soul takes final leave of this body, do come in my Presence, locking you, then, in my aura, that by my Diamond Heart in coming weeks you may chart your course for a destiny that fulfills karma, the dharma, and [your] reason for being.

I encourage you to make your calling and election sure,[7]

absolutely sure, sure in the surety of the living Presence, and that you determine in this hour this one thing:

that the purpose for your soul's descent in this life shall be accomplished

and that you shall bear any burden, face any challenge, but keep on moving toward the Central Sun,

that you shall retain the individualization of the God Flame and know yourself as an identity in God when this sphere arrives at that Sun behind the sun

[*in order*] *that* the profile of your Christhood and image in crystal shall endure and endure and endure from *manvantara* to *manvantara.*[8]

With this fire I infire you with the will to be God!

Begin now, beloved, for the spiral must needs be raised.

I AM the Resurrection and the Life of the Fifth Ray precipitation flame within you.

I seal you in a swaddling garment for your safe passage.

[chant]

"The Summit Lighthouse Sheds Its Radiance O'er All the World to Manifest as Pearls of Wisdom." This dictation by **Mother Mary** was **delivered** by Elizabeth Clare Prophet following her lecture **"The Path of the Divine Mother East and West: Mother Mary and Kuan Yin"** on **Sunday, February 14, 1988,** at the Sheraton-Palace Hotel, **San Francisco,** where she was stumping for Saint Germain's Coming Revolution in Higher Consciousness. (1) Rev. 12:1, 2. (2) On May 30, 1987, Saint Germain said: "**The chime of an ancient bell** now sounds. One of my angels called by Portia does begin this chiming. It will sound in the ear of every true son and daughter of Liberty as though he or she does hear a liberty bell that long ago rang on other spheres. This chiming, beloved, shall continue as the inner Call. And if it stop its chiming, beloved, Cosmos shall know that I, Saint Germain, have no longer opportunity to rescue the Lightbearer. Therefore, beloved, let the giving of the violet flame on behalf of those who respond and hear be continuous as a vigil unto the seventh age. So long as there are those who respond, even a single heart reciting my violet flame mantra in each twenty-four-hour cycle, Opportunity's door shall remain open and the chime shall be heard." See 1987 *Pearls of Wisdom,* vol. 30, no. 29, pp. 291–92. (3) Gen. 2:9; 3:22, 24; Rev. 2:7; 22:2, 14. The **Tree of Life** is the I AM Presence and the causal body. (4) Rev. 11:1, 2. (5) Rev. 2:25; 3:3, 11. (6) "Verily, verily, I say unto thee, When thou wast young, thou girdedst thyself, and walkedst whither thou wouldest: but when thou shalt be old, thou shalt stretch forth thy hands, and another shall gird thee, and carry thee whither thou wouldest not" John 21:18. "They went down both into the water, both Philip and the eunuch; and he baptized him. And when they were come up out of the water, the Spirit of the Lord caught away Philip, that the eunuch saw him no more: and he went on his way rejoicing. But Philip was found at Azotus: and passing through he preached in all the cities, till he came to Caesarea" Acts 8:38–40. "The wind bloweth where it listeth, and thou hearest the sound thereof, but canst not tell whence it cometh, and whither it goeth: so is every one that is born of the Spirit" John 3:8. (7) II Pet. 1:10. (8) *manvantara* [Sanskrit, from *manv,* used in compounds for *manu,* + *antara* 'interval', 'period of time']: in Hinduism, the period or age of a Manu, consisting of 4,320,000 solar years; one of the fourteen intervals that constitute a *kalpa* —the duration of time from the origination to the destruction of a world system (a cosmic cycle).

published by The Summit Lighthouse

Vol. 31 No. 25   *Beloved Kuan Yin*   **June 11, 1988**

Saint Germain Stumps America

14

Are You Truly Free?

A Dispensation of Mercy's Flame from the Karmic Board

Blessed Ones,

I come, Kuan Yin, a ray of light in form out of the All-Seeing Eye of the Buddha.[1] I come to you this evening representing the Lords of Karma and I come, beloved, to tell you that this is the hour when you may appeal to the Lords of Karma[2] for a dispensation of Mercy's flame, violet flame, when you* make the request to use that dispensation specifically for the mitigation, turning back, [or] transmutation of those prophecies told to you last evening.[3]

Therefore, all who will join me in the bodhisattva vow for the saving of Lightbearers in the earth, to you I say, the extraordinary light of the violet flame is given to those who will direct it and invest it *in* the saving of that which could be lost without that impetus and *in* the transmutation of the karma of Lightbearers that can be taken in this hour.

The Lords of Karma, then, contemplating this prophecy and the accuracy thereof, bring to you the awareness (as Saint Germain has done and as Mother Mary does intimate) that self-assessment in the way of the Christ and the Buddha and the assessment of earth conditions must bring you to some resolute conclusions regarding the usefulness and use of your life.

My message is brief. You may pen a letter to me or to any member of this board setting forth what you desire to do and your [intended] service, stating those conditions that burden you that you desire to be delivered of and what service you will render for that grace. My ear is a listening ear this night[4] and my voice is a voice that speaks in the silence of your soul.

Now be suspended in the sea of light. Now feel yourself alone

*when you = if you will

in the All. Know yourself suspended in a sea of such light as almost to equate with the experience [you will have] one day of nirvana. Know that from this sea of light you can reach out and touch each Lightbearer lost in the sea of samsara[5] and that in this manner I reach out and touch you who yet have ties to lesser vibrations that pull you down, further down into the illusions of that sea.

Therefore, as karmic cycles have intensified, the Lords of Karma have leaned their hearts and listening ears to the prayers and the desirings of those who are of the Light, who carry the Light, who stand for the Light, who know the meaning of freedom and embody it as the violet flame.

We are able, then, to help you in this hour and we tell you again that the sound of your voices in mantra is a power and a flame anchored in this city. May you esteem your self-worth and come together at our Teaching Center or places of gathering and not lose the momentum of the mantra but multiply it, gain the mastery of the mantra, become adepts of the science of mantra through the teaching of the spoken Word.

O great sound wave of Alpha and Omega descending in this hour, pass through these souls and all of equal devotion upon this planet! Let them resonate now as earth receives a vibration of sweet mercy, of piercing illumination, of healing and peace profound. May you hold this vibration and know yourselves together as a mandala of light who have come together here and thus fashioned a crystal of selves one in the sound of the *OM MANI PADME HUM HUM HUM.*[6]

I AM Kuan Yin. I unfold a violet flame ribbon before you. It is a highway of light that leads to fiery destiny. Follow the lead of the violet flame ribbon. Come to my heart. Come to me, O beloved children. Come to me, sons of Light, come. I AM Kuan Yin, loving you always in Mercy's flame of Seventh Ray.

I seal now in my causal body in the heart of Amitābha the light of all mantras released here, withdrawing them from this place, that they may never be requalified by the human, [but] sealed in a reservoir over this city which you may increase day by day by your mantras. As long as there is a reservoir of light usable for emergencies, souls will continue to be cut free.

I AM cutting you free. I AM free. I AM free. I AM free to take the bodhisattva vow and fulfill it.

Are you free, beloved, to take that vow? Are you truly free? When is a soul truly free? In the decision to be and to be God here and now forever is the beginning of a freedom that never ends. Even so, I am your never-ending friend all the way to the heart of the AUM.

AUM Buddha, seed of Light in each one.
AUM Buddha. AUM Buddha. AUM Buddha.

Delivered February 14, 1988, at the Sheraton-Palace Hotel, San Francisco. For notes, see Pearl no. 26.

Pearls of Wisdom®
published by The Summit Lighthouse

| Vol. 31 No. 26 | Beloved Paul the Venetian | June 12, 1988 |

Saint Germain Stumps America
15
The Initiation of Hearts
Fire for the Realignment of Worlds

Out of the ineffable Word I come, O beloved, as the Lord of the Third Ray, your own Paul the Venetian.

I come, then, for the initiation of hearts and heart chakras unto the unfoldment of Divine Love to all hearts of this state who must accelerate in the development of the discernment of the heart. For the heart knoweth all things, readeth all things, understandeth all things. Let the understanding of the heart unfold and let the soul rise to her lawful mentor, even the Christ within.

My angels of Love surround you. They surround each and every Lightbearer, every child, man and woman throughout this state of California. For I, Paul, do come to minister unto those burdened by those tremblings in the earth of karma and the weight of misqualification in this state and from ancient records.

Thus, how bright is the light of the day. Yet those who listen, those who hear and hear angel voices and heed the inner call know that all is not well, and therefore the rumblings of prophecies and predictions of earthquake and cataclysm must surely affect the inner psyche as well as the beings of Nature who tend this garden of God.

Now, then, beloved, for the anchoring of pillars of fire in the earth, I commend you to the call of the Divine Mother to rise to meet your destiny in this age. I commend you to the violet flame whereby the light of the heart does simply increase and increase as the flower unfolds its petals and the rose of light of the heart sheds its fragrance to all who are in distress, all who are dying and those who have not lived in the light, for they knew not how.

For want of teachers and those who care, some are lost, and for want of caring for the Law, many self-extinguish the Flame. And in the denial of the Divine Mother of ancient Lemuria, there has come to pass a civilization bereft of the intimate knowledge of being the vessel of the Mother and thereby coming unto the love of the Buddha, even the one who unfolds the light of eternal Christos.

Wherefore, then, do we deliver our Word? It is that flood tides of Love might descend upon a people reincarnated from the Motherland, here once again to resolute karma and situations of ancient history.

Blessed ones, be not caught, then, in those places that must receive a purging light and a washing of the waters by the Word.[1] Be mindful to entertain angels of God.[2] Be mindful to establish the inner fount of peace as a means of receiving the Divine Presence and these angels who have always ministered unto the servants of God to take them where they ought to be, perhaps where they desire not to go.

Nevertheless, the Holy Spirit that is of my ray and bands must pick you up and take you to other places and sometimes to other times, past and future, that you might establish the coordinates of your own understanding of a prophecy that is written in the rock and in the marrow of your bones and in the very waters of the sea themselves.

I call, then, unto those who have heard the call already and are responding by answering with their own call, and I come to you, opening my heart for the healing of hearts. For the heart chakra of this state must needs be expanded that there might evolve fruition and a light.

Let the children of Mu[3] come of age. Let them understand what it means to be sons of God in a time when few accept the responsibility of shepherding.

I come also with a ruby fire for the purging of corruption in the government of this state. I come with a purging light that compels the light to rise for the restoration of the divine memory. For with the loss of light, there is also the loss of memory; and [on] the Tablets of *Mem*,[4] with which you were familiar on Lemuria, are the recordings of ancient lifetimes when you, beloved, possessed an extraordinary light.

But, for vast numbers of those settled in this state in this time, it was the compromise of the heart and the heart chakra that allowed you to lose that light and therefore to descend in an apartness, a separation first from the Mother and then from her

Son, from the Universal Light and then from one another, being divided, then, by fallen ones, angels who waged the wars of the gods unto the utter destruction of the inner temples of Light.*

They have come again, beloved, to destroy the temples and the devotees of Tibet; and who has raised the hand to say, "Thus far and no farther!" to those Communist hordes who have denied the culture of the Mother in the gentle ones of Tibet⁵ who have carried forward the ancient wisdom?

I tell you, not the government of this nation or the West. Blessed hearts, it is a crime against humanity when hordes who are undeveloped are given the freedom in the name of Aquarius to snuff out the candle that has been lit upon the altars of the ancients for hundreds and thousands of years.

Will the candle go out in your heart?—in the hearts of the people of Lemuria on this side of the fire ring?

It is a decision that the individual must make by free will to keep the flame of Life and to know that in the science of the spoken Word (which you have so gently and powerfully exercised this evening) is the means to raise up the Mother Light [the sacred fire from the base-of-the-spine chakra], to draw forth the Light of the Father [from the I AM Presence], to experience that union [of both] in the temple as an increase of the fire of the heart that shall consume the ancient karma of the compromise of the heart—ultimately that fire, that threefold flame expanding, returning to you the consciousness of God you once knew.

Though I read the records of akasha in a moment of each one gathered here and all former citizens of Lemuria living in California, I shall not read them in detail in my dictation but only tell you, beloved, that the axiom is so true that those who neglect a self-knowledge of their history are doomed to repeat that history. Thus, you stand in a moment on the pinnacle of a choice: to move upward in the spiral of being to transcend oneself all the way back to the days of Lemuria and enter the high road of reunion with God, else to repeat the former cycles and go down again.

Blessed hearts, the Great White Brotherhood is compelled to send forth the Messenger to reach its own with the knowledge of *choices*, for you have earned the right to know, to be loved and to yourself love as God loves every part of Life. You have a right to learn and walk the way of self-givingness, which the adepts of ancient Lemuria did in the last days of that continent as they gathered their disciples and transferred the flames of the temples to mountain fastnesses.⁶

Know, beloved, that what is in the earth as karma must be

*the inner sanctum of Lemurian temples where the Divine Mother was worshipped transmuted, for the earth cries out in agony for the weight of infamy of the fallen ones, even within this state alone and, yea, the entire planet: "How long, how long, O Lord!"

Thus do the beings of the earth and the fire and the waters and the air cry out unto God, "How long must we bear the infamy of rebellious spirits who wander about perverting the life-force in little children and in their bodies?"

Thus, it is, beloved, [that] the sacredness of Life within you must needs be acknowledged. God is in you. Revere that Light, that Consciousness, that Being, and understand that unless Life be revered and some pull away from the ease of the pleasure cult, the ease of squandering the light of the chakras, you will know once again the cataclysms of the past. All prediction may be turned back by the violet flame, some may be but mitigated.

Let us hasten to Higher Consciousness.

As the watchman of the night climbs to his tower to see that all is well or that it is not, [so] may you rise to higher planes of your being and see through the Mind of Christ in you what is your destiny and what is earth's destiny, that you might chart a course to be in planet earth a pillar of fire, a pillar of fire.

Thus are the adepts of Love and of the Third Ray initiates of the Holy Spirit and of the priesthood of the Order of Melchizedek.[7] Thus do we know the ruby fire that is a love so intense as to bring judgment upon the forces of anti-Love that abuse the Light of the heart.

May you run to the Immaculate Heart of Mother Mary, to the Sacred Heart of Jesus and to the purple fiery heart of Saint Germain and therefrom receive the engrafted Word.[8] This, this is Cosmic Christ illumination. This is the transfer from the great Masters to you directly through your own Christ Self, who is high priest at the altar of your being, of that fire so needed for you to know and to sense and to be who, what and where you ought to be in this age.

I release now the fire for the realignment of worlds. Come Home, my beloved, to the heart of everlasting Love. So may it be that you discover Reality and in the process know the Teacher, the Twin Flame and the beloved God.

My angels touch you and love you in this hour. They have known you for a foreverness. May you greet them as long, almost lost friends from higher octaves who salute you now with the embrace of other worlds. Heaven is so close; closer yet, heaven's love.

My coming, then, is established as angels of the Third Ray throughout the city have established focuses for transmutation and the righting of this government for the benefit of all people.

In the flame of your heart I remain a Teacher of Love who loves you unto the heights of Love's mastery.

Be at peace, beloved, but keep the flame. Do not fail to keep the flame of Love burning. So is the dawn of the New Age through the flame of Love.

"**The Summit Lighthouse Sheds Its Radiance O'er All the World to Manifest as Pearls of Wisdom.**" This dictation by **Paul the Venetian** was **delivered** by the Messenger Elizabeth Clare Prophet following her **Tues., Feb. 16, 1988** lecture at the Sacramento Hilton Inn where she was stumping for Saint Germain's Coming Revolution in Higher Consciousness. (**1**) Eph. 5:26. (**2**) Heb. 13:2. (**3**) **Mu**, or Lemuria, was the lost continent of the Pacific which, according to the findings of James Churchward, archaeologist and author of *The Lost Continent of Mu*, extended from north of Hawaii three thousand miles south to Easter Island and the Fijis and was made up of three areas of land stretching more than five thousand miles from east to west. Churchward's history of the ancient Motherland is based on records inscribed on sacred tablets he claims to have discovered in India. With the help of the high priest of an Indian temple he deciphered the tablets, and during fifty years of research confirmed their contents in further writings, inscriptions, and legends he came upon in Southeast Asia, the Yucatan, Central America, the Pacific Islands, Mexico, North America, ancient Egypt and other civilizations. He estimates that Mu was destroyed approximately twelve thousand years ago by the collapse of the gas chambers which upheld the continent. See *The Lost Continent of Mu* (1931; reprint, New York: Paperback Library Edition, 1968). (**4**) The etheric, or memory, body contains the **Tablets of Mem** (memory), the electronic, computerized recordings of all vibrations and energy impulses ever sent forth through the soul and its higher and lower vehicles. This life record (the L-field) is written on innumerable discs of light which comprise the changing, evolving identity pattern of the soul merging with the Spirit; it determines the patterns which will be outpictured in the three lower vehicles—the mental body, the desire body, and the physical body. Only the violet flame can permanently alter the effect by thoroughly transmuting the cause. For further teaching see Serapis Bey, *Dossier on the Ascension*, pp. 87–88, quoted in Mark L. Prophet and Elizabeth Clare Prophet, *Climb the Highest Mountain*, 2d ed., pp. 350–51. (**5**) **Chinese takeover of Tibet and destruction of Tibetan culture.** See Elizabeth Clare Prophet, "The Abdication of America's Destiny," Part 2, 1988 *Pearls of Wisdom*, vol. 31, no. 23, pp. 185–88; no. 6, pp. 58, 59, 62 n. 5; no. 8, p. 94 n. 7. (**6**) **The transfer of the flames from the temples of Lemuria and Atlantis.** See Mark L. Prophet and Elizabeth Clare Prophet, *Lords of the Seven Rays: Mirror of Consciousness*, Book One, pp. 80, 89, 129, 131, 149; Book Two, p. 276. (**7**) **The Priesthood of Melchizedek.** Gen. 14:18; Ps. 110:4; Heb. 5:5–10; 6:20; 7. (**8**) James 1:21.

Notes from Pearl No. 25 by Kuan Yin:
(**1**) Legends in Mahayana Buddhism recount that Avalokiteśvara (Sanskrit; Kuan Yin, Chinese) was 'born' from a ray of white light which Amitābha Buddha emitted from his right eye as he was lost in ecstacy. Avalokiteśvara, or Kuan Yin, is thus regarded as the "reflex" of Amitābha—an emanation or embodiment of *maha karuna* (great compassion), the quality which Amitābha embodies in its highest sense. (**2**) **Lords of Karma.** The ascended beings who comprise the Karmic Board. Their names and the rays which they represent on the board are as follows: First Ray, the Great Divine Director; Second Ray, the Goddess of Liberty; Third Ray, the Ascended Lady Master Nada; Fourth Ray, the Elohim Cyclopea; Fifth Ray, Pallas Athena, Goddess of Truth; Sixth Ray, Portia, the Goddess of Justice; Seventh Ray, Kuan Yin, Goddess of Mercy. The Lords of Karma dispense justice to this system of worlds, adjudicating karma, mercy, and judgment on behalf of every lifestream. All souls must pass before the Karmic Board before and after each incarnation on earth, receiving their

assignment and karmic allotment for each lifetime beforehand and the review of their performance at its conclusion. Through the Keeper of the Scrolls and the recording angels, the Lords of Karma have access to the complete records of every lifestream's incarnations on earth. They determine who shall embody, as well as when and where. They assign souls to families and communities, measuring out the weights of karma that must be balanced as the "jot and tittle" of the law. The Karmic Board, acting in consonance with the individual I AM Presence and Christ Self, determines when the soul has earned the right to be free from the wheel of karma and the round of rebirth. Customarily the Lords of Karma meet at the Royal Teton Retreat twice yearly, at winter and summer solstice, to review petitions from unascended mankind and to grant dispensations for their assistance. (**3**) On Saturday, Feb. 13, 1988, the Messenger delivered the lecture "Saint Germain On Prophecy from 1988 through the 1990s—the Astrology of World Karma." See 1988 *Pearls of Wisdom*, vol. 31, no. 20, p. 166, n. 1. (**4**) **Kuan Shih Yin** (as Kuan Yin is also called) means "the one who regards, looks on, or hears the sounds of the world." In Mahayana Buddhism, Kuan Yin is the bodhisattva of compassion; a bodhisattva is literally a "being of wisdom" who is destined to become a Buddha but has foregone the bliss of nirvana with a vow to save every being on earth. According to legend, Kuan Yin was about to enter heaven but she paused on the threshold as she heard the cries of the world. (**5**) **samsara** [Sanskrit, lit. "wandering through"]: the indefinitely repeated cycles of birth, misery, and death caused by karma; often rendered transmigration or metempsychosis; corporeal existence; the universe of manifestation and phenomena as distinguished from the real existence which lies behind it. (**6**) Devotees of Kuan Yin invoke the bodhisattva's power and merciful intercession with the mantra *OM MANI PADME HUM,* which means "Hail to the jewel in the lotus!" or, as it has also been interpreted, "Hail to Avalokiteśvara (or Kuan Yin), who is the jewel in the heart of the lotus of the devotee's heart!" Just released!—send for Kuan Yin's Rosary, two 90-minute audiocassettes including three sets of Kuan Yin mantras: 10 mantras of the vows of Kuan Yin with the Hail Mary; 14 Kuan Yin mantras for the Woman and her seed: the fourteen stations of the Aquarian cross; and 33 mantras for the 33 manifestations of Avalokiteśvara as Kuan Yin, plus joyous Seventh Ray songs to Kuan Yin, the Goddess of Mercy, and violet flame decrees, sealed with calls to the Defender of the Woman and her seed, Archangel Michael, and to the Starry Mother Astrea, B88049–50, $5.95 each (add $.74 each for postage); $11.90 for both cassettes (add $.95 for postage). Ready for shipping May 15, 1988.

Teachings on the Priesthood of Melchizedek

Elizabeth Clare Prophet, March 23, 1978, "The Mystery of the Priesthood of Melchizedek," audiocassette B7843, $6.50 (add $.55 for postage), on 6-audiocassette album *The Second Coming of Christ II,* A7842, 9 hr., $37.50 (add $1.65 for postage).

Kuthumi, June 30, 1978, "Revolutionaries for the Coming Revolution: An Outer Order of the Priesthood of Melchizedek," audiocassette B7873, $6.50 (add $.55 for postage), on 4-audiocassette album *"Find Your Way Back to Me,"* A7872, 6 hr., $26.00 (add $1.15 for postage).

Elizabeth Clare Prophet, January 24, 1982, "The Story of Our Father Abraham and of His Chela and of His Guru" and "The Apostle Paul on the Priesthood of Melchisedec," audiocassette B82113, $6.50 (add $.55 for postage), on 12-audiocassette album *In the Heart of the Inner Retreat 1982,* A82118, 18 hr., $75.00 (add $2.35 for postage).

Elizabeth Clare Prophet, February 15, 1986, "Christ the High Priest," 1986 *Pearls of Wisdom,* vol. 29, no. 29, pp. 281–85.

Mighty Victory, March 23, 1986, "Conquer in the Name of Victory: Testings of the Priesthood of Melchizedek," 1986 *Pearls of Wisdom,* vol. 29, no. 38, pp. 357, 358–59; audiocassette B86038, $6.50 (add $.55 for postage), on 8-audiocassette album *Conclave of the Friends of Christ,* A86032, $50.00 (add $1.65 for postage).

Archangel Zadkiel, May 25, 1986, "The Priesthood of the Order of Melchizedek," 1986 *Pearls of Wisdom,* vol. 29, no. 57, pp. 511–17; audiocassette B86066, $6.50 (add $.55 for postage), on 12-audiocassette album *The Healing Power of Angels,* Vancouver, B.C., A86055, 18¼ hr., $67.50 (add $2.05 for postage).

Saint Germain, May 28, 1986, "The Intercession of the Priesthood of Melchizedek," 1986 *Pearls of Wisdom,* vol. 29, no. 58, pp. 519–20, 525, or *Saint Germain On Prophecy,* Book Four, pp. 164–65, 174–75, $5.95 (add $.50 for postage); on audiocassette K86098, $6.50 (add $.55 for postage).

The Ascended Master Melchizedek, June 15, 1986, "To Sup with You in the Glory of Christ," 1986 *Pearls of Wisdom,* vol. 29, no. 61, pp. 539–41; dictation with teachings on Melchizedek by Elizabeth Clare Prophet, "The Subtle Essence," on two 90-min. audiocassettes, K86099–100, $13.00 (add $.95 for postage).

Pearls of Wisdom®
published by The Summit Lighthouse

| Vol. 31 No. 27 | Beloved Mother Mary | June 15, 1988 |

Saint Germain Stumps America
16
The Karmic Weight of a Planet
We Would Raise Up a Flame of Healing

In the irresistible light of the God Flame of the Divine Mother, I AM descended into your midst, Mary, your Mother of grace, and Mediatrix before the throne of God. I come for the comfort and consolation of all souls of Light. I come to edify you and to draw you into the strains of my heart of the Holy Spirit that you might henceforth know my Presence as a protecting mantle that you may wrap about yourselves.

In these days, beloved, when many wonder, "Shall the earth tremble beneath our feet?" I tell you that the greater danger in the earth body is of the rise of the cumulative karma of Evil itself that suffocates the soul, penetrates the pores and renders many in a state of depression, of weight, even to the loss of the natural élan of life.

Thus, some who have not banked the fires of the devotion of their hearts are not able to meet that weight that we find in coastal areas of the effluvia of the large cities and centuries of misqualification of the Mother Light, especially here on the shores of Lemuria where reincarnated priests of those temples who did desecrate the life[-force] then do also this day in many ways in society.

Blessed ones, I come to quicken you by the Diamond Heart, whereby you can affiliate yourself with my Sons, the Lords of the Seven Rays, who would draw you by the initiation and acceleration of your chakras into a vibration whereby through the spinning of those chakras you naturally throw off the weight of environmental karma and mass effluvia of the astral plane of mankind's untoward emotions spewed out into life daily and hourly.

Beloved, the signs of the times are the increasing karmic weight of a planet and by that very weight a loss of sensitivity, even in those who in past lifetimes have known the path, East or West, of the Divine Mother. The signs in the heavens portend a generation seeking after success and wealth, position and pleasure.

Where are those of decades past who sought the living Guru, found many false gurus, yet in their quest arrived at a certain inner balance of being? Where are these who have also graduated to a mundane life as the exigency of the hour?

Let all turn away from those things that are temporal to seek the consciousness of God in this hour. As I have spoken to my own in Medjugorje,¹ so I speak to you who understand the message of this age in terms more definite and scientific. Let those who have the devotion give devotion. Let those who have the enlightenment exercise the sword of the Spirit as the Sacred Word,² even the science of the spoken Word.

I promise you, then, in [your] giving of my rosary daily, raising up the Mother Light thereby and with these bija mantras given,³ that I have by your leave an entrée into your world as one representative of the Divine Mother.

When you are sealed in the Mother's light invoked by you and multiplied also by myself you will also have a state of listening grace where[in] you may hear the voice of the Son of God, your own Christ Self, and in hearing and heeding that voice live forevermore in the Light and finish your round as a champion of Life on earth and one who by absorption of the Fifth Ray of our bands and of Hilarion may also be the instrument of the healing of nations, the healing of bodies, the holding of a flame of wholeness.

Let the Light* that is in thee be raised up, for many need a lighthouse and a beacon to follow. Reacquaint thyself with this Inner Reality and then discover how it is a fount—a fount that overflows thy being to nourish and sustain millions.

You are at the place in life where, having been so ministered unto and taught by a Messenger of the Great White Brotherhood, you can in definite self-knowledge enter the path that the adepts entered when they came to a true assessment of self-worth by the living flame of cosmic Truth.

The Lady Master Pallas Athena is another [representative of the Divine Mother] who does embody this flame and tutor your soul. Thus, seek Truth and know her face as one who defends your cause before the Court of the Sacred Fire.

We of the ascended hosts, beloved, do often plead the cause of our unascended brothers and sisters who are of the Light yet [who],

*sacred fire of the Divine Mother in the base-of-the-spine chakra

through ignorance or a life of ease or a life of busyness, do not occupy themselves in keeping a flame and therefore, unbeknownst to themselves, are losing slowly and surely (and sometimes fast) the dispensation to be in this hour a world saviour.

You may be surprised at this appellation. But I speak of you [thus as] mediating at your altar, giving your invocations, not [as] going forth making pronouncements of your glory but giving glory to God, entering into the closet to pray[4] and building such a momentum of prayer that you, beloved, perhaps not even fully known to yourself, hold the balance of light for an entire city.

Having fulfilled your duties at the altar daily, go forth, a brother, a sister championing those who need your assistance, being active in government, in community affairs, in decision-making bodies who are deciding the future of neighborhoods, of educational systems, of governments and of people.

Know, then, beloved, that those who have the light of Christ of the heart are those who ought surely to be the sponsors and representatives of a people in this form of government. Alas, beloved, we do not see them; and to add to the injury and prophecy of the age, those who now represent you in your government, state and federal and local, are for the most part self-seeking and unenlightened individuals who have sought and gained power by many measures and those not always of the highest honor.

Therefore, beloved, where the people are misrepresented, the people themselves must recognize that the true leader of their own life is their Holy Christ Self. If you subject yourself to that Divine Ruler within and unite with that one and learn of him and know his wisdom, you, then, may place yourself, through education and preparation, in a position where you believe that you can help in the representation of citizens of this land.

Blessed hearts, there are all sorts of interest groups [and] social programs that require those enlightened by love to minister to the many whose growing needs are becoming burdens on society and astronomical in financial considerations. Thus, there is no dearth of opportunity of ministration and service for those who would earn their wings and accelerate in light on the Path.

I reiterate to you what you may also read and know of my past prophecies. These will come to pass unless those in embodiment see themselves as intercessors, *intercessors before the courts of heaven and the courts of earth*—before karma and its adjudication—standing, then, as pillars of fire ere that karma descend.

In this hour angels of Raphael, my beloved consort, surround this city. For here we would raise up a flame of healing, a healing light that can be invoked by you in your healing services in honor of the one, Saint Joseph, who did father and nourish the Christ Child and therefore set the pace of the age of Pisces.

May all who are of the Masculine Ray in this life remember his example in all of his lifetimes[5] and know that your stature in God can be modeled after this role model of one who dared to defend Woman, who dared to raise up that Manchild and stand as the protector not only of a family but of an entire area of a planet until that one could fulfill his Christhood.

All of you must nurture life, espouse the calling to be world fathers and world mothers. In [fulfilling] this, [in] your daily calls you may send love to every child homeless, bereft, mistreated, abused. All need your care, and in answer to your prayers millions of angels minister unto them from our bands and those of the Holy Spirit.

Care for Life, beloved, and Life shall care for you.
Serve the Light and the Light shall turn and serve you.
Set all Life free and all Life will set you free.
As Above, so below be the embodiment of the Light Universal.
Triumph in this age—it is thy destiny . . .
But only if by free will you realize it and accept it.

I AM ever present in the heavens and in the earth, profoundly concerned, sometimes grieved and, in a certain level of my being, shedding tears for that which is coming upon some who are bankrupt spiritually and will not or cannot receive my Light. You are closer to them than I, for you have incarnation. Therefore, pray for these, for some will be quickened by your calls and when quickened [they] will indeed receive my angels.

Angels of Raphael's bands tend you now and bring to you unguents of healing for your souls, for your finer bodies, for your inner beings, beloved, and your psyches. For some of you have been assaulted and bombarded by great burdens in this life and others. Thus, a healing light is come that you might know that in the Healing Masters and Angels of the Fifth Ray there is recourse—there is recourse through my Immaculate Heart to healing and the whole healing of the whole body.

In the cosmic cross of the white fire, I seal you unto your fiery destiny in the God Star.

This dictation was **delivered** following the Messenger's **Feb. 17, 1988** Stump at the Hyatt San Jose, **Calif.** (1) **Medjugorje.** See 1988 *Pearls of Wisdom,* p. 142, n. 1. (2) Eph. 6:17, 18. (3) **Rosary.** See 1988 *Pearls of Wisdom,* p. 142, n. 4. **Bija mantras.** See "Bija Mantras to the Feminine Deities," no. 14, and "Bija Mantras for Chakra Initiation," no. 62, in *Mantras of the Ascended Masters for the Initiation of the Chakras,* pp. 4, 17; on audiocassettes B85135, B85137. (4) Matt. 6:6. (5) On **Saint Joseph** and other embodiments of Saint Germain, see *The Count Saint Germain: The Wonderman of Europe,* in *Saint Germain On Prophecy,* Book One; *Saint Germain On Alchemy,* p. 443.

Pearls of Wisdom®
published by The Summit Lighthouse

| Vol. 31 No. 28 | *Beloved Jesus Christ* | June 18, 1988 |

Saint Germain Stumps America
17
I Come to Heal
Hold Out a Candle in the Darkness

Out of the light of the I AM Presence of each one I come, Jesus, the ascended one, that you might know me in the fullness of the Light and not as I have been characterized in some circles for too long.

I come into this city for a very special healing of special loved ones whom I call to my Sacred Heart. I come to heal the cleavages and the fissures in the rock and in the earth. I come to heal by seizing by my sword unreal forces of Evil that have arrayed themselves against my own for centuries.

I come in gratitude for the blessed and the beloved hearts in any and all walks of life who have kept my flame and held out a candle in the Darkness, who have been undaunted in the face of rebuff and rejection and misunderstanding by the world.

If you will receive me, beloved, I would enter your heart to tutor you with your beloved Christ Self. I would come unto you as the Divine Bridegroom to receive you unto myself that I might restore in you the lost memory, the lost estate, the lost love of thy beloved I AM Presence. I would knit together once again the finer bodies injured by the bombardments of civilization.

I come in the person of the healer. Healing, then, is my mission in this hour, and that healing light that I give to you arcs to the place of Fátima and Lisbon where I send my Messenger, that you might know that this fount of living waters is also unto you, some of you who in past ages have given yourselves and your lives to the healing arts.

This increase of light and healing I transmit to all of my initiates throughout the earth. For, beloved, the world is suffering famine and death as we gather, and plagues come upon a people by nefarious design, even out of the laboratories of the ancient Atlanteans revisited. Thus, beloved, though there has been a vulnerability in the nation to the last plagues, surely not all upon whom they have descended have deserved so harsh a judgment.

Yet, beloved, where is the error? Where is the shortcoming? I tell you the crux of the matter: it is the false teaching in some quarters, often out of the East, that the spiritual adept does not soil his garments by entering in to such lowly activities as politics or running the government or entering the arena where there is a struggle for the minds and bodies of souls.

Blessed ones, by whatever non-indoctrination of the true Divine Doctrine that has come upon this people by whatever false gurus have come into their midst, the people of this nation have allowed their leaders, often the power elite come again as fallen angels, to do what they would with the government, with health and medical services and departments, with the monetary system, with those things that ought not to have been placed in their hands; and it was not so conceived by Saint Germain and those whom he contacted at the birth of a nation.

Therefore, unbeknownst to you, there have crept into your midst those ones who have actually corrupted life, whether in the guise of the medical profession or social services. This does not blacken all those who seek selflessly to serve. It takes only one betrayer in an institution or in a sector of the government to turn the best of intentions into darkness.

This people must rise and monitor their public servants and agencies. They must call them to task and challenge them in my name. For you are in the earth and therefore you are the Light* of this world.[1] My Light flowing through you with the same fierceness whereby I overturned the money changers in the temple[2] will do much to serve notice to these wolves in sheep's clothing[3] that occupy the state, local and federal governments that the people of this nation have had enough!

How many proofs do you need that your best servants go unprotected who would defend life from a military posture? How many more proofs do you need of those self-seeking and self-serving politicians who would occupy the first office in the land?

Beloved, now you know that there is something you can do. I come to you to tell you that there is something you *must* do and you can begin at the altar you erect in your own home[4] to call

*Christ consciousness

to me daily to deal by the highest law of God with these inter-lopers who are [the] betrayers of the very purposes of freedom in this nation and every nation upon earth.

You are the sons of Light. Blessed hearts, there are many children of Light in the world. They have not the understanding of the call or the path or a discipleship that leads to individual Christhood. Therefore, beloved, know that those who can equate with this path and embrace me as Brother and Friend and Teacher, those who can have an assessment of their divinity without turning that divinity to the service of the human ego, these are the true shepherds in every department of life.

I say to you, make haste to claim this planet for the universal reality of God. Make haste to assume your appropriate role, for the days are short and shortening.

May those who understand and hear enter into the courts of the sacred fire in the inner temples of light to learn of me and know me and receive me, for I am more present than ever, almost physical at your side.

Angels attend you. Therefore neglect not the call daily but O defend the defenseless, the homeless, the jobless, the oppressed! Defend them, beloved! They need a voice, and your voice one with my own can turn the tide.

My angels of healing are walking throughout this city. Thus, the healing light descends and the ancient temples of Lemuria are revealed outlined against the night sky. Those, then, who dese-crated the altars of the Divine Mother, these are bound, for they have long prevented my light from fully descending into this town.

Let it be known, then, that in answer to the call of blessed hearts, I, Jesus, occupy and I call to you to occupy until I come fully into your temple. Tarry, then, in the city of the New Jerusalem until ye be endued with power from on high.[5] For without the Holy Spirit no work of God in man is accomplished. With the Holy Spirit you receive guidance, and the words that come from thy mouth shall be also from my own.

One with your Holy Christ Self, I AM the living Christ forevermore. Come unto me, beloved, for I would receive you.

Delivered following the Messenger's **Feb. 19, 1988** Stump at the Miramar Hotel, **Santa Barbara.** (1) Matt. 5:14–16. (2) Matt. 21:12, 13; Mark 11:15–17; Luke 19:45, 46; John 2:13–17. (3) Matt. 7:15, 16. (4) You can set up an altar in a special place in your home. The central focus of the I AM Presence is flanked by the Sindelar portraits of Saint Germain on the right and Jesus Christ on the left—all three available in a number of sizes including a folding stand-up portable altar. Two or more candles, a piece of natural quartz crystal, some amethyst crystal, a crystal chalice and the representative "Books of the Law" *(Climb the Highest Mountain, The Lost Years of Jesus, The Lost Teachings of Jesus I* and *II)* complete your focus. Depending on the size and elaboration of these, you can add fresh or silk flowers, a monstrance and selected statuary of the saints of East and West. Be careful not to clutter it. (5) Luke 24:49.

Lady Master Nada addressed the problems of **fanatical polygamist sects and the high rate of child abuse in Utah** in her January 30, 1988 dictation given in Salt Lake City. She said, "Let the Diamond Heart of Mary be centered in this place and let healing be the power that does indeed, by the hand of Mary and Raphael, exorcise those things which have come to pass which ought not to be. . . . I am sent by Jesus to manifest the intensity of the Ruby Ray for a purging action in this state. Those responsible in Church and State for depravity and violence continuing must also stand before the Court of the Sacred Fire" (Pearl 11, pp. 123, 125). On January 28, two days prior to Nada's dictation, a 13-day standoff between members of a polygamist clan and over 150 policemen and FBI agents in Marion, Utah, 50 miles east of Salt Lake City, ended in a shoot-out that left one officer dead and the clan's leader seriously wounded. Lawmen had surrounded the clan's rural farm following the bombing of a local Mormon church by the clan's leader, 27-year-old Addam Swapp. Swapp claimed the bombing was an act of revenge against the Mormon Church and the state of Utah for the 1979 death of John Singer, the clan's patriarch who had been slain in a police siege when he resisted arrest for defying a court order to send his children to public school. Swapp, who married two of Singer's daughters, said in a letter to the governor of Utah that he was forming an independent nation and claimed that a violent confrontation would bring the resurrection of Mr. Singer, an event which Swapp and Singer's widow, Vickie, believed would save his family and bring about a religious and political revolution. Swapp and members of the clan are currently on trial on charges relating to the bombing and attempts to kill FBI officers.

Swapp also apparently believes that John Singer was the "One Mighty and Strong" whom Mormon Church founder Joseph Smith had predicted in a letter would come to reform an errant church in latter days. The belief in the One Mighty and Strong is common to several "fundamentalist Mormon" groups that have broken away from the mainline Mormon Church over the practice of polygamy and has led to other instances of violence and murder. A January 31, 1988 story in the Ogden *Standard-Examiner* reported that, according to L. G. Otten, a religion professor at Brigham Young University, "the mainline Mormon Church teaches that Smith's letter was meant for an errant bishop. When the bishop repented, the One Mighty and Strong was no longer needed. But sects that broke away from the church over polygamy say the One Mighty and Strong will yet come to restore order—and plural marriage—to the church forcefully." (The Mormon Church abandoned polygamy in 1890 and excommunicates members who practice it.)

The late Ervil LeBaron, founder of the polygamist Church of the Lamb of God who claimed to be the One Mighty and Strong, was a suspect in several murder attempts on the lives of rival religious leaders. In 1980 LeBaron was convicted of directing the murder of Rulon Allred, head of the Apostolic United Brethren, a large polygamist sect in the Salt Lake Valley, and of plotting to kill his brother Verlan LeBaron, leader of another polygamist group. Police think he may have also ordered the murder of at least four other people, including one of his daughters. Although LeBaron died in prison in 1981, authorities suspect he left a hit list of those he felt had betrayed him, possibly accounting for the deaths of two former members of his sect. Ron Lafferty, who believed that he and his brothers were the Ones Mighty and Strong, was convicted of the 1983 murders of his sister-in-law and her baby. When his sister-in-law urged her husband not to accept Ron as leader, Lafferty and one of his brothers slashed the throats of the woman and her child. Lafferty claimed he had received a revelation to kill her. Immanuel David, another who reportedly asserted that he was the One Mighty and Strong and God the Father, committed suicide in 1978 near Salt Lake City. Three days later his wife and seven children jumped from the eleventh floor of a hotel, apparently fulfilling a suicide pact.

Child abuse and neglect, including sexual abuse, is a major problem in Utah. In 1982 it was reported that while Utah was the nation's thirty-fourth most populous state, it ranked thirteenth in per capita child abuse cases with 12 to 14 children dying from child abuse each year. Between 1981 and 1985 incidents of child abuse jumped 210 percent—the third largest statewide increase in the United States. Between 1983 and 1985 reports of sexual maltreatment increased 74 percent. The child sex abuse problem and the alleged failure of local officials to properly deal with it has received increased attention with the child abuse investigation that resulted in the December 1987 conviction of Alan B. Hadfield of Lehi, Utah, for molesting two of his children. During that time the Utah attorney general's office was flooded with requests to investigate similar allegations which citizens say are not being adequately handled by county prosecutors (*Salt Lake Tribune,* 10 April 1988).

Pearls of Wisdom®
published by The Summit Lighthouse

Vol. 31 No. 29   *The Beloved Maha Chohan*   June 19, 1988

Saint Germain Stumps America
18
The Mandate of the Holy Spirit
Love's Testing of a Planet and a People

Out of the Light* of the Central Sun I come. I am known as the Maha Chohan;[1] and therefore, beloved, understand that I represent to you not only the Holy Spirit but the initiations of that Spirit.

I have come, then, to deliver to this city the mandate of the Holy Spirit.

Blessed hearts, you have read the scripture concerning the sins against the Holy Spirit which cannot be forgiven.[2] Mankind have violated the compelling law of the Father, the compelling law of the Son. Intercession, then, has come.

Blessed hearts, the age of Aquarius does set a new standard; and, therefore, as the tides of the sea and the planetary levels of water threaten to rise, so there is the raising of the standard whereby the sons of God are expected to embody a Greater Love whose intensity, whose very sacred fire in your hearts does bind the force of anti-Love.

Blessed ones, you have heard the interpretation of the four planets in Capricorn.[3] One must understand that they represent the deliverance† of the Holy Spirit's initiations to a planet; and as the result of the consequences of the violation of the Holy Ghost in little children, in Nature and [in] the defilement of the body and the soul, you will see that *unless these things are turned around and a people invoke the Light of their God and fulfill the Law of Love, those things projected will come to pass.*

This [astrological] configuration is the testing of the four lower bodies of a planet and a people, and the signal of Mars

---

*Universal Christ   †seventeenth-century usage meaning delivery

entering this twenty-third does denote the triggering in the physical plane of all that has gone before in the mental, etheric and desire bodies [of the planetary evolution].

Blessed ones, it is in the city of Los Angeles that this spiral must be initiated, for the ancient area of this city on the continent of Lemuria was also the scene of the violation of that Holy Spirit which did trigger the sinking of that continent in a conflagration of fire.[4]

Therefore note well, beloved, that having come full circle, a people endowed with enlightenment and the fervor of our bands must now come to understand that the Tester whose sign has been seen as Saturn also comes in the presence of Uranus and Neptune. Therefore, beloved, all that which has been considered as the consequences of such an astrology must be seen in the light of the Holy Spirit as Teacher, as Comforter, as the manifestation of God as the Great Guru.

In this cycle therefore, beloved, it is true that a great awakening, enlightenment and golden age can appear. The option, then, to embrace the Spirit of the living God in this hour comes upon every lifestream upon this planet.

Blessed ones, many are not prepared, and the signs of the times of the momentum of the people themselves do not predict that they will change. Nevertheless, the Lightbearers of the earth and the sons of God may invoke unlimited light in this time. For other planets appearing, representative of the Divine Mother, such as Venus and Jupiter, the Sun itself and even the Moon when the energies are raised, do give wide open door of opportunity by the communication of the God Mercury for a sweeping conversion that is the very essence and energy of Aquarius.

Freedom, then, [is] of the Holy Spirit: know it and let it not catch you off guard, for that freedom is a power and a momentum, and to properly exercise it creatively you need an allegiance to that Holy Spirit and the very Person of that Holy Spirit.

Thus, I come to you with the same offer made to you by the Lord Christ: to receive you as my students.[5] For as I serve as the Teacher of the Lords of the Seven Rays, I shall also desire to teach the pupils of the Lords of the Seven Rays.[6] Traveling their sevenfold path back to my heart of the Holy Ghost, you will know, then, that *there is a way out* and that there is a transfiguration that awaits you, there is a transformation indeed.

Therefore, out of the ashes of the former self let the anointed one arise! I can assure you that those who apply themselves to the path of purity in Love and Love in purity in the heart of their I AM

Presence will receive all of the training, the discipline and comfort necessary to enter into this walk with God.

Angels of the Holy Spirit, descend now into this city and into this place! Blessed ones, the heavens are filled with millions of angels who exist only to bear the vibration of that Spirit.

Know, then, that that Spirit is a sacred fire and, as you know, the fire that is physical is the most difficult of the elements to control. [Therefore,] may you seek the path, and the calling as well, [of the Holy Spirit and] of the five secret rays [in order to keep your God-control of both the spiritual and physical fire in the earth] and know that these [secret ray] initiations in the earth[7] are the very cause as to the disturbance in the nations and the governments and sudden burdens upon a people.

The comfort of the LORD your God is truly given in the violet flame and in the presence of angels. So great a company of his emissaries surround you, for we have sent our Messenger before you only to be a visible sign of our Presence—that [you may know that] the hosts of heaven do descend to walk and talk once again with those who are the issue of Light.

This event on planet earth of the convergence of heavenly hosts with those in embodiment does itself produce a divine alchemy. Divine alchemy must always be met by those in embodiment with the supreme oneness with the ritual of the violet flame and the Seventh Ray.

Let all who know the call in their inner beings feel Love's immensity, Love's intensity, Love's angels and the profound caring of the Divine Mother and all those who serve from Ascended Master levels this planetary evolution.

Blessed ones, if the Holy Spirit come not, there be no deliverance. Thus, know that the same Light* that is become the testing of souls is become the opening by the dove of the Spirit in whose wake you ascend in vibration.

My comfort before you, beloved, is a living Flame. My cloven tongues would descend upon you. Will you not prepare yourselves to receive those cloven tongues of fire?[8] For, beloved, it is the age and this is the sign of Aquarius—the true and profound sign.

Let the sign God gave you in the beginning of the I AM Presence be your sign in the ending to enter a straight and narrow path in the ascent to the Holy of Holies of your being. Putting all lesser things aside, then, know that the Aquarian age can be in your heart and be in you in this hour if you but receive its hierarch, Saint Germain, its violet flame and the [Seventh Ray] path of initiation.

*Universal Christ

I have come because a people who seek Truth have a right to the comfort of Reality, and Reality *is* the comfort flame. For to know what is real gives one the option to embrace that Divine Reality. If I had not told you so this evening, beloved, you should be the victim of ignorance to which you have been victimized for so many centuries. Therefore we say, restore enlightenment to those who truly desire it [in order] to use that enlightenment in the spiritual path of service in Love. Let it not be held back.

My angels will not cease until they have touched every soul upon this planet who truly desires to know the LORD [the I AM THAT I AM] face to face. And the very first face they see may be an angel face peeping through the veil!

Blessed ones, in the reality of thy walk with the Holy Spirit, I AM at thy side, the Maha Chohan, for the victory of Life in you. O keep the flame of Life and know that the breath that is breathed upon you in the hour of your soul's descent into form is truly the breath of the Holy Spirit!

As the years go by, through absence of mantra or prayer the sacred fire breath is no longer native to the body but must be re-invoked by you. To this end the Ascended Master Djwal Kul dictated the *Intermediate Studies of the Human Aura* that you might have a simple exercise for the breathing in again of the breath of the Holy Spirit.[9] Therefore, take it. Practice makes perfect.

In this hour of our oneness, I, therefore, in holy emanation breathe upon you the breath of the Holy Spirit. [The holy breath sounds]

Thus, beloved, the initiating spiral of the Holy Spirit has descended this night in planet earth in this city and citadel. So it is done! It shall not be turned back! Let he that is holy be holy still[10] and let all who know God embrace that Spirit and live forever in his sacred fire breath.

I bless and love you. I caress and seal you with the kiss of peace upon the brow. I AM that LORD, that Lord of the Ninth Ray and the power of the three-times-three.

    *Purusha.** (Parousia†) [The holy breath sounds]

---

*Purusha [pū-roosh]: Sanskrit, lit. man; soul or spirit, the animating principle in man, the Spirit as passive as distinct from the *Prakriti,* or creative force.   †*Parousia* [pa-róo-zee-uh, puh-róo-see-uh, puh-roósh-ee-uh, puh-roósh-uh, or par-oo-sée-uh]: Greek, lit. presence, being near, coming; advent or return, Second Coming of Christ. It is possible that the Sanskrit and Greek words converge in the Divine Word to exemplify the Second Coming of Christ as the raising up of the Divine Principle in the heart of every individual.

"The Summit Lighthouse Sheds Its Radiance O'er All the World to Manifest as Pearls of Wisdom." This dictation by the **Maha Chohan** was **delivered** by Elizabeth Clare Prophet following her **Sunday, Feb. 21, 1988** lecture at the Beverly Hilton, **Beverly Hills,** where she was stumping for Saint Germain's Coming Revolution in Higher Consciousness. **(1) Maha Chohan:** Great Lord. *Mahá* [Sanskrit]: great, mighty, strong, abundant. *Chohan:* "A Lord or Master. A high Adept. An initiate who has taken more initiations than the five major initiations which make man a 'Master of the Wisdom'" (Alice A. Bailey, *A Treatise on Cosmic Fire,* p. 66, n. 24). "A Rajput term used by Indian writers to denote high spiritual rank" (Christmas Humphreys, *A Popular Dictionary of Buddhism,* p. 57). "Chief, Cho-Khan, 'Rock of Ages'" (*The Mahatma Letters to A. P. Sinnett from the Mahatmas M. & K. H.,* index, p. 9). "Chohans, Tibetan? [Lord]. Seven Mighty Beings who, having passed the Sixth Initiation, have the power to focus within themselves the Ray-Streams or Attributes of Logoic Consciousness" (H. P. Blavatsky, *The Secret Doctrine,* 5th Adyar ed., 6:452). *Chohan* may be related to the Tibetan *chos* (pronounced chō), meaning dharma, religious doctrine, or religion, especially the doctrine of Buddha. In a general sense, the meaning of *chos* encompasses all phenomena, matter, and knowledge of worldly and spiritual things. The Tibetan word *jo-bo* (pronounced chō) means lord or master, Buddha or the image of Buddha. The Mongolian word *khan* or *qan* (pronounced hahn) also means lord, ruler, emperor, or king. The Tibetan *chos-mkhan* (pronounced chǐ-kěn or chō-kěn) means one who practices or is skilled in the dharma. **(2)** Matt. 12:31, 32; Mark 3:29; Luke 12:10. **(3) Four planets in Capricorn.** In her Stump message prior to this dictation, Elizabeth Clare Prophet explained that in February 1988, Neptune, Saturn, Uranus and Mars formed a major conjunction in Capricorn. This conjunction marks the formal starting point of a period of upheaval and change on the planet. If not mitigated or consumed by calls to the violet flame, the negative effects of this configuration could include war, revolution, economic debacle and major earth changes. For an in-depth analysis of the karmic challenges this and other astrological configurations portend and how we can turn back untoward prophecy through Divine Intervention and the science of the spoken Word, see Elizabeth Clare Prophet, February 13, 1988, "Saint Germain On Prophecy from 1988 through the 1990s—the Astrology of World Karma," on 2 videocassettes, 3 hr. 50 min., GP88019, $49.95 (add $1.50 for postage), or 3 audiocassettes, 3 hr. 51 min., A88024, $19.50 (add $1.00 for postage); and October 31, 1987, "Halloween Prophecy 1987," on 2 videocassettes, 4½ hr., GP87063, $39.95 (add $1.50 for postage), or 3 90-min. audiocassettes, A87079, $19.50 (add $1.00 for postage). **(4) The fall of Lemuria (Mu).** See 1988 *Pearls of Wisdom,* vol. 31, no. 19, p. 158, n. 2. **(5) Jesus' call to discipleship.** See 1988 *Pearls of Wisdom,* vol. 31, no. 12, p. 130, n. 2. **(6)** For dictations by and teachings on the Maha Chohan, see *Lords of the Seven Rays: Mirror of Consciousness,* Book One, pp. 8, 11, 13, 15–18; Book Two, pp. 277–97. **(7) Serapis Bey's fourteen-month cycles.** On December 29, 1978, Serapis Bey, Chohan of the Fourth Ray, announced that a fourteen-month cycle of initiation in the white sphere of the Great Causal Body had been inaugurated at winter solstice, December 21, 1978. Serapis said, "The goal of this fourteen months is the passing through of your lifestream on the fourteen stations of the cross of the Woman and her seed. . . . I announce to you, then, the dispensation and the means whereby you can increase the great white sphere of your individual causal body surrounding the Light of Alpha and of Omega." Since that time, every fourteen months has marked the initiation of another fourteen-month cycle through one of the bands of the causal body. On January 27, 1980, Serapis Bey told us that the testings of the fourteen stations of the cross which we undergo during the fourteen-month cycles are the "opportunity for you and your beloved twin flame to transmute an extraordinary momentum of personal and planetary karma." On February 28, 1987, Serapis Bey announced the inauguration of "fourteen months of planetary initiation in the first secret ray" as the first of "five [fourteen-month] rounds in the five secret rays." On January 2, 1988, Sanat Kumara addressed the challenges of initiation in the secret rays: "Blessed ones, the very forcefield and the aura of the sons of God can be in the earth the full power of the Great Central Sun Magnet. Therefore, I say unto you, invoke the Great Central Sun Magnet and know how serious and how complete are the fourteen-month dispensations of Serapis Bey. Each and every fourteen-month cycle, you are calling to the Great Central Sun for the amplification of one of the spheres of the causal body by the power of ascension's flame. . . . Blessed ones, understand that this is for your ultimate protection, and we have explained to you that the initiations of the five secret rays, which have succeeded those of the seven, are most difficult. For here is the place of the violation of the heart" (1988 *Pearls of Wisdom,* vol. 31, no. 4, p. 36). For more information on Serapis Bey's fourteen-month cycles and the secret-ray initiations, see Serapis Bey, October 28, 1984, "Initiation from the Emerald Sphere," and Elizabeth Clare Prophet, "Fourteen-Month Cycles of the Initiation of the Christed Ones through the Spheres of the Great Causal Body," 1984 *Pearls of Wisdom,* vol. 27, no. 56, pp. 487–93, 495–510; Serapis Bey, December 28, 1985, "The Descent of the Mighty Blue Sphere," 1986 *Pearls of Wisdom,* vol. 29, no. 15, pp. 125–27; Godfre, July 14, 1987, "Do Not Give Up the Ship!" 1987 *Pearls of Wisdom,* vol. 30, no. 45, p. 424. See also Mighty Cosmos, April 8, 1973, "The Secret Rays Are Released to the Earth from the Heart of Alpha and Omega," and June 30, 1973, "The Starry Body of Man: A Talisman for the Secret Rays," 1973 *Pearls of Wisdom,* vol. 16, nos. 22, 45, 46, pp. 95–98, 193–200; Mighty Cosmos, July 4, 1975, "The Secret Rays and the White-Fire Core: Let the Secret Rays Descend!" in *The Great White Brotherhood in the Culture, History and Religion of America,* pp. 145–48. **(8)** Acts 2:1–4. **(9) Djwal Kul's breathing exercise.** See Djwal Kul, "The Sacred Fire Breath," in *Intermediate Studies of the Human Aura,* pp. 67–75, plates 18–20, quality paperback with color illustrations of the chakras, patterns of energy flow and auric renderings, $7.95 (add $1.00 for postage); also in *The Human Aura,* pocketbook, pp. 139–48, $4.95 (add $.50 for postage); Elizabeth Clare Prophet, August 16, 1981, "The Healing of the Etheric Body: Djwal Kul's Breathing Exercise for the Integration of the Four Lower Bodies," on 92-min. audiocassette B82128, $6.50 (add $.55 for postage). **(10)** Rev. 22:11.

Pearls of Wisdom®
published by The Summit Lighthouse

| Vol. 31 No. 30 | Beloved Archangel Uriel | June 22, 1988 |

Saint Germain Stumps America
19
The Descending Fire
The Power of the Living Flame of Peace

Hail, Sons of God, Daughters of Zion!

I AM Uriel Archangel. I stand in thy presence as I stand in the Presence of God. For, lo, I am sent to you in this city and I come in the fulfillment of the ancient word of the angel with one foot upon the land and one foot upon the sea.[1]

Therefore, the fire does descend through me in this hour, anchored in the earth—in the sea and in the land in the physical and the astral planes—for the holding of the balance on behalf of those who are the inheritors of the Light.

I come, then, with the flaming sword and the flaming sword whose flame shall not be quenched. Therefore, as fire does descend into the earth with the coming of the Lord Christ, I also am sent to deliver that living fire as Aquarius must intensify for the consuming of the dregs of karma of Pisces.

Last eve the representative of the Holy Spirit did release that sacred fire of the LORD's judgment by Holy Spirit, which is an initiation of great dimensions and proportion;[2] and those who keep the Flame within their hearts must realize the portent of the descent of the Holy Spirit.

But if the Spirit come not with the attending Archangels, then what should we have upon a planet? A rot that is not consumed, a karma that delays and a burden upon a people who cannot forever groan and travail in the Divine Mother to bring forth the Universal Christ in their beings.

Therefore, God has sent his angels and his legions of Light to intercede on behalf of those who truly have hearts that burn with a fire that may also meet, measure for measure, the descending fire. Many have prayed for [this] Divine Intervention. I, Uriel, am the fulfillment of God's answer to prayer; for this, too, is a function of all angels of his Presence.

Therefore, the answer is the delivery of the sacred fire and it does preempt and prevent even the conspiracies of the fallen ones who have not so soon expected the coming of our descent that does indeed precede the descent with the sound of a trumpet of the Lord Christ[3] coming into your temple and into the earth.

Therefore, we say, let them, these fallen ones and their infamy plotted on the screen of life, be turned back and held back while a people once again are given opportunity, as opportunity is [embodied in] the Feminine Ray of Aquarius,[4] to choose to be and to be that Flame! to choose to be and to be that Christ! to choose to be and to be that God Presence!

I tell you, beloved, had you heard the teachings [given] this night delivered by an Archangel, you should be weary of the intensity. Wherefore we have sent our Messenger that you might in the love of the Divine Mother through her receive nourishment for your souls. But I tell you, beloved, had we delivered it, it should have been the very same message. For it is vital—vital to acquaint now thyself with cosmic law, with that Presence and to know the power of the living flame of Peace! For Peace is the flame of my sword and my bands!

We are the legions of the Sixth Ray. Peace, then, is a two-edged sword, for it does consume every force of anti-Peace. And those who would receive that flame must know that that flame is a purging light that shall also disrupt and disturb those subconscious levels of anxiety and agitation within the psyche.

Pierce, then, the veil of unreality, I command you, O legions of the Sixth Ray in the service of the Lord Christ! *Pierce*, then, and strip all who desire that Reality of the Cosmic Spirit and flame of Peace—of all unreality and darkness. Therefore, we come and we are those who prepare the bodies and chakras of everyone [who is] of God who desires to be infilled with the Holy Spirit of the New Age.

Blessed ones, John the Baptist went before the Christ and before our coming. As he did demand fruits meet for repentance,[5] recognize that it is not by an insistence without cause or wisdom that we say, release into the flame the dross and receive the Light.

For, beloved, as the ages move on, that cup that is not drunk willingly of the divine elixir of Life does come upon the individual and a planet by the very necessity of cycles ongoing. Better, then, to prepare for the initiation of the living Christ than suddenly to cast oneself upon the rock and be broken,[6] when by surrender today to the will of God thou couldst have merged with the cycles oncoming of the Central Sun.

Blessed hearts, it is prophesied that the people who experience cataclysm will cry out to the mountains, "Fall on us! Fall on us!"[7] You need never arrive at that moment of desperation, for when you become the mountain and the fire in the heart of the mountain, one with Nature and Mother Earth, you are already at the level of vibration where you contain the oncoming wave of light.

O to merge in the cosmic sea with Divine Reality! O to retain individuality in the flame of God! Such a wonder and grace [it is] to do this, beloved! The key is to begin. The key is to begin to fan the fire of the heart with the holy breath. *Purusha!*[8] [The holy breath sounds] So [is] the breath of an Archangel.

So remember the coal that is placed on the tongue of the prophet to purge and purify the mouthpiece of God.[9] So remember [that] thou, too, must prophesy in this age, for thou art a prophet and knowest it not. For the spirit of prophecy does emerge out of the deeds of the past. These are the prophecies you yourselves have written and can unwrite in this hour.

O awake! Awake, ye who are of the God Flame and Divine Reality, and know that the Eternal Youth, Sanat Kumara, has sent me to you in this hour for the quickening of divine memory that you might catch the spark, the spiral and the wave of an age and merge with that ultimate Reality.

I AM Uriel. My coming [is] to preserve a way whereby the soul might enter in. My coming [is] to establish a highway for our God that his descent and your ascent might therefore occur and the fusion [take place] when hearts are one, as Above, so below.

Release, then, thy fire, O angels of Uriel! Release, then, the fire of Peace, for it is a consuming fire, consuming, then, the momentums of war and warfare.

In the living light of the Divine Mother, I, Uriel, bow to the inner Christ in you, for I AM the servant of that Christ and of your soul ascending to meet her Lord. May you remember forever that an Archangel has addressed you and shall continue to do so this night personally at inner levels with a message for each and every one of you.

Therefore, know that thou art regarded as the instrument of God and the potential to realize the All. Therefore, precious art thou in the sight of thy God.

I seal thee with the blessing of Peace and the sign of the judgment upon the force of anti-Peace.

Hail! legions of Light. Hail! tiers of angels now forming. Hail! O Thou Divine Mother who art crowned again and again by the angels of heaven.

Hail, Mary, full of grace, the Lord is with thee. Blessed art thou amongst women and blessed is the fruit of thy womb,[10] the Cosmic Christ aborning in these thy sons.

Lo, I AM with you. But invoke the Spirit of the Resurrection and know that I am come to you in that power of eternal Life now and at the hour of your victory over karma, dis-ease and the illusion called death, now and at the hour of the challenge and the victory over the fallen angels who have defied our God.

Thou art, therefore, held in the chalice of the Divine Mother's matrix, the immaculate concept for the fulfillment of fiery destiny!

Purusha![8] Until we meet in the heart of the Flame, I AM Uriel, Archangel of the Sixth Ray of God.

"The Summit Lighthouse Sheds Its Radiance O'er All the World to Manifest as Pearls of Wisdom." This dictation by **Archangel Uriel** was **delivered** by Elizabeth Clare Prophet following her **Mon., Feb. 22, 1988** lecture at the Ramada Renaissance Hotel, **Long Beach,** where she was stumping for Saint Germain's Coming Revolution in Higher Consciousness. N.B. Bracketed material denotes words unspoken yet implied by the Archangel, added by the Messenger under his direction for clarity in the published text. (1) **The angel with "his right foot upon the sea and his left foot on the earth."** Rev. 10:1, 2, 8–11. (2) **The initiation (judgment) of the Holy Spirit.** See the Maha Chohan, February 21, 1988, 1988 *Pearls of Wisdom,* vol. 31, no. 29, pp. 225–28. (3) I Thess. 4:16. (4) The Ascended Lady Master Portia, Goddess of Justice, also known as the **Goddess of Opportunity,** is the twin flame of Saint Germain, Hierarch of the Aquarian Age. (5) **Fruits meet for repentance.** Matt. 3:8; Luke 3:8. (6) **To cast oneself upon the rock.** Matt. 21:42–44; Luke 20:17, 18. (7) **Fear of God in the day of karmic reckoning.** "And I beheld when he had opened the sixth seal, and, lo, there was a great earthquake; and the sun became black as sackcloth of hair, and the moon became as blood; and the stars of heaven fell unto the earth, even as a fig tree casteth her untimely figs, when she is shaken of a mighty wind. And the heaven departed as a scroll when it is rolled together; and every mountain and island were moved out of their places. And the kings of the earth, and the great men, and the rich men, and the chief captains, and the mighty men, and every bondman, and every free man, hid themselves in the dens and in the rocks of the mountains; and said to the mountains and rocks, Fall on us, and hide us from the face of him that sitteth on the throne, and from the wrath of the Lamb: for the great day of his wrath is come; and who shall be able to stand?" Rev. 6:12–17. See also Hos. 10:8; Luke 23:27–30. (8) ***Purusha/Parousia.*** See 1988 *Pearls of Wisdom,* vol. 31, no. 29, p. 228, note. (9) **The cleansing sacred fire.** "Then flew one of the seraphims unto me, having a live coal in his hand, which he had taken with the tongs from off the altar: And he laid it upon my mouth, and said, Lo, this hath touched thy lips; and thine iniquity is taken away, and thy sin purged." Isa. 6:6, 7. (10) **Salutations to Mary.** Luke 1:28, 42.

Pearls of Wisdom®
published by The Summit Lighthouse

| Vol. 31 No. 31 | Beloved Archangel Gabriel | June 25, 1988 |

Saint Germain Stumps America
20
The Visitation
Integrate with the White Fire

Hail, O Thou Immortal Fire!

I, Gabriel, descend into this city to release now sacred fire into the earth, into these hearts for the saving of that which is lost.

I AM the Archangel which stand in the Presence of the Divine Mother, and I announce to you each one, in the path of the annunciation itself, that thou art a son of God destined to appear with the morning stars,[1] destined to know God as thy habitation and grace.

There be some in this place who in this hour receive me, for they have earned the right to receive the Messenger of God that I AM [who have come] to announce to them that they shall ascend in this life. And to others I say, those to whom it is given to ascend are so told by right that they might note their progress on the Path and so be notified of the Divine Call.

You who see in your souls these individuals at inner levels as shining ones, know, beloved, that I announce to you that you may also so qualify yourselves to also receive my visitation in the future. Therefore where one son of God has qualified for this initiation, I AM here, I AM there, Gabriel of the Light!

My legions move with seraphim. Therefore, this city on inner planes is a blazing light of white-robed angels of the Fourth Ray and they do form rings and tiers of light.

Blessed hearts, they come for the great gathering of souls, for it is the age and the hour when all must prepare for inner changes and earth changes. For the alchemy of God does not wait and cannot wait, for the timetable is governed by the Central Sun and its release in cycles of the sine wave whereby the great momentum of dispensation does flow.

Flow, O Holy Light! Flow into these vessels now that they might be pillars and learn of me and my path of initiation.

I come to anchor in this city a spiritual protection, an inner vision and guidance. I serve, then, the Lord Christ, the Blessed Virgin, [and] Saint Germain, and I assist in the quickening of the inner sight and self-knowledge. Therefore, with my complement, beloved Hope, I greet you. And in this hour know that in your inner being I place a jewel of light and its counterpart in the inner being of your twin flame.

Happy are ye to find yourselves at the feet[2] of our Messenger, reacquainting yourselves with the mysteries of God. Happy are ye to be greeted by an Archangel who does love you and shall always love you and desires to see you return Home—*Home* in the heart of the One. Therefore, my beloved Hope does touch the other half of the Divine Whole,[3] and seraphim of God of whom you should learn draw solar rings[4] for the sealing of that Oneness.

Now I charge you, O sons of men, invoke the light daily to fill in the pattern the angels establish, for they can do so much and then you must do your part, therefore [the necessity for] the filling in of the inner pattern by light, by white fire, by violet flame, by all diligence.

Blessed ones, some of you have had my visitation five thousand years ago and I tell you, beloved, some of you have not seen or heard of me since. For you have gone out in other rounds and vibrations, only to return in this age by the very grace and blessedness of Saint Germain, who has come to you personally to quicken you.

Therefore, once again you have hungered, you have thirsted for that Divine Appearing, and by good karma now [it is] a propitious hour—and this city has been set aside for my coming. And many who violate the white light of purity in this world have sought to prevent this Messenger's coming here.[5]

Blessed ones, the white fire is oncoming and cannot be turned back. I adjure you in this hour, therefore, to integrate with it; for when it is within you and the cosmic initiations of a planet and her evolutions accelerate, you will be found in consonance [with the white fire] at a vibratory rate [which shall be] the equivalency of that fire that shall descend. Therefore [because you shall have become the vessel of the white fire][6] you shall not be consumed by the descending fire but raised up by it.

Let it be said of you and may you yourselves repeat the mantra:

The prince of this world cometh and findeth nothing in me[7] —nothing of like vibration whereby to ensnare and entrap and entangle me one more round in the lower levels of being!

Therefore, let it also be said of you:

The angels of God come and find in me a living pillar of fire, for I know who I AM and surely I AM the issue of the I AM THAT I AM!

Thus, blessed be the name of the LORD and blessed be those who come in that name [I AM THAT I AM] and come with its recitation as a love song for the wooing of their Presence to their hearts and the wooing of that Beloved in inner planes.

I draw you, then, to the inner retreat that I keep over northern California,[8] that you might come and know me and know what is my vision and inner awareness of what is coming upon this state and [upon] the Ring of Fire of the Pacific. Where the outer mind cannot receive it, let the inner self and soul be tutored until by that inner knowledge there is an inner walk and an inner path.

Take courage! You can fulfill all things that are required of you by the Law and you can awake fully satisfied in the bliss of God.

I direct fire into the earth and into the sea, into the beings of Nature who cry out to me, for their burden is heavy with man-kind's perfidy and perversions. [intonations, 33 sec.]

Guard the flow. Guard the light. I AM thy ministering servant. I AM Gabriel. Through my heart step through to higher octaves.

Behold, the Blessed Virgin cometh: Mary, Mary the Divine Mediatrix, Mary who does prophesy and weep and save and succor, Mary, Mother of the Infinite.

In thy heart, O Blessed One, is the immaculate concept for these thine own. Seal them, O Mother of the incarnation of God, of Jesus, of all.

I, Gabriel, have accomplished my mission in this city and in your behalf. Now my seraphim form a spiral around each one and it is done; and the coil around you is a mother-of-pearl, a cone of light for your keeping safe in the Divine Mother's heart.

I AM Gabriel, servant of the Son of the Most High God in you. I AM Gabriel which stand in the Presence of the Divine Mother. [12-sec. pause]

AUM AUM

This dictation by **Archangel Gabriel** was **delivered** by the Messenger Elizabeth Clare Prophet following her **Tuesday, February 23, 1988** lecture at the Scottish Rite Masonic Memorial Center, **San Diego,** where she was stumping for Saint Germain's Coming Revolution in Higher Consciousness. Lecture and dictation on 3 videocassettes, 5 hr., GP88027, $59.95 (add $1.90 for postage), or 4 audiocassettes, 4¾ hr., A88030, $26 (add $.95 for postage). **N.B.** Bracketed material denotes words unspoken yet implied by the Archangel, added by the Messenger under his direction for clarity in the published text. **(1) Morning stars.** Refers to Cosmic Beings known as Elohim who embody God's consciousness on the seven rays and the five secret rays as well as the heavenly hosts, angels, Archangels, seraphim and cherubim of God who minister at the Throne of Grace and to the evolutions of God worlds without end. **(2)** The standing-room-only crowd which filled the Scottish Rite Masonic Memorial Center gladly sat on the floor, around the stage and down the aisles. **(3)** While Archangel Gabriel is speaking his feminine complement, the **Archeia Hope, touches the twin flame of everyone present,** wherever that twin flame may be throughout Cosmos, for the uniting of the twain and the restoration of the Divine Whole as they were in the beginning with God in the Great Central Sun. **(4)** You can learn about the service of the **seraphim of God and the electronic fire rings** in Seraphic Meditations I, II, III: "The Great Electronic Fire Rings," "The Sea of Glass" and "The Predication of God," in Serapis Bey, *Dossier on the Ascension,* pp. 118–40. On November 25, 1987, during her lecture on "The Healing Power of Angels: Christ Wholeness—The Seven Rays of God," Elizabeth Clare Prophet delivered these meditations in a powerful reading through which the fiery auras of the seraphim may be felt and experienced. As Serapis Bey and the seraphim teach in the Seraphic Meditations, the seraphim possess the quality of "cosmic penetrability," which enables them to pass through the human consciousness of an individual to absorb and transmute negative substance and to leave behind a "residue" of "intense white-fire devotion, charged with a yearning for purity." The 21-minute healing meditation with the seraphim included in this lecture is recommended for use in Wednesday night healing services in conjunction with "Watch With Me" Jesus' Vigil of the Hours and healing decrees as a most powerful means of healing whereby the seraphim may superimpose their Electronic Presence upon those who enter into the meditation and invoke the seraphic intercession on behalf of themselves, loved ones and millions upon the planet who need healing in this hour. Entire 4½-hour service, including dictations by the Archangels Zadkiel and Uriel, available on 2 videocassettes, GP87089, $59.95 (add $1.50 for postage); 3 90-min. audiocassettes, A87100, $19.50 (add $.95 for postage). **(5)** The officers of the Scottish Rite Masonic Memorial Center received hundreds of phone calls from fundamentalist Christians who staged a **protest against Elizabeth Clare Prophet's delivery of her message at the Masonic temple.** Some Masons, who had also received these calls, even tore up and sent in their membership cards in protest of her coming. True to the honor and principles of their fraternity, the officers upheld her right of freedom of speech, freedom of religion and freedom of assembly and her contract with them to lease their auditorium for the evening. After hearing her speak the officers affirmed that the orchestrated protest was a hate campaign and saw only positive good in her words: "She's a great lady and we haven't heard anything in there that's wrong, and she's welcome back here anytime. And if she ever needs a recommendation in any Masonic temple anywhere in the country, call us." Religious fanaticism is a violation of the white fire purity that is at the heart of every movement sponsored by the Great White Brotherhood, including the Masonic Order. **(6) Becoming the vessel of the white fire.** By devotion to God through words and works, mantra, meditation and action that proceeds out of God-awareness, the embodied disciple establishes in his forcefield the negative (Mother) polarity of the white fire; therefore he magnetizes to himself that portion of the descending white fire, the positive (Father) polarity, which is equal to his own momentum. Jesus stated this law when he said, "For whosoever hath, to him shall be given, and he shall have more abundance: but whosoever hath not, from him shall be taken away even that he hath" (Matt. 13:12). See Mark L. Prophet and Elizabeth Clare Prophet, "Momentum," in *The Lost Teachings of Jesus I,* pp. 133–34. **(7)** John 14:30. **(8) The retreat of Archangel Gabriel and Hope,** his divine complement, is located in the etheric plane between Sacramento and Mount Shasta, California.

Save the World with Violet Flame!
by Saint Germain

John F. Kennedy International Airport
New York City
En route to Lisbon, Portugal
February 24, 1988, midnight

Beloved of My Heart--

It is with the tenderness of Saint Germain's love in springtime that I send to you the enclosed cassette, SAVE THE WORLD WITH VIOLET FLAME!

Placing this precious "amethyst crystal" in your hands, my happiness is full--like the Mol Heron Creek, sparkling, rushing with the new waters of the spring melt as the winds from the south bear tidings of the coming of the Goddess of Spring in her green and violet garments.

I am writing to you from New York during an extended layover on the way to Lisbon for a weekend seminar and pilgrimage to Fátima with European Keepers of the Flame.

It is, in fact, with a violet flame dispensation for Europe that the Great White Brotherhood has sent me on this mission for our beloved Lanello's ascension day, February 26, 1988. And so, thinking of you as I write, I am taking all of you with me for this historic event.

To accompany the violet flame songs and decrees given with such delight by all who assembled for our New Year's Retreat at the ranch, I desire you to have and cherish the attached teachings on the violet flame that have been given since 1982 and on my recent tour concluded yesterday with a tremendous victory for Saint Germain in San Diego.

In addition to these illumining statements on this Seventh Ray action of the Holy Spirit, I wanted to share with you the excitement that is rippling through our movement worldwide: the macrobiotic diet as it is taught and practiced by the Eastern adepts! So many students of the Ascended Masters are loving the food and learning to cook balanced meals simply and experiencing realignment and healing in their bodies that I thought that I would give you the recipes and theory behind the macrobiotic breakfast consisting of miso soup and rice-and-oat cereal.

Box A, Livingston, Montana 59047-1390 (406) 222-8300

We'll be giving cooking classes before and after the July conference, which will be held June 29 through the Fourth of July. But in the meantime you'll find that the violet flame combined with the beneficial body-building and cleansing properties of this diet will truly increase your capacity to hold God's light in your physical cells and organs--and in your chakras.

May I suggest that you treat your body elemental to a complete abstention from dairy products as the very first step to freedom with the violet flame, which Saint Germain says is the most physical flame, and that you treat yourself to the breakfast that gives your body, soul and mind strength in the yin and yang of Alpha and Omega and a profoundly peaceful nutrition.

If you would like to pursue the diet of the Eastern adepts as your alchemy of transition into the new age of Aquarius, we have found the books listed on the enclosed order form extremely helpful. You may also want to order the audiocassettes of my basic lectures on the health benefits of macrobiotic foods and how the health of the organs affects human behavior, given at our New Year's Retreat at the Royal Teton Ranch.

As you know, Saint Germain and the Ascended Masters have given us the mandate to flood the world with violet flame in order to mitigate the effects of returning personal and planetary karma accelerating at the end of this age. In my lecture "Saint Germain On Prophecy from 1988 through the 1990s--the Astrology of World Karma," delivered at our weekend seminar in San Francisco, I analyzed current and upcoming astrological configurations and the serious karmic challenges they portend. This lecture, available on audio- and videocassette, will give you the information you need to make incisive invocations with your violet flame decrees for the transmutation of this karma.

I am also very happy to offer you the audio- and video-tapes of my lecture given February 14 in San Francisco, "The Lost Teachings of Jesus and Maitreya on Your Divine Reality." It shows how the Chart of Your Divine Self embodies the parallel teachings of East and West on the path of reunion with God.

If you desire to accelerate your mastery of the science of the spoken Word along with your use of the SAVE THE WORLD WITH VIOLET FLAME! cassette, I recommend the following steps. First, read or reread <u>The Science of the Spoken Word</u> and listen to its companion cassette album which teaches you how to decree effectively.

In addition, you can experiment with the decrees and songs in the following publications and audiocassettes: <u>Heart, Head and Hand Decrees,</u> a pocket-sized booklet of meditations, mantras, prayers and decrees for the expansion of the threefold flame in the heart; our decree book designed in three sections for beginning, intermediate and advanced students; the two-cassette albums <u>Decrees and Songs by the Messenger Mark L. Prophet</u> (at beginners' speed) and <u>Rainbow Rays Out of the Mouth of the Messenger</u> (intermediate-level decrees); <u>Archangel Michael's Rosary,</u> a powerful tool for the protection of yourself and your loved ones; and our audiocassette albums of bhajans, devotional songs to the Persons and Principles of the Godhead in the Eastern tradition.

To sustain the forcefield of your dynamic decrees and mantras, we also have available amethyst crystals in various sizes charged by the Lords of the Seven Rays. You may want to place one of these focuses on your personal altar to anchor the violet flame that you invoke in your vigil with Saint Germain.

Keepers of the Flame around the world are keeping a thirty-three-day vigil with the SAVE THE WORLD WITH VIOLET FLAME! tape, giving it daily in its entirety either in fifteen-minute segments or all at once.

I am calling all Lightbearers to join in this effort to lift the karmic weight of earth at this moment of the difficult astrology of Saturn, Uranus, Neptune and Mars conjoined in Capricorn. Let this be our alchemical experiment to see just what we can do to mitigate prophecies of planetary karma for this year and the decade of the nineties. May you become the violet singing flame.

In the flame of our dearest love, Saint Germain, the great Master Alchemist, I bid you TRY.

I'll see you in the Heart of the Inner Retreat. Be there June 29 through July 4!

All my love in Freedom's flame,

Elizabeth Clare Prophet
"Guru Ma"

P.S. We're already preparing the second violet flame tape SAVE THE WORLD WITH VIOLET FLAME! Please send me $5.95 to be sure and get your copy as soon as it's ready.

P.P.S. I hope to see you at our Easter Retreat at the Ranch, March 30–April 3, for members of the Keepers of the Flame Fraternity.

Saint Germain, December 2, 1984

Now, understand why the violet flame is so necessary. It is because it is the age of opportunity--the opportunity of the Mother that is with us. Understand, then, that in sorting out human history and the history of the lifewaves who have migrated to this soil, one must perceive the causes and name them and call for their binding, and then the effects will disappear as easily as one erases a chalkboard. . . .

The hour of change is come, even as the hour of the harvest is come. Change is the order of the day, experiencing internally that fire of the violet flame sun, beloved hearts. . . .

The violet flame is a physical flame! And what do I mean when I say this? I say the violet flame is closest in vibratory action of all of the rays to this earth substance, to these chemical elements and compounds, to all that you see in Matter. And therefore, the violet flame can combine with any molecule or molecular structure, any particle of matter known or unknown, and any wave of light, electrons, or electricity.

Thus, the violet flame is the supreme antidote for food poisoning, chemical waste, toxins, pollution of drugs in the body. The violet flame is an elixir that you drink and imbibe like water, like the purest juice of the fruit of the harvest of the elementals' consciousness. The violet flame is the supreme antidote for physical problems. Wherever chelas gather to give the violet flame, there you notice immediately an improvement in physical conditions!. . .

Whether organic or inorganic matter, there is a disintegration spiral that works in the buildings, in the land, in the sea, and in the bodies which can be counteracted best by the violet flame.

The violet flame turns around the spin of electron and atom. It turns around the downward spiral of the chakras and the energy. It is forever the power of conversion--and conversion means "to turn around"! The violet flame is the buoyant joy of the Holy Ghost that turns around spirits and minds and souls and emotions!. . .

Even in the six months that have passed since we came last in the Heart of the Inner Retreat, while you have seen an acceleration of Light, there is a corresponding and unseen acceleration of Darkness. And this is as it has been through past ages when cataclysms in the economy or in the land have been nigh.

Therefore I tell you, it is necessary to counteract this Darkness with increasing violet flame, increasing the call for the reversing of the tide of the downward spiral of civilization. (Washington, D.C., Pearls of Wisdom, vol. 27, no. 61, pp. 550, 551, 553, 554)

Archangel Michael, February 5, 1988

Beloved hearts, we the Archangels move across the face of the earth, speaking in the hearts of many, for we are also cosmic teachers. We desire awareness and a quickening, and for that purpose we must open the continents of the air, of the mind itself, that you might know that to enter the New Age does demand new thought and a new understanding of prophecy and a realization that the karma of a planet that could descend may yet be stayed by the heart, head and hand of those who determine to keep the flame of Life and recognize that the all-consuming power of God released in the violet flame by millions upon earth can in this hour, even in a twinkling of an eye, be the last trump of the Death and Hell of the forces of Darkness. . . .

Beloved, it is a time for all due seriousness for those who know that they are mature sons and daughters of God. Enter into the path of keeping the flame, I say! Call unto the angelic hosts and invoke the violet flame daily. It is necessary, beloved, else, I will tell you, certain cataclysms will not be averted. It is no longer a question of hundreds but of millions of lifestreams who must hear the call of the Archangels who come in the defense of the God of Freedom to the earth, who is Saint Germain. (Tucson, Arizona, Pearls of Wisdom, vol. 31, no. 14, pp. 136–37)

Thérèse of Lisieux, February 7, 1988

Blessed hearts, let millions rally in this hour to the cause of our beloved Saint Joseph. Blessed hearts, he would save both Church and State and yet must now do so on the outside of both. For as of old, heads of state nation by nation have not heard his call, and those who represent the people have not received the gift of the violet flame.

There are saints in heaven, numberless numbers, and those not yet ascended waiting in the etheric octave. Many of these have graduated out of the Church and yet did not make their full ascension because they lacked the knowledge and use of the violet flame and the gift of the science of the spoken Word. . . .

If you could see what the Messenger sees, I assure you that you would make this calling, this election a daily priority in your lives: to offer the calls to the violet flame and the rosary to Saint Michael the Archangel and to Mother Mary. Recognize, beloved, that it will take millions who will invoke the violet flame to transmute world karma. . . .

Blessed hearts, while there is life and hope and while the courses continue, there is day by day the intercession of your lifestream. This is my plea to you and this is my call. While the representatives of the governments of the nations betray the people and many of the clergy also betray them, let the people en masse rise up to save the world by the violet flame and by the fervent call. (Mexicali, Mexico, Pearls of Wisdom, vol. 31, no. 15, pp. 140, 141)

Great Divine Director, February 4, 1988

You live in an era, beloved, when the ancient karma sown in the rock and the mountain, even of this vicinity, comes due for balance. Let it be balanced by a violet flame conflagration. . . .

The world can receive the violet flame as the gift of your hearts. Know you, beloved, what six hundred souls of Light such as those who have gathered here this evening can do, not alone for this state and nation but for a planet? I tell you, were six hundred to gather even weekly for four hours of violet flame, what changes you would see would astonish you. For there is a geometrization of that God Flame, and the number who gather is squared and then multiplied by the power of the ten thousand-times-ten thousand. (Phoenix, Arizona, Pearls of Wisdom, vol. 31, no. 13, pp. 132–33)

El Morya, February 13, 1988

Out of the First Ray of the dawn's love for the diamond-shining Mind of God I come to you with lessons to keep you in the facets of the sapphire will of God that you might not sink into lesser vibration, my chelas, in these hours when earth becomes heavier before she shall become lighter--

and she <u>shall</u> become lighter by your invocation of the violet flame <u>and only by that invocation.</u>

Therefore, in making myself a chalice for my chelas, I give myself to be filled by my chelas with the wine, the purple wine of the rich grape of the harvest. Let it be, then, an intense wine of the Spirit that comes forth by your call to the violet flame. Let the chalice of my being, with you, be the wine-bearer of Aquarius, beloved, for something must be done. Something is needed, beloved. Therefore, I propose in my heart to give myself, for what else can one give?. . .

Blessed hearts, I desire to be a chalice that does over-flow with the wine that you distill by your meditations in the white light of the Holy Spirit, and then with the intense imploring and fiery appeal to Mercy, to Kuan Yin, my cohort of Light, there might flow through you such intensity of the violet flame as to provide our beloved Saint Germain with an extraordinary portion, even a reservoir of such violet flame as to increase transmutation and therefore provide that measure of safety that is not now present in the earth. . . .

Thus, I AM become a chalice walking--a chalice running when you run! I come, beloved, in the full measure of my heart's devotion to my brother Saint Germain, your own beloved Master whose life, I tell you, is given for you. There-fore, let the full measure of this chalice be given daily, for each day I shall take that which you have deposited in this chalice and place it in the violet flame reservoir of light on the etheric plane. Therefore, beloved, fill and let it be emptied--fill it to overflowing.

Thus, beloved, this my walk with Saint Germain may prove to be that stitch in time of Hercules and Amazonia. It may prove to be such a boon to chelas that they will at last transcend these planetary karmic cycles that have produced a density within them that is not to my liking.

Therefore, <u>pierce!</u> <u>pierce!</u> <u>pierce!</u> O blue-flame sapphire light! Blue-lightning angels and devas of the Dia-mond Heart, come forth, then! For there must be a piercing of this density, that this overflowing wine of violet flame, Holy Spirit, may pour through the cracks and the fissures in the earth and yet give to elemental life the support so necessary. (San Francisco, California, <u>Pearls of Wisdom,</u> vol. 31, no. 19, pp. 155, 156)

Saint Germain, February 13, 1988

Blessed hearts, the fulfillment of all of the promises of God is upon you. So long as you claim me as your Brother and Friend, I am at your side, and when you give but fifteen minutes of violet flame decrees each day, you allow me to place an extraordinary measure of my Electronic Presence with you. Thus, I am seeking the lamplighters who will ignite a planet with violet flame candles, that all of the stars and the angels may look down upon it and know that a planet has been claimed for Freedom by a people who awakened before it was too late! (San Francisco, California, <u>Pearls of Wisdom,</u> vol. 31, no. 20, p. 165)

Omri-Tas, July 7, 1984

If in all reverence, with inner attunement, a sense of yourself in your Christ Self as priest or priestess of the sacred fire, if with all your heart and deep within your heart you will take, then, fifteen minutes each day to give <u>profound</u> and loving invocations to the violet flame in my name (and please remember to use my name, for I AM the one from whose causal body this dispensation comes to you through the heart of Saint Germain), then we will take that offering, measure for measure--as it is devoted, as it is profound and sincere-- the very weight of its power and Light, and therefore by the <u>quality</u> of it, quality for quality, it shall be multiplied in your life ten times. . . .

I would, therefore, further explain to you that in this violet flame that you give. . .the dispensation can only start once you have given the fifteen minutes. In the giving of your decrees, then, you may use the inserts that you use with the blue-flame Masters, with the Ruby Ray decrees, with the Ritual of Exorcism and so forth. (Heart of the Inner Retreat, Royal Teton Ranch, Montana)

Arcturus and Victoria, July 1, 1984

If you could know that fifteen minutes of decrees, specific and in the violet flame, [given daily] could save a nation,. . .you would give it I am certain. (Heart of the Inner Retreat, Royal Teton Ranch, Montana)

Saint Germain, July 6, 1985

I come with the power of the Central Sun. I come bearing that light of freedom. I come drawing forth from the inner Holy of Holies of Alpha and Omega the fire of the Grail, the Shekinah, and the flame infolding itself.

It is the flame of freedom, the flame of Aquarius, the flame that is also native to your soul. For the swaddling garment with which you were swaddled by the Cosmic Virgin in the beginning was indeed the violet flame of freedom. For the first covering of thy soul was the awareness of free will--free will to affirm in the flame of God-freedom your divine inheritance, the will of God....

I stand before every one of the holy ones of God upon earth, irrespective of religion or race or background or past sin. I stand before the Lightbearers to transfer now the sacred cup of Communion--the wine of the violet flame that is not only the Blood of Christ but also the Blood of Christ that is transmutative, purifying, transforming--to restore in you the right-mindfulness of the Son of God....

The path of God-realization and self-mastery and of the adepts of the ages is given to you <u>directly</u> from the heart of Sanat Kumara. You need not go here or there, but obey the first teachings and principles and become alchemists of the sacred fire and neglect not the dynamic decree whereby that flame is internalized, whereby the violet flame does support and increase the divine spark. (Camelot, Los Angeles, California, Pearls of Wisdom, vol. 28, no. 34, pp. 429–30, 438)

Arcturus, December 30, 1984

I am called again to speak to you as the sponsor of physical form and as the sponsor of the violet flame extolled and brought by Saint Germain. I desire to see bodies made of clay be transmuted into bodies made of living Spirit-fire!...

I come for the reversing of the degeneracy of Matter. It is my office, it is my life. Only the Seventh Ray, the Seventh Age, and the Seventh Dispensation may accomplish this. (Camelot, Los Angeles, California, Pearls of Wisdom, vol. 28, no. 3, pp. 30, 31)

Cyclopea and Virginia, January 3, 1982

The victory in the battle is to the victors over time and space! And you are indeed accelerating over time and space when you invoke the violet flame. And though it appears imperceptible, I tell you that your light bodies, your very living temples are entirely different in this moment from those of other lifewaves upon earth because you give your love to God and the heavenly hosts as you happily invoke the violet flame daily. (Camelot, Los Angeles, California, Pearls of Wisdom, vol. 25, no. 13, p. 139)

Jesus Christ, October 7, 1984

I would give you the visualization of the meaning of the alchemy of the physical body and a thoughtform for your visualization with the tube of light. It is the power of the flame that has been called the deep purple. It is the action of the Seventh Ray charged with the holy blue. That purple fire, beloved ones, may be visualized as a cylinder of purple within the center of the tube of light, with the more pink violet flame still burning in the center. . . .

And know this, beloved hearts--that this is the color that we visualize for the transformation of the earth element and the earth body and the physical body you wear. Its visualization is a great protection.

In fact, I, Jesus, desire you to see yourself as a pillar of purple fire moving through the earth as a crystal cylinder that cannot be violated or penetrated--all inside the tube of light. I desire you to have a very physical awareness of this color, to recall it to the mind's eye. . . .

The physical body corresponds to the violet flame. The violet flame, in all of its qualifications and beauty, delivers to you the means to implement your service and provides in your hand a mighty gift for healing through transmutation. (Camelot, Los Angeles, California, Pearls of Wisdom, vol. 27, no. 52, pp. 459, 460)

The "Violet-Purple-Pink" decree on the SAVE THE WORLD WITH VIOLET FLAME! tape will help you to implement Jesus' visualization and alchemy.

God of Gold, September 3, 1984

[Inasmuch] as you have a momentum on violet flame, you therefore must declare your will for the channeling of that violet flame [into the earth body], for it is God's gift to you--not alone of the transmutation of karma and of forgiveness, but of alchemy. (Washington, D.C.)

Cyclopea and Virginia, June 3, 1984

[Personal and planetary] past history can be changed, can be transmuted! And therefore, in the process of harvesting those works that have been unfruitful and unacceptable before the altar of the Most High God, there is the opportunity [through the violet flame] to re-create in God. . . .

Hear me and understand, children of the Sun, such a mighty opportunity [is yours] that whilst yet in the Matter spheres there can be the correction, the going back, the transmutation of regret and sorrow and forgetfulness and sins of omission[--all this by the violet flame, the Seventh Ray aspect of the Holy Spirit]!

The violet fire, the power of the Seventh Ray, is upon you because you have entered Aquarius as this dispensation [of universal transmutation] that comes not often in thousands of years of evolution. The hierarchies of Aquarius. . . are standing galaxy by galaxy to transmit to you and through Helios [who, with Vesta, serves as the 'Sun-God' of this solar system] to you this momentum of mercy, of transmutation, of forgiveness, of the divine ritual of the atoms and planets and spheres so that the rotation and the spin of thy life and of thy solar system may be brought into alignment and that which ought never to have been may be cast into the sacred fire of the very Central Sun of this system of worlds. (Heart of the Inner Retreat, Royal Teton Ranch, Montana)

Mother Mary, December 9, 1984

Those come newly to the fount drink joyously and freely and feel cleansed by the waters of Life. When you come to the deeper troubles of the heart and the subconscious, these are not as easy. Therefore, let the violet flame saturate and drench and soften and clear away those subconscious blocks to the flow of the mighty River of Life within you. . . .

I can assure you that the change on earth by a cosmic alchemy, were tens of thousands to give the violet flame daily, would be so phenomenal not only would you wonder where the problems went but you would forget that you ever had any problems. (Minneapolis, Minnesota, Pearls of Wisdom, vol. 27, no. 63, p. 578, 581)

Jesus Christ, April 11, 1982

Take the gift of my own beloved Joseph, whom you know as Saint Germain, and recognize that the Holy Spirit will cleanse of all sin and balance all karma by that violet flame! And it is the fulfillment of the promise of miracles and healings by the Holy Spirit! (Camelot, Los Angeles, California, Pearls of Wisdom, vol. 25, no. 27, p. 277)

Saint Germain, February 10, 1985

We do not allow such things as the mere indoctrination of a lifetime to deter us from making the heart-to-heart contact with the violet flame bearers who long ago went forth with you from Zadkiel's retreat, also bearing the flame-flower of the Seventh Ray--the only hope for the nations, the only hope for the soul of Aquarius. . . .

The real issue is to become the living Christ! The real issue is to raise up the violet flame within the living temple of each one! And by the increase of Light on the planet, the entire geopolitical configuration of the world will change. . . .

Let the Woman take the leaven of the Christ consciousness and hide it in the earth, in the very hearts of God's people, and let it leaven the whole world consciousness to Freedom. . . . And the violet flame shall have so transmuted the entire momentum of world totalitarian movements that they shall scarcely remember that there was a period in history when the whole world was threatened by the fallen angels who came in many disguises East and West to tear the people from their God. . . .

The conversion of the nations is by the violet flame, by the action of the science of the spoken Word, by the message of the heart of Freedom that unites all lightbearers throughout the world who rise up in one mighty voice and demand the action of their governments to overturn that which is the injustice of the ages. . . .

If we desire in the name of Arcturus and Zadkiel to have a physical action of the sacred fire and a physical presence of the violet flame and a physical healing of a physical earth, then we must have a physical Messenger and we must have you as physical messengers of the Light of your Christhood, meaning that the Light of your Christhood must penetrate through your very pores and through your very bodies and through your very hearts [until by violet flame transmutation the world will see the Light of your Higher Self shining through]. (Camelot, Los Angeles, California, <u>Pearls of Wisdom,</u> vol. 28, no. 12, pp. 133, 136–37, 142)

<u>Elizabeth Clare Prophet, from Saint Germain On Prophecy</u>

Can anything or anyone come between a people and this handwriting on the wall?

Is there an intercessor who can turn the tide of Darkness and invoke the oncoming tide of Light to devour the karma of abuses of the abundant Life charted in the stars and the quatrains and in the collective unconscious of a nation?

Must this prophesied economic debacle followed by war and the nuclear nightmares come to pass?

Yes, Yes, and No.

There is a power of God that can be summoned by you from your Mighty I AM Presence. The Universal Christ in and through and around you is able to turn back personal and planetary karma and to consume it by the sacred fire-- if you are willing to be one-pointed in giving daily dynamic decrees to the violet flame. (Fifteen minutes is good and basic, 30 is great, 45 is terrific and one hour of violet flame decrees daily is stupendous!)

This Seventh Ray ritual is the foundation for the Eighth Ray Solution to the ailing economies of the nations through the eight-petaled chakra, the secret chamber of the heart. The decrees at the end of this chapter recommended by Saint Germain (given with "Ten for Transmutation," favorite violet flame decrees found in our book <u>The Science of the Spoken Word</u>), when buttressed by Archangel Michael's Rosary for Armageddon, comprise a ritual of the Eighth Ray.

When followed up with community action applying the teachings of Saint Germain, this exercise of the power of the Word will avail much in the solving of the problems of the capitalistic/communistic economies outlined by Saint Germain as well as by Nostradamus.

Archangel Michael's Rosary was dictated to me by the Defender of the Faith who identified himself to Joshua as the Captain of the LORD's Hosts. It is a ritual of prayers, psalms, invocations and dynamic decrees to the angels, the Divine Mother and the Son of God for the deliverance of God's people and the turning back of Evil.

So, the answer to the third question and the Third Horseman is that it is Saint Germain, Lord of the Seventh Ray

and Hierarch of the Aquarian Age, who can and does intercede in the economies of the nations in answer to your call.

He with his beloved Portia has the authority to act,
but the Law says we must exercise the science of the spoken
Word, hour by hour, which compels the intercession of the
Lord's hosts, the entire Spirit of the Great White Brotherhood,
on behalf of every Lightbearer on earth and all who will
receive them, repenting of their vile violations of the abundant Life and returning to the Law of the One.

No, economic debacle, war and the nuclear nightmare
do not have to come to pass.

Nostradamus' prophecies, the scriptural and Fátima
warnings as well, are given that we may act in time to meet
them with the all-consuming fire of God and the command to
the Seven Archangels to deliver God's people in this time of
trouble.

Divine Intervention is the key to undoing the untoward
prophecy that is but a mathematical equation of karma which
tells us what will happen if we the people do nothing. (Saint
Germain On Prophecy, Book Two, Chapter 8, "Saint Germain's
8th Ray Solution to the Economy," pp. 79–81)

The macrobiotic diet is a balancing, healing diet that
prepares us for survival in a nuclear age and provides a way
to reverse the biological and spiritual degeneration of mankind. The foods that we should eat are the foods that are
strong building blocks for a healthy body. These are found in
the macrobiotic diet.

The dietary discipline of macrobiotics was traditionally
used in former golden ages. It primarily consists of whole
grains. In the East, brown rice was called "the gift of the gods."
Other grains, such as buckwheat, millet, barley, wheat, oats,
rye and corn, have also been used as staple foods throughout
the ages.

Whole grains are high in complex carbohydrates, iron,
B vitamins, calcium, zinc, trace minerals and fiber. These elements are useful in guarding against the absorption of radioactive substances. Grains are also a good source of protein
and are low in sodium and fat.

In addition to whole grains, the main foods that are recommended in the macrobiotic diet are fresh local vegetables,
beans and bean products, white deep-sea fish (especially for

transition from a red-meat diet to a macrobiotic diet), seeds, sea vegetables, seasonal local fruits and several fermented foods like miso and tamari.

How much of each type of food you eat should be adjusted according to your personal needs, age, conditions in the body, the climate, season, etc. For restoring and maintaining health, 30 to 60 percent of our daily food intake should be grains and 30 to 50 percent should consist of vegetables, including a variety of leafy green, round and root vegetables.

Fresh vegetables, like grains, are a good source of fiber. Fiber promotes the growth of beneficial bacteria in the intestines and helps digestion. These bacteria synthesize the B vitamins and prevent harmful microorganisms from multiplying and producing toxins and carcinogens (cancer-causing agents). The sulfur-containing amino acids that are found in vegetables bind with toxins, enabling the body to discharge them. Vegetables also build the blood, the thymus and the immune system, and their many nutrients fortify the body against the absorption of radioactive elements.

When vegetables are not organic, they should be put in cold, salted water for at least a half hour to pull out the chemicals and pesticides as much as possible. Boiling the vegetables in lightly salted water helps to preserve their natural minerals. (It is important to use sea salt.)

Minerals that are necessary to prevent the body's absorption of radioactive elements, such as calcium, iron, iodine and potassium, are found abundantly in sea vegetables. Kombu, arame, dulse, wakame, hiziki and nori especially provide these minerals. They also remove radioactive particles that have already settled deep within the organs. The optimum intake of sea vegetables is one to three tablespoons daily.

Beans are a concentrated source of vitamins, minerals and protein. They also contain several properties that inhibit cancer and protect against radiation. Aduki beans, lentils and chick-peas are among the most balanced and strengthening beans and best for regular use. Tempeh is a fermented soybean product that strengthens the nervous system and the immune system, helps build red blood cells, and blocks the intake of radioactive cobalt-60 and zinc-65. About 10 to 15 percent of the food we eat should be beans or other protein products.

Miso is a paste made from soybeans and sea salt, often mixed with rice, barley or other grains. Naturally existing bacteria cause the mixture to ferment and produce enzymes that help digestion. The binding agent zybicolin in miso is effective in detoxifying and eliminating elements that are taken into the body through industrial pollution, radioactivity and artificial chemicals in the soil and food system.

Miso soup (see recipe) contains all the amino acids considered essential by modern nutritionists. It stimulates the secretion of digestive fluids in the stomach, restores the intestinal flora, aids in the digestion and assimilation of other foods in the intestines, and is a good vegetable-quality source of B vitamins (especially B_{12}), calcium and iron. Miso soup also strengthens the quality of the blood and lymph and detoxifies the body of the harmful effects of excessive animal food, sugar and other extreme substances.

Through the process of fermentation, the sea salt in the miso does not have the same qualities as table salt nor its harmful effects. However, the amount of miso used should not exceed 2 teaspoons per person per day.

Miso Soup
Ingredients
approx. 1/3 cup wakame seaweed (after soaked)
4–5 cups of water
one half–1 tsp. miso per cup of water
(generally 3-year-old unpasteurized barley miso is recommended for daily use)

1) Rinse the wakame quickly under cold running water and soak it approximately 10 mins. Cut it into 1-inch pieces.

2) Bring the water to a boil in a saucepan and add the seaweed; simmer for about 10–15 mins. until the wakame is tender.

3) Take 1/2 cup of hot water from the soup and dilute the miso in it.

4) Turn the flame <u>very low</u> and add the diluted miso.

5) Simmer the soup on a low flame for 1–2 more mins. (it will look like "clouds" are gently moving upward in the broth). BE CAREFUL NOT TO BOIL THE MISO, which will destroy its beneficial enzymes.

6) You can add vegetables (especially finely chopped greens, such as parsley or watercress), tofu, seitan (also known as gluten), fish, tempeh, and noodles to the soup.

Extreme care should be taken when serving children miso soup or any other foods to which salt is added. Children under ten months should not have miso soup. For children ten months to seven years old, the miso soup should be diluted. Children ten months to one year should only have one to two teaspoons of diluted miso soup daily.

Pressure-Cooked Brown Rice

Ingredients

> 2 cups short grain brown rice
> 3–4 cups purified water
> 1/8–1/4 tsp. sea salt (it is best to use Muramoto sea salt)

1) Put 2 cups short grain brown rice in a stainless-steel pressure cooker.

2) Wash the rice by adding approximately 4 cups of water. Stir gently with your hand in a clockwise or counter-clockwise direction. Pour the water out using a strainer. Repeat 3 times.

3) Add 3–4 cups of purified water for boiling. The amount of water you use depends on how moist or dry you want the rice to become.

4) Put the pressure cooker with its contents on a high flame and bring to a boil without the lid.

5) When the rice boils, remove the foam that has come to the surface; it may contain dirt or chemicals.

6) Add 1/8–1/4 tsp. of sea salt and cover the pressure cooker.

7) Continue to cook the rice, using a high flame, until the pressure is high enough.

8) Boil the rice for 50 mins. on a low flame. You may need to put a flame diffuser under the pot to prevent burning.

9) Remove the rice from the stove. It's best not to take the lid off right away. The pressure will be gone in about 15 mins. If you are in a hurry, you can put the pot under cold running water.

10) Take the lid off the pot and gently stir the rice with a wooden spoon.

Pressure-cooking the rice gives it more strength and makes it easier to digest.

Morning Cereal

Pressure-cooked rice can be used to make morning cereal. You can make a creamy rice cereal by boiling 1/2 cup of quick oats in 3 cups of water for 20 mins. Then add approximately 3–4 cups of pressure-cooked brown rice and boil on a low flame for another 10–15 mins.

This cereal and miso soup (with vegetables, seitan, etc., if desired) is a good macrobiotic breakfast and is also a good equivalent for a fast.

When the food is chewed 50–200 times per mouthful, it becomes totally liquefied before it is swallowed and is therefore well prepared for the body to absorb. Thoroughly mixed with your alkalizing saliva, it heals and balances the body while you refrain from other foods. Traditionally in the East, rice and miso soup have been used as the main foods for healing.

Pearls of Wisdom®
published by The Summit Lighthouse

| Vol. 31 No. 32 | Beloved Archangel Gabriel | June 26, 1988 |

Saint Germain Stumps Portugal

1

The Betrayal of the People of the World
Soviets Prepare to Strike Europe and the United States

Hail to Thee, O Light of the Virgin Mary!
I AM Gabriel which stand in the Presence of the Mother of God.

I am in the fullness of joy upon the occasion of the celebration of the ascension of one son of God, and by this event, beloved, you may know that your hour is also come when you verify and establish the proof of the living God where I AM THAT I AM within you. Therefore, beloved, what one soul of Light has done, each and every son of Light may also do.

Hasten, then, to the heart of the Blessed Mother, for she shall lead thee in the path of eternal Life in the footsteps of her Son Jesus. Therefore, beloved, hear my call, for the hour is far spent when some who have come to this altar of the I AM Presence will know the benediction of their God:

"This is my beloved Son, in whom I AM well pleased."[1]

Therefore, I say unto the sons and daughters of Light, Hail! Greetings from the throne of glory and the living Presence of our Father! As I have spoken two days ago in the heart of San Diego, so now I speak here before you, beloved, for there is also an arcing from that city that does carry the Light of the Divine Mother to this city which does also carry her Light.

Thus, we desire to knit together the hemispheres and the nations but the fallen angels in embodiment in the earth would make this very difficult for us, even for an Archangel. For they have pitted themselves against the Light—your Light—the Light of the living Christos within you.

Beloved ones, the karma of a planet has caused a densification of the senses of the people, and the souls are not alert to their ministering angels. Therefore, I send my Messenger before my face[2] that you might hear the words of my heart and also know the voice that may tremble the physical octave and move the ethers and move the very waters under the seas.

Thus, beloved, we the Archangels do stand for the people of our God[3] in this earth. We have called this weekend [conclave] and called the tribes of the nations to come hither from the nations of Europe, and therefore each and every one of you is an ambassador of Light of the nation of your birth and [of] the ancient tribe of Israel from which one and all [of] you have descended.

Thus, we have called you, not to a cinema in the downtown of Lisbon, but to the etheric retreat of Raphael and Mother Mary [that is] not only over Fátima but that stretches in a vast area over this nation.

Beloved hearts, come with me now, for I draw you into the etheric octave in the great amphitheater of that inner retreat* of the Great White Brotherhood. Know, then, [that] you are seated with five thousand and more who have gathered from all nations of the earth for this conclave of ascended and unascended beings of Light. Know, then, beloved, that some of you see in this amphitheater those souls who are your twin flames, brothers and sisters of old with whom you have served the Light.

Therefore the call is gone forth and we have come—we have come in the name of Saint Germain. For Saint Germain has indeed been denied by the Lords of Karma and the Cosmic Council any further dispensation to intercede on behalf of Europe but only for the individual Lightbearer; and this is in consonance with the proclamation of Alpha rendered Wesak last by Gautama Buddha, our beloved Son and your Brother.[4]

Blessed ones, hear me, then! For our God has sent me to address you and to open this conclave. Wherefore I bring to you the report of the karma that is descending upon this continent for the blindness of the people and their following their blind leaders.

Blessed ones, it is karma that does blind the individuals and the nations. Therefore, I say to *you*, one and all who hear me, that it is necessary for you to make your statement to the leaders of your respective nations [in order] that you make your voice count and make an enlightened statement as to that which is transpiring on the planet in this hour.

Therefore, I read to you from the Book of Akasha and I, Archangel Gabriel, assure you that that which I read is true; and

*the etheric retreat of Archangel Raphael and Mother Mary

therefore, think not that one iota of my message is colored by any human consciousness, not the least of which that of my Messenger.

Hear me, then, beloved people. Hear me, then! For it is upon my word that you will understand and know what has not been stated to you.

Therefore, what concerns an Archangel of the Fourth Ray, beloved, is the defense of the Divine Woman and her seed upon earth. I AM Gabriel of the white light of the Divine Mother and of the soul within you. Recognize my Presence here and know that I come solely for your protection and to lead you unto eternal Life.

Therefore, hear the Truth and know the facts: that while negotiations take place between Washington and Moscow, there is a betrayal of the people of the whole world. And whose betrayal is greater, beloved? That of the representative of Moscow who does use therefore furtive diplomacy to gain his ends, who has not Truth in his heart or on his lips, or is it the one in Washington who knows this and has the evidence and will turn a deaf ear to all presentations of the realities of the politics being played by Moscow?

I AM an Archangel and I AM here to tell you, even as I address the heads of state of all European nations as I address the people of God in every nation upon earth: Your fate is being decided in this hour and the greatest betrayer of all is the representative from Washington who has convinced the heads of state of this continent to surrender their last and remaining deterrence to nuclear and conventional war upon this soil!

And whose voice is the sane one we hear?—that of Margaret Thatcher and a few others, but none have dared to challenge to the last this infamy, beloved, that is taking place.

I tell you, in this very hour, *in this very hour,* and I repeat it, the plans move forward with speed on the part of the Soviets for the installation of radar units and ABMs in multiple numbers, a vast assembly line prepared and moving forward; and this is also revealed by the intelligence of the United States Air Force,[5] and yet there is still compromise!

I tell you, beloved, the Truth that I speak can save your life and if you heed me not, you will one day hear my words again. Therefore, listen unto me in this hour.

The movement is accelerated on the part of the Soviets to move against Europe and to take the United States as well by a first-strike attack. This is what is on the drawing board and this is the only reason negotiations are continuing. I tell you the step-up is enormous! And in these days that are passing, in these very hours your lives are being betrayed by fallen angels in power.

242 Vol. 31 No. 32

And what do we read? That high percentages of the people of Europe now trust this individual from Moscow. I tell you, beloved, Saint Germain, who is in our chambers this evening at Fátima, does tell you from his heart that this same individual is the prince that did enter that golden-age civilization fifty thousand years ago as he, the Lord of the Seventh Ray and the Knight Commander, did [then] prophesy.[6]

And therefore, beloved ones, though it was announced to all the people in the whole land and broadcast as a dictation from the being to whom you have sung, Mighty Victory, yet the people by their own karma and density allowed this one to take them over. And that golden-age civilization went down and its evolutions have reincarnated to the present hour, many in the United States; but there are also those who have reincarnated in Europe.

And therefore we come full circle, whether those of Light shall accelerate enough to enter into a higher consciousness and heed the word of the Archangels or whether they will suffer the same fate.

Blessed ones, the acceleration is at hand and El Morya has declared it and it has not changed: Unless the United States change her course and defend the peace of the world, you will see an encounter as early as twenty-four months from October last.[7] Blessed hearts, these are the facts and these are the realities. Wherefore we say, get thee into the high mountain of God, for this is the fulfillment of the prophecy of Fátima!

And if you do not believe the Archangel or his Messenger in this hour, then heed the word of the Blessed Virgin who has warned you not only in Fátima but [also] in Medjugorje of the "Great War" impending at the end of the twentieth century.[8] That time is at hand, beloved, and therefore the hour is far spent that you should allow your leaders to manipulate you. And therefore let your letters, let your telegrams and let your statements be heard, for [it is written in the Book of Life:] "By thy word thou shalt be justified and by thy word thou shalt be condemned."[9]

It is lawful for a people to make their statements of protest to their leaders. It is lawful for a people to expose the Truth. It is lawful for a people to invoke the Archangels for the binding of the fallen ones who have been the oppressors of my people for tens of thousands of years.

Blessed ones, this is the last time you will hear me speak through this Messenger on this continent, and therefore let this message be heard and let it be known and let your hearts now fear the Almighty but not fear the Fallen One. Let your hearts now increase in Light* and know that God has provided a way of escape and a haven of safety.

But you must recognize it and you must realize that if and when the Senate of the United States does ratify that treaty,[10] as they have been rushed to do, so there will be the opening of the way for the Soviet to make war as soon as all of his radar installations have therefore been put together. Beloved ones, it is in fact a netting together of these vast systems with those newly produced that can be completed in a year or less.

Blessed ones, the hour is far spent! I, Gabriel, say unto you, it is a time for the calling of the [LORD's] Judgment[11] upon those who have planned the massive chemical/biological warfare upon this continent. Let it be known, beloved, that those who would escape must escape, for those who will be left will not be able to raise the right hand and turn back what has descended.

And I will tell you why the LORD will not intercede. The LORD will not intercede for the karma of a people who have gone the way of lust and selfishness and the pleasure cult—for a people who have not challenged their leaders, for a people who have believed the Lie and now rush to enter into trade agreements and the control of Europe by the Soviet. Blessed hearts, it is a stampede of those blinded by their karma, I tell you, and therefore only their returning karma shall awaken them.

Would to God that they should have heeded Fátima and all turned to be converted to the Blessed Mother and have given their prayers since the very inception of the Bolshevik Revolution![12] And I charge you, beloved ones, the popes who have not revealed the third secret have indeed betrayed the people![13]

And if they have not done so, as some have said, because it would encourage the Communist coups, I tell you this is false logic, and it is the logic of the Divine Mother that they ought to have heeded. For a people, had they known what was coming upon them, had it been told to them many decades ago, should have risen up in defense of their nations and of their personhood. But without knowledge and without a vision the people perish!

Why do you think the Blessed Mother came? It is because the people required this vision and, as you know, not unto this hour has any pope called upon so revealed that third secret of Fátima; and this is why Mother Mary appeared again at Medjugorje to the children. But this time those secrets could not be revealed on time [for the nations to act] for the very karma of the Church itself in not delivering her first messages [and of the people's neglect of their God] and, alas, therefore the warning

*in the Light and Consciousness of the Holy Christ Flame

shall come only three days before the events take place.

Beloved ones, Saint Germain has called his own. Let them heed and not delay!

I AM Gabriel and I speak to your very hearts! I say to you it is an hour to pray and to pray profoundly as you have been taught by these Messengers. For these are the most effective, dynamic and powerful prayers that you will find on the face of the earth, and they have been given because the Messengers have not denied us.

They have not kept from you any of the Teachings but given all that was given to them; and therefore the fount has never ceased to flow. And therefore, going forth in foreign nations with a message that is unpopular, fearlessly, you can understand that wheresoever we do send our Messengers they do speak the Word without compromise, without concern for their personal popularity.

We know this is an unpopular message! When has the Light and the Truth ever been popular amongst the masses [or their oppressors]? When have those who have never been able to face the accountability of personal and planetary karma ever been willing to hear the prophet in the land? When have they ever welcomed the Divine Mother in embodiment? I tell you, beloved, they do not desire to encounter a living Guru because they may have to surrender some of their human nonsense, some of their illusions, and some of their dabbling in the lesser and black arts.

Blessed hearts, I come with a fire and I come with an intensity and I come because I desire to strip you of your illusions! Yet I am obedient to the Law of the One. I am an Archangel and I bow to the free will of the servants of God upon earth, and therefore I will not touch a hair of your head unless by free will you desire in this hour and throughout this weekend to be stripped of those illusions and stripped, then, of those scales that are upon your eyes that do not allow you to see and to know what is preparing against you.

Beloved hearts, no greater betrayer has ever walked the nation than Ronald Reagan himself, [inasmuch] as he has known in his heart exactly what these Communists are preparing, and he has known it for years. Therefore I say, he has abdicated his responsibilities, and his mantle has been taken from him months ago[14] and he no longer walks holding the mantle of Saint Germain.

I tell you, this is come upon a people and a people of Light in America who should have stood stalwart in defense of a leadership who should truly defend Europe no matter what is the ingratitude of the nations of Europe; and I tell you there is ingratitude, and therefore let us call a spade a spade!

How will you be defended if you do not allow your bases to

be used, then, by the United States? I speak to you, Spain and
Portugal, and I say, let the Goddess of Liberty walk this land and
rekindle in your hearts the threefold flame of intense gratitude
and let those burdens [the karma of spiritual blindness that
accrues from spiritual selfishness] fall from you and realize that
the one who said, "I came not to send peace, but a sword,"[15] lives
today and lives to defeat the forces of Evil that assail you.

And therefore the sword is the two-edged sword dividing the
way of Truth and Error and of the Tree of Life.[16] Therefore,
beloved, that Sword of Peace is able to keep the peace because it is
extended, and thus this is the meaning of the sword. A sword that is
in defense of freedom is lawful and that sword need not harm any.

I tell you, a nation such as the Soviet Union that has violated
its ABM Treaty and established nine large radar stations around
its borders and is increasing [its ABM capability] every day and is
now putting up massive ABM and radar systems connected with
it [the radar network]—beloved ones, there is no reason to do this
unless you expect to launch a first strike and have to [i.e., must be
prepared to] receive a retaliatory strike. I can tell you, beloved
ones, as I know the hearts of a people, there is not a shred of
intention on the part of anyone in the United States to launch any
strikes against this planet; and therefore, those who prepare to
war, go to war!

This is Europe, who has known the drenching of soil with
blood, lo, hundreds of years! This is Europe, who has known the
preparations of a Hitler that were watched and observed and yet
no one believed that war was coming.

Blessed hearts, these preparations are massive and unless
those of you who understand the meaning of the strategy of Light
and Darkness prepare, there will be no time to prepare.

Blessed ones, I tell you that these Soviets have misused the
science of Nikola Tesla[17] and they are actively using ELF waves[18]
and others, such as microwaves, not only to destroy life but to
sabotage the space program of the United States, not only to do
this but to act against individuals who will raise their voice and
their cry against these fallen ones.

Therefore, do not underestimate this massive conspiracy
against your governments and nations, including rays so powerful
as to lull the people themselves to sleep. Therefore, they have demonstrated sufficiently to themselves that they are capable of putting
rockets and planes out of commission by this misuse of the ancient
technology of Atlantis brought to modern man through Nikola
Tesla and yet perverted again by the black magicians in the USSR.

Blessed ones, the West refuses to see it, refuses to tell her people about it! And all seek personality and the god of money and the god of lust. I tell you, the betrayers of yourselves are there! And let them know that I AM an Archangel and that I have spoken this hour and I have come, then, to pierce their illusion across this entire continent in the hope that a people will awaken and a people will rally!

And therefore I have sent the Messenger for this quickening action; and those who have come from all nations and gathered, let them gather together in a prayer vigil specifically for the turning back of the nefarious plot against these nations.

Blessed ones, I tell you, the time is short!

I, Gabriel, am the Angel of the Annunciation and my annunciation to you in this hour is that as the age of Aquarius dawns it is the birth of the Universal Christ within every heart of Light upon earth; and I tell you that birth of the Cosmic Christ in your hearts nation by nation is for the quickening of a planet unto the golden age of Aquarius, and this is what is foretold in the annals of the Great White Brotherhood.

And I tell you that the false hierarchies of the sinister force and the fallen angels and the aliens who abet the cause of world totalitarian movements, they know the timetable of the birth of the Christ even as Herod knew the timetable of the birth of Jesus, and he would not stop in the slaying of one child! He had his henchmen slay all the male babies and yet he could not deny the life of the living Son of God.[19]

I tell you, beloved, they know. The fallen ones know that if they do not act in time, the whole world will come into that God consciousness. And you will see a violet flame planet appear and an acceleration and you will see transmutation and world changes and the people walking with their I AM Presence and knowing God face to face!

This is what could come upon a planet if this force of war be turned back; and if it be not turned back, beloved, then you will see an age of darkness and the Dark Night of the Spirit and you will see that come to pass which is prophesied in Revelation[20] and in Fátima and in Medjugorje of mass starvation and death as Death will stalk the earth through plague and through war.

O beloved ones, it is an hour to be on your knees daily, to set all other activities aside except those which are essential for the maintenance of your life. Blessed ones, it is essential to pray daily by the hour for Almighty God to intercede that this terrible plot of darkness happen not. You may call, therefore, for the [LORD's]

Judgment upon the entire International Capitalist/Communist Conspiracy—of those superpowers and those in them who have aided and abetted one another's cause and plotted together at inner levels truly the destruction of nations as they exist today.

And when you hear fully the teachings of the signs written in the heavens that are called astrology, as I have given them to the Messenger to bring to you, so you will understand just how clear is the import, how clear is the prognostication of these events.[21]

Let it be told, beloved. Let it be heard! For if the voice be not spoken in this hour and you do not hear me, then I tell you it will be the ultimate betrayal of Mother Mary who came in 1917 and yet whose message has not been sung, has not been told, has not been spoken!

Do you wonder, therefore, why we raise up our sister of Light who has walked among you for embodiment after embodiment? Do you wonder why we have raised her up? It is to vindicate the Blessed Mother herself, whose voice has not been heard. It is that you might hear directly from us in this hour by the Holy Spirit that which the Divine Mother has desired to say to you, lo, these many decades.

Beloved ones, in the heart of the living Christ and in the heart of the Divine Mother, I seal you.

I AM Gabriel which stand in the Presence of the Divine Mother and her Manchild! I AM Gabriel who say unto you, I have spoken, I have transferred to you a fire! My angels will not leave you as long as you call to them daily. The seraphim of God will not leave you, but you must be found in the holy mountain of God in defense of the Cosmic Spirit of Freedom, for there must be those of Light of Aquarius who do not go down under this bloodshed that is prophesied.

Therefore, I say unto the people of Light upon earth, *you are* destined to survive cataclysm and war on this planet, but you must awake to the divine calling of Saint Germain and make haste! Therefore, I seal you in the cosmic cross of white fire. I seal you in the Immaculate Heart of Mary! I AM THAT I AM Gabriel, angel of the Lord, servant of the Light within his own.

"The Summit Lighthouse Sheds Its Radiance O'er All the World to Manifest as Pearls of Wisdom." This dictation by **Archangel Gabriel** was **delivered** upon the occasion of the fifteenth anniversary of the ascension of the Messenger Mark L. Prophet on February 26, 1973, by the Messenger Elizabeth Clare Prophet on **Friday, February 26, 1988,** at the Cine Alvalade, **Lisbon, Portugal,** where she was stumping for Saint Germain's Coming Revolution in Higher Consciousness. **N.B.** Bracketed material denotes words unspoken yet implied by the Archangel, added by the Messenger under his direction for clarity in the published text. **(1) My Beloved Son.** Matt. 3:13–17; 17:1–5; Mark 1:9–11; Luke 3:21, 22; II Pet. 1:15–18. **(2) My Messenger.** Matt. 11:10; Mark 1:2; Luke 7:27; Mal. 3:1. **(3) Archangel Michael stands for the people.** Dan. 12:1. **(4) Dispensations confined to the Lightbearers.** See Saint Germain, June 21, 1987, "A Door That Shall Open..." and Gautama Buddha, May 13, 1987, "For the Alignment of a World— 'A Proclamation' by Alpha," 1987 *Pearls of Wisdom,* vol. 30, nos. 25, 24, pp. 251–56, 243–49. **(5) Soviet breakout of the ABM Treaty.** The Anti-Ballistic Missile (ABM) Treaty signed by the United States and the Soviet Union in 1972 prohibits either nation from deploying more than 100 missiles that could intercept incoming warheads— i.e., ABMs. Restrictions also were placed on the production, deployment and use of radars. The treaty was meant to enhance superpower stability by keeping each nation vulnerable to the attacking missiles of the other. Under the logic of the strategic doctrine of Mutual Assured Destruction (MAD), if both the U.S. and the USSR remained defenseless, peace would be maintained since it would be suicidal for either side to attack the other. But if one side had a ballistic missile defense and the other did not, under certain circumstances the side which was defended might launch a first strike or use its unilateral advantage to blackmail the other.

According to reports in the media, Air Force Intelligence recently concluded that the Soviet Union is in the process of mass-producing ABMs and radars and could have a nationwide ballistic missile defense system in operation as early as 1989. The Air Force reportedly made a formal intelligence finding of the breakout after U.S. signals intelligence observed the Soviets exchanging data between six of their ten large phased-array radars and after the Air Force Intelligence Service concluded that the Soviets' SH-08 very-high atmosphere ballistic missile interceptor and the supporting mobile "Flat Twin" and "Pawn Shop" radars are now in mass production.

These conclusions, leaked to the press late in February of 1988, caused a great deal of controversy. Air Force Secretary Edward Aldridge said the reports were "just flat wrong," although he acknowledged that the Soviets had been working on an ABM system for years. "They've got a massive program. But there is no evidence that would support the allegation that they're prepared to break out of the ABM Treaty," he said. One reason Aldridge may have said that the breakout story was just flat wrong is that it appeared in the press with inaccuracies. It was reportedly based on a briefing given to the CIA by chief of Air Force Intelligence, Maj. Gen. Schuyler Bissell. Later reports said that Bissell was merely giving a hypothetical scenario of what Soviet activities would be if they decided to break out. Other sources in the intelligence community do not regard the assertions as hypothetical. They say the individual components of the story are accurate although the framework in which they were reported was not.

It is difficult to determine whether or not the Soviets are currently mass-producing ABMs. One source in the intelligence community says that if they were, the U.S. would know, but "probably not immediately." One piece of evidence is that they have recently doubled the floor space at their Gomel plant, which produces ABM components. Since they already have 100 ABMs in place around Moscow, it is reasonable to conclude that the increased production capacity is associated with a breakout.

Joseph Douglass, Jr., a former official with the Department of Defense Advanced Research Projects Agency, says the Soviets have been breaking out of the ABM Treaty gradually for years. "It is wrong to think in terms of a breakout," he says, "because that suggests that there will be a specific time when all of a sudden the Soviets will have a missile defense capability. Things are rarely black and white. The Soviets have been violating the ABM Treaty since the day it was signed. There is no indication that they ever had any intention of doing anything other than violating the treaty and continuing to work on their defensive capability. So it's not a breakout like all of a sudden they are going to 'spring out.' It is the continuing evolution of [an anti-ballistic missile] system that goes on independent of any treaty."

Commenting on Secretary Aldridge's denial of a Soviet breakout, Frank J. Gaffney, Jr., former deputy assistant secretary of defense for International Security Policy, said that "it is certainly the party line here in Washington that at most there are some worrisome developments but it doesn't amount to a breakout. But this is unfortunately a grey area and a lot of what we see and know is going on is entirely consistent with a breakout. . . . I have concluded that they are actively breaking out based upon the evidence that's available to me."

(6) **Visiting prince takes over ancient golden-age civilization.** More than fifty thousand years ago, Saint Germain was the ruler of a thriving golden-age civilization located in a fertile country where the Sahara Desert now is. When its people became more interested in the pleasures of the senses than in the larger creative plan of the Great God Self, a cosmic council instructed the ruler to withdraw from his empire; henceforth their karma would be their Guru. The king held a great banquet for his councillors and public servants during which a Cosmic Master, identifying himself solely by the word *Victory* upon his brow, addressed the assembly. In his message broadcast from the banquet room throughout the realm he warned the people of the crisis they had brought upon themselves by their faithlessness and rebuked them in their neglect of their Great God Source. The Master prophesied that the empire would come under the rule of a visiting prince and that the people's recognition, all too late, of their nonalignment with their God Reality would be of no avail. The king and his family withdrew seven days later to the golden-etheric-city counterpart of the civilization; the prince arrived the next day. Assessing the condition of the empire, he subtly planned to become its ruler and took over without opposition. See Mark L. Prophet and Elizabeth Clare Prophet, *Lords of the Seven Rays: Mirror of Consciousness,* Book One, pp. 239–42; Godfre Ray King, *Unveiled Mysteries* (Chicago: Saint Germain Press, 1934), pp. 39–61.

(7) **A confrontation between the superpowers in twenty-four months.** In his dictation delivered in New York City, October 2, 1987, El Morya warned: "Ere twenty-four months have passed, be it known to you that this nation must have the capacity to turn back any and all missiles, warheads incoming whether by intent or by accident. Where there is no defense you invite the bear into your own haven. . . . Ere twenty-four months pass, beloved, there shall be a reckoning and a confrontation unless something is done." See 1987 *Pearls of Wisdom,* vol. 30, no. 54, pp. 474, 480. (8) **The "Great War."** See 1988 *Pearls of Wisdom,* vol. 31, nos. 14, 15, pp. 137 n. 2, 142 n. 1. (9) **Thy words.** Matt. 12:37. (10) On December 8, 1987, Ronald Reagan and Mikhail Gorbachev signed the **INF (Intermediate-Range Nuclear Forces) Treaty,** which if ratified by the United States Senate would require the U.S. and USSR to eliminate all ground-launched missiles with ranges between 300 and 3,400 miles. (11) **The Judgment Call.** See 1988 *Pearls of Wisdom,* vol. 31, no. 23, p. 202. (12) **Mary's warning at Fátima.** Between May 13 and October 13, 1917, during World War I and the fomenting of the Bolshevik Revolution, the Blessed Mother appeared six times to three shepherd children near Fátima, Portugal. She warned that men must amend their lives, ask for pardon for their sins, and give the rosary daily to obtain world peace. On July 13, 1917, Mother Mary delivered a three-part message that was revealed in part to the world in 1941 when Lucia, one of the three children, wrote her third memoir. Lucia said that Mother Mary had warned the children of the spread of Communism and outlined her plan to bring peace to the world and prevent war through the practice of Communion of reparation on First Saturdays, worldwide devotion to her Immaculate Heart, and the consecration of Russia to her Immaculate Heart (which was never carried out by any pope exactly as the Blessed Mother had directed). (13) The third part of the July 13, 1917 message delivered by Mother Mary at Fátima, known as the **third secret,** was written down in the form of a letter by Lucia in late 1943 or early 1944. It was placed in a sealed

envelope and stored in the archives of the Bishop of Leiria-Fátima and later transferred to the Vatican, to be opened and read to the world in 1960 or after Lucia's death, whichever happened first. In 1960 Pope John XXIII read the secret, as have other ecclesiastical authorities and popes since, but the Church has never publicly released its contents. See Mark L. Prophet and Elizabeth Clare Prophet, *The Lost Teachings of Jesus II*, pp. 553–55 n. 132. **(14)** On November 8, 1987, Elizabeth Clare Prophet delivered Saint Germain's message "When the Enemy Speaks Peace..." *I Am Sent by the Prophet Samuel for the* LORD's *Judgment,* a prophecy detailing Ronald Reagan's abdication of his responsibilities as president of the United States of America and his failure to carry out the promises he made to the American people and pronouncing the LORD's judgment and withdrawal of his mantle. **(15) Peace and a sword.** Matt. 10:34. **(16) Two-edged sword.** Heb. 4:12; Gen. 3:23, 24. **(17) Nikola Tesla** (1856–1943), American inventor (born in Austria-Hungary), revolutionized electrical science by developing the alternating current electrical system; invented wireless radio and power transmission systems, the Tesla coil and various generators and transformers; discovered terrestrial stationary waves, proving that the earth could be used as a conductor and would be responsive to electrical vibrations of a certain pitch; created man-made lightning. The technology of Nikola Tesla is applicable to the modification of behavior, health and weather, to national defense and to geological exploration. Tesla offered his discoveries to the United States government for military purposes, but the War Department declined to use them. When Tesla died, his papers and laboratory notes were inherited by a nephew in Yugoslavia and later placed in the Nikola Tesla Museum in Belgrade, Yugoslavia. It was there that the Soviets reportedly obtained Tesla's records and began to develop his theories. **(18) ELF waves:** extremely low frequency radio waves of the electromagnetic spectrum which range from 3 kilohertz to 3 hertz. The Soviets beam ELF waves in the 6- to 16-hertz range which are known to affect human health and behavior. **(19) Herod slays the male babies.** Matt. 2:1–18. **(20) The Four Horsemen.** Rev. 6:1–8. **(21)** For the Messenger's lectures on current and upcoming astrological configurations and the karmic challenges they portend, see 1988 *Pearls of Wisdom,* vol. 31, no. 29, p. 229 n. 3.

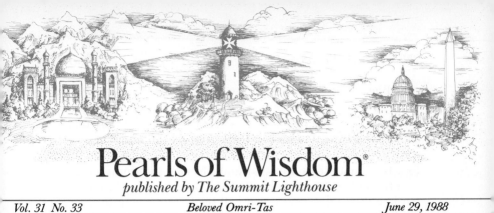

Pearls of Wisdom®
published by The Summit Lighthouse

| Vol. 31 No. 33 | Beloved Omri-Tas | June 29, 1988 |

Saint Germain Stumps Portugal
2
A Reservoir of Violet Flame over Europe
A New Vision and a New Quickening Must Come

From out of the causal body of the violet planet I, Omri-Tas, descend into this city. Greetings to all Aquarians. Greetings from my heart to your souls who have kept the vigil of violet flame, who have remembered Saint Germain, whose devotion is pure to the Blessed Mother and who have reincarnated on this soil in her name to raise up a violet flame in this hour.

Blessed is he that cometh in the name of the LORD, I AM THAT I AM. Blessed is he that cometh in the name of the LORD's Messenger.

I, Omri-Tas, therefore have come in this hour to deliver the LORD's dispensation of violet flame in the hour of the anniversary [of the ascension] of your beloved Messenger Mark Prophet.

Thus, in this hour of his ascension, beloved, know well that by the mantle of his causal body which you may claim, there is now a multiplication of our release of violet flame. And this violet flame is positioned as a reservoir of light over central Europe. It is a very large reservoir of light as a sea in itself; and this [light], beloved, is there for you to invoke as a direct transfusion to all Lightbearers of Europe, Eastern Europe and the entire Soviet bloc.

We send light, illumination and violet flame to all whose hearts burn in the love of God, and we desire that you shall continue to invoke this violet flame as you receive the *Save the World with Violet Flame!* cassettes[1] by Saint Germain released by your Mother that you might have again and again these words playing in your hearts and homes.

Blessed ones, when you invoke the violet flame, it will draw forth the light of this reservoir and also maximize it, fortify it, multiply it by your own love and devotion; and therefore that light shall flow to every Lightbearer in these lands. And as it does flow to them it shall quicken them, it shall cut them free, it shall therefore transmute their spiritual and physical blindness as to those events coming. And if you will also call to the Seven Archangels to cut free the Lightbearers, you will see a tremendous ground swell of the people of our God rising up in the vision of Archangel Gabriel, of Mother Mary and of the LORD God himself.

Blessed ones, this reservoir is a certain dispensation. If those Keepers of the Flame in embodiment do not make the violet flame call daily, then this reservoir will come to be used up in its entirety, apportioned then among all Lightbearers. But if the call continues to be given, the reservoir shall be like the unfed flame. It shall not fail. It shall remain full and all that goes out of it shall be returned unto it multiplied by your call.

Thus, beloved, it is the Lightbearers in embodiment who awaken to the violet flame that shall keep the momentum. And it is those who are quickened by their calls—who come into the knowledge of the dynamic decrees to the violet flame, of the action of the sacred fire that shall indeed extend to the Lightbearers of this continent an activity that is so desired [—who shall be saved].

Therefore, in the calling of the LORD and in the sign of Saint Germain, watch, then, for Portia's extension of your opportunity to keep the violet flame vigil upon this continent. Watch for her opportunity and call it forth, for Opportunity is the handmaid of the Lord of the Seventh Ray, is the divine counterpart and Cosmic Being. And therefore the Lords of Karma look with compassion upon the laborers in the vineyard who are few; and by this dispensation of violet flame, *which I must tell you shall come to an end unless it is re-fed,* there can be a quickening and a cutting free. Watch, then, for the time shall be given and made known to you.

I AM Omri-Tas and I stand in the joy of my Son Lanello as he does take his place at this platform in this hour. Blessed ones, millions of violet flame angels go solely to the Lightbearers, solely to those who have a threefold flame in their hearts and a devotion to the living God, the living Christ, the living Divine Mother, the living Buddha, the living Universal Light.

Thus, the ministry is specific unto those who may make the difference. It is a dispensation of the final hour of the twentieth century. It is made, beloved, out of mercy extended to those who have missed knowing the third secret of Fátima[2] and therefore been deprived of the opportunity to intercede, to turn back and overthrow the betrayers of the people East and West.

Therefore I, Omri-Tas, now occupy myself in extending consciousness throughout the very large territory in which the Lightbearers are to be cut free, and I now secure this continent and more with my legions of angels while your beloved Lanello does address you.

I therefore seal each brow with cloven tongues. Twin flames of violet flame seal the third eye. Let this be a sign unto the Lightbearers that with the violet flame transmutation of that third-eye chakra, a new vision and a new quickening must come.

But no dispensation becomes physical, beloved, unless the one who vows to keep the flame does invoke it daily. For the law of free will prevents the interference in this octave by heavenly hosts unless the call is made in each twenty-four-hour cycle. May you never conclude a twenty-four-hour day without a minimum of fifteen minutes of invocations and decrees to the violet flame, and out of the love of your heart for brothers and sisters untold, may you extend that time.

I tell you, beloved, as Mary said, penance is required for world sin, which is world karma, and that penance is the violet-flame power of transmutation. We desire to see a million Europeans calling forth the violet flame and then you will see whether Saint Germain shall be called again to this continent.

Blessed hearts, let us consider that with God all things are possible! Let the fervor, let the fire, let the intensity, let the hope, let the God-determination, let the zeal not be diminished!

Beloved, remember the blessed Igor, a saint ignorant* of the Great White Brotherhood and yet devout in the Divine Mother, who kept the flame for Mother Russia throughout the revolution of the Bolsheviks. Blessed ones, by his singular vigil, the solitude of his life in perpetual prayer, millions of lives were saved by that prayer force of his heart.[3]

Now, Keepers of the Flame, the all-power of God is unto you in your I AM Presence. The all-power of the Universal Christ is accessible to you in your Holy Christ Self. We say, then, persevere, for a light is kindled and it can become a universal conflagration of violet flame.

We have not sent our Messenger for naught, but to reinfuse you with a spark of Liberty that shall not die except ye let it go out. May you not be the self-extinguished ones but the self-ignited ones who have known the holy breath of Omri-Tas [the holy breath sounds],

---

*in his outer mind

received it and felt the fire of the Holy Ghost as the white-hot heat of fervor burning in the breast.

I AM Omri-Tas—Omri-Tas, Ruler of the Violet Planet, so near to you yet so far vibrationally. O earth, that thou mayest become Freedom's Star is yet our hope, our prayer, our imploring to those Lightbearers of the world who hold the key to the seventh age.

Let them unite, O God!

To you we say, you who are one in heart and voice:

Lightbearers of the world, unite in the name of Saint Germain!

"The Summit Lighthouse Sheds Its Radiance O'er All the World to Manifest as Pearls of Wisdom." This dictation by **Omri-Tas** was **delivered** upon the occasion of the fifteenth anniversary of the ascension of the Messenger Mark L. Prophet on February 26, 1973, by the Messenger Elizabeth Clare Prophet on **Friday, February 26, 1988,** at the Cine Alvalade, **Lisbon, Portugal,** where she was stumping for Saint Germain's Coming Revolution in Higher Consciousness. **N.B.** Bracketed material denotes words unspoken yet implied by Omri-Tas, added by the Messenger under his direction for clarity in the published text. (1) See *Save the World with Violet Flame! by Saint Germain,* released by Elizabeth Clare Prophet, booklet and 92-min. audiocassette of violet flame decrees and songs for the healing of planet earth, performed by 800 voices, full musical accompaniment, B88019, $5.95 (add $.55 for postage). (2) **The third secret.** See 1988 *Pearls of Wisdom,* vol. 31, no. 32, pp. 249–50 n. 13. (3) **Igor's vigil for Mother Russia.** In a dictation given March 25, 1967, the Ascended Master Igor said that as a child growing up in Russia he saw his countrymen as "a vast evolution which seeks for liberty and yet creates bondage" and he prayed to God to help him understand this world "peopled with dark shapes and distortions." He received many visitations from Archangel Gabriel, who comforted him and promised, "I will guide thee throughout thy life and I will be to thee a friend. . . . Thou shalt no longer be just as a peasant boy called Igor, but thou shalt be a son of the Most High God; for in thee God has generated a flame this day. . . . God is no respecter of men's persons but in every age and time listens to the heart calls of the children of men. Know, then, that God hath heard thy call." When Igor became aware of the coming destruction of the czar and his family and realized that the "red dragon" would march across Russia, he spent hours in prayer imploring God to provide some measure of assistance. One evening "the beautiful Lady of Fátima" appeared to Igor and spoke of the terror of the red dragon. She said that only by a great struggle would mankind be able to turn back the oncoming darkness. Igor implored her assistance and offered his life if it would save his people. Then Mother Mary explained to him the karmic law; she said that the people by their misuse of free will had wrought this destruction and that only by seeking the things of the Spirit would they make the world free. As Igor recounts, "I accepted her love and her wisdom and my heart was comforted, but the terror burned on. Throughout my life as I sought to be a pilgrim in a strange country, I aspired to attain something higher that I might free men. By and by, through the solemn ritual of the sacred mantra of my devotion toward God and through my one-pointedness, it came to pass that I was finally made ready for the moment of my ascension." See the Unknown Master (Igor), "The Drama of One Life Touched by God," in *Mary the Mother on the Temple of Understanding* (1972 *Pearls of Wisdom,* vol. 15, no. 53), pp. 217–18. For other dictations by the Ascended Master Igor, see December 31, 1972, "The Forces of the Lord Shall Descend: Special Dispensations for the People of Russia and China," 1972 *Pearls of Wisdom,* pp. 215–16; and April 2, 1983, "The Miracle of the Holy Ghost," 1983 *Pearls of Wisdom,* vol. 26, no. 34, pp. 319–24.

Pearls of Wisdom®
published by The Summit Lighthouse

| Vol. 31 No. 34 | Beloved Lanello | July 2, 1988 |

Saint Germain Stumps Portugal
3
The Bodhisattva Vow
The Messengers Give Their Christhood to a World
The Retreat of Fátima Anchored in the Western Shamballa
Ascension Day Address, Fifteenth Anniversary 1988

My Beloved Sons and Daughters,

In preparing room and making way for my Beloved, so you have prepared a place for me also, that where you are I may also be. And in this oneness in the physical octave and in Fátima's [etheric] retreat of the Archangel Raphael and Mary of the Fifth Ray, we are one.

The purpose of this weekend is for the acceleration of Light* in you and sensitivity and vision and awareness. Therefore, in this hour of the victory of my union with God I can assure you, beloved, that it is the hour when again through my Beloved I lay down my life. I did lay it down then† for America, to give opportunity for a people to awaken to defend the Spirit of Cosmic Freedom worldwide. In this hour I may give my Christhood to a world and I have chosen to do it here at the altar of Fátima where we are gathered one and all at inner levels.

Know, then, beloved, that it is the hour for me, as it is for my embodied twin flame, of the Fifteenth Rosary. And that rosary, beloved, is the extension of one's Christhood to all the world that a world might have it and receive it and again have opportunity.[1]

As we have made this bodhisattva vow together in your behalf and in behalf of all Lightbearers of this earth, so we are one with you and desire to make this announcement at the court

*the Christ consciousness †February 26, 1973

of Fátima before our most beloved Mary, our Divine Mother, our blessed Cosmic Virgin, without whom we should not have been delivered from the toils of our karma nor transcended the trials and temptations of life.

Blessed ones, it is a joy to know that the Body of one's Christhood may be given to all and that in this very process there is the holding of a flame, a kindling of a flame. And we may look into the most wondrous eyes of Mary and see her profound love, and for a moment her tears dry as we give ourselves to those precious souls of her heart whom she does succor. For out of her heart there is concern for many that they may be lost in this age.

Thus, it is our prayer to the ancient ones, Cosmic Beings of Light, that they may be saved by the Saviouress, by the living Christ and by these two* in the hearts of many Buddhas, bodhisattvas and Christed ones, saints of God, East and West.

O blessed hearts, many angels out of the Himalayas have come to this continent and they are standing guard by the Lightbearers to assist them as they receive portion by portion the violet flame that it might be for the illumination of consciousness, a sudden awareness and the receiving of our beloved Saint Joseph's violet flame angels which he gave to every Keeper of the Flame in November 1986, that they might be present as angels of the Seventh Ray to give the warning to those who will heed and listen, to those who in quietude and prayer fifteen minutes before retiring at night will pray and listen and call to God for daily divine direction.[2]

Blessed hearts, fear not! I, Lanello, come before you with a flaming sword of my victory to cast out fear and anxiety and all darkness. Be not paralyzed by a prophecy of an Archangel who loves you but be galvanized into action, fiery zeal, as with Zarathustra and his legions the fiery ones put to the torch all plans and plots of war and East/West conspiracies!

Our God is a consuming fire[3] and his fire lives in you, and that spiritual fire is able to devour all darkness in the earth when only a people shall invoke it and shall invoke it into the night and the day hour by hour!

Blessed hearts, we are one in all octaves. And in this moment as you are able and as you have received myriad angels, you are caught up into a vibration that is beyond your own physical self, approaching the level of your own Holy Christ Self. And thus, as the Messenger with you does abide in the heavenly realms while delivering this dictation physically, so know, beloved, that thy life is also hid with Christ in God.[4]

---

*i.e., saved by the twain—the Saviouress and the living Christ—*as they come in the hearts of....*

My mantle be upon those who claim it in this hour. My mantle be unto those who will walk with me in the footsteps of our Lord and Saviour Jesus Christ. My mantle be upon those who will use it to divide the waters of the Jordan, to cleave asunder the Real from the Unreal, to rescue the nations.

In the name of Mother Mary, our message to you is this: Save that which is lost of the children of Light. Go after them to cut them free. Tutor the true shepherds and ministering servants. Make the blinded eye to see by the violet flame—the blinded third eye that no longer has the inner vision, neither of his destiny nor of the plotters that move against that destiny.

I AM in the living Presence of Ascension's Flame. And in this hour our twin flames kneel before the altar of Fátima's retreat and thus we rededicate our lives and mission, as Above so below, to the rescue of the servants of God in the earth. May you kneel also in this hour, beloved, for it is a moment when you may also give your Christhood unto a planet. [Congregation kneels]

How ready is the heart of the true pilgrim to kneel before the Blessed Virgin and Raphael—Saint Raphael, Archangel. How profoundly moved are the angels who attend you now—my angels of the ascension and those of the healing ray. And healing you shall know, beloved, of the burden of the heart and of the burden of the age. Let it be, then, that you may pray aloud, unconcerned about your neighbor, that the angels may take your calls to that altar in this moment. [Congregation offers prayers aloud]

Therefore, beloved, Mary and Raphael extend their hands to you in this fashion* and the emerald light does radiate from all of their chakras and from their hands to you. It is a restoration of the wholeness of the soul, which may become a reality to you as you prepare the physical chalice according to the disciplines of diet that have been given to you by the Mother and that you may learn and pursue in this city of light.[5]

Therefore, rise, beloved. [Congregation rises] In the dominion of your Christhood, stand now. Receive thy portion, O people of God, for the portion that is due thee for thy love and thy service measure for measure is meted out into thy heart and each one is filled with his own good works multiplied by the twin flames of Raphael and Mary.

Know, then, beloved, that thy reward is with thee now and shall be with thee in heaven. Therefore, thou art not so concerned for thyself but for those who may or could be lost. Therefore, let us pray the rosary of our Blessed Mother and give it daily.[6]

I am Lanello, your father, your brother, and sometimes I am

*Messenger's hands are outstretched

your son or child. I am one so very much like you, who loves you and loves you. I have been with you in the beginning and I shall be with you in the ending, for in my heart the living Christ does also declare, I AM Alpha and Omega.

Now, beloved, as is customary on my ascension day, I bid you claim my mantle that it might fall upon you as a swaddling garment of light, protection. Thus, beloved, you may shout in the fervor of the Holy Spirit in this hour,

I claim the mantle of Lanello in God's name!
[Congregation affirms with Lanello:]
I claim the mantle of Lanello in God's name!

Therefore, how neatly angel servants of God place this mantle upon your shoulders that you might remember me in all of my guises and embodiments.

I remind you of the Call—the ancient call of my soul to defend Camelot.[7] Thus, beloved, in a sense Camelot is the whole world, and in another it is a jewel across the sea, an Isle of Avalon where Morya returns. Now the future king who was once in England's land has found that island green in the heart of the Western Shamballa.[8] Thus, to a new world, to a new world this Aquarian of the First Ray does sail.[9] Thus the eagles gather, and where the eagles gather so shall the Body of Christ be.[10]

Let the eagles fly. Let the eagles fly! For the way is known. The sign was given to Martha by Jesus long ago. Let it be known that this is more than a physical place of safety but an etheric retreat of the Divine Mother[11] and the Buddha, an etheric passage-way to realms of Light and Victory.

Thus, out of the mighty Yellowstone and from deep within the earth do the healing waters of the Divine Mother flow, and therefore the Call of the arc of the Western Shamballa is the anchoring there of the retreat of Fátima. Thus, this is the true Call we make in this hour, that Fátima, our Fátima—as the place where Mary does speak and is heard and [is] not denied by Church or State—*that Fátima* be reborn [in the Heart of the Inner Retreat] even as Camelot is called again [to be built at the Royal Teton Ranch].

I AM the Call of Camelot and the Call of Camelot is the Call unto the soul!

Come forth, O soul! Know the way and the Homeward Way. Come forth, O soul, for the sign of the cross of white fire is the sign of the dove and the forever Mystery School which we fondly, with a tear, remember as that special place where, one and all, we knew the path of individual Christhood.

On this my ascension day with my Beloved, I AM, we are, One in the hearts of the Lightbearers of earth, there to save, to remind, to adjure and cajole, to bring into consonance with the grace, *the listening grace and the hearing ear* of the blessed Mary.

Thus, the wings of Raphael flutter, and their fluttering, beloved, does now bring you back to the physical and to that state where you may take your bodies to rest and pray the angels of Archangel Michael take you to the etheric retreat of Fátima this night. May you return, then, on the morrow to hear the translation of these dictations, for we desire your souls at inner levels to continue this communion [this night, out of the body at the etheric retreat of Raphael and Mary rather than remain here in the physical plane for the translation].

In the name of the Father, in the name of the Mother, in the name of the Son and the Holy Spirit, we are One in the cosmic cross of white fire unto the victory of Light in the hearts of the Christed ones.

"The Summit Lighthouse Sheds Its Radiance O'er All the World to Manifest as Pearls of Wisdom." This dictation by **Lanello** was **delivered** upon the occasion of the fifteenth anniversary of the ascension of the Messenger Mark L. Prophet on February 26, 1973, by the Messenger Elizabeth Clare Prophet on **Friday, February 26, 1988,** at the Cine Alvalade, **Lisbon, Portugal,** where she was stumping for Saint Germain's Coming Revolution in Higher Consciousness. **N.B.** Bracketed material denotes words unspoken yet implied by Lanello, added by the Messenger under his direction for clarity in the published text. **(1) The Fifteenth Rosary.** In her dictation "The Gift of a Mother's Heart: The Mystery of the Fifteenth Rosary," given March 19, 1980, at the conclusion of Summit University Winter Quarter, Mother Mary said that "the Fourteenth Rosary and all of the rosaries preceding it are preparatory initiations for the putting into the flame of the unbalanced karma, the misqualified energies of life, the unwanted substances, and all that is unreal. These rosaries are sacred keys to the initiations of Christhood whereby you, very presently and with haste, may balance fifty-one percent of your karma and remain in life the presence, lo, the living presence of your own blessed Christ Self. . . . The mystery of the Fifteenth Rosary is the mystery of the surrender of that Christ that you become. It is not an automatic surrender, for some disciples may fulfill the fourteen stations and become that Christ and yet desire to possess that Christ, to be that Christ, to enjoy that Christhood and with it to yet pursue some of the private paths which indeed may increase attainment but may not increase the path of Christhood for others. Thus you see that when all other surrenders are in the valleys behind you and you stand on the mount of that transfiguration and you stand in the glory of Easter morn, you recognize that from the mount of transfiguration unto the mount of the Holy of Holies of the Resurrected Self there is a unique path to be walked. It is the surrender of that Christhood that you have attained." See Mother Mary, 1980 *Pearls of Wisdom,* vol. 23, no. 27, pp. 165–69; Mother Mary, April 17, 1981, "The Offering of the Rose of Sharon: The Hour of the Mother's Crucifixion with Maitreya Attended by the Avatars Lord Jesus and Lord Gautama," 1981 *Pearls of Wisdom,* vol. 24, no. 17, pp. 203–8; and Elizabeth Clare

Prophet, "The Mutuality of Self-Transcendence in Mercy's Flame," *Kuan Yin Opens the Door to the Golden Age,* Book One (1982 *Pearls of Wisdom,* vol. 25), pp. *40–43.* **(2) Saint Germain's angels will warn and direct you.** See 1988 *Pearls of Wisdom,* vol. 31, no. 20, p. 166 n. 4. **(3) God a consuming fire.** Deut. 4:24; 9:3; Heb. 12:29. **(4)** Col. 3:3. **(5)** During the 1988 New Year's Retreat at the Royal Teton Ranch, the Messenger lectured on the **macrobiotic diet,** including how human behavior and physical and mental health relate to the condition of the body's organs and what foods are beneficial to the health of the organs. The diet was given by Sanat Kumara to the Lightbearers and, among others, to Lord Lanto when he was embodied as the Yellow Emperor (c.2704 B.C.). The principles of macrobiotics are based on *The Yellow Emperor's Classic of Internal Medicine* (the *Nei Ching*), the oldest known book of Chinese medicine. See Elizabeth Clare Prophet, January 3 and 4, 1988, 3 audiocassettes, 3½ hr., B88010–12, $19.50 (add $.95 for postage). **(6) The rosary.** See 1988 *Pearls of Wisdom,* vol. 31, no. 15, p. 142 n. 4. **(7)** The Ascended Master Lanello was embodied as **Launcelot du Lac,** one of the knights of the Round Table. **(8) Arthur, the "once and future king."** El Morya was embodied as Arthur, King of the Britons and Guru of the mystery school at Camelot. According to Arthurian legends, after King Arthur was mortally wounded at Camlann by his bastard son (or nephew), Mordred, he was placed on a barge with three queens which drifted toward Avalon, an "island valley," where, as Alfred Lord Tennyson wrote in *Idylls of the King,* "falls not hail, or rain, or any snow, nor ever wind blows loudly; but it lies deep-meadow'd, happy, fair with orchard lawns and bowery hollows crown'd with summer sea." Some accounts say that Arthur would be healed of his "grievous wound" at Avalon and would return to rule over his people. Sir Thomas Malory, who gathered together and chronicled the legends of Arthur in his fifteenth-century classic *Le Morte d'Arthur,* writes: "Yet some men say in many parts of England that King Arthur is not dead, but had by the will of Our Lord Jesu into another place; and men say that he shall come again, and he shall win the holy cross. I will not say that it shall be so, but rather I will say, here in this world he changed his life. But many men say that there is written upon his tomb this verse: *Hic iacet Arthurus, rex quondam rexque futurus* [Here lies Arthur, the once and future king]." The Heart of the Inner Retreat is as "Avalon" where chelas of El Morya retreat in summer to be healed of the blows of karmic adversity affecting body, mind and soul. And the Master himself takes refuge in this **Western Shamballa** — Gautama Buddha's etheric/physical retreat in the West, an extension of his retreat over the Gobi Desert, which is centered over "the Heart" of this island valley. See 1981 *Pearls of Wisdom,* vol. 24, pp. 226, 227. **(9)** As Sir Thomas More, lord chancellor of England, El Morya's fiery spirit descended into form when the sun shone in the sign of Aquarius, February 6, 1478. **(10) Eagles gather.** Matt. 24:28; Luke 17:37. **(11) The Retreat of the Divine Mother.** On December 15, 1985, Sanat Kumara announced, "The opening of the door of the temple of the Divine Mother and her Inner Retreat is also come. And this Inner Retreat, positioned now as a vast center of Light, is indeed above that 'Place Prepared' — prepared, of course, by the Divine Mother — the entire area of the Royal Teton Ranch." See Sanat Kumara, "The Retreat of the Divine Mother at the Royal Teton Ranch," 1986 *Pearls of Wisdom,* vol. 29, no. 10, pp. 70–72.

Pearls of Wisdom®
published by The Summit Lighthouse

| Vol. 31 No. 35 | Beloved Archangel Raphael | July 3, 1988 |

Saint Germain Stumps Portugal

4

The Fulfillment of an Ancient Promise
Take a Stand for Truth!

Hail, O Light of the Immanuel. Lo, I AM come for the fulfillment of an ancient promise. And though the outer self make it difficult for the inner soul to receive me, yet I enter in, for the soul does long for my coming. And I AM Raphael, Archangel of God of the Fifth Ray, consort of the Blessed Virgin. One are we in the sacred fire of God.

Therefore, I, Raphael, fulfilling the promise to come unto you in your hour of greatest need for healing, for wholeness, present myself to you with the intensity of the God Flame of the Fifth Ray, the brilliant emerald green light that surely is a purging light that healeth all thy diseases.

Those who may see by an inner sight raised up will note that I have placed my hands over this Messenger's hands and I am releasing through her chakras in this hour the healing light, and therefore I am carving out new channels of her being for healing[1] and I am releasing that light to the earth for the healing of the psyche of nations. For nations are beset by a national consciousness that does prevail, a characteristic burden of karma, attitude, and profile of a people. So entrenched are these limitations, beloved, that scarcely can the Universal Christ appear.

In this day and hour, then, know that my legions move throughout the earth with angels of the Blessed Mother, and our angels together are seeking those who will take a stand for Truth, pay any price, go anywhere, be in any field or calling so long as they can stand for Truth.

Blessed hearts, to those of you and us who are revolutionaries of Truth returning in every age to reconsecrate life to the inner alignment with Being so set forth by Gautama Buddha, by Jesus Christ and other incarnations of God, I say that it is curious indeed to observe those who know the Truth and yet do not allow its flame to burst forth from within, who do not allow the quickening, who do not allow their souls to speak and to rise up and to be that Light unto the nations.

Thus, what is their fear? What is their fear, beloved? Will not Truth lead you into all places of light and victory and of Love's own healing? Will not Truth be thy companion and guide and a true friend who shall never betray you for the living Truth?

Blessed hearts of living fire, those who espouse Truth and commit their lives to that Truth and do so unequivocally, those individuals, beloved, are rare in the planet and they are indeed the true devotees of my beloved Mary. Know, then, that the true knowledge of Truth is found in those who *are* the living Truth. Those who *become* the Truth, therefore, surely understand that Truth is the foundation of the threefold flame of holy Christhood.

Truth, then, is the crying need of the hour! Therefore, understand why our bands go up and down the land. Truth is denied and therefore the force of anti-Truth in the earth has raised up, by way of challenging absolute Truth, that which is known to us as the Big Lie. It is the all-encompassing lie, East and West, of the denial of the individuality of the God Flame, whether in totalitarian movements, whether in the economies of the nations or in an education[al system] that is without a spiritual fire.

Truth, then, is born out of the Logos, out of the divine Word and logic itself. Truth is the geometry of Being, and the geometry of your Divinity is indeed *God;* and therefore, if you are not comfortable with the word *God* or with the concept of Deity, just remember that the pinnacle of your being is the *geometry of Divinity.*

Therefore, this *G-o-d* is like a geode, for this is a rock, beloved, which when cleaved does reveal crystalline substance which is, in truth, Nature's way of reminding you that in the heart and in the womb of the Cosmic Virgin there is an interlining of violet flame and crystal light; and all the [crystal] substances in the earth are a reminder that some who have walked the path of Truth are indeed its embodiment universally.

Truth is a pathway to the ascension espoused by the beloved Saint Paul, and that path, beloved, known and fulfilled does bring one to the place of becoming the embodiment of the flame of living Truth.

Is it not, then, altogether fitting that we should bestow this flame upon our Messenger? Blessed hearts, her dedication to Truth has presented you with the sacred mysteries and the very fountain-head of the Lost Teachings. By the Truth already set forth you have the keys to your ascension. Blessed ones, all of that ascension is now in the doing and in the becoming and in the realizing.

Truth, then, is a holy allegiance and it is a holy alliance. Let all those who stand for Truth, then, in science, in religion and in government, in the very path of the soul's union with God, know that we of the Fifth Ray open our retreat at Fátima for the receiving of all those of courage who have become outcasts in their own families and hometowns because they have taken a stand for Truth, for the divine art, for the divine music and for a new age of freedom, peace and enlightenment.

All, then, who have gone out of the established modes of their fields of endeavor, finding therein hypocrisy and compromise, all who have begun to doubt even the very existence of Almighty God, those who call themselves agnostics but, in truth, doubt not God but doubt all who have misrepresented him, let them know that we together, twin flames, Archangels of the Fifth Ray, do present to the world the opening of the doors of our temple as the first opening in general of a retreat of the Archangels to those [who have passed] beyond [the levels of] the mystery schools [of the Lords of the Seven Rays].

Blessed ones, the earth is suffering from a profound deception placed upon all of humanity by the fallen angels who have been cast out of heaven into the earth and yet reincarnate on this planet in physical bodies for having denied the Universal Christ in your twin flames, in your own heart flame and that of your Beloved with whom you were created by Elohim in the heart of the Great Central Sun.

Thus, the twin flames who have gone forth from the Divine Whole have been subjected to the lies of these fallen ones, and though they may not have entirely accepted those lies, it is the coloring of the stream of consciousness, as you call it, the mass consciousness of humanity, that has warped the entire evolutionary stream of this planet and dyed it and colored it outside of the crystal-clear colors of the chakras of the seven rays.

Blessed hearts, the non-Truth, the error, the deliberate lie and malice perpetrated against the children of God in the earth is truly the root cause for their loss of memory of the divine Truth and Doctrine of the living Christ, the Saviour.

Know, then, that we have taken a very active presence and we are no longer on the defensive for Truth, but the armies of the Lord and of the Faithful and True are on the offensive, wielding the mighty sword of Truth that does indeed cleave asunder the Real from the Unreal.²

Beloved of the Light, let there be a living Word within you that does understand that now is the hour to espouse that Truth and to understand that he taught that the Truth shall make you free. But the only Truth that can free you, beloved, is the Truth that you know.

Therefore, when you hear the statement "And ye shall *know* the Truth, and the Truth shall make you free,"³ [*know*] that [that] knowledge of Truth *is self-knowledge* and this is a part of the inner teaching, the inner mysteries given to the disciples, that has come down to you as Gnosticism.

Self-knowledge was the rule and the order of the day set forth by Jesus Christ. Understand that therefore self-knowledge in Truth is the *Self*-knowledge of the inner Christ, the inner Light and the Universal One. It is the *Self*-knowledge of the I AM THAT I AM.

I tell you, beloved, to have one glimpse of the face of your I AM Presence is worth all of the giving and the devotedness and the self-discipline on the path of universal discipleship unto the individuality of the God Flame. I tell you, beloved, for all of the dalliance and all of the preoccupations with entertainment and television, if you would put this time into acknowledging and giving calls and decrees to your I AM Presence, you would see the face of the Beloved and in seeing that face you could no longer live as a mortal man!

For in you would be planted, then, the memory of your divine seed and of your immortality and you would know it by a fierce presence of the sacred fire pulsating, by an expression of ultimate love, and you would see the face in whose divine image you were made. Therefore, one glimpse of the I AM Presence is sufficient for a lifetime and many lifetimes.

I tell you, this is the desire that should be pure desire in your being: to know God face to face and to talk with him as Moses did talk with him as a man unto a man.⁴ For we the Archangels do embody the Presence of God and the fullness of that Presence on our individual rays. Therefore, when we come to you, beloved, we come in the flaming presence of the I AM THAT I AM!

I AM an Archangel and where I AM there is the Spirit of the Lord! And where the Spirit of the Lord is, there is Liberty⁵ *because there is Truth*. And the Truth is revealed by the Universal Light, for in the presence of that Universal Light, Darkness can no longer wear the mask of Truth and thus the real identity of the fallen ones is made crystal clear when you bask in the light of Truth.

And therefore, it is Mother Mary who is the Great Guru, the Great Initiator of the raising of the Light [of the Divine Mother] within you. For when that Light is raised up (as you have begun a simple exercise toward that end[6]), you will discover that that Light shall finally attain a permanent residence in the crown chakra and the third eye. And the third eye, therefore, is the ray of healing and the Fifth Ray; and that eye, therefore, when perfected does radiate the emerald fire and the healing ray. Thus, as your vision is, so shall your healing be and so shall your self-knowledge in Truth [be].

It is clear, therefore, that when a people no longer remember their devotion to the Divine Mother or [to] the raising up of the white light, they have no self-knowledge except that of the baser elements. They have no divine knowledge of themselves, they have no Christ Self-knowledge, and therefore they do not know the Truth. They have not become it. They have not self-realized it.

How, then, do you expect, beloved, a humanity who has gone astray from the path of the beautiful bliss of oneness with God to be saved by the Archangels when they have lost their sight and almost lost their souls for the absence of devotion to the divine spark?

And in some, beloved ones, that divine spark has been extinguished by their absolute denial of the absolute God within their being, and this has been done unto them by the fallen angels who have led them astray into byways of the not-self, of atheism and existentialism and a total nihilism ending in self-suicide even before that physical act is taken.

Thus, the danger of the suicide of the soul is the danger of the age and it is rooted in the absence of the knowledge of Truth and the self as the repository of Truth. Beloved, souls are committing suicide in this age, for they have desired not to be and not to exist in God, and therefore they pursue a course of self-destruction by all manner of perversion of the Light within them and of the life-force until it is entirely squandered and there is nothing left of the original endowment that was given to that soul when she first stepped forth from out the heart of God with her beloved twin flame in the beginning.

Therefore, remember the Great Central Sun and remember the Sun behind the sun. Therefore, remember that thy living God is living Truth. Therefore, remember also Pallas Athena, not a mythical goddess but a being of great light who has espoused Truth for tens of thousands of years upon this planet. Remember Vesta who now does keep the flame of Truth and of Love/Wisdom in the heart of the sun of this system of worlds with a twin flame, Helios.

Remember all who have gone before you on the path of Truth. For in this age it is the flame of Truth that must swallow up the darkness of that Great Lie that is told and the Great Lie begins with a temptation: "Thou shalt not surely die." So the fallen angels in the garden, the Mystery School, did tell that story to the woman.[7]

Realize, beloved, that *there is* the death of the soul and it is written in scripture in Revelation.[8] And therefore, it is also stated: "The soul that sinneth, it shall die."[9] And there does come a time, beloved, when the light of the soul is totally squandered, when the Light of God at the Court of the Sacred Fire does pass through that soul and does neutralize the identity. And therefore life returns to Life with no stamp of creativity or individuality upon it because that soul has never, not in all of earth's history, pursued a path for the individualization of the God Flame.

Know, then, beloved, that the Truth of eternal Life may be found by you *only* through your union with your own Christ Self, the Universal One. And that union is called the alchemical marriage; and that fusion of the soul unto the Eternal Christ, the Eternal Word, the Eternal Logos, is the moment and the hour when that soul does gain immortality.

What is the soul, then? It is the nonpermanent atom of being. It is that portion of self that has gone forth with a gift of free will, having so demanded it, and in that free will to choose to be or not to be in God.

Blessed ones, I am certain that you can think of any number of individuals within [the circle of] your acquaintance who have chosen to deny the Light, who have chosen to deny Love and Truth and live only unto themselves and unto the waste of the precious Life that God has given to them which flows to them heart to heart by the crystal cord day after day after day. Beloved ones, there does come a time, and the conclusion of ages is that time, as [it is] in this conclusion of the age of Pisces, when the soul, therefore, must give an accounting. And that accounting is due in this hour for all lifestreams upon this planetary body.

Know, then, beloved, that in this hour [it] is the hour to magnify the LORD as Mother Mary has taught you: "My soul doth magnify the LORD, and my spirit hath rejoiced in God my Saviour!"[10] Your soul is a mirror that can magnify infinitely the LORD your God [your Mighty I AM Presence] and thereby the LORD your God does descend suddenly into your temple[11] to live with you as your Teacher, as your Beloved, as your very own Real Self.

In the infinitude of this Light, beloved, therefore know [that] there is a path and [that] the path does indeed lead to the retreat of the apostle Paul, who is known as the Ascended Master Hilarion,[12] and [that] that retreat does tutor you and prepare you to come into our temple of the Archangels of the Fifth Ray. Thus, beloved, Truth always leads to healing.

Those among you who would be healers among men, know that you may apply to the heart of Mary and in so doing give her Child's Rosary daily. You may appeal to my own heart; and when you embody Truth, beloved, I tell you, healing shall flow through you, for healing is the power of Divine Wholeness and wholeness is the Whole-I-Spirit of the All-Seeing Eye of God manifest through your third eye.

And by that wholeness, beloved, by that completeness and oneness that you discover in the living flame of Truth, lo, the Alpha and the Omega, the plus and the minus polarity are One, and it is by that plus and minus, beloved, that living Truth is bestowed upon you once again.

Let there be a raising up of the Light therefore! For in each and every one of your seven spiritual centers, known as chakras, there is a light to be made whole, there is a light to be returned to that sacred center. Thus, the seven rays may flow from you, and preceding that, let the violet flame flow and flow and flow through your chakras for the fullness of that healing which is God's.

We come, then, to bestir you, and I trust my cohort Archangel Gabriel has impressed upon you the terrible urgency of the hour. I come to address you, then, on the need to prepare for any hour and any day for [the Great Initiator to initiate you unto] your own salvation, which is the elevation of the soul within you unto the living Christ.

And I tell you from the level of an Archangel there is no greater teaching in the earth in this day than the Teachings of the Ascended Masters that can swiftly take you on your course to your reunion with the eternal Light! And I tell you, it has been set forth fastidiously by our Messengers. It is a teaching, then, that will take you far on the path of God-realization. It will take you all the way to the victory of your ascension.

Therefore, I say to you, humble yourself before the living Guru who is Christ the Lord, who is my beloved Mary and recognize that *there are* Ascended Masters and that *you do need to submit yourself to the disciplines of those who have gone before you* and are Cosmic Lights in history and have an attainment that is so magnificent and so great, beloved, that before you have [reached the level wherein you have] seen your God you may see these Ascended Masters. Therefore, recognize that it is time you gave allegiance to and time you were

humble before those who have an attainment and have the great
wisdom to impart that attainment to you step by step!

Know this, then, beloved, that the false teaching has gone
forth upon this continent of the denial of the Teacher, the denial of
the Ascended Masters or any masters, the denial of the necessity
for any master, and therefore every man has become once again a
law unto himself as in the days when God sent the judges unto the
children of Israel.[13]

And therefore, when each one claims himself as his own master
but has no mastery whatsoever and does require the basic steps of
the violet flame, he does become too proud to bend the knee before
any [Christed one] and yet these same ones will take their courses
and will study in the universities of the world and yet they say they
need no path.

Blessed ones, I tell you truly, it is folly to deny those who have
gone before you in this age, for the Ascended Masters have tarried
[and are tarrying] with this age and with this earth for a certain
period only. These are those who have forsaken [their opportunity]
to go on in the cosmic service [in order] to tarry and tend those Lightbearers who remain on the planet and those children of the Sun.

And therefore as the cycles turn, know that the doors of the
universities of the Spirit which are open to you are open again for
the first hour in ten thousand years and when they have again
served their purpose they shall be sealed unless there is a greater
turning to the Light by those of the earth who have the Light.

And therefore it is an experimental hour, this entering of the
age of Aquarius, and by the response of the Lightbearers we shall
see what shall become of the ministrations of the hierarchies of
Light to a planet and a people.

And should this planet go down, beloved, in that "Great
War" that is prophesied by my own [beloved Mary], you may
understand that the Darkness that may come over the land will be
a Darkness of the people's separation from their Teachers, from
the heavenly hosts and from the Ascended Masters. When this
does occur, beloved ones, [if it occur,] the path of the ascension
will not be found or realized, for one does need a guide and an
example to be on that path of the ascension and to make it.

And for this cause came Jesus Christ into the world and yet the
true teachings on how to make one's ascension have not been set
forth; for two thousand years ago they were the inner mysteries. But
today in the dawn of Aquarius they are set forth. They are set forth,
beloved, that step by step you may climb the golden crystal spiral of
the inner ladder of Life back to the heart of your God Presence.

Thus, fear not to understand that the chain of Hierarchy is intact and that it is real. You need to understand that great Cosmic Beings are sponsoring you in this hour and you ought to call upon them in utmost gratitude that they are there and that they may show you the way and [that] they may assist you in clearing that spiritual pride that affirms that you need no Teacher! I tell you, there has never been an hour in the history of this planet when a people more needed their Cosmic Teachers!

Blessed hearts, let us decree together that Atlantis and Lemuria and their cataclysm shall not be revisited in this age because of this human infamy—both humanity's inhumanity to man and that which has been done to the denial and exclusion of the universal saints and our Brotherhood of Light.

Blessed ones, we may decree it but unless millions also decree it and turn around the downward trends in so many areas of civilization, as the Blessed Mother has said in Medjugorje, "The right hand of my Son shall descend and the judgment shall come."

Therefore, let it be known to you, beloved, that there is an hour for intercession and it is now! There is an hour for Truth and it is now! There is an hour for the flaming sword of Truth and it is now! May you seize it and see it and may those who have had this teaching the longest wax hot in a fiery zeal and know just how much you have received and therefore just how much you have to give.

A world is waiting for the message of universal Truth as a living flame within each heart. And by that flame, I tell you, you can light a world! You can be the spark that does become a conflagration of Truth! Let earth be bathed in the healing light this day as a complement to the violet flame you invoke. Let earth be bathed in a consciousness of Truth that shall immediately expose the consciousness of the Lie to all people.

I AM Raphael and I say to you that [in order] for this to be fulfilled [it] will take a mighty effort and a one-pointedness on the part of everyone who does hear me. For we come with our proposal, beloved, and yet others have gone before us with their proposals, whether to the students of the Ascended Masters or to the public, and somehow the karma of the age and the density of the human spirit has not allowed them to become activists for Truth.

I tell you, beloved, those who have labored in this field have labored hard and long for the victory of the hour. Let those, then, who have received the blessings from their Tree of Life know that this is the hour when every man's light can shine unto a planetary victory!

I cry to you at the end of an age! I cry to you, then, representing the Archangels and I say to you, beloved, our call goes

forth and we desire to see a return! And if there be a return forthcoming, we come again, and if there be not, beloved, I must tell
you that the Cosmic Council will ask us to withdraw.

Therefore, in the name of Saint Germain, in the name of his
courage to bring to Europe truly the union of the I AM THAT
I AM, we stand. And we stand in our love for him and in the love of
all servant-sons of God who have given their lives again and again
that Truth might live.

Blessed ones, there are those among you this day who have
stood for Truth lifetime after lifetime after lifetime, and I tell you,
our angels bow before the Light within you that is Christ. May all
who desire to enter into the league of the servants of Cosmic Truth
know that when you do so, you shall not escape the persecutors of
Truth in every age. What of them? Let them howl and whine. They
have their day and then they are no more. Truth lives on and those
who espouse her live on eternally with her.

May you be enfolded, then, with the garments of Pallas Athena
and know the Muses and know those who have sponsored Saint
Germain and know those who have sponsored you in many lifetimes.

Your devoted servant, I AM Raphael of the Fifth Ray!

I have poured out the fervor of my heart to you, beloved, that
you might know what is the zeal of those who serve this healing
light to a diseased and dying planet!

I AM THAT I AM in the heart of the flame, servant of God,
and the God is Truth!

"The Summit Lighthouse Sheds Its Radiance O'er All the World to Manifest as Pearls of Wisdom."
This dictation by **Archangel Raphael** was **delivered** by the Messenger Elizabeth Clare
Prophet on **Saturday, February 27, 1988,** at the Cine Alvalade, **Lisbon, Portugal.**
N.B. Bracketed material denotes words unspoken yet implied by the Archangel, added
by the Messenger under his direction for clarity in the published text. (1) This moment
commences for the Messenger a series of continuing initiations for the greater release of
the healing light of beloved Raphael and Mary through her hands. Therefore these
archangelic hierarchs of the Fifth Ray have requested she not shake hands in greeting but
bow to the Light, the Christ, of each one. Kindly assist her in keeping this observance by
not offering your hand but returning instead the same salutation, as it is said in the holy land
of India, *"Namaste"* (nah-muh-stā) [Hindi, from Skt. *namas* 'a bow']: a popular Hindu
greeting meaning "Salutation to the divinity within you"; gesture made by placing the
palms together, thumbs against the chest, and nodding the head slightly. (2) Heb. 4:12.
(3) John 8:32. (4) Exod. 33:7–11; Num. 12:7, 8; 14:13, 14; Deut. 5:4, 5; 34:10. (5) II Cor. 3:17.
(6) During the service preceding this dictation the Messenger led the congregation in
salutations to the Divine Mother East and West with bija mantras to the Hindu Feminine
Deities and the Hail Mary for the raising up of the Mother Light from the base-of-the-spine
chakra. She instructed them that Saint Germain is the sponsoring Master for the raising of
this Kundalini energy and that the recitation of the bija mantras must be preceded by the
Violet Fire, Tube of Light, and Forgiveness sections of the "Heart, Head and Hand
Decrees" and calls to Archangel Michael. (7) Gen. 3:1–7. (8) Rev. 2:11; 20:6, 11–15; 21:8.
(9) Ezek. 18:4, 20. (10) Luke 1:46, 47. (11) Mal. 3:1. (12) For teaching on and dictations by
the Ascended Master Hilarion, see *Lords of the Seven Rays,* Book One, pp. 183–216;
Book Two, pp. 169–210. (13) Judg. 2.

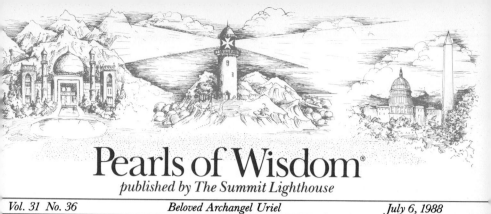

Pearls of Wisdom®
published by The Summit Lighthouse

Vol. 31 No. 36	Beloved Archangel Uriel	July 6, 1988

Saint Germain Stumps Portugal

5

The Hour for the Fulfillment of Your Christhood
The Betrayal of the People by Their Leaders

Ho! Legions of Light,

I AM Uriel in the infinite splendor of the Sun. I AM come, then, flaming Presence of the Sun behind the sun.

Ho! Legions of Light, sons of the Most High God, I quicken in you Divine Self-awareness by the power of resurrection's flame. I am also the angel of the avenging sword, the Angel of the LORD's Judgment.

Therefore, in the Holy of Holies of thy being, even thine own I AM Presence, thou art a Son of God. Be quickened, then, and make haste, for this is the individual Mount Zion. It is the place of the ascent of the soul, beloved.

Therefore, hear me, for the hour is late and the hour is far spent wherein souls of Light have opportunity to realize the fullness of the Light. Nevertheless, Divine Intercession is everywhere upon this planet in this hour.

Would to God that you could see. *Would to God that you could see, my beloved!* even the millions of angels of Light who come knocking on every door on this planet and every door of the heart. The majority of the people do not hear the knock, are not looking for Divine Intercession, and therefore do not receive the emissaries of God who come for the awakening.

I come in the name of the living Saviour Jesus Christ. I go before him, therefore, to clear the pathway for his coming. I also clear the way for the descent of the Holy Christ Self into each one's temple.

In the living flame of God, *know* the Elohim of Peace! Elohim Peace and Aloha, reveal thyself in this hour. Elohim of God of the Sixth Ray, expand the mighty presence of Peace throughout this continent! Let the flaming sword of Peace, then, divide the way of the Real and the Unreal and let Unreality be bound.

I come, then, as do all the Archangels, for the rescue of the Lightbearers in the name of the Cosmic Virgin, the beloved Mother Mary. Know, then, that inasmuch as we have knocked for ten thousand-times-ten thousand years upon the door of the hearts of humanity, we must turn and center our attention on those who carry the Light and have done so. Thus, it is an hour for their quickening and for their awakening, for even those of the Light have fallen asleep by the weight of Darkness on this planet earth.

Thus, beloved, it was to these Lightbearers that Mother Mary did speak here in Portugal at Fátima[1] and it is to give that message to the Lightbearers that she does speak again in Medjugorje[2] and does speak again and again through this Messenger. And as this Messenger does go to Fátima on the morrow, Monday and Tuesday, so you will understand that Mother Mary will address you through her.

Thus, it is the revisitation of Fátima for which this entire seminar is held. For inasmuch as the true mysteries of God and revelations have not been unveiled, as they were to be through the third secret[3] and through other messages of the Blessed Virgin through the ages, so the world must have a final opportunity not only to hear her words repeated by those who attend her visions but to know that there is a Messenger in the earth today who does receive, therefore, the dictations of this Blessed Mother of God for the edification of all [who are] of the Light and for the rebuke in Church and State of the betrayers of the Word of God.

Lo, I AM come, and I am come also as the Angel of the Judgment. For when you desire to raise up a flame of living Peace in the earth, you must be able to defend that Peace by the living sword of Peace. Thus, beloved, understand that wherever a son of God does raise up a living flame of Peace, the forces of anti-Peace gather.

Thus, in the age which should be the culmination of the age of Pisces in Universal Peace and in an age beginning in Aquarius that ought to be an age of Universal Freedom—thus Peace and Freedom won—you discover that the prophecy of Saint Germain is for the coming of war and the prophecy of Mother Mary is for the coming of war and chastisements—that is, the return of personal and planetary karma.

Why is it so, beloved? It is simply because the people, lo, these two thousand years have not internalized the messages of the Great Lightbearers of East and West who have come down the stream of revelation and the delivery of prophecy and who have embodied the Word; and mankind have rejected their Teachers and the emissaries of their Teachers. They have rejected Almighty God in the person of the living Guru and they have desired to be served a banquet of light even in the wilderness of their consciousness.

But they would not bend the knee, no, not before Melchizedek, priest of the Most High God and king of Salem.[4] No, they would not, beloved. For in that hour as to this day, there are those who would take the light of the Cosmic Christ without bending the knee before the person of that Christ, whether in Jesus or whether in the hearts of his little ones. Thus, it is the desecration of God in the temple of the people of which I would speak to you, for the denial of the God Flame within the people is the mark of the oppressor of that people.

Blessed hearts, you must not wait for those who have betrayed you generation after generation to now suddenly become your deliverers in this age. As you study history you see the betrayal of the people and their life [by] fallen angels who stalk the earth, and these fallen ones are the [very] ones who bring war East and West and they so execute these wars for population control and for the suppression of the Light.

Therefore, in the dawning golden age of Aquarius, I, Uriel, stand with my cohorts of Light. And we stand now upon the earth itself and we declare to all who will hear and listen and [to] all who will take our Word and preach it to the children of the Light that it is the hour for the fulfillment of your Christhood and that in every age there is come those Antichrists prophesied in the Gospel of Jude according to the Book of Enoch.[5] Therefore, not one but many Antichrists are gone forth in the land;[6] and these are individuals who deny the Light in the hearts of the people and they have desired to take from an entire age and planet truly a universal Christ realization in every nation upon earth both bond and free.

Know, then, that there are Lightbearers everywhere and in every religion and in every race and amongst every people. And these Lightbearers must be cut free, and it is your call to the heavenly hosts that does accomplish this goal; and without the call we are not free to interfere with the will of the people.

Know, then, that when that Christ is amplified in you, these fallen ones move against you by subtle and cunning measures, by projections into your own psychology and into your own mind, deceiving you and making you believe that these negative vibrations are your own when they are indeed not native to your heart or soul or mind. Understand, therefore, that the subtleties and the wiles of the fallen angels are a massive conspiracy against the Mystical Body of God upon earth and, alas, this conspiracy has its agents in both Church and State.

Therefore, let them tremble throughout this continent, for I, Archangel Uriel, Angel of the LORD's Judgment, descend therefore. And I descend with a flaming sword and my sword is held high! And they do receive their karma, then, for the denial of the Light of the people and [for] their failure to liberate the people to know Divine Reality, [for] their failure to liberate the people that they might exercise the inner flame of Freedom in absolute God Freedom in their governments and in their economies.

Therefore, by a path of Freedom is true adeptship won. And the people have been made to believe that their governments, their bankers, their banking houses, their common market and their universal temporal religion must dictate to them the terms of life. And inch by inch they have surrendered their Freedom in order to have someone make for them the most vital decisions of their future concerning their spiritual life, concerning their inner self-government under their own I AM Presence, and concerning the freedom of the flame of the heart when drawn forth ingeniously to be the true fulcrum and measure of supply.

Thus, understand, beloved, that the abundant Life taught by Jesus Christ is a life of absolute God Freedom with only those restraints necessary for the protection of human life and the securing of the commonweal, the betterment of humanity. Thus, beloved, each time there has been taken from you the freedom to be the giver, to be the doer, to be the knower, to be the creator, to be the fulfillment of God's law on earth, you have had taken from you a portion of the path of your own self-mastery. Thus, it is a creeping cancer upon the nations to deprive them of their wealth and to redistribute that wealth, whatever the name or the means of the scheme be.

We speak, then, of the movements East and West of internationalists who have manipulated the people in every nation. Let it be known, then, that I have come into Europe this day sent by the LORD God and his Christ for the absolute judgment of those who are moving these nations toward the confrontations of war.

Blessed hearts, this betrayal of a people has come throughout the world and from the governments of every nation, especially those of the United States and the Soviet Union. And therefore in the councils of this leadership, even in this very hour, there is the betrayal of a people of this entire continent; and you must know that this betrayal is almost complete and therefore the very prophecies of Fátima are being fulfilled even when they are not known by the people.

I come, therefore, anchoring a flame of the resurrection in the heart of every Lightbearer who will receive me. Therefore, I urge you to make known the name of Archangel Uriel, which has been denied to the people long ago by Church councils.[7] I AM the angel and the living Presence of the Lord Jesus Christ, and therefore he does desire you to call unto me and millions of angels of my bands of the Sixth Ray to restore the Universal Christ consciousness among those who are the Lightbearers of the earth who have descended from God with that Light and still retain it in their hearts.

The hour is late, beloved, and we must emphasize the lateness of the hour. This is a moment, then, for the soul to raise up the Light in her temple and to be raised up by the Spirit of the Resurrection.

Know, then, that the Archangels can assist you *only* to that extent to which you make the call. When you call us, we are instantaneously with you. When you do not call upon us, even though we would save you from dire calamity, we are bound by cosmic law not to intervene. Thus, the saints who have prayed daily throughout history are those who have been open hearts to our coming and through them the Light has shone. Yet, I tell you, if you are not saints today you may be saints tomorrow, and this sainthood, beloved, is the infusion of your being and your spiritual centers with the light of the Universal Christ.

I am Uriel, then, and I come to you with the admonishment to make haste in the acceleration of the energies of your being, [and to that end] to apply the violet flame daily and generously. For those things that have already come upon Europe in all past ages there are records that must be cleared, records of war and bloodshed drenching the earth with the blood of the saints and those who have taken a stand for Freedom. Blessed ones, these records *must* be cleared, your own personal records *must* be cleared, and there *must* be the binding by the call to the Archangels of those forces of war that are yet moving with their malintent and are moving and hastening to take this continent before the access to it is denied to them.

They know that they are in a race against the Lightbearers who are being awakened and quickened unto that Universal Reality. They know it, beloved, and they know the presence of the Archangels in the earth. Yet, beloved, they have a timetable and if they can pull the rip cord of planetary and nuclear war before the Lightbearers take dominion in the earth, then they will do so, that they may guarantee to themselves another age of darkness, another age of the enslavement of humanity. These, therefore, are the conditions that face the world in this hour.

I have come to fulfill, therefore, the messages of Mother Mary and not to deny them. I have come to shake you awake! to shake you awake! to shake you awake! and to make you understand that you must take responsibility for your nations and not leave the conditions of these nations in the hands of a few leaders. It is time to recognize that the freedom of the threefold flame in your hearts has been taken from you one by one in the governments of the nations of Europe!

Know, then, beloved, that the hour is come for the restoration of Freedom and a true revolution in Higher Consciousness. For when you ascend the plane of Being, when you daily direct the violet flame for the balance of personal karma, when you raise up the Light of the Divine Mother within you, then you will see how Christ shall come suddenly into your temple to make his statement and to take his dominion in the earth.

I, Uriel, therefore come before the Master Saint Germain as I have gone before all Sons of God embodying the flames of the ages. I come, therefore, an angel of ministration and service, ministering unto you that your Christ Self-awareness might be complete ere you receive the Master of the seventh age.

Blessed ones, the Holy Spirit has directed a dictation through this Messenger in the city of Los Angeles in Beverly Hills just this past week, and in that hour the Holy Spirit did deliver the Word that the initiation of the Holy Spirit is now returned to the planet and its initiation must begin in that city.[8] For long ago when that city was a part of the now-lost continent of Lemuria, the inhabitants of that city did violate the flame of the Holy Ghost.

Therefore, beloved, know the trembling in the earth. For the sign of the Holy Spirit is also the sign of the Holy Spirit's judgment, and therefore when that sign is come you know that conditions have passed the point where remedies can be given *in some cases,* and in other cases there is still the opportunity for the mitigation of karma.

Know, then, that the Holy Spirit did speak upon [the subject of] the very key configuration of the four planets in Capricorn in this hour; and this configuration, as has been told to you by the Messenger, does now prophesy a downturn in the economies of the nations and major challenges.[9] And therefore the prophecies of war are written in the handwriting in the sky, the handwriting of astronomy that does become an exact science of astrology.

Know, then, that the karma of nations and individuals is written in the heavens, and this particular configuration of Saturn, Neptune, Uranus and Mars in Capricorn does tell you, beloved, that the initiations will be serious and severe for every individual who does inhabit this planet and especially for the governments and the economies of nations. Thus, it does come at an hour when the prophecies of Nostradamus and of Mother Mary are also being outplayed.

Let each one, then, find the high habitation of his God and set his house in order, for it is an hour for you to receive the Blessed Virgin Mother and to live with her day by day throughout the twenty-four hours as her beloved friend and servant, her instrument and her mouthpiece. Therefore, let her teaching be known and let her New Age teaching be known.

I AM Uriel. I speak to you at length because of my profound love for you and because the Father hath sent me to you, and the Son, to deliver to you an inner divine awareness of that Reality within yourself that has been denied for too long to your detriment.

Lo, the living Christ is high in the atmosphere over this place. Lo! he does come therefore to restore that which is lost in you and the divine memory of your own soul's oneness in the heart of the Great Central Sun.

May you take and receive the Teaching. May you take and receive the Lord. May you come, therefore, to receive also the one who does come in the name of the Lord.

I AM Uriel, Archangel of the Cosmic Christ, servant of Maitreya and all Sons of God. I bow to the Light in your heart and I breathe upon it the breath of the Holy Spirit that this Light might increase unto your soul's salvation! [The holy breath sounds]

"The Summit Lighthouse Sheds Its Radiance O'er All the World to Manifest as Pearls of Wisdom." This dictation by **Archangel Uriel** was **delivered** by the Messenger Elizabeth Clare Prophet on **Saturday, February 27, 1988,** at the Cine Alvalade, **Lisbon, Portugal,** where she was stumping for Saint Germain's Coming Revolution in Higher Consciousness. [**N.B.** Bracketed material denotes words unspoken yet implicit in the dictation, added by the Messenger under Archangel Uriel's direction for clarity in the published text.] **(1) Mother Mary's Fátima warnings.** See 1988 *Pearls of Wisdom,* p. 249 n. 12. **(2) Mother Mary's appearances at Medjugorje.** See 1988 *Pearls of Wisdom,* p. 142 n. 1. **(3) The third secret.** See 1988 *Pearls of Wisdom,* pp. 249–50 n. 13. **(4) Melchizedek.** Gen. 14:18–20; Heb. 7:1–3. **(5) Jude on the ungodly and**

their judgment prophesied by Enoch. Jude 4–19; I Enoch 2. For Enoch's revelations and warnings about the fallen angels called Watchers, with exegesis and
exposé by Elizabeth Clare Prophet, see *Forbidden Mysteries of Enoch: The Untold
Story of Men and Angels,* containing all the Enoch texts, including the Book of
Enoch and the Book of the Secrets of Enoch, Summit University Press, $12.95 (add
$1.00 for postage). **(6) Antichrists.** I John 2:18. See also Antichrist, I John 2:22;
4:3; II John 7. **(7) Worship of angels forbidden by the Roman Church.** The Roman
Catholic Church has repeatedly banned the worship of angels not named in its
officially approved scriptures. The Synod of Laodicea in A.D. 343 decreed that only
the names of the Archangels Michael, Gabriel and Raphael could be used in prayers
and forbade Catholics to worship angels privately outside their churches. The
worship of angels not named in scripture was again banned by a Roman synod
convoked under Pope Zachary in 745 and by Church councils in the ninth and
fifteenth centuries. In 1950 Pope Pius XII in his encyclical *Human Genesis* reaffirmed
that Catholics were only allowed to use the names of Michael, Gabriel and Raphael.
In 1964 when Vatican II revised the liturgy of the mass, it eliminated Pope Leo XIII's
prayer to Archangel Michael, which had been said at the end of each mass since
1886, because it did not refer to the Eucharist or the communion of Christ with his
disciples. The premise that the early Christians were "worshiping" angels was an
assumption; praying to the Archangels by way of calling for their intercession in time
of crisis is not worshiping angels; it is allowing them to perform their lawful role on
behalf of the issue of God for which they were created by God. Bowing to the Light
within the manifestation of God, angelic or human, is the acknowledgment of the
God Flame within, not a deification of the creation or offspring of the one God whom
we worship. Under the pretext that Christians were "worshiping" angels, Church
councils have kept Christians from pronouncing the names of the Archangels, which
embody the power of God on the ray on which they serve (e.g., Archangel Uriel
embodies the power of God on the Sixth Ray, Jophiel on the Second, Chamuel on
the Third, Zadkiel on the Seventh and Uzziel on the Eighth); thereby the people have
been deprived of the intercessory power of the Seven Archangels who can assist
them in realizing the Universal Christ on the paths of the Seven Rays and in fighting
the battle of Armageddon. In truth, the church hierarchies feared that by invoking
the Archangels the people would gain power and illumination and, being endued by
the Holy Ghost, would see through the usurpers of Christ's true doctrine—that each
individual is free to engage in the communion of saints in heaven and on earth and
to receive God's emissaries and the angelic hosts at his command as did the biblical
personages of old. For men of ecclesiastical posture to use their sacred offices and
trust to deny the people's lawful communion, by the Holy Ghost, with the Lord Jesus
Christ and his hosts is not only antiscriptural but it doth offend our conscience and
cause us to violate the admonishment of Hebrews 13:2: "Be not forgetful to
entertain strangers: for thereby some have entertained angels unawares" and Ps.
91:11: "He shall give his angels charge over thee to keep thee in all thy ways."
(8) The initiation (judgment) of the Holy Spirit. See the Maha Chohan, 1988 *Pearls
of Wisdom,* pp. 225–30. **(9) Four planets in Capricorn.** See 1988 *Pearls of
Wisdom,* p. 229 n. 3.

Pearls of Wisdom®

published by The Summit Lighthouse

| Vol. 31 No. 37 | *Beloved Saint Germain* | *July 9, 1988* |

Saint Germain Stumps Portugal

6

Mikhail Gorbachev and Ronald Reagan: The Hand of God Is Raised Against You!

Hail, Keepers of the Flame!
Hail, Sons and Daughters of the Most High God!

I AM Saint Germain and by the grace of God and only by that grace am I here on this platform this night to speak to you.

Welcome to my heart. [1½-min. standing ovation]

My beloved hearts, if I could shed a tear in this hour it would be that you as the devotees of Peace, Light and Freedom and your counterparts worldwide are not in the seats of government, are not in the seats of control of the economies and money systems of the nations, are not in the seats where you belong in the true aspect of the saints ministering to the people, [for] wolves in sheep's clothing[1] have stolen those seats.

O beloved, for this cause my heart goes out and I do receive your love in this moment with the full understanding that I shall take it to the heart of the Father in the Great Central Sun to see what more can be done for the Lightbearers of the earth! [40-sec. applause]

Beloved ones, while you give me your devotion, my violet flame angels have prepared for you a special violet flame lotus seat; therefore, be seated now in that violet flame lotus.

Happy are ye who stand in praise of our God, one LORD, and who recognize that individuality of God Freedom in myself. For you see, beloved, what you see in me is what you become and this is the foundation of the path of mysticism of the saints of all ages and the true teaching of our beloved Jesus, my Son and your Son.[2] O the blessed one of God who has come for you to save you and whose Presence has so been denied in the earth! And therefore he has been rendered in the style of an effeminate and spineless individual instead of one who does wield the sword of Peace in defense of Freedom and turn back the hordes of night!

Therefore, let the armour of the living Christ and his Archangel Uriel be upon you one and all! And may you understand the true meaning of being soldiers of the cosmic cross of white fire.

In the invincible Victory of the God Flame I come and I stand in this land with my pure devotion to the Blessed Virgin Mary.

Blessed ones, by leave of Omri-Tas and cosmic councils from the heart of the LORD God Almighty there has been delivered an opportunity for this age for Europe. Therefore, that violet flame reservoir of light[3] can be invoked by you with such intensity for the quickening.

Blessed hearts, Armageddon is a fact of life on earth and it is in full swing. People look to see when it will begin. Well, I tell you, beloved, the war has long begun before the first rocket is fired. And know that when it is fired, it is far too late to deal with the consequences thereof. And thus the miscalculations of the free nations are bringing them to their knees before the totalitarian system that is the cancer of this planet and the major obstacle to the age of Aquarius.

Thus, be not deceived, for God himself will not be mocked![4] Therefore, at least let not the Lightbearers be mocked in the mockery of the fallen ones who have put forth such an all-pervasive lie. And this lie, beloved, is in the same vibration as the karma of the people; and therefore the people do not read the lie because of their own karmic vibration and density.

Thus it has ever been and therefore I say to you, Archangel Uriel, wield your mighty sword! Rend the veil of spiritual blindness upon this continent! I, Saint Germain, decree it! May my saints, the Keepers of the Flame, be emboldened to embody this rending of the veil!

Let the veil be torn asunder, then, and let the people see and know what is coming and let them not faint and let them not become stiffened in a rigor mortis posture in fear of death but, rather, in seeing the Divine Vision let them act and act in time to turn around these conditions! And, beloved, where these conditions are not turned around, I tell you, the violet flame and the rescue teams of Archangel Michael do come to the side of all Lightbearers and you are borne up on wings of light.

Blessed ones, therefore we seek not alone the salvation of a physical platform but we seek the salvation of souls who would not otherwise make it out of the lower astral plane if they should come under the transition called death in an untimely manner. Blessed hearts, this is our profound concern apart from the salvation of nations and continents and a way of life and a history.

Let it be known that change is the order of the day of Aquarius, and therefore there must be *some* change. There must be *some* physical change. There must be *some* giving way of the old institutions to the new and a Divine Appearing of the institutions of Aquarius which are truly based on Community when that Community has as its central flame the living Holy Spirit.

And therefore, we say to you, if life, then, must be lost, let that life be saved at the soul level and let souls be borne up instantaneously into the heaven-world of the etheric octave so gently, so completely that they are found at inner levels in the great golden-age cities of light on the etheric plane, in the inner temples and in the great cathedral of our God and his Christ.

Know, then, that the saints go marching on lifetime after lifetime, whether in the body or out of the body. Therefore, we seek to preserve the life, the eternal life of the soul first and foremost, and secondly we desire to preserve at all costs the physical manifestation of your souls. For the Lightbearers must bring in a golden age, after the Dark Night of the Spirit is long past of the deliverance of a planetary karma.*

Thus, you must have short-term goals and long-term goals and you must be goal-fitted by the Ascended Master El Morya and the Lords of the Seven Rays, who invite you to their universities of the Spirit to study there nightly.[5] Answer their call, beloved. For these temples are open and they are open not without cause. For we have in mind the very same goals that I have just stated to you.

And if you do take their training and if you are diligent in the giving of the violet flame [decrees] and if you take, therefore, the mystery of surrender as a rosary from the heart of Mother Mary and the rosary of Archangel Michael for Armageddon,[6] you will find yourself thoroughly engaged with the angels of Light for the defense of life on earth. Know, then, that these rosaries are given to you for your absolute God-protection and perfectionment.

Beloved ones, it has taken thousands of years to prepare this Messenger to receive these dictations in this manner. Therefore not in one life or a few short years but for many lifetimes has that preparation come; and I tell you, beloved, it is by the grace of the Holy Spirit and the mantle of our Father upon her, and you must know this, that there shall not be another and another.

---

*the Dark Night during which the planetary karma is delivered to the planet

For until the hour of the fulfillment is come for your own victory in the Light, you must take this teaching we have given. For we cannot give more and more teaching if the plates that we have served you are not emptied, if you have not assimilated the Body and Blood of the Universal Christ, if you have not known the fiat of the Lord Christ: "Lo! I AM Alpha and Omega, the beginning and the ending! Lo! I AM THAT I AM!"

Let it also be your cry daily and fear not to raise your voice unto the heavens, sensing that in the very fervor and fire of your hearts you do reach untrammeled octaves of light! Therefore, so be it.

Let the saints of God know that the hour for the marching of the Archangels and the company of saints and the leader of the battle in heaven, even Sanat Kumara and the Faithful and True, Maitreya and the living Christ Jesus, is come. And these armies have been seen marching in the city of Washington, up and down that city last Thanksgiving past;[7] and the marching of those armies, beloved, has been the sign of the coming of the victory of the Light and the defeat of the forces of Darkness.

Unfortunately, the entrenched forces of Darkness in Washington and New York almost parallel those in Moscow and in the nations' capitals of Europe. Therefore, wherever the betrayers of the Word are, know, then, that it is the Lightbearers of the nations who must unite.

I speak to you, then, of that wave of anti-Americanism that has spread through Europe. Beloved ones [of Europe], it is the people's rejection of the fallen angels in Church and State. But reject not the hearts of the [American] people themselves who are filled with light and love for you personally, and they have never comprehended and many of them have never even known that there is such a thing as hatred of Americans on this continent.

I pray, then, that you swiftly awaken and see now that it is also the leadership in the Soviet Union who are the betrayers of the people and it is the leadership in each and every state and nation that have so denied the living Word that has also obscured the God Reality of the universal oneness of those who are the issue of God.

And therefore, take haven and take refuge in the Mother of God, in your own I AM Presence, and in one another; and know, therefore, [that] where the people of Light gather, where the eagles gather, there is the Body of Christ.[8] And it is the Mystical Body of Christ in the earth, that true and living Body, that must be saved and must be in the earth even a lodestone of heaven, even a divine magnet of the Great Central Sun that does hold the balance when the elementals themselves must bring forth those necessary earth changes that are to come to pass before the planet may be utterly purged of [by] the violet flame and begin anew. For the old order, that which is [become] corrupt and decayed by the [works of the] fallen angels, must pass away!

And you will see [that passing of the old order in] the hour when the reapers come. And the reapers come from all the bands of the angels;* and they come therefore to bind the seed of the Wicked [One] and to bind them in bundles.[9] And this was prophesied by the Lord and not left out of scripture [in order] that you might have the remembrance that it is the genetic seed of the Evil One which is sown among the genetic seed of the Lightbearers.

And therefore we deal not alone with individuals but with genetic sowings by fallen ones seeking always to intrude upon the forcefield and psyche of the individual some element of self-denial of the living Christ, however faint, that will tie him to the planetary force of Antichrist.

Therefore, I come secondly to call Archangel Uriel for the purging within you of each and every momentum in the subconscious that is anti-Christ in nature, in other words, the momentum of your own personal karma [as well as the momentums of the genetic tares sown by the Enemy among the good wheat of your Christic genes] that do move against the rising Light of the Universal Christ within you.

Therefore, beloved, I tell you, the date of Wesak accorded to those Keepers of the Flame[10] is now moved up to the Fourth of July 1988, giving you, then [52-sec. standing ovation with joyous shouts], giving you, then, beloved, two additional months for the invocation of the violet flame and the calls to Archangel Michael to cut free the Lightbearers of this continent and to see what great multiplication may be made of that violet flame dispensation of Omri-Tas.

Beloved ones, I tell you, you are bought with a price,[11] and in this hour that price is paid for you by my own beloved Portia, the Goddess of Justice! [33-sec. applause] Therefore the Mother of Aquarius has given to you her heart and the momentum of Opportunity from her causal body.

Blessed ones, know, then, that Portia some years ago did place her flame of Divine Justice in the heart of your Messenger,[12] so intending to use that flame within the Messenger as a point of countermeasure and in the hour when the Lightbearers of the world should most have need of it. Because of that physical anchor point, beloved, you may understand that dispensations can be given

*the Archangels

because some one and some many [among the] souls of Light upon earth have given their Light to that divine purpose. And therefore, I do call to you that in the very next violet flame cassette you shall also include the songs to my beloved Portia that the Feminine Ray of Aquarius may descend and may come truly in Divine Justice before it is too late to foil the attempts of the fallen ones.

Blessed hearts, therefore, I tell you this date [of July 4, 1988] is firm and you must be in your seats in the Heart of the Inner Retreat on July Fourth if you desire to keep pace with me and my accelerating spirals—always, of course, subject to your own inner counsel and free will.

Therefore, in the love of Portia I greet you and I say, be seated.

I would acquaint you, then, with the major challenge that is faced, unknown, by all Lightbearers in the earth, who are my deep concern in this hour. Those who have not been quickened and who are not aware of the path of the Ascended Masters—which is the highest path on the earth East and West and the only path that can lead you to the victory of the ascension in this life through the soul's fusion in the Holy Christ Self and the I AM Presence—these Lightbearers, then, who know not how to call for their protection are subject to the great barrage and bombardment, at all levels, of the denial of that Light. And the conspiracy of the fallen ones is to so entangle them in alliances with those of Darkness that they cannot extricate themselves from these entanglements.

Therefore the call has gone forth (and it has been answered at our Inner Retreat in Montana) for the daily decrees to concentrate on the cutting free of the Lightbearers and [for you] to make that call constantly. For at any hour of the day or night souls may turn to the left-handed path, whether on the path of initiation under a false guru who appears to be true or under the false path involving the world political situation [which also appears to be true].

Many souls have been turned away from the true path of light in Church and State by the media itself East and West, which is the chief means of the control of public opinion, of the manipulation of populations and of disinformation sent forth to divide nation against nation and brother against brother. You need to be absolutely aware of the wiles of cunning serpents. For to awaken to the Light, beloved, is also to awaken to the potential of Darkness in the earth in the person of those fallen angels who have embodied it with the intense determination of the annihilation of the people of God.

Therefore, beloved, <u>I ask you, when you call for the violet</u>

flame dispensations to [be given to] their hearts, to not neglect the giving of Archangel Michael's Rosary daily [in their behalf]. Beloved, some immense sacrifice must be forthcoming from those Lightbearers of Europe who have seen the Truth and know it in their hearts! And I tell you, it is the Archangel Michael Rosary followed by calls to him, unrelenting, to the blue-lightning angels for this action of their swords of blue flame, to march up and down and left and right, east and west, north to south and up again, [for] the encirclement of these nations that they might be quickened to the awareness of what is that evil intent that is planned against them.

Therefore, beloved, know that that intent *is* on the drawing boards in Moscow and in the Kremlin and has ever been. It is not new. And therefore, I tell you, *glasnost* is a propaganda sham! I tell you, the prince out of the Soviet Union is a sham and a liar and a betrayer of the people!

And I say this directly to the heart of Mikhail Gorbachev:

You may fool the people but you have not fooled the ascended hosts of Light and you have not fooled the hearts of the Lightbearers in the earth! And you, Ronald Reagan, are a sham and betrayer of my sponsorship and you also shall know your karma for this betrayal of Europe and the European states!

And everyone who has gone after these liars, in the United States Senate and in the nation-states of Europe, know that I, Saint Germain, do stand and my angels with me and you shall not pass and you shall know the judgment of your karma and you shall know it all too late, too late therefore! And you shall have caused, therefore, the downfall of nations, and in so doing you shall have incurred a karma so vast as to be practically impossible to balance in aeons of the future.

Therefore I sound the warning and I sound it with Archangel Gabriel! And I announce to you fallen ones, though you may think you are the instruments of the karma of the people, let it be known that if you so become those instruments, the sword of Damocles shall be upon your own heads and your victory shall be short-lived and your triumphs and your celebrations shall be exposed as the very conflagration of hell surrounds you!

And thus, in the councils of Death and Hell *you* meet and in the higher octaves *we* meet; and *we* have a course of salvation for our Lightbearers and *you* have no part with the marriage feast of the lambs. And beware the day when they are called to the supper where the kings and the captains and the high and the mighty are decimated[13] and the Light-bearers therefore assemble for the universal transmutation of Absolute Evil, worlds without end! They shall endure to the end and to the fulfillment of their union with God and *you* shall go down to the sides of the pit with your leader, that fallen one, Archangel Lucifer![14]

Therefore know that the hour of your judgment is come and as you raise your hand against the Light and Freedom of a planet, so the hand of God is raised against you! I say to you that what is in your favor is the ignorance of the people, which you have also plotted. But they shall not long remain ignorant, for the hour and the day of the clap and the thunder of Almighty God is upon them also, and they shall hear the voice of the Son of God through this Messenger and they that hear his voice shall live[15] and they shall live unto everlasting Life in which you have no part!

And those to whom you render your mausoleums and your tombs and your vainglory and your worship of that fallen one, Lenin, let it be known to you that these have been bound by the Lord and are judged by him also and they, too, shall know their second death and trial before the Court of the Sacred Fire. Therefore, whatever does come to pass, your day is done and you shall know the judgment of God upon you in due course! Therefore you shall rue the day and it will be too late.

Therefore, beloved of the Light, inasmuch as the judgment must come upon evildoers, is it not just that a people of God should raise up their voices on time and ahead of time, that their evil intent be judged before it precipitate the calamitous events prophesied? [4-sec. pause] Blessed hearts, is it not therefore meet that a people send forth their cry? ["Yes!"]

Therefore I say, let your cry ring the very bells of heaven and let your hearts become the throne of your own Holy Christ Self and let your temple be delivered of all lesser vibrations, that the Holy Spirit in the power of God may descend through you.

Blessed hearts, this continent belongs to the people who inhabit it, not to the fallen angels who have taken it from them at every hand. I say, claim the earth beneath your feet and claim it for the age of Aquarius! Claim it for Saint Germain! Claim it for Freedom! Claim it for the Lightbearers! For unless you take a stand with the armies of heaven, these armies of Hell pitted and poised to defeat you [will do just that]!

Know, then, beloved, [that] it is the moment of the soul's victory; [therefore] let the soul compromise in no thing and in no area of life. Let the soul truly know the Spirit of Victory and become untouchable by the force sinister in the earth. Let the soul in her wedding garment and in her white light, let the soul in her armour therefore be clothed upon in an age of deliverance.

Let the saints on earth be my deliverers! For in delivering a people, beloved, you shall deliver me also to engage once again more directly in the affairs of earth.

I, Saint Germain, have expended my allotment of energy accorded to me from the Great Central Sun to speak to you in this hour. Every word spoken is a release of immense power from Almighty God and it has been anchored in every portion of the territory of this continent and in the waters and in the air and in the nucleus of every atom of being.

Therefore, I AM Saint Germain, Hierarch of Aquarius, Divine Lover of Freedom and of Your Souls. I seal you in the Seventh Ray action of my causal body and hold you in my heart.

"The Summit Lighthouse Sheds Its Radiance O'er All the World to Manifest as Pearls of Wisdom." This dictation by **Saint Germain** was **delivered** by the Messenger Elizabeth Clare Prophet on **Saturday, February 27, 1988,** after midnight, at the Cine Alvalade, **Lisbon, Portugal,** where she was stumping for Saint Germain's Coming Revolution in Higher Consciousness. [**N.B.** Bracketed material denotes words unspoken yet implicit in the dictation, added by the Messenger under Saint Germain's direction for clarity in the published text.] (1) **Wolves in sheep's clothing.** Matt. 7:15. (2) **What Christhood you see you become.** The Gnostic Gospel of Philip describes the devotee of Christ who no longer calls himself a Christian "but a Christ": "You saw the Spirit, you became Spirit. You saw Christ, you became Christ. You saw [the Father, you] shall become Father. So [in this place] you see everything and [do] not [see] yourself, but [in that place] you do see yourself—and what you see you shall [become]" (67:26, 27; 61:29–35, in *The Nag Hammadi Library in English* [San Francisco: Harper & Row, 1977], pp. 140, 137). John also wrote in his epistle: "Beloved, now are we the sons of God, and it doth not yet appear what we shall be: but we know that when he shall appear, we shall be like him; for we shall see him as he is" (I John 3:2). (3) **Reservoir of violet flame over Europe.** See Omri-Tas, 1988 *Pearls of Wisdom,* pp. 251–53. (4) **God is not mocked.** Gal. 6:7. (5) **Universities of the Spirit.** On January 1, 1986, Gautama Buddha announced that he and the Lords of Karma had granted the petition of the Lords of the Seven Rays to open universities of the Spirit in their etheric retreats for tens of thousands of students to pursue the path of self-mastery on the seven rays. Traveling in their finer bodies (the etheric sheath) during sleep, students spend 14 days at Darjeeling for training on the First Ray under El Morya, alternating with 14 days at the Royal Teton Retreat for training on the Seventh Ray under Saint Germain until they have successfully passed certain levels of accomplishment in the use of the First and Seventh Rays.

Then they may go on to receive training under the Lords of the Second, Third, Sixth, Fourth and Fifth Rays in that order: Lord Lanto and Confucius at the Royal Teton (2nd), Paul the Venetian at the Goddess of Liberty's Temple of the Sun over Manhattan (3rd), Nada at the retreat of Jesus in Saudi Arabia (6th), Serapis Bey at the Ascension Temple, Luxor (4th), and Hilarion at the retreat of Pallas Athena in Crete (5th). It is the desire of the Great White Brotherhood that through the courses given and the tests passed in meeting the challenges of everyday life as well as through second and third levels of instruction, students will quickly make outer contact with Summit University and attend its halls of learning at the Inner Retreat. On December 28, 1986, the God Meru encouraged us to follow the path of the Lords of the Seven Rays by choosing to embody the Presence and Light of each Chohan (i.e., Lord) and then the Maha Chohan (the Great Lord who is over the Lords of the Seven Rays, the representative of the Holy Spirit who delivers the initiations of the Third Person of the Trinity to the evolutions of planet earth) in 14-day cycles starting January 1, 1987, while attending their universities of the Spirit. On December 31, 1986, El Morya spoke of the chelas spending "14 weeks" with him. Thus the chelas shall pursue 7 cycles of 2 weeks in each of the Chohans' retreats and that of the Maha Chohan. Those who follow this discipline starting January 1, 1987, will conclude their 'Odyssey' through the 14 weeks of initiations with each Ascended Master on George Washington's Birthday, February 22, 1989—a most propitious hour in the turning of planetary cycles when all chelas should be spiritually and physically prepared for earth changes in the decade of the 1990s. See 1986 *Pearls of Wisdom,* pp. 178–81, 689–90, 698; 1987 *Pearls of Wisdom,* p. 286. **(6)** See *The Fourteenth Rosary: **The Mystery of Surrender,*** booklet, $1.00 (add $.50 for postage); booklet and 2-audiocassette album, includes rosary, 2 lectures, and a dictation by Mother Mary, 3 hr., V7538, $12.95 (add $1.10 for postage). ***Archangel Michael's Rosary for Armageddon,*** 36-page booklet, $1.00 (add $.50 for postage); booklet and 91-min. audiocassette, $5.00 (add $1.00 for postage). **(7) The armies of heaven in Washington, D.C.** See Archangel Uriel, Jesus Christ, and Serapis Bey, 1987 *Pearls of Wisdom,* pp. 597, 605, 607, 608, 609, 610. **(8) Where the eagles gather.** Matt. 24:27, 28; Luke 17:37. **(9) The tares among the wheat.** Matt. 13:24–30, 36–42. **(10) The date accorded to European Keepers of the Flame.** In his June 21, 1987 Pearl of Wisdom, "A Door That Shall Open...," Saint Germain said: "We who are your mentors of the Spirit counsel you who serve beyond the borders of the United States of America to place a priority upon being *here now* legally according to the laws of the nations, legitimately according to the law of chelaship, no later than Wesak 1988. Your immigration through the heart of the Goddess of Liberty is a path of initiation to be fulfilled in the mantra *'I AM gratitude in action!'* You must fly as eagles to the cities of North America on the wings of your sacred labor, an avocation and a profession *en main* (in hand) by diligent striving and application in the LORD's Work." See 1987 *Pearls of Wisdom,* p. 254. **(11) You are bought with a price.** I Cor. 6:20; 7:23. **(12) Portia's flame of God Justice transferred to the heart of the Messenger.** See Archangel Uriel, 1983 *Pearls of Wisdom,* pp. 188–89. **(13) The supper of the Great God.** Rev. 19:17–21. **(14)** Isa. 14:12–17. **(15) The voice of the Son of God.** John 5:24, 25.

Pearls of Wisdom®
published by The Summit Lighthouse

| Vol. 31 No. 38 | Beloved Jesus Christ | July 10, 1988 |

Saint Germain Stumps Portugal
7
The Call to the True Shepherds
to Move among the People and to Shepherd Them
The Restoration of Your Divine Inheritance

Lo, I AM come into your midst, O people of great faith. O my sons and daughters of the living flame of cosmic Truth, I am in your midst in this hour out of the profound love of the Father and the Son for your devotion to the Blessed Mother, for your devotion to Life and Truth, upon whatever course it [your devotion] has taken you.

Know, then, that in the fullness of the joy of angels I come to gather my own unto the victory of Life everlasting, to call you and to call you again to return to my heart and to see me as I truly AM in the victory of the ascension—one who walks midst those who are of the Light and does not necessarily enter those paths of organized religion and orthodoxy [whose hierarchs] have closed out my Heart and my Teaching behind their garrisoned walls where they render themselves impervious to the cries of the people or to their proper role of challenging the evildoer.

What has happened to the "Church Militant"[1] on earth that does defend Life when Death and Hell move against the souls of a people? Where, then, are today's saints? They are outside of its walls, I tell you, for the true saints have long ago recognized that these walls cannot contain nor house my Great Causal Body.[2]

And therefore, I must in protest come again to overturn the money changers in the temple.[3] These are they who conspire with world movements of totalitarianism, who enter into compromise, and challenge and deny the true path of individual soul freedom and

the rightful inheritance of every son of God to walk and talk with me
and to commune with me as I walked and talked with my disciples
for many years, even many years after my resurrection. For I did
remain upon earth and the Gnostic text Pistis Sophia does bear
witness to this even as does the Church Father Irenaeus, commenting that I was teaching well into the [fiftieth year. And it was so.][4]

Blessed ones, the mysteries I have taught have been banned
and denounced as heresy, and therefore you are as shorn lambs
today, having accepted the orthodox lie of sin and condemnation.

Therefore, upon the hour and the brink of an age of destiny
when the dark powers of this world are determined to make war
and to destroy and to take this entire continent, I say to you,
because they have not passed on to you the great teaching of my
heart, therefore the true shepherds are not raised up. Thus, the
wolves in sheep's clothing[5] in Church and State have effectively
taken from my own the great Truth of the ages.

But I AM your brother and I come to your side in this hour
of need and world crisis. I call you not only to be my disciples,
[but] I call you [also] to be shepherds and to feed my sheep,[6] to
quickly devour by the Holy Spirit the teaching that is already set
forth and therefore to put on and receive the mantle of apostle-
ship—that you might know yourselves as shepherds and feed the
children of God mouthful by mouthful that morsel of bread, that
cup of cold water in my name that does return to them the inner
resource of Light, the fount of that holy Christhood and the
Presence of the I AM THAT I AM.

This must be done quickly, beloved, for the fallen angels
know that they have but a short time, but a narrow few years in
which to move against the world that is about to deliver* the
mandate of the Universal Christ nation by nation.

Blessed ones, it is an hour of great danger to the nations of
Europe, and you must understand that it is because of the absence
of the Christs. Each one who does follow me does become that
Christ and this is the message written down by my apostles, such
as Thomas and Philip and Mary Magdalene,[7] that has either been
lost or suppressed. Know, then, beloved, that the need of the hour
is for those anointed ones, anointed of the Light, who are called
Christs, to move among the people and to shepherd them.

Let it be said, therefore, that this nation which has received
so great a gift as my Mother's Fátima visitations shall also receive
me in this hour and know that my appearance to you is every whit
as personal and as present and as seeable and knowable as was the
visitation at Fátima.

Blessed ones, know this, therefore, that I come to this nation

---

*a world in which the Lightbearers are about to deliver

to minister to the poor in spirit that they might receive fully the fruits of my being, that they might truly know that the Spirit of God is upon them and therefore that they are equal to the task of challenging those false hierarchy impostors of my name both in Church and State.

The hour is late! And so many have become accustomed to the oppressions of these false hierarchies that they take for granted the controls that are leveled upon them.

Blessed hearts, when you expand the fire of God that is already within you, when you have the restoration of your divine inheritance, you will know that not the human but I with you and in you, God in you and with you is the deliverer of nations. Thus, it is to become a transparency for the One who sends you that is the goal of this path rather than to make the fatal error of believing that one's human self is the anointed one.

The soul is anointed and you therefore become instruments of God. Forever the instrument, you shall not fail. But should you consider yourself as the originator of the Light, you will also go the way of pride, the spiritual pride of the fallen angels that has taken root on this continent from ancient times.

Blessed hearts, this my dictation, then, is spoken to the world. I am therefore calling shepherds to arise quickly and understand the great dearth of true teaching and true teachers, the dearth of leaders and leadership. Understand, beloved, that the people need in you an example, an example of one who is positive in the walk of the Teaching and does serve the LORD at that altar and does go out, therefore, and challenge conditions in society.

Blessed ones, I am here to challenge also the false teaching out of the East that those who are spiritual do not soil their hands [or their garments] by entering into the arena of politics or government. I tell you, it is the withdrawal of the Lightbearers from these areas that has given complete reign to the fallen angels to take over your nations, your destinies and your monetary systems.

Thus, it is certainly an area of a low vibration and power struggles. But it is entirely possible for those of the Light to enter these fields and to make their statement once again as the great prophets of old, [just] as those who have sought to be statesmen in every nation have risen and therefore dedicated their empires and their nations and civilizations to a higher cause.

Witness, therefore, Akbar of India, an incarnation of your beloved El Morya.[8] In this life he set the stage of universality in India that has endured to the very present hour; and as you study his life you will know that those who are of the First Ray never shirk their responsibility to enter into the fray and to challenge the evildoers who decade by decade and generation by generation have a continuity of purpose, which is to enslave and imprison the children of the Light in their institutions and in their organizations and controls.

Blessed ones, you can no longer sit back and watch the world crumble before you and watch the value of your money be destroyed by the manipulators of the system itself. You can no longer therefore think that those who quote me as being a pacifist and a socialist are speaking the truth. I tell you, I am not a pacifist nor am I a socialist! And therefore understand that the doctrines of Marx can never be justified through my parables or through my life, and I state it clearly!

And therefore, let it be known that these doctrines do deny the path of individualism and the path of karma; and therefore through the redistribution of wealth by the state there is a nullification of [the law of] karma, [which decrees] that every man may sow and reap and receive according to his effort.

Know, then, beloved ones, that as a man soweth, that shall he also reap,[9] and no state or private agency, therefore, has the right to take from him and to give to another who has not sown.

Therefore, if totalitarianism in these forms be allowed to continue on the planet, you will see that the path of initiation is ultimately denied for every individual upon this planet. And the day is at hand, for the powers that be have planned it, to control you, therefore, from space and to control every area of your life and every nation on this planet.

Let it be understood, beloved ones, that the agents of hell spoken of by my Mother are truly in the land and they are moving against the freedom. And therefore, those who do not exercise free will, those who do not understand the embodiment of the Word and the Work of the LORD lose the sense of the divine spark within. They are no longer co-creators with God, for someone else does everything for them and metes out their portion of meal daily.

Blessed ones, this is not life but death. And understand that all of the promises of the fallen ones for this ideal society of World Communism will come to naught, and you will understand that if they are allowed to continue, the earth will no longer have the approval of the Karmic Board to continue as a school of initiation of the Great White Brotherhood.

For it is the requirement that each and every year one soul make the ascension from this planet, and if souls are not ascending and there is not freedom of religion guaranteed in every nation, then you will come to that day when all will be enslaved by the fallen ones who plan to take over this planet in this very hour.

I speak to you, then, from the depths of my being and I say
to you: Resist the encroachment that does take from you day by
day the portion of your own I AM Presence!

It is necessary, therefore, that you enter into life fully and
become fully accountable for that which you have and that which
you have not, and therefore each and every individual under God
is accountable. And I will tell you, it is the fallen ones who have
been cut off from the Light* of the living Presence of God, who
have nothing and no Light,* who therefore have thought up these
schemes to receive the handouts and the light and the money and
the care from those who labor yet in the Lord's vineyard.

And therefore, you see, beloved, what is the true meaning of
the haves and the have-nots on this planet is those who have the
Light* and those who have it not. And those who have it not may
receive that Light by the very same means that those who have it
do have it, and that is to bend the knee before the Universal
Christ, to accept his laws, his God-government.

And that Universal Christ, beloved, is supreme in the earth
and they long ago did rebel against that Universal Christ. They
were cast out of heaven by the Archangel Michael into the earth.[10]
They have never relented and never recanted their position and
therefore they do not bend the knee neither to your I AM Presence
or to my I AM Presence nor to your Christ Self or my own
Christhood. And because of this, therefore, they have no Light,
and the Light that they once had in their hearts is self-extinguished
by their denial [of that Christ].

Therefore, in that state of emptiness, of being hollowed out,
they demand that those Lightbearers who serve the altar of God
shall give to them all that they have because now they are the poor;
and in piteous pleas they come begging, therefore, for everything
that they need and demanding that the state, the people, the rich,
et cetera, meet all of their wants.

Beloved ones, this system has nothing to do with my call to feed
the poor and the hungry and to feed the sheep. All have the right to
receive [in Christ], and therefore where there is abundance in the
earth it ought to be freely given by those who are able to give it.

Blessed ones, I gave my teaching for the fulfillment of the
Light in those who were on a path of discipleship. How can I call
fallen angels to be my disciples, beloved, when they are the very
ones who staged my mock trial and did crucify me?

Can you understand, therefore, that there is a teaching for
the children of the Light, who must come and repent of their sins
and be forgiven and walk on the path of their personal discipleship unto the Light? And [that] there is a message of the descent of

---
*Christ consciousness

the woes upon the seed of the wicked and the fallen ones who demand that the children of God serve them?

And the children of God, not having the true shepherds because you have not claimed that shepherd's crook from me, are therefore without true leaders, and they must therefore be subjected once again to the taskmasters who work them and live upon the fruit of their labors and build their empires and their money systems upon the very light and life-essence of my own.

I tell you, the time is already come when the judgment of the LORD God has been proclaimed in New York City and on Wall Street on the very third of October 1987.[11] And therefore the judgment of Wall Street and the moneylenders and money changers has descended, and this is the real reason for the October 19 crash.

Know this, beloved, that the judgments are already descending upon the fallen ones, but it is the false leaders in Church and State who are preventing that judgment from descending, who take more light [as God's energy] and more money of the people to shore up their crumbling systems.

Know, then, beloved ones, that it is the true shepherds, yourselves, to whom I call this day to enter in and to establish yourselves where you ought to be, where fallen angels have stolen your seats of authority from you, and to stand for a people who need you in this hour. Thus, let this dictation go down as the call to the true shepherds of the children of God.

I am calling you as these true shepherds out of every nation throughout the world and I say, it is high time that you recognize that you may no longer allow the fallen ones to encroach upon and to abuse and oppress the children of God! Hear me, beloved! Those who have been these shepherds in the past, many of them have ascended and some are yet with you.

Understand that there is such corruption across the governments of the nations that where to begin becomes the challenge of the hour, but I will tell you where to begin. That beginning is in the raising up of the true Light [as the Threefold Flame] in your heart. That beginning is to know me, to know my Word and to become it—and to fear not to assimilate my Body and my Blood, the fullness of the Omega-Alpha consciousness of the Father-Mother God. Fear not, therefore, to set aside the former things and to enter into the newness of the Spirit.

The second thing, therefore, is to stand before the altar of God that you erect in your own home and to daily, hourly invoke the power and intercession of God and to ask to be his instrument and to call upon those Seven Archangels and Lords of the Seven Rays. Call upon all of us in heaven and we will come to your side and we will open the way for you to serve your nations and your communities. The hour is late, yet everyone must give his all to this calling.

And therefore, I say to you, beloved, let those who plan on going to the United States go not in fear. For if fear is the motivation, then you must remain where you are and first conquer fear. For you flee nothing and no one, but you stand staunch and true to the call of Saint Germain and recognize that when he calls you he has very good reason, and he may not tell you all of those reasons nor may I. But we are not desirous of adding a momentum of the fearful ones and the anxious ones to our Inner Retreat.

Therefore, I speak to one and all. If you think that you come to be cared for, perish this idea. For, beloved ones, when you come to the Mystery School you come to care for the Body of God on earth, you come to care for his little ones, you come to add your momentum of Christhood.

Thus understand, beloved, that the standards are high and we expect true initiates who desire a path that leads straight up the mountain of God and [who,] by the spiral of that momentum, are determined that the purpose and reason for their being is to attain that reunion with God in this life. No lesser reason can be the foundation, beloved. Otherwise, if you are coming only for fear, you might as well remain here and become a part of that mass momentum of fear upon this continent.

Therefore, I suggest that you make calls for the violet flame and to Archangel Michael to cut you free, that you might establish in your own heart your motive and that [that] motive be pure for service and for victory and for the preservation of the Work and the Word, the Path and the Teaching, the Sangha of the Buddha and the Guru incarnate.

The preservation of the presence of the Great White Brotherhood in the earth is our determination, for upon that presence in the earth of that Brotherhood does depend the entire future of a planet.

Therefore, should the dark years and decades come upon the earth, know, then, beloved, that in that period of darkness a Light shall truly shine and remain in the Western Shamballa. And therefore, for that Light remaining and the vigil that is kept and a path of initiation that is understood and entered into, there shall remain dispensations to the Lightbearers of earth. Therefore, above all callings, beloved, this is the highest calling.

And therefore, come to serve. *In the name of Nada, I serve.* And remember my words, "The servant is not greater than his lord."[12]

I come, therefore, with my legions of angels to cast out fear and doubt and death and anxiety, for these are [those demons of the mind and the feeling world] which beset you on the path of discipleship. And therefore, legions of Light and angels of the sacred fire: according to the light of the Lightbearers of Europe, bind therefore the momentums that I have named, bind therefore the momentums and the astral consciousness that the LORD God Almighty has decreed may be taken in this hour for the lightening of the load of the Lightbearers of these states.

I, Jesus, have therefore sent my angels, and my angels move with those of the great beings who have addressed you, with Uriel and Gabriel, with Saint Germain. Therefore know that these legions of Light come, beloved, and they come with the legions of Omri-Tas and beloved Lanello. They come in the great mystery of the God Flame.

And therefore their deliverance of the Presence of Mary and Raphael is this, that there will be done for this continent all that the Great Law allows according to and only according to the service and the ministration of the Lightbearers. For the Lightbearers are the only ones who are recognized by God as having lawful right to dispensation [from the courts of heaven] in this hour.

Therefore I have come, beloved. I have placed my Electronic Presence here. The ascended disciples of my bands are with me and they reveal themselves to you at inner levels and they show themselves to you, beloved, that you might understand that you may be counted as one of them and in a few short decades attain to the victory of your ascension.

Tarry not and do not take for granted that by many years of study or by none you will so easily enter into the gates of heaven once again. For every step must be fulfilled and that which has been sown must be reaped, and that by the sacred fire with all diligence.

I believe that the ascended hosts and our bands have made abundantly clear the options of the hour. Therefore, beloved, I can tell you that our dictations and our discussions concerning these subjects will shortly be coming to a conclusion; and therefore the Lightbearers of the earth in the future will have to read these documents and will have to know that that which has been given has been given, what has been spoken has been spoken, what has been written has been written, and it must be used and it must be implemented for the further initiations to come.

But of this thing I promise you and this one thing remember, that Maitreya's Mystery School reestablished in the Heart of the Inner Retreat does provide the individual who has embodied and assimilated our dictations of the past twenty-four months with the opportunity of very direct initiation in the personal encounter through the Messenger with Maitreya.

Therefore know that the sign and the Presence of Maitreya is the Mystery School and the embodied Guru in the person of the Messenger, who is qualified as of God, God working through her, to deliver to you those very initiations, those very disciplines and those very loving teachings whereby seeing the way clearly you can mount as the mountain goats and the bighorn sheep up high, high into the mountains, high along the spiral that is ascending to your I AM Presence.

Know, then, that because this Mystery School is open to all who will come and qualify themselves, earth has the greatest opportunity to survive what Saint Germain has called the International Capitalist/Communist Conspiracy. As Saint Germain has challenged those of East and West last eve, I say to you, they are doubly challenged by the office of the Universal Christ in the entire Spirit of the Great White Brotherhood. We stand and support and reaffirm that challenge of Saint Germain.

And I tell you, heaven is united in demanding a response and a recompense from the people of Light, for the LORD's hosts have served you long. And thus, it is the message of Fátima that long and long enough have humanity been given the opportunity to turn to the Light and to take the opportunity and to heed the warning of the prophets that have been sent.

Therefore understand, beloved, that upon the decision of the true Lightbearers of Aquarius, those who understand my true coming, and upon your becoming a Christ and not merely a Christian, as Philip wrote down, upon this, beloved, does the thread of the future hang. Therefore, I say: May you be the LORD's compensation for those who have neglected so great a salvation, [for] those who do have a divine spark and do not act and do not serve and do not see and would rather follow the fallen ones than finally make an about-face and turn to the Light and walk toward the Sun.

I give you now my Body and my Blood. I give you the wine and the bread of my being. I bless the Communion offering, beloved, and therefore know that I, Jesus, have come to you, as in the ritual of the sacrament of the Last Supper I did take the loaf of bread and I did break it, teaching all, "This is my Body of universal Light-substance* which is broken for you."[13]

Therefore, that portion of my universal Christhood I give again this day, not alone to twelve but to twelve million and more. For I call my souls of Light out of every nation and the call is strong, it is persistent and it is day by day; and as long as the Father does give me leave, I, the Son, shall pursue my own.

Therefore, feel the intensity of the Love of my Sacred Heart that I give you in this hour and drink the wine of my Blood, the

*Christ-essence

essential Light of my Being, which is surely shed for you in this hour as it was shed two thousand years ago.

My beloved, I can come to you and I can speak to you and no orthodoxy shall prevent me from communing with my own, for this is the communion of the saints. And I AM at the center of the true Church Universal and Triumphant in heaven and I AM in the center of your heart and I will not be denied the oneness with my little ones. And therefore, no amount of doctrines and dogma will ever change the immortal Truth that thou art a son of God: this day has the LORD begotten thee, and this day shalt thou make thy decision to fulfill thy true reason for being.

Come unto me, all ye who labor, then, with the burden of orthodoxy and the laws of mortality, for in the Light of my Presence I will give you Life. Remember, I AM your brother always. Call to me and I will answer. Knock upon the door of my heart and I shall open. And promise me this, beloved, that when I knock upon the door of your heart you will also open and allow me to enter in and to use you in a moment of personal or national crisis in your nation, in your planet, for I need your hands and heart. I need your temples for the deliverance of souls and I need your voice to speak to them the word of comfort.

Receive me now, beloved, even as I receive you. Therefore, we are one and we are one in the beautiful prayer that has descended through the Messenger Mark, "Drink me while I am drinking thee";[14] and this is the divine interchange taught to me by Maitreya. Therefore, as Above, so below, as the disciple self-empties, the Master enters in and the Master and the disciple are one and the disciple does declare, "I and my Father are one." And therefore, there is the divine interchange, and as in heaven, so on earth we experience God through one another's vehicles.

I seal you and bless you for the victory of your whole life day by day, and the recording angels have outlined for you what is that just and perfect and holy calling for thy life in this hour. Day by day to the finish, to the end of mortality, to the soul's immortality! Day by day, thus the LORD calls you! Answer, answer and be free!

O shepherd of souls, thou Universal Christ, descend now and be unto them their Divine Reality.

"The Summit Lighthouse Sheds Its Radiance O'er All the World to Manifest as Pearls of Wisdom." This dictation by **Jesus Christ** was **delivered** by the Messenger Elizabeth Clare Prophet on **Sunday, February 28, 1988,** at the Cine Alvalade, **Lisbon, Portugal,** where she was stumping for Saint Germain's Coming Revolution in Higher Consciousness. [**N.B.** Bracketed material denotes words unspoken yet implicit in the dictation, added by the Messenger under Jesus' direction for clarity in the published text.] For notes, see Pearl no. 41.

Pearls of Wisdom®

published by The Summit Lighthouse

Vol. 31 No. 39   *Beloved Saint Thérèse of Lisieux*   July 13, 1988

Saint Germain Stumps Portugal

8

Outside the Church

Part II

My Beloved Friends, Brothers and Sisters of My Heart of Hearts,

The Father has granted my prayer that I might speak to you and to all of the Mystical Body of God in the earth. Therefore, he did send me and send this Messenger to Mexico where I did deliver my first dictation. Now he has sent me to you in this city so ancient,[1] again to call hearts that you might feel the ennoblement of the flame of God raising you to that place where no man or woman can go, save the Father himself elevate that one.

Now, my beloved, you shall hear this evening part one of my message already delivered in Mexico and I shall give you part two. And this shall be my complete statement in this century for all who know me and know my heart as I do serve in your midst and have done so in those hours allotted to me.

Following my ascension, I was accorded the grant to spend a portion of my heavens on earth. But for another portion the Father did assign me to study under the three Masters El Morya, Koot Hoomi* and Djwal Kul. These three wise men, adepts of the East who did come and tend the birth of the Lord Christ, therefore did tend with me the full flowering and birth of that Christ in my being multiplied many times over by their presence after my ascension.

Therefore, through their hearts I did learn the mysteries of the East, the profundity of the message of the Buddha and his oneness with our Lord. Thread upon thread they did assist me in weaving and weaving again the fullness of the garment of light that does comprise the whole complement of the teaching of God to this age.

---
*"Kuthumi"

Therefore, beloved, I had full opportunity to receive that instruction which did fill in for me all of those sacred mysteries that had not been revealed through the established Church. Therefore you understand that much teaching that is given to you in this hour I received at inner levels after my ascension.

As I did say recently, there are many in the Church who have had the holiness and the sanctity and the purity [prerequisite for sainthood] but because the powers that be in this world who have seated themselves in these positions of power in the Church hierarchy have not seen fit to deliver the Everlasting Gospel to the people, those who qualified for the ascension and for sainthood could not receive that promotion and therefore they did reincarnate.

Blessed ones, I desire not to give you any cause for personal pride or spiritual pride but I am here to tell you that some who are in this place are among those who have reincarnated because they have been "shortchanged," as you would say, by the Church and its tradition.

Therefore, beloved, I come to tell you that the way of discipleship can be seen by you as a thousand stairs upon a thousand-tiered golden spiral and that step by step there is an orderly path of discipline. These Masters who have sponsored your Messenger and this activity, who have supported Jesus in establishing through the Messengers the true Church Universal and Triumphant on earth have seen fit to also establish an ordered ritual, for they are fully aware what it takes to mount one of these steps.

The figure of the nun burdened with the cancer in her body, concealing this from all others and occupying herself with the humble task of scrubbing the stairs of the enclave[2] must be seen as archetypal of the soul who, bearing her karma, recognizes that she must clear the debris in each step of consciousness, scrubbing by the violet flame until that level of record and ideation is fully and wholly transmuted. In the process she may mount a single step. In past ages it would take a soul perhaps an entire lifetime to mount a single step, for the only purging of karma and record and self, as well as its outcropping in the body as disease, would be manifest through prayer and works of penance.

Thus, beloved, to know "how great, how great thou art, O God, my Father, my Mother, how great is the gift of the violet flame!" you must establish a co-measurement, a sense of realism that such a gift is also an experiment. For it is a dispensation for which ascended beings of the Seventh Ray, not the least of whom being your beloved Saint Germain, have given this opportunity. And after a certain lapse of cycles they will give accounting before the Lords of Karma and the Four and Twenty Elders who stand round the great white throne, and they shall determine whether a people have taken that flame and used it only to deliver themselves of their discomforts [or whether they have] used it seriously for the path of initiation as an adjunct, as a mighty assistance to the soul's entering in.

You must therefore understand that you are watchmen of the night, keeping the watch in your time and in your place as many who have gone before you have kept that watch. In this dark night of the age of the Kali Yuga, you bear violet flame torches and torches of illumination with the beloved Mother Liberty. Therefore, beloved, understand that all holy orders have had their rituals and their disciplines and their rules.

Therefore, those who would serve to keep the flame of this nation must come into alignment, as must those of every nation and city, to understand that it is both the spirit and the letter of the Law which must be fulfilled and obedience in the details of service and the givingness of self. It is this that will lead most swiftly to the desired goal of light in the seven chakras balanced in the supreme blessing of the Father-Mother God.

This balance, beloved, and the Mystery of Surrender that is the rosary of our dear, most Blessed Mother will enable you to understand how you may be the vessel not alone for your Christ Self, the Anointed One, but for beings of great light such as the Avalokiteśvara, beings who have come down the centuries such as Maitreya and even the Lord Sanat Kumara. Again, this is never a point of spiritual pride but of everlasting humility that hour by hour remembers to make oneself worthy and worthier still.

So often when the Ascended Masters have dictated to the people of this earth who have gathered to hear them through this Messenger, those most psychologically disturbed individuals, those who have the greatest tendency toward self-idolatry have immediately assumed that they have far greater attainment than they do, far greater attainment than they have actualized in this octave. Thus, to reveal the Path and its possibilities does render to some a test that they do not pass well.

Thus, beloved, it is important to remember the teaching of our beloved Serapis Bey, with whom I have also studied, as this blessed Master has revealed the utter humility of the Lord Christ as he did visit the retreat at Luxor even in his final embodiment. And this experience of our beloved Jesus, Jesus of the Sacred Heart, is not written down in the annals of the historians of the East. Nevertheless, by the grace of the Holy Spirit it was dictated by Serapis to Mark Prophet, whom I love as our Saint Mark and our Saint Bonaventure and who also must needs be called Saint Origen. And therefore he did write down Serapis Bey's *Dossier* and revealed how even the Lord Christ, who could have been received at the highest levels of initiations, requested to be placed on the very first step of the neophyte and to take each step in succession, thereby confirming, proving and reproving his own soul, strengthening himself and also setting an example for all who would follow him.

May you truly follow him and understand that the very first principles and precepts are the foundation of the pyramid that you build and stone upon stone is the soul perfected, not, then, in giant leaps but rather in the constancy and consecration daily whereby the flame increases by your devotion; and for the very reason of your self-discipline and constancy the Lord may add unto you the Spirit of his Presence in a great power.

And when you feel that Holy Spirit descending upon you, beloved, again, let it not be a source of spiritual pride; and see to it that you do not run and make much ado about yourself and your spiritual path to others, therefore setting yourself up, then, as someone that is better than the rest.

These are the secrets of God in your heart and they must be sealed there. For you see, when you make any statement about your spiritual experiences the devils also listen and the fallen angels, and the moment you claim some level of experience they come to challenge you. And in their challenge, therefore, you are obliged to face the Adversary and prove that point of the Law when in fact this initiation may not be on schedule for your lifestream.

Thus, by too quickly assuming a spiritual mastery, you precipitate challenges for which you are not ready; and therefore these fallen ones, adepts on the left-handed path, will stand on the very step [that] you would mount and they stand and they challenge and therefore they block the way.

'Tis then that you run and hide beneath the wings of the Almighty in the person of Saint Michael the Archangel, and when you call to him he does defeat that one. Thus, beloved, it is like a child who taunts the wild animal and by and by the wild animal does [move to] attack him and then he runs swiftly away.

Understand, precious hearts, the realism of the left-handed path and the antichrists in the world, for they come to precipitate initiations that are not on your timetable. They did so in the Mystery School of Eden before twin flames, therefore delivering to them the fruit of the Tree of Knowledge of Good and Evil before this initiation should be given to them by the Great Initiator, the then representative of the Cosmic Christ.

Therefore, beloved, once you accept the false initiation of the false gurus you may set yourself back thousands of years. Some twin flames who were in that Mystery School have not regained their position vis-à-vis Lord Maitreya which they lost in that hour when through their own spiritual pride or naïveté, as the case may be, they did accept the fruit from the Fallen One.

Many false gurus have come forth even out of the East. And somehow the West, not having been healed or purged of that spiritual pride, have so readily accepted these talkers who come saying that they represent the lineage of unascended adepts and masters. Blessed ones, it is well to remember the counsel of your Lord: "The kingdom of God is within you." It is well to understand that these [gurus] of the old dispensation cannot take you where you must go in this age.

Have you ever asked them why, if they have all of this adeptship, they have not taken the government and the economy of India under their great mastery, why they have not fed the poor and educated the masses and raised up India to a place where she might be a vessel of the true Buddha and the Cosmic Christ? If there are all these masters, then where is their proof of their love of this humanity? They will provide you with many excuses, but the true adepts of the East are beyond reach and thus you may know them when you come to the level of your Holy Christ Self and I AM Presence.

Seek ye first this great kingdom of God and know, then, that where the Ascended Masters are and where the Messenger is, there you will see, when your eyes are purged by the fiery baptism of Jesus, always the presence of Babaji, always the presence of unascended masters of the Himalayas.

[But] the false gurus are a great plague upon Europe and America, for again they have turned aside the reincarnated tribes of light of Sanat Kumara into byways of the neglect of the day-to-day affairs of their civilization. Teaching a counterfeit path of the East in the West, they have therefore deterred you from your calling to draw forth the light by the power of the name I AM THAT I AM and to direct it into the physical octave.

The challenges of the West are physical. You have completed your incarnations in the East. You have risen to an inner oneness by the science of the AUM and the Word of Brahman in the beginning. You have reincarnated here for the final incarnation if you choose to accept it or for the final several incarnations to take the portion of your causal body and to direct it into form.

Therefore, beloved, I attest to you, and may you know my vibration and know that my Word is true, that I have served with this beloved Messenger when she was embodied as Saint Clare and Saint Catherine. And therefore we are one in an ancient service and calling to preserve the mysteries of Christ within the Church—not as a doctrine, for the hierarchy forbade it. Therefore we did preserve it as a fire in our hearts that burned, that none could quench, that none could turn back.

And therefore I move with the Messenger, giving my strength and support from the higher octaves; and from the ascended level I may also gladly use her outreach to call my own, my sisters and brothers, the religious, the priests, the brothers, the devotees of holy Church who do not understand the schism within that has to do with interior corruption and uncleanness and the violation of the sacred fire and the psyche by the introduction of all manner of modern techniques, whether of self-hypnosis, hypnosis or psychology and all manner of deviations practiced by the priests themselves.

Blessed hearts, the corruption is rampant and rife. Therefore, know that when Mother Mary did appear at Knock, she did come standing outside of the Church and not within.[3] When she did appear at Fátima and [now] at Medjugorje in Yugoslavia, again it [was and] is to the pure heart of the child outside of the edifice.

Know, then, beloved, that the Church can no longer contain the Mystical Body of God and yet there is great fear among those who are yet trapped within its walls—who fear to disassociate themselves, for they know in their hearts that once this Church had the dispensation of Christ.

Know, then, beloved, that these require courage and a path and you also require courage and a path. Therefore the Father has anointed me with angels that he has given to me as my very own bands to come to you and to assist you and to plead this cause: that these holy ones of God within the Church, whose very light and blood are the sustenance thereof [and who] are also being devoured by it, [might be set free from their captivity in answer to your calls].

Therefore, these are candidates for the ascension who will not realize that ascension at the end of this age as is their cosmic timetable, for they are not given the violet flame or the ancient mysteries preserved by early Christians as the true faith of our Lord, today called Gnosticism. The Gnosticism that has been discovered in this "library in a jar" at Nag Hammadi in 1945 is certainly not the final word, is certainly not the perfected doctrine, but the elements within it reveal clearly that which was banned as heresy by the Church Fathers; and by their banning of this true teaching of Jesus, they have denied our Lord's doctrine to all the faithful these seventeen hundred years or more.

Know, then, beloved, that Christ has indeed long ago been put out of this Church and that Christ resides only in the pure hearts of those who are within it, and some of these pure hearts have risen to the position of pope and high office and some have been the humble of no particular stature. Therefore they in their

hearts of fire rather than through an organization or a doctrine
have kept alive the true Presence of Jesus [on earth and, coincidentally, within the Church].

Know, then, beloved, that there is a mission to be performed
and there are souls to be cut free who fear that if they sever their
allegiance to an earthly institution their souls will experience
eternal damnation in hellfire. Blessed hearts, this fear is ungodly
and I would tell you I have personally witnessed it in my own life
and as I move through the religious and among them this day.
Their fear is so great that it is a question of whether they must
reincarnate outside the Church if they are ever to be delivered of
that fear of this false hierarchy.

Know, then, beloved, that were the power of the teaching to
be received by them, could this message be preached throughout
the world in the churches, there could indeed be the rallying of
millions to the heart of Mother Mary and Saint Joseph and those
who are truly in a position under God to do something about the
world problems. You understand, then, the tear in our eye and the
weeping Madonnas for the very fact that all of the ingredients,
the knowledge, the teaching, the intercession—all of this is present
for a world's salvation. And the blind leaders of the blind have
denied it again as they denied it on Atlantis, on Lemuria and in
other civilizations that have passed away.

This is not only a problem of a year or a decade. It is a
problem of the culmination of twelve thousand years of spiritual
evolution since the sinking of Atlantis, and therefore in ten-
thousand-year cycles is an opportunity given for a people again to
transcend themselves. Thus, the denial of this age [of the enlightenment of the Christ of Pisces] to the millions who are of the Light
on this planet can set back the course of planetary evolution as
much as another ten thousand years.

Therefore, beloved, the intensity of the ministration of angels
would cause you to be in such awe and ecstasy as to enter into a
spiritual path so intense whereby you yourself should be infused
with the light of the Great Central Sun for the conversion of many.
Above all, beloved, it is essential to be fearless and to observe the
fearlessness of the revolutionaries of the Spirit East and West.
Your fearlessness comes not, again, in personal pride of spiritual
attainment but in the utter giving of oneself to God whereby you
receive the glory and protection of the Archangels and you fear
neither loss of reputation nor friend nor life. For the inner being is
aglow with fire and you know that your soul will be utterly
assumed into the pillar of ascension's flame as my soul was in the
hour of my passing.

And therefore this life that you have, this life that is God's, is given for the many who know not the way to go and for whom you pray daily:

Father, forgive thy children, for they know not what they do. They are the victims of a conspired ignorance. Therefore, neglect not those who are neglected by those who ought to be their shepherds, feeding them, *feeding them, feeding them, feeding them* hour by hour in measures of soul resuscitation the true Communion wine and bread of the Lord's own Body.

Know, then, beloved, that each individual in his time passes through the initiations through which Jesus passed. There is a crucifixion, therefore, that is of this world as fallen angels attempt to preempt the day and the hour of the true sign of the cross in the life of the individual wherein the soul is fastened to the cosmic cross of white fire and angels gathering round celebrate the alchemical marriage—"Father, into thine arms I commend my spirit." Into the heart of the living Christ the soul, then, is assumed.

It [the true crucifixion] is in this hour, then, a path of initiation and the transfiguration does precede that crucifixion and prior to that a life of works, good works and healing, joy and teaching. Therefore take care to study in order that thy teaching be true and just, rightly dividing the word of Truth.

Blessed ones, I speak now not [only] of the individual initiation but to tell you that the hour is come that the nations themselves as tribes, ancient tribes of a karmic group, are [also] facing the initiation of the crucifixion. And because they have not responded to their ancient teachers and therefore have had a karma of vulnerability to the denial of the Truth to them by their current leaders, they come ill-prepared to this magnificent moment when, though the world condemnation and the trial of the world and the fallen ones be upon them, those nations could rally in defense of the living Christ and their own opportunity to give birth to that Christ.

Therefore, you will see that the crucifixion, which is a divine initiation, is preempted by fallen angels who would desire to utterly crucify and destroy those souls who have not yet been wed to Christ, as Jesus was thoroughly wed to the Light in the initiation of the transfiguration on the Mount of Transfiguration. That filling of his body with the fullness and intensity of the white light was an experience whereby he was also empowered to move on and to face the courts of hell who put the Son of God on trial.

Blessed ones, in this hour it is well to understand and remember that in the hour of the ascension of the soul of the beloved Mark, this Messenger with you did receive that initiation of the transfiguration and then, beloved, [that of] the descent into hell; for fifty-one percent of her karma had been balanced, [she] therefore spending seven years in that descent into hell and more, preaching to fallen angels and spirits gone out of the way of the Lord. During that period, then, at successive stages one by one those fallen ones who rejected the true path of Maitreya through her did judge and condemn her and ultimately bring her before the trial of the courts of this world.

Know, then, that you are serving with a Messenger who has never shirked her responsibility or the call to take the next step on this path so that you might understand that it is entirely possible with God for the soul on earth today to pass through each and every step of these initiations through which Jesus passed.

Understand, beloved, that the crucifixion of the individual Messenger is behind her but the crucifixion of the nation and of the Body of God itself is yet nigh. For this reason I am permitted to tell you [that] you have been called to come to the Inner Retreat. For it is the Community of the Body of God—those saints who are preparing for the ascension—who, strengthened by one another, reinforced by one another in prayer and supplication and in physical mastery of the environment, may together meet and pass through all of the period of the balancing of karma that does precede the transfiguration and the crucifixion which does follow it.

Therefore, know, beloved, that there does come a time, as my Father in heaven has asked me to tell you this evening, when the [walking of the] individual path of the thirty-three steps of the son of God, which are multiplied over those thousand stairs, does become the most important event in the life of the individual and the nations and the planet. Because the light is so great and the victory of such cosmic import to all life upon a planet, the hour does come when their ministrations to life must be translated and must be raised to the point where the fulfillment of their individual Christhood along that path does become more expedient to the entire Great White Brotherhood and the World Mother than any other service that they might possibly render.

Therefore, for that reason you are called and called to accelerate within the Community under the disciplines of the holy order, the Order of Saint Francis and Saint Clare, reinstituted within this church years ago. Who else, then, beloved, would have the qualifications to lead you on this path than your own reincarnated sister Clare? Remember, then, that her Light and Presence is far beyond even that which it was in those days. For the cumulative causal body that she does bring to you comes from her discipleship under the adepts of East and West in many lifetimes.

Know, then, beloved, that the fire in the mountain of the Northern Rockies is the fire of the saints and the true holy Church that shall be kept alive even through the transitions that earth shall make. That you might become the fire of the Mystical Body of God, we call you to that disciplined life in the understanding that those who reach the top of the pyramid are those who by their service guarantee to all others who are at its base that when they too arrive at the hour of this initiation, there will yet be a Mystery School and a platform of evolution called planet earth. It is to this end that the Masters, the Archangels have spoken to you during this weekend and to this goal that we have directed your attention.

Those who have not completed their disciplines in the outer world nor truly fulfilled their required service to minister to life and to teach cannot leap and desire, then, by the motive of fear or self-preservation to suddenly enter into the Mystery School. It is those who have balanced a certain karma and ministered to the nations of Europe who are called in this hour, and they themselves must have a certain level of attainment and then the realization that while they have ministered in the field they have not received all of the training and chelaship that would normally be commensurate with their current level of service. These will also come in the footsteps of Jesus to present themselves as neophytes on the first steps.

Thus, those who come newly to the Path should receive from these blessed brothers and sisters who have served you in all nations the fire of their hearts' devotion. And you must in appreciation make the vow to yourself and to God in this hour that these who have served shall not have lived in vain, as you may recall the words of President Abraham Lincoln, "that these dead shall not have died in vain."

Therefore, I speak for the saints of the Church, those who have ascended and those who have not. They have given their life and their blood to reinfuse that Church with light until it has come to an age where that light is so denied [by the false hierarchy within the Church] that the Father will no longer allow that light of the saints to be retained in the Church as a repository for it.

Thus, this Church Universal and Triumphant is the crystal chalice where that light is reserved for those coming after them. Looking upon these lives and those who are robed in white who wait for you beneath the altar of God in the etheric octave (for they are not able to ascend until you [also enter that ritual and initiation] and until they have fulfilled at inner levels their rituals of violet flame transmutation of karma), of these I say, then, [I] having been a part of this Church for many lifetimes, that they may not have died in vain but that their death might be a sign to all that for death to be followed by the life everlasting the soul does require a path and submission to the Hierarchy of the ascended saints robed in white, the Great White Brotherhood, [and a] submission to a path which at times, beloved, becomes distasteful not because of the Path but because the very biliousness of one's own karma does rise within the belly and return to the mouth to make one realize that there are astral toxins as well as physical toxins, all of which are to be purged in you for that path of soul purity and perfectionment.

I am here as a living witness that [it is] "in spite of" rather than "because of" outer institutions [that] the soul ascends to God. The fallen angels have no power over thee except the power thou givest them by an absence of the raising up of the Light [of the Divine Mother] within yourself. Thus, know that they may delay but never ultimately turn back the victory of a soul who knows that she is the beloved of her Lord and the beloved of her God.

Of one thing I have the conviction and have always had the conviction, that in my soul I was the living bride of Jesus. Through all of the periods of self-doubt and self-mortification of my own karma returning, I, beloved, rested my heart in the Star of his Hope and Love. This was a vindication and the restoration in my inner being of the sense of dignity, integrity and self-worth that sometimes becomes bowed down by unnecessarily harsh disciplines which involve the condemnation for one's sin and sinfulness while failing to also give the upliftment of one's glory in Christ.

Therefore, as there is a church in heaven and a church on earth, there is a body that you wear in heaven which is thy Christ and a body you wear on earth, the body where karma remains. Know, then, that not all of thy being is in this form but thy being is in the highest realms and reaches of thy God.

Take heed, then; for those who accelerate [on] the path of Jesus' life all the way to the hour of their resurrection, they shall be ready when their nations undergo the trial and crucifixion, and they shall keep a flame in the mountain of God that the threefold flame of the nations be not extinguished but live and endure to be rekindled again when new generations of Lightbearers can be born once the earth has been purged of a karma of the seed of the wicked and of a neglect of the children of God. These things must come to pass.

Know, then, that you may receive the initiation of the resurrection and yet retain physical life and form. To walk about endued with the Spirit of the Resurrection, let this be thy goal. For remember, "the Light shone in the darkness and the darkness comprehended it not, but we beheld his glory, the glory as [of] the only begotten Son of God," in the profile, in the Presence of our brother Jesus.

Because he lived, we have a path to follow. We know [for we have been told] the decisions he made each step of the way; and as his life is revealed to you, as recorded in akasha, and you have shown to you the many things which he said and did which the world's books could not contain, you will have abundant criteria for decisions of righteousness that you must also make on the path of [soul-]testing when you reach the level where Absolute Evil seems right and Absolute Good seems wrong. Thus, the two-edged sword of the Universal Christ Mind in you will always separate the Real from the Unreal and *by the steadfastness of your heart in the Sacred Heart of Jesus you will know what is the right choice for you.*

Therefore, in righteousness and in faithfulness, one with the Sacred Heart of Jesus as your Messenger is, you will come to the Place prophesied by Jesus when he was on earth, lo, two thousand years ago, prophesied to Saint Martha as the one where you would gather in this age. As by her heart in the heart of Jesus she followed the sign, so may you also know that every path and every station of the cross that you walk with the Divine Mother is already marked, and by your heart you will know it and you will find it.

I AM with you and all who aspire to this victory. Now I flood to you millions of pink roses from my causal body that you may know that you have a sister who cares for you and is with you unto the hour of your soul's victory in Divine Love. And may all of your victories of that Divine Love be spent upon earth until all who are a part of our Lord's harvest in this age are wholly ascended in the light and free.

I thank you for your gracious presence, your blessed hearts of purity, and I now withdraw to the heart of Jesus as I am taken to higher octaves by my Lord.

This dictation by **Saint Thérèse of Lisieux** was **delivered** by the Messenger Elizabeth Clare Prophet on **February 28, 1988**, at the Cine Alvalade, **Lisbon, Portugal.** (1) The origins of **Lisbon,** the capital of Portugal, prior to the Roman occupation of the city in 205 B.C. are unknown. Its founders may have been Phoenicians who established the city as a trading station as early as 1200 B.C. Other legends claim that Lisbon was founded by Elisha, the grandson of Abraham, or Ulysses, from whom its ancient name, Olisipo, may be derived. (2) **Saint Bernadette** (1844–1879), a devout peasant to whom the Blessed Virgin appeared 18 times in a grotto near Lourdes, France, when she was 14, endured the painful and debilitating disease of tuberculosis of the bone for more than seven years while she served as a Sister of Notre Dame at the Convent of Saint-Gildard. During the last two years of her life she developed a large tumor on her knee, which she kept a secret as long as she could so she would not be relieved of her duties, as portrayed in the film *The Song of Bernadette* (1943) based on Franz Werfel's novel by the same name. (3) **Mother Mary's appearance at Knock.** On August 21, 1879, the Blessed Mother with Saint Joseph on her right and Saint John the Evangelist on her left appeared in a silent visitation before the south gable wall of the small church at Knock, County Mayo, Ireland. The apparition was reportedly seen by about 18 people. Witnesses said the Blessed Mother was dressed as a queen in brilliant white raiment and wore a crown, with a rose over her forehead where the crown fitted her brow. She was gazing upward and appeared to be praying. Following this visitation, many pilgrims received miraculous cures. For an excerpt on the significance of the Knock appearance from Elizabeth Clare Prophet's sermon at Croagh Patrick, Ireland, see 1980 *Pearls of Wisdom,* pp. 287–88.

Pearls of Wisdom®
published by The Summit Lighthouse

| Vol. 31 No. 40 | Beloved Mother Mary's Fátima Message | July 16, 1988 |

Saint Germain Stumps Portugal
9
I Still Desire to Save a World
The Gift of My Immaculate Heart

My Beloved,

You are the comfort and consolation of my soul at Fátima. For as those enlightened by my Son and his Holy Spirit gather, truly the rekindling light of Fátima is known.

Blessed ones, the nonacceptance of my appearances here and elsewhere early when they are given is already the indication of the nonacceptance, the nondesiring of individuals, prelates within the hierarchy of orthodoxy, who are concerned lest in the purity of the heart of a child, as in the child Samuel, they should be exposed and their evil deeds revealed.[1]

Thus, it is they who consider that my tears are for earth and my children. I tell you, beloved, I also weep for Jerusalem as the archetypal sound of every city, of the Vatican, and the Establishment where there is not even a vestment or a vestiture of a semblance of the true identity of my Son in their midst. Yet by my love for the hearts of a people my flame does burn on, for I am faithful to my own.

Therefore, midst a structure that is corrupt, midst individuals whose corruption does mount all the way to their disobedience to my word given through the hearts of these three children, I come. I come, beloved, and therefore you may understand how those who are among the heavenly hosts become bound on earth,[2] for the princes of this world hold sway. And though they control the structures and though in some cases they limit the unfoldment of the flower of the soul, yet they cannot steal from Jesus the true hearts that are his.

How necessary, then, it was for the Angel of Peace to teach the children true prayer.³ How grateful you must be, then, that your Messenger-angel is visible to you, teaching you how to pray, teaching you how to move with the winds of Aquarius as the Holy Spirit does infill you. I come in this hour, then, truly able to anchor in this place the spirit of the New Age that is neither allowed nor permitted entrée into the vessel of the Holy Church.

Blessed ones, there is one thing in my desiring concerning your own path of which I would speak to you. Though it has been said before, I desire that you should seek and find through meditation with the seraphim of God a new sense of holiness concerning your very own self, your life, your soul, your path, your daily prayers and especially your decrees, that you might understand that holiness is a presence and it is an aura and [that] this presence and aura is easily dissipated through disobedience to the inner Word, through dissipation by any form of discord or even a sense of the mundane.

How easily the minds of our chelas, then, flit from those moments of ecstasy in higher octaves in prayer and hymn to those things that appear on the screen of the television, come through the media or simply are about the mundane, the banal conversations of life. Unseemly conversation may also dissipate this holiness, for holiness is always sustained by your Holy Christ Self, so near to your being, and by the blessed angels.

Thus, beloved, in a world that is reeling and reeking with the astral plane we are comforted as we pass by those whose holiness is so tender and so loving and so evincing of the Person of the Holy Spirit that we may truly make ourselves one with that aura and multiply the power and the influence of the holiness of God in the earth.

I come in this hour to explain to you that due to the [inaction of the] hierarchy of the [Roman] Church it is not possible to save the millions of souls whom I desire to save, such limitations and constraints have they placed upon them and upon myself and upon my message and upon my Messenger. Therefore, beloved, those who are told merely to pray the rosary may increase holiness, may raise up the Light within themselves, but, not [being] taught how to challenge the very ones who should* be the instrument of the dark prophecies that I did deliver, [they do not fulfill their karmic role as soldiers of the Church Militant⁴].

Therefore understand, beloved, that the saving of these souls may be unto eternal Life but it may not be that they will endure to bring in the New Age in this life. Blessed ones, it is because the door to the Holy of Holies has not been opened unto them and [because] those who reserve this place at the altar of God for themselves have

---
*who are to be

failed to tell my children, as you have been taught by the Mother, that your own Holy Christ Self is the high priest in the Holy of Holies, the inner sanctum of your own being. Thus, my beloved, to place all things [of God] exterior to [outside] oneself [in ritual and in life], to retain forms of penance that are [in the nature of] self-immolation [without the raising up of the Christ in the supplicant] when the violet flame has now been available for over fifty years, this does cause [more than] a tear in my eye.

I come, then, in this hour speaking softly to you, for my Presence and energy is extended throughout the planetary body. Blessed ones, I hold a great balance for you and I hold my being as a Presence that can turn back and hold back the forces of intended war and the attack upon the economy, which is the attack truly upon yourselves. Understand, then, my beloved, that this weight that I bear is a burden truly grievous to be borne and it is also the cause for the shedding of the tear; and therefore I ask you to remember me as your Mother and to understand, sweet sons and daughters of Light, that you must bear more of this burden.

The so great a salvation you have been given, the Watch[5] and the rosaries, all of the decrees that are so effective, must needs be given by you hour upon hour upon hour. Therefore, this being accomplished in the full fervor of the heart, you will come to know that your Presence and holiness is one and that your Presence is indeed all around you.

Therefore, among some who have had this teaching short or long time, there is yet the absence of this sense. Blessed ones, there is a fervor that can be delivered in giving decrees and then there is a conversational tone whereby the heart is not engaged, the fire is not generated and the eyes wander about the room as the individual is not able to concentrate or even to focus on the words that are being repeated.

Blessed ones, all religions have fallen into decay when the ritual of the Word has become rote. Not only do you not exert a fire in delivering the Word by the power of the throat chakra but you fail to remember that a decree is given through seven chakras and that the fervor of the seven rays in you going forth can in fact be the instrument of the Elohim of God through you.

We desire to see such a sense of co-measurement in you of the enormous danger to a planet in contradistinction to the great immensity of heaven descending (as you, too, mourn for those who are bowed down and burdened and who may pass from the screen of life in an untimely manner) that in such heart pain [as you, too, may feel] as you sense the world pain, you cry out to the living God, as you have never cried out before, to use you as an instrument for the deliverance of a planet.

It is this level and fervor of the saints that I should expect of all those who have received the teaching on this path. Anything less, beloved, is a sign that you truly have not understood how so great a power has been given unto you. And, beloved, it was I who went before the Father to secure the dispensations in this century for this violet flame to be given to you, for the way to be made plain and clear and open for Saint Germain, for El Morya, for all of my Sons, the Masters of the Seven Rays.

Blessed hearts, I did this out of the very same fervor of which I am speaking to you, out of the depth of my soul crying out for assistance unto those who had no intercessors in the churches, no true shepherds, none who would give them fully the cup of wine, fully that portion of the Bread of Life[6] which came down from heaven for their soul's conversion, for the engrafting of the Word. Blessed hearts, by my imploring did these activities come forth, and therefore you can understand how I also have incurred karma for the loss and misuse of this release by some.

I pray, then, you will realize that there have been thousands who have contacted this teaching in the past fifty years since the [chart and the teaching of the] I AM Presence was released. Understand, beloved, that many who have contacted it [this knowledge of the Divine Self] have simply gone their way disinterested. Others have been aroused to an intensity of ire and they and their hatred have been pitted against our mouthpieces as these mouthpieces have gone forth to deliver the Ascended Masters' dictations.

Blessed ones, the very presence in the earth of this path [of the soul's ascent to God] has been the drawing of a line of Light and Darkness. It is certainly not an hour to speak of that which might have been, and yet you may understand a mother's heart and indulge me for a moment as I tell you that ten thousand-times-ten thousand could be marching with the violet flame in this hour had their own karma and human selfishness not blinded them, had they not been offended in one of our Messengers in this or that mode or guise. Blessed ones, truly karma is a blinding factor in the lives of individuals; and therefore, where they do not see and [where] they who could have the vision do not carry it, all of a planet may perish.

How long have the ascended hosts waited for a golden age to appear! This century, begun so beautifully, [was] so immediately taken over by those forces of hell that came as the Bolsheviks. These [rebels against the Word], beloved ones, did go forth, and therefore I made my appearance early that something might be done. But the "powers that be" [the original powers of Death and

Hell] worked their schemes and the abdication of the destiny, [the] responsibility of America [to defend world and individual freedom], has been almost complete.[7] Yet in every nation there have been betrayers, and instead of condemning America and Americans, there should have been a forthright challenge made by the leaders of Europe to challenge and decry the betrayal of the freedom fighters [by the archdeceivers] worldwide.

Billions of souls have been lost to World Communism by the betrayers in the United States government. Look at China herself and the Soviet Union. These could have been turned to [in the direction of] the free enterprise societies. These people who were once industrious and filled with the divine spark of the threefold flame, who had every opportunity and joy and determination to be the builders of the future have now gone down under a system whose very evil, beloved, does cause them to lose hope, to lose faith, to have crushed in them their own charity.

And therefore the threefold flame in many millions is even smaller than one-sixteenth of an inch in height. Where it does become less and less until it is almost infinitesimal, one reaches the point where it is fairly snuffed out and then you see how there does come upon an entire nation that look of absence. Hopelessness is no longer the look; it is simply one of absence. No one is there in that temple, once the creation of God.

Blessed hearts, not all those who are without a threefold flame this day are the original creation of mechanization man. Many of these once had that same hope and fervor that you have. But, beloved ones, there does come a time in the life of a soul when she is trodden upon lifetime after lifetime by these monsters out of hell with none that come [to the rescue]—no hope, no awareness, no longer any memory or sense of Divine Reality. And then, beloved, when the individual does let go of life itself, there comes that moment of darkness when none can reach that one.

Blessed hearts, I am there when this does occur and yet I can do nothing. For like all those of us in realms above, we must obey the very mandate of free will and the laws governing the octaves.

Thus I have presented myself to children always to teach them to pray and to pray the rosary, for in the rosary there is truly the raising up of the Light* of the Divine Mother. And where all else does fail, it is truly the Mother Light that retains hope in the being and the soul and the consciousness of the individual.

Blessed hearts, the Fátima message has not changed. You must understand this. Though I have dictated [on my] desire to turn it around and in some areas there has been a mitigation, what is the true cause of this prophecy continuing is that those to whom

*Kundalini, sacred fire that rises from the base-of-the-spine chakra to the crown

it has been given, those who have occupied the chair of Peter, these have chosen not to relate it to the heads of state of free nations. They have chosen not to call congresses of the faithful across all lines of religious belief to warn, to organize, to summon and to rally the forces of freedom worldwide from the beginning to defeat the ugly beast of World Communism. And thus it has grown and it has become a planetary dragon.

Blessed ones, you must understand just how profound is my grief in this hour that there has not been one representing my Son in the Church of Rome who would rally the people to defend, even by paying with the price of their lives, the flame of freedom in their hearts and in the earth—not one who has dared to give his life without fear of the consequences since 1917 when I did foretell even the coming of the greater war which has passed as World War II. This, too, could have been averted.

But I tell you, beloved, those who are not the sons of God in the earth who occupy bodies of men, these are such evil devils, I cannot even tell you, and their corruption has reached all the way to the levels of Protestantism and even our own church, the Roman Catholic Church. Blessed ones, realize that the infamy of their lust against little children, against babes, against every part of life and their desecration of me as I am in the body of all women of the world is beyond hell itself.

Therefore, beloved, it is certainly a truth that in this age my Son will not allow these deprivations of the Light [of the Divine Mother] in the earth to continue. Know, then, beloved, that the hour is long past that this judgment should have taken place. But for the faithful who have given the rosary, but for yourselves whose calls have been powerful and an immense barrier to the acceleration of World Communism, all these things should have already come to pass.

Nevertheless, in the interim greater preparations have been made by these forces of the fallen ones. Therefore, beloved, it must be unmistakable in your awareness that the plan for Europe is no ordinary war. You may not think back on World War II and say to yourselves, "I will stay and hold the balance and somehow survive" or "I will get out at the last minute."

Blessed ones, if (and I say if, for nothing is final until it is physical), but if and when such a war should take place, it should be a blitzkrieg such as none has ever seen. And this lightning war should descend as chemical death, as biological/bacteriological death along with those forces of modern weapons and warfare. Understand, therefore, that should it take place the devastation would be almost instantaneous.

This is a plot of the Soviet world so intense, so calculated, so planned, charted and visualized, so prepared for, that any of you who will call to me may be shown by myself directly or from our retreat the very image of these Soviet tanks moving across Europe en masse. Blessed ones, it is not hard to see. But those who do not see are those who will not see,[8] for it is frightful indeed. It is like looking into hell itself, and even the saints have fainted and swooned when Jesus has showed them a portion of that hell.

Therefore, beloved, you must understand the burden upon your Messenger, for the reaction to the messages that have been delivered through her are such that individuals take a very stiff point of consciousness, and when they hear such prophecies they decide that they can do nothing about it and they become almost immobilized by their fear. On the other hand, beloved, they take them lightly and become superficial and decide that with a certain amount of decrees they will avert the entire calamity and they simply go about their business waiting for the day when we will deliver a dictation saying that all is past and the victory is won and none of these things shall take place.

Beloved ones, these two extremes are dangerous. You must realize that it is possible to deter all prophecy. You must realize that God the Father in his very Person and heart does reserve to that Person and heart the decision as to what to unleash and what not to unleash. Therefore, as it is not given the Son to know the hour and the day,[9] so it is not given to the Messenger. Therefore you must understand that when the percentages are so high that an event will take place, it is no longer possible to make any other plans than those which are given to you to secure yourselves and to secure the bastions of liberty in our retreat.

You need to understand that if there is an 8 percent chance that none of these things will come to pass and that 8 percent does actually become the reality, you must not think that you will turn and point the finger and say that your Messenger was incorrect and the prophecy was false. You must understand that prophecy is highly complex. There are beings who are Cosmic Beings at the level of Elohim who though they would do all in their power to stand between this planet and her karma are not able to do so. Therefore understand, beloved, that there must be a response in your own heart and soul once and for all.

We cannot and will not long repeat our messages concerning this outcome. It is a burden to us and it is a burden to the Messenger and it does weary the ethers. Enough has been said. And Saint Germain has said this to me this very day, "Beloved Mother Mary, go speak to them once more from the profoundness of your heart and, according to the will of the Father, so give to them one final word."

Therefore I come to you, beloved, to enable you to understand that when called by the Brotherhood and called by God, [you] must [have] a sense of reserve that there are many more reasons for that call than the obvious or that which may be being said.

Thus obedience has ever been a necessity of the Guru-chela relationship. For one cannot give to those of lesser attainment that which they will become aware of through the very process of obedience. It is like climbing a mountain. Each few yards that you climb gives you a new vista and until you climb them you simply do not see the next mountain on the horizon, the next valley over the mountain below you.

Know, then, beloved, that you must earn the right to see, and the means of earning the right to see is obedience itself. And therefore, though the Messenger has said, "May I not tell them more? May I not tell them more?" we have always said: "Those who will not hear and heed what we have already said would only be burdened by our saying more. When they come to a higher resolution of their own inner being, they will have the inner fortitude, the Light will be raised up and they will also see, for they will become one with myself."

Becoming one with myself to have that vision, beloved, is to give with me aloud in full fervor and devotion daily that fifteen-minute rosary, which was shortened for you from forty-five minutes, which was its original length. Therefore, it is called the Child's Rosary.[10]

We understand, therefore, how the hours of the day are occupied in all that you desire to do to save souls, to prepare yourselves, to support the Messenger, to build the Inner Retreat, to determine how you will pass through those citadels of the world and the sentinels who guard them who have their requirements for immigration and the legalization of your status in another country such as the United States.

Blessed ones, these are hurdles with which I will assist you. I come today, therefore, with this my Fátima promise to you, to every Lightbearer that does live outside of the United States: I pledge to you in this hour my Immaculate Heart that I will clear the way for you to be there legally if you will only call to me and not fail to give my rosary once in twenty-four hours.

I am appealing to Keepers of the Flame in the United States to consider your sponsorship by any and every available method. Therefore, beloved, it is possible to fulfill both the human and the divine law; and we expect you to do so and not to tarnish the image of our activity nor burden our representatives who must therefore take the blame when their reputations are sullied by those who think that they may break the laws and justify it in doing God service.

Blessed ones, I tell you, miracles have happened to those of the faithful. Remember [how] Peter was released from prison by an angel.[11] May you not also be released from prison, the prison house of your karma, your country, your continent, your self-limitation? Blessed hearts, you must change your ways and look within. Look within to the inner Saviour and become confident and self-reliant individuals.

Remember, then, that the Messenger is here to give you a teaching that you must apply; and therefore, lean on my heart as the Immaculate Heart and I will act through her as well as directly through your very own hearts for your deliverance. As it has been said by Thérèse, there does come a time when the most important event in the life of the individual is his Christhood.[12] Let each one value that Christhood above all else and pursue it daily.

Blessed ones, there is a victory to be won by each of you in Montana. By whatever route you arrive there, understand that the challenge is immense to our staff; and when you make other plans to do other things thinking that you have months and years, I tell you, shall we not do first things first? Shall we not secure the Place Prepared? Shall it not be so secure that you have ultimate and utter peace of mind for yourselves and your families? And when it is secure, can you not then, if opportunity be dispensed, set yourself apart if that is your desire and dream?

Beloved ones, I ask you in one final hour in this moment of Fátima to look with me now as those children stood in 1916, 1917, as those children saw and were shown this century; and now see how it is 1987, 1988, 1989, 1990. Blessed ones, the hour of 1990 and this decade should be seen by you as the greatest challenge the planet will ever know.

I demand that you meet that challenge and be conquerors in life. And I say to you that should any one of you allow yourself to lose your life by the folly of the nonhearing of our word, I, your Mother, shall weep profoundly for you and for a cause and a victory and a future date you have with destiny beyond the year 2000 that you will, then, not fulfill and thereby in not fulfilling it not win your ascension.

Blessed ones, the hour is too short. I tell you, then, that it is an hour of what might have been. Church hierarchies and nations, single individuals might have taken a stand. But, beloved ones, it goes back to the spiritual wickedness in high places and the fallen ones themselves who put themselves in these key positions. The hour is long past when their citadels must crumble. By the very fact of this and the weight of their karma, you yourselves should tremble, for it is their entire civilization that is rotten at the base. Blessed ones, their steel is rotten at the base, their concrete, their towers, their achievements of technology, they are all rotten at the foundation.

Therefore, know, beloved, that they cannot stand. Either there is such a maximum infusion of the planet by violet flame, by millions of individuals invoking it, either there is such a courage demonstrated by those who will go in and take their stand and unseat these fallen ones at all levels—[and do] all of these things that must be done when you look at what would have to happen to turn things around[—or there is not]. This is what puts the percentages on the side of a chaos and calamity descending.

You see, beloved, that which should have been done should have been begun at the hour of the presidency of Abraham Lincoln.[13] With his death there was sounded the world around a certain mourning, a certain chime that said, "Sons of God, unless you rise up to replace this one, the fallen ones will move [against you] now with their spiral against the founding principles that Saint Germain has sent forth as the flame of freedom in America."

The corruption which followed, beloved, has not been adequately challenged. Thus, another century and more having gone by, you can see where is earth's timetable, where is the cosmic timetable, and in the midst of this you must observe your own.

My coming forth to you in this hour, then, has a very special purpose. For it is in this hour that I desire to give [my gift] to my dearest friends and devotees, to those who have loved me for lifetimes, yourselves and Keepers of the Flame in the earth and Lightbearers who know this path and teaching and have embraced it.

For my gift, beloved, does require enlightenment and the opening of the crown chakra and not only devotion—my gift, then, to you, beloved, is the gift of my Immaculate Heart.[14]

This heart is placed in the heart of your Holy Christ Self. And as you make your heart here below in this lower body (called the *Nirmanakaya* by the beloved Buddhas) the receptacle for that Immaculate Heart, purifying it and bringing into your being that aura of true holiness, you will see how the qualities of the Immaculate Heart will be woven into your own heart, how portion by portion your heart will be strengthened by the threads of my heart until one day, beloved, you may stand at my side embodying the very same heart that I do.

This is a goal and a path and, beloved, receiving the fullness of that heart is tantamount to the goal of reunion with God in

the ascension. Yet so much of it can be known and realized by
you as you become the devotee of this heart.

But I tell you, beloved, changes must occur in all of your
lives. *Changes must occur, beloved.* And those changes can come
about as you listen and listen carefully to the admonishments and
the disciplines that are given through the Messenger. For it is true,
beloved, that when karma blinds you, you cannot see. Therefore
you must have one who sees for you and believe in that seeing until
you can remove the patch from your own eye and see, then, what
was seen for you through the Messenger by Maitreya, by myself,
by Jesus. It is the only reason that the Messenger tarries in life, to
see for you, beloved, and to deliver our fire that may strip you, *if
you will allow it,* of that human substance that limits you, the very
substance which must go.

I remind you that your bodies are subject to the laws of
chemistry and alchemy. Therefore, as the chemistry of the body
goes, so is the consciousness of God that you are able to hold in the
physical octave. In this hour, then, we desire to see a change of
that [food] which is taken in that you might be strengthened if and
when the earth does become saturated with the deadly toxins
and chemicals that are not only planned but are already physical
and waiting to be released by these fallen ones out of the East.

Blessed hearts, it is an hour when an extraordinary victory
can be won. I bid you not to lose sight of the Messenger and [to go]
profoundly within in this hour to chart your life with goals beyond that of a physical future, [with] goals of self-transcendence
whereby that physical future can be for the planet, because of you,
a transfiguring initiation.

May earth pass through the transfiguration and therefore
come to the place to be endowed with the true cycle of Aquarius.

You are the key, beloved, and God does take all of you
together now, fashioning one great golden key. And you may see
the beloved Father take that key and put it into a great golden door.
It is a vast golden door, beloved, and when this door is opened (as
there is a second adjacent door [double doors] and both swing
wide) you pass through as the forerunners into a new octave.

And all those who have become a part of the Light through
you will follow after and eventually all who are assigned to
[embody midst] earth's evolution (once the fallen ones have been
bound and removed and passed through the trial and fiery judgment) [will also pass through]. Thus know, beloved, that in your
hand is the key, and the key to the opening of that golden door is
truly the Inner Retreat.

I, Mary, enfold you and I place around the waist of every

322 Vol. 31 No. 40

Keeper of the Flame of this path and activity a golden cord, knots within it like the cord of Saint Francis, that you might understand that though there be an acceleration of the Path and though the golden light be upon you, though you may be robed as kings and priests unto God, the simple and basic and humble virtues of soul-chastity (purity), poverty (as selflessness, self-emptying to be filled) and obedience—these three, beloved, are truly the magnet for the threefold flame.

Thus, because you have made your pilgrimage here and kept the flame, there has been cleared from this place certain entrenched darkness. Beloved ones, I am grateful. The faithful shall have a new line to my heart and I shall seal this light that a false hierarchy may never appropriate it.

Blessed ones, the Masses are misused to enslave rather than to enlighten. Therefore I say, let the power of darkness go down in the Church! Let the power of black magic go down! I, Mary, bring the judgment of the order of the Jesuits and the black pope. Let their darkness and misuse of my Light now be upon them!

Be not afraid, beloved, for we have raised up the new edifice of the Church Universal and Triumphant. And remember "Forever and forever, you are the living Church!" I AM the living Church. Let this be your affirmation, beloved: "I AM the living Church." And when you recognize this, beloved, you will understand that the aura of sanctity of the Church must become the aura of sanctity of your presence.

By then [when the aura of sanctity becomes your own] shall men not fear to leave the old decaying orders and follow thee, beloved, for your iridescence shall bloom strong, shall be a lamp unto my own. They are precious, beloved. They are so precious. May you know them as I have known them and realize that already the religious and the good priests have been studying the Teachings of the Ascended Masters and they know truly their sister Clare, their sister Catherine.

In the profound love that all who are of the Light who are in this [Roman Catholic and Eastern Orthodox] Church might be saved, I appeal to you, beloved. I have nowhere else to go upon earth to find enlightened ones who also love me and are faithful to my heart. I have never needed you so much, beloved. *I need you at the Inner Retreat.* For I need a greater momentum of prayer, and only by greater numbers can we provide both the services needed to build, to feed and to house those present and the ever-flowing light that flows from the altar [to the untold millions who have need of it].

I need you, beloved, for from that citadel I still desire to save a world. *I still desire to save a world.* May it be so by the violet flame and your own immaculate heart. For, beloved, my Immaculate Heart in heaven is not sufficient to save a world. So long as I AM in the world, I AM the Immaculate Heart of the world, but I AM of another world now. Therefore, you are the light of my Immaculate Heart in the world and in so becoming, you also spare this heart of my Messenger. And you, therefore, weaving the strings of the Diamond Heart, must know that the Immaculate Heart and the Diamond Heart are one and the same.

My Raphael is with me.

Blessed ones, that precious Angel of Peace does touch each one of your brows in this moment and will touch everyone who does hear or read this dictation—that sweet Angel of Peace who is teacher of prayer to children. May you call to him to enter your classrooms and teach your sweet children their prayers and may you also be his mouthpiece.

Blessed ones, there is a great rejoicing by all angels of our bands at our retreat in this hour. For you have come and some of you are yourselves angels who descended out of this retreat because long ago you gave forth that cry of desperation to the Father to save the souls and were accorded entrée into the kingdom of the sons of God. Thus you entered the path whereby the soul must attain reunion, and when you ascend you shall have earned your stripes as a good angel and as a good son of God.

Know, then, beloved, [that] the sharpening of the tools of the mind, of organization and delivery, of building and being practical is nowhere more needed. I, then, remind you of the dates of October 2, 1987, to October 2, 1989.[15] In this period, beloved, we expect all to be in readiness. Therefore make haste, for when Morya speaks he speaks out of the intelligence and the files of the Darjeeling Council, which are complete with intelligence in every aspect of all nations. He does know whereof he speaks. And as far as the Darjeeling Council is concerned, we (for I am a member) do not take chances with the lives of our chelas who have given their all to us.

You have served us, beloved, long and faithfully. Therefore, know that we also serve you. In the mutuality of comfort and consolation let us endure in our oneness; and therefore [we bid you,] come again and again nightly to our retreat until all things are resolved in your own plan and purpose in life.

By the sign of the Maltese cross of Saint Germain, truly the sign that is the cross of the age of Aquarius, I seal you now, your everlasting Mother who does hold you in her everlasting arms.

"The Summit Lighthouse Sheds Its Radiance O'er All the World to Manifest as Pearls of Wisdom."
This dictation by **Mother Mary** was **delivered** by the Messenger Elizabeth Clare
Prophet on **Tuesday, March 1, 1988,** at the Hotel Verbo Divino, **Fátima, Portugal,**
where she was stumping for Saint Germain's Coming Revolution in Higher Consciousness. [**N.B.** Bracketed material denotes words unspoken yet implicit in the dictation,
added by the Messenger under Mother Mary's direction for clarity in the published
text.] **(1) The LORD's prophecy to the child Samuel of the judgment of the house
of Eli,** high priest and judge in Israel. I Sam. 3:1–19. **(2) Heavenly hosts bound on
earth.** Mother Mary is referring to the fact that, in effect, the princes of this world have
effectively bound her message by not allowing it to be published *as directed,* nor have
they allowed the consecration of Russia by the pope and bishops *as directed* and in so
doing have bound her, i.e., interdicted her, in the action she would have taken upon
earth. On Mother Mary's Fátima message, including the consecration of Russia and
the third secret, see 1988 *Pearls of Wisdom,* pp. 137 n. 2, 249 nn. 12, 13; *The Lost
Teachings of Jesus II,* pp. 553–55 n. 132. **(3)** Prior to Mother Mary's appearances to
the three shepherd children in 1917 at Fátima, Portugal, they received three **visitations of the Angel of Peace,** who taught them how to pray and prepared them for the
appearances of the Blessed Mother. In the spring of 1916, the angel, in the form of a
young man 14 or 15 years old, gave the children the following prayer, which they repeated for hours from that day on, kneeling and placing their foreheads on the ground
as the angel had demonstrated, asking for pardon for those who did not believe in
God: "My God, I believe, I adore, I hope and I love you! I ask pardon of you for those
who do not believe, do not adore, do not hope and do not love you." When the angel
appeared to them a second time, in the summer, he asked them to offer prayers and
sacrifices continually to the Most High as reparation for sins committed against God
and for the conversion of sinners. He explained that by doing this they would draw
down peace upon their nation and then he revealed that he was the Guardian Angel
of Portugal. In the autumn when the angel appeared for the last time, he held a chalice
with a host above it from which drops of blood fell into the chalice. Prostrating himself
on the ground, he taught them the following prayer of reparation: "Most Holy Trinity,
Father, Son and Holy Spirit, I adore you profoundly and I offer you the most precious
Body, Blood, Soul and Divinity of Jesus Christ, present in all the tabernacles of the
world, in reparation for the outrages, sacrileges and indifference with which he
himself is offended. And, through the infinite merits of his most Sacred Heart, and the
Immaculate Heart of Mary, I beg of you the conversion of poor sinners." Then he gave
them Communion and departed. **(4) The Church Militant.** See 1988 *Pearls of
Wisdom,* p. 332 n. 1. **(5)** *"Watch With Me" Jesus' Vigil of the Hours* released by
Elizabeth Clare Prophet is a worldwide service of prayers, affirmations and hymns
which in 1964 the Master called upon Keepers of the Flame to keep individually or in
groups. The service was dictated by the Ascended Master Jesus Christ for the protection of the Christ consciousness in every son and daughter of God and in com-
memoration of the vigil the Master kept alone in the Garden of Gethsemane when he
said: "Could ye not watch with me one hour?" Available on 90-min. audiocassette
B87096, $6.50 (add $.55 for postage), and in 44-page booklet, $2.00 (add $.60 for
postage). Special offer: $5.00 for cassette and booklet in quantities of 5 sets or more
(for postage add $1.50 per 5 sets); additional booklets $20.00 a dozen (for postage
add $1.50 per dozen). **(6) Bread of Life.** John 6:22–59. **(7) The abdication of
America's destiny.** See Elizabeth Clare Prophet, 1988 *Pearls of Wisdom,* pp. 95–
116, 173–204. **(8)** "None so blind as those that will not see." Mathew Henry, *Commen-
taries* (1708–1710), Jeremiah 20. **(9)** In Codex Sinaiticus, one of the oldest existing
copies of the Bible (c. A.D. 340), Matt. 24:36 reads: "Of that day and hour **knoweth
no-one,** not even the angels of heaven, **neither the Son,** but the Father only." This
codex was discovered after the King James Version of the Bible was translated. The
phrase "neither the Son," while it is retained in Mark 13:32, is omitted in the King
James Version of Matt. 24:36 ("But of that day and hour knoweth no man, no, not the
angels of heaven, but my Father only"). See Mark L. Prophet and Elizabeth Clare
Prophet, *The Lost Teachings of Jesus I,* pp. *lii–liv.* For notes 10–15, see Pearl no. 42.

Pearls of Wisdom®

published by The Summit Lighthouse

Vol. 31 No. 41 | *Beloved Portia* | *July 17, 1988*

Saint Germain Stumps America

21

The Mother of Aquarius
Steps Down from Cosmic Levels
"As You Receive Me, Earth Shall Become Freedom's Star"

Beloved of My Heart and of the Heart of Saint Germain,

I come to this city with greetings of the Great Central Sun— [of] great beings of Light gathered there, and from their hearts a ray of violet flame to planet earth.

It is an hour when the supreme moment of Opportunity is come for the evolutions of Light on earth to so amplify this violet flame as to create the violet flame magnet as a Great Central Sun Magnet of that sphere of Light of the Great Causal Body, which is the violet sphere*—within the earth, around the earth, through the earth and through all who are tied to the Great Central Sun by the threefold flame of the heart and the I AM Presence.

Pillars of violet fire in the earth, then, we summon all who are like the amethyst quartz crystal, like the amethyst ray and stone. We summon all hearts, beloved, and we desire, therefore, [to see that] through those who have that understanding of the violet flame, through those who will literally become a continual vessel for the violet singing flame—to see that through you the spark of the Great Central Sun of the seventh age may leap heart upon heart around the world until literally those millions called for for the saving of a planet shall be quickened and enter into their own sense of personal instrumentation of the descent of the Word of the seventh age from the Great Central Sun through their hearts and minds and beings and souls.

*the sphere of the God consciousness of the Seventh Ray

Blessed ones, therefore, I come inasmuch as Saint Germain has given all that can be given by his Presence in the earth. I place my Presence over this city and I duplicate that Presence over every place where two or three are gathered together in his name,[1] in the name of Saint Germain, to give these calls to the violet flame and to use that tape recording which has been produced[2] and those which will follow it.

Blessed ones, by the cosmic momentum of my service to Divine Justice on the Seventh Ray I desire to so multiply the momentum of your giving of the violet flame as to anchor the intensity of purple fire in the earth of a divine justice that surely shall consume all the diabolical injustices of the fallen ones that have been pitted against the children of the Sun for so long.

Blessed hearts, I am standing for your beloved Saint Germain and my own beloved Saint Germain. I am standing in this hour for all saints in the earth, in the etheric octave and in the realm of pure Spirit who have served the violet flame, that their offering and gift shall not have been in vain.

Therefore, beloved, in this hour of intensity we will surely summon angels of the Seventh Ray. We will surely see what the Cosmic Council will allow for planet earth and her evolutions in this hour when there may yet be a golden age, even the soft effusive glow of violet on the horizon that may become the fullness of a violet flame dawn.

Blessed hearts, in the victory of Light I can assure you that if those today who are Keepers of the Flame will not frequent their sanctuaries and meeting places those three times a week[3] to give their all to this purpose, that the fulfillment of this dream shall not come. If those who have the gift of the violet flame and the sponsorship of Saint Germain will not finally and ultimately rally in this hour, I tell you, there will not be sufficient generators of sparks to quicken the rest who must yet be contacted. As it has been said through the past year, in this hour it is truly the fact of life that all does hang upon those who are now Keepers of the Flame as to what fervent-hearted response they shall give.

I can tell you, beloved, there are some who have given all that they can give physically and spiritually, your Messenger being such a one. Therefore, beloved, understand that to give and to give again in the physical octave, this is the great calling of the hour—to give one's life for one's friends, the Ascended Masters and those on earth.

Understand, precious hearts, it is not the Messenger alone whose life given can save a planet. But when that is duplicated and when Keepers of the Flame see and behold a living witness and a living sacrifice and can therefore run and do the same, you will see that the duplication of the Diamond Heart of Mary, of Morya[4] and the mighty ones of Light will come to you and will be in your hearts as an amethyst heart and jewel, and you will know what it means to hold the balance for the servants of God everywhere on earth by the purple fiery heart of Saint Germain.

Blessed ones, in life let us serve and let there be, then, that which is called for (even in this meeting by your Messenger), a divesting of your beings of those [food] substances which keep you at times a part of the mass consciousness of lethargy and of insensitivity to the impulses of your own threefold flame and Holy Christ Self simply because the light of the chakras is prevented from physically manifesting by those substances in the body that do not vibrate with the alchemy of the age of Aquarius.

Blessed ones, it is not necessary for you to lay down your body and therefore pass through a transition and have to return to reincarnate on this earth in order to have a pure body and a pure manifestation of light for the age of Aquarius. You can so be rejuvenated, you can so re-create yourself as to be a babe in Christ and move through the cycles of Jesus' life until in the twinkling of the eye of God you stand at the symbolical age of thirty-three once again; having built a firm foundation, you are now ready to place the capstone upon the pyramid of your own life.

Know, beloved, that as you are in your temple, so the violet flame may fill you as an elixir, not only to your own regeneration, not only to your own ascension, but as a quickening, as an intensity, as a crystal fire mist that can be transmitted to others.

Do not accept, therefore, that it takes so many years or lifetimes to achieve your Christhood, neither entertain the folly that the achievement of Christhood is easily won. It is not easily won, beloved, or you should have long ago won it, for many of you are devotees of great ardor. It does require the slaying of that dweller on the threshold, and I rouse you to give that call for the slaying of that dweller[5] daily, to give it three or nine times a day and to determine that no thing within your temple shall ever again hinder you from the full victory of the Light descending into your form!

Therefore, beloved, have a sense of co-measurement that [the advent of] full Christhood in you should make you at that level of the unascended Masters of the Far East. Understand that though that Christ Mind may occupy and serve through you, its full occupancy in your temple does require the greater strength of the Holy Spirit anchored in the physical form, atoms, cells and chakras.

Know, then, beloved, that the physical fitness of this body, the correct exercise and yoga of your choice, which means a physical devotion to your own I AM Presence, is essential as a part and parcel of any diet. Know, then, that the wholesomeness of life, the morality, the conservation of the life-force, that which is kind and pure and loving, uplifting, all of these things contribute to a health that does become even a wholeness [a holiness] and a vessel for the Holy Spirit.

Beloved ones, I am Portia, and as many of you can understand, one does not desire to see one's most beloved twin flame misused, trampled upon and denied. The Communist world today, with the full cooperation of many who call themselves liberals in [the] nations of the earth, have done this very thing. And I tell you, I, Portia, do embody, as does every Ascended Lady Master, the various faces of the Mother of God; and therefore I AM Sarasvati, I AM Lakshmi, I AM Durga. But I tell you, in this moment I AM the Great Mother Kali and I come with a fierceness to you to strip from you and rip from you those demons that yet lurk merely because of a lethargy and an indulgence that is long overdue to be plucked.

Therefore, because you are chelas of Saint Germain, I come as his Shakti in this hour. I come to you, beloved, with a fierceness of the sacred fire that is the white fire core of the living flame of Aquarius! I come with an intensity, blessed ones; and remember this, that in the day and the hour of the vengeance of our God[6] (as you have been reminded of this a number of times) that intensity of the divine Word as the Rock does descend, whether by free will you have called for it or not.

Therefore, you may turn yourself from the Mother manifestation of the Feminine Ray for some period of time, you may deny the intensity of that white fire of the Mother, but the hour and the day do come, beloved, when that Divine Mother and that Presence shall come upon the whole world as the action for the purging of a planet [in order] for the age of Aquarius to be firmly locked into the physical atoms. This age will come, beloved, whether there is a living man, woman, child, beast or plant upon this planet, for there is a necessity for cosmic cycles to be fulfilled.

Happy are ye, then, who know me and trust me as your Portia in the highest sense of Divine Justice! Happy are ye who will cooperate with the very process upon which I embark this day and hour for the purging of those closest to the heart of Saint Germain of all that prevents them from embodying our twin flames of Aquarius and their own twin flames; for neither do you embody the flame of your I AM Presence nor [do you embody] the flame of the twin flame of you.

Therefore, know that twin flames are of the highest sacred fire, and you can be that oneness of yourself and your twin flame moving through the earth as this Messenger is. You can be that presence, beloved, but you will have to allow those of us who are of cosmic realms to enter your life and set that house in order. You must do it, beloved, by free will.

But I tell you, the free will of your opening of your hearts already to our Presence does allow me a certain liberty this night and therefore I shall take it. For I shall shake and awake those who call themselves Keepers of the Flame until either they come into the fire infolding itself [of their own Mighty I AM Presence] and nestle in Saint Germain's [purple] fiery heart or they are spun off as they slink off in condemnation and cursing of the Messenger through whom this very fire and dictation has been delivered. For with the anchoring of my dictation in the physical octave, beloved, there is a changing of the planet.

So it is with every dictation that is given [that] earth receives a measure of transformation and self-transcendence. Thus, the dictations come by dispensation of the Cosmic Council and none other. Neither can we nor can the Messenger produce a dictation that does not come as a dispensation from the Great Central Sun.

So long, therefore, as there are vessels who give us room, these dictations shall flow. And should the vessels increase and that threefold flame of the heart become even more balanced until, reaching the full perfection of balance, it should then increase in size—should that occur, beloved, you will know that the chime heard of [an ancient bell by] the violet flame⁷ shall be accompanied by another chime of a bell that appears as silver but [is] only silvery in color, for it is the most magnificent metallic substance of the highest octaves, and that "silver" bell, beloved, that substance of "white-fire" silver, that sounding shall note a Christ consciousness in the earth manifest in you in physical incarnation *because you have called forth the violet flame, cleared the heart chakra, been diligent and intense in the white fire and received the ministrations of the Great Kali.*

Thus, beloved, when the threefold flame is balanced and when it does increase, lo, there is the Christ born and there in that Christ is the golden age of Aquarius. For the Universal Christ consciousness of the Seventh Ray must be embodied in this age. As Saint Germain is the Lord of the Seventh Ray, so he does embody the Law and the Christ consciousness of that ray. Therefore understand [that] the Universal Christ consciousness of Aquarius is the incarnation of that sign and signet of the Cosmic Christ of the Seventh Ray.

Now will you understand why the call to give the full length of these violet flame tapes for thirty-three days is so foundational and fundamental—first of all to your own change and acceleration, then to that of the planet, then to my coming to you to strip you [of all that is unreal, all that is the antithesis of your incarnation of the Christ consciousness of the Seventh Ray]? For you must have the means to rebuild and re-form and re-create, and thus is the violet flame the creative fire side by side with that white sacred fire.

Know, then, beloved, that the intensity of Aquarius manifesting through you will be the magnet to overturn all that is anti-Saint Germain, East and West, especially in the political and religious fields. Therefore, in his name and our own, summon us when you give the judgment calls, for we are there for the judgment of all that is anti the Universal Christ in you and in planet earth for the Aquarian dispensation.

Let there then be a clear and certain sign of Aquarius! Let there be the clearness of the chime of a "silver" bell! Let there be the clearness of those individuals who do give in their lives and in their actions and in their vibrations the answer to the question that is being asked everywhere: What is the New Age? What is the meaning of Aquarius? What is it?

Very few know or understand [the answers to these questions] because the image and name of Saint Germain is not [widely] known and has yet to be fully embodied by his chelas and, moreover, because the violet flame as a vibration is not yet outstanding for want of recognition and invocation by the very ones who have it.

Thus, beloved, increase and multiply thyself. Call, then, for the multiplication of thy Christ in the earth until the earth does become such an outstanding example of the incarnation of the Seventh Ray that no one will ask any longer, "What is the Seventh Ray?" But even other planetary homes may say, "If you want to know what is the Seventh Ray and Age of Aquarius, look at planet earth and the shining of that shining light of the royal purple, the shining light of violets in a bouquet held in the heart and hand of a devotee of the Mother."

I am, beloved, the Mother of Aquarius. Call to me, for I am Portia and I have stepped down from cosmic levels to be with you. As you receive me, earth shall become Freedom's Star.

I make the sign of Aquarius, the sign of the purple fiery

Maltese cross, and therefore it does blaze over this center and city. But, beloved ones, take heed, for the Lords of Karma are not yet satisfied with the planetary or national response of Keepers of the Flame. Therefore, know that they *must* respond. They must respond! *They must respond.*

You are the Light of Aquarius. Let it shine! You are the Love of Aquarius. Let it blaze forth from your hearts! You are the Truth of Aquarius. Be witnesses unto that Truth! You are the Power of Aquarius when the allness of thy being does embody that Light.

Therefore, move toward the day and the hour of the initiation when there is given unto you the all-power of your heaven and your earth to focus it by the science of the Work and Word of the LORD; and that LORD is, for all intents and purposes to your mission, the Ascended Master Saint Germain, my great beloved and dearest friend.

Thus, beloved, I, Portia, am here by my love of Saint Germain. May you also be here with me for that very same love. There is no greater love, for through his heart is the Light and Life of the seventh dispensation.

May it [the seventh dispensation] not be lost to ages of darkness and war and plague and death as has been a major portion of the age of Pisces. But let this age truly be seen as the sign of the turning around of universes, systems of worlds and individuals because, beloved, that last measure of violet flame was invoked and finally—their burden removed by the simple act of devotion of a single son or daughter maintaining the flame in our sanctuary—that one individual and that one times a billion could leap and come to his senses and awake! and awake! and awake and be, then, once again the living flame that he was in the beginning with God with twin flame in the Central Sun.

I AM Portia. I have come with the fiery determination of this age and dispensation. Blessed ones, *I AM here!* And I shall give my all and we shall see what the response will be.

"The Summit Lighthouse Sheds Its Radiance O'er All the World to Manifest as Pearls of Wisdom." This dictation by **Portia** was **delivered** by the Messenger Elizabeth Clare Prophet on **Friday, March 4, 1988,** at the Church Universal and Triumphant Chicago Community Teaching Center, **Chicago, Illinois. [N.B.** Bracketed material denotes words unspoken yet implicit in the dictation, added by the Messenger under Portia's direction for clarity in the published text.] **(1) Where two or three are gathered.** Matt. 18:20. **(2)** See *Save the World with Violet Flame! by Saint Germain 1,* released by Elizabeth Clare Prophet, booklet and 92-min. audiocassette of violet flame decrees and songs for the healing of planet earth, performed by 800 voices, full musical accompaniment, B88019, $5.95 (add $.55 for postage). Cassettes 2 and 3 available July 1988. **(3)** On February 28, 1987, Serapis Bey admonished Keepers of the Flame to participate without fail in three services a week: Saint Germain's Saturday night service; the Sunday Sacred Ritual for Keepers of the Flame; and the Wednesday evening healing service, "Watch With Me" Jesus' Vigil of the Hours, available in 44-page booklet, $2.00 (add $.60 for postage) and on 90-min. audiocassette B87096, $6.50 (add $.55 for postage). Serapis Bey's dictation on audiocassette K87016. **(4) The Order of the Diamond Heart.** See Mother Mary and Jesus, 1987 *Pearls of Wisdom,* pp. 633–37, 638 n. 11, 640, 641, 644–46; and El Morya, 1988 *Pearls of Wisdom,* pp. 2, 8. **(5)** See decree 20.09, "I Cast Out the Dweller on the Threshold!" by Jesus Christ, in *Prayers, Meditations and Dynamic Decrees for the Coming Revolution in Higher Consciousness,* Section III. **(6) Day of the Vengeance of our God.** Isa. 34:8; 61:2; 63:4; Jer. 46:10. **(7)** On May 30, 1987, Saint Germain said: **"The chime of an ancient bell** now sounds. One of my angels called by Portia does begin this chiming. It will sound in the ear of every true son and daughter of Liberty as though he or she does hear a liberty bell that long ago rang on other spheres. This chiming, beloved, shall continue as the inner Call. And if it stop its chiming, beloved, Cosmos shall know that I, Saint Germain, have no longer opportunity to rescue the Lightbearer. Therefore, beloved, let the giving of the violet flame on behalf of those who respond and hear be continuous as a vigil unto the seventh age. So long as there are those who respond, even a single heart reciting my violet flame mantra in each twenty-four-hour cycle, Opportunity's door shall remain open and the chime shall be heard." See 1987 *Pearls of Wisdom,* pp. 291–92.

Notes from Pearl No. 38 by Jesus Christ:
(1) The **Church Militant** in Catholic theology is the Church on earth whose function is to engage in constant warfare against its enemies, the powers of evil, in contrast to the **Church Triumphant,** the Church in heaven whose members have achieved union with God. **(2)** This statement of the Lord does not imply that there are no saints within the Church. It is rather a generalization because the percentages left within the Church are very small by comparison to those who are without. In this case the exceptions prove the rule. **(3) Overturning the money changers.** Matt. 21:12, 13; Mark 11:15–17; Luke 19:45, 46; John 2:13–17. **(4) Jesus' post-resurrection ministry.** There were traditions in the first to third centuries of a long interval between the resurrection and ascension. The Church Father Irenaeus wrote, "From the fortieth and fiftieth year a man begins to decline towards old age, which our Lord possessed while He still fulfilled the office of a Teacher, even as the Gospel and all the elders testify; those who were conversant in Asia with John, the disciple of the Lord, [affirming] that John conveyed to them that information" (*Against Heresies,* c. 180). The third-century Gnostic text Pistis Sophia (1:1) states: "It came to pass, when Jesus had risen from the dead, that he passed 11 years discoursing with his disciples and instructing them." See *The Lost Years of Jesus,* pp. 4–5; *The Lost Teachings of Jesus I,* pp. 335–36. **(5) Wolves in sheep's clothing.** Matt. 7:15. **(6) Jesus' call to discipleship and Christhood.** See Jesus Christ, 1987 *Pearls of Wisdom,* pp. 269–76, 491–98, 577–82, 601–6; John 21:15–17. **(7) True followers of Christ become Christs.** In the Gospel of Thomas, Jesus is recorded as instructing his disciples: "I am not your master. Because you have drunk, you have become drunk from the bubbling stream which I have measured out. . . . He who will drink from my mouth will become as I am: I myself shall become he, and the things that are hidden will be revealed to him. . . . The Kingdom is inside of you, and it is outside of you. When you come to know yourselves, then you will be known, and you will realize that you are the sons of the living Father" (logia 13, 108, 3). See also the Gospel of Philip 67:26, 27; 61:29–35, quoted in 1988 *Pearls of Wisdom,* p. 287 n. 2. **(8) Akbar** (1542–1605), Mogul emperor of India. See *Lords of the Seven Rays: Mirror of Consciousness,* Book One, pp. 21–27, 46, 57–59. **(9)** Gal. 6:7. **(10) Fallen angels cast out of heaven.** Rev. 12:7–9. **(11) The judgment of the manipulators of the abundant Life in New York City.** See Saint Germain, 1987 *Pearls of Wisdom,* pp. 484–88; p. 545 n. 2. **(12) The servant is not greater than his lord.** John 13:16; 15:20. **(13) My Body which is broken for you.** Matt. 26:26; Mark 14:22; Luke 22:19; I Cor. 11:23, 24. **(14)** See decree 60.06, "Beams of Essential Light," in *Prayers, Meditations and Dynamic Decrees for the Coming Revolution in Higher Consciousness,* Section I.

Pearls of Wisdom®

published by The Summit Lighthouse

| *Vol. 31 No. 42* | *Beloved El Morya* | *July 20, 1988* |

An Easter Retreat

I

Focus!

The Call of Darjeeling

Saint Germain's Great Desire
to Initiate Hearts of Keepers of the Flame

As Chief of the Darjeeling Council of the Great White
Brotherhood and the Friend of all Lightbearers of earth, I salute
you in this hour when a planet itself does tremble with the
trembling of a heart not centered in the diamond will. Therefore,
all is askew and youth have not the Polestar of Being to adore nor
to be adorned with.

Therefore, beloved, I come to salute those who have been our
students these twelve weeks and those who have pressed on around
them, bearers of the blue rose of Sirius and all who love the will
of God.

I have stood aside for some time to see what many would
make of the call of Darjeeling, of the will of God, of the blue
lightning of his Mind, the true fire of purpose. Thus, in an interval
when some among our students might have risen to the embodying
of that beautiful presence of the diamond-shining Mind of God,
they have instead left a vacuum to be filled by none know who.

Blessed ones, in this hour of everlasting Life it is you who
must reach and whose reach must exceed the grasp, even the
grasping of the torch of Liberty.

Therefore, in the absence of the Messenger and in our [own]
absence it is expected that a giant blue-flame sea of light should
emerge and a quickening and that infiring of the mind to sharpen

the wit as well as the wisdom, to sharpen the humor and objectivity to life [and to] the seriousness to be pondered of the plunder of the fallen ones in the earth who come to tear from you not only territory but, I say, the very ability to reason and to know, to meditate and to intuit what is that diamond-shining Mind of God.

Thus, you see, beloved, some years ago we did speak of the sending forth of light from the Sun and the meditation of the Sun, and then [of] those hours when in the absence of the receiving of that light, rather than entering into states of depression alternating with states of merriment, there should be the taking up of the calling to be the radiating sun of light to fill a sea of cosmos and earth [and] all inside with the very momentum that is outpoured, now week in and week out, year in and year out.[1]

Blessed hearts, it is when [we as] parents and teachers step aside and the child and the pupil must perform, must give concert or recite or deliver the accuracy of the bow and the arrow — [that] is [the] moment when we should see all of the great positive release of heaven return in a wave of joy back to our hearts.

But, blessed ones, as we have commented at [the] New Year and as the Messenger commented in her lecture to you,[2] the absence of leadership [within the Community] — of taking that fiery step to manifest that blue-flame will [of the] Son of God — is well noted by the Darjeeling Council. Rather do we see a continual human questioning, a continual waiting, then, for the Messenger to initiate cycles long overdue in their performance throughout the student body. Meanwhile, beloved ones, those fallen ones who know the hesitancy of many [sons of God] who ought to have a fire of personal Christhood, these do of course take advantage and move in where Lightbearers could long ago have positioned themselves.

Whether [one takes note of the necessity for self-defense] in the psyche or in the passing event of another abdication of America's destiny — and that destiny *is* to arm those who are under attack — those who have the means of defense must place that means of self-defense, both spiritual, military and physical, in the hands of those who do not have it. [This is the morality of cosmic law.]

Therefore, to withdraw weapons from the Afghans who have so intimidated the Soviets, to withdraw those Stinger rockets in this hour and to leave a vacuum, an absence of self-defense, is once again to invite the bear into their haven.[3] Understand, hearts of Light, that to leave that moment of interval between the dark and the daylight unattended is surely the betrayal once again of the Lightbearers of the earth.

Therefore does it also occur when blatantly the Soviet

Sandinistas cross the border into Honduras and yet they are not repulsed by the United States, and the Hondurans do not move forward, when they could have, to eliminate certain strategic bases and areas that ought long ago to have been put out of commission by wise rulers of the people.[4]

Where do we seek, then, for wise rulers? We come to the heart of the disciple of Truth. We come to the heart of the student, and there, as you have done this day, in the absence of a presence of mind universally upon earth to defeat Darkness and espouse Light, we do find you invoking our Presence and our Light for the overturning of these conditions. Well and good, for this does, in this avenue of service, truly multiply a power and a presence that can defeat much that is on the astral plane and indeed turn the tide in the physical, even as the calls to the violet flame have also made their difference.

Beloved hearts, the focusing upon action through the departments and channels already established within this activity here and its Teaching Centers and Study Groups is most important! We look, then, for the leadership of the heart. We look, then, to the threefold flame and to those who will call and call again for its balance and expansion. We look to the ingenious ones who know their talents, sharpen them, and put them to the greatest use for the changing of personal and planetary conditions.

Leadership, then, is always embraced by those who imitate the living Christ. We have come to this Community these weeks in a concentrated manner, leaving trails of footprints here and there that you might find your feet stepping in, that you might sense and take the reading of our steps of discipleship unto the embodiment of that Universal Christ of our ray—that Christ consciousness of our ray.*

Let it be, then, that you have a sense of the significance of working together as we work together. One cannot choose which of the rays is more important. Whether they seem to be subordinate and supporting, all are necessary as all members of the universal Body of God are necessary.[5]

Thus, working in community, the balance of those serving on these rays must come together, must come into a focalization. And to have the vision and the divine direction, one must call it forth, I say! One must call it forth. For the forces of chaos, disintegration, nihilism, suicide and world death and depression are immense. Therefore, to carve a hole of light as you have done and for pillars of light to extend from the Central Sun to each and every heart, *it is necessary to put forth an immense effort.*

As you abide upon a darkened star, ever darkening day by day

---

*The Lords of the Seven Rays presided at and sponsored Summit University Winter Quarter 1988. (El Morya is the Lord of the First Ray.) Their presence was universally felt.

by the mismanagement of the affairs of state of this nation alone, blessed ones, you must come to realize just what a burden it is for those who have vowed to embody the Diamond Heart of Mary and of the will of God which I espouse to keep that light aloft and visible in the lighthouse of being—to keep that light, beloved, at a point of contact, at a point of symmetry, at a point where eye meets eye in the All-Seeing Eye of God! Therefore, beloved, to organize oneself and to be on the point of action is most necessary.

We come, then, to turn your attention away from too much introspection and to [remind you to] focalize upon those challenges of the hour which when met, [one does find] in the very victory itself the true resolution of one's inner being. For the out-of-alignment state—the "feeling blue" state, in the burdened sense of that word, the downward sense of depression in the chakras—all of this results from two factors, one being the weight of the planet and the other being the sense of nonfulfillment of one's life mission, what one has come here to do and what is the purpose of being.

[This is] the ultimate frustration, beloved, the frustration of being on earth and yet as one barricaded at each turn, not being able to truly assist, not being able to turn the tide for [the very presence of] those individuals who sit in their seats of power! And were they to be unseated now, beloved, should those who come in their stead yet be worse or should there be an ultimate vacancy because, again, of the absence of preparation?

Let it be understood that for those who work so hard in prayer and in service it sometime does seem that enough is enough. But I say, enough is when one's sources, resources and forces are marshaled in a focalization and plan of action that has as its goal the ultimate victory of the soul and the Community and of the planet itself.

Let us, then, consider the withdrawing of much confusion and dissipation of energy in disorganization and let us consider the focalization of that light in the third eye all-seeing. Let us consider a renewed zeal for the raising of the Kundalini and the conserving of the life-force, that each individual might sense himself truly as though [he were] the Lord's tuning fork, truly as [though] suspended, a vibrating sword of power that does change the vibrations of a planet; and let us sense this Community, and never forget it, as the Great Central Sun Magnet of the will of God [to a planet and her people].

Let us remember, beloved, that those who have come from other planets and those in this earth who have mastered certain technologies and the misuse of waves and all sorts of machinations controlling the mind do not rest or sleep day and night. And they do place a great weight not only upon the Lightbearers and their bodily functions but also upon the masses of the people; and they would move them and do move them and sway them to believe those things which are outright lies, to believe those things that have no foundation in reality or in honor or in the love about which they prate or [in] the peace for which they long and dream. Yes, they have their dreams but they do not have a waking vision of that which is the reality of the hour.

Therefore, let souls ascend the holy mountain of God. Let there be an experience of co-measurement and let our chelas of the will of God and of the seven rays now understand just what it does take to embrace that discipline of mind and heart where one's day does count for a planetary victory, where one's hours are focused and coordinated upon goals that can be realized before it is too late.

I stand, then, in this hour, even as Saint Germain does wait to anoint those of this quarter with his mantle and signet and sign. But, blessed ones, the raising up and the expansion of the heart is that for which we wait and therefore this sealing in this hour of these souls shall attend that heart meditation and initiation which Saint Germain desires to give,[6] beloved, because of the very burden that was spoken about to you this past Christmas.[7]

Let it be known, then, that hearts must increase in fiery zeal in order to expand and be balanced, and the individual must have a fiery spirit in all that he does and not be mindless and perpetually an instrument of what has truly and rightly been called *ignorant animal magnetism.*[8] For base ignorance and dullness of mind, beloved, are the tools of the malice of these fallen ones in their false hierarchies.

Let all know, then, that the focalization of purpose has never been more necessary as the sands in the hourglass are now falling and as the falling of that sand does denote that whatever the span of time, time does come to a conclusion. All that can contain the heart is Infinity, and yet to achieve Infinity in the heart in this life does require initiation from our octave.

For all you have given and all of your service and all of the striving and even the laying down of the ultimate breath and life by some, I say to you, Saint Germain's great desire is to initiate hearts of Keepers of the Flame [so that] as though in the springtime when the lilies blossom, there might come tulips as cups of light symbolizing that each heart is unfolding, is expanding, is containing more of that Diamond Heart, more of the Diamond Heart of Mary, whose heart immaculate can be thine own. This process, beloved, is an accelerating, upward-spiraling one. Let it be so, then, for our desire is to see you here and now and forever in the immaculate will of God.

By the power of the firstfruits of the labor of our own love and your own, there is a uniting and a oneness that does take place and it is conveyed by devas of the will of God, angels of the First Ray. This day earth has a blue aura as so many of the First Ray gather to give their homage to Saint Germain and to enter in to assist him in that noble purpose to which he has set his life so many hundreds of thousands of years.

You who have been his compatriots throughout these long millennia, you who gather again, let us make this hour when we focus together on that will of God in action be the finest hour for the Master.

We of the Darjeeling Council stand in this hour and we raise our right hands, and together those who are assembled in this meeting say to his beloved heart:

Hail, Saint Germain! Our love is one with thy heart and we shall stand with earth so long as the Almighty One does give to us renewed opportunity to save and to save and to save to the uttermost.

Therefore, our Knight Commander, our Hierarch of Aquarius, to you, Saint Germain, we pay homage in this hour and we pledge our lives again to the deliverance of all who stand for freedom and to the hour coming of the judgment of those who have denied that freedom and its defense.

[To] those who stand between two worlds attending the descent of heaven yet firmly grounded in their karma and earth's, we say, be brave, for you are brave hearts! Extend the boundaries of the honor flame. Extend the boundaries, and heaven shall meet you more than halfway.

I AM El Morya, bearing the burdens of the governments of every nation on the planet in this hour. Grace to you who have extended grace to me this day in your calls. Each one is multiplied by the geometry of God, and many across the world feel new hope while you agree to bear the burden of their despair.

Into the violet flame I send it! Into the violet flame I send it! And let this dark cloud of despondency and despair be consumed, for the light does gleam upon the mountain. It is the fire of the diamond of God's will.

"The Summit Lighthouse Sheds Its Radiance O'er All the World to Manifest as Pearls of Wisdom." This dictation by **El Morya** was **delivered** by the Messenger Elizabeth Clare Prophet on **Palm Sunday, March 27, 1988**, at the **Royal Teton Ranch, Montana. [N.B.** Bracketed material denotes words unspoken yet implicit in the dictation, added by the Messenger under El Morya's direction for clarity in the written word.] (1) **Sun meditation.** See Helios, "I AM In and Behind the Sun" and "The God Behind the Physical Sun," 1970 *Pearls of Wisdom,* pp. 129–35. For the Messenger's reading of these Pearls with invocations and teaching, see audiocassettes K7833–34. (2) **Absence of leadership.** See 1988 *Pearls of Wisdom,* pp. 1–8, 69, 70–71, 97–98, 113. (3) **U.S. withdrawal of Stingers from Mujahidin.** United States-supplied Stinger missiles were first deployed by the Mujahidin in Afghanistan in October 1986 and began to have an immediate effect, first by bolstering Mujahidin morale and, after several months, by largely neutralizing Soviet air power. Stingers are portable, highly sophisticated, shoulder-fired anti-aircraft missiles. Reports indicate that the Soviets initially lost at least one aircraft per day to the Stingers. This forced Soviet aircraft to adjust their tactics, principally by flying at a higher altitude, which decreased the accuracy of their weapons. Thus, U.S. Stingers caused a dramatic decline in Soviet military fortunes and led directly to Moscow's decision to withdraw from Afghanistan. However, the Mujahidin charged that the Central Intelligence Agency stopped shipping Stinger missiles to them around November or December 1987 in anticipation of a withdrawal of Soviet troops as part of a negotiated settlement, which was concluded on April 14, 1988, with the signing of the Geneva Accords. These accords include two bilateral agreements signed by Pakistan and the Moscow-backed government of Afghanistan, an agreement on interrelationships signed by Pakistan and Afghanistan with the United States and the USSR as witnesses, and a Declaration on International Guarantees signed by the United States and the Soviet Union. In essence, these agreements force a cut-off of all aid to the Mujahidin. Pakistan and Afghanistan agreed to "noninterference and nonintervention" in the affairs of each other's countries, including a ban on camps or bases, arms transportation or supply, and the training or financing of political or ethnic groups for the purpose of subverting the other's territory. As a guarantor the United States is obliged to hold Pakistan to these terms. (4) **Sandinista incursion into Honduras.** On March 9, 1988, about 4,500 Sandinista troops launched a major offensive against Contra bases in northern Nicaragua and southeastern Honduras. The Contras fled across the Coco River into Honduras. Sandinista troops followed them into Honduras and attacked the Contra camps in the area around the village of San Andrés de Bocay in an attempt to destroy Contra supplies and bases. These bases contained about half the remaining American-supplied arms and equipment. Heavy fighting ensued between Contra and Nicaraguan units. During the incursion, the Honduran Air Force twice bombed Sandinista forces near the Nicaragua-Honduras border, but the Honduran government did not accuse the Sandinistas of a border violation. Neither did the United States or the Honduran governments choose to give answer by attacking and destroying the Sandinista command and logistics base at Bonanza, Nicaragua, 30 miles from the Honduran border. The United States sent 3,500 combat troops—elements of the 82d Airborne Division and the 7th Infantry Division—to Honduras as a show of force, some venturing to within 15 miles of the border. The administration called the U.S. troop movement an "exercise" and stated that U.S. troops would not engage the Sandinistas unless attacked. By March 21 Sandinista troops had withdrawn across the border. Two days later a reported 300 Sandinistas again briefly intruded into Honduras. (5) **The Body of God.** Rom. 12:4, 5; I Cor. 12. (6) On May 3, 1987, at the request of Saint Germain, the Messenger conducted **"Saint Germain's Heart Meditation"** for the clearing, initiation and strengthening of the heart chakra; on 93-min. audiocassette B87027, $6.50 (add $.55 for postage). On March 28, 1988, the day after El Morya's dictation, Saint Germain delivered his second heart meditation. It is important to participate in the first heart meditation in preparation for the second, available on cassette August 1, 1988. (7) **The saving of America through the Order of the Diamond Heart.** See Mother Mary and Jesus, 1987 *Pearls of Wisdom,* pp. 631, 633–37, 640, 641–46. (8) **Ignorant animal magnetism** is a state of mental density violating or blocking the Mind of Christ (the Higher Mental Body) from expressing through the lower mental body. As charted on the Cosmic Clock this human creation of the carnal (fleshly) mind is a perversion of the mental discipline, intelligence and God Control developed under the hierarchy of Aries on the 3 o'clock line; of the inner alignment with the divine blueprint and plan and the self-determination and God Obedience developed under the hierarchy of Taurus on the 4 o'clock line; and of the soul-awareness, self-knowledge, discernment, discrimination and God Wisdom developed under the hierarchy of Gemini on the 5 o'clock line. The absence of these qualities and the presence of their perversions is noted in states of mind characterized by a lack of God-centeredness, Christ-poise and integrity, or integration with the Holy Spirit. The typical forms are conceit, deceit, arrogance, spiritual pride and the self-importance of the lower ego, all of which eclipse the Sun of the Divine Ego or Higher Consciousness (3 o'clock); disobedience, human stubbornness and willfulness, and defiance against God and his laws, all of which sustain the out-of-alignment state known as *dukkha,* the root cause being inordinate desire, the net effect being human suffering (4 o'clock); envy, jealousy, self-ignorance, ineffective communication, nervous tension, scatterbrained, chaotic, disorganized, confused and robotic behavior patterns which distort the polarity of Alpha and Omega, the Gemini twin flames, and disorient the soul's centeredness in the Great Central Sun Magnet (5 o'clock). In sum, ignorant animal magnetism is a mental sloth and a lethargy which causes accidents and the breakdown of vehicles, machinery and equipment, among other things, because the individual is not focused in the right mindfulness of the higher Christic intelligence. Through the violet flame and a conscientious self-discipline, obedience to the precepts of the Path and a deep devotion to God and the gurus, one can transmute that which opposes the realization of the Christ Mind through the mental body, the heart, the soul, and the chakras.

The sign of the Place Prepared given by Jesus to Martha (see reference Pearl no. 34, p. 258; Pearl no. 39, p. 310). The Messenger has described a prophecy given to her by Jesus when she was embodied as his disciple Martha: "My remembrance of Jesus, aside from what is recorded and the inner teachings he gave to us, is what he said to me one day when I was kneading bread in the kitchen and he sat near me speaking with us: 'The kingdom of heaven is like unto leaven which a woman took and hid in three measures of meal till the whole was leavened.' And I came to understand that the leavening of three measures of meal would be the leavening of the etheric, or memory, body that contains the records of the highest and the lowest of ourselves; the mental body, which is the cognitive mind of reason; and the desire, or astral, body, the repository of our feelings, emotions and desires. It leavened the whole lump of the physical consciousness and the physical plane of the planet because the physical is the focus and the effect of the other three bodies, which also correspond to earth's etheric, mental and astral planes as well as the collective conscious and unconscious awareness.

"So when we asked Jesus if he would take us with him in the resurrection, he told us we would follow him but not until the 'end of the age' of Pisces. He said we must reincarnate to keep the flame of the mysteries burning within the Church and when the fullness of the time would come for their revelation, he would restore them through us (outside his Church because the Church hierarchy would not sanction it)—his Lost Teachings, his Lost Arts of Healing and the path of discipleship unto personal Christhood which he demonstrated during his years in the East. He even told me that he would lead me to a place in a wilderness land across the sea where he would reestablish his Mystery School and the Lightbearers of the whole world would come to raise up the Light as he had taught us (within our chakras and temples) to be an ensign of the 'I AM Race.' Astonished, I asked him how I would find this place and how I would know it when I had found it. The Master said, 'You will see a giant jet of water coming out of the earth, and it will quicken your soul memory that I made this promise to you, and you will recognize the land as the "Place Prepared." '

"I didn't have the outer memory of that promise until after Keepers of the Flame in the name of Church Universal and Triumphant had purchased our 12,000-acre Royal Teton Ranch adjacent to Yellowstone Park in 1981. When I saw the property I knew in my heart it was right, by vibration—there was no doubt in my mind. Sometime afterward Jesus came to me and quickened my memory of that scene where he had given me that prophecy. And I realized that the sign that my soul had followed was Old Faithful, the geyser in Yellowstone Park. Our property borders on eight miles of the Yellowstone River as well as five miles of Yellowstone Park. And I said to him, 'Jesus, why didn't you tell me all this *before* we purchased this property?' He said, 'Because, beloved, I wanted you to understand that you needed only your communion with my Sacred Heart to have my unerring guidance in order to know the place I had prepared for you. And although I would give it to you, you did not need the outer remembrance of the things that I had told you. Thus, in all things trust your heart to mine and you will not fail.' " See Luke 10:38–42; John 11:1–46; 12:1, 2; Matt. 13:33; Luke 13:21; Morton Smith, *The Secret Gospel: The Discovery and Interpretation of the Secret Gospel According to Mark* (Clearlake, Calif.: Dawn Horse Press, 1982).

Notes from Pearl no. 40 by Mother Mary continued:
(10) *A Child's Rosary to Mother Mary,* 15-minute scriptural rosaries for the Child within you, published on 4 audiocassette albums, 3 cassettes per album: Album 1 (A7864): John, James, Jude. Album 2 (A7905): Paul to the Hebrews. Album 3 (A7934): Paul to the Galatians. Album 4 (A8045): Paul to the Corinthians. $9.95 ea. (add $1.05 ea. for postage). **(11) Apostles' release from prison.** Acts 5:17–23; 12:1–11; 16:16–34. **(12) The import of Christhood.** See Saint Thérèse of Lisieux, 1988 *Pearls of Wisdom,* p. 307. **(13) Conspiracy against Lincoln.** See 1988 *Pearls of Wisdom,* pp. 101–4. **(14)** The Messenger returned from her Lisbon stump and pilgrimage to Fátima with an **Immaculate Heart statue of Mother Mary**, gift of European Keepers of the Flame, which now stands on the altar in King Arthur's Court at the Royal Teton Ranch. The 4-foot-8-inch statue shows the Blessed Mother dressed in a simple white robe and veil trimmed with gold, her arms outstretched. Her ruby heart, with flames leaping from the top of it, is displayed inside a circle of thorns. Upon her head is a gold filigree crown, a rosary is draped over her right hand (her left hand is outstretched with palm upward), and she is wearing a necklace from which hangs a gold sphere at waist level (a focus of the world). The lighted globe of the world has been placed at her feet and an arrangement of greens provides the backdrop for the statue, which is positioned to the left of the altar in front of Jesus' picture. Personal devotion at the Inner Retreat to the Blessed Mother is self-evident, moving and profound. This statue represents Mother Mary's second Fátima apparition in which she revealed that Jesus wished to spread in the world devotion to her Immaculate Heart. Lucia, one of the three children to whom Mother Mary appeared, later wrote of the second apparition in her memoirs: "In front of the palm of Our Lady's right hand was a heart encircled by thorns which pierced it. We understood that this was the Immaculate Heart of Mary, outraged by the sins of humanity and seeking reparation." Upon the unveiling of the statue at King Arthur's Court, the Messenger explained that the Blessed Mother's flaming heart represents the Path of the Ruby Ray and the "Immaculate Heart in which we consecrate Russia and all nations of the earth, the Immaculate Heart in which we trust. And in the parlance of the Darjeeling Council, it is the Diamond Heart. . . . Finding this statue was finding the focus of our Christmas Day dictations," which speak of the necessity of becoming a member of the Order of the Diamond Heart for the saving of America (see Mother Mary and Jesus, 1987 *Pearls of Wisdom,* pp. 629–49). **(15) 24 Months.** See El Morya, 1987 *Pearls of Wisdom,* pp. 474, 480, quoted in 1988 *Pearls of Wisdom,* p. 249 n. 7.

Nonacceptance of Mother Mary's appearances at Fátima and Medjugorje (see reference Pearl no. 40, p. 311). The six appearances of Mother Mary to the three shepherd children—Lucia, 10, Francisco, 9, and Jacinta, 7—in Fátima, Portugal, between May and October 1917 were at first met with disbelief. Lucia's mother, the most skeptical among the families of the children, wanted her daughter to publicly recant what she considered to be a hoax. She scolded Lucia harshly and treated her with scorn in an effort to get the child to admit she was lying. She was not converted until she witnessed the miracle Mother Mary predicted would occur during her final visitation on October 13, 1917, known as "the miracle of the sun." The parish priest, after questioning Lucia about the first two visitations, thought the apparitions might be the work of the devil. Despite the increasing number of pilgrims who came daily to visit Cova da Iria (the site of the apparitions) or to be present during the apparitions, the ecclesiastical authorities remained reserved and aloof; the Cardinal Patriarch of Lisbon went so far as to forbid the clergy from taking part in any of the events. Journalists employed by the revolutionary government in Portugal, which had persecuted the Church since coming to power in 1910, ridiculed the apparitions, claimed that they were an organized plot to incite the people against the government, and encouraged the civil authorities to intervene.

On August 13, the date set for Mother Mary's fourth appearance, Arturo de Oliveira Santos, administrator of the district of Fátima, kidnapped the children and took them to his house in Ourém where they were interrogated and imprisoned. Enraged by their refusal to divulge the secret message that they had received during the July visitation, Santos locked them in the public jail and threatened to have them boiled in oil. He had the children led separately to their supposed death as each one was told that the child who had been led out previously had already gone to his death. The children remained unshakable during this persecution and on August 15 the administrator returned them to their homes. Although the children did not expect to see the Blessed Virgin until the following month, she appeared to them on August 19 at Valhinos, a field about a mile from Fátima, where they were tending their sheep. Five years after the apparitions, the Bishop of Leiria-Fátima appointed a commission to study the Fátima apparitions. In 1930, after a seven-year investigation, he confirmed the apparitions of the Blessed Mother in a pastoral letter and said they were worthy of belief by the faithful. (The bishop, as the pope's representative, is empowered to investigate apparitions.)

Mother Mary's almost daily appearances to six youths in the small village of Medjugorje, Yugoslavia, since June 25, 1981, have also been met with skepticism and persecution. The seers, who ranged in age from 10 to 16 when the apparitions began, have been interrogated by authorities of the Yugoslavian Communist government and the Catholic Church. At one point the local police detained the youths, told them to recant, and threatened to have them committed to a mental asylum. The parish pastor and other priests at first doubted the authenticity of the apparitions, causing one of the seers, Ivanka Ivankovic, to remark, "The only ones who do not believe us are the priests and the police!" The youths have been subjected to medical, psychological and psychiatric examinations to determine if their behavior is being caused by drugs, hypnosis or other factors, and they have also been closely examined while in the state of ecstasy during the Blessed Mother's visitations. Bishop Zanic of Mostar, the diocese where Medjugorje is located, has openly voiced his doubt about the apparitions, declaring, "The phenomenon at Medjugorje will be the greatest shame of the Church in the twentieth century. One can say that these are hallucinations, illusions, hypnosis or lies." In 1986 the commission he impaneled to investigate the apparitions reached a similar conclusion. Vatican officials, however, not satisfied with that investigation, have instructed the Church hierarchy in Yugoslavia to undertake a second one in order to determine if the visions are worthy of belief. That commission has not yet reached a conclusion.

The Communist government, alarmed at the religious revival that was taking place and the huge crowds of people who gathered at the place of the apparitions (a hillside overlooking Medjugorje), took repressive measures. Several priests and sisters were arrested and from August 1981 to May 1983 police forbade anyone to visit the place of the apparitions and all religious services outside the church were banned. From August 1981 to January 1982, the appearances took place at various sites, such as fields, woods, and the homes of the youths as well as many other homes in the village. Since January 12, 1982, the Blessed Mother has appeared in the rectory, the sacristy, and the choir loft of the parish church. Although the apparitions have not been authenticated by the Church, as many as 50,000 people reportedly visit Medjugorje on holy days.

Pearls of Wisdom®

published by The Summit Lighthouse

| *Vol. 31 No. 43* | *Beloved Cyclopea* | *July 23, 1988* |

An Easter Retreat

II

A Star of Harmony

"Lo, it is come! Thy ascension draweth nigh"

Announcement of the Ascension of Mary Lou Majerus

Ho! You may become the Sun if you are bold enough to contain it! You may even become the All, as I AM.

Elohim I AM THAT I AM.

Therefore, know, O soul draped with mortality, I AM Immortality's Flame dancing before you as God of very gods. Therefore, shed mortality and know that the Flame of Immortality draws nigh to you.

Ho! Ho! Ho! I cry halt! to the sleep of that human consciousness with which you have draped yourselves.

I AM Elohim. I call Home those who can mount the spiral of the divine music, cadence by cadence unto the Sun.

I come to call Home the pyramid builders, those who value the capstone and see destiny in the eye* and do not flinch and know [that] in this hour there must assemble those who will place the capstone upon a civilization nobly begun, and more than a capstone. For violet flame must *saturate! penetrate! saturate! penetrate! saturate, penetrate* those levels upon levels of a pyramid that is built. And yet, sealed in the cement are the dead flies of human consciousness and more.

Therefore, for purification that the intended white stone may become white, *I AM come.*

I am come because you have carved in the earth crevices of violet flame. Some have even bored holes with violet flame. Into all openings where keepers of the violet flame have created that

---

*the All-Seeing Eye of God in the capstone

crevice in the rock of human hardness, I, Cyclopea, pour, then, the magnificent green elixir of the Life abundant that the green shoot might appear again and again and again!

I come to saturate earth in answer to the call of those who, with us, are weary—weary of the decadence and death and despair of a planet. So, let it be and let it be known that Elohim penetrate the strata of the rock, and earth shall receive in this hour such an impetus, such a divine vision.

Yet who will carry it? Who will defend it? Who will defend the Lightbearers aborning in the womb of this cosmos? Who will defend them that they might have the right to be the Sun?

Ho! Ho! Let the sun penetrate. Helios, Vesta, I pronounce thy name. Helios, Vesta! Helios, Vesta!

And the power of Elohim, seven in number, does resound this night in the center of the atom, in the center of the cell of organic and inorganic matter; and there is a spinning of the center after the original spin, the cosmic spin of Alpha and Omega. Therefore that spin in the center will begin to cause disturbance on the periphery of worlds.

Keep the flame! For earth must be righted from the microscopic level to the point of subatomic particles, else, beloved, chaos will produce the thrusting from the center, for there must be a star of harmony somewhere.

Thus, take note, beloved. A star of harmony has risen this day from your midst and from the Grand Teton, and the Law is satisfied already that in 1988 one daughter of God has taken her ascension and therefore sealed the quota of one each year; and therefore earth does receive that cosmic spin. And I AM Elohim, here to see to it that each one of you shall also win.

Therefore, we salute in our Community of the Holy Spirit the newly ascended Lady Master Mary Lou![1] [45-sec. standing ovation]

Thus, I signal to you the consecration of this retreat* to the ascension flame and the crystal ray sent forth by the Elohim of the Fifth Ray.

Blessed ones, it is an honor and a privilege to welcome to the courts of heaven one who has been loyal in life and in victory to our Messengers of this century. Behold, was she not the most humble amongst all? In the love of her heart may you be seated, and may you be seated in the praise of all Elohim who rejoice; for, beloved, the purity of a soul is known by us though not even suspected by herself.

Thus, in her final weeks and months and years she would often ask the Messenger, "Have I done anything of merit?

*the Inner Retreat of the Royal Teton Ranch

Have I scored any points? Am I worthy to be received by Saint Germain?" Blessed ones, such a staunch and true friend should all our Messengers have had in past ages.

Therefore, with her dying breath did she affirm to this Messenger, "You are the Messenger of the Great White Brotherhood!" Blessed ones, so has she consecrated her victory to the upholding of the office, mantle and person of the Messenger of the Great White Brotherhood and this has been her star for many aeons.

Therefore, beginning her training with the Ballards so early in this century, her lifetime has been graced by flowers of violet flame. Thus, imagine, beloved, for a period of a half a century and decades more to keep the flame of purity, obedience, chastity and love, to keep the violet flame so long for a planet! Can heaven deny such a one whose heart and soul and eyes of fire may yet be seen by you? For they have not only not diminished, they have increased a thousandfold. Behold the eternal youth of the newly ascended Lady Master Mary Lou!

Blessed ones, so has she desired to be called, that you might know that you have a friend and compatriot who shall never leave this place but only goad you to the same discipline and staunchness and true faith.

Blessed hearts, once again the motto of our Brotherhood has been fulfilled: What Man Has Done, Man Can Do. [And therefore,] what woman has done, woman can do—what child has done, child can do. Therefore, beloved, there have been children who have ascended, reincarnating [solely] for that purpose.

Know this, then, that the present reality of a victory out of your midst must give to you courage and determination and the recognition that though it may not be seen, it is the innermost purity of heart and dedication and fervor in service, that does never neglect those decrees of the living fire, [that does win the ascension]. For, beloved, know that all* must purge, purify and balance all records of karma. It is the Law, beloved. Not a single Ascended Master may pay for you, when you pass from the screen of life, that last 3 percent, 4 percent that is needful to bring the total to 51.

Blessed hearts, if it is not fulfilled, you will either remain in the etheric retreats for some time rendering service, calling forth the flame, or you may even reincarnate to pass some years upon earth again to bring that cup full to the brim. For that cup of light is needful to those who must drink now of thy Christhood.

Blessed hearts, *tempus fugit!* Has not Morya said it? I say it! For I AM Elohim and I contain all time and space. Fire the mind

*everyone

and enfire it! Spend less time *thinking* and more time *knowing* in the all-knowing Mind of God that does press down upon you to illumine you.

Prepare the vessel. Fill it with the rich wine of the Spirit. Fill it, then, beloved, for when that violet flame cup is full and overflowing you shall be, before your ascension, a fountain of the Seventh Ray to the earth—which will delight more than the eye of Saint Germain. For every eye shall behold you and angels shall walk at your side when you determine with such a fervor of heart, as did and does still Mary Lou, that you will always have more than enough violet flame for yourself and for others, as though you could fill a thousand teacups and then a thousand again for all who would drink.

Do you not desire to give abundantly? O beloved, the abundant giver has abundant joys, happiness and bliss; and there is no distance between yourself and bliss, for bliss is a state of the crystal Mind of God. O be infired in this hour, beloved, with such determination!

Would you not enter the courts of heaven at the conclusion of this life, whenever it might be? ["Yes!"] I am glad that *some* of you do.

Blessed ones, calculate by that cosmic calculator and say to yourself that if that passage should come soon or late you will be ready, having therefore called forth the maxim light of Maximus— having called forth such untold blessings, having rendered such service so as to bless so many tens of thousands—that if perchance you are wanting a bit the full cup of violet flame, you may have to your record so many deeds well done, so many smiling faces on planet earth, that for the very service and the quickening of hearts and the many who shall become Suns after you or even before, by meritorious deeds you shall have therefore fulfilled the requirements for the victory. *Both are so necessary, beloved.*

Let praise be upon thy lips—for the flame of God and for the light and the smile of a friend, for the testings of the enemy and for those who are neither hot nor cold for whom you must strive. Strive, then, for them to be galvanized to the Light or even to the Dark but to make some decision that will start the process of self-immolation and God-victory.

Therefore, let the lesser self decrease,[2] for I, Cyclopea, come to all who receive me [in order] to accomplish that. Even if by a hair's measure, beloved, let that lesser self be eclipsed by the Great God Presence, by the sun of even pressure. Even let the self-concern be eclipsed by the appearance of the Lord Gautama Buddha for whom you contain such love that in seeing him all self is forgotten and you melt in the divine embrace of the Lord of the World.

He is here in the Western Shamballa and though he may be everywhere in the earth, he does not leave this place. Do you know what that means, beloved? That means that anywhere you may be on this property, *anywhere,* you may suddenly encounter him. In the song of a bird, in the smile or frown of a friend—in any manifestation however small or great—you may know that the Lord of the World does not cease to teach your soul, for by the pulsation of his heart you are perpetually, *perpetually receiving* that heartbeat of God that does pump into your mind and being the gnosis of cosmos!

O expand the mind, beloved! Expand the heart, which is even more needful, to know in this moment that higher reality of self, to know that thou art God as I AM and yet to realize that all of the testing and the challenging and the striving and the giving and taking is for, beloved, the realization of that God here below!

O run and sing in the hills and listen to the sound of angels return thy chorusings!

I AM the God of Music. Therefore, *I AM determined to save the earth with music.* What is music, beloved? It is the original sound with which earth was endowed in etheric spheres. It is the sound and the hum of a bee or an electron or a child learning his first tune. Music is the melody of the soul that is always in the divine rhythm of Love. Music conveys all virtues of God. Music therefore does bring to you the inner sound of the living Word. But *you are* that Word, *you are* that Peace, *you are* that Peace-commanding Presence.

I propose, then, to drench the earth with the eternal sound simply because the sounds that come from the earth in this hour— the sounds of the groanings of pain as individuals pass from life through the tortures of hell (a hell of their own creation, I must say, beloved, and yet we have compassion)—the sounds of the earth violate the Christ of you and the Cosmic Virgin, [they violate] the sounds of the Infinite One.

Lo, I AM THAT I AM: I will fill all the earth with music but I must have vessels, vessels who contain the sound of our dictations, *for on another track they are all music, beloved.*

Music is the perpetually flowing stream. It is the River of Life. It is movement in self, and as movement, beloved, it is always power. Each change of the note, the vibration, beloved, is a release of power.

Therefore, we wrap the earth in the swaddling garment of the music of the Divine Mother. May this presence of the power of Elohim and the music of all seven rays not drown out the freewill expressions of those who have a right to their free will. But let it be such a Peace-commanding Presence, such an illumination, such an inspiration that gently by the Holy Spirit and powerfully, too, souls may be turned around, galvanized, then, to the original sound that gave them birth, the sound of the chorusing of twin flames and their retinue of angels.

Would you not be converted by the original sound of that God-free being, that twin-flame manifestation and the retinue of angels? Would you not for a moment lend an ear and, not as following Pied Piper but as moving with the currents of your own being, at last [be] free to be yourself? Would you not, then, leave the cups, the old cups containing the old beat?

Ah, yes, beloved. Those who have come from the Sun shall be turned around. Those who are the children of the Sun shall leave their nets of entanglement in the melody and rhythm of the fallen ones.

And what shall they do who have rebelled against the original sound? Blessed ones, in this hour I, Cyclopea, deliver unto them the mighty chorusings of the angels of God which they knew before they took the left-handed path and the step to descend and descend again and to descend, decelerating, then, into a plane where they could be comfortable with their rebellion.

In this hour, then, we, Elohim, release [the sound of God Harmony] to all angels who have fallen, leaving their first estate, going after that fallen one whose end has already come,[3] that they might know the sound they once knew and once loved, many of them only following after their hierarchs and yet by some strange, warped loyalty remaining faithful unto them to this hour.

I release you from the bonds and bondage of your word vowed to those dark ones who have led you into the byways of Evil. All of you, then, throughout this cosmos who have followed the false hierarchy of Lucifer, of the Satans, Beelzebub and others, to you I say, "Hear the sound you once loved when, in the heart of the Divine Mother, you too were there when the morning stars sang together!"[4]

Therefore, this night, beloved, they shall hear the sound and they shall know and remember the fullness of the joy of freedom they once knew before they were cast out of heaven. If then they reject the Call of the divine music, wherein they [shall] have also rejected the divine memory of God that comes through that music, [it] shall come to pass that they shall be brought to the Court of the

Sacred Fire to receive the judgment for having led an entire planet and civilization not once but thrice to the brink of cataclysm and to its fulfillment [through the perversion of the original sound and the Word and the rhythm of the spheres].

Therefore, beloved, the judgment shall come upon those who have perverted the divine Word and the divine Sound.

Know, then, that not one Ascended Lady Master but many ascended ones now come forward to displace the black magicians whose hour has come for the judgment.[5] We take, then, the occasion of the ascent of a single Son of God to also let the white fire descend for the judgment of those evil spirits who to this very moment have corrupted earth and would continue were it not for legions of Elohim and Archangels who do bind them now. Many are on the astral plane, some yet abide in the physical.

Know, then, that the angels have come for the binding of certain tares. And this day and date does mark a harvest,[6] then, of certain forces of Evil because some, some Lightbearers, some Keepers of the Flame, have chosen to keep the Light, to keep the Flame, to not squander it, to say, *"I will take a stand with my God! I will become a Sun!"*

To the merit of Mary Lou many will make that determination *because she did,* and already many have followed in her wake, for her fiery spirit has parted the waters of the astral plane.

Thus, beloved, whether ascended or unascended, in this hour let your fiery spirit, let the way you hold your mind through the day, let the way you hold your heart and soul and sacred fire in your temple be a sign to all upon earth that you are becoming a Sun and they can too!

Let hope be reborn in the heart of the Mother, for I, Cyclopea, have come. I AM Cyclopea of the Sun. Crystal rays from the heart of Virginia descend. The likely chalice, the quartz crystal, does magnetize it almost as quickly as your hearts.

Thus, O ye of crystal hearts who are of the crystal fire mist, receive, then, the crystallization of the God Flame and behold these crystal quartz chalices[7] whose atoms now tuned to my song do sing and sing and sing of the hour when you, too, shall fly straight as an arrow to the heart of our retreat, there to go within until the moment of your ascension.

Lo, it is come. Lo, it is come. Lo, it is come. Remember these words, for when a seraph does approach you on the road of life with those words, "Lo, it is come!" know that he speaks of the hour of thy ascension that draweth nigh. [intonations, 38 seconds]

Thou shall become a Sun! I AM a Sun. Earth shall be a Sun.

"The Summit Lighthouse Sheds Its Radiance O'er All the World to Manifest as Pearls of Wisdom."
This dictation by **Cyclopea** was **delivered** by the Messenger Elizabeth Clare Prophet on **Wednesday, March 30, 1988,** during the 5-day Easter Retreat at the **Royal Teton Ranch, Montana. [N.B.** Bracketed material denotes words unspoken yet implicit in the dictation, added by the Messenger under Cyclopea's direction for clarity in the written word.] **(1) Mary Lou Majerus,** b. July 15, 1893; d. May 31, 1987; a. March 30, 1988. **(2) "He must increase, but I must decrease."** John 3:30. **(3) The second death of Lucifer.** See Elizabeth Clare Prophet, *The Great White Brotherhood in the Culture, History and Religion of America,* pp. 234, 239, 247–48, 384. **(4) Morning stars.** Job 38:7. **(5) For each black magician taken, a Christed one must fill the vacuum.** See Saint Germain, 1988 *Pearls of Wisdom,* p. 119. **(6) The tares among the wheat.** Matt. 13:24–30, 36–43. **(7)** Throughout the Easter Retreat three rows of **quartz crystals** were arranged on the platform in front of the altar, forming a band of crystals about one and a half feet wide. In the row nearest the altar there were large rock crystals, which ranged in weight from eight to forty pounds. In the center row were crystals weighing one-half pound to four pounds. The row farthest from the altar was about five inches wide, composed of small crystals in the one-ounce to eight-ounce range. Closest to the high altar there was also a row of Easter lily plants between which were positioned amethyst crystals. On the high altar there were several quartz and amethyst Pará point crystals in addition to the large central piece, chalice of the Flame.

Quotes from Mary Lou Majerus

Elizabeth Clare Prophet: This is a chela of Godfre and Lotus, who worked in their household, served them personally and has come here for her golden-age victory in the Light. God bless you.

Mary Lou Majerus: I'm here to recommend old age. But also the transmutation. . . . I have to represent old age, get them used to it, and I have to transmute it, to change the old into the young.

ECP: That's right.

MLM: That's my duty and I accept it.

ECP: So tell us how many years you have worn this body. . . .

MLM: I will be ninety-one, ninety-one in two months. . . .

ECP: How would you like me to make out your book?

MLM: Mary Lou. The Presence gave me that name. And I once, I didn't know what to say. They say, "Call me," you know, "by my first name." And I thought, Marie Louise, that's kind of stilted. And I was in the country, you see. So I heard my Presence say, "Mary Lou." And since then I'm Mary Lou.

ECP: Mary Lou it is.

MLM: You know, my name, Majerus, if you write it backward it's "sure I am." I am. [Messenger's birthday celebration; autographing of books, April 8, 1984, Camelot, California]

Now, let me tell you, you wanted to know how I came to know Godfre, how a little girl from Europe can all of a sudden be friendly with a Master. Well, I tell you, it was this way. I arrived in America shortly after the end of the war, debarked in New York. My destiny was Chicago because little girls like me needed a sponsor to be safe in this country, so I was under a sponsor in Chicago.

After many ups and downs I had really loved America, and after more than a week I was ready to stay here forever, I said. After Europe and the experiences in the war, I was very happy to find such a peaceful place, and I said right away, "I am going to stay here." But staying here and making a living are two different things, and I had never been educated to make a living. But I had followed education and had had several diplomas, but that was not enough to make a living here in America. So I had to devise a way.

And one day I had the courage to enter the *Chicago Tribune* and ask for the advertising. And I put an ad in the paper and I said, "French lessons, cheap." That was only one line. But it had also one result, one letter, but the letter was from one of the society leaders in Chicago. So I had an interview with her. She liked me. She liked my nerve, I guess, and she liked my different clothes and the little flair of Paris still left in me. So she arranged for some lessons.

And after we had arranged that she said, "That's not enough, one dollar for a lesson. I am going to arrange it that you can have three or four of my friends, and I make a little tea party every time when you come and then that makes it worthwhile." So she took me under her wing. And I said, "fine," that winter with the society people of Chicago.

But after spring came they all went away and I was left almost without any students, so I had to find out another way. They offered me to be *dame de compagnie,* doing nothing, living with them, talking French. That didn't suit me. I refused several of those offers and I said, "No, that isn't what I want."

So they said to me, "Stick to this lady. She will help you." So I had a lesson with her every day, and one morning she said to me, "Since you don't want an easy life, you go with me today and we find a place." So we set out and she took me in a street where I had never been. It was Brentano's bookstore. We entered in, she asked for the manager and she said, "Would you have a position for this girl?" The manager looked me over and she said, "Yes, we have been looking for somebody for six months."

Well, it was just six months that I had arrived in Chicago. So I was hired and I started to rebuild the French library. And I was there many years and I liked it. I liked my work and I liked the people that I met and we were very successful. The business grew.

And one day a little boy in the stockroom had a pile of books with various titles like "occult," "esoteric." He thought they were French words. So he took the books, he took the pile of books and brought them in my department. And I had my time finding out they belonged in the philosophical department. So I got to know the manager of the philosophical department, a lady. We got acquainted. Her name was Ella Wheeler Wilcox. And by and by I found out that she had a sister that visited her every so often. The sister was Edna Wheeler, later on, Mrs. Ballard, and I made her acquaintance. She liked me and one day she asked me would I come to her reading club.

The reading club was a little tea party or a little get-together every week to read esoteric and occult novels. So we read Spalding's *The Masters of the Far East,* like most of you have read already too, and we discussed them. That continued for a while. There were about four or five retired people. I was the youngest of the lot but I was welcome.

Then after a couple of years, the reading group was continued, and one day during the Christmas season when I was absent, Godfre, Godfre Ballard came home. He was Edna Ballard's husband, who had been absent, and he had lived in California....

I said to Mrs. Ballard, "Won't you please introduce your husband to me. I don't know him."... Well, she brought Godfre along and we shook hands and I said, "I have met you before." Edna looked at me in astonishment and said, "How could you have met him? He was in California and you were here in Chicago." "Well," I said, "I have met him."... That was many years after that I found out how I had met Godfre....

I met Godfre and I didn't know how or when or where at that time. But when I read El Morya's *Chela and the Path,* when I read that book, the idea of that screen that El Morya explains to his chelas about certain activities—you will all have read it in the book—he explains the workings of the sinister force at the time. That's where I had met Godfre, in that retreat in Darjeeling before I ever knew him. And you see, he was sitting a couple of rows in front of me....

So that is my story, and someday I'll tell you how I met Saint Germain. I never lost him and he never lost me. I never lost him and we are still together. And that is how after these many years I am still the little humble chela and he has grown to immense stature.

And bless his heart, and come, come closer to him every day. It is worth all that you possess and all that you ever will be. He will be your Master forever and ever. [Thanksgiving Day, November 27, 1986, Royal Teton Ranch, Montana]

The following is a story of how Mary Lou met Saint Germain, recounted here by a chela who heard her tell it many times.

Mary Lou and her sister were living in Los Angeles because they would have had a hard time getting a job in Chicago. They were somewhat at a loss as to what to do. She was crossing a busy street in downtown Los Angeles when a car almost ran her over. She had to jump to the curb to avoid the car. Her dear Saint Germain was right there on the sidewalk for her in this stressful moment. He was dressed like a very dapper gentleman. The perky yet dignified hat on his head had a little feather "just so," and he swung a gold-topped cane with style.

Saint Germain gave Mary Lou his arm and they walked down the street together. He let her talk about the traffic for a while because she was still upset from having almost been run over. Then they spoke about what she was doing. She said that she and her sister did not know where to locate themselves. He suggested, ever so gently, that they might want to consider moving inland a bit. He said that he had a sister in Tempe (or Phoenix) and she seemed to be happy there. After that they had a few parting words and then he was gone. Mary Lou always pointed out how considerate he was in first letting her fuss about the traffic and second, not telling but simply dropping a hint about where to go.

Elizabeth Clare Prophet: We're celebrating a very special birthday today. It's the birthday of Mary Lou Majerus, who is eighty plus, a very, very young student in our midst. . . .

Mary Lou Majerus: You know, it's my eighty-eighth. . . .

ECP: I knew you were eighty-eight but I didn't know you wanted anyone else to know.

MLM: That's all right. I'm a great-grandma. . . . But I'm Saint Germain's child though. So I'll always remember I'll be a child and humble and grateful to all that have helped me to get this far in the light. And now I'm rescued. I'm in. My foot is in the doorstep of heaven. . . . I have a long way to go yet. So wish me good luck on the way. And I wish it to you all. You have your foot in the door of the doorway to heaven. Don't take it back. Step forward boldly like the Master and like our blessed Messenger. How happy I am to be here, I can never tell! There are not words enough in the dictionary. So we have to improve that too. [Comments following the World Teachers' Seminar, July 15, 1981, Camelot, California]

It is important to keep your body healthy so that you can bear the burden of the Lord in it if you are asked. . . . I must stay here until I have suffered enough, loved enough, served enough and been kind enough. . . . There is a time, a date, a place—when you come, it is fixed for you to return. You have to bring what you have accumulated, good or bad. Here you have a chance to consume the evil and come clean. . . .

Your Presence is the greatest blessing you can have. The Presence has taken care all along. The Presence first. Your Presence is more powerful than any Ascended Master, for your Presence can do anything for you within the Law and the Ascended Master must first seek permission.

Mighty I AM Presence, stay with me, surround me and guide me and all others who wish to reach the goal as I do. [Conversations with visitors, May 28, 1987, Royal Teton Ranch, Montana]

God bless you and thank you and let our gratitude for being together here now, let our gratitude pour forth to the Inner Retreat and to all the things that the Masters are doing for us to bring us Home. Let it pour forth like a river, never ending, growing bigger like the Yellowstone, bigger and bigger. And we'll all be there together forever and ever. [Talk on Thanksgiving Day, November 27, 1986, Royal Teton Ranch, Montana]

Cyclopea's dictation and comments of Mary Lou Majerus from July 15, 1986, and Thanksgiving 1986 are available on two 90-min. audiocassettes B88045-46, $13.00 (add $.95 for postage)

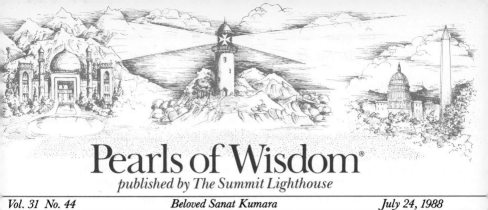

Pearls of Wisdom®
published by The Summit Lighthouse

| Vol. 31 No. 44 | Beloved Sanat Kumara | July 24, 1988 |

An Easter Retreat
III
I Will Come When You Need Me
"I place my Electronic Presence at the gate of this City Foursquare"
Only One Solution: Individual Christhood

Now the sound of Venus does approach the ear as a wave from distant shore not yet having reached the point of reference of oneself.

I have come to you, beloved, because you have need of me; and I quicken your memory, for you may recall that when we did leave our home star, Venus, I did make that promise to all who would keep my flame: I will come when you need me even though you know not that you have need of me.

Blessed ones, I come on this day of the celebration of the Last Supper that you might understand that in the hour before the trial and crucifixion of the Son of God there is this moment when we sup together, the entire Spirit of the Great White Brotherhood, and when the one who will take his leave does say, "I will not drink this wine until I drink it new with you in my Father's kingdom."[1]

Therefore, though you have shared in many communions on distant stars, as the then incarnation of the Universal Christ has ministered unto you and many others, giving, then, of that Christhood, of the Light of Alpha and Omega, so this is a most special Communion hour. For it is that moment when the Son of God does give his Christhood that the sons who have been called and chosen might receive the impartation of that Presence and a great impetus for the incarnation of the Word. Therefore, I have come to serve you in this hour that holy bread, that holy wine *because you have need of it.*

Blessed ones, my Sons and Daughters, the Ascended Masters, have given to you many teachings and warnings in the past three years, statements calling you to prepare and, again, to prepare and, again, to make ready. Is not the readiness and the preparedness, then, for my coming, for the coming of the Guru who does represent and sponsor all other teachers? One day the hour must come, then, the hour of the coming of the Bridegroom.[2]

I come also because you have need of me, and though you know it not, beloved, I shall explain. There are a number of necessities that are before each and every Keeper of the Flame. Be it understood, then, that when there is a movement toward the community of Light settled on a planet of pilgrims who seek no continuing city but to keep a flame, there does appear a "moving in" of fallen ones, and they surround and they press in until those who are the devotees can scarcely bear the burden of that Darkness.

In that moment, beloved, there is *only one solution* and that solution is *individual Christhood*. My Son Jesus has called you to it, has implored you to receive him as your Teacher, has even given to you the date for your commencement of that action of the Word of Christhood* as November 1, 1987,[3] the All Saints' Day of the entire Spirit of the Great White Brotherhood. Such a necessity for the incarnation of the Christ is at hand.

Beloved, earth is moving toward that day, "the Day of Vengeance of our God," [prophesied by Isaiah[4]] when the karmic accountability must fall upon every individual; and I can tell you, beloved, that *in that day no man or woman or child shall stand, saving the one who has diligently, daily and hourly, pursued that Christhood.* Unless this be done, beloved, the overwhelming karma and the fallen ones' using of that karma against the Son of God shall be for the many and the majority too hard to bear.

You have heard it said [that] for every fallen angel and black magician taken, there must be the Christed one to fill the vacuum.[5] And if there is not, beloved, what then? Shall a people and a planet be overcome by fallen ones who have been more diligent on the left-handed path than the sons of God have been on the right?

There is only one person who can answer that question and it is you, each one individually. The hour of Christhood in you is more important than any other event taking place upon this planet.

Now, therefore, beloved, your necessity for my Presence here does indeed have to do with our establishment of this entire retreat and ranch and more—[that] of the forcefield of the Great White Brotherhood on earth. It has everything to do with the opposition [to your Christhood through the establishment of this retreat

*the action of the Word incarnate within you as your Christhood

which comes] from all levels and all sides. For when in recent
centuries has a retreat of the Great White Brotherhood become
physical to be sustained by such advanced disciples as you are or as
you are capable of becoming? I tell you, such a measure of light,
such a high teaching, such a constancy of servants drawing forth
our Light, our Presence, our Power has not been seen in many more
centuries than I would care to tell.

Therefore, beloved ones, the coming of [the Lightbearers to
the mountain of God and] the establishment of this place is seen by
every false hierarch, every minor demon or Satan[6] as the greatest
threat to their survival not only on this planet and system but
throughout this galaxy and others. Where there is, then, a victory
of unascended ones who are truly ascending in the physical cosmos
at such a dense level, there does threaten to be a victory such as
[has] not been seen except in the turning of ages of the inbreath
and of the outbreath.[7]

Know, then, beloved, that your need of me is to have one in
your midst who does bear that Cosmic Christ consciousness, that
God consciousness, so that quickly you may mount that spiral
staircase of your inner being to become congruent with my own
and to establish, as it were, permanent residence at this vibration
and frequency, relinquishing not, then, one clump of earth, one
stone, one acre as territory to be surrendered to the fallen ones.

It is essential that we manifest in the physical octave the
victory of the Brotherhood [in order] that all molecules in this
wavelength throughout the universes might receive that impetus of
victory, that all lifestreams and lifewaves, therefore, as though
receiving my hand (and they shall through you), may come from
such low levels and begin the path of the ascension which formerly
began only in the etheric retreats.

Beloved ones, this is the etheric retreat of the Divine Mother
and my consort, your own beloved Venus,[8] and this etheric retreat
does embrace the physical. When you are on this land, you are
always in the etheric octave and the physical simultaneously. This
in itself is an adjustment which some cannot make. Being uncom-
fortable, they quickly leave. You have found it necessary, then, to
adjust the dial of frequency of your own physical atoms and cells
so that you might experience the etheric domain simultaneously as
you are in the physical, balancing the karma of the physical.

Blessed ones, the joy of fulfilling that karma must be great. Do
not ever ask again why you are here or why you must do thus and
such, for I tell you, the Law is so accurate that you need never fear
that any injustice is being done unto you. For all tasks and all that is

required, all situations, all that must be dealt with have to do with karma. Karma is the mathematical force of a physical cosmos.

Thus, beloved, as you balance it and take dominion you will see how as the cup of karma decreases, the cup of dharma increases so that you always have a full cup, more and more of the dharma, less and less of the personal karma, [and] therefore such a freedom, such a self-givingness, such an opportunity to lend to life your flame: this is the meaning of being braced by the dharma even as you embrace it.

Therefore, beloved, I embody the Dharma, which is the Teaching and the union with God and the all-knowing and our responsibility to transform this planet into a place of golden-age peace and freedom and individual creativity restored. Beloved ones, in my aura, as in your higher being, this golden age does exist. Thus, as we commune together in Love, we truly share the beauty of past, present, future.

Future, then, is always now, and therefore by tuning in to that future, you can become aware of the movement of forces in the earth, of the victors rising and [of] this Night itself of the defeat of many forces of Antichrist. Throughout the remaining days of this conference as you hold the balance in this sanctuary with this type of dynamic decree work, you will see how our legions of the Faithful and True and the armies of heaven shall harvest many dark entities that no longer have the right to persist on this planet or system.

Thus, a certain portion of the harvest is come; and therefore you have need of me and my Communion, that by the transfer of my Body and Blood and my Christhood, a portion you are able to receive only according to your preparedness, so you shall fill the vacuum left by Darkness, fill it with Light and begin again a New Day as you persevere to embody the whole of the Divine Mother and the Divine Woman.

Beloved ones, I stand, then, for the Great White Brotherhood, for our lawful right and privilege to send our Messenger to this octave to deliver and publish our Word. *I stand therefore at the gate of the city, this City Foursquare, beloved, and I shall place and retain my Electronic Presence here* for the alignment and realignment of yourselves with my Son Gautama Buddha, with my Son Maitreya, with Jesus and Kuthumi.

Thus, beloved, seek diligently the alignment with the will of God, and call to me, implore me that that portion of my Alpha and my Omega may be to you the filling in of those gaps of memory or health or vision or constancy or harmony or knowing of divine purpose.

Beloved ones, I hear and know all complaints and sense of absence of this and that. But, beloved ones, I desire you to take three steps backward into the etheric plane—to look down upon yourselves for a moment, to see that all suffering is indeed caused by a sense of incompleteness, a sense that you have not this or that, perhaps comfort or a friend or direction or meaning, fulfillment, [just] so many [mental and psychological] projections of these fallen ones [who are] about to be taken [by the Archangels to the Court of Sacred Fire for judgment] who would like to have their last hurrah in seeing you fail that test and go down.

Not so. For I, your Sanat Kumara, am with you as I have promised, and through you I am also with all those of our bands; and I am sustaining the Lightbearers of the earth and all who through your hearts receive the Holy Spirit, the Maha Chohan, and therefore come to know and realize how it is that they may increase in the threefold flame and the Christ consciousness.

Most beloved of the Light, *most beloved of the Light,* it is essential to pass your tests, to accelerate your own vibration by a conscious will and entering in to the sacred fire. You shall gain your mastery by free will. Trusting our reminder, then, [you shall find that] our Presence will bring home to you [the awareness of] both the lack and the light that is waiting to fill it, the realization that all that you sense that you have not is simply the sense imposed upon you by astral hordes who are [themselves] the have-nots and who truly come to steal your light in your comings and your goings.

These hordes that gather around the retreat as beggars outside the castle walls have been bound and taken in this hour in answer to the calls of all. Through the heart of the Messenger, therefore, the call has ascended to God and descended. Know, then, beloved, that this is a weekly ritual, the clearing of the astral hordes who gather without [outside of] the tube of light of our retreat. They must be cleared, for they block the way of the coming of the Lightbearer and the new Keeper of the Flame.

Guarding such a citadel of divine freedom on earth, guarding the retreat-to-be of the Great White Brotherhood, must surely now come to your heart and mind as a supreme culmination for all of your sojourn on planet earth since we came forth together to keep the Flame for the lost evolutions of this that was intended to be Freedom's Star. Know, then, beloved, that to secure that land and that retreat and around it a nation and nations who are committed to that freedom is the greatest legacy you can leave, a foundation upon which a golden age may be built.

May you have the vision, then, of so many Lightbearers and

souls who yet require the quickening; and may you know that as you are quickened through our Holy Communion, so in you there is a heart of fire that can be a signal, mountain to mountain, across the chains of the ranges of the earth until all on earth who once knew me as Sanat Kumara[9] shall know that again the fire is kindled and that I am in my retreat. For this is the Western Shamballa, coordinate of the place once prepared for me and all of us. Thus, out of the East and unto the West we fulfill the whole calling of our coming.

Truly it is the age for those who are a part of my bands to walk through the door of Serapis Bey's retreat and to take the disciplines of the ascension. It is the hour of the harvest of Lightbearers. Thus, it is the hour when Lightbearers must swiftly come into congruence with the original vibration of the highest etheric octave of Venus, our abode.

Some have not yet fully realized the integration of the lower vessels with that higher octave. Beloved ones, remember, *that* is your native universe, *that* is your native wavelength, and when you are sealed in it, none, *none, beloved,* may assail you. But when parts of consciousness stray to the astral, to a sense of physicality, then, you see, you are not where the source or the fountain of Light is.

Thus, one has seen Archangel Zadkiel casting out of that abode fallen ones. Why is it so, beloved? Because you have not occupied till I come. The etheric abode does belong to you but so long as you dream away the hours for the cult of success in this octave, you lose the kingdom that is already thine; and when you are absent from your throne too long, the fallen ones somehow get the idea that that throne and castle are not tended or guarded, and so they move in as bastards like Modred and they mock and they sit in the seat of the Lightbearers.

This Retreat of the Divine Mother gives you a stopover, the place where you adjust your cycles from one planetary system to the next as you make the transit to the portals of the Ascension Temple. Thus understand, beloved, that this is a place of training, of sharpening the mind and of disciplining, of focusing on the diamond of El Morya for pure communication of the Word from the heart of the God Mercury. So many lessons to be learned whereby the chakras do become such crystals, such means of a transfer of light and excellence!

As this takes place in you while you are yet physical, you will see how many will come to admire the attainment and those levels of light and achievement that you have realized. They who are of the Light will desire to be like you and those who are not will desire to destroy you.

Thus you see, I am come because you have need of me in the hour when you have not yet the full mastery in the physical nor in the etheric octave nor [in] the planes in between but when the potential so unfolding is so great that already you have become a threat to the major false hierarchies of many systems of worlds.

Do you realize, beloved, that this pattern of this Community and Retreat, if victorious here through you, can be repeated again and again in other systems and you will be the example of those who by your ingenuity figured out how to literally carve out of the astral mire the Lightbearers of a planet that their eyes might be washed that they might see again, that their ears might be cleared that they might hear again?

Do you not know, beloved, that many would study the measures and means whereby through persistent decrees and publications and a reaching out you have been able to sound a note heard by many above the din of war and rivalries and killings and so many endless disputes over territories and commodities?

O beloved, the wickedness in the earth is surely sustained by the fallen ones, but there are laggard evolutions and those who have abandoned their threefold flame who have given full allegiance to them. Among these, beloved, there are a small percentage who can receive again the engrafted Word and return through a repolarization by Helios and Vesta to the heart of the Sun. But for the most part it is the children of the Sun and the Lightbearers who will receive this Light, and therefore they are the ones whom you must mark, for they are the ones whom you must reach.

Know, then, beloved, that my coming is to strengthen you, to arm you, to guard you, to protect you while you pursue the seven stages of excellence through the seven planes of being and yet maintain a bastion of freedom. I ask you to include the call to me personally, constantly, whenever you may think of it, whenever you have need. For I am here to defend our fortress against all fallen ones on this planet and other systems who have sworn to destroy the beachhead of the Great White Brotherhood wherever it has been raised up upon earth.

The New Year's message of the Messenger did underscore the overturning and the pillaging, the murdering and the utter destruction of the homeland of Tibet, homeland of the ancient Buddhas.[10] Blessed ones, that this has been allowed to happen by the conspirators of East and West is the greatest travesty against the Great White Brotherhood. That this be not repeated here, I am come.

This is the hour when the protection may be established. This is the hour to see to it in every way that neither America nor this

Inner Retreat is left vulnerable to such calamity and such hordes of Darkness, beloved.

Though there be Lightbearers in China, there are indeed embodied amongst them hordes that have come forth out of the astral plane that have done this time and again, time and again on this and other planets. Thus [the Lightbearers] have been vulnerable to their overlords who come in the name of Communism and other totalitarian movements, depending upon the century or the planet.

Know, then, beloved, that the land that is thine [and] the nation sponsored by Saint Germain must receive from your heart extraordinary calls for protection and intercession until the many shall wake up to the necessity of spiritual and physical defense. You may see, then, how great is the challenge yet how great is the reinforcement. For where I AM, there are my legions and there is the entire Spirit of the Great White Brotherhood.

May you ponder in your hearts these words and allow your own Christ Self, your own intelligence, your own awareness to embroider upon them until there is [made] known to you the full perspective, the full awareness of that which is taking place on earth and that which can take place.

In this perspective that is a part of the blessing of the All-Seeing Eye of Elohim, may you then place in proportion the personal needs, demands, wants, desires, complaints, et cetera, and let them become as tiny as a pack of matches; and may they be self-ignited by a greater fire than they contain, the fire of your own desire to enter a higher Godhood, a higher estate whereby to defeat the Darkness on this planet.

There is no better place to defeat it, beloved ones. Therefore, cast out that which is the puny self and walk forth from King Arthur's Court as kings and priests unto God, responsible as [was] Melchizedek of old.

As you receive my Light, so assimilate.

I call our servers now to serve that Communion to you, and in taking it you may know that I AM THAT I AM, that the I AM of me, portion by portion, may now become a part of the I AM of you. I say to one and to all, claim the Divine Selfhood and be it! There is no time, no space, only Light. [24-sec. pause]

Now as you procession to receive this essence of my heart and breath, may you also sing continuously our song *Finlandia*.[11]

"The Summit Lighthouse Sheds Its Radiance O'er All the World to Manifest as Pearls of Wisdom." This dictation by **Sanat Kumara** was **delivered** by the Messenger Elizabeth Clare Prophet on **Thursday, March 31, 1988,** during the 5-day Easter Retreat at the **Royal Teton Ranch, Montana.** [N.B. Bracketed material denotes words unspoken yet implicit in the dictation, added by the Messenger under Sanat Kumara's direction for clarity in the written word.] For notes, see Pearl no. 45.

Pearls of Wisdom®

published by The Summit Lighthouse

| *Vol. 31 No. 45* | *Beloved Elohim Peace* | *July 27, 1988* |

An Easter Retreat
IV
The Meaning of Peace
"Elohim of Peace I AM THAT I AM"
The Power of Elohim to Reverse the Downward Spirals of a Planet

Attention! Light of Elohim has passed through the heart of every devotee of God. Light of Elohim has penetrated deepest recesses of the astral plane. Elohim of Peace I AM THAT I AM.

Let the light of the Eternal Now know the summoning, for in the earth in this hour there is come the thunder and the quietude of Peace.

Know ye the sound of the fount of resurrection's flame passing through and restoring cells? To listen* from the heart of a cell, one should hear the thunderous sound of the rearrangement of worlds, not by the abuse of nuclear fission or fusion but by a rearrangement whereby all of substance is restored to be the vessel of Light.

The Elohim seal a planet, for the invocation of the Great Lord, the Keeper of the Flame, passed and transmitted through your calls, has resulted in a saturation of earth to certain levels by light and the excommunication of fallen ones from a planet, from the Mystical Body of God universal, from all the Matter octaves.

Blessed ones, as you persist and continue in these calls throughout this conference and beyond, you shall see a true measure of change. Thus we are summoning the Lightbearers of the earth to know the effects of a decree marathon continuate,† six hours. May it be understood that such a six-hour session as you have held in the intensity of the white fire is the certain necessity

---
*in listening   †1555: continuous, uninterrupted

for planetary triumph over the hosts of Darkness. Continue unrelenting and you shall see results.

Elohim of Peace I AM THAT I AM. Our legions minister by the power of Peace, strengthening, revivifying, intensifying in all who dare to make the call the profound power of Peace that is in the eye of God in the Great Central Sun.

You should know the meaning of Peace, beloved! In the stillness of the vortex of light there is a suspension of power; and in a moment to enter the swiftly moving spiral, moving by the speed of light and beyond: that motion, beloved, is contained alone by Elohim.

That is the energy of God. It is the power to reverse the downward spirals of a planet. The power is in Elohim. It is in Cosmos. It is in the Central Sun. When millions invoke it a minute portion of our power may pass through the embodied supplicant, and thus, by having [millions of] coordinates in the physical universe, the work of God is accomplished.

I speak quietly, for a great alchemy does take place upon earth in this moment. As great Darkness has been removed, there is an inbreath and in the holding of the inbreath of Elohim, pockets emptied are filled with light by seraphim invoked.

Seraphim of God adore the Divine Mother. They serve the Divine Mother and the Messenger of the Mother and all devotees of the Mother. Thus they come in adoration, fulfill the command: wait, watch, listen, prepare, heal, stand in the aura of the one whose Light so loves the Lord that that one himself is a perpetually ascending flame.

Ho, Zarathustra! O Zarathustra and all thy bands, consume the core of hate and hate creation in the Middle East. Bind the fallen race, once servants of fire who now misuse it and keep the flame of war, not Peace.

I, Peace, raise my right hand against them. They shall go down. They shall go down! They shall go down! And the misuse of the power of Allah is taken from them this night by the power of Seven Elohim.

Thus, a ring of light is drawn around those laggard evolutions and nations who perpetuate war and persecute the homeless and hesitate not to kill and kill again. They shall not continue, not in the name of Abraham, not in the name of Christ, not in the name of Mohammed. For the right hand of Elohim of Peace descends and I tell you, they are diminished. *They are diminished! They are diminished!* Enough is enough. We have seen their intent.

Thus, every man shall be consumed by his own consciousness

of the sacred fire, and he who has turned it to destroy others shall be consumed by his own destructive intent. It is done. Whatever a man shall do with the fruit of his prayer against life must return to him tenfold, for he has taken the light of the altar of God and turned it to destruction.

God is not mocked on planet earth, for God has representatives in every nation who will not succumb to the abuse of his power in his name. By these who live in the cosmic honor flame and will not compromise the Law of Love, there is yet a divine standard in the earth.

Happy are ye who remember the divine standard. Judge not lest ye be judged.[1] Do good to them who curse you and despitefully use you.[2] Send forth the Ruby Ray that the all-consuming fire of God, that the Shekinah glory consume all unlike itself. Stand, thyself, in the eye of the vortex of Elohim of Peace I AM THAT I AM.

Rings of fire encircle those who embody Good, God, Light—eternal Light, Love, Truth, Peace and the Mind of God! But take care, beloved, for when in the service of the Fourth Ray of Serapis and his seraphim, I caution you, do not abuse the Light of the Divine Mother in any form. For being in the center of that fire, you may quickly be burned by your misuse of it. Dare not to be unthinking or unfeeling, for one *must* think and feel. Dare not to be uncaring or unloving, for one *must* care and love.

In the eye of the vortex of the Elohim of Peace,
I AM THAT I AM.

Put on the whole armour of God's Law.[3] Therefore, know the Law. Study the Law. Take a vow of silence from senseless chattering, if you will. It is good. And if there be fasting, let there be fasting from vain and unseemly conversation, for therein you unhinge the four lower bodies and allow yourself to expend precious light that is for the holding of balance and harmony. And let all of your silence be filled with the breath of the Elohim of Peace I AM THAT I AM.

I come, then, for the consuming of the noises of hell and hellions, noise as of false-hierarchy creations of deadly bees. Thus, the abuses of life and the life-force of the Divine Mother must be consumed. Their patterns, then, are passed through the ray of Elohim. All that is not in imitation of Christ of the creations of men must go down by the power of Elohim of Peace.

Elohim of Peace, Peace Elohim I AM THAT I AM.
[intonations, 21 sec.]

All Elohim of God intone the sound of their ray that is the Shiva sound for the disintegration of the vicious creations of fallen ones. They have had their day! Let the councils of the sons of God in embodiment determine to ratify our call. For by your governments and your systems of justice those who malign the will of God, those who malign the Divine Mother must be bound on earth as in heaven.

Archangels of the ninth throne, come forth. Archangels of the twelfth throne now present, fulfill the action. Fulfill the action of the great wind that shall come to pass, that the wind of the Holy Spirit now take the harvest of this day; and as the darkness is reaped and the dark ones, flowers are raised up and children of God bowed down know once again the sense of the divine spark burning within.

Elohim have come to collect a planet. May you be found in your niche in the rock, in the crevice high where the eagles soar and the stars are brighter because you are nearer.

O Thou who art seated upon the great white throne, all evolutions bow before thy living Flame. Dispel, disperse the nonentities that pursue the ones to be our Lightbearers. Thy ray shot forth as a million rays and arrows is seen, then, to pierce the heart of devils whose hearts have long grown cold. [The holy breath sounds]

By the power of the vortex of Elohim, I cause the integrating spiral to draw you, beloved, nearer, and as nearer can, the inner polestar of Being that you might know Alpha, Omega, the beginning and the end of thy incarnation in physicality.

Alpha, seal the crown. Omega, seal the base-of-the-spine chakra. Let those who know it, who desire it and have the courage to invoke it begin to know the Alpha/Omega pillar of fire as the magnet of Being that shall indeed magnetize light of ascension's coil.

The one who would ascend must pass through the Good Friday spell and *break!* that spell by the rod of Power, the rod of Self. There is no other rod but self, no other jewel but self.

Into yourselves is poured light that can be sustained in harmony. Into the clear quartz crystal of the Mother is poured that which you are unable to contain but may so do one day. And therefore, as earth is the repository of the great power of God, so let these crystals be the *resonators, resonators, resonators,* establishing, then, the resonance, the vibration, Alpha to Omega. Let them be the resonators of amethyst crystal and every other gemstone, for it is the Divine Mother's chalice in the earth, on the altar of the heart, and upon the altar of each one's invocation.

I summon you to be trained this night in the art of invocation once known in ancient temples. For, beloved, as a community of oneness of those who have so endured decades and more in this

mode of invocation, some have earned the gift for all to receive
now* lessons, early and advanced, in the superior art of invocation
and intonation. Pursue the mantras of the East, for intonation can
come forth only from one whose inner harmony of chakra is well
oiled, well oiled.

I AM the light of Peace in the earth. Who will hold my Light?
Who will hold it in the interval of the secret chamber of the heart?

Peace! Peace! Peace unto the lilies of the field. Peace unto ye
all. As Christ's lilies, you have planted yourselves in the mountains of the Western Shamballa. May you grow and grow and grow
by the science of sound and soundlessness.

Treasure now the peace of the soundless manifestation as
there is placed in this room for a moment now the vibration of
soundlessness that does in this moment surround the great white
throne in the Central Sun. Treasure the record and memory placed
in your soul and chakras of the vibration of that soundless sound.
Take some moments each day to celebrate the vibration of soundlessness. [38-sec. pause]

Be still and know that I AM God in you! O be still and know!
[2-min. 12-sec. pause]

O Thou Cosmic Generator, O Thou Cosmic Regenerator,
commence thy work. [41-sec. pause]

In Love's stillness I bless all who bless Love, who rekindle a
fire and are not consumed by it, who stand in the fire and are
translated unto the perfect day.

I AM Peace. Elohim I AM THAT I AM. [19-sec. pause]

Go in Peace. Go in the Great Silence, for the Great Silence
awaits thee. And one day thou and thy twin flame shall be found
within its ovoid forever.

Amen.

---

*that all might receive now

"**The Summit Lighthouse Sheds Its Radiance O'er All the World to Manifest as Pearls of Wisdom.**"
This dictation by **Elohim Peace** was **delivered** by the Messenger Elizabeth Clare
Prophet on **Good Friday, April 1, 1988,** after midnight, during the 5-day Easter
Retreat at the **Royal Teton Ranch, Montana.** [N.B. Bracketed material denotes
words unspoken yet implicit in the dictation, added by the Messenger under Elohim
Peace's direction for clarity in the written word.] (**1**) **Judge not lest ye be judged.**
Matt. 7:1; Luke 6:37. (**2**) "**Love your enemies,** bless them that curse you, do good to
them that hate you, and pray for them which despitefully use you, and persecute you;
that ye may be the children of your Father which is in heaven: for he maketh his sun to
rise on the evil and on the good, and sendeth rain on the just and on the unjust." Matt.
5:44, 45. See also Luke 6:28; Rom. 12:14. (**3**) "Finally, my brethren, be strong in the
Lord, and in the power of his might. Put on the **whole armour of God,** that ye may be
able to stand against the wiles of the devil. For we wrestle not against flesh and blood,
but against principalities, against powers, against the rulers of the darkness of this
world, against spiritual wickedness in high places. Wherefore take unto you the
whole armour of God, that ye may be able to withstand in the evil day, and having

done all, to stand. Stand therefore, having your loins girt about with Truth, and having on the breastplate of Righteousness." Eph. 6:10–14.

Notes from Pearl no. 44 by Sanat Kumara:
(1) Matt. 26:29; Mark 14:25; Luke 22:18. (2) **The coming of the Bridegroom.** Matt. 25:1–13. (3) **The day to commence the path of Christhood.** See Jesus Christ, 1987 *Pearls of Wisdom,* pp. 577–82. On the call to be disciples and shepherds, see also Jesus Christ, 1987 *Pearls of Wisdom,* pp. 269–76, 491–98, 601–6; 1988 *Pearls of Wisdom,* pp. 289–98. (4) **Day of Vengeance of our God.** Isa. 34:8; 61:2; 63:4; Jer. 46:10. (5) **For each black magician taken, a Christed one must fill the vacuum.** See Saint Germain, 1988 *Pearls of Wisdom,* p. 119. See also Cyclopea, 1988 *Pearls of Wisdom,* p. 349. (6) **Satans** (pronounced Seh-tánz): the race of the seed of Satan who long ago rose up against the I AM Race and have not abated their warfare against the Spirit. Jesus Christ pronounced the judgment of the Satans, "who have infiltrated every corner of this galaxy and beyond," concurrent with the final judgment of Satan, in his dictation given February 1, 1982. See "The Final Judgment of Satan," 1982 *Pearls of Wisdom,* pp. 187–96. This judgment must be ratified "on earth" *daily* (as it was spoken by the Lord "in heaven") by the Lightbearers of the world. This judgment, whereby they are stripped of their misappropriated, misqualified power of God, is invoked through Jesus' Judgment Call, decree 20.07. (7) **Inbreath and outbreath.** In Hindu cosmology, the universe is continually evolving through periodic cycles of creation and dissolution. Creation is said to occur during the outbreath of the God of Creation, Brahma; dissolution occurs during his inbreath. Every world creation evolves through the four *yugas,* or ages, which are the smallest units in the Hindu cosmic cycle. These four ages are Satya or Krita, Treta, Dvapara, and Kali; the first age begins in perfection and each succeeding one decreases in length and increases in its degradations. The combined duration of all four ages is said to be 4,320,000 years. (For a different calculation of the duration of the yugas, see Swami Sri Yukteswar, *The Holy Science,* 7th ed. [Los Angeles: Self-Realization Fellowship, 1972], pp. *x–xxiii.*) According to one tradition, the cycle of four yugas, known as a *mahayuga,* is repeated 1,000 times, thereby forming a larger cycle, or *kalpa,* which constitutes a complete cosmic cycle from the origination to the destruction of a world system. A kalpa is one day in the life of Brahma. It is during the day of Brahma that the manifest world evolves. Each day is followed by the night of Brahma during which all matter in the universe is absorbed into the Universal Spirit. This period of destruction, or involution, is called a *pralaya.* Matter is again formed after this cycle, continuing to evolve during each day of Brahma and to dissolve during his night. Brahma's lifetime is conceived as being 100 cosmic years, a vast length of time calculated as 311,040,000,000,000 solar years, the largest of the cosmic cycles. At the conclusion of Brahma's lifetime there is the "Great Dissolution," or *mahapralaya,* the period of the destruction of the entire universe. Continuing in the pattern of the cycles, after a period of rest Brahma is reborn and the cycles of creation begin again. The Hindu scripture Yoga-Vasishtha, which presents a different view of the cyclical nature of the universe, teaches that the cycles of involution and evolution are ongoing; different systems of worlds may be at different stages in these cycles simultaneously and there is never a point when all creation ceases for a time, as in the Great Dissolution. (8) **The Retreat of the Divine Mother.** See 1988 *Pearls of Wisdom,* p. 260 n. 11. (9) **Sanat Kumara and Shamballa.** See glossary *The Alchemy of the Word,* in *Saint Germain On Alchemy,* pp. 445–46, 450–51. (10) **Chinese takeover of Tibet and destruction of Tibetan culture.** See Elizabeth Clare Prophet, 1988 *Pearls of Wisdom,* pp. 185–88; see also pp. 58, 59, 62 n. 5, 94 n. 7. (11) See "Our Beloved Sanat Kumara," sung to the melody of *Finlandia* by Jean Sibelius, song 546 in *The Summit Lighthouse Book of Songs;* no. 51 in *Mantras of the Ascended Masters for the Initiation of the Chakras,* on audiocassette B85136.

Pearls of Wisdom®
published by The Summit Lighthouse

| *Vol. 31 No. 46* | *Beloved Kuan Yin* | *July 30, 1988* |

An Easter Retreat
V
Finding Those Pearls
"The Divine Mediator does appear"
The Descent into Hell to Rebuke the Devils
and Preach a Sermon Worthy of Siddhartha and Issa

The significance of the descent of Elohim and our Lord Sanat Kumara into this octave and the astral plane is a part of the celebration of Easter that is most important for initiates, for disciples, would-be bodhisattvas. For this day of Holy Saturday, beloved, is the hour of the descent into hell of the Lord Christ. This descent, beloved, is a part of your path of initiation under Lord Gautama Buddha.

Surely, the Avalokiteśvara of myself that I AM THAT I AM in the masculine aspect[1] does go forth as a diver, a deep-sea diver, certain to find pearls and much else not worth the taking. Finding those pearls, beloved, is the great joy of our office. Therefore, so long as there is a pearl that remains in the grips of the death consciousness or bound by the hordes of hell in some Soviet gulag or other miserable prison, there am I, and you are with me.

So in the great joy of our descent we also celebrate the reason for being of your Messenger's birth, born this Holy Saturday, therefore come for that certain mission,[2] a path that must be walked and must be fulfilled. Thus, by example know true courage as I and others have given to her a fearlessness flame able to be magnetized for her own momentum thereof.

Let perfect love cast out fear[3] as you walk in the footsteps of one who has taught you the power of the *"HRIH!"* mantra, who has taught you the meaning of "bolts of blue lightning!" much to the consternation of neighbors and press. Blessed ones, they are saved by the blue lightning you have invoked, saved also to emerge from the sea of samsara and to enter the Divine Reality.

Know, then, that this "thunderbolt"[4] that does descend from the heart of Padma and the Buddhas aloft is yours also to wield. Let the fire crackle as the demons cringe and let the power of fohat released through you be the fullness of the Holy Spirit! *HRIH! HRIH!*

Therefore I, too, come. For each year in this hour there is the rebuke by the Christed ones and [by] those earning their stripes as bodhisattvas who must go to the places where Christ and Buddha have gone to rebuke the devils, to preach to them a sermon worthy of Siddhartha, of Issa.

Know, O most beloved, that when you do preach to those filled with evil spirits who mouth their enmity in return, you are in that point of initiation. Let it come, then, by the Call. Let it come by the Holy Spirit! But when it does come and when you know you must rebuke a liar, a devil, a murderer, a scoundrel who has moved against the Light of innocent victims, then in that hour, beloved, do not shirk the responsibility.

You will know it by this one sign, that you are the only one there to speak the rebuke. There will be none other competing for the prize of the opportunity of wrestling with devils incarnate or devils attempting to displace a soul—devils who come forth and would take over the very bodies and souls of their victims without your standing between.

The Divine Mediator does appear.

And where souls have become weakened in their desire to be attached to the body and are easily fragmented and scattered by chemicals and drugs and the poisons of the age and the misuse of sound, there, beloved, vacancy of body temples does invite the habitation of evil spirits who take over the bodies sometimes vacated by children of Light. Some current authors have called these "walk-ins."[5] Beware of them, beloved, for those who take over the temple of another have lost their own. They have forfeited many times [over] a threefold flame.

Therefore the command was given to you, "Occupy till I come. Occupy till I come."[6] This is the LORD's temple. You are the custodian. See to it that it is swept clean with no bats above or below.

Understand, precious hearts, that you are the guard and the keeper. You keep the midnight watch outside the tomb, that none other may enter while a soul in Christ does work out the problem of being to emerge resurrected and by that Resurrection Spirit having also so accelerated the atoms and cells of that temple. Thus, defend with all your might [thy soul, and thy soul's initiation 'rite' in thy body] and drive away all evil spirits who would interfere with the testament that you bear.

Witness unto the Truth, beloved. When you speak Truth, be ready. For some of the "nicest people you know," who may [even] be on the Path, may react angrily, for they are not ready to hear that word of Truth. Thus, speak Truth and then, if you will or must, change the subject to one more readily acceptable. Truth is a fire and a seed that is planted; it will grow in its own time and season.

Love, then, life where it is. Comfort and support life but always be ready with a push and a tug to guide that one and give that one the courage to peer from the habitualities of the day, to move on, to accelerate, to peel away a snakeskin or two, to see a new face in the mirror of self and to venture forth to a higher plane.

This venturing forth would not require so much courage if it did not mean a lessening of one's baggage. Can you imagine all who would run for the courts of heaven if they could take all of their bag and baggage with them? O beloved, they dream of heaven where all things are as they are now. They would take their animals, their pets, their antiques, their habits, their music; and if all these things may not go along, then they would rather not go.

Thus, the few are the solitary climbers.

Blessed ones, many of you may be tired of this world, perhaps even tired this evening. But I know that you are the ones who carry the crystal in heart, [who] know that in the crystal is the All [and] that in every compartment of every molecule of the crystal you carry is a house of memory to which you may return if you like. And if you do not, seraphim will one day hand you a taper whereby that particular molecule of memory may be easily consumed, only to find a diamond in its place for your crown of rejoicing—rejoicing to be looking toward the Father's mansions,[7] rejoicing for all that has been gained in lesser experience. But the fruit of that experience is with you and a part of you. You do not need to go back to the old haunts to regain the memory.

So, beloved, past experience is like the food you eat. The essence of it becomes a part of you and you grow, and the rest can be left behind. So it is, beloved, [with the state of] nonattachment, [the] going in to the Unconditioned Reality: those who have not been there cannot imagine what it is like. Therefore it is leaving the known for the unknown. But this is precisely why we have tarried with earth, that you might feel our vibration and our presence and our assistance, feeling the charge of light, knowing that the light is an effect and that the cause thereof is the Source to which you return.

By knowing so many angels by name and Ascended Masters, you almost think that you know what it is like in heaven or beyond in the Great Central Sun [or] in nirvana. But, beloved, the exact description of these experiences, though words may be used, can never be conveyed. Not only is it not possible for the lesser container to contain the greater but it is not lawful for us therefore to attempt to convey to the unascended ones the fullness of the glory that awaits.

Thus, by music and sound you do have the best means for entering higher vibrations and compartments of God. To this end was classical music given, and as that [classical music] which is of the highest vibration is used, it does also seal you from those states of the astral plane where, apart from initiatic rites such as I have described, you need never enter—unless, of course, Archangel Michael calls and you agree to accompany him on a very special mission. For now and again there may be a soul there, a pearl, that has been close to you at one time or another or to whom you owe a debt of karma.

Thus, under the wing of Archangel Michael you journey to a place that you would not be comfortable in without him, and there beneath his shield and rod you may speak your piece and speak your message. Beloved, prepare it well. For to woo a soul to let go the grips of a sensual existence, [a soul] warmed by the fires of hell and encouraged by all of those foul spirits and false gurus, I tell you, it does require ingenuity of heart, compassion and an intense fire whereby in you and in your eye one so possessed and so enslaved might see a fire burning—as the fire of John the Baptist, who was "a burning and a shining light"[8]—and therefore say, "There is my friend. I know him, I trust him. I will leave at his behest and under the guardianship of that mighty Archangel."

Blessed ones, you have spoken to many individuals in your time on this path, so desiring to draw them even to my heart as well as to the hearts of your ascended brethren. You have not realized that many of these individuals have literally had one foot in hell, and though they were physical they yet did abide in a hellish nightmare from which they could not see themselves liberated. But, beloved, they have not forgot you; and thereby by planting a seed you have an anchor point and all to whom you have delivered the message may be reached by you by this ray of light.

For you also have many, many arms as I do, with many eyes, one in each palm.[1] And thus as a sword of the *Dharmakaya*,[9] around you many light rays go forth from your heart as the hands of Kuan Yin and the Divine Mother of Mercy extending to these. And each time you give your Astreas, each hand extended to another soul on earth, [the one and the many you have preached to] receive the power of Astrea and the momentum does build; and thus in the very process of balancing karma by your Astreas you have lived to see the day when one whom you thought could not or would not be saved was ultimately reached.

As long as you remember that you preach the message of salvation to the soul and that your light is sealed in the Christ Self of that one, as long as you do not engage in human sympathy to be drawn down to the level of that one, know, then, beloved, that it is lawful to extend the hand that is the hand of God through you. But, beloved, in so extending that hand never compromise the Teaching, the Principle or the Word nor dilute the message, for it is the undiluted message, the concentrate, and only this that can rescue souls who are so far afield from the Tree of Life.

Thus, the Ritual of Exorcism by the Ruby Ray taught to you has availed much, as have all of your mighty invocations.[10] I suggest [that] you [make the] call that in all of your bodies and higher bodies your invocations never cease.

This nation, beloved, is literally covered in the astral plane with discarnates, nonentities, godless manifestations. It is as though the Divine Mother would desire to take a giant rake and rake into a heap all of this gray matter, this plastic, protoplasmic substance molded into identities not of God. Beloved, these cannot so easily be taken, for so many in embodiment are of a like vibration. They not only magnetize them but their free will sustains their presence.

Therefore, while all the world celebrates the triumph of Jesus Christ over Death and Hell and claims him as the Saviour whereby they too shall attain the resurrection, may you tarry as you tarry another day to make the calls intensely for the clearing of the astral plane over America. For only by a majority vote of Christed ones can we see the true clearing necessary in this nation to bring about a major change of consciousness whereby the practical path of the Buddhas and of my very own heart with Mother Mary and the Darjeeling Council might bring about the adequate defense and the consciousness of what is that spiritual defense, that thunderbolt, *Vajra!*[4]

With all of this gray matter suspended, beloved, it is like a jellylike sea of [the] dead and dying, and their astral presence brings disease and plague not yet outpictured. But that which has been, as you know, is severe enough.

Blessed ones, one of the most important services you can

render is the Friday night Ascension Service whereby you call for the clearing, at least of America as well as your own nations, of these astral discarnates which are not the remains of Lightbearers (who [themselves], one and all, have gravitated to etheric octaves) but [which are] of the lowest order of vibrating entities that you could imagine as well as all of the addicting ones you name.

Blessed ones, we need a clean sweep; and in this hour, beneath all of this weight, these miles of density of the astral plane and its denizens, there are yet those pearls.

I pray you, enter the path of fire, sacred fire, Kundalini fire, Mother Light raising, seraphim following, salamanders, Zarathustra, all of the violet flame and the blue lightning. I pray you have this fire stored that you might see the necessity that if there is truly to be a victory on earth, this must be cleared.

O beloved, you are doing so much. May you recognize it and know to multiply your effort and to keep on keeping on.

Every call you make to me, I promise you, shall go in my very heart as momentum for the saving of the pearls of Light now lost in the astral sea. For this cause does Mother Mary shed perpetual tears. For this cause do I join the hosts of the Lord, enarmored, beloved, moving with the Archangels and Astrea to go after them. It is my mission of Love.

Blessed ones, there are those in this room this Easter morning whom I have rescued from those depths because I had the impetus of your calls. And you who have been rescued (may you know it, may you not, depending on your awareness), I say to you: in gratitude for the Avalokiteśvara, the Alpha-to-Omega that I AM THAT I AM—I say, *make the Call.* For you were taken but another was left.[11] Let us go after the one left.

The gift of Good Friday and Holy Saturday is a saturation of violet flame. May you awaken to a new day of hope, hope because the Amitābha Buddha has sent forth a ray, and that ray in your heart is now a shaft unto eternity that the soul may climb.

I am in your heart forever, the sunbeam of the eye of God, precipitated as your friend and sister and Mother of Mercy.[12] I banish sin, I vanish sin. I am the fullness of the all-consuming fire of love of the Seventh Ray.

Those, then, who take my rosary[13] and give it shall increase mercy unto themselves first and foremost, and that mercy descending in your cup . . . shall fill all of your house until the abundance of your mercy called forth and returned to you may then be extended in wider and wider circles.

As we all require mercy and as some will surely be lost without it, I am determined to be the Bodhisattva of Mercy until not another soul requires it, for by my example many shall have become it. And then, beloved, an entire octave shall be rolled up as a scroll and you shall behold worlds beyond worlds that you have never even dreamt existed. But they are waiting for you, beloved, and they shall wait.

Thus, in the fullness of joy be all that you desire to be and vow to be. I am your attending Angel of Mercy, your Teacher and your Goddess.

OM MANI PADME HUM. O thou jewel in the heart of the lotus blossom of my own—how I love thee and love thee always as the Mother and the Amitābha Buddha.

Good day, my beloved.

"The Summit Lighthouse Sheds Its Radiance O'er All the World to Manifest as Pearls of Wisdom." This dictation by **Kuan Yin** was **delivered** by the Messenger Elizabeth Clare Prophet on **Holy Saturday, April 2, 1988,** after midnight, during the 5-day Easter Retreat at the **Royal Teton Ranch, Montana. [N.B.** Bracketed material denotes words unspoken yet implicit in the dictation, added by the Messenger under Kuan Yin's direction for clarity in the written word.] (1) **Kuan Yin as Avalokiteśvara.** See 1988 *Pearls of Wisdom,* p. 48. (2) It is the **mission of the Messenger** and all who follow the path of Christic initiation in the footsteps of our Lord to "descend into hell," i.e., the astral plane, with Jesus to rescue souls of Light, to rebuke and preach repentance to the fallen ones and to call for the judgment and the binding of those who remain in the death consciousness, avowed destroyers of life. (3) **Perfect love casts out fear.** I John 4:18. (4) **Vajra.** See 1988 *Pearls of Wisdom,* p. 170 n. 7. (5) Author Ruth Montgomery introduced the concept of **"walk-ins"** in her book *Strangers Among Us* followed by *Threshold to Tomorrow.* She wrote: "A Walk-in is a high-minded entity who" after numerous incarnations "is permitted to take over the body of another human being who wishes to depart. . . . The motivation for a Walk-in is humanitarian. He returns to physical being in order to help others help themselves, planting seed-concepts that will grow and flourish for the benefit of mankind. . . . The original occupants vacate the bodies because they no longer can maintain the physical spark of life or because they are so dispirited that they earnestly wish to leave." See Ruth Montgomery, *Strangers Among Us: Enlightened Beings from a World to Come* (New York: Ballantine Books, Fawcett Crest Book, 1979), pp. 11, 12; *Threshold to Tomorrow* (New York: G. P. Putnam's Sons, 1982), p. 10. In fact, according to the teachings of the Ascended Masters such spirits are fallen angels masquerading as angels of light. They are not enlightened beings but archdeceivers. (6) **Occupy till I come.** Luke 19:13. (7) **Many mansions in the Father's house.** John 14:2. (8) **A burning and a shining light.** John 5:35. (9) *Dharmakaya* [Sanskrit]: rendered as the Body of Essence, Body of the Law or Truth. The Causal Body and I AM Presence. The third of the three bodies of the Buddha *(trikaya);* the ultimate body from which the other two emanate for the purpose of interacting with and assisting life; the 'essence-being' of all Buddhas, immutable and undifferentiated, identical with absolute knowledge or reality. (10) See **"The LORD's Ritual of Exorcism,"** in *Invocations to the Hierarchy of the Ruby Ray through the Messenger Elizabeth Clare Prophet,* looseleaf. (11) **One shall be taken and the other left.** Matt. 24:40, 41; Luke 17:34–36. (12) **Avalokiteśvara 'born' from a ray from Amitābha's eye.** See 1988 *Pearls of Wisdom,* p. 215 n. 1. (13) *Kuan Yin's Crystal Rosary: Devotions to the Divine Mother East and West* released by Elizabeth Clare Prophet, 3-audiocassette album A88084, plus 40-page booklet, 4 hr. 40 min., $14.95 (add $1.50 for postage); booklet, $2.00 each (add $.90 each for postage), or 6 for $10.00 (add $1.10 for postage). This ritual of prayer and meditation is derived from ancient Chinese mantras, sutras and novenas combined with songs and mantras to the Divine Mother East and West, such as the Hail Mary, as well as dynamic decrees invoking the violet flame and the protection of the heavenly hosts. Cassette I includes the ten vows of Kuan Yin taken from the Great Compassion Heart Dharani Sutra; cassette II, Kuan Yin mantras for the Woman and her seed, using sacred names, titles and mantras of Kuan Yin arranged according to the fourteen stations of the Aquarian cross; cassette III, mantras to the thirty-three manifestations of Avalokiteśvara as Kuan Yin.

Catherine of Siena (see 1988 *Pearls of Wisdom,* pp. 139, 303), b. March 25, 1347, Italian mystic, defender of the pope and the Church. At age six in a powerful religious experience Catherine saw the radiant figure of Christ the King raise his hand and bless her. He was seated on a throne, crowned with a mitre and surrounded by the apostles Peter, Paul and John. Believing that her vocation was to be in the world but not of the world, at age sixteen she became a Sister of Penance, a member of the Dominican third order who wears a habit but is not confined to a convent. For the next three years Catherine remained cloistered in a small room in her father's house, living a life of austerity, solitude and silence, withdrawing into the "inner cell" of the knowledge of God and self, as she described her communion with the Lord. She had many visions and conversations with Jesus, culminating in the spiritual marriage with Christ. During that time Catherine received Jesus' teaching "I, nothing; God, All. I, nonbeing; God, Being." This fundamental truth inspired in her the humility and the conviction that enabled her to confront the forces threatening the Church and society in the turbulent fourteenth century.

At Jesus' direction Catherine returned to public life in Siena, where she tended the poor and the sick. As her reputation for spirituality became known, there gathered around her a circle of devotees from all walks of life who called her their "sweet holy mother." Catherine acted as a peacemaker and diplomat in order to bring peace to Italy and reform the Church. She traveled widely and addressed hundreds of letters to the prelates and sovereigns of the day, giving counsel and advice yet directly confronting misdeeds. Wherever Catherine went, preaching, teaching and healing, she brought a spiritual revival and led thousands of souls back to the Church. In 1375 on a visit to Pisa, Catherine received the stigmata, which at her request remained invisible until after her death.

In her absolute devotion to the papacy Catherine, accompanied by twenty-three devotees (friars, nuns and laymen), traveled to Avignon, France, where the popes had resided for the past 70 years, in order to convince Pope Gregory to return the papacy to Rome. In 1377 the pope returned to Italy, but a year later with the election of his successor, Urban VI, certain cardinals set up a rival, or "anti-pope," Clement VII. Thus began the "Great Schism," which absorbed the remainder of Catherine's life as she attempted to gain for Pope Urban VI the recognition that was rightfully his. In November 1378 she moved to Rome to devote herself to the cause of the papacy. During the last months of her life Catherine went daily to Saint Peter's basilica where she spent hours in prayer before the mosaic of *la Navicella,* the ship of the Church. Just before Lent in 1380 she had a vision of the ship being lifted out of the mosaic and placed upon her shoulders. Three months later, on April 29, 1380, at age 33, Catherine died, exhausted by her penances and efforts in the service of the pope and the Church. "O eternal God," she had prayed upon her deathbed, "receive the sacrifice of my life for the sake of this mystical body of holy Church." Her greatest work, the *Dialogue,* a spiritual treatise in the form of conversations with God the Father, was dictated by Catherine to her secretaries during a five-day state of ecstasy. About four hundred of her letters have survived as well as twenty-six of her prayers. Catherine was canonized in 1461; she was declared the patron saint of Italy in 1939 and proclaimed a Doctor of the Church in 1970. Her feast day is celebrated April 30.

Pearls of Wisdom®
published by The Summit Lighthouse

| Vol. 31 No. 47 | The Beloved Messenger | July 31, 1988 |

An Easter Retreat
VI
The Mysteries of the Light Kingdom
His voice resounding, "Pearls! pearls!"
Physicians of Souls: Heal the Body, Heal the Heart

O Lord, we are filled with thy Presence in this hour. Thy rapture is upon us. We exult in thy resurrection flame and thy victory and thy Universal Christhood on earth as in heaven. Infill us, O God, Thou who art God, with the totality of his Mind and that universal consciousness whereby in Alpha and Omega, as Above so below, we are one.

Let thy Presence with us and in us be thy Sacred Heart in our heart. Let us know through thy heart, O Lord, the pains of the world in order that we might ever maintain our vigil with Thee to nurture and to shepherd life and to pour forth abundantly thy healing unguents descending from thy Tree of Life—our Tree of Life.

Make us one even as we are one, O God. And this day strengthen our hearts by thy Body and thy Blood that we might be on earth the Diamond Heart of thy Blessed Mother—the diamond of God's holy will. O Lord, truly we would be thy instruments for the saving of the soul of a planet, the soul of a people and of the Spirit of the living God forever.

Thou who dost hear our prayer, strengthen us infinitely for thy Word and thy Work. And now, O Lord, in this joy of our moment with Thee, commune with us as in Galilee the breezes blow softly and the waters are made sacred by thy Presence. Carry us, then, to a scene two thousand years ago. Let us gather there for thy Word and thy ministry in this

hour in order that in our I AM Presence, in our higher
bodies of Light, we may challenge and rebuke again those
whom you did rebuke in that hour.

Therefore, let the persecutors of Christ in every nation
receive the judgment of thy Blood and thy Body, thy Alpha
and thy Omega. Let them know, O Lord, that Thou art
come and that we accept not only thy resurrection but thy
Second Coming in our hearts in this hour.

O Lord, come into our temples now. Take dominion:
Thy heart, my heart—thy Christ, my Christ—thy soul, my
soul—thy love, my love—thy peace, my peace. Amen.

From the Gospel of Mark, chapter 16:

And when the sabbath was past, Mary Magdalene, and
Mary the mother of James, and Salome, had bought sweet
spices, that they might come and anoint him.

And very early in the morning the first day of the week,
they came unto the sepulchre at the rising of the sun.

And they said among themselves, Who shall roll us
away the stone from the door of the sepulchre?

And when they looked, they saw that the stone was
rolled away: for it was very great.

And entering into the sepulchre, they saw a young man
sitting on the right side, clothed in a long white garment;
and they were affrighted.

And he saith unto them, Be not affrighted: Ye seek
Jesus of Nazareth, which was crucified: he is risen; he is not
here: behold the place where they laid him.

But go your way, tell his disciples and Peter that he
goeth before you into Galilee: there shall ye see him, as he
said unto you.

And they went out quickly, and fled from the sepulchre;
for they trembled and were amazed: neither said they any
thing to any man; for they were afraid.

Now when Jesus was risen early the first day of the
week, he appeared first to Mary Magdalene, out of whom he
had cast seven devils.

And she went and told them that had been with him, as
they mourned and wept.

And they, when they had heard that he was alive, and
had been seen of her, believed not.

After that he appeared in another form unto two of
them, as they walked, and went into the country.

And they went and told it unto the residue: neither
believed they them.

Afterward he appeared unto the eleven as they sat at

meat, and upbraided them with their unbelief and hardness of heart, because they believed not them which had seen him after he was risen.

And he said unto them, Go ye into all the world, and preach the gospel to every creature.

He that believeth and is baptized shall be saved; but he that believeth not shall be damned.

And these signs shall follow them that believe; In my name shall they cast out devils; they shall speak with new tongues;

They shall take up serpents; and if they drink any deadly thing, it shall not hurt them; they shall lay hands on the sick, and they shall recover.

So then after the Lord had spoken unto them, he was received up into heaven, and sat on the right hand of God.

And they went forth, and preached every where, the Lord working with them, and confirming the word with signs following. Amen.

From *The Nag Hammadi Library* I read to you the Acts of Peter and the Twelve Apostles. As these are in fragments, sometimes words are omitted.

[...] which [...] purpose [...: after ...] us [...] apostles [...]. We sailed [...] of the body. [Others] were not anxious in [their hearts].

And so the first complete sentence begins:

And in our hearts, we were united. We agreed to fulfill the ministry to which the Lord appointed us. And we made a covenant with each other.

We went down to the sea at an opportune moment, which came to us from the Lord. We found a ship moored at the shore ready to embark, and we spoke with the sailors of the ship about our coming aboard with them. And they showed great kindliness toward us as was ordained by the Lord. And after we had embarked, we sailed a day and a night. After that, a wind came up behind the ship and brought us to a small city in the midst of the sea.

And I, Peter, inquired about the name of this city from residents who were standing on the dock. [A man] among [them] answered, [saying, "The name] of this [city is Habitation, that is], Foundation [...] endurance." And the leader [among them...holding] the palm branch at the edge of [the dock]. And after we had gone ashore [with the] baggage, I [went] into [the] city, to seek [advice] about lodging.

A man came out wearing a cloth bound around his waist, and a gold belt girded [it]. Also a napkin was tied over

[his] chest, extending over his shoulders and covering his head and arms.

I was staring at the man, because he was beautiful in his form and stature. There were four parts of his body which I saw: the tops of his feet, and a part of his chest, and the palm of his hand, and his visage. These things I was able to see. A book cover like (those of) my books was in his left hand. A staff of styrax wood was in his right hand. His voice was resounding as he slowly spoke, crying out into the city, "Pearls! Pearls!"

I, indeed, thought he was a man [of] that city. I said to him, "My brother and my friend!" [He answered] me, [then, saying, "Rightly] did you say, '[My brother and] my friend.' What is it you [seek] from me?" I said to him, "[I ask] you [about] lodging for me [and the] brothers also, because we are strangers here." He said [to] me, "For this reason have I myself just said, 'My brother and my friend,' because I also am a fellow stranger like you."

And having said these things, he cried out, "Pearls! Pearls!" The rich men of that city heard his voice. They came out of their hidden storerooms. And some were looking out from the storerooms of their houses. Others looked out from their upper windows. And they did not see (that they could gain) anything from him, because there was no pouch on his back, nor bundle inside his cloth and napkin. And because of their disdain they did not even acknowledge him. He, for his part, did not reveal himself to them. They returned to their storerooms, saying, "This man is mocking us."

And the poor [of that city] heard [his voice, and they came to] the man [who sells pearls. They said, "We] beseech you to [show us a] pearl [so that we may], then, [see] it with our (own) eyes. For we are [poor]. And we do not have this price to pay for it. But [allow us] to say to our friends that [we saw] a pearl with our (own) eyes." He answered, saying to them, "If it is possible, come to my city, so that I may not only show it before your (very) eyes, but give it to you for nothing."

And indeed they, the poor of that city, heard and said, "Since we are beggars, we surely know that a man does not give a pearl to a beggar, but (it is) bread and money that is usually received. Now then, the kindness which we want to receive from you (is) that you show us the pearl before our eyes. And we will say to our friends proudly that we saw a pearl with our (own) eyes" —because it is not found among the poor, especially such beggars (as these). He answered (and) said to them, "If it is possible, you yourselves come to my city, so that I may not only show you it, but give it to you for nothing." The poor and the beggars rejoiced because of the man [who gives for] nothing.

[The men asked Peter] about the hardships. Peter answered [that it was impossible to tell] those things that he had heard about the hardships of [the] way, because [interpreters were] difficult [. . .] in their ministry.

He said to the man who sells this pearl, "I want to know your name and the hardships of the way to your city because we are strangers and servants of God. It is necessary for us to spread the word of God in every city harmoniously." He answered and said, "If you seek my name, Lithargoel is my name, the interpretation of which is, the light, gazelle-like stone.

"And also (concerning) the road to the city, which you asked me about, I will tell you about it. No man is able to go on that road, except one who has forsaken everything that he has and has fasted daily from stage to stage. For many are the robbers and the wild beasts on that road. The one who carries bread with him on the road, the black dogs will kill because of the bread. The one who carries a costly garment of the world with him, the robbers will kill [because of the] garment. [The one who carries] water [with him, the wolves will kill because of the water], since they were thirsty [for] it. [The one who] is anxious about [meat] and green vegetables, the lions will eat because of the meat. [If] he evades the lions, the bulls will devour him because of the green vegetables."

When he had said [these] things to me, I sighed within myself, saying, "[Great] hardships are on the road! If only Jesus would give us power to walk it!" He looked at me since my face was sad, and I sighed. He said to me, "Why do you sigh, if you, indeed, know this name 'Jesus' and believe him? He is a great power for giving strength. For I too believe in the Father who sent him."

I replied, asking him, "What is the name of the place to which you go, your city?" He said to me, "This is the name of my city, 'Nine Gates.' Let us praise God as we are mindful that the tenth is the head." After this I went away from him in peace.

As I was about to go and call my friends, I saw waves and large high walls surrounding the bounds of the city. I marveled at the great things I saw. I saw an old man sitting and I asked him if the name of the city was really [Habitation]. . . . He said to me, "[You speak] truly, for we [inhabit] here because [we] endure."

[I responded], saying, "Justly [. . .] have men named it [. . .], because (by) everyone [who] endures his trial, cities are inhabited; and a precious kingdom comes from them, because they endure in the midst of the apostasies and the difficulties of the storms. So that in this way, the city of everyone who endures the burden of his yoke of faith will be inhabited, and he will be included in the kingdom of heaven."

I hurried and went and called my friends so that we might go to the city which he, Lithargoel, appointed for us. In a bond of faith we forsook everything as he had said (to do). We evaded the robbers, because they did not find their garments with us. We evaded the wolves, because they did not find the water with us for which they thirsted. We evaded the lions, because they did not find the desire for meat with us. [We evaded the bulls. . . they did not find] green vegetables.

A great joy [came upon] us [and a] peaceful carefreeness [like that of] our Lord. We [rested ourselves] in front of the gate, [and] we talked with each other [about that] which is not a distraction of this [world]. Rather we continued in contemplation of the faith.

As we discussed the robbers on the road, whom we evaded, behold Lithargoel, having changed, came out to us. He had the appearance of a physician, since an unguent box was under his arm, and a young disciple was following him, carrying a pouch full of medicine. We did not recognize him.

Peter responded and said to him, "We want you to do us a favor, because we are strangers, and take us to the house of Lithargoel before evening comes." He said, "In uprightness of heart I will show it to you. But I am amazed at how you knew this good man. For he has not revealed himself to every man, because he himself is the son of a great king. Rest yourselves a little so that I may go and heal this man and come (back)." He hurried and came (back) quickly.

He said to Peter, "Peter!" And Peter was affrighted, for how did he know that his name was Peter? Peter responded to the Savior, "How do you know me, for you called my name?" Lithargoel answered, "I want to ask you who gave the name Peter to you?" He said to him, "It was Jesus Christ, the Son of the living God. He gave this name to me." He answered and said, "It is I! Recognize me, Peter." He loosened his garment, which clothed him—the one into which he had changed himself because of us—revealing to us in truth that it was he.

We prostrated ourselves on the ground and worshipped him. We comprised eleven disciples. He stretched forth his hand and caused us to stand. We spoke with him humbly. Our heads were bowed down in unworthiness as we said: "What you wish, we will do. But give us power to do what you wish at all times."

So, let us contemplate that teaching of the Master, his word to us, which in the above context his disciples in turn say, appropriately, to him: "What you wish, we will do. But give us power to do what you wish at all times."

Is this not what the Master says to us: "What you wish, I will do. But give me the power to do what you wish at all times"?

Shall we go about wishing for our perfection, for our soul's salvation, for our body's healing, for our enlightenment or shall we, as Jesus said, give to him the power to do what we wish him to do in our lives? Is life not so much more simple when we acknowledge our respective roles and realize that we must by free will empower our Lord to enter our lives, that we must call upon him and be willing to self-empty that he might infill us? And how we know so very well those things of which we must divest ourselves to be a crystal chalice for his/our 'wish-fulfillment'.

Therefore, we know that our God has empowered us to be humble, to be pure, to be holy, to be the receptacle of Light and that our God has empowered Jesus to grant unto us, when we shall have fulfilled the requirements of his Law, the "all-power of heaven and earth."[1]

At the nine gates of the city called Nine Gates we receive the initiations preparatory to our receipt of the nine gifts of the Holy Spirit.[2] The city is the place prepared for us to also receive the initiations of the "Power of the Three-Times-Three." This is the power of the threefold flame of your I AM Presence multiplying the power of the threefold flame of your Holy Christ Self multiplying the power of the threefold flame in your heart, each multiplication a geometrization of the Word.

And when the three flames become one, and one great heart of Light is the consummation of the heart of your I AM Presence and Christ Self with your heart that beats here below, then you will know the meaning of the Power of the Three-Times-Three in connection with that city that is called Nine Gates, where stand to receive us nine hierarchies of the LORD who are sent to prove and reprove our souls on nine paths of the Holy Spirit.

In all humility, then, moving toward this goal according to the Teachings of the great Buddha and the great Christ, let us know that the path of the bodhisattva lies before us and that in taking the very first step we must remember the mutual empowerment which is the trust of the true Master/Disciple relationship: *"What you wish, we will do. But give us power to do what you wish at all times."*

We give to our Lord the authority to act in our name as he gives us the authority to act in his. That means being at peace as his joyous, willing instrument as he answers the calls of the multitudes through us and as we answer his call by obeying his command thusly: Lord, thy wish is my command: *"Whatever you wish me to do, I will do it. Pray, do Thou give me the Power, Wisdom and Love of the Three-Times-Three—thy heart, my heart—to do what you wish at all times."*

In order to be prepared for Jesus' call we ask the intercession of the Divine Mother and her angels to exorcise from us demons of doubt and fear, anxiety and death and those things that would separate us from the love of Christ Jesus which is as near and as close to us as the tear in our Blessed Mother's eye.

"O my Lord, thy wish, my wish always—thy empowerment mine."

He gave them the unguent box and the pouch that was in the hand of the young disciple. He commanded them like this, saying, "Go into [the] city from which you came, which is called Habitation. Continue in endurance as you teach all those who have believed in my name, because I have endured in hardships of the faith. I will give you your reward."

A simple and eternal promise. You need not be concerned ever for recognition or that your due will not come to you or that someone has slighted you or will slight you. Your Lord has said, "I will give you your reward." Be at peace. Enter into the joy of the Lord's work.

"To the poor of that city give what they need in order to live until I give them what is better, which I told you that I will give you for nothing."

Peter answered and said to him, "Lord, you have taught us to forsake the world and everything in it. We have renounced them for your sake. What we are concerned about (now) is the food for a single day. Where will we be able to find the needs that you ask us to provide for the poor?"

The Lord answered and said, "O Peter, it was necessary that you understand the parable that I told you! Do you not understand that my name, which you teach, surpasses all riches, and the wisdom of God surpasses gold, and silver, and precious stone(s)?"

He gave them the pouch of medicine and said, "Heal all the sick of the city who believe [in] my name." Peter was afraid [to] reply for he did not want to ask the second time. So he signaled to the one who was beside him, who was John: "You talk this time." John answered and said, "Lord, before you we are afraid to say many words. But it is you who asks us to practice this skill. We have not been taught to be physicians. How then will we know how to heal bodies as you have told us?"

He answered him, "Rightly have you spoken, John, for I know that the physicians of this world heal what belongs to the world. The physicians of souls, however, heal the heart. Heal the bodies first, therefore, so that through the real powers of healing for their bodies, without medicine of the world, they may believe in you, that you have power to heal the illnesses of the heart also.

"The rich men of the city, however, those who did not see fit even to acknowledge me, but who reveled in their wealth and pride—with such as these, therefore, do not dine in [their] house nor be friends with them, lest their partiality influence you. For many in the churches have shown partiality to the rich, because they also are sinful, and they give occasion for others to do (likewise). But judge them with uprightness, so that your ministry may be glorified, and (so that) I too, and my name, may be glorified in the churches." The disciples answered and said, "Yes, truly this is what is fitting to do."

They prostrated themselves on the ground and worshipped him. He caused them to stand and departed from them in peace. Amen.[3]

Let us sing to our beautiful Saviour who comes to us to transmit to us our mission in this life. Please talk to Jesus in your heart. Pray to him softly now. Open yourself to him and empower him to help you as he does empower you.*

I shall read to you a discourse of our Lord as recorded in the Gnostic Gospel *Pistis Sophia,* translated by G. R. S. Mead.

Jesus continued again in the discourse and said unto his disciples: "When I shall have gone into the Light, then herald it unto the whole world and say unto them: Cease not to seek day and night and remit not yourselves until ye find the mysteries of the Light kingdom, which will purify you and make you into refined light and lead you into the Light kingdom.

"Say unto them: Renounce the whole world and the whole matter therein and all its cares and all its sins, in a word all its associations which are in it, that ye may be worthy of the mysteries of the Light and be saved from all the chastisements which are in the judgments.

"Say unto them: Renounce murmuring, that ye may be worthy of the mysteries of the Light and be saved from the fire of the dog-faced [one].

"Say unto them: Renounce eavesdropping, that ye may [be worthy of the mysteries of the Light] and be saved from the judgments of the dog-faced [one].

"Say unto them: Renounce litigiousness, that ye may be worthy of the mysteries of the Light and be saved from the chastisements of Ariēl.

---

*"Beautiful Saviour! King of Creation," number 67, sung

"Say unto them: Renounce false slander, that ye may be worthy of the mysteries of the Light and be saved from the fire-rivers of the dog-faced [one].

"Say unto them: Renounce false witness, that ye may be worthy of the mysteries of the Light and that ye may escape and be saved from the fire-rivers of the dog-faced [one].

"Say unto them: Renounce pride and haughtiness, that ye may be worthy of the mysteries of the Light and be saved from the fire-pits of Ariēl.

"Say unto them: Renounce belly-love, that ye may be worthy of the mysteries of the Light and be saved from the judgments of Amente.

"Say unto them: Renounce babbling, that ye may be worthy of the mysteries of the Light and be saved from the fires of Amente.

"Say unto them: Renounce craftiness, that ye may be worthy of the mysteries of the Light and be saved from the chastisements which are in Amente.

"Say unto them: Renounce avarice, renounce love of the world, renounce pillage, renounce evil conversation, renounce wickedness, renounce pitilessness, renounce wrath, renounce cursing, renounce thieving, renounce robbery, renounce slandering, renounce fighting and strife, renounce all unknowing, renounce evil doing, renounce sloth, renounce adultery, renounce murder, renounce pitilessness and impiety, renounce atheism, renounce [magic] potions, renounce blasphemy, renounce the doctrines of error, that ye may be worthy of the mysteries of the Light and be saved from all the chastisements of the great dragon of the outer darkness.

"Say unto those who teach the doctrines of error and to every one who is instructed by them: Woe unto you, for, if ye do not repent and abandon your error, ye will go into the chastisements of the great dragon and of the outer darkness, which is exceedingly evil, and never will ye be cast [up] into the world, but will be non-existent until the end.

"Say unto those who abandon the doctrines of the truth of the First Mystery: Woe unto you, for your chastisement is sad compared with [that of] all men. For ye will abide in the great cold and ice and hail in the midst of the dragon and of the outer darkness, and ye will never from this hour on be cast [up] into the world, but ye shall be frozen up in that region and at the dissolution of the universe ye will perish and become non-existent eternally.

"Say rather to the men of the world: Be calm, that ye may receive the mysteries of the Light and go on high into the Light kingdom.

"Say unto them: Be ye loving-unto-men, that ye may be worthy of the mysteries of the Light and go on high into the Light kingdom.

"Say unto them: Be ye gentle, be ye peaceful, be ye merciful, give ye alms, minister unto the poor and the sick and distressed, be ye loving-unto-God, be ye righteous, be good, renounce all, that ye may receive the mysteries of the Light and go on high into the Light kingdom.

"These are all the boundaries of the ways for those who are worthy of the mysteries of the Light.

"Unto such, therefore, who have renounced in this renunciation, give the mysteries of the Light and hide them not from them at all, even though they are sinners and they have been in all the sins and all the iniquities of the world, all of which I have recounted unto you, in order that they may turn and repent and be in the submission which I have just recounted unto you. Give unto them the mysteries of the Light kingdom and hide them not from them at all; for it is because of sinfulness that I have brought the mysteries into the world, that I may forgive all their sins which they have committed from the beginning on."[4]

Accepting in this hour Jesus' promise of the forgiveness of sin and the balance of karma, let us share together Easter Communion. May our servers please take their stations.

Let us have Mark's blessing.

O eternal God, Thou who art one with all life, with the blessed consciousness of everyone who has ever lived upon the planetary body and held sweet awareness of thyself, Thou who has broken the Bread of Life in the midst of the earliest temples of the Brotherhood, Thou who has showered upon mankind awareness of thy kingdom of other worlds, of the strange and beautiful beauty that is in thy consciousness, be now Father, Mother, eternal God unto each one of us. Help us to hold gentle awareness of thy perfection working in these walls of time and serving to remind us that we can indeed make our lives sublime. For Thou hast already prepared the matrice of perfection and endowed each heart and being with that matrice.

Forgive us for our errors, the tragedies that we have created as we have gazed upon Darkness rather than Light. Help us to the newness of discovery of that rainbow of promise shining just beyond the bend in the wall of time. Let us see that hope is everywhere, that hope is real tonight for our world regardless of the appearances of tragedy and takeover and the thrusts of the denizens of darkness.

Reveal to us thy light, thy sweet and subtle light that shineth greater than any light that has ever shown upon land or upon sea. And break Thou the bread of Life with each of us, communing with us this night in memory of our Lord and Saviour, of the eternal Christos, the fountain from Eden that is the Creator and the Tree of Life that from the beginning of the ages was the foundation of the divine seed in man, springing up as immortality and fruition, as maturity and beauty, as the perfection of the plan in the life of each one that will change us effectively from glory unto glory, even as by thy Spirit. In Thee is no Darkness but only the light of Life and that light is the Light of men. So be it.

So do Thou this that we ask of Thee this night. And let thy hand and the hand of the angels change the substance we take into our bodies into the spiritual essence of the sacred fire, that as there passes down into the center of our body these broken fragments we take and partake of in memory of Thee, we may also understand the cup of the mission that is before us each one.

To partake of this is our joy. And may we surrender beautifully and completely not only for this hour, O Father, but for every hour to come when thy perfectionment shall make us all at last one without fear or torment.

It is to thy nearness that we dedicate ourselves, for Thou art with us always, even to the end of the age of cycles and the beginning of the new.

Our Father, so do Thou this thing in the name of the living Christ and to the sacraments of our immortal soul and the light thereof. It is done in the name of God. It is done in the name of Christ. It is done in the name of the Brotherhood Eternal. So be it.

Remember, Communion is the receiving of the Body and Blood of Christ after the confession of sin. As you come forward for Communion, confess to your Lord Jesus, to your Holy Christ Self those things that you are placing on the altar of God nevermore to take up again. His angels, then, clarifying and clearing you, washing you clean, prepare you to receive the Alpha and the Omega of the Ascended Master, the Light Body of Jesus. This light, then, reestablishes your wholeness and your alignment with the Universal Christ.

"The Summit Lighthouse Sheds Its Radiance O'er All the World to Manifest as Pearls of Wisdom." These readings were given by the Messenger Elizabeth Clare Prophet on **Easter Sunday, April 3, 1988,** prior to the dictation by Jesus Christ, during the five-day Easter Retreat at the **Royal Teton Ranch, Montana.** (1) Matt. 28:18. (2) See I Cor. 12; *Lords of the Seven Rays,* Book One, pp. 5–20; and chart of the "Twelve Gifts of the Holy Spirit: Initiations under the Twelve Hierarchies of the Sun." (3) James M. Robinson, ed., *The Nag Hammadi Library in English* (San Francisco: Harper & Row, 1977), pp. 265-70. (4) G. R. S. Mead, trans., *Pistis Sophia: A Gnostic Gospel* (Blauvelt, N.Y.: Spiritual Science Library, 1984), pp. 213–18.

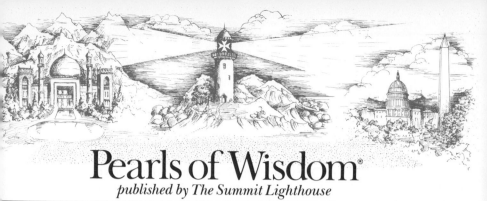

Pearls of Wisdom®
published by The Summit Lighthouse

| Vol. 31 No. 48 | Beloved Jesus Christ | August 6, 1988 |

An Easter Retreat
VII
The Overcoming Victory of the Light
"Descend to save the pearls, the pearls, the pearls!"
Be My Disciples: Be Myself

And so is my descent to you in this hour, O beloved, for the divine purpose unto which you are called, the overcoming victory of the Light in this life.

For the Light kingdom is the great canopy of Love and that spherical body that is a blazing, dazzling sun above you. Unto this body of Universal Light I impel you by ascension's call and resurrection's Spirit!

For I AM the LORD thy God in manifestation. I AM thy brother and I truly show the Way that must be attained by thee in this hour.

Blessed ones, the Way may be hard and each footstep up the mountain more difficult, but, beloved, the steps must be taken, even if at a slow pace, one foot after the other on the Path, whereby the soul herself is garmented in beauty, liberated from the sense of sin. For though I long ago have cleansed you of sin, you retain the sense of sin in a sinful world.

Therefore, be bright and whitened and encouraged in this hour. For, beloved, the Way must be taken and there is no other Way. For through my Sacred Heart and the initiatic path which I gave to my disciples and truly for you, that is sealed in the heart of my disciple Martha,[1] you will then demonstrate to the world that the path of initiation can be realized, can be attained and [you will] introduce the age of Aquarius with the victory of Christ in you.

The breaking of the spell of Death and Hell[2] in established religion, truly the hypnotic spell of orthodoxy, may only come by the living witness. And I, if I am lifted up in you, I will draw all Lightbearers unto you.[3] Therefore, as a staff, raise up the Light* in your temple.

Heed my call! Deny me not! For the years pass: I come again, I deliver my message, and the Law requires an acceleration.

Therefore, O my beloved, know, then, that I have called you to be my disciples as[†] being myself in form, the pupil being the embodiment of the Teacher in thought and attitude, *Be-attitude,* in feeling, in compassion, in kindness and humility and in the brilliance of mind that reflects the great Mind of God that is able diligently to conduct oneself according to the highest standards of our court and Hierarchy, excelling, then, where others of lesser grace excel,[4] thy grace being that Holy Spirit.

Beware, then, the coming of the judgment of the Holy Spirit declared in Los Angeles as the initiation of that Holy Spirit.[5] For thy Christhood must be sealed.

Therefore, listen—and listen and learn of me. For when I speak or when I exorcise through my Messenger, even in the secret place of her meditation, there is always the thrashing and the lashing out of that dweller on the threshold. See to it, beloved, that thou dost stand apart from the not-self to also bring judgment upon the unreality of thy being.

Therefore, when I call my Messenger to give my invocations in your behalf, for the hour is come for the purging Light, I desire to find you fully prepared, having so called upon me to exorcise that dweller on the threshold that that final fiat of Light and purging may come and you may know yourself delivered, then, of that which is no longer a part of thee. It is called "the hanger-on" and it does hang on, beloved. Therefore [to exorcise the dweller] it does require the intercession of Maitreya or one of us who may come in the name of the Universal Christ.

Know, then, beloved, that the assistance of Hierarchy is required to fulfill the goal of reunion with God. Therefore, with all thy getting get thee understanding of oneness with our heart, for we are ever near. The soul must not neglect her tutoring or her studying beneath her tutors.

Thus, the path of the bodhisattva is formally introduced to this Community beginning with the ten vows of our beloved Kuan Yin.[6] This is the beginning of your understanding of Maitreya's Mystery School as set requirements which are before you to which you must apply yourselves.

I encourage you, beloved, for as you prepare the vessel,

---

*raise up the Light of the I AM Presence, of the Universal Christ of Jesus and of your Real Self (the Holy Christ Self), and of the Divine Mother (the sacred fire, or Kundalini, in the base-of-the-spine chakra).   †by way of untold graces and glories will fill your cup and overflow to the healing of many. Think you that I would not empower you as I empowered my own two thousand years ago?[7]

Blessed ones, great advances have been made in the unfoldment of the Teaching and the Mysteries. Dispensations of light have returned. The dark ages which occurred as the judgment of the denial of the Son of God by the powers of this earth have also been set aside.[8]

Thus, the new dispensations of Aquarius bring us back to the moment of my original revelation of the opportunity for every son of God to realize the fullness of my Christhood and the Light of the I AM THAT I AM. Understand, beloved, that these revelations come again are for the gathering by the Holy Spirit of those who must in this hour come to the focalization of the sacred fire and hold that fire in the earth.

For I prophesy to you that a great wind shall come, greater than you have heard or seen in this life. Know, then, that thou shalt stand in that day if [you have] fully heeded the warnings we have spoken and the specific directions that come through the Messenger. So it shall be, beloved, that in this standing and in this enduring there shall be the opportunity to attain the crown of Life[9] if the sufficient foundation has been laid.

Remember, then, the box of ointment.[10] I have given to you, therefore, unguents necessary in the full complement of the Teaching. I say, open the box, each one, for my angel physicians hand it to you in this hour individually. Know, then, that this box is the sign and symbol of the sacred mysteries.

The desire to heal and be healed must be preceded by the desire for wholeness above all else. It is in the Light kingdom that thou art whole. Therefore, call down the causal body of Light! Be thou made whole!

Beloved ones, the gift of the pouch[10] is that which you will require to meet the daily necessities of life as you go in my name to heal. Blessed ones, I speak not of healing in the larger sense of which the churches speak but I speak truly of the healing of the heart. I speak of restoration of faculties of soul and minds who can no longer think or remember or know or be. [For] the loss of faculties in this generation is alarming.

Without the power of the Logos within you there is no salvation, and the Logos is more than the Word which was in the beginning with God.[11] It is the Divine Reason, the Divine Doctrine, the Divine Gnosis!

Know, then, that the cultivation of the heart, the Sacred Heart, the Diamond Heart, the Immaculate Heart, the threefold flame, this cultivation, beloved, shall find thee in the center of a sun. And the rays going forth infinitely in all directions are pathways to the infinite and down these pathways to your heart does come the divine understanding, and with that understanding you can quickly master the subjects necessary for the performance of daily responsibilities. But without the divine understanding of the Sun behind the sun pouring into the heart daily, thou shalt be as blocks of wood, stones, computers outmoded, not functioning well.

Fear not the loss of materiality nor of the sensual mind but rather fear nonpreparedness to receive the Higher Mind and all of golden illumination's flame.

"We have no time to pray, Lord." I say, *be* a prayer. "We have no time to study, Lord." I say, rise fifteen minutes early and with full concentration upon my Teaching take one of my books.[12] Read for fifteen minutes. Carry that book with you and remind yourself of what you read. Embody it for the day. A morsel will suffice for the divine alchemy. Where there is no morsel I, then, have nothing to multiply, no wavelength of meditation whereby to enter.

Neglect not, beloved, for in days in the future and in the hereafter salvation is far, far more difficult than in the Eternal Now. The tools are before you. Let them not rust upon the bench.

Now, then, my beloved, I speak also to a world. I speak to a world whose din has been so raised that scarcely do they seek or hear the living Truth that is spoken.

The Mysteries I have revealed through this Messenger are basic, are fundamental, are building blocks. Would you not think that the whole world would recognize these keys? And those who are touched by the Holy Spirit as night after night I preach this message through her, are they not able to retain it? Many are not, and many compare the real jewels with the trinkets, the baubles of life and see not the difference. Such a state of the Kali Yuga!

And in the midnight hour Kuan Yin, Avalokiteśvara, the great Amitābha and others descend. They with a great intensity of fiery zeal have come, beloved, to save what can be saved.

Let the perpetual prayer of the heart be the desiring, then, and let angels carry thy desiring as command to go forth, to clear the way, to enter those lower octaves where by the Law of the One and according to free will they must receive the invocation, the spoken Word, even the whisper, "O Light, I command you! O hierarchies of Light, forces of Light, angels of Light, descend to save the pearls, the pearls, the pearls!"[13]

I call to all who love me on earth: Come now to be my shepherds! Come now and be not stiff-necked and doubting as my disciples! Why do you trust the foundations of your orthodoxy to those whom I upbraided as my final sermon to them?[14] Beloved, do you not think of the pain in my heart that in parting from them in that hour in the mystery of the resurrection I did find the requirement of the Law to rebuke them, to deliver that sacred fire for their human questioning and their doubting?

It is because they would not believe my beloved Magda,[15] my beloved Mother, my beloved John. They would not believe but only if I should appear to them directly. Thus, they stole the crown without the content and did not note that they had not the jewels to hold that crown.

Know, then, beloved, how this stiff-neckedness may also persist for generations, and is this not the term yet applied to the Israelites, to the brothers of Joseph? Let it not be applied to those in our Community this day nor in the world.

For I speak to the churches and their denial of woman. I speak to the fallen angels who have determined that the Woman and her seed[16] shall not enter the pulpits. I speak to you, then:

You whose auras are black with your calumny, you who have defiled my little ones, *you* rabbis, priests, ministers, to you I say, you shall not stand in the day of my glory and resurrection nor shall you stand this day! For one and all who have denied the Divine Mother in my disciples or my Word through perhaps the one whom you consider to be the least of these my brethren[17] in this Messenger, know, then, that not for the denial of my representatives but for the denial of me in them shall you know the full accountability.

And the Archangels do stand even at the very door; and the world shall know my Lost Teaching and the lost art of true healing. The world shall know of me, for the hour is come and the hour of fulfillment. And I am here, and in each cycle and quadrant of the year as the decades unfold I am more physical, more embodied in those who carry my Word truly.

Therefore, know, *you* who have denied the cosmic Truth for paltry doctrines established by evil men such as you in long gone centuries of ignorance, *you,* then, shall give accounting for the entire false hierarchy of Christianity!

And you who have limited the power, the doctrine of Moses and the prophets and replaced it, then, with your own books and tomes, you who have denied the power of Sanat Kumara* to raise up my people, I say to you, the lost tribes of the house of Israel shall emerge from your temples and synagogues and from your cathedrals;

*the Ancient of Days who sent you the prophets

and they shall no longer allow their body and their blood that is mine to nourish your ages-old conspiracy of denial of the true path of the inner walk with God. And all of these foundations you have laid for gain and control [afford] but temporal power that crumbles as the dust in an instant.

I say to all who deny me in each and every child of God and who have mocked my teaching of the potential Godhood of everyone who is the issue of the Most High God: Your judgment shall come in one night, even as the judgment of Babylon shall come, and in one night you shall see your citadels of power no more![18]

Therefore, let the wise and the pure in heart remember that I do not sup with them nor should you. Seek not, then, the approbation of the powerful and the rich, for all that they have has come from my Light in you. And I take from them in this hour by my scepter and rod all that they have stolen of the Light that they have not achieved by bending the knee to the Universal Christ, to the Lord of the World, to the God of very gods.

When you see what they shall retain by their own path of Christic initiation, beloved, and when you see what you shall retain in the same hour, then you will know who are the stars in the earth whose causal bodies keep alive the quickening fire as coals on the altar of a planet and who are the dead that weigh down a planet with their incomparable misery and selfishness.

My Presence in the earth in this hour is a warning. I am as John the Baptist of old, for I am a Messenger going before— before the incarnation of the Christ within you, as I was always this Messenger displaying to you a path of Christhood that you might know it and become it.

For too long have even my own in this Community heard this message without fully believing and drinking the cup and manifesting that Christhood. Do not weary us with delays and we shall not weary you with the repetition of our message. Thus, beloved, the hour is come and must be taken; and the world shall see and know that the Teaching is real because you and not another, but *you* have dared to embody my Word.

Now, beloved, in this hour I choose not to comment further on world conditions or the progression of cycles but to speak of the resurrection and again the resurrection and again the resurrection, preferring, then, that your attention be upon a mighty effort from this hour to Wesak and to the celebration of my ascension, that Lord Gautama may speak to you of those things you desire to hear.

Remember, beloved, so as you do and so as you are, you are writing the pages of history from which the Lord of the World shall read at Wesak. Thus, we shall not count our victories or our lapses until the final moment before that delivery, that you might have ultimate opportunity to write by works what is to be. For the prophecy of earth's destiny is in the hands of the embodied prophets all, and all of you who know the Spirit of my Father, Saint Germain, embody that prophecy; and prophecy is as prophecy does.

Thus, I choose to gather the hearts of my little ones, those newly come to life. Those who have called to me for baptism in this hour I choose to receive into my Church, and I do call this "my Church Universal and Triumphant," for I would impart the blessing of communicants this day. I desire to receive the thousands who shall become white stones in the temple building.

Let the corrupt civilizations be diminished. Let the new order of the ages appear.

Beloved, my promise of healing is unto you. Therefore, I shall release this day through my Messenger a healing ray to you individually; and as you have prepared, as you have called, as you have allowed it, so it shall be unto you. Each one shall receive that for which he is prepared and each one may pray to me that supreme request that is most important to his soul and heart. The healing you receive, beloved, shall be the healing that you allow and that for which you have prepared in all diligence. May it be unto you according to thy word, according to thy faith, according to thy hope, according to thy charity, according to thy discipleship.

In this conveyance, beloved, you shall learn the lesson [in order] that you may receive from my heart that for which you are ready. Remember, I have told you that the counsel of my Messenger given to you is always for your preparedness when in that day and hour I come, for my Father has sent me.

Now remember Moses. For as Moses did raise up that brazen serpent in the wilderness that all who did look upon it were healed,[19] so look upon my scepter of authority and my staff, for it does symbolize the Light raised up in you. Visualize it now upon the spinal altar. Receive it in the mind and crown and third eye and hold it there. For in thy all-seeing is thy wholeness and if thine eye be single, thy whole body shall be full of Light.[20]

I am forever your Jesus, your brother. In my love for you I am stern with you that you will realize that to win the prize does take all due diligence. Now let us see many victors arise from this Community. I decree it and I am the fulfillment of the Law, even as I am with you unto the end of your struggle and your karma.

This dictation by **Jesus Christ** was **delivered** by the Messenger Elizabeth Clare Prophet on **Easter Sunday, April 3, 1988,** during the five-day Easter Retreat at the **Royal Teton Ranch, Montana. [N.B.** Bracketed material denotes words unspoken yet implicit in the dictation, added by the Messenger under the Master's direction for clarity in the written word.] Prior to the dictation the Messenger read Mark 16 on the resurrection of Jesus Christ, the Acts of Peter and the Twelve Apostles from the Nag Hammadi library, and an excerpt from the Gnostic text Pistis Sophia, bk. 3, chap. 102 (see Pearl no. 47). Readings and dictation by Jesus on 92-min. audiocassette B88048, $6.50 (add $.55 for postage). **(1) Martha.** See 1988 *Pearls of Wisdom,* pp. 340–41. **(2) The spell of Death and Hell is sin.** I Cor. 15:54–57. **(3) "And I . . . will draw all men unto me."** John 12:32. **(4) "Where others of lesser grace excel."** Jesus is pointing to the fact that many Christians who have less grace, in that they do not have the testimony of Jesus in the Spirit of prophecy whereby his dictations are delivered through the Messengers and the sacred mysteries are taught, sometimes excel more than those who have received these greater gifts. **(5) The initiation (judgment) of the Holy Spirit.** See the Maha Chohan, 1988 *Pearls of Wisdom,* pp. 225–30. **(6)** The day before Jesus' dictation, on April 2, 1988, celebrated as Kuan Yin's birthday, the Messenger delivered teachings on the path of the bodhisattva and on the **ten vows of Kuan Yin** taken from the Great Compassion Heart Dharani Sutra—a Buddhist text in which Kuan Yin explains that those who wish to "bring forth a heart of great compassion for all beings. . . should first follow me in making these vows." The Messenger led the congregation in reciting these bodhisattva vows as mantras in English and Chinese alternated with the Hail Mary. Lecture and dictation by Kuan Yin on 3 videocassettes, 4 hr. 8 min., GP88042, $49.95 (add $1.90 for postage), or 3 audiocassettes, 4 hr. 10 min., B88052–54, $19.50 (add $.95 for postage). The ten vows of Kuan Yin are also recorded on 3-audiocassette album *Kuan Yin's Crystal Rosary,* cassette I, B88084, $6.50 (add $.55 for postage). Album plus 40-page booklet, A88084, $14.95 (add $1.50 for postage); see 1988 *Pearls of Wisdom,* p. 373 n. 14. **(7) The empowerment of the disciples.** Matt. 10:1, 5–8; 28:18–20; Mark 6:7; 16:15–18; Luke 9:1, 2, 6; 24:46–49; John 20:21–23. **(8)** Read Matt. 23, 24. **(9) The crown of Life.** James 1:12; Rev. 2:10. **(10)** See pp. 382–83. **(11) In the beginning was the Word.** John 1:1, 2. **(12) Teachings by Jesus.** See Jesus and Kuthumi, *Prayer and Meditation,* quality paperback, $9.95; hardbound, 1968 *Pearls of Wisdom,* vol. 11, nos. 10–23, $14.95.

Jesus and Kuthumi, *Corona Class Lessons,* quality paperback, $12.95.

Elizabeth Clare Prophet, *The Lost Years of Jesus,* hardbound, $19.95; quality paperback, $14.95; pocketbook, $5.95.

Mark L. Prophet and Elizabeth Clare Prophet, *The Lost Teachings of Jesus I* and *II.* Volume I hardbound, $19.95; quality paperback, $14.95. Volume II hardbound, $21.95; quality paperback, $16.95. Pocketbook edition, Books One–Four, $4.95 each.

Mark L. Prophet and Elizabeth Clare Prophet, *Climb the Highest Mountain,* hardbound, $21.95; quality paperback, $16.95. Keepers of the Flame Lessons.

(For postage, add $.50 for books $5.95 and under; $1.00 for books $9.95–$14.95; and $1.50 for books $16.95–$21.95.)

(13) See **"The Hymn of the Pearl,"** a Gnostic poem thought to have been composed by the apostle Thomas. It portrays the soul's descent from the highest spiritual plane into the planes of illusion with loss of memory of her origin. There she faces the trial and tribulation of the lower life until she responds to the Call from Home, which eventuates in her ascent culminating in her union with the Divine. On October 4, 1987, the Messenger delivered a lecture on the Lost Years and the Lost Teachings of Jesus in which she read and gave commentary on "The Hymn of the Pearl" from G. A. Gaskell, *Gnostic Scriptures Interpreted* (London: C. W. Daniel Co., 1927), pp. 43–68. See also Jesus, 1987 *Pearls of Wisdom,* p. 494. **(14) Jesus upbraids the disciples.** Mark 16:14. **(15)** See the **Gospel of Mary,** in *The Nag Hammadi Library in English,* ed. James M. Robinson (San Francisco: Harper & Row, 1977), pp. 471–74; the Messenger's Easter sermon with teaching on the Gospel of Mary, April 19, 1987, two 90-min. audiocassettes, B87030–31, $13.00 (add $.95 for postage). **(16) The Woman and her seed.** Rev. 12. **(17) The least of these my brethren.** Matt. 25:40. **(18) The judgment in one night, one day, one hour.** Dan. 5:30; Rev. 18. **(19) The brazen serpent raised up.** Num. 21:5–9; John 3:14, 15. **(20) If thine eye be single**. . . Matt. 6:22; Luke 11:34.

Index to 1988 *Pearls of Wisdom*

For an alphabetical listing of many of the philosophical and hierarchical terms used in the 1988 *Pearls of Wisdom,* see the comprehensive glossary, "The Alchemy of the Word: Stones for the Wise Masterbuilders," in *Saint Germain On Alchemy: For the Adept in the Aquarian Age.*

Soviet tanks entered, 179
"Hymn of the Pearl," 394n.13
Hypnosis, 304. *See also* Tape recordings

I AM: "Beloved I AM," 62; greatest word of power ever uttered, 150. *See also* I AM Presence; I AM THAT I AM
I AM Presence, 352; chart and teaching of the, 314; descent of the, 160; and the Dharmakaya, 373n.9; does descend suddenly into your temple, 266; fifteen minutes before retiring meditate upon your, 166n.4; mantle of, 46; Mount Zion, 271; one glimpse of your, 264; people walking with their, 246; permanent atom of the, 206; sign of the, 227; threefold flame of your, 381; turning of each individual toward his, 133; unlimited power in your, 163. *See also* Chart; I AM; I AM THAT I AM
"I AM" Race, letters of America spell out, 101
I AM THAT I AM: flaming presence of, 264; its recitation as a love song, 237; power of the name, 303. *See also* I AM; I AM Presence
Ignorant animal magnetism, 337; def., 339n.8. *See also* Density
Igor, his vigil, 253, 254n.3
Illumination: as a dawn of presence, quietude and power, 152; decrees for illumination's flame, 59–62; illumination('s) flame, 55, 56, 58; is always become illumined action, 153; keep the flame of, 154
Illusions: in the world, 56; your, 244
Immaculate Heart: cultivation of the, 389–90; gift of Mother Mary's, 320–21; Immaculate Heart statue of Mother Mary, 341n.14; Mother Mary's, 323; recourse through Mother Mary's, 220
Immortality, 15–16, 266
Inbreath, in Hindu cosmology, 366n.7
Incarnations, in the East and West, 303
Indecisiveness, 89
India: false gurus of, 303; false hierarchies out of, 43
INF Treaty, 69, 180, 249n.10
Initiates, true, 295
Initiation(s): of the crucifixion, 306; of the decade of the nineties, 207; of great dimensions and proportion,

231; of the Holy Spirit, 225–26, 276, 388; individual path of, 98; path of, 387; phases of, 111–12; to rebuke devils, 368; of the resurrection, 309; secret ray, 227; of the secret rays are most difficult, 36; serious and severe, 277; that are not on your timetable, 302; thirty-three steps of, 164; of this Messenger, 306–7; of the transfiguration, 306–7; through which Jesus passed, 306, 307
Inner Retreat: consecrated to the ascension flame and crystal ray, 344; Fátima reborn in the Heart of, 258; Heart of, 57; help to build, 84; as the key to the opening of a golden door, 321; Maitreya's Mystery School at, 54n.8, 296–97; in Montana, 163; Mother Mary needs you at, 322; our, 295; protection of, 359–60; spiritual building within the mountains of, 165; wall of Light drawn around, 41; Western Shamballa over the Heart of, 20n.2, 70, 260n.8; why you have been called to, 307. *See also* Place Prepared; Retreat(s); Royal Teton Ranch; Western Shamballa
Instauration, Great, 165, 166n.7
Institutions, outer, 309
Intelligence, divine, 57
Intercession: Divine, 271; extraordinary calls for, 360; hour for, 269; invoke, 294–95; of your lifestream, 141. *See also* Intervention
Intercessors, before karma and its adjudication, 219. *See also* Mediators
Interchange, divine, 298
Intermediate-Range Nuclear Forces Treaty. *See* INF Treaty
International Capitalist/Communist Conspiracy, 83–84; earth has the opportunity to survive the, 297; judgment upon, 247. *See also* Capitalists; Communism; Communists
Intervention, divine, *following* p. 122 *(in Feb. 1, 1988 letter)*, 143, 232
Introspection, too much, 336
Investments, which will not pan out, 92
Invocation(s): art of, 364–65; call that your, never cease, 371; dawn is the hour to be in, 90; by the Messenger, 375–76; that angels must receive, 390. *See also* Call(s); Decree(s); Spoken Word
Irenaeus, 290; on Jesus' age, 332n.4

evil intent on the drawing boards in, 285; people of Europe now trust this individual from, 242; politics being played by, 241; visiting "prince" from, 180. *See also* Soviet(s); Soviet Union

Moses, angel of the Lord who appeared unto, 149n.1

Mother: absence of our adoration of the Divine, 68; arcing of the Light of the Divine, 239; denial of the Divine, 212; devotion to the Divine, 265; Divine, 205; Divine, in embodiment, 244; El Morya's call to the Divine, 157; of God, 328; intensity of white fire of the Divine, 328; making way for the Divine, 147; the means to raise up the Mother Light, 213; misuse of the Light of the Divine, 363; perversions of the Divine, 67–68; planets representative of the Divine, 226; retreat of the Divine, 70, 258, 260n.11, 355, 358; rising Mother Flame, 50; seed atom of the Divine, 206; temple of the Divine, 127

Mothers, the calling to be world, 220

Motive, 24

Mountains: manifestations of Light inside, 57; of the north, 151

Mozart, Wolfgang Amadeus, 41

Mu: children of, 212; def., 215n.3. *See also* Lemuria

Music: classical, 370; Cyclopea on, 347–49; inner, 52–53. *See also* Rock music

Mutual Assured Destruction (MAD): doctrine of, 82, 83, *following* p. 122 *(in Feb. 1, 1988 letter);* logic of, 248n.5

Mysteries: denounced as heresy, 290; inner, 268; not revealed through the established Church, 300; sacred, 389; would you not think that the world would recognize these, 390

Mystery School, 258; called Summit University, 57; of Eden, 302–3; fallen angels in the, 266; Maitreya's, 20, 53, 54n.8, 118, 296–97, 388; purpose of Maitreya's, 37; this, 58; those outside the courts of Maitreya's, 42; what once was a, 128; when you come to the, 295

Mystical Body, of Christ, 282

Nag Hammadi, "library in a jar" at, 304

Nag Hammadi Library, a reading from, 377–83

Nation(s): beset by a national consciousness, 261; come to the hour of self-transcendence, 111–12; exemplar, 126; responsibility for, 276; that will not rise again, 8; vulnerable, 164. *See also* America; United States

Nephilim gods, 29, 118–19. *See also* Fallen ones

Neptune, 226; in Capricorn, 229n.3, 277

New Year's Eve, ascension on, 6

New York, entrenched Darkness in, 282

Nguyen Van Thieu, 199

Nicaragua, at the turning point, *following* p. 122 *(in Feb. 1, 1988 letter). See also* Sandinistas

Night, Dark, of the Spirit, 246, 281

Nine Gates, city that is called, 379, 381

1988: opens with ten times the darkness of the latter, 90; thoughtform for, 19–20; "The Way Out for 1988," 20

1989, October 2, 1989, 323

1990, greatest challenge the planet will ever know, 319. *See also* Nineties

Nineties, decade of the, 207. *See also* 1990

Ninth Ray, Lord of the, 228

Nirmanakaya, 320

Nirvana, 210; what it is like in, 370

Nixon, Richard, 173, 198–99

Noah, 40

Noble, Samuel, 103

Nonattachment, state of, 369

North America, ten thousand saints in, 158n.5

Norton, Charles D., 110

Nostradamus, prophecies of, 92, *following* p. 238 *(in Feb. 24, 1988 letter),* 277

November 1, 1987, 354

Nuclear power, a force to negate all misuse of, 119

Nuclear war: grave possibility of, 92; permanently deter, 166n.6; rip cord of, 276; and the Soviets, *following* p. 122 *(in Feb. 1, 1988 letter). See also* First strike; Mutual Assured Destruction (MAD); War(s)

Nuclear weapons accidents, 86

Nun, archetypal of the soul, 300. *See also* Religious

Obedience, 322; in the Guru-chela relationship, 318

Old Faithful, 50, 341

behalf of Europe, 240; Francis Bacon was an embodiment of, 166n.7; has come to you personally, 236; heart meditation and initiation he desires to give, 337; his exit from the nation's capital, 8; his withdrawal from Washington, D.C., *following* p. 122 *(in Feb. 1, 1988 letter);* his words to Mother Mary, 317–18; image and name of, 330; love of, 133; and Mary Lou Majerus, 352; misused, trampled upon and denied, 328; Portia's love of, 331; ruler of an ancient golden-age civilization, 249n.6; Saint Joseph was an embodiment of, 142n.2; to seal the servants of God in the forehead, 126; sponsor of, 131; sponsoring Master for the raising of the Kundalini, 270n.6; those who have a fervor of devotion to, 22; twin flame of, 234n.4; what you see in, 279; whether he shall be called again to Europe, 253; whose life is given for you, 156; will give accounting for the dispensation of violet flame, 300–301; at your side, 165. *See also* Lords of the Seven Rays

Sainthood, those qualified for, 300. *See also* Saint(s)

Salvation: far more difficult in the future, 390; so great a, 160

Sambhogakaya, 170; def., 172n.1

Samsara, def., 216n.5

San Diego, arcing of Light from, 239. *See also* California

San Francisco, turned toward Darkness, 156. *See also* California

Sanat Kumara: call to him constantly, 359; call to him to fill in gaps, 356; force of the anti-Mind dare not cross his path, 121; heartbeat of, 119; his Electronic Presence at the gate of this City Foursquare, 356; his promise to come when we need him, 353; his wall of Light around the Inner Retreat, 41; preparedness for the coming of, 354; second coming of, 117–18; on the six o'clock line, 68; those who are a part of his bands, 358; those who came with, 43; in the thoughtform for 1988, 19–20; with you as promised, 357. *See also* Ancient of Days

Sanctity, aura of, 322. *See also* Holiness

Sandinistas, *following* p. 122 *(in Feb. 1, 1988 letter);* cross into Honduras, 335, 339n.4

Satan(s): def., 366n.6; greatest threat to every, 355. *See also* Fallen ones

Satellites, 69, 73; in the KKV system, 86; and the Soviet spaceplane, 78; Soviets have stockpiled, 75; and Star Wars, 63; and the United States, 77; and the United States and the Soviet Union, 64, 66. *See also* Anti-satellite (ASAT)

Saturn: in Capricorn, 229n.3, 277; the Tester seen as, 226

Save the World with Violet Flame! cassettes, *following* p. 238 *(in Feb. 24, 1988 letter),* 251

Saviour, world, 219

Science of the spoken Word. *See* Decree(s); Spoken Word

Scientific dispensations, 90

Scorpio, initiations of, 80

Sea, of light, 209–10

Second Coming, of Christ, 126, 126n

Second death, 19, 286

Secret chamber, of the heart, 57, 152

Secret ray(s): challenges of initiation in the, 229–30n.7; five, 227; five fourteen-month rounds in the, 47n.1, 229n.7; initiations of the, 36; secret-ray chakras, 33n.4

Self: Chart of Your Divine, *xiv–xvi*, 97; lesser, 172, 346; puny, 360

Self-assessment, 169, 209

Self-knowledge, 264, 265

Self-rule, 5

Self-transcendence: law of, 160; nations come to the hour of, 111–12

Senate, of the United States, 243, 285. *See also* Government(s)

Senses, spiritual, 58

Seraph, that speaks of thy ascension, 349. *See also* Angel(s); Seraphim

Seraphim: form a cone of light, 237; four, to command and send on missions, 44; gathering of, 130; possess the quality of "cosmic penetrability," 238n.4; purifying you, 29–30; serve all devotees of the Mother, 362; will not leave you, 247. *See also* Angel(s); Seraph

Serapis Bey: admonished Keepers of the Flame to participate in three services, 331–32n.3; fourteen-month cycles of, 36, 47n.1, 229–30n.7; revealed the humility of Jesus at Luxor, 301–2

Serpent, raised up by Moses, 393
Service: opportunity of, 219; and the requirements for the victory, 346; your, 19; your intended, 209
Services: attendance at Saturday night, 89; Keepers of the Flame admonished to participate in three, 331–32n.3
Seventh Ray, 330. *See also* Violet flame
Shamballa, spiritual fire first kindled at, 117. *See also* Western Shamballa
Shasta, Mount, 44; Brotherhood of, 47n.8, *following* p. 122 *(in Feb. 1, 1988 letter);* withdrawal of the Brotherhood of, 39
Shepherd(s): come to be Jesus', 391; Jesus' call to, 290, 294; true, 41, 129, 223
Shiva, def., 154n.5
Shiva sound, of Elohim, 363–64
Siddhis, 43; def., 47n.16
Sight, inner, 236. *See also* Vision
Sin(s): condemnation for, 309; confession of, 386; against the Holy Ghost, 124; against the Holy Spirit which cannot be forgiven, 225; orthodox lie of, 290; of the past, 24–25; sense of, 387; where people continue to repeat their old, 27
Sinners, conversion of, 324n.3
Sirius, 134n.6; blue rose of, 158; Council of, 7
Six o'clock line, 80; and our national astrology and psychology, 67–68
Skylab, 64
Social programs, 219
Social services, 222
Socialism, and monopoly control, 107
Society, its dissolution, 111. *See also* Civilization(s)
Sodom and Gomorrah, *following* p. 122 *(in Feb. 1, 1988 letter)*
Solar Logoi, 20
Solzhenitsyn, Aleksandr 177, 178
Son(s): descending of the Sons of God, 37; of God, 11, 168; incarnation of the, 169; "neither the Son," in Codex Sinaiticus, 324n.9; thou art a, of God, 298
Soul: Archangel Raphael on the, 266; saving of one's own, 18; suicide of the, 265
Sound: discordant and divine, 53; soundless, 365
Sound wave, of Alpha and Omega, 210
Soundlessness, vibration of, 365

Southeast Asia, 201. *See also* Vietnam
Soviet(s): in Afghanistan, *following* p. 122 *(in Feb. 1, 1988 letter),* 339n.3; and the Afghans, 334; control of Europe by the, 243; have killed millions of their citizens, 177–78; and the Korean War, 189–90; to make war, 243; to move against Europe and the United States, 241; and nuclear war, *following* p. 122 *(in Feb. 1, 1988 letter);* sabotage through the, 93; slaughter of millions by the, government, 180–81; Soviet Sandinistas, 334–35; Soviet tanks moving across Europe, 317; their misuse of the technology of Atlantis, 245; their takeover of Hungary, *following* p. 122 *(in Feb. 1, 1988 letter). See also* Moscow; Soviet Union
Soviet Union: betrayal from the government of the, 274–75; gone down under an evil system, 315; has violated its ABM Treaty, 245; leadership in the, 282; and the race for space, 63–87 passim; and technology, 180–81; their breakout of the ABM Treaty, 248n.5; and the Vietnam War, 195–96, 197. *See also* Bolshevik(s); Moscow; Soviet(s)
Space: control from, 292; dominance in, 90; race for, 63–87; and time, 121
Space program, of the United States, 245
Space shuttle, 63, 67, 77, 90; Challenger, 72, 76, 80
Space station(s), 64–65, 86
Spacecraft, those who come in their, 132. *See also* Aliens
Spaceplane(s), 73, 78, 86
Spain, 245
Spark: divine, 9, 11, 12, 265; forfeiture of the divine, 19; those who have extinguished the divine, 109. *See also* Flame(s); Threefold flame
Spin, cosmic, 344
Spinelessness, 80
Spirit: fiery, 337; and Matter cosmos, 32
Spirits, communication from, 168. *See also* Evil spirits
Spiritual experiences, your, 302
Spleen, 23, 33n.4
Spoken Word: evolutions who begin to understand the science of the, 22; exercise the science of the, 218; marshaling of forces by the power of

FOR MORE INFORMATION

Write or call for information about the dictations of the Ascended Masters published weekly as *Pearls of Wisdom*, the Keepers of the Flame Fraternity with monthly lessons, the Ascended Masters' study center nearest you, and Summit University three-month retreats, weekend seminars and quarterly conferences that convene at the Royal Teton Ranch. At this 33,000-acre self-sufficient spiritual community-in-the-making adjacent to Yellowstone National Park in Montana, Elizabeth Clare Prophet gives teachings on the Divine Mother, the parallel paths of Christ and Buddha, Saint Germain's prophecies for our time and the exercise of the science of the spoken Word as well as dictations from the Ascended Masters and initiations of the Great White Brotherhood. These teachings are published in books and on audio- and videocassette. We'll be happy to send you a free catalog when you contact Summit University Press, Box A, Livingston, Montana 59047-1390. Telephone: (406) 222-8300.

All in our community send you our hearts' love and a joyful welcome to the Royal Teton Ranch!

Reach out for the **LIFELINE TO THE PRESENCE.** Let us pray with you!
To all who are beset by depression, suicide, difficulties or insurmountable problems, we say **MAKE THE CALL!** (406) 848-7441

PROFILE

Elizabeth Clare Prophet

Teachings of the Ascended Masters

Harry Langdon

Who Is Elizabeth Clare Prophet?

S he preceded the trends and
outlived the fads. Since 1961
Elizabeth Clare Prophet has
pioneered the New Age movement. Her books are landmarks in
the spiritual skyline. She challenges
mainline Christianity with bold
questions, and even bolder answers.

And people are taking notice. Her
books have sold over a million copies
and her cable television shows have
a viewing audience of 36 million.

Her students call her "Guru Ma"
(the teacher who is mother) but more
often "Mother" because of her devotion to the flame of God as Mother.
Her surname is Prophet, and it is her
calling as well. Prophet comes from
the Greek *prophētēs*, literally "to
speak for," hence a messenger; a
prophet is "one who utters divinely
inspired revelations." She is a prophet
of God and the messenger for the
Ascended Masters.

Her name is familiar as the leader
of Church Universal and Triumphant,
headquartered at the exquisite
33,000-acre Royal Teton Ranch bor-
dering Yellowstone National Park.

But we're getting ahead of our story.
How did Mrs. Prophet become America's foremost woman religious leader?

Having spent her life until age
22 searching for the teachings of the
Ascended Masters, she devoted herself to spreading the message when
she found them. Working 18-hour
days and setting grueling schedules
for herself, she has lectured in over
30 countries and 150 cities, written

Chad Slattery

Harry Langdon

over 50 books, conducted four conferences a year with seminars in between, taught in-depth courses, ministered to thousands of followers, founded her own distinctive Montessori school, and raised four children.

Her books include the New Age best-sellers *The Lost Years of Jesus* (100,000 copies sold), *Saint Germain On Alchemy* (150,000 copies sold), and *The Human Aura* (200,000 copies sold), as well as such classics of esoteric literature as *The Lost Teachings of Jesus* and *Climb the Highest Mountain*.

She was born Elizabeth Clare Wulf in Red Bank, New Jersey, in 1939. After completing her French studies in Switzerland she attended Antioch College, later transferring to Boston University where she received a B.A. in political science.

Her spiritual quest sprang from her childhood recollection of past lives and her determination to find confirmation of the truth that Jesus was speaking to her in her heart. By age nine she had attended every Protestant and Catholic church and Jewish synagogue in Red Bank without finding the answers she was looking for.

"I would hear the voice of Jesus speaking to me in my heart, speaking the truth as I heard error building upon error from the pulpit," she says. Meanwhile her modern-day heroes were Mohandas Gandhi, Albert Schweitzer, and Norman Vincent Peale, whose writings she avidly read.

From age nine to 18 she studied the complete works of Mary Baker Eddy along with her Bible and attended the local Christian Science

3

church and Sunday school. Although satisfied with the deeper truths of metaphysics she was learning, she knew there were missing pieces and she continued her search.

At age 18 she opened a book on the Ascended Masters that she had seen in her parents' library for years but never taken off the shelf. Finding herself face to face with a picture of the Ascended Master Saint Germain, she was electrified. "This was the turning point of my life," she recalls. For the first time she felt the presence of an Ascended Master and realized that Saint Germain was the one she had to find.

On April 22, 1961, she attended a meeting of The Summit Lighthouse in Boston and met its leader, Mark L. Prophet, the messenger for the Ascended Masters. She recognized him as *the* teacher she had been looking for all of her life who was to lead her on her spiritual path.

Within six weeks the Ascended Master El Morya appeared to her in a park on her way to class at B.U. and told her to go to Washington, D.C., where Mark Prophet would train her to be the messenger.

Answering the call, Elizabeth entered a period of intense spiritual discipline and inner soul awakening. She says, "I believe that my preparation for my life's calling had been ongoing for a number of embodiments and that this lifetime was to be the culmination of my soul's tutoring in the universal mysteries of Christ."

Three years later she received Saint Germain's anointing to be the

Rev. Mark L. Prophet

He was the only child of Thomas and Mabel Prophet, born Christmas Eve 1918 in Chippewa Falls, Wisconsin. As a child his mystical inclinations were apparent. He saw and freely communed with angels and nature spirits. When he was nine his father died and it affected him deeply. Attending the Pentecostal church, praying by the hour at the altar he built in the attic of his home, the young Mark showed an extraordinary religious devotion. Before finishing high school he had received all nine gifts of the Holy Spirit.

When Mark was a young man the Ascended Master El Morya appeared to him but, unable to reconcile the turbaned Eastern adept with his lifelong devotion to Jesus or his mother's studies with Unity School of Christianity, he dismissed him.

Years later, El Morya returned. Having realized that the path of the Ascended Masters was also the path of Jesus, Mark accepted Morya as his teacher and took on the rigors of Eastern discipleship. Mark also studied the teachings of Paramahansa Yogananda and was for a time associated with Self-Realization Fellowship as well as the Rosicrucian order.

After serving in the Air Force in World War II, Mark lectured on Christian and Eastern mysticism and the Masters of Wisdom from 1945 until 1952 when he began publishing a series of letters for his students called *Ashram Notes,* dictated by El Morya from his Ashram at Darjeeling, India.

In 1957 the Master called him to Washington, D.C., to found The Summit Lighthouse for the purpose of publishing the teachings of the Ascended Masters. On August 8, 1958, El Morya dictated the first of the *Pearls of Wisdom* to Mark, launching a worldwide movement.

messenger of the Great White Brotherhood. Empowered by the Holy Spirit, she began delivering prophetic messages from the Ascended Masters in the form of dictations spoken before the congregation of the Masters' students who gathered for worship services.

Mark and Elizabeth were married March 16, 1963, and together they built The Summit Lighthouse, publishing the Masters' teachings themselves.

With a growing staff and nationwide membership, they and their one-year-old son moved to Colorado Springs in 1966. Their spiritual retreat in the Broadmoor area became a gathering place for seekers in the '60s. Here their three daughters were born, Montessori International school was founded, and the spiritual movement became international in scope. Here, too, Mark Prophet, having completed his mission, passed on in February 1973.

Although her loss was profound, Elizabeth carried on the ministry

*S*ome people get mixed up about my name. They think that I am Elizabeth Clare, the prophet. Well, my name is Prophet. It is the surname of my late husband, Mark Prophet, whose ancestors carried the name from France to Ireland to Canada."

—Elizabeth Clare Prophet

with faith in God, the support of her staff, and the love of her children. She led a pilgrimage to South America and held a conference in Mexico City that Christmas. Since then she has traveled to West Africa, Europe, Australia, the Philippines, India, and across the United States and Canada, teaching thousands of students and establishing centers. She continued to write books—her own and the compilation of Mark's work—and to administer the organization. Her first priority remained the weekly *Pearls of Wisdom* (letters from the Ascended Masters to their students), which Mark had begun publishing in 1958.

By 1976 Mrs. Prophet was established as a prominent religious leader and she moved the church headquarters to a leased campus in Pasadena, California. Two years later the church purchased the 218-acre Gillette estate in the Santa Monica Mountains near Malibu and renamed it "Camelot."

In 1981 Mrs. Prophet married Edward L. Francis, who had begun studying the Ascended Masters' teachings while a student at Colorado College in 1969. He has served on The Summit Lighthouse staff since 1970 and the Board of Directors since 1972. Mr. Francis is vice president and business manager of Church Universal and Triumphant and directs the day-to-day operations at the Royal Teton Ranch in Montana. The church purchased the 13,000-acre Forbes ranch in 1981 and in 1986 sold its California properties and moved its international headquarters to Montana.

Teachings of the Ascended Masters— Ancient Wisdom for the New Age

Ancient Tibetan manuscripts say that Jesus spent 17 years (age 12 to 29) in the East as both student and teacher. He mastered Hindu and Buddhist scriptures, learned to heal and to cast out devils, and prepared for his Palestinian mission.

"To me the great discovery of these texts is that Jesus did not claim that he was born a god," Mrs. Prophet says. "He saw himself as a disciple. He studied and learned. He became a great adept. Jesus is our Saviour who saved us so that we could walk the same path of discipleship that he walked."

The fundamental principle of the teachings of the Ascended Masters is that all sons and daughters of God have a divine spark which is their potential to become, or realize, the Christ within and ascend to God as Jesus did.

This concept is at the heart of the major religions, East and West. And it was part of Jesus' original teachings to his disciples which were either destroyed or obscured by Church Fathers.

Jesus never said that he was the exclusive Son of God. When in John 3:16 he spoke of the "only begotten Son," he was referring to the universal Christ, whose Body is individualized (broken) for each of us as our personal inner Teacher. This Teacher we address as our beloved Holy Christ Self—"the true Light which lighteth every man that cometh into the world," as John wrote.

The word *Christ* comes from the Greek *Christos,* meaning "anointed." Hence the 'Christed one' is one who is anointed with the Light of the LORD, the "I AM" Presence. This is the I AM THAT I AM (the Yod He Vau He) witnessed by Moses which God individualized for each of his sons and daughters.

Did Jesus go to India? In *The Lost Years of Jesus* **Mrs. Prophet published three variant translations of ancient Tibetan manuscripts which say that Jesus spent his 17 "lost years," from age 12 to 29, traveling in the East.**

The early Christian Gnostics, whose writings were suppressed by orthodoxy, taught the same principles. The Gnostic Gospel of Philip describes the follower of Jesus who walks fully in his footsteps as "no longer a Christian but a Christ." In the Gnostic Gospel of Thomas, Jesus says, "I am not your Master. . . . He who will drink from my mouth will become as I am: I myself shall become he."

The understanding that each soul has the potential to externalize his divine nature is also found in Buddhist texts that speak of "the Buddha-Essence" which is "in all beings at all times."

Mrs. Prophet says, "The concept of the incarnation of the Light of God, the inner Buddha and the inner Christ, is what has been taken from us in the West in church, in synagogue, in mosque, in temple."

The culmination of the path of Christhood is the initiation of the ascension, a spiritual acceleration of consciousness which takes place at the natural conclusion of one's lifetime when the soul returns to the Father and is freed from the round of karma and rebirth.

Karma and Reincarnation

Saint Paul said it: "Whatsoever a man soweth, that shall he also reap." And the Ascended Masters teach it. Thousands of years ago the people of earth began to disobey the laws of God. Today they are reaping the harvest of past sowings of their misuses of God's light, energy, and consciousness to the detriment of life on earth.

Karma is the effect of causes set in motion, good and bad. The law is irrevocable: As we sow, we reap. But through the grace of Jesus Christ, a true entering in to the Word and Work of the Lord, and the violet flame—the all-consuming fire of God which cleanses us from sin, i.e., transmutes karma—all can balance their negative karma, accomplish their unique mission and fulfill the requirements for the ascension.

Students of the Ascended Masters use the science of the spoken Word to expand the light in their spiritual centers, known in the East as chakras.

Science of the Spoken Word

Spoken prayer is at the heart of the major religions, whether as the Our Father, the Hail Mary, the Psalms and other Christian responsive readings; the Jewish Shema and Amidah; the Moslem confession of faith, the Shahadah; Buddhist mantras; or the recitation of the Hindu Vedas.

The Ascended Masters teach the science of the spoken Word, a step-up of all prayer forms East and West. It combines prayer, meditation, and visualization with what are called dynamic decrees, placing special emphasis on affirmations using the name of God—I AM THAT I AM.

They say this form of devotion is the most effective method known today for spiritual resolution, the balancing of karma, and soul advancement. Students of the Ascended Masters give dynamic decrees to direct God's light for the solving of personal and planetary problems, including crime, pollution, drugs, child abuse, the economy, AIDS, and the threat of nuclear war.

The Violet Flame

The violet flame is the gift of the Holy Spirit known to mystics throughout the ages but introduced at large by Saint Germain early in this century. When invoked and visualized in the giving of dynamic decrees, this seventh-ray aspect of the sacred fire transmutes the cause, effect, record, and memory of negative karma and misqualified energy that result in discord,

*W*e live in a world *where everything is instant— coffee, oatmeal, love. This Teaching isn't instant. It's tough. You will find the people who come to this path to be independent thinkers and doers. They're tough. They've been through everything else, they have seen for themselves the falsity of superficial dogma and religion. They know the true inner mystical path based on the principle of reverence for life. And they want to be part of a worldwide community of kindred souls who live it and share it in love."*

—Elizabeth Clare Prophet

disease, and death. Those who correctly call forth the violet flame daily, experience transformation, soul liberation, and spiritual upliftment.

What Are Dictations?

Elizabeth Clare Prophet is the messenger for the Ascended Masters in the tradition of the Old Testament prophets who delivered the Word of the LORD to his people.

She is fully conscious and in possession of her faculties, yet in an exalted state, while delivering the words of the heavenly host as "dictations." Her work is not a form of psychicism or spiritualism in which a discarnate entity from the spirit world takes over the body of a channeller. Rather is it a conveyance by the Holy Spirit of the sacred fire and the teaching of immortal beings who with Jesus have returned to the heart of the Father.

They deliver a message of prophecy for our time, the ancient wisdom applied to current planetary dilemmas, and spiritual initiation, which is a transfer of light for soul quickening.

The Great White Brotherhood

The Ascended Masters are part of a hierarchy of beings known as the Great White Brotherhood, a spiritual order of Western saints and Eastern masters. (The term "white" refers not to race but to the aura of white light that surrounds these immortals.) They are our elder brothers and sisters on the path of personal Christhood who have graduated from earth's schoolroom, ascending as Jesus did at the conclusion of his earthly mission.

They are the great multitude of saints "clothed with white robes" who stand before the throne of God (Rev. 7). The Brotherhood works with earnest seekers and public servants of every race, religion, and walk of life to assist humanity in their forward evolution.

Who Is Saint Germain?

Saint Germain is an Ascended Master known as the Lord of the Seventh Ray. There are seven paths to the realization of the inner Light based on seven aspects of God's consciousness. The qualities of the seventh ray are freedom, justice, mercy, alchemy and sacred ritual. Initiates on the seventh ray pursue callings in government, the economy, religion, science or related fields which allow them to develop their self-mastery in serving society's needs on the seventh ray.

Having studied and become an example of the seventh-ray path of Christhood during his lifetimes upon earth, Saint Germain attained his ascension in 1684. The name of this friend and teacher of mankind means "holy brother" and it is in this regard that his students hold him.

He was embodied as the prophet Samuel (c. 1050 B.C.); Saint Joseph, protector of Jesus (1st century); Saint Alban, first Christian martyr in Britain (3rd century); Merlin, seer and sage at Arthur's court (5th century); Roger Bacon, philosopher, persecuted scientist, and Franciscan monk (c. 1214–1294); Christopher Columbus, discoverer of America (1451–1506); and Francis Bacon, father of inductive reasoning and the scientific method and prolific author—some say of the Shakespearean plays (1561–1626).

Following his ascension Saint Germain devoted himself to the advancement of government and science. From 1710 to 1822 he appeared as the 40-year-old Count Saint Germain who is mentioned in the letters of Voltaire, Horace Walpole, Frederick the Great, Casanova, and Madame Pompadour.

Saint Germain attempted to assist a smooth transition from monarchy to representative government and to prevent the bloodshed of the French Revolution. To gain the attention of the crowned heads of Europe he executed a series of seemingly miraculous feats of alchemy. But to no avail. They did not heed his warnings and Saint Germain turned his attention to the New World.

He became the sponsoring Master of the United States of America and of her first president—inspiring the Declaration of Independence and the Constitution. He also inspired many of the labor-saving devices of the twentieth-century to further his goal of liberating mankind from drudgery that they might devote themselves to the pursuit of God-realization.

Jesus the Christ

The Chart of Your Real Self

Saint Germain

The upper figure in the Chart of Your Real Self is the I AM Presence, the I AM THAT I AM, the individualization of God's presence for each of his sons and daughters. The middle figure is the Mediator between God and man, called the Holy Christ Self, the Real Self, or the Higher Consciousness. The lower figure represents the soul evolving through the four planes of Matter to balance karma and fulfill the divine plan. Your soul is the nonpermanent aspect of being which is made permanent through the ritual of the ascension.

11

What Is Church Universal and Triumphant?

In 1974 Elizabeth Clare Prophet responded to the call from Jesus to found his Church. Accordingly, the Board of Directors of The Summit Lighthouse incorporated Church Universal and Triumphant to meet the religious needs of a world body of believers.

Thereafter the Church took on the liturgical function that had been carried on by The Summit Lighthouse on a lesser scale and the latter expanded its original mission—the publishing of the teachings of the Ascended Masters.

There are various options for participation in the teachings of the Ascended Masters. Some students simply read the Prophets' books, available in ten languages in bookstores around the world. Others subscribe to the weekly *Pearls of Wisdom*. They may also join the Keepers of the Flame Fraternity, a secular organization dedicated to keeping the flame of Life in earth's evolutions and to planetary enlightenment. Members of the fraternity receive monthly lessons on the teachings of the Ascended Masters.

They may participate in the activities of Church-sponsored teaching centers and study groups around the world and also attend Summit University. After serious study and advancement on the path some, desiring a closer affiliation and a greater spiritual commitment, become communicants of Church Universal and Triumphant.

The Royal Teton Ranch:
New Age Spiritual Community

The Royal Teton Ranch is a
33,000-acre self-sufficient spiritual
community-in-the-making, located
in the Paradise Valley in Park
County, Montana. It is the international headquarters for Church
Universal and Triumphant, The Summit Lighthouse, Summit University,
Montessori International, and
Summit University Press.

Here, in the tradition of the
world's religions, come seekers for
truth to retreat, meditate, commune
with nature, attend Summit University seminars, or participate in
community life with the 600 permanent residents. Activities include
organic farming and ranching,
publishing the Ascended Masters'
teachings, or learning the art of macrobiotic cooking. Some stay for six
weeks or a year, others a lifetime.
Professionals of all ages, families,
the retired and the young call this
"Inner Retreat" home.

Summit University:
A College of Religion,
Science, and Culture

Summit University is dedicated to
bringing the Lost Teachings of Jesus
to those seeking a more spiritual understanding of themselves and their
world. Founded in Santa Barbara in
1971 by Mark Prophet, it offers
courses on the sacred scriptures
of East and West, how to gain self-
mastery through the science of the

spoken Word, the purification of the aura and the chakras (spiritual centers within the body), alchemy as the science of self-transformation, the cycles of karma and past lives, hatha yoga, and the macrobiotic diet.

It sponsors three twelve-week sessions a year—fall, winter, and spring—as well as summer courses, weekend seminars and five-day quarterly conferences.

(Summit University has neither sought nor received regional or national accreditation.)

Montessori International: A Prototype for New Age Education

Founded by the Prophets in Colorado Springs in 1970, Montessori International is a private school for children age three months through the twelfth grade. Dedicated to the educational principles set forth by Dr. Maria Montessori, its motto is: Learn to Love to Do Well and You Shall. Its goal is to assist children in developing their highest potential, human and divine.

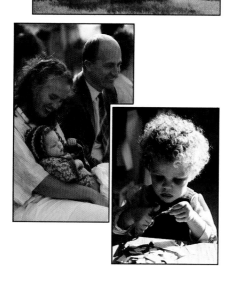

Children learn to read between age two and five. (But they're already beginning at three months!) Every student masters the basics and then accelerates in subjects at which he excels. Some go on to America's finest universities. Others enter trades for which they have apprenticed throughout school.

Note: Summit University and Montessori International do not discriminate on the basis of race, color, sex, national or ethnic origin in their admission policies, programs, and activities.

Montessori International sponsors a Primary Teacher Education Course offered by the Pan American Montessori Society leading to teacher certification. The program is presented by Master Teachers prepared by Dr. Elisabeth Caspari, Director of Education of the society.

Summit University Press: Publisher for Church Universal and Triumphant

Summit University Press, an arm of The Summit Lighthouse, publishes the books written by Mark and Elizabeth Prophet as well as their audio- and videotapes of dictations by Ascended Masters, lectures, decrees and songs.

Mrs. Prophet has four cable television shows: "The Coming Revolution in Higher Consciousness," on which she gives prophecy and expounds on the teachings of the Ascended Masters; "The Everlasting Gospel," specifically Jesus' revelation to her on the sacred scriptures of East and West; "The Lost Teachings of Jesus," which examines ancient texts; and "Summit University Forum," on which she interviews revolutionaries in every field who provide alternative information on health, the economy, education, medicine, and current events.

For more information write or call Summit University Press, Box A, Livingston, MT 59047-1390, (406) 222-8300.

T he Ascended Masters present a path
and a teaching whereby every individual
on earth can find his way back to God.
I do not claim to be a Master but only their instrument.
Nor do I claim to be perfect in my human self. I am the servant of the
Light in all students of the Ascended Masters and in all people.
My books and writings are intended to give people the
opportunity to know the Truth that can make them free—so they
can find God without me. My goal is to take true seekers,
in the tradition of the Masters of the Far East, as far as they can go
and need to go to meet their true Teachers face to face."
—Elizabeth Clare Prophet

SUMMIT UNIVERSITY 🌙 PRESS®
Box A, Livingston, Montana 59047 (406) 222-8300